PEARSON ALWAYS LEARNING

Lodging Management

Custom Edition for Florida Gulf Coast University
HFT 3253

Taken from:
Check-In Check-Out: Managing Hotel Operations, Ninth Edition
by Gary K. Vallen and Jerome J. Vallen

Foundations of Lodging Management, Second Edition
by David K. Hayes, Jack D. Ninemeier and Allisha A. Miller

Managing Front Office Operations, Ninth Edition
by Michael L. Kasavana

Managing Housekeeping Operations, Revised Third Edition
by Aleta A. Nitschke and William D. Frye

Cover Art: Courtesy of Photodisc, Stockbyte/Getty Images.

Taken from:

Check-In Check-Out: Managing Hotel Operations, Ninth Edition
by Gary K. Vallen and Jerome J. Vallen

Upper Saddle River, New Jersey 07458

Foundations of Lodging Management, Second Edition
by David K. Hayes, Jack D. Ninemeier and Allisha A. Miller

Published as Prentice Hall

Managing Front Office Operations, Ninth Edition
by Michael L. Kasavana

Lansing, Michigan 48906-4221

Managing Housekeeping Operations, Revised Third Edition
by Aleta A. Nitschke and William D. Frye

Lansing, Michigan 48906-4221

This special edition published in cooperation with Pearson Learning Solutions.

Pearson Learning Solutions, 501 Boylston Street, Suite 900, Boston, MA 02116
A Pearson Education Company
www.pearsoned.com

Printed in the United States of America

2 3 4 5 6 7 8 9 10 V092 16 15 14

000200010271896211

SK

ISBN 10: 1-269-93823-1
ISBN 13: 978-1-269-93823-5

TABLE OF CONTENTS

Chapter 1 Outline

Competencies

1. Explain what a mission is, and describe how goals, strategies, and tactics are used to accomplish a hotel's mission. (pp. 3–6)
2. Describe how hotels are organized and explain how functional areas within hotels are classified. (pp. 6–10)
3. Describe the functions performed by departments and positions within the rooms division. (pp. 10–19)
4. Identify the functions performed by other divisions and departments within a full-service hotel. (pp. 19–22)
5. Describe the organization of the front office, including traditional work shifts, alternative scheduling practices, and the purpose of job descriptions and job specifications. (pp. 23–26)

Taken from *Managing Front Office Operations,* Ninth Edition, by Michael L. Kasavana

Chapter 1

Hotel Organization

A PERSON ENTERING A HOTEL LOBBY for the first time might never guess the complexities underlying the day-to-day operation of the property. He or she might not recognize that the courtesy of the door attendant, the competent and friendly manner of the front desk agent, and the tidiness of the guestroom reflect hours of planning, extensive communications, ongoing training, and a coordinated effort to create the workings of an efficient organization. The actual network of a hotel's divisions, departments, and personnel in a smoothly operating hotel should be invisible to the casual observer. But the services that result from a hotel's smooth operations are highly visible. Providing those services presents hotels with a unique challenge.

For a hotel to run effectively and efficiently, every employee must understand the property's mission and work to achieve it. Every employee must ensure that guests are so impressed by the property's facilities and services that they will want to come back and will enthusiastically recommend the property to others.

Teamwork is the key to success. All employees must have a spirit of cooperation both within and between their departmental areas. While every department and division should strive to offer and improve quality guest service, it is especially important that good service be emphasized in high-profile locations like the front office. The ability of front office employees to answer questions, coordinate services, offer choices, and satisfy guest requests is critical to the hotel's mission.

This chapter examines the relationship of hotel employees, departments, and divisions, as well as how each of these components contributes to achieving the property's mission. Several sample job descriptions for front office staff positions are shown in the appendix to this chapter.

Organizational Missions

Every organization has a reason or purpose for existing. Its purpose forms the basis for the organization's mission. An organization's mission can be expressed in a **mission statement,** which defines the unique purpose that sets one hotel or hotel company apart from others. The mission statement expresses the underlying philosophy that gives meaning and direction to hotel policies. While employees learn the tasks involved in their jobs—or the *what to do* of the job—the mission statement communicates the *why we are doing it* of the job. Hotel employees may derive a sense of purpose from a well-conceived mission statement. For example, a hotel's mission may be to provide the finest facilities and services in the market while providing a good place for its employees to work and a reasonable return on investment to its owners. From such a mission statement, employees know what is expected of them (providing the finest facilities and services in the market, thus helping the owners to earn a reasonable return on their investment), as well as what they can expect (a good place to work).

A hotel's mission statement often addresses the interests of its three main constituent groups: guests, managers, and employees. First, a hotel's mission statement can address the basic needs and expectations of the hotel's guests. Regardless of a hotel's size or service level, it is safe to assume all guests have the following basic expectations:

- Safe, secure accommodations
- A clean, comfortable guestroom
- Courteous, professional, knowledgeable, and friendly service
- Well-maintained facilities and equipment

Hotel guests generally anticipate a particular level of service at a given property type. If a hotel clearly defines its markets and consistently delivers the level of service those markets expect, it can satisfy its guests, encourage repeat business, and improve its reputation.

Second, a hotel's mission statement can reflect its management philosophy. Since styles of operation differ, mission statements often vary from property to property. In fact, a hotel's mission is one of the principal means it uses to distinguish itself from other hotels. A mission statement guides managers in their jobs by identifying the property's basic values.

Third, the mission statement can help the hotel's employees meet or exceed both guest and management expectations. A mission statement can also serve as a basis for job descriptions and performance standards and as an introduction to the property for new employees. The property's mission statement should appear in employee handbooks and training manuals, and should accompany job descriptions.

Consider this example of a hotel mission statement:

> The mission of our hotel is to provide outstanding lodging facilities and services to our guests. Our hotel focuses on individual business and leisure travel, as well as travel associated with group meetings. We emphasize high quality standards in our rooms and food and beverage divisions, as well as the finest service available in our market. We provide a fair return on investment for our owners and recognize that this cannot be done without well-trained, motivated, and enthusiastic employees.

Goals

Once the hotel has defined and formulated its mission statement, the next step is to set goals. **Goals** are those activities and standards an organization must successfully perform or achieve to effectively carry out its mission. A goal is more specific than a mission; it requires a certain level of achievement that can be observed and measured. Measurable goals encourage hotel employees to perform effectively while enabling management to monitor employee progress. Many organizations evaluate their goals frequently. Yearly goal planning is common, and sometimes these goals are broken down by month or quarter. Some goals are financial and are linked to the hotel's budget and forecasting cycle. Other goals may deal with the quality of guest service, frequency of guest or employee accidents, property security, or the number of new corporate clients the hotel has obtained. Even more important, goals often become part of the management team's evaluation process. Salary increases, bonuses, awards, and other forms of recognition are often linked to specific goals. Management and staff should be periodically evaluated on their progress toward meeting the hotel's goals. Management can determine whether goals are being achieved or whether corrective action is necessary. A properly written goal includes an action verb followed by a specific form of measurement such as a time interval or a level of quality, quantity, or cost.

The following are examples of measurable front office goals:

- Increase the hotel's average occupancy level by 2 percent above the previous year's level.
- Increase the volume of repeat guest business by 10 percent.
- Reduce average check-in and check-out times by two minutes.
- Reduce the number of guest complaints by 20 percent.
- Respond to all guest maintenance requests within one half hour.

It is very common for more than one department to be involved in achieving a goal. For example, in order for the front desk to achieve a goal of checking every guest in within a two-minute period, it is necessary for the housekeeping department to keep the inventory of clean and vacant rooms current. For this reason, some hotel goals are stated as property-wide goals, not simply as departmental or divisional goals. Achieving goals is often the result of close coordination between departments. The goals of various departments can be tied together, and the success of one department often leads to the success of others. Joint goal-setting also fosters cooperation and *esprit de corps* among departments.

Strategies and Tactics

By establishing property-wide, measurable goals, a hotel enables its managers and employees to concentrate on specific strategies that will help the property achieve its goals. Goals define the purpose of a department or division; they direct the actions of managers and employees and the functions of the department or division toward fulfilling the hotel's mission. To achieve its goals, a department or division establishes **strategies**—the methods a department or division uses to achieve its goals. **Tactics** further define how goals will be achieved. Tactics are the day-to-day operating procedures that implement successful strategies. It is important that goals and strategies set at the departmental and divisional levels complement and support the property's mission and its property-wide goals.

Examples of goals, strategies, and tactics involving areas within the front office are:

- Registration—*Goal:* Operate the front desk efficiently and courteously so that guests may register within two minutes of arrival. *Strategy:* Preregister all expected guests with reservation guarantees as rooms become available from the housekeeping department. *Tactic:* Preprint registration cards for arriving guests and separate the cards of all guests with a reservation guarantee.

- Guest Cashiering—*Goal:* Post all charges reaching the front desk within thirty minutes (for properties using a non-automated system). *Strategy:* Provide sufficient staffing to enable rapid and accurate posting of guest charges when they are received. *Tactic:* Review occupancy forecasts weekly to develop proper staffing guidelines.
- Bell Stand—*Goal:* Respond to every check-out luggage request within ten minutes. *Strategy:* Keep a log of when bell attendants are dispatched and when they return from each guest call. *Tactic:* Enter guest name, room number, bell attendant assigned, and time out and time in for each luggage request.
- Telecommunications Department—*Goal:* Answer every telephone call within three rings of the telephone, regardless of whether it is an inside call or an outside call. *Strategy:* Perform telephone traffic studies periodically, reviewing the number of calls received, to ensure that the proper number of telephone lines are available for both incoming and outgoing telephone calls. *Tactic:* Print a daily traffic report from the telephone switchboard and record volume by time on a spreadsheet.

Hotel Organization

The people authorized by a hotel's owner to represent his or her interests are called hotel management. In small properties, hotel management may consist of just one person. Management guides the operation of the hotel and regularly reports the general state of the hotel's financial health to its owner. The major duties of a hotel management team include planning, organizing, coordinating, staffing, directing, controlling, and evaluating hotel activities and/or personnel. Management performs its duties to reach specific objectives and goals. These duties involve the activities of various hotel divisions and departments.

The top executive of a property is usually called the managing director, general manager, or innkeeper. For discussion purposes, this chapter refers to the top executive as the general manager. The general manager of an independent hotel normally reports directly to the owner or the owner's representative. The general manager is ultimately responsible for the success of the hotel and supervises all hotel divisions, either through a resident or assistant manager or through division heads. Chain organizations usually have a district, area, or regional executive who supervises the general managers located at the properties within his or her jurisdiction.

While the general manager is responsible for supervising all hotel divisions, he or she may delegate responsibility for specific divisions or departments to an assistant general manager, resident manager, or director of operations. When the general manager is absent, the assistant general manager, resident manager, or director of operations usually serves as the acting general manager. When these four managers are all off the premises, a manager-on-duty (MOD) is often appointed to assume overall managerial responsibility. Front office managers are often called upon to be the MOD when more senior managers are not on the property.

Historically, resident managers actually *lived* in the hotel. Essentially, it was the resident manager's job to be available twenty-four hours a day, seven days a week. Over time, more authority has been delegated to other managers. While many resident managers are still responsible for the rooms division, it is rare for a property to require its resident manager to live on the premises.

To qualify for a department head position, an individual must thoroughly understand the functions, goals, and practices of a particular department. Front office managers are usually considered department heads.

Organization Charts

An organization requires a formal structure to carry out its mission and goals. A common way to represent that structure is the **organization chart.** An organization chart is a schematic representation of the relationships between positions within an organization. It shows where each position fits in the overall organization, as well as where divisions of responsibility and lines of authority lie. Solid lines on the chart indicate direct-line accountability; dotted lines indicate relationships that involve a high degree of cooperation and communication, but not a direct reporting relationship.

An organization chart should be flexible. It should be reviewed and revised yearly, or more often if business conditions significantly change. Employee responsibilities may change as individuals assume more duties, depending on their qualifications and strengths. Some organizations list each employee's name on the chart along with his or her title. A copy of the property's organization chart should be included in the employee handbook distributed to all employees.

Since no two hotels are exactly alike, organizational structures must be tailored to fit the needs of each individual property. The charts in this chapter illustrate several organizational possibilities: a full-service property, a property with separately owned food and beverage operations, and a rooms-only hotel.

A full-service property that offers both lodging and food and beverage service will probably have an extensive organizational structure. Exhibit 1 shows an organization chart outlining the management-level positions in a large full-service property. All but two of the lines on the chart are solid, indicating reporting relationships. The dotted lines connecting the sales director to the catering director and the reservations manager represent the close working relationships among these positions.

Some hotels may lease food and beverage outlets to another company. This means that food and beverage operations and guestroom operations are separately owned and managed. When another company operates food and beverage, it is essential that both companies communicate closely, as their goals may not be shared at all times. Exhibit 2 shows a typical organization chart for a hotel with leased food and beverage operations. In this example, informal consulting relationships exist between the managers and owners of the two businesses. The restaurant manager and the hotel's sales department manager must also work closely together. These relationships are indicated by dotted lines.

Exhibit 1 Organization Chart: Management Positions in a Full-Service Hotel

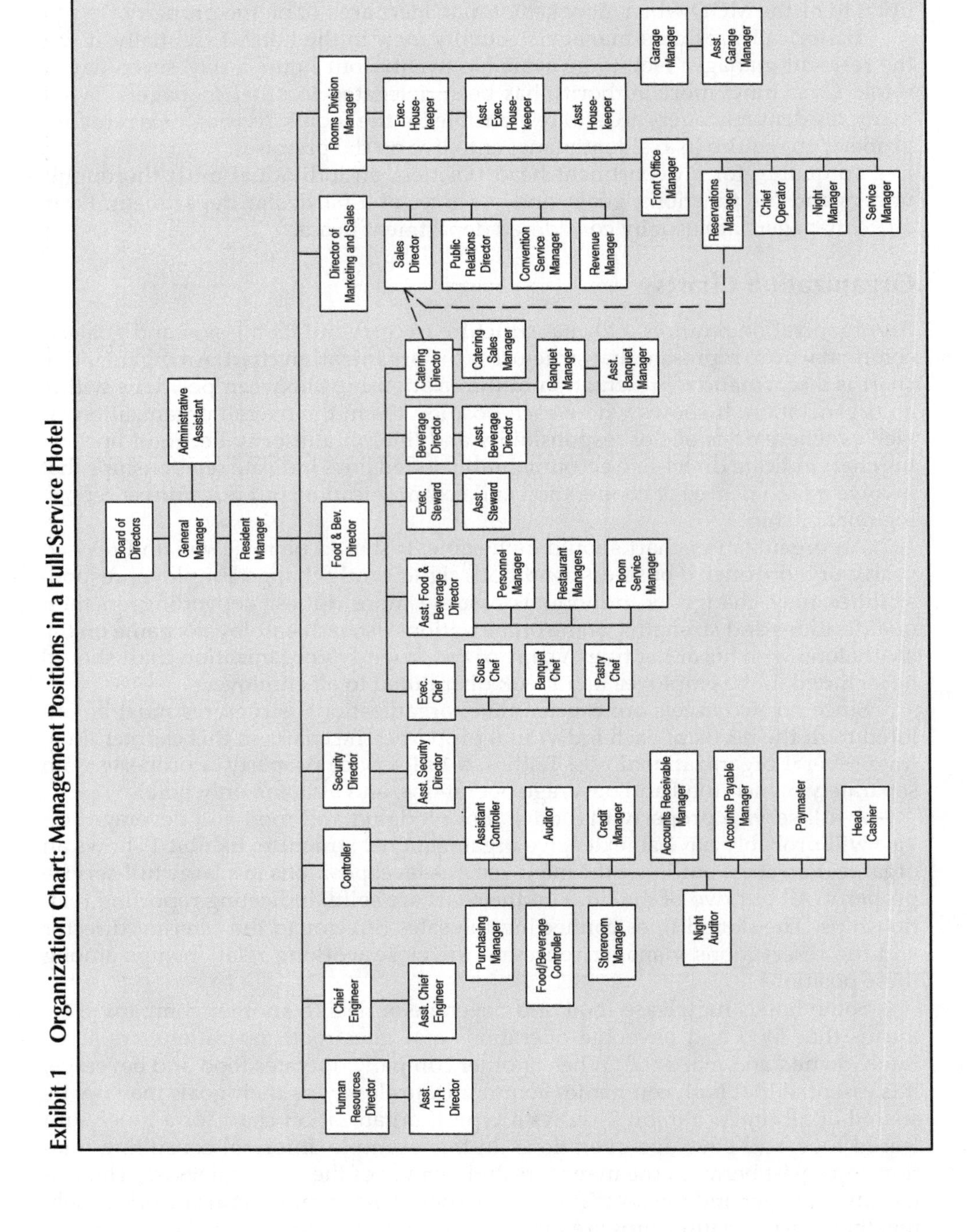

Exhibit 2 Organization Chart: Hotel with a Leased Food and Beverage Operation

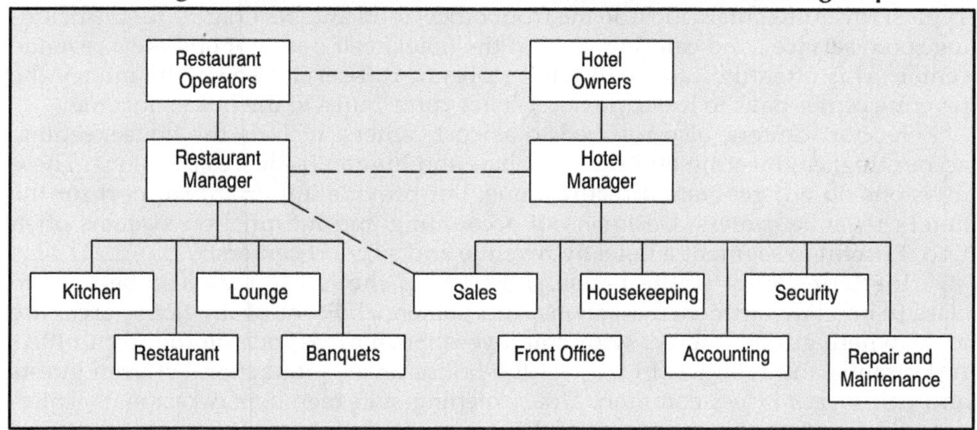

Exhibit 3 Organization Chart: Rooms-Only Hotel

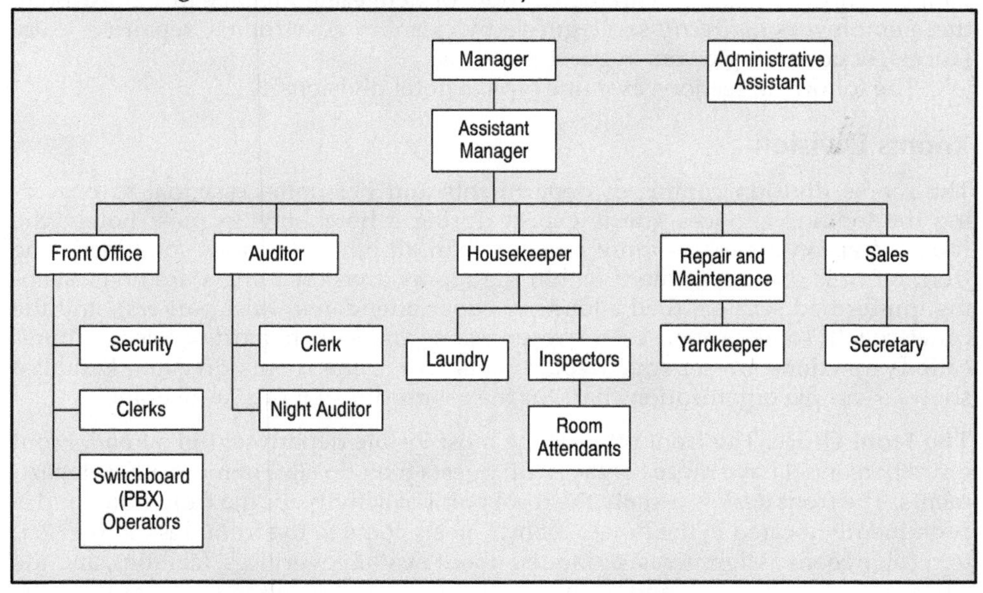

Exhibit 3 presents a possible organizational structure for a hotel without a restaurant. The charts in Exhibits 1–3 illustrate some of the many organizational variations possible among lodging properties.

Classifying Functional Areas

A hotel's divisions and departments (its *functional areas*) can be classified in almost as many ways as the hotel itself. One method involves classifying an operating division or department as either a **revenue center** or **support center.** A revenue center sells goods or services to guests, thereby generating revenue for the hotel. Typical revenue centers include the front office, food and beverage outlets (including room service), and catering. Even if the hotel itself does not operate a revenue center (as is often the case with retail stores or full-service spas), the money the revenue center pays to lease the hotel space contributes to the hotel's income.

Support centers, also referred to as cost centers, include the housekeeping, accounting, engineering and maintenance, and human resources divisions. These divisions do not generate direct revenue, but provide important support for the hotel's revenue centers. Designers of accounting and information systems often find it useful to segment a hotel by revenue and support centers.

The terms **front of the house** and **back of the house** may also be used to classify hotel departments, divisions, and personnel. Front-of-the-house areas are areas where guests interact with employees. Such areas include the front office, restaurants, and lounges. In back-of-the-house areas, interaction between guests and employees is less common. Housekeeping staff members occasionally interact with guests, but it is not part of their primary duties as it is for front desk and bell staff. Although back-of-the-house employees may not *directly* serve guests by taking an order, assisting with registration, or delivering luggage to a guestroom, these employees *indirectly* serve guests by cleaning guestrooms, repairing leaky faucets, or correcting errors in guest accounts.

The following sections examine typical hotel divisions.

Rooms Division

The rooms division comprises departments and personnel essential to providing the lodging services guests expect during a hotel stay. In most hotels, the rooms division generates more revenue than all other divisions combined. The front office is one department within the rooms division. Others are housekeeping, uniformed services (bell attendants, door attendants, valet parkers), and the concierge. In some properties, the reservations and switchboard or telecommunications functions are separate departments within the rooms division. Exhibit 4 shows a sample organization chart for the rooms division of a large hotel.

The Front Office. The front office is the most visible department in a hotel. Front office personnel have more contact with guests than do staff in most other departments. The front desk is usually the focal point of activity for the front office and is prominently located in the hotel's lobby. Guests come to the front desk to register; to receive room assignments; to inquire about available services, facilities, and the city or surrounding area; and to check out. The front desk often serves as the hotel control center for guest requests concerning housekeeping or engineering issues. International guests use the front desk to exchange currency, find a translator, or request other special assistance. In addition, it may also be a base of operations during an emergency, such as a fire or a guest injury.

Other front office functions include receiving and distributing mail, messages, and facsimiles (faxes), as well as guest cashiering. Cashiers post charges and payments to guest accounts, all of which are later verified during an account auditing procedure (often called the *night audit*). Front desk personnel also may verify outstanding accounts receivable, and produce daily reports for management. Some

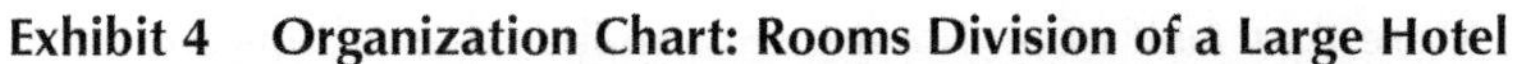

Exhibit 4 Organization Chart: Rooms Division of a Large Hotel

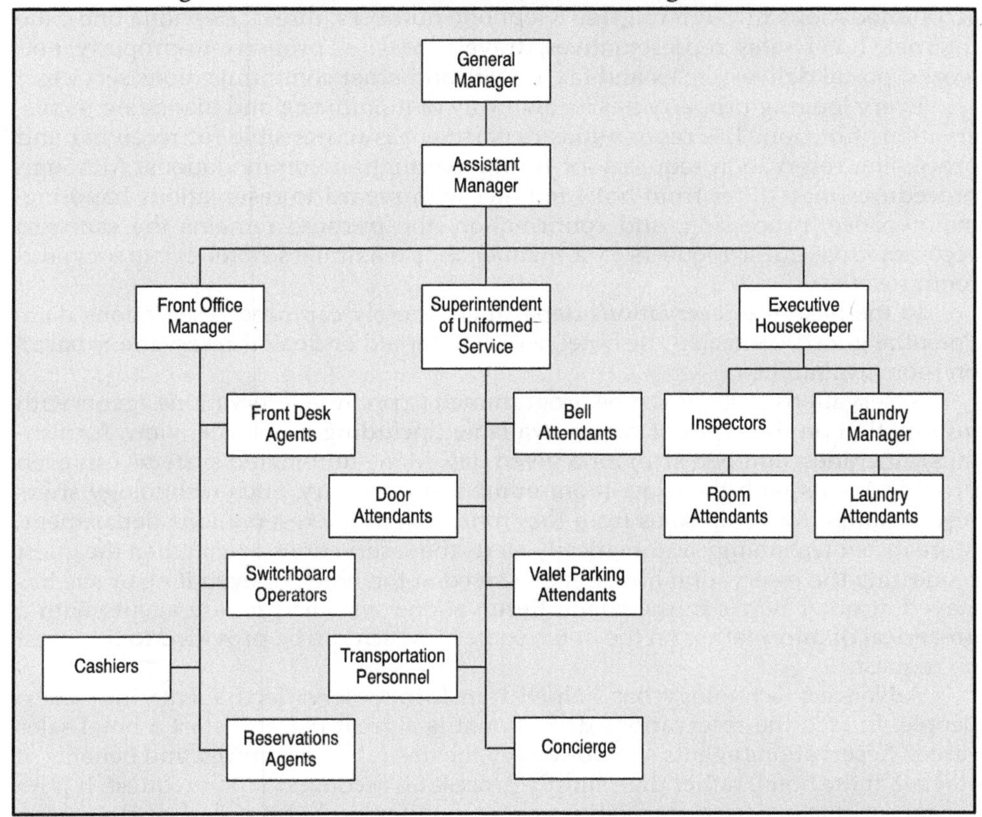

hotels have added concierge services to their list of front office functions. In a sense, concierge services are simply an extension of the guest services provided by front office personnel.

The functions of the front office are to:

- Sell guestrooms, register guests, and assign guestrooms.
- Process future room reservations, when there is no reservations department or when the reservations department is closed.
- Coordinate guest services.
- Provide information about the hotel, the surrounding community, and any attractions or events of interest to guests.
- Maintain accurate room status information.
- Maintain guest accounts and monitor credit limits.
- Produce guest account statements and complete proper financial settlement.

Reservations. More than half of all hotel guests make reservations for hotel accommodations through toll-free telephone numbers, direct telephone lines, the Internet, hotel sales representatives, travel agencies, property-to-property networks, postal delivery, telex and fax, e-mail, and other communications services.

Every lodging property has its own way of monitoring and managing its reservations function. The reservations department is responsible for receiving and processing reservation requests for future overnight accommodations. Although procedures may differ from hotel to hotel with regard to reservations handling, maintenance, processing, and confirmation, the purpose remains the same: to accommodate guest requests in a manner that maximizes hotel occupancy and room revenue.

In the past, the reservations department merely captured reservations data. Potential guests contacted the hotel, which accepted or denied reservations based on room availability.

Reservations systems can be programmed to provide reservations agents with information on the types of rooms available (including room rate, view, furnishings, amenities, and bed size) for a given day. Many automated systems can even provide agents with the exact room number if necessary. Such technology shifts responsibility for room sales from the front desk to the reservations department. More recent technology automatically alerts the reservations agent when the guest requesting the reservation has already stayed at the hotel, or even if he or she has stayed at other hotels in the chain. Reservations systems provide agents with a great deal of information on the hotel, some of which can be provided to the guest on request.

Advanced technology has helped transform reservations agents into salespeople. In fact, the reservations department is a great place to start a hotel sales career. Reservations agents should convey the desirability, features, and benefits of staying at the hotel, rather than simply process an accommodation request. It is no longer satisfactory for a reservations agent to defer to the front desk to determine a room's rate at registration. This shift in responsibility away from the front desk to the reservations department is important because it allows management to accurately forecast not only occupancy but revenue as well. Whenever possible, reservations agents should confirm the rate at the time the guest makes the reservation. In fact, most guests requesting a reservation will not book a room without receiving a confirmed rate. The reservations system should reinforce the guest's decision to stay at the property and provide sufficient information to satisfy guest inquiries.

It is essential for reservations department personnel to work closely with the hotel's sales and marketing division when group reservations are being solicited or processed. In fact, some hotel companies now place the reservations functions under the direction of the sales department instead of the front office. In any case, sales department representatives must be kept informed of room availability to ensure they know how many rooms are available in the reservations system on any given day. On a day-to-day basis, reservation managers must review reservations system reports and room availabilities to avoid *overbooking*. Overbooking can create bad feelings and contribute to lost business in the future. The management of reservations is further complicated by the fact that several states have enacted legislation prohibiting overbooking.

An additional dimension of reservations is the reservations department's coordination with the chain or referral group's reservation center, sometimes termed a *call center.* In most cases, reservation centers provide a significant portion of a hotel's occupancy. This is one of the most important reasons hotel owners affiliate with a chain or referral group. Reservation centers do much more than provide a convenient and inexpensive way for potential guests to make reservations. They have become communications hubs for the company, coordinating room availability and rates for airline reservation systems, Internet reservation sites, and other reservation channels.

Telecommunications. The telecommunications switchboard area or department maintains a complex communications network similar to that of any large company. The telecommunications department may also be called a **private branch exchange (PBX).** Hotel switchboard or PBX operators may have responsibilities that extend beyond answering and distributing calls to the appropriate extension. Switchboard operators may also place wake-up calls, answer questions about the hotel, monitor automated systems (such as door alarms and fire alarms), and coordinate emergency communications. Operators also protect guests' privacy, thereby contributing to the hotel's security program by not divulging guestroom numbers. Some hotels now instruct guests to call the hotel operator or a special guest service department for all service requests, including housekeeping, room service, and even bell service. Another recent trend involving guest safety with telephone systems is to have all house phones (telephones in public areas of the hotel used for calling within the hotel) ring the operator for call processing. This reduces the risk of unwanted or mistaken guestroom telephone calls. Many hotels also provide guest paging services over a public address system.

Recent technological advances have considerably decreased the responsibilities and workloads of telephone switchboard operators. Hotels have installed technology that allows guests to place their own room-to-room or outgoing phone calls. Most guestroom phones offer touchtone convenience and may feature call waiting or caller ID. Also available is guest voice mail, which reduces the reliance on hotel operators to record messages for guests and turn on message waiting lights in guestrooms. Call accounting systems can place direct-dialed calls over the least costly route available. Call accounting systems, which automatically price calls, also enable hotels to add surcharges and access charges to local and long-distance calls. Call accounting systems communicate with a front desk system to automatically post telephone charges to a guest's account. This reduces disputes at the front desk over charges for calls that were not actually completed.

Some hotels have installed answering devices for calls coming from outside the hotel. These automated answering devices, or AADs, direct callers to guest reservations, dining reservations, group sales, or other departments without the intervention of an operator. Voice messaging technology also can help improve the efficiency and effectiveness of incoming telephone traffic. In addition, voice messaging can allow callers to leave guest messages in their own voice, a service many guests appreciate.

Technology can also automatically place wake-up calls to guestrooms at preprogrammed times. With an automated system, when a front desk agent or switchboard operator receives a request for a wake-up call, he or she enters the room number and the desired time into the auto wake-up system. Some hotels have systems that allow guests to program the telephone to wake them up—without the assistance of a hotel employee. The system then places the wake-up call as specified, and plays a recorded message when the guest answers the phone. This can be especially helpful in large hotels where hundreds of wake-up calls for the same time may be requested. In world-class hotels, the system may alert the hotel operator to make the wake-up call at the requested time.

Uniformed Service. Employees in the hotel's uniformed service department generally provide the most personalized guest service. Given the high degree of attention this department pays to guests, some properties refer to uniformed service simply as *guest service.* Among the primary positions within the uniformed service department are:

- *Bell attendants,* who provide baggage service between the lobby area and the guestroom.
- *Door attendants,* who provide curb-side baggage service and traffic control at the hotel entrance.
- *Valet parking attendants,* who provide parking service for guests' vehicles.
- *Transportation personnel,* who provide transportation services for guests.
- *Concierges,* who are very knowledgeable about the local area and assist guests by making restaurant reservations; arranging for transportation; getting tickets for theater, sporting, or other special events; and so on.

While personnel in reservations, front desk, and communications areas affect guest perceptions, it is often employees in uniformed service who make a lasting impression. This is especially true in world-class or luxury hotels that offer a broad range of guest services. Uniformed service employees are usually classified as tipped employees, since a portion of their income is derived from guests' gratuities. To some degree, uniformed service personnel can affect their income through the quality and frequency of service they provide. While uniformed service jobs may not appear complex, they are critical to the smooth operation of a hotel. Quite often it is the ability of uniformed service staff to properly anticipate guest needs and communicate effectively with guests that makes the difference in the hotel's service quality.

Among the major challenges the manager of the uniformed service department faces are: setting the proper service standards, recruiting and training employees, and ensuring that employees successfully provide quality service. Since uniformed service employees generally receive among the lowest hotel wages, keeping them trained and motivated can be an enormous job. Without a doubt, well-motivated uniformed service employees can enhance the hotel's image while earning a good income through a combination of wages and tips. Providing excellent service can be personally rewarding as well.

Bell attendants. Many guests arrive at a hotel with heavy baggage or several pieces of luggage. Guests receive help handling this luggage from probably the best-known employee on the uniformed service staff: the bell attendant.

Bell attendants should be carefully selected. Since most hotels have carts for transporting baggage, the physical ability to actually *carry* the baggage is not a critical job qualification, although heavy lifting is often involved. More important, bell attendants should have strong oral communication skills and should display genuine interest in each guest. Depending on the size and complexity of the hotel, bell attendants may be counted on to:

- Transport guest luggage to and from guestrooms.
- Familiarize guests with the hotel's facilities, services, and safety features, as well as the guestroom and any in-room amenities.
- Provide a secure area for guests requiring temporary luggage storage.
- Provide information on hotel services and facilities, as well as group functions.
- Deliver mail, packages, messages, and special amenities to guestrooms.
- Pick up and deliver guest laundry and dry cleaning.
- Perform light housekeeping services in lobby and entry areas.
- Help guests load and unload their luggage in the absence of a door attendant.
- Notify other departments of guest needs, such as informing the housekeeping department if a guest requests a crib or extra towels.

While many of these tasks appear simple, they all require a degree of professionalism. For example, to assist a guest with his or her luggage, the bell attendant must know how to properly load a luggage cart. Fragile items must not be placed below heavy items. The cart must also be properly balanced so that it does not tip over or become difficult to steer.

Due to their direct contact with guests, bell attendants have an opportunity to communicate vital information to them and help them feel welcome at the hotel. A bell attendant who consistently and clearly conveys a warm welcome and proper information to each guest is a very valuable employee. One of a hotel's best marketing opportunities arises when the bell attendant escorts the guest to his or her room. Familiarity with the area outside the hotel, as well as with the hotel's restaurants, entertainment lounges, recreational activities, meeting rooms, and safety and security measures, is an important part of the job. It is through informal conversation that bell attendants become key players in the hotel's sales and marketing efforts. Bell attendants should make an extra effort to learn guests' names and perhaps the purpose of their stay. This makes guests feel especially welcome and allows bell attendants to provide more personal service.

Door attendants. Door attendants play a role similar to bell attendants: they are dedicated to welcoming guests to the hotel. Door attendants are generally employed in hotels offering world-class or luxury service. Some of the duties door attendants perform include:

- Opening hotel doors and assisting guests upon arrival.
- Helping guests load and unload luggage from vehicles.

- Escorting guests to the hotel registration area.
- Controlling vehicle traffic flow and safety at the hotel entrance.
- Hailing taxis, upon request.
- Assisting with valet parking services.
- Performing light housekeeping services in the lobby and entry areas.

Like bell attendants, door attendants must be well informed about hotel facilities and the local community. Guests frequently ask door attendants for directions to businesses, government offices, transportation centers, restaurants, and local landmarks and attractions. One of the most challenging responsibilities for a door attendant is controlling vehicle traffic at the hotel entrance. Controlling vehicle traffic can be a very demanding job, especially when the hotel is busy.

Experienced door attendants are capable of handling all these tasks with aplomb. A skilled, experienced door attendant learns the names of frequent guests. When these guests return to the hotel, the door attendant is able to greet them *by name* and can introduce them to other front office staff. Such personal service enhances the reputation of the hotel and provides the guest with a unique experience.

Valet parking attendants. Valet parking is generally available at hotels offering world-class or luxury service. Specially trained employees park guest and visitor automobiles. The personal attention and security of valet parking service is considered both a luxury and a convenience. Guests do not have to worry about finding a parking space, walking to the hotel in inclement weather, or finding their vehicles in the parking lot. Hotels generally charge a higher fee for valet parking than for self-service parking. In addition to paying the higher fee for valet parking, guests are also likely to tip the valet parking attendant.

Valet parking attendants are also responsible for the security of vehicles being moved to and from the hotel entrance. Attendants should not take a car into their care without issuing a receipt to the guest or visitor, usually in the form of a ticket. On the hotel portion of the ticket, the attendant should note any existing damage to the vehicle. Vehicle keys must be kept in a secure area and issued only by qualified personnel. Cars should not be issued to guests or visitors without proper documentation; in most cases, guests or visitors must return the receipt or ticket issued by the attendant before they can receive their keys. If a key is lost or given to the wrong person, the vehicle can be rendered inoperable or considered stolen and the hotel may be held financially responsible.

The uniformed service department is responsible for all vehicles under its care, and reports information to the front desk each night so that parking charges can be posted to guest accounts. In addition, when the vehicle entrance to the hotel is busy, valet parking attendants should help keep the area running smoothly by providing traffic control assistance.

Transportation personnel. Already common at most airport hotels, transportation services and departments are gaining in popularity at other types of properties. Many airport hotels offer complimentary bus service between the airport and the hotel on a regular schedule. In some cases, a guest can simply step from an airport's baggage claim section to a conveniently located courtesy van area. In other cases, the guest must telephone the hotel before being picked up. Some hotels provide direct-connect phone lines through a courtesy board at the airport for guest convenience.

Bus or courtesy van drivers must be well trained and properly licensed to operate hotel vehicles. Since these drivers are sometimes the first contact the guest will have with the hotel, it is important that they be polite, efficient, and knowledgeable about the property. It is generally customary for drivers to provide some information about the hotel while in transit, either through a live spoken presentation or a pre-recorded audiotape. Drivers should also help guests entering and exiting the vehicle. An experienced driver efficiently and carefully loads guest luggage into the van. As a result of such assistance, guests won't have to wrestle with heavy bags while entering and exiting the vehicle. Many hotels have equipped vans with two-way radios. While these radios are provided primarily for safety and scheduling reasons, drivers may ask guests for their names and relay the information to the hotel. This allows the hotel to prepare for guests before their actual arrival.

Another recent addition at many hotels is providing courtesy transportation service to local business, shopping, entertainment, sporting, and dining establishments. At some properties, limousines may be made available to VIP guests. Transportation personnel may be classified as either tipped or non-tipped employees.

In all cases, drivers must present the proper image of the hotel. Guest privacy must be maintained, especially in limousines. Any conversations among guests must be considered confidential and should not be discussed with hotel employees, family, or friends. Also, traffic safety is a critical concern. Drivers must be licensed according to state and federal laws. They must know how to check their vehicles to ensure that all equipment is working correctly. Safety equipment, such as flares and fire extinguishers, must be checked regularly, and drivers must be familiar with their use.

Concierges. Even though this guest service position has existed for quite some time, the concierge is perhaps the least understood position in the uniformed service area. In the distant past, the concierge was the castle doorkeeper. The concierge's job was to ensure that all the castle occupants were secure in their rooms at night. The concierge often accompanied traveling royalty to provide security and to travel ahead of the royal party to finalize food and lodging arrangements. As hotels became more common in Europe, the concierge eventually became part of the staff that provided personalized guest services. It is common to find a concierge at a world-class or luxury hotel.

Certified concierges may display prominent crossed gold keys on their jacket lapel. To earn these keys, a concierge must be certified by the international association of concierges, known as **Les Clefs d'Or** (Golden Keys). This concierge association has established high standards for its members. While many hotels employ experienced staff to assist guests with special needs, the title concierge technically applies only to members of Les Clefs d'Or.

Concierges may provide custom services to hotel guests. Duties include making reservations for dining, securing tickets for theater and sporting events, arranging for transportation, and providing information on cultural events and local attractions. Concierges are known for their resourcefulness. Getting tickets to sold-out concerts or successfully making last-minute dinner reservations at a crowded restaurant are expected of a good concierge. Most successful concierges have developed an extensive network of local, regional, and national contacts for a variety of services. Especially important, however, are the local contacts the concierge has established at restaurants, box offices, car rental offices, airlines, printers, and other businesses. Some hotels actually encourage concierges to visit appropriate businesses and organizations to establish and strengthen such relationships. Finally, a highly successful concierge should speak several languages.

With the implementation of advanced technology throughout the hotel, guests may require assistance in accessing and using such devices, networks, or systems. For this reason, some hotels employ a *technology concierge,* a staff member who specializes in assisting guests with technology issues. For example, if the hotel offers in-room high-speed Internet access and the guest is unable to access the network, the technology concierge may be dispatched to help resolve the issue.

The concierge position is generally a salaried position, but gratuities from guests are common expressions of gratitude for exemplary service. In some hotels, the head concierge is the manager of the uniformed service department. When this is the case, the head concierge assumes additional responsibilities for supervising all uniformed service personnel. In large hotels, the head concierge is often too busy to undertake such tasks and supervises employees in the concierge department only.

As mentioned in the introduction to this chapter, service is becoming more important in attracting guests and maintaining their ongoing loyalty. In many hotels offering world-class and mid-range accommodations and services, the role of the full-service concierge or guest-service staff is becoming a key to establishing the reputation of the hotel.

Housekeeping. Housekeeping is perhaps the most important support department for the front office. Like the front office, housekeeping usually is part of the rooms division of the hotel. In some hotels, however, the housekeeping function is considered an independent hotel division. This is especially true in very large or convention hotels, where the housekeeping staff may number several hundred employees. Effective communication among housekeeping and front office personnel can contribute to guest satisfaction while helping the front office to effectively monitor guestroom status. Housekeeping employees clean occupied and vacated rooms, inspect rooms before releasing them for sale, and communicate the status of guestrooms to the front office. At most properties, a front desk agent cannot assign a guestroom until the room has been cleaned, inspected, and released by the housekeeping department.

The housekeeping department often employs a larger staff than other departments in the rooms division. Normally, an executive housekeeper is in charge of the department, aided by an assistant housekeeper. In large hotels there can be several assistant housekeepers, each responsible for specific floors, sections, or, in very large hotels, entire buildings. The department also includes inspectors, room attendants, housepersons, lobby and general cleaners, and laundry personnel. Room attendants are assigned to specific sections of the hotel. Depending on the hotel's service level, average guestroom size, and cleaning tasks, room attendants may clean eight to eighteen rooms per shift. If the hotel has its own laundry, housekeeping department staff may clean and press the property's linens, towels, and uniforms, and may also launder guest clothing.

Housekeeping personnel (usually executive housekeepers) are responsible for maintaining two types of inventories: recycled and non-recycled. Recycled inventories are those items that have a relatively limited useful life but are used repeatedly in housekeeping operations. These inventories include such items as linens, uniforms, and guest amenities like irons and hair dryers. Non-recycled inventories are items that are consumed or worn out during the course of routine housekeeping operations. Non-recycled inventories include cleaning supplies, small equipment items, and guest supplies and personal grooming items. Guest amenities and linens are among the items and conveniences most often requested by guests.

To ensure the speedy, efficient rooming of guests in vacant and inspected rooms, the housekeeping and front office departments must promptly inform each other of any change in a room's status or availability. Teamwork between housekeeping and the front office is essential to effective hotel operations. The more familiar housekeeping and front office personnel are with each other's departmental procedures, the smoother the relationship.

Food and Beverage Division

The hotel's food and beverage division generally ranks second to the rooms division in terms of total revenue. Many hotels support more than one food and beverage outlet. There are almost as many varieties of hotel food and beverage operations as there are hotels. Possible outlets include quick-service, table-service, and specialty restaurants, coffee shops, bars, lounges, and clubs. The food and beverage division also typically supports other hotel functions such as room service, catering, and banquet planning. Banquets, normally held in the hotel's function rooms, may represent tremendous sales and profit opportunities for the food and beverage division. Hotels that appeal to group and convention business typically generate large amounts of banquet and catering revenues. In group hotels, catering opportunities may extend to the guestrooms, where suites often serve as settings for special hospitality parties given by companies. These are often upscale events, providing good opportunities for creativity on the part of the catering department. Catered functions, such as weddings and anniversaries, may also provide significant revenue opportunities for the food and beverage division.

Sales and Marketing Division

The size of a hotel's sales and marketing staff can vary from one part-time employee to more than a dozen full-time employees. In small properties, the general manager often fulfills all of the sales and marketing roles. In large hotels, the sales and marketing responsibilities are typically divided into five functions: sales, **revenue management,** convention services, advertising, and public relations. The primary goal of the division is to promote the sale of hotel products and services. To this end, sales and marketing staff members need to coordinate their efforts with the front office and other hotel divisions to effectively assess and communicate guest needs.

Marketing employees strive to attract guests to the hotel. They research the marketplace, competing products, guest needs and expectations, and future demand. Based on their findings, they then develop advertising and public relations programs for the hotel. Sales staff, on the other hand, strive to create revenue through the direct sale of hotel products to guests and groups. Front desk agents also may act as salespersons, especially when negotiating with and registering **walk-in** guests. In many hotels, the reservations office works very closely with the sales department, and serves in a sales role when guests call the hotel to make reservations.

Revenue Management. The revenue manager is responsible for ensuring that the hotel is maximizing its revenue by balancing the room rates guests pay with hotel occupancy. The challenge the manager faces is to secure the highest possible room rate for each potential guest, while not turning away any potential guests simply because room rates are too high. The revenue manager works cooperatively with the sales department, the reservations department, and often other departments to determine which room rate strategies should be applied to ensure that the hotel achieves its room revenue goals. Hotel sales team members often check with the revenue manager before quoting room rates for groups or local business associates. The revenue manager also establishes room rates for the reservation office and works with the hotel's many distribution channels, which include the hotel's website, corporate Internet sites, third-party websites, airline reservation systems, visitors' bureaus, and others. Revenue management often extends beyond room rates, and considers non-room revenues in order to optimize the property's total revenue opportunities. In small hotels, the front office manager, the reservations manager, or the general manager may also serve as the revenue manager. Often hotels of the same brand are "clustered" geographically and assigned to a single revenue management department designed to effectively serve multiple hotels.

Accounting Division

A hotel's accounting division monitors the financial activities of the property. Some hotels use off-premises accounting services to complement the work of their internal accounting division. In this case, the hotel's staff collects and transmits data to a service bureau or chain headquarters. A hotel that performs its accounting work on the premises will employ a larger accounting staff with a higher level of responsibility.

Accounting activities include paying outstanding invoices, distributing unpaid statements, collecting amounts owed, processing payroll, accumulating operating data, and compiling financial reports. In addition, the accounting staff may be responsible for making bank deposits, securing cash loans, and performing other control and processing functions as required by hotel management. In many hotels, the night audit and the food and beverage audit are considered accounting division activities.

The accounting division's success depends on close coordination with the front office. The front office cashiering and guest accounting functions include monitoring cash, checks, payment cards, and other methods of guest account settlement. The most common financial transactions handled by front office staff members are receiving cash payments, verifying personal checks, processing payment cards, tendering change, and monitoring guest account statements. In small hotels, the front office is also responsible for monitoring the credit status of registered guests.

Engineering and Maintenance Division

A hotel's engineering and maintenance division is responsible for maintaining the property's structure and grounds, as well as its electrical and mechanical equipment. This division may also be charged with swimming pool sanitation, parking lot cleanliness, and fountain operations (some hotels, however, may have a separate grounds department or an outdoor and recreation department for these tasks). Quite often, the operation of the hotel's safety equipment comes under the engineering and maintenance division as well.

Not all engineering and maintenance work is handled by the hotel's staff. Often, problems or projects require outside contracting. For example, special skills may be needed to calibrate building controls, charge fire extinguishers, and test and adjust building fire alarms. The special equipment that cleans kitchen duct work, disposes of grease and other refuse, or removes snow from parking lots may require that these tasks be contracted. Since some of the work of the engineering and maintenance division must be done in cooperation with the housekeeping department, some hotels have combined housekeeping and engineering into a single unit called the Operations Department.

The front office must efficiently exchange information with a representative of the engineering and maintenance division to ensure guest satisfaction. A guest complaint about a leaky faucet, malfunctioning lamp, or sticking lock shouldn't rest with a front desk agent but should be written up and quickly relayed to engineering and maintenance staff for corrective action. Conversely, front desk staff must be informed quickly about maintenance problems that render a room unsuitable for sale. They also must be informed when the room becomes ready for sale again.

Security Division

While all employees at every hotel should be concerned about the safety and security of hotel guests, visitors, and employees, many properties have a security division that is dedicated to these responsibilities. Security staff may include in-house personnel, contract security officers, and off-duty or retired police officers. Security responsibilities may include patrolling the property; monitoring surveillance equipment; and, in general, ensuring that guests, visitors, and employees are safe and secure. Critical to the effectiveness of the security division is the cooperation and assistance of local law enforcement officials.

A hotel's security program is strongest when employees outside the security division participate in security efforts. For example, front desk agents play a critical part in key control by issuing guestroom keys to registered guests *only*. Room attendants practice security when they verify a guest's room key *before* allowing that guest to enter a room they are cleaning. All employees should be wary of suspicious activities anywhere on the premises, and report such activities to the security staff. A key role of the security division is to ascertain that the hotel staff is strongly aware of safety issues through training and enforcement of standards. Hotel management should maintain strong, positive relationships with the local safety agencies as part of its ongoing safety and security program.

Human Resources Division

Hotels have increased their investment in and dependence on human resources management. The size and budgets of human resources divisions have grown steadily, along with their responsibility and influence. This expanded role is mirrored by the growing preference for the broader term *human resources management* over *personnel management.* In properties that are not large enough to justify a separate human resources office or division, the hotel's general manager often supervises the human resources function. When a hotel company has several properties in an area, it may choose to "cluster" the human resources function. With this arrangement, the hotel company has one main office and a skilled human resources manager to serve all the properties in the area. This reduces the cost for each hotel and brings a higher level of knowledge to all of the hotels.

Recently, the scope of the human resources division has changed in response to new government legislation, a shrinking labor pool, and growing pressures from competition. Although techniques have changed, the basic functions of the human resources division remain the same: employment (including external recruiting and internal reassignment), training, employee relations (including quality assurance), compensation, benefits, administration (including employee policies), labor relations, and safety.

Other Divisions

Many hotels staff a variety of other divisions to serve their guests. The range of possibilities reflects the diversity of hotels.

Retail Outlets. Lodging properties often establish gift shops, newsstands, or other retail outlets in their lobbies or other public areas. These outlets generate revenue for the hotel based on a percentage of sales or a fixed space rental fee.

Recreation. Some hotels—primarily resorts—staff a division dedicated to providing group and individual recreational activities for guests. Some recreation divisions also undertake landscaping the property's grounds and maintaining the swimming pool. Golf, tennis, bowling, snorkeling, sailing, walking tours, bicycle trips, horseback riding, hikes, and other activities may be arranged by recreation division staff. The division may also plan and direct activities such as arts and crafts shows or children's programs. Typically, recreation employees collect fees for organized activities or arrange for charges to be posted to guest accounts.

Casino. Casino hotels have a casino division that operates games of chance for guests and protects the property's gambling interests. The casino division may offer various forms of entertainment and other attractions to draw customers into the property and its gambling facilities. For casino hotels, revenues derived from gambling are usually larger than revenues from hotel operations. Therefore, casino priorities may take precedence over hotel priorities.

Front Office Operations

Traditional front office functions include reservations, registration, room and rate assignment, guest services, room status, maintenance and settlement of guest accounts, and creation of guest history records. The front office develops and maintains a comprehensive database of guest information, coordinates guest services, and ensures guest satisfaction. Employees in diverse areas of the front office perform these functions.

While no industry standards exist for front office positions, front office organization charts can help to define departmental reporting and working relationships. The highest level of employee and guest satisfaction can be ensured through a carefully designed front office organization, together with comprehensive and well-planned goals and strategies, work shifts, job descriptions, and job specifications.

Organization of the Front Office

Large hotels often organize the front office according to functions, with different employees handling separate areas. This division of duties can enhance the control the front office has over its own operations. Front office personnel can provide more specialized attention if each area is responsible for only one segment of the guest's stay. Such a separation of duties may not be practical in a small hotel, where it is common for one or two individuals to handle all front desk operations.

The front office in a large hotel supports many positions with a considerable separation of duties. These positions typically include, but are not limited to:

- *Front desk agents,* who register guests and maintain room availability information.
- *Cashiers,* who handle money, post charges, and oversee guest account settlement.
- *Information clerks,* who take messages, provide directions to guests, and handle facsimiles (faxes) and packages.
- *Telephone operators,* who manage the switchboard and coordinate wake-up calls.
- *Reservations agents,* who respond to reservation requests and create reservation records.
- *Uniformed service agents,* who handle guest luggage and escort guests to their rooms.

If a hotel is automated, each employee may be restricted to accessing only those electronic records pertinent to his or her function.

The front office of a mid-size hotel performs the same functions, but with fewer employees. Staff members are often cross-trained, and job duties are typically combined. For example, a front desk agent may also serve as a cashier and information clerk. He or she may also be trained to assume the duties of a switchboard operator and a reservations agent in their absence. During busy periods, several agents may work at the same time. Although each agent may be assigned identical duties, the agents may informally divide the functions among themselves. For example, one agent may register guests and handle the switchboard, another may function as a cashier, and a third may handle reservations and information requests.

Small hotels may have a single front desk agent who performs nearly all the functions with little assistance. If the front desk agent becomes overwhelmed by the workload, the general manager or accountant, if properly trained, can help relieve the burden. In a small property, the general manager and accountant often become more directly involved with front office operations.

Work Shifts

A forty-hour workweek is the typical workload for front office employees in most hotels. Federal and state wage and hour laws apply to the front office, and, in addition, some properties may be bound by union contracts and rules. A front office employee may work any one of the property's work shifts, depending on the front office's needs and the staff member's availability. Traditional front office work shifts are:

- Day shift   7 A.M.–3 P.M.
- Evening shift   3 P.M.–11 P.M.
- Night shift   11 P.M.–7 A.M.

A recent trend in front office operations is to provide a limited level of guest service during late night hours, thereby reducing the number of employees required on the night shift. In mid-size and smaller hotels, the night auditor also serves as the front desk agent.

Front office work shifts may vary with guest business patterns. A program of flexible work hours, or **flextime,** allows employees to vary the time they start and end work. Certain busy hours during a work shift, however, may require the presence of a majority of the staff. For example, one front desk agent may work from 6 A.M. to 2 P.M. so that wake-up calls and check-outs can be handled more efficiently through the 7 A.M. shift change. On the other hand, scheduling a front desk agent to work from 10 A.M. to 6 P.M. may allow for smooth processing of late-morning check-outs and guest arrivals during the time when evening shift personnel are scheduled for a meal break.

Other types of alternative scheduling include variations on the traditional workweek of five 8-hour days. A **compressed work schedule** occurs when an employee works 40 hours in fewer than five days (for instance, four 10-hour days). **Job sharing** is an arrangement in which two or more part-time employees share the responsibilities of one full-time position. Each worker may perform all aspects of the position on alternate days, or divide the duties while the employees work simultaneously.

Part-time employees are an increasingly important source of labor for the hospitality industry. Many potential workers, such as students, parents of young children, and retirees, may not be available to work full time. Part-time workers give the front office the flexibility to respond to fluctuating guest demands while reducing overall labor costs. Alternative scheduling programs, however, require careful planning and evaluation before implementation.

Job Descriptions

A **job description** lists all the tasks that are required of a work position. A job description may also outline reporting relationships, additional responsibilities, working conditions, necessary equipment and materials, and other important information specific to the place of employment. To be most effective, job descriptions should be customized to the operational procedures of a specific lodging property. Job descriptions should be task-oriented; they should be written for a position, not for a particular employee. Job descriptions will become dated and inappropriate as work assignments change, so they should be reviewed at least once a year for possible revision. Typically, front office managers write job descriptions. Employees should also be involved in writing and revising their job descriptions. Properly written job descriptions can minimize employee anxiety by specifying the chain of command and the responsibilities of the job.

Well-written job descriptions can also be used:

- In evaluating job performance.
- As an aid in training or retraining employees.
- To prevent unnecessary duplication of duties.
- To help ensure that each job task is performed.
- To help determine appropriate staffing levels.

Each front office employee should receive a copy of the job description for his or her position. Final job candidates may also receive a copy of a job description, even before receiving a job offer. This is better than having someone accept a job offer and then decline it because he or she was unaware of the job's requirements.

A word of caution about job descriptions is appropriate. In the United States, job qualifications, and, therefore, job descriptions, are subject to certain federal laws. The Americans with Disabilities Act (ADA) states that people with disabilities are considered qualified for a position if they can perform the position's **essential functions** with or without **reasonable accommodation.** Job descriptions should be created before an open position is advertised, and they should list essential functions. Management must not discriminate against an applicant with a disability merely because the applicant cannot perform a non-essential function. Improper job descriptions may not only lead to improper hiring decisions, they may also expose the hotel to liability for illegal discrimination. At the same time, proper job descriptions may open opportunities for qualified applicants who have disabilities covered under the ADA.

Job descriptions play many roles in an organization. They should be used in the job interview, so that the person applying for a position understands what is expected of him or her. Job descriptions can also be used for promotion, transfer, or—in certain cases—disciplinary action. Therefore, having complete and accurate job descriptions is an essential part of managing front office operations, as well as any other hotel department. (The appendix at the end of this chapter presents a sampling of front office job descriptions.)

Job Specifications

Job specifications list the personal qualities, skills, and traits an employee needs in order to successfully perform the tasks outlined in a job description. Basically, front office job specifications spell out front office management's expectations for current and prospective employees; they are typically prepared by the front office manager with input from front office employees. Job specifications are usually developed after job descriptions, since a particular job may require special skills and traits. Factors considered for a job specification are: formal education, work experience, general knowledge, previous training, physical requirements, communication ability, and equipment skills. Job specifications often form the basis for advertising job opportunities and identifying eligible applicants; they may also help to identify current employees for promotion. A sample job specification for a generic front office staff member is shown in Exhibit 5.

Although standardized job specifications do not exist throughout the industry, certain traits and skills likely appear in job specifications in most hotels. Because of their high degree of guest and visitor contact, front office employees often must possess extraordinary interpersonal skills. Evaluating an applicant on the basis of these traits may be highly subjective. Nonetheless, traits important to front office work include:

- Professional demeanor
- Congenial, outgoing personality
- Helpful attitude
- Good diction, grammar, and speaking voice
- Flexibility
- Well-groomed appearance
- Willingness to learn
- Orientation to detail

Successful performance of front office procedures usually requires general skills acquired through education and experience. Valuable employees possess practical skills, knowledge, and aptitude. Mathematical abilities (for cashiering and accounting tasks) and keyboarding (for recordkeeping and computer operation) are often necessary in front office work. Some hotels may find it beneficial to have employees in the front office who speak more than one language, to better serve international guests.

Front office personnel must be team players. They must be willing to work together for the benefit of the entire operation.

Summary

The services that result from a hotel's smooth operation are highly visible to guests. Guests are more likely to return to or recommend a lodging property if they enjoy their stay. For a hotel to run effectively and efficiently, every employee must understand and work to achieve the property's mission. The hotel's mission

Exhibit 5 Sample Job Specification: Front Office Positions

Job Specification
Front Office Personnel

Our property considers the following traits important for the successful performance of front office work.

1. *Professional Demeanor*
   - Reports to work on time
   - Has a positive attitude toward the job and the hotel
   - Recognizes positive and negative aspects of the job
   - Possesses maturity in judgment
   - Appears businesslike
   - Maintains control and composure in difficult situations
2. *Congenial Nature*
   - Smiles readily
   - Exhibits cordial and pleasant behavior
   - Is a people person
3. *Helpful Attitude*
   - Is sensitive to the guests' needs
   - Possesses a sense of humor
   - Responds and speaks intelligently
   - Demonstrates creativity
   - Practices good listening skills
4. *Flexibility*
   - Willing and able to accept a different workshift if necessary
   - Understands others' points of view
   - Willing to try new ways of doing things; innovative
   - Works well with guests and hotel staff; a team player
5. *Well-Groomed Appearance*
   - Dresses appropriately; meets property standards for personal grooming, wearing jewelry, and the wearing of and caring for his or her employee uniform (if applicable)

statement expresses the underlying philosophy that gives meaning and direction to hotel policies. The mission statement should address the interests of three diverse groups: guests, management, and employees. A sound mission statement should address guests' expectations, reflect management's philosophy, and provide hotel employees with a sense of purpose.

The front office is typically responsible for developing and maintaining a comprehensive database of guest information, coordinating guest services, and ensuring guest satisfaction. Large hotels tend to organize the front office by functional areas in order to enhance control over operations. In a computerized property, each employee may be restricted to accessing only those electronic records pertinent to his or her function.

A hotel operating department can be classified as either a revenue center or a support center. By definition, a revenue center sells goods or services to guests, thereby generating revenues. A support center does not generate direct revenue, but instead provides important backing for the hotel's revenue centers. The terms *front of the house* and *back of the house* also refer to hotel operational areas. Areas in the front of the house are those in which guests and employees directly interact. In back-of-the-house areas, there is little direct contact between guests and staff members. Although back-of-the-house employees may not directly serve guests (by, for example, taking an order, assisting with registration, or delivering luggage to guestrooms), they indirectly serve guests by cleaning guestrooms, repairing leaky faucets, or correcting errors in guest accounts. Typical hotel operating divisions and departments include rooms, reservations, food and beverage, sales and marketing, accounting, engineering and maintenance, security, and human resources.

A job description lists a majority of the tasks assigned to the position. A job description may also outline reporting relationships, additional responsibilities, working conditions, equipment and materials to be used, expected standards of performance, and other important information specific to the property. To be most effective, job descriptions should be customized to the operational procedures of a specific lodging property. Job specifications list the personal qualities, skills, and traits a person needs to successfully perform the tasks outlined in a job description. They can be used in promotions, transfers, and disciplinary actions. Several sample front office job descriptions are presented in the chapter appendix.

Key Terms

back of the house—The functional areas of a hotel in which staff have little or no direct guest contact, such as the engineering, accounting, and human resources divisions.

compressed work schedule—An adaptation of full-time work hours that enables an employee to work the equivalent of a standard workweek in fewer than the traditional five days.

essential functions—A term used in the Americans with Disabilities Act; according to government guidelines, the essential functions of a job are those functions or fundamental job duties that the individual who holds the position must be able to perform unaided or with the assistance of a reasonable accommodation.

flextime—A program of flexible work hours that allows employees to vary their times of starting and ending work.

front of the house—The functional areas of a hotel in which staff have extensive guest contact, such as the food and beverage facilities and the front office.

goals—Those activities and standards an organization must successfully perform or achieve to effectively carry out its mission.

job description—A detailed list identifying all the key duties of a job as well as reporting relationships, additional responsibilities, working conditions, and any necessary equipment and materials.

job sharing—An arrangement in which two or more part-time employees share the responsibilities of one full-time position.

job specification—A list of the personal qualities, skills, and traits necessary to successfully perform the tasks outlined in a job description.

Les Clefs d'Or—The international association of concierges; the title "concierge" technically applies only to members of Les Clefs d'Or.

mission statement—A document that states the unique purpose that sets a hotel apart from other hotels, expresses the underlying philosophy that gives meaning and direction to the hotel's actions, and addresses the interests of guests, management, and employees.

organization chart—A schematic representation of the relationships among positions within an organization, showing where each position fits into the overall organization and illustrating the divisions of responsibility and lines of authority.

private branch exchange (PBX)—A hotel's telephone switchboard equipment.

reasonable accommodation—A change in the usual way of doing a job so that a qualified person with a disability can participate, but a change that does not impose "undue hardship" on the employer.

revenue center—A hotel division or department that sells products or services to guests and thereby directly generates revenue for the hotel; the front office, food and beverage outlets, room service, and retail stores are typical hotel revenue centers.

revenue management—The practice of maximizing revenue by balancing the room rates guests pay with hotel occupancy. The challenge is securing the highest possible room rate for each potential guest, while not turning away any potential guest simply because room rates are too high.

strategy—A plan of action a department or division uses to achieve its goals.

support center—A hotel division or department that does not generate revenue directly, but supports the hotel's revenue centers; includes the housekeeping, accounting, engineering and maintenance, and human resources divisions.

tactics—The day-to-day operating procedures that staff members use to implement strategies.

walk-in—A person who arrives at a hotel without a reservation and requests a room.

Review Questions

1. What is the purpose of a hotel's mission statement? What are the three groups of people whose interests should be addressed in a hotel mission statement?
2. How do a hotel's goals relate to its mission statement and to departmental and divisional goals and strategies?
3. How does an organization chart show employee reporting and consulting relationships? Why should an organization chart be flexible?

4. Which hotel departments and divisions are typically classified as revenue centers? Why?
5. Which hotel departments and divisions are typically classified as support centers? Why?
6. What main divisions are typically found in the organization of a full-service hotel?
7. How may a limited-service hotel differ in its organization from a full-service hotel?
8. How does the front office interact with the rest of the rooms division and the other main divisions in a full-service hotel?
9. Why is it impossible for some front offices to divide employee duties according to function?
10. What are the three traditional front office work shifts? What variations on the traditional workweek might a hotel adopt?
11. How are job descriptions typically used? How do they differ from job specifications?

Internet Sites

For more information, visit the following Internet sites. Remember that Internet addresses can change without notice. If the site is no longer there, you can use a search engine to look for additional sites.

Americans with Disabilities Act (ADA)
www.ada.gov

Les Clefs d'Or (USA)
www.lcdusa.org

Case Study

Dark Days at Sunnyvale: Can Teamwork Part the Clouds?

The Sunnyvale Resort is a 300-room luxury property with a lake on one side and a golf course, riding stables, and tennis courts on the other. Once considered the premier resort of the South, the rich (both old and new money) considered it fashionable to winter at Sunnyvale back in the twenties and thirties. However, by the sixties, its glory had begun to fade and so had its revenues. In 1978, the resort added fifty suites and 20,000 square feet of meeting space in an effort to attract group business. This helped for a time, but in the last five years both occupancy and room rates were caught in a seemingly unstoppable decline. Recently, the resort lost a star in the travel guides and was now listed as a three-star property.

Losing a star spurred Thomas Redgrave to take action. Mr. Redgrave was the resort's owner, and he was not happy that a property that should be making $15 to $16 million a year in revenue had grossed less than $12 million in each of the last two years. He gave the general manager, who had been with the resort since 1977, a nice farewell dinner and a gold watch, then hired Ken Richards, an experienced general manager from a convention hotel in Richmond, to come in and turn things around.

At a meeting with Ken, Mr. Redgrave summed up the situation as he saw it. "I'd like to renovate Sunnyvale and really bring it back to where it ought to be. As a businessman, I know sometimes you have to spend money to make money. But I'd have to put several million dollars into the place to do it right. The way things are going at Sunnyvale right now, I'm not sure I'd get the kind of return on investment that I should.

"The last general manager was here long before I bought the place and he didn't communicate with me very much. I try to be a 'hands-off' owner and I gave him plenty of room, but for the last few years the numbers have been bad and getting worse, and he didn't seem to know what to do about it. I'll be honest—I don't know that much about the hotel business. But that's why I hired you. I want you to find out what's wrong and get the revenues back up to where they should be. If I see signs that you've got Sunnyvale back on track, I'll open the purse strings. It'll take some time, but we'll make everything at Sunnyvale first-class again. That'll make me happy, and down the road it'll make your job a whole lot easier."

From his experience at other properties, Ken knew that low occupancy and low rates were not the resort's real problems, only the symptoms. His first inspections of the property revealed quite a few minor blemishes—walls that needed painting, leaky showerheads, thin carpets, and so on. In fact, the entire resort, even the relatively new suites and meeting spaces, had an air of genteel shabbiness. But, more importantly, Ken took time during his first week to meet one-on-one with all of Sunnyvale's managers. He especially wanted to learn all he could about his department heads before calling his first executive staff meeting next Monday morning.

Skip Keener, the resort's director of sales, had been with Sunnyvale for over forty years and fondly remembered the resort's glory days. "When I first got here, the property sold itself," he told Ken. "Never had a problem filling the place up. We were featured in *Southern Living* magazine practically every year. But all of a sudden we fell out of fashion, and then in the seventies they put in all that meeting space that I have to sell to groups like vacuum-cleaner salesmen, the Kentucky Aluminum Siding Association, and the North Carolina Association of Used Car Dealers. This is the kind of business that keeps us going now. I tell you, the place sure isn't what it used to be."

The resort's executive housekeeper, Ruth Harless, had been with the property for almost thirty years and she missed the glory days, too. "It was a slower pace back then," she said. "Guests stayed longer—ten days, two weeks, even a month or more. You got to know them and they got to know you. Now, most guests are here for a big meeting and are out in two or three nights. It's 'rush, rush, rush.'" Ken learned that Ruth's reputation for upholding cleaning standards was not what it used to be. The comments he heard were: "She used to be a real stickler for detail—every room was spotless, but there's no denying that the rooms just aren't as clean anymore." Ken also learned that Ruth had stopped attending executive staff meetings years ago. "I don't have time," was her excuse.

Bob Ruggles was the resort's chief engineer. Since he had been with the property for "only" eleven years, Skip and Ruth still considered him "the new guy." "I don't know why, but I just never hit it off with them," he lamented to Ken. He also lamented the fact that, because the resort was old, every day he faced a large number of minor maintenance problems. "If it's not the plumbing, it's the electrical. If it's not the electrical, it's the HVAC system acting up. It's always something. I run to put out one 'fire' and two more take its place. I can't catch up."

The reservations manager, Teresa Mansfield, had been with the resort for three years and she was also considered a "newcomer." No one on the executive staff went out of the way to talk to her. One assistant manager from another department told Ken that "she seems angry about something all the time, but she never says much." Her complaint was that she was left out of the decision-making at the resort and was expected to just do as she was told. Skip frequently sold more rooms than were allocated to group sales, for example, without telling her. "I don't know exactly what rooms I can sell from one day to the next," she lamented.

The last, and newest, member of the executive staff was Jon Younger, the resort's food and beverage director. He had arrived at the property just six months ago, after the previous F&B director of twenty-eight years, Abe Williams, had retired. Unfortunately, Abe had chosen to coast into retirement, and the department's performance had declined during the last three years of his tenure. Smart and ambitious, Jon had tried to whip the F&B staff back into shape and restore the resort's reputation for F&B excellence, but his opportunities to shine had been few. Skip, the director of sales, had received so many F&B complaints from clients during Abe's last years that he had begun to book most of the big F&B group functions off-site, and "comp" a lot of the minor ones he allowed the resort's F&B department to handle (a complimentary cocktail party for a group's first night was a favorite giveaway). Jon had asked Skip to book more F&B functions in-house and had lobbied the previous general manager for support, but had made no headway. In his early thirties and feeling the pressure of his first job as a department head, Jon had become defensive and abrasive in his dealings with Skip and the others.

By Friday of Ken's first week, Sunnyvale's major difficulties were coming into focus. The sales department was so busy bringing in business that it wasn't communicating with the rest of the staff like it should. The result was confusion, poor service, and dissatisfied guests. To entice dissatisfied guests back to the resort, the sales staff was constantly lowering room rates. It was a downward spiral that Ken had to find a way to stop.

Next Monday morning, Ken began his first staff meeting by reassuring his department heads that the owner was committed to the resort's long-term health. "Mr. Redgrave wants to put a lot of money into the place and make it a four-star property again, but first he wants to see that we can turn the rates and occupancy around and beef up the bottom line. I'm committed to taking action quickly and I know all of you want to makes things better, too." Ken picked up a pen and a legal pad and surveyed the managers gathered around the table. "I've looked at the reports," he nodded toward a stack of papers on the table in front of him, "but I'm interested in hearing what all of you think. Does anyone have any ideas about why the revenue's been down the past few years?"

Silence hung over the room while the department heads looked at the table or shot sidelong glances at each other. Finally, Jon Younger spoke up. "I think a big problem is that we're giving too much F&B business away." Another silence descended on the group.

"Yes," Ken agreed after a while, trying to prompt more comments, "I noticed in the financial statements that the F&B lines seem very low for a resort of this size. What's going on there?"

"Well, I hate to say it," Skip said, "but I got so many complaints from clients that I finally decided I'd better send them off-site for F&B. I've lined up a few outside caterers that do a good job for me, and just up the road there's the Mountainview Gourmet Steakhouse. I send groups up there and they get steaks bigger than their plates, servers in Wild West costumes, skits and 'gunfights' and other entertainment while they eat—they love it."

"The problem with that," Jon said sharply, "is that Skip's not giving me a chance to show what I can do. Those complaints he's talking about happened back when Abe was here. And we're getting killed with all the comps he's giving away. Every group that comes in gets a comp cocktail party the first night, which wipes out the restaurant's dinner sales because everybody goes to the party and scarfs down the heavy hors d'oeuvres and free booze. Why not a banquet the first night? That's high-profit business that we really need."

"What about that, Skip?" Ken asked.

"Well, all I can say is that it's hard when a client looks you in the eye and says, 'Last time we booked here, the banquet was terrible—eight of my people stood around embarrassed because you under-set by eight places, you forgot the ice sculpture, the soup was cold, the entrées were late and most of them were cold, too, and I had to listen to my people griping about it the entire time I was here. So if you want me back you're gonna have to do something different.' A lot of my clients come back every year or two, and they remember the things that went wrong the last time."

Ken made a note on his pad. "But the problems your clients refer to didn't happen on Jon's watch, is that right?"

"True," Skip said. "But I still have to fight the perception that we can't deliver quality F&B."

Another silence descended on the group. Ken turned to Teresa. "What problems do you see in the reservations area?"

Teresa swallowed hard. It wasn't her usual style to speak up, but this might be the best time to get things out in the open with the new general manager. "Well, one thing that could be better," she began, "is that I'm never sure how many rooms Skip has sold, so occasionally I've had to turn guests away because of overbookings. But much more often we've suffered from 'underbookings.' That's when Skip asks for more rooms than he really needs, rooms I could have sold, but they stand empty because he blocked them off and then didn't need them for his groups. That happens a lot more than it should.

"It's also hard to have to sell the less-desirable rooms all the time," Teresa continued. "Skip tends to use up the suites and the nicer guestrooms—even the ones allocated to me—with his groups. To make it worse, I'm under pressure to sell those less-desirable rooms at a premium. The budget calls for a group rate of $150, but a lot of the time Skip gives groups a $120 rate. This pressures me to sell my allotment of rooms at an even higher rate than my budgeted target of $170 per room. That's hard to do when all the rooms that are left are at the end of the hall, or next to the laundry, or the ones with no view."

Skip crossed his arms over his chest. "Groups should get a break, especially with the kind of service they usually get around here. And part of your paycheck isn't riding on how many rooms you sell, like mine is. If you think it's easy selling ten thousand rooms a year, try it sometime!"

Ken turned to Skip. "You had to meet a 'rooms sold' target, not a revenue target?"

"Correct. No bonus unless I sold ten thousand rooms. It's not easy, especially when there's problems—VIPs standing in the lobby because their suites aren't ready, for example. Do you have any idea how hard it is to sell somebody the next time, when the first thing that happens to Mr. Bigshot is that he has to cool his heels in the lobby while his room is cleaned? Instead of getting ushered up to his nice suite and feeling pampered, he gets ticked off."

"Wait a minute," Ruth interrupted. "Whenever that happens, I always pull room attendants off their regular rooms so they can blitz through the suites and get them ready."

"Ready?" Skip snorted. "They're never as 'ready' as they should be! If I had a nickel for every time the fresh flowers and fruit baskets weren't placed in the suites like they're supposed to be—"

"I get them in the rooms every time I'm notified," Jon interjected.

"You're right, Jon, sometimes I forget to tell you," Ruth said defensively, "but I have my hands full just trying to 'rush rush rush' to get everything clean and get my crew back on their regular duties. It disrupts the entire day."

"What about the cleaning problems?" Skip asked Ruth. "It's embarrassing when the president of a state association comes to me—this happened just two weeks ago—and tells me his wife found a hairball in the bathtub drain and is afraid to take a shower now."

"What do you expect when you tell people they can check in at noon, when check-out time is noon, too?" Ruth said. "We're not given time to do a proper job."

"Does that happen a lot?" Ken asked. "I mean, people wanting to check in to suites that people have just checked out of?"

"All the time," Ruth said.

"So you have to do these 'cleaning blitzes' pretty often?" Ken laid a hand on the reports in front of him. "I noticed that housekeeping's labor costs are pretty high—all those blitzes helps explain that."

"They certainly happen more often than they should," Ruth replied. "And you're right, it's costly, because my crew has to stay later to finish their regular assignments. The overtime adds up."

"The guest complaints add up, too," Teresa said. "When Ruth pulls her crew from their regular assignments to blitz the suites, the regular guestrooms aren't getting done. So they get cleaned late, and those guests end up inconvenienced and unhappy. So the guest dissatisfaction ripples down through the entire resort."

"Also," Ruth added, "when you have ten minutes to try to whip a room into shape, you intentionally skip over some things and miss others, so the constant blitzing doesn't do my housekeepers any good, either. They start to get sloppy even when they aren't rushed. Some of them figure if a quick touch-up is okay for a VIP suite, it's okay for a regular guestroom, too. I really have to fight that attitude with some of my crew."

"We've got to plan a little better in the future," Ken said, scribbling in his legal pad.

"It's hard to plan when you don't get much advance notice about groups coming in or what their needs are," Teresa said pointedly, looking at Skip.

"It's one of the reasons I can never catch up," Bob chimed in. "I never know what's going on, either. I just get calls all the time: 'Leaky toilet in Room 113.' 'The guest in Suite 27 turned on the air conditioning and nothing happened.' Fine. I ask for the rooms for five days, then suddenly they have to be sold because a big group's coming in. The repairs aren't made, guests complain, and I get chewed out."

"And I have to lower the rates next time for that group," Skip said. "I call the client and he says a bunch of my people were unhappy last time, why should I come back? So I give him a break on the rates, comp the coffee breaks, breakfasts, what have you, to try to get him to come back for another year. Sometimes it works, and sometimes I lose a group."

"And my housekeepers are unhappy because they keep reporting maintenance problems that never get fixed," Ruth said. "They ask me why, and I don't know what to tell them, because I'm never told why either."

"If you would talk to me once in a while, I'd be glad to tell you," Bob said. "It's not all my fault. I can't get any cooperation out of anybody."

"Do you really need five days every time?" Teresa asked. "Cooperation is a two-way street, you know. Sometimes it's hard to keep a room 'out of order' that long."

"I'd like to have five days. I don't see why it's such a big deal."

"One room out for five days is not a big deal," Skip said, "but you keep adding rooms to your list, so eventually it gets to be a big deal."

Ken held up his hands to halt the discussion, then surveyed the group over steepled fingers. "Obviously there's a lot of frustration in this room. You're frustrated because you want to get your jobs done, but your co-workers—instead of helping you—are sometimes getting in the way. This not only frustrates you, it frustrates our guests as well, because they're not receiving the service they should." Ken paused. "You're not getting in each other's way on purpose, or because you want to make someone else's life miserable," Ken smiled. "I just think you're all too focused on your own areas and aren't seeing the big picture.

"From what I've heard today, I'd say our biggest problem is that we're not talking to each other. We've got to learn to communicate better so we can serve each other and our guests better. More communication will help bring the bigger picture into focus for everybody.

"I want to show Mr. Redgrave some positive changes within ninety days," Ken continued. "With that in mind, I'd like all of you to come to next Monday's staff meeting with ideas on how you can improve communication and work together better as a team. I'll think about it as well, and come to the meeting prepared with recommendations for each of you. I think teamwork will be the key to doing a better job of satisfying our guests and moving revenues in a positive direction."

Discussion Questions

1. What are the problems that each department experiences because of poor communication among the executive staff?

2. What recommendations can Ken make to each of the resort's department heads to help them work together as a team?
3. What actions should Ken take if his department heads, after a suitable period of time, don't seem to be coming together as a team?
4. What can Ken show Sunnyvale's owner in the next ninety days to demonstrate that the resort is making progress?

Case Number: 3322CA

The following industry experts helped generate and develop this case: Richard M. Brooks, CHA, Vice President, TWE Group; and S. Kenneth Hiller, CHA, General Manager, Holiday Inn, Beachwood, Ohio.

Chapter Appendix

Selected Front Office Model Job Descriptions

Cross-training front office employees has helped standardize procedures in many hotels. In a small hotel, for instance, one employee may handle reservations, registration, switchboard, and check-out tasks. Lines of responsibility have also blurred, as more and more properties adopt computerized front office recordkeeping systems. These systems can combine information required for most front office tasks in a common database that can be accessed by many front office employees.

Many hotels refer to front office employees as *front office agents, guest service representatives*, or something similar. Even in hotels with a traditional division of duties, the titles for each position may change over time. These changes may reflect a reevaluation of the tasks involved or an attempt to avoid the negativity associated with certain titles. The position titles that were used in this chapter represent trends in the lodging industry. This appendix presents generic model job descriptions for typical front office positions found in a mid-size hotel.

JOB DESCRIPTION

POSITION TITLE: FRONT OFFICE MANAGER

REPORTS TO: Assistant Manager or General Manager

POSITION SUMMARY: Directly supervises all front office personnel and ensures proper completion of all front office duties. Directs and coordinates the activities of the front desk, reservations, guest services, and telephone areas.

DUTIES AND RESPONSIBILITIES:

1. Participates in the selection of front office personnel.
2. Trains, cross-trains, and retrains all front office personnel.
3. Schedules the front office staff.
4. Supervises workloads during shifts.
5. Evaluates the job performance of each front office employee.
6. Maintains working relationships and communicates with all departments.
7. Maintains master key control.
8. Verifies that accurate room status information is maintained and properly communicated.
9. Resolves guest problems quickly, efficiently, and courteously.
10. Updates group information. Maintains, monitors, and prepares group requirements. Relays information to appropriate personnel.
11. Reviews and completes credit limit report.
12. Works within the allotted budget for the front office.
13. Receives information from the previous shift manager and passes on pertinent details to the oncoming manager.
14. Checks cashiers in and out and verifies banks and deposits at the end of each shift.
15. Enforces all cash-handling, check-cashing, and credit policies.
16. Conducts regularly scheduled meetings of front office personnel.
17. Wears the proper uniform at all times. Requires all front office employees to wear proper uniforms at all times.
18. Upholds the hotel's commitment to hospitality.

PREREQUISITES:

Education: Minimum of two-year college degree. Must be able to speak, read, write, and understand the primary language(s) used in the workplace. Must be able to speak and understand the primary language(s) used by guests who visit the workplace.

Experience: Minimum of one year of hotel front-desk supervisory experience, experience handling cash, accounting procedures, and general administrative tasks.

Physical: Requires fingering, grasping, writing, standing, sitting, walking, repetitive motions, verbal communications, and visual acuity.

JOB DESCRIPTION

POSITION TITLE: **FRONT DESK AGENT**

REPORTS TO: **Front Office Manager**

POSITION SUMMARY: Represents the hotel to the guest throughout all stages of the guest's stay. Determines a guest's reservation status and identifies how long the guest will stay. Helps guests complete registration cards and then assigns rooms, accommodating special requests whenever possible. Verifies the guest's method of payment and follows established credit-checking procedures. Places guest and room information in the appropriate front desk racks and communicates this information to the appropriate hotel personnel. Works closely with the housekeeping department in keeping room status reports up to date and coordinates requests for maintenance and repair work. Maintains guest room key storage, and maintains and supervises access to safe deposit boxes. Must be sales-minded. Presents options and alternatives to guests and offers assistance in making choices. Knows the location and types of available rooms as well as the activities and services of the property.

DUTIES AND RESPONSIBILITIES:

1. Registers guests and assigns rooms. Accommodates special requests whenever possible.
2. Assists in preregistration and blocking of rooms for reservations.
3. Thoroughly understands and adheres to proper credit, check-cashing, and cash-handling policies and procedures.
4. Understands room status and room status tracking.
5. Knows room locations, types of rooms available, and room rates.
6. Uses suggestive selling techniques to sell rooms and to promote other services of the hotel.
7. Coordinates room status updates with the housekeeping department by notifying housekeeping of all check-outs, late check-outs, early check-ins, special requests, and part-day rooms.
8. Possesses a working knowledge of the reservations department. Takes same day reservations and future reservations when necessary. Knows cancellation procedures.
9. Files room keys.
10. Knows how to use front office equipment.
11. Processes guest check-outs.
12. Posts and files all charges to guest, master, and city ledger accounts.
13. Follows procedures for issuing and closing safe deposit boxes used by guests.
14. Uses proper telephone etiquette.
15. Uses proper mail, package, and message handling procedures.
16. Reads and initials the pass-on log and bulletin board daily. Is aware of daily activities and meetings taking place in the hotel.

(continued)

FRONT DESK AGENT *(continued)*

17. Attends department meetings.
18. Coordinates guest room maintenance work with the engineering and maintenance division.
19. Reports any unusual occurrences or requests to the manager or assistant manager.
20. Knows all safety and emergency procedures. Is aware of accident prevention policies.
21. Maintains the cleanliness and neatness of the front desk area.
22. Understands that business demands sometimes make it necessary to move employees from their accustomed shift to other shifts.

PREREQUISITES:

Education: High school graduate or equivalent. Must be able to speak, read, write, and understand the primary language(s) used in the workplace. Must be able to speak and understand the primary language(s) used by guests who visit the workplace.

Experience: Previous hotel-related experience desired.

Physical: Requires fingering, grasping, writing, standing, sitting, walking, repetitive motions, hearing, and visual acuity, and may on occasion have to lift and carry up to 40 pounds.

JOB DESCRIPTION

POSITION TITLE: RESERVATIONS AGENT

REPORTS TO: Front Office Manager

POSITION SUMMARY: Responds to communications from guests, travel agents, and referral networks concerning reservations arriving by mail, telephone, telex, cable, fax, or through a central reservation system. Creates and maintains reservation records—usually by date of arrival and alphabetical listing. Prepares letters of confirmation and promptly processes any cancellations and modifications. Tracks future room availabilities on the basis of reservations, and helps develop forecasts for room revenue and occupancy. Additional duties may include preparing the list of expected arrivals for the front office, assisting in preregistration activities when appropriate, and processing advance reservation deposits. Knows the types of rooms the hotel has as well as their location and layout. Knows of all hotel package plans—meaning status, rates, and benefits.

DUTIES AND RESPONSIBILITIES:

1. Processes reservations by mail, telephone, telex, cable, fax, or central reservation systems referral.
2. Processes reservations from the sales office, other hotel departments, and travel agents.
3. Knows the types of rooms available as well as their location and layout.
4. Knows the selling status, rates, and benefits of all package plans.
5. Knows the credit policy of the hotel and how to code each reservation.
6. Creates and maintains reservation records by date of arrival and alphabetical listing.
7. Determines room rates based on the selling tactics of the hotel.
8. Prepares letters of confirmation.
9. Communicates reservation information to the front desk.
10. Processes cancellations and modifications and promptly relays this information to the front desk.
11. Understands the hotel's policy on guaranteed reservations and no-shows.
12. Processes advance deposits on reservations.
13. Tracks future room availabilities on the basis of reservations.
14. Helps develop room revenue and occupancy forecasts.
15. Prepares expected arrival lists for front office use.
16. Assists in preregistration activities when appropriate.
17. Monitors advance deposit requirements.
18. Handles daily correspondence. Responds to inquiries and makes reservations as needed.
19. Makes sure that files are kept up to date.

(continued)

RESERVATIONS AGENT *(continued)*

20. Maintains a clean and neat appearance and work area at all times.
21. Promotes goodwill by being courteous, friendly, and helpful to guests, managers, and fellow employees.

PREREQUISITES:

Education: High school graduate or equivalent. Must be able to speak, read, write, and understand the primary language(s) used in the workplace. Must be able to speak and understand the primary language(s) used by guests who visit the workplace.

Experience: Previous hotel-related experience desirable.

Physical: Requires fingering, grasping, writing, standing, sitting, walking, repetitive motions, hearing, visual acuity, and good speaking skills.

JOB DESCRIPTION

POSITION TITLE: FRONT OFFICE CASHIER

REPORTS TO: Front Office Manager

POSITION SUMMARY: Posts revenue center charges to guest accounts. Receives payment from guests at check-out. Coordinates the billing of credit card and direct-billed guest accounts with the accounting division. All guest accounts are balanced by the cashier at the close of each shift. Front office cashiers assume responsibility for any cash used in processing front desk transactions. May also perform a variety of banking services for guests, such as check cashing and foreign currency exchange.

DUTIES AND RESPONSIBILITIES:

1. Operates front office posting equipment.
2. Obtains the house bank and keeps it balanced.
3. Completes cashier pre-shift supply checklist.
4. Takes departmental machine readings at the beginning of the shift.
5. Completes guest check-in procedures.
6. Posts charges to guest accounts.
7. Handles paid-outs.
8. Transfers guest balances to other accounts as required.
9. Cashes checks for guests following the approval policy.
10. Completes guest check-out procedures.
11. Settles guest accounts.
12. Handles cash, traveler's checks, personal checks, credit cards, and direct billing requests properly.
13. Posts non-guest ledger payments.
14. Makes account adjustments.
15. Disperses guest records upon check-out.
16. Transfers folios paid by credit card to each credit card's master file.
17. Transfers folios charged to the non-guest ledger to each company's master file.
18. Balances department totals at the close of the shift.
19. Balances cash at the close of the shift.
20. Manages safe deposit boxes.

PREREQUISITES:

Education: High school graduate or equivalent desired. Must be able to speak, read, write, and understand the primary language(s) used in the workplace.

Experience: Previous hotel-related experience beneficial.

Physical: Requires fingering, grasping, writing, standing, sitting, walking, repetitive motions, hearing, and visual acuity. Must possess basic computational ability.

JOB DESCRIPTION

POSITION TITLE: HOTEL SWITCHBOARD OPERATOR

REPORTS TO: Front Office Manager

POSITION SUMMARY: Speaks clearly, distinctly, and with a friendly, courteous tone. Uses listening skills to put callers at ease and obtains accurate, complete information. Answers incoming calls and directs them to guestrooms through the switchboard (PBX) system or to hotel personnel or departments. Takes and distributes messages for guests, provides information on guest services, and answers inquiries about public hotel events. Provides a paging service for hotel guests and employees. Processes guest wake-up calls.

DUTIES AND RESPONSIBILITIES:

1. Answers incoming calls.
2. Directs calls to guestrooms, staff, or departments through the switchboard or PBX system.
3. Places outgoing calls.
4. Receives telephone charges from the telephone company and forwards charges to the front desk for posting.
5. Takes and distributes messages for guests.
6. Logs all wake-up call requests and performs wake-up call services.
7. Provides information about guest services to guests.
8. Answers questions about hotel events and activities.
9. Understands PBX switchboard operations.
10. Provides paging services for hotel guests and employees.
11. Knows what action to take when an emergency call is requested or received.
12. Monitors automated systems including fire alarms and telephone equipment when the engineering and maintenance department is closed.

PREREQUISITES:

Education: High school graduate or equivalent. Must be able to speak and understand the primary language(s) used by guests who visit the workplace.

Experience: Previous hotel-related experience desirable.

Physical: Requires fingering, grasping, writing, standing, sitting, walking, repetitive motions, hearing, visual acuity, and good verbal skills.

JOB DESCRIPTION

POSITION TITLE: NIGHT AUDITOR

REPORTS TO: Front Office Manager or Accounting Department

POSITION SUMMARY: Checks front office accounting records for accuracy and, on a daily basis, summarizes and compiles information for the hotel's financial records. Tracks room revenues, occupancy percentages, and other front office operating statistics. Prepares a summary of cash, check, and credit card activities, reflecting the hotel's financial performance for the day. Posts room charges and room taxes to guest accounts including guest transactions not posted during the day by the front office cashier. Processes guest charge vouchers and credit card vouchers. Verifies all account postings and balances made during the day by front desk cashiers and agents. Monitors the current status of coupon, discount, and other promotional programs. Is able to function as a front desk agent especially in terms of check-in and check-out procedures.

DUTIES AND RESPONSIBILITIES:

1. Posts room charges and taxes to guest accounts.
2. Processes guest charge vouchers and credit card vouchers.
3. Posts guest charge purchase transactions not posted by the front office cashier.
4. Transfers charges and deposits to master accounts.
5. Verifies all account postings and balances.
6. Monitors the current status of coupon, discount, and other promotional programs.
7. Tracks room revenues, occupancy percentages, and other front office statistics.
8. Prepares a summary of cash, check, and credit card activities.
9. Summarizes results of operations for management.
10. Understands principles of auditing, balancing, and closing out accounts.
11. Knows how to operate posting machines, typewriters, and other front office equipment and computers.
12. Understands and knows how to perform check-in and check-out procedures.

PREREQUISITES:

Education: Minimum of a two-year college degree. Must be able to speak, read, write, and understand the primary language(s) used in the workplace. Must be able to speak and understand the primary language(s) used by guests who visit the workplace.

Experience: Minimum of one year of hotel front desk supervisory experience, experience handling cash, accounting procedures, and general administrative tasks.

Physical: Requires fingering, grasping, writing, standing, sitting, walking, repetitive motions, verbal communications, and visual acuity.

JOB DESCRIPTION

POSITION TITLE: GUEST SERVICES MANAGER

REPORTS TO: General Manager/Front Office Manager

POSITION SUMMARY: Oversees all guest services operations, including front desk, reservations, PBX, bell staff, and transportation services to ensure quality and guest satisfaction.

DUTIES AND RESPONSIBILITIES:

1. Answers letters of inquiry regarding rates and availability.
2. Trains new Guest Services department personnel.
3. Maintains a thorough knowledge of the room rack locations, types of rooms, room rack operations, package plans, and discounts.
4. Maintains a detailed knowledge about the hotel's services and hours of operations.
5. Oversees servicing and security of the safe deposit boxes.
6. Knows all safety and understands emergency procedures and how to act upon them. Understands accident prevention policies.
7. Knows cash handling procedures. Files and posts all changes to guest master and city ledger account.
8. Possesses a thorough knowledge of credit and check-cashing policies and procedures and adheres to them.
9. Anticipates and intervenes in all incidents of guest dissatisfaction and attempts to satisfy all such guests, within hotel policy.
10. Develops and maintains all aspects of the hotel's reservations system directed toward the maximization of profit.

PREREQUISITES:

Education: Minimum of a two year college degree. Ability to speak and understand the primary language(s) used by guests who visit the workplace. Ability to speak, read, write, and understand the primary language(s) used in the workplace.

Experience: Minimum one year of hotel front-desk supervisory experience, experience handling cash, account procedures, and general administrative tasks.

Physical: Requires fingering, grasping, writing, standing, sitting, walking, repetitive motions, verbal communications, and visual acuity.

JOB DESCRIPTION

POSITION TITLE: CONCIERGE

REPORTS TO: Front Office Manager

POSITION SUMMARY: Serves as the guest's liaison for both hotel and non-hotel services. Functions are an extension of front desk agent duties. Assists the guest, regardless of whether inquiries concern in-hotel or off-premises attractions, facilities, services, or activities. Knows how to provide concise and accurate directions. Makes reservations and obtains tickets for flights, the theater, or special events. Organizes special functions such as VIP cocktail receptions. Arranges for secretarial services.

DUTIES AND RESPONSIBILITIES:

1. Develops a strong knowledge of the hotel's facilities and services and of the surrounding community.
2. Provides guests with directions to attractions or facilities in or outside the property.
3. Provides guests with information about attractions, facilities, services, and activities in or outside the property.
4. Makes guest reservations for air or other forms of transportation when requested. Obtains necessary itinerary and tickets.
5. Makes guest reservations for the theater and other forms of entertainment when requested. Obtains necessary tickets and provides directions to facilities.
6. Organizes special functions as directed by management.
7. Arranges secretarial and other office services.
8. Coordinates guest requests for special services or equipment with the appropriate department.
9. Contacts roomed guests periodically to ascertain any special needs.
10. Handles guest complaints and solves problems to the degree possible.

PREREQUISITES:

Education: Minimum of two years college education with emphasis in business, sales, or marketing. Must be able to speak, read, write, and understand the primary language(s) used in the workplace and by guests who visit the workplace.

Experience: Minimum of two years sales experience with a minimum of one year supervisory experience.

Physical: Requires bending, stooping, climbing, standing, walking, sitting, fingering, reaching, grasping, lifting, carrying, repetitive motions, visual acuity, hearing, writing, and speaking. Must exert well-paced mobility to reach other departments of the hotel on a timely basis.

Chapter 2 Outline

Competencies

1. Summarize front office operations during the four stages of the guest cycle. (pp. 49–56)
2. Describe front office recordkeeping systems and front office documents. (pp. 56–61)
3. Describe the front desk and its support devices, and describe the services and equipment of a hotel's telecommunications area. (pp. 61–68)
4. Identify and describe property management systems used by the front office. (pp. 68–75)

Taken from *Managing Front Office Operations,* Ninth Edition, by Michael L. Kasavana

Chapter 2

Front Office Operations

ALL THE FUNCTIONS, ACTIVITIES, AND AREAS of the front office are geared toward supporting guest transactions and services. Critical to the success of the department and the hotel are appropriately designed and used front office work areas, equipment, forms, and reports. Also paramount is the accurate planning and monitoring of front office transactions.

To many guests, the front office *is* the hotel. It is the main contact point for nearly every guest service the hotel provides. This chapter examines front office operations in terms of the various stages of a guest's stay, referred to as the guest cycle. Discussion focuses on the various forms, work space designs, equipment, related tasks, and automated applications appropriate to each stage.

The Guest Cycle

The financial transactions a guest makes while staying at a hotel determine the flow of business through the property. Traditionally, the flow of business can be divided into a four-stage **guest cycle.** Exhibit 1 diagrams these four stages: pre-arrival, arrival, occupancy, and departure. Within each stage, important tasks related to guest services and guest accounting can be identified and analyzed.

The guest cycle in Exhibit 1 is not an inflexible standard. Since activities and functions tend to overlap between stages, some properties have revised this traditional guest cycle into a sequence of pre-sale, point-of-sale, and post-sale events. For automated properties, this revised sequence significantly improves coordination among hotel operating departments. Regardless of the number of stages, the guest cycle identifies a logical sequence of hotel-guest interactions.

Front office employees need to be aware of guest services and guest accounting activities at all stages of the guest stay. Front office employees can efficiently serve guest needs when they clearly understand the flow of business through the hotel. Exhibit 2 indicates which front office personnel are most likely to serve the guest during each stage of the guest cycle. The guest cycle also suggests a systematic approach to managing front office operations.

Pre-Arrival

The guest chooses a hotel during the *pre-arrival stage* of the guest cycle. The guest's choice can be affected by many factors. The type of travel is often an important factor. People traveling on business may be more concerned about convenience than price. People traveling for vacation or personal reasons are more likely to be cost-conscious, since they are paying the bill. They also may be more flexible

Exhibit 1 The Guest Cycle and Related Front Office Functions

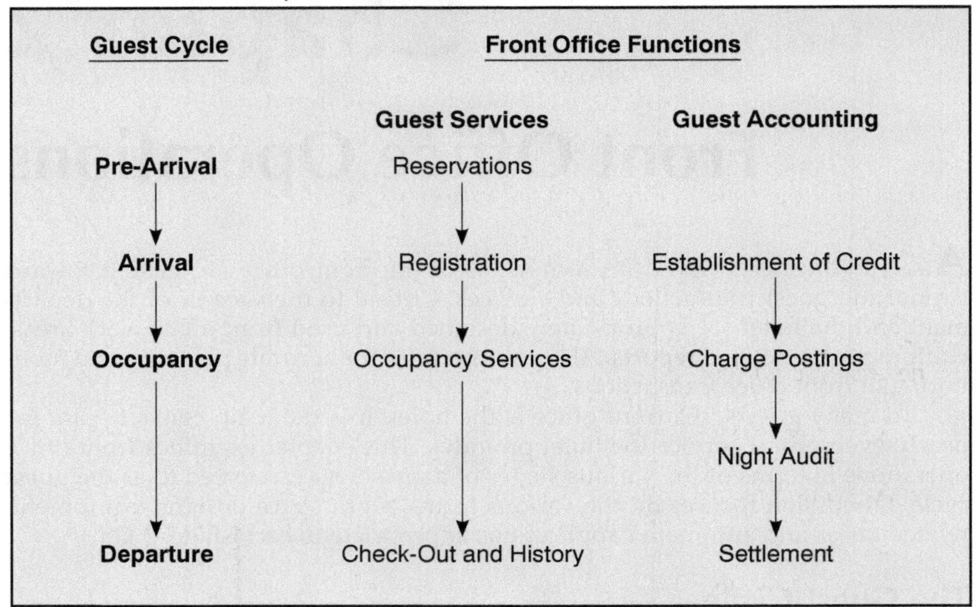

Exhibit 2 Interaction During the Guest Cycle

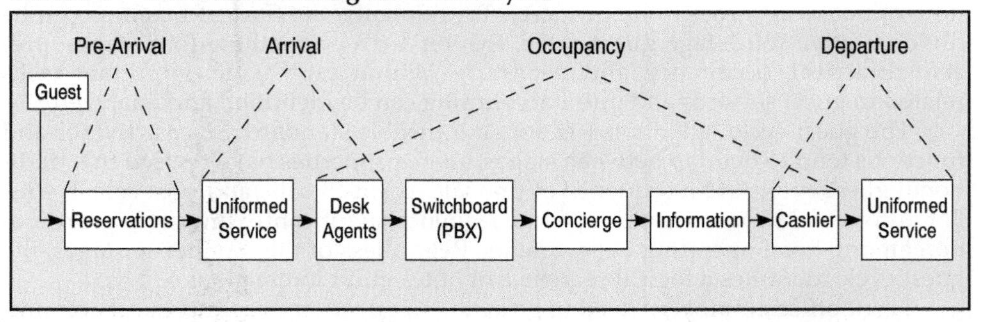

about where they travel and the hotels they stay in; the popularity of Internet sites offering deeply discounted hotel rooms for vacation travelers willing to be flexible about where and when they travel is certainly evidence of that. In addition to the type of travel, guests must consider such factors as previous experiences with the hotel; advertisements and promotions; company travel policy; recommendations from travel agents, friends, or business associates; the hotel's location and reputation; frequent traveler rewards programs; and preconceptions based upon the hotel's name or chain affiliation. The guest's decision may also be influenced by the ease of making reservations and how the hotel's reservations agent or website describes the hotel and its facilities, room rates, and amenities. In reality, the reservations department is the sales office for the hotel's non-group business.

Its employees must be sales-oriented and present a positive, strong image of the hotel. The front office staff's attitude, efficiency, and knowledge may influence a caller's decision to stay at a particular hotel. Similarly, the ease with which a guest can navigate the hotel's website can be a contributing factor in property selection.

A reservations agent must be able to respond quickly and accurately to requests for future accommodations. The proper handling of reservation information can be critical to the success of a lodging property. Efficient procedures allow more time for the reservations agent to capture needed information and to market hotel services.

If a reservation request matches room availability in the reservation system, the request can be accepted, and the reservations agent creates an electronic **reservation record.** The creation of a reservation record initiates the hotel guest cycle. This record enables the hotel to personalize guest service and appropriately schedule necessary staff and facilities. By confirming a reservation, the hotel verifies a guest's room request and personal information, and assures the guest that his or her lodging needs will be addressed. Using the information collected during the reservations process, a **property management system (PMS),** the term used for a hotel's main computer system (discussed in more detail later in the chapter), may be able to initiate pre-registration applications. Such pre-registration functions include automatically assigning a specific room and rate to guests who have not yet registered, and creating an electronic **guest folio.** A guest folio is a record of the charges incurred and credits acquired by the guest during the guest cycle.

An automated reservation system helps maximize room sales by accurately monitoring room availabilities and forecasting rooms revenue. (To further maximize room sales, some of these systems are supplemented by revenue management systems.) By analyzing reservation transaction reports, front office management can develop a better understanding of the hotel's reservation patterns. Data collected during the reservations process become especially useful in subsequent front office functions. But, without a doubt, the most important outcome of an effective reservations process is having a room available when the guest arrives.

Arrival

The *arrival stage* of the guest cycle includes registration and rooming functions. After the guest arrives, he or she establishes a business and legal relationship with the hotel through the front office. It is the front office staff's responsibility to clarify the nature of the guest-hotel relationship and to monitor the financial transactions between the hotel and its guests.

Many guests arrive at the hotel entrance by private automobile, taxicab, or shuttle bus. The entrance is often the first place guests directly interact with hotel staffers. It is for this reason that world-class, upscale, convention, casino, and resort hotels typically station attentive uniformed staff there. Door attendants direct traffic in the hotel entrance, help guests unload luggage, open doors for arriving and departing guests, and provide directions and information about both on-premises and nearby points of interest. Valet parking staff members are often available to provide automotive parking assistance to guests not using self-park. Bell attendants, who are often stationed near the front door, escort guests with luggage to the front desk for registration. While a mid-scale, economy, or limited-services hotel might employ a small number of staff members to provide similar service, most do not.

The front desk agent should determine the guest's reservation status before beginning the registration process. Persons with reservations may have already undergone pre-registration activities. Persons without reservations, known as "walk-ins," present an opportunity for front desk agents to sell guestrooms. To sell successfully, the front desk agent must be very familiar with the hotel's room types, rates, and guest services and be able to describe them in a positive manner. A walk-in is not likely to register if he or she is not convinced of the value of renting a particular hotel room. Once a person has registered, whether they have a reservation or are a walk-in, they legally become a guest. Often, the hotel's property management system can be used to quickly identify available rooms and amenities. An electronic reservation record, created during the pre-registration application or at the time of check-in, is essential to efficient front office operation. A registration record includes information about the guest's intended method of payment, the planned length of stay, and any special guest needs such as roll-away bed or a child's crib. It should also include the guest's billing address, e-mail address, and telephone number.

When the guest presents a form of identification, it serves as proof of intent to establish an innkeeper-guest relationship. Presenting a valid payment card during registration, for example, is deemed evidence of the traveler's intent to become a guest. The innkeeper-guest relationship has many legal benefits for both the hotel and the guest. For example, the hotel obtains legal assurance of payment for the room and services provided, while the guest obtains legal assurance of personal safety while on the premises.

Gathering all requisite information in detail at the time of reservation and registration enhances the front office's ability to satisfy special guest needs, forecast room occupancies, and settle guest accounts properly. At check-out, the guest's registration record may also become the primary data source for creating a guest history record. This record is a collection of personal and financial information about a guest that can help the hotel in its subsequent marketing and sales efforts. It also provides a basis for facilitating online reservation or registration at the time of a return stay. The hotel's property management system has a predetermined formula (algorithm) that applies registration information to automatically assign a room type and rate for each guest. Room and rate assignment depend on reservation information (long-run availability) and room status (short-run availability) information. The housekeeping status of a room must be communicated to the front desk as soon as possible so that the property management system can maximize room assignments. Some common room status terminology is defined in Exhibit 3.

Hotel room types may range from a standard single guestroom to a luxurious suite. Exhibit 4 defines some typical hotel room types. Furnishings, amenities, and location within the property will tend to differentiate room rates within the same room type.

Front desk agents must also be sensitive to accessibility issues for guests with physical impairments. The Americans with Disabilities Act requires new

Exhibit 3 Room Status Terminology

During the guest's stay, the housekeeping status of the guestroom changes several times. The various terms defined are typical of the room status terminology of the lodging industry. Not every room status will occur for each guestroom during every stay.

Occupied: A guest is currently registered to the room.

Complimentary: The room is occupied, but the guest is assessed no charge for its use.

Stayover: The guest is not expected to check out today and will remain at least one more night.

On-change: The guest has departed, but the room has not yet been cleaned and readied for resale.

Do not disturb: The guest has requested not to be disturbed.

Sleep-out: A guest is registered to the room, but the bed has not been used.

Skipper: The guest has left the hotel without making arrangements to settle his or her account.

Sleeper: The guest has settled his or her account and left the hotel, but the front office staff has failed to properly update the room's status.

Vacant and ready: The room has been cleaned and inspected and is ready for an arriving guest.

Out-of-order: The room cannot be assigned to a guest. A room may be out-of-order for a variety of reasons, including the need for maintenance, refurbishing, and extensive cleaning.

Lock-out: The room has been locked so that the guest cannot re-enter until he or she is cleared by a hotel official.

DNCO (did not check out): The guest made arrangements to settle his or her account (and thus is not a skipper), but has left without informing the front office.

Due out: The room is expected to become vacant after the following day's check-out time.

Check-out: The guest has settled his or her account, returned the room keys, and left the hotel.

Late check-out: The guest has requested and is being allowed to check out later than the hotel's standard check-out time.

and renovated properties to be barrier-free in design. The term *barrier-free* means that facilities and accommodations must be designed with the disabled guest and visitor in mind. Some of the more prevalent features of barrier-free guestrooms are extra-wide doorways for wheelchairs (both entry doors and bathroom doors), extra-large bathrooms, grab bars beside the toilet and inside the bathtub area, roll-in showers for wheelchairs, lowered vanity countertops and extra height (knee space) under the sink, handles on doors and bathroom fixtures instead of knobs, and strobe lights and pillow shakers as part of the smoke and fire detection systems (for the hearing impaired). Other aspects of barrier-free design are addressed later in the chapter.

Exhibit 4 Room Type Definitions

The following room type definitions are common throughout the lodging industry.

Single: A room assigned to one person. May have one or more beds.

Double: A room assigned to two people. May have one or more beds.

Triple: A room assigned to three people. May have two or more beds.

Quad: A room assigned to four people. May have two or more beds.

Queen: A room with a queen-size bed. May be occupied by one or more people.

King: A room with a king-size bed. May be occupied by one or more people.

Twin: A room with two twin beds. May be occupied by one or more people.

Double-double: A room with two double (or perhaps queen) beds. May be occupied by one or more persons.

Studio: A room with a studio bed—a couch that can be converted into a bed. May also have an additional bed.

Mini-suite or junior suite: A single room with a bed and a sitting area. Sometimes the sleeping area is in a bedroom separate from the parlor or living room.

Suite: A parlor or living room connected to one or more bedrooms.

Connecting rooms: Rooms with individual entrance doors from the outside and a connecting door between. Guests can move between rooms without going through the hallway.

Adjoining rooms: Rooms with a common wall but no connecting door.

Adjacent rooms: Rooms close to each other, perhaps across the hall.

Once a registration record is created, the front desk agent turns his or her attention to identifying the guest's method of payment. The hotel guest accounting cycle depends on captured information to ensure deferred payment for rendered services. Whether the guest uses cash, personal check, credit card, debit card, travel voucher, smart card, or some alternative method of payment, the front office must take measures to ensure eventual payment. A proper credit check at the outset of a transaction greatly reduces the potential for subsequent settlement problems. If a guest has not secured management approval of credit before arriving at the property, the hotel might deny the guest's request for credit at the time of check-in.

Registration is complete once the guest has established his or her method of payment and departure date. The guest is issued a room key and allowed to proceed to the room without assistance, or a uniformed service employee may escort the guest to the room. When the guest arrives at the room, the occupancy stage of the guest cycle begins.

Occupancy

The manner in which the front office staff represents the hotel is important throughout the guest cycle, particularly during the *occupancy stage.* As the center of hotel activity, the front desk is responsible for coordinating guest services.

Among many services, the front desk provides the guest with information and supplies. The front office should respond to requests in a timely and accurate way to maximize guest satisfaction. A concierge may also be on staff to provide special guest services.

A major front office objective throughout the guest cycle is to encourage repeat visits. Sound guest relations are essential to this objective. Guest relations depend on clear, constructive communications between the front office, other hotel departments and divisions, and guests. The hotel must be aware of a guest complaint in order to resolve it. Front desk agents should carefully attend to guest concerns and try to seek satisfactory resolutions as quickly as possible.

Security is a primary front office concern throughout all stages of the guest cycle, especially during occupancy. Security issues likely to apply to front office employees include verifying guest identify and other information, and protecting guest funds and valuables.

Various transactions during the occupancy stage affect guest and hotel financial accounts. Most of these transactions will be automatically processed through property management system interfaces to revenue centers according to established posting and auditing procedures.

The room rate of the guestroom is usually the largest single charge on the guest's folio. Additional expenses can be charged to a guest's account if he or she established acceptable credit at the front desk during registration. Goods or services purchased from the hotel's restaurant, lounge, room service department, telephone department, transportation areas, gift shop, spa, and other revenue outlets may be charged to guest accounts. Many hotels establish a maximum limit on the amount that guests can charge to their accounts without partial settlement. This amount is usually referred to as the **house limit** and can be automatically monitored by the property management system. Guest accounts must be continually monitored to ensure that the house limit is not exceeded.

Front desk accounting records must be periodically reviewed for accuracy and completeness through a system audit, which can be programmed to run automatically at any time during the day. Even though automated properties *can* perform the audit at any time, they almost invariably follow the hotel tradition of performing the audit at night, since transaction volumes tend to be lower then, and most transactions occur earlier in the day.

Regardless of when the system audit takes place, room charges (room rates and room tax) are automatically posted to guest accounts as part of the audit routine. Other system audit tasks usually include: online verification of account postings, monitoring of accounts and credit limits, identification of discrepancies in room status, and the production of operating reports.

Departure

Guest services and guest accounting aspects of the guest cycle are completed during the cycle's fourth phase: *departure.* Effective front office monitoring includes processing the guest out of the hotel and creating a guest history file. The final element of guest accounting is settlement of the guest's account (by bringing the account to a zero balance).

At check-out, the guest vacates the room, receives an accurate statement of the settled account, returns the room keys, and leaves the hotel. Once the guest has checked out, the front office system automatically updates the room's availability status and closes the account.

During check-out, the front office staff should determine whether the guest was satisfied with the stay and encourage the guest to return to the hotel (or another property in the chain). The more information the hotel has about its guests, the better it can anticipate and serve their needs and develop marketing strategies to increase business. In addition, it is important for guests to leave with a positive impression of the hotel—it will definitely affect how they talk about the hotel to others and may be the determining factor in whether they return to the property in the future.

Most property management systems use registration records to automatically construct a **guest history file** when a guest checks out. A guest history file is a collection of guest history records. Information in a guest history file allows the hotel to better understand its clientele and provides a solid base for strategic marketing. Guest histories, including details of the guests' spending at the hotel, are usually sent electronically to the company's central database management system for processing and storage.

The purpose of account settlement is to collect money due the hotel before guest departure. Depending on the guest's credit arrangements, the guest will pay cash; use a credit card, debit card, or smart card; or apply pre-established direct billing instructions. Account balances should be verified and errors corrected before the guest leaves the hotel. Problems may occur in guest account settlement when charges are not posted to the guest's account until *after* the guest checks out. These charges are called **late charges.** Even if payment is eventually collected, the hotel usually incurs additional costs through billing the guest. In addition, this can irritate guests, who may have to submit incomplete expense accounts to their employers. The task of settling accounts with outstanding balances for departed guests is generally transferred to a back office system to be handled by the accounting department, not the front office. However, the front office is responsible for providing complete and accurate billing information to assist the accounting department in its collection efforts.

Once the guest has checked out, the front office can analyze data related to the guest's stay. System-generated reports can be used to review operations, isolate problem areas, indicate where corrective action may be necessary, and highlight business trends. Daily system reports typically present information about cash and charge transactions and front office operating statistics. Operational analysis can help managers establish a standard of performance that can be used to evaluate the effectiveness of front office operations.

Front Office Systems

Before the 1970s, technology in the front office was almost nonexistent. Manual operations were the rule in lodging operations. The semi-automated operations through the early 1970s laid much of the groundwork for the development of automated operations in the 1980s. The implementation of comprehensive automated applications became prevalent in the 1990s and beyond. The first decade of the twenty-first century introduced analytical metrics, revenue management, online purchasing programs, and e-commerce solutions. Technology has become affordable, allowing lodging properties to manage many of their operations with automated applications that may rely on portable devices, wireless networks, and remote access, including select self-service applications.

Front Office Activities

Front office recordkeeping in an automated property management system (PMS) is mostly the result of programmed routines. Computer systems designed for use in the hospitality industry at first were not considered functionally viable or generally affordable. These initial systems tended to be expensive, making them attractive to only the largest hotel properties. As hardware, software, and netware became less expensive, more compact, and easier to operate, implementation became more commonplace. User-friendly applications that did not require sophisticated technical training evolved for various hotel functions and applications over the next several years. The development of versatile portable and wireless devices enabled system vendors to approach all classes of lodging properties. Systems are now cost-effective for hotels of all sizes. It is important to note that the addition of wireless mobile devices to the technology toolbox enabled applications in areas previously considered impractical.

Pre-Arrival Activities. The reservations software of a property management system usually interfaces with a central reservations system or other distribution network and may automatically quote rates and reserve rooms according to booking engine protocol. The reservations software may also automatically generate e-mail confirmations, produce requests for guest deposits, handle pre-registration activities, and establish the credit status of the traveler if a credit card, debit card, or smart card number is provided as part of the reservation record. Electronic folios can be used to track pre-registration transactions for guests with confirmed reservations. A reservations software package may also generate an expected arrivals list, occupancy and revenue forecast reports, and a variety of auxiliary reports.

Arrival Activities. Guest information collected during the reservation process is automatically transferred as a reservation record to the property management system's front office software. A front desk agent enters similar guest information for walk-in guests into the front office system. The agent may then present a computer-generated **registration card** to the guest for verification and signature. The installation of online payment authorization terminals enables front desk personnel to receive timely payment card approval. Registration data, stored electronically, can also be retrieved whenever necessary, thereby making a room rack unnecessary. Electronic guest folios are maintained and accessed through the system's application software.

Some properties offer self check-in/check-out terminals in the hotel's lobby area, onboard a shuttle van, or via mobile devices. In addition, the availability of automated teller machines (ATMs) and self check-in kiosks at airports and other off-premises locations has had a positive impact on guests willing to accept self-service technology in lodging establishments.

To use a self-service terminal, the guest inserts a credit card, debit card, frequent traveler card, or smart card into the machine, which reads the encoded card data and communicates with the property management system. The central system locates the guest's reservation and returns the information to the terminal. The guest may be asked to verify name, departure date, rate, and room type on the display. Some systems allow changes to this information, and some require that the guest be on property at the front desk if any changes are necessary. If the information is correct, the system assigns an available room within the lodging management system and may dispense a walking map to the room along with a downloadable guestroom door-lock code or guestroom key.

Some hotels may not employ self check-in/check-out terminals, as a means to keep personal contact between the hotel staff and the guest. Typically, self check-in terminals work especially well in large convention hotels where long check-in and check-out lines can undermine a guest's experience. These terminals are used to accelerate the check-in process and get guests to their rooms quicker. Other hotels, such as economy-priced hotels and some mid-range hotels that do not provide extensive personal service, often install and rely on self-service terminals. One additional advantage of these devices in economy and mid-range hotels is that they may reduce the size of the work shift at the front desk, since the equipment may be capable of processing check-ins and check-outs independently.

Some hotel companies allow guests to register via the Internet prior to arrival at the property. Guests access the hotel's website registration area and confirm their arrival information. When they arrive at the hotel, they simply stop by a convenient pre-registration desk, show identification, and pick up their room keys. The entire process takes only a few seconds once they arrive at the hotel. With the extension of wireless technologies, guests can also pre-register through a laptop computer, personal digital assistant (PDA), or smart phone.

Occupancy Activities. A hotel property management system typically includes work stations and related devices located throughout the hotel facility. These devices may include point-of-sale (POS) terminals, data workstations, smart identification tags, handheld units, pagers, and other formats. As guests charge purchases at revenue outlets, the charged amounts are electronically transferred to the property management system, and the appropriate guest account is automatically updated. Most automated devices are capable of supporting two-way (duplex) interfaces, so the status of each guest is verified before the system accepts the charge for posting. For example, if a guest checks out of the hotel and then attempts to purchase a gift shop item and charge it to his or her room account, the point-of-sale terminal notifies the gift shop clerk that the item cannot be charged to the guest's account because the account has already been settled and closed. Instantaneous postings, simultaneous guest account and departmental entries, and continuous trial balances free front office staff to spend time reviewing, rather than focusing on data entry and balancing guest accounts.

Departure Activities. An electronic or printed folio presented at check-out or e-mailed helps assure the guest that the statement of account is complete and accurate. Depending on the method of settlement, the system may automatically post the transactions to appropriate back office accounts. For a guest account that requires third-party billing, the system is capable of producing a bill to be sent to the sponsor or credit-granting agency. Once the guest's account is settled and the postings are considered complete, departed-guest information may be used to create an electronic record in the hotel's guest history file.

Off-premises outsourcing, application service providers (ASPs), and cloud computing networks enable hotels to implement automated applications without having to support a complete on-premises system. Such system solutions require the hotel to provide the servicing bureau with data for processing. A popular hospitality industry outsourced application has been payroll accounting. Employee time records are sent to the service bureau to convert into paychecks and payroll reports for management. However, service bureaus, which focus primarily on back office functions, are not always a feasible option for front office activities. On the other hand, cloud computing is capable of supporting aspects of both front office and back office operations.

Front Office Documents

The front office relies on various documents to monitor the guest's stay. This section discusses front office documents employed in the four stages of the traditional guest cycle. It is important to note that many of these reports may only be available initially in electronic format.

Pre-Arrival Documents

Since reservations initiate the guest cycle, capturing and maintaining reservation data is critical to effective front office operations. Regardless of the reservation's point of entry (in-house, the hotel's website, or the reservations office), reservations are formulated into an electronic **reservation file.** The guest may be sent a system-generated confirmation to indicate that a reservation has been made and that its specifications are accurate. The confirmation process permits errors to be corrected prior to guest arrival and verifies the guest's correct contact information for future communication. Digital confirmations have the advantages of lower costs to the hotel and a rapid response to guests.

Arrival Documents

The front office may use a front desk or concierge location for guest check-in. A registration record indicates the guests' personal data, including length of stay and method of settlement. Registration records may also provide guest information related to on-premises and in-room amenities and hotel policies. Additionally, registration records indicate the room rate and length of stay, allowing the guest to reconfirm this information. This reduces questions about the price of the room or intended length of stay at check-out.

Credit must be established, verified, or authorized during check-in as well. Most payment card companies require an online authorization of electronic data capture by a recording device to establish credit. A front desk agent will acknowledge online approval against the guest's method of payment for a pre-established amount. Should the balance exceed that amount during the stay, additional requests are made to the payment card company. Often, the front office system automatically requests the credit approval during check-in and, when the balance approaches or exceeds the approved level, the system may automatically request additional approvals from the payment card company.

Occupancy Documents

Once the guest is registered, the front office system creates an electronic guest folio to capture guest charges and credits. While folio information is comparable across front office recordkeeping systems, folio formats tend to vary. In nearly all electronic systems, information from guest registration data is used to create the folio. This is an example of data interchange within the flow of electronic records. The front office may retain a copy of the guest folio as a record of the guest's stay, and present a hard copy or electronic equivalent to the guest following check-out. Additional folio copies may be used for such purposes as assistance in direct billing after departure, for creating e-mail receipts, and to help reconcile departmental sales reports.

Electronic folios simplify transaction posting and handling. Once the information is captured, the system assigns a unique account number or carries forward the reservation number. In a property management system, an electronic folio is automatically created and available for immediate transaction posting. Electronic folios are stored internally and can be printed on demand.

A **voucher** is a support document detailing the facts of a transaction. A voucher does not replace the *source document* created at the point of purchase. Common types of vouchers include charge vouchers, allowance vouchers, transfer vouchers, and paid-out vouchers. During a system audit routine, vouchers help ensure that all transactions requiring account posting have been processed correctly. Automated properties require few paper vouchers, or, in some cases, no paper vouchers at all. This is because remote revenue centers are electronically connected (interfaced) with the front office system, thus reducing the need for support documentation.

Automated front office systems replace traditional filing techniques with desktop and mobile terminals, thereby eliminating the need for information racks and rack slips. These terminals can quickly access guest records and display comprehensive information. Interfacing technology enables other electronic equipment, such as point-of-sale terminals, electronic locks, call accounting devices, and energy management systems, to also be connected to the front office system.

Departure Documents

Guest folios are kept current throughout occupancy to ensure an accurate account balance for settlement at the time of departure. In addition to the guest folio, other documents may be required for account settlement. A payment card voucher, for example, may be necessary if the guest elects to settle the account with a payment card. In some hotels, a cash voucher is used to document a cash settlement. A transfer voucher may be necessary if the guest's account is direct-billed—that is, transferred from a guest receivable account in the front office to a non-guest receivable account in the back office. The property management system typically generates several records and reports that may be used to prove transactions and provide a basis for comprehensive front office auditing.

During the departure stage, the property management system may create a guest history file. As stated earlier, a guest history file stores information that can be used for marketing and sales efforts, and can be helpful in registering and serving the guest during a return visit. Most systems automatically create an electronic guest history file as part of the check-out process. A collection of guest history files forms a database of invaluable marketing information.

The Front Desk

Most front office functions are performed at the front desk. The front desk is where guests register, request information and services, relate complaints, settle accounts, and check out.

Most front desks are prominently located in the hotel lobby. A typical front desk surface is a counter approximately three-and-a-half feet high and two-and-a-half feet deep. Its length may vary according to the design of the desk area, the duties performed at the front desk, and the size of the hotel lobby. Signs may be placed on or above the desk to direct guests to the proper activity center for registration, cashier, check-out, information and mail handling, and other guest services. Front desk designs usually screen front office forms and equipment from guests or visitors standing at the desk, since much front office information is considered confidential and proprietary.

Functional Organization

The functional efficiency of a front desk configuration depends on the organization of the work stations located at the desk. The design and layout of the desk should provide each front desk employee with easy access to the equipment, forms, and supplies necessary for his or her assigned tasks. (Exhibit 5 presents a sample front desk design.) Ideally, the front desk layout is planned and its furniture and fixtures situated according to the functions performed at designated activity centers along the desk. However, as lines of responsibility overlap among front desk personnel, largely because of cross-training and automation, more front desks are being designed with position flexibility in mind.

Efficiency is an important concern in front office design. Whenever front office employees have to turn their backs to guests, leave guests unattended, or take too long to complete a process, front desk design could be improved. Studies that examine how front office personnel interact with guests and equipment often suggest changes in front desk design.

Design Alternatives

Various hotel companies have researched industry needs and redesigned front desk areas to make them more aesthetically appealing. For instance, there is general agreement that traditional mail, message, and other filing or compartment organizers visible to traffic in the lobby are unnecessary at the front desk, not to mention unwise from a security standpoint. Mail, messages, and other materials can be stored in drawers or slots located under or away from the front desk, thereby making the front desk area appear more streamlined.

Exhibit 5 Sample Layout of a Front Desk

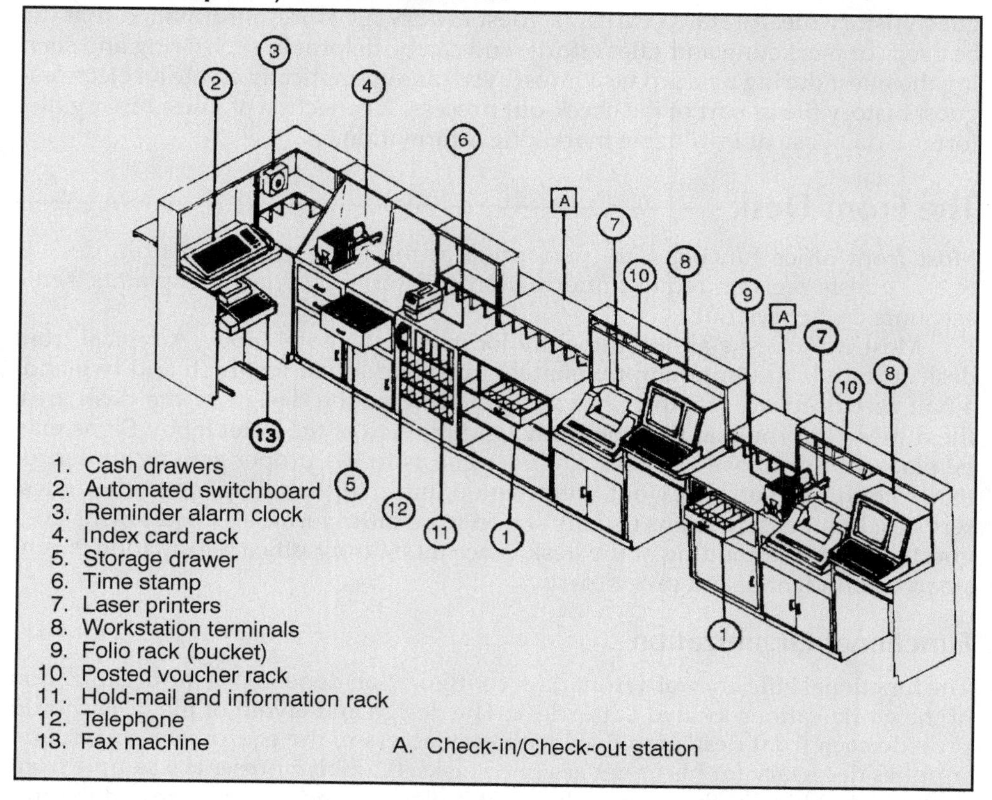

Some hotels have circular or semicircular front desk structures. The circular desk encloses the front desk staff with its counter. In a semicircular arrangement, there is normally a straight wall at the back of the desk with a door leading to front office support services. Circular and semicircular desks allow greater service to more guests at the same time, and also tend to appear more modern and innovative than the traditional straight desk. This design, however, may present potential problems in the sense that guests can approach the desk from all angles, even though front office work stations and equipment are situated in specific spots. Extra care may be necessary to ensure the success of these and other innovative desk designs.

Some hotels have experimented with a lobby arrangement that includes no front desk at all. In a desk-less environment, registration and room assignment may be handled at a small table or personal desk in a low-traffic area of the lobby. A concierge, receptionist, or special guest service employee may serve as guest host. Although a guest host may perform many of the same functions as a front desk agent, the service is intended to be more personal and informal. Guests often enjoy a casual, seated registration instead of a long wait standing in line at a front desk counter.

Other hotels use self check-in terminals, with a small reception desk for those guests who are uncomfortable using technology or who may have questions. Also available are options for remote check-in.

Accessibility. The traditional standards for front desk design may not satisfy the physical needs of all hotel guests. Accessibility is an important consideration in the general design of a hotel, especially its front office area. The Americans with Disabilities Act stipulates that companies that serve the general public must make public areas and services readily accessible to the disabled. This means that public areas and accommodations in new and renovated lodging properties must be barrier-free, including front desk areas. According to the law, existing businesses will be required to make architectural and physical changes that are "readily achievable" given the company's size and financial resources. This may require changes in the size and setup of doorways, as well as the removal of architectural barriers such as curbs and steps. The law may also require that a portion of the front desk be of a more accessible height and design to accommodate people using wheelchairs or people with other special needs. When the front desk design cannot be changed, it is customary for front desk agents to go, when necessary, to the guest side of the desk to accommodate disabled travelers.

Point-of-Sale System. In some hotels, the front desk also serves as a place where guests can purchase items they may need while traveling. A front desk point-of-sale (POS) terminal is used to record cash transactions and maintain cash balances for front desk sales not associated with the guest cycle, such as the sale of newspapers, personal grooming items, sundries, or other items. In some limited-service properties, the hotel may offer a pantry of items that guests can purchase, such as sandwiches, canned food items, breakfast foods, toiletries, and snacks. Guests are expected to pay for these items at the front desk; the items may be paid for in full or posted to the guest's folio via the front desk POS terminal. Many specialized functions can be built into a POS system to facilitate close monitoring of front office transactions. The POS system is normally interfaced with the property management system to provide more complete control over financial transactions, folio postings, and other settlements.

POS systems possess the capabilities to produce transaction records, generate sales receipts, capture electronic settlement data, monitor inventory levels, and maintain item pricing. POS systems typically record the:

- Amount of the transaction
- Description of the transaction
- Affected departments
- Type of transaction
- Identity of the cashier
- Amount tendered
- Method of payment

A POS terminal may also feature a cash drawer divided into several money compartments, or may have removable drawers for individual cashier banks.

Support Devices. The front office may have numerous pieces of automated and manual support equipment. These devices can help simplify cumbersome procedures with logical information handling and adequate storage capacity for data and files. The following paragraphs describe just a few of the support devices found at a front desk.

An *electronic payment reader* captures the account type and number, expiration date, and select additional information assigned to the account. These devices may operate in a stand-alone or online mode connected to an automatic call-out transaction authorization network. In many cases, they are integrated with the property management system and can be used for several functions involving electronic data capture and settlement. Data that is magnetically encoded and stored on the magnetic stripe on the back of a plastic card or contained in a contactless signal exchange is transmitted to a clearinghouse or authorization service. On the basis of the transaction data and the cardholder's account status, the clearinghouse or authorization service either approves or disapproves the transaction. The technology integrates the reader and the front office system and may allow more information to be exchanged between the authorization service and the guest's electronic record. Guest loyalty programs can include a plastic membership card with a magnetic stripe that may also be read by the payment device. Membership information, including reward points, may be verified when guests check in by swiping or tapping the card.

In addition to credit and debit cards, guests may present gift cards or smart cards for partial or full account settlement. Gift cards represent a prepaid amount that can be applied against an outstanding folio balance. Smart cards differ from credit and debit cards in that they usually contain an integrated circuit on a silicon chip imbedded in them (instead of, or in addition to, a magnetic stripe) to store account information. A smart card is capable of storing much more information than a magnetic stripe card.

The front office area may also feature security monitors, such as closed-circuit television screens, allowing front office management or security personnel to monitor certain areas of the hotel from a central location.

Telecommunications

Hotels must be able to support a broad range of telephone traffic with adequate technology to ensure an efficient, effective telecommunications system. There are many types of calls a guest may place during a hotel stay:

- Local calls
- Direct-dial long-distance calls
- Pre-payment card calls
- Collect calls
- Third-party calls
- Person-to-person calls
- Billed-to-room calls

- International calls
- Toll-free calls
- 900 or premium-price calls
- Voice over Internet Protocol (VoIP) calls

While all of these calls can be completed without operator assistance, guests sometimes ask front office staff for assistance in placing calls. In addition, a single call often fits into more than one call category. For example, a direct-dial long-distance call could also be a pre-payment card call; a person-to-person call could also be a collect call; a local call could be to an Internet service provider; and an international call could be a person-to-person call. For many of these types of calls, the hotel may charge guests a surcharge for use of its telephone technology.

A hotel's telephone equipment may include a "call accounting" billing system. The system detects how the call is being placed (direct dial, calling card, etc.) and then calculates the amount the hotel needs to bill the guest once the call is finished. The charge is then posted to the guest's folio in the hotel property management system. Since a majority of guests carry a cellular phone, the volume of billable guest telephone traffic has been significantly reduced.

International calls typically not within the scope of a guest's cell phone plan can be direct-dialed or placed with operator assistance. To direct-dial an international call, the guest typically dials an international access code, a country code, a city code, and the telephone number. The hotel bills guests for direct-dialed international calls and may apply a fee in addition to the price of the call.

Toll-free calls can be direct-dialed from a guestroom as either local calls or long-distance calls. In either case, the guest receives access to an outside line and dials the toll-free access number (such as 800, 888, 877, etc.). The hotel may apply a surcharge or other fee for this service.

Calls made to businesses that charge callers a fee for the call (a fee separate from the one the telephone company charges for placing the call) may be 900 or premium-price calls. Problems can arise when these types of calls are made from guestrooms. Guests may be shocked and mistakenly blame the hotel upon receiving premium call charges. The businesses involved in premium-price telephone services charge widely varying rates. One business might charge $1.50 per minute; another might charge $3.50 for the first minute and $2.00 for each additional minute; a third business might charge a flat rate of $9.00 a call. Another problem that arises is that the hotel's telephone system may be able to track only the costs involved in placing the call and not the premium charged by the premium service company. A guest could settle a phone charge of $2.50 at check-out and the hotel could later receive a premium call bill of $40.50 for the same call. It is for these reasons that some hotels choose to block premium-price calls from guestrooms.

Calls placed and connected over Internet technology, as opposed to common carrier networks, tend to be less expensive. Use of the Internet for telecommunications is termed *Voice over Internet Protocol (VoIP)* and represents a viable alternative to traditional phone lines and switching equipment.

Telecommunications Equipment

To serve guests efficiently and price calls properly, hotels need the right mix of telephone equipment and lines. There are many types of telephone lines or *trunks*. Each type of line is designed to carry certain types of calls. There are lines dedicated to incoming calls, others dedicated to outbound calls, and two-way lines as well. Based on its level of guest service, each hotel must determine the types and number of lines it needs to install. Systems and equipment that hotels use for placing and pricing calls include the following:

- Telephone switchboards (also known as PBX or PABX systems)
- Call accounting system
- Guestroom phones
- Pagers and cell phones
- Related technology

Telephone Switchboards. Historically, an important piece of equipment controlling phone service at hotels was the switchboard or private branch exchange (PBX), now automated and often labeled the PABX (for "private automated branch exchange"). This equipment routes inbound calls to the hotel telephone operator's console. The hotel operator, in turn, connects these calls to particular extensions or station lines. These might be at the front desk or in guestrooms, administrative offices, hotel departments, or other areas. This arrangement allows the hotel to have a large number of telephones share a limited number of telephone lines. Outbound calls are usually placed without the hotel operator's help, although they often go through the same equipment. Some hotel PBX/PABX systems have advanced features enabling them to handle data as well as voice communications. For example, room attendants can update the status of guestrooms by dialing a code from guestroom phones.

Alternatively, some hotels have implemented voice over Internet protocol (VoIP) that conducts communications over the property's high-speed Internet connection without requiring any PBX/PABX equipment. The telephone traffic for VoIP calls is handled by automated network devices and routers.

Call Accounting System. A **call accounting system (CAS)** enables hotel-based technology to place, price, and post telephone calls to electronic guest folios without assistance from phone company personnel or front desk staff. A CAS is a set of software programs that initiates the routing, rating, and recording of calls emanating from guestroom and/or administrative office telephones. The CAS interfaces with a hotel's property management system to electronically post charges to guest folios or to print charge slips for the front desk staff to post appropriately. Some CASs have a least-cost-routing component that routes a dialed call to the type of line that can carry the call at the lowest cost to the hotel. Prior to folio posting, the CAS may add a surcharge or other property-imposed fee (PIF) to the telephone company's call pricing.

Guestroom Phones. Along with other telecommunications equipment, guestroom phones are increasing in sophistication and capabilities. For example, guests can connect a personal computer or other compatible portable device into a guestroom phone supporting an input jack or port for connectivity. Many hotels provide two-line guestroom phones, so one line can accommodate an electronic interchange while the guest talks on the other line. Other features found on some guestroom phones include: conference calling, caller ID, speed dialing, hold buttons, call-waiting, hands-free speakers, voice messaging, and a message-waiting alert. Some phones combine voice, data, e-mail, fax, and other technologies so guests can retrieve messages, order room service, receive text documents, and place wake-up call requests. In addition, some hotels place cordless phones in guestrooms. A cordless phone uses a radio frequency to connect to the telephone system. Although guests like the convenience of cordless, these phones are not as secure or reliable as wired telephones. Alternatively, a computerized device may be used for guest communication with a VoIP system.

Pagers and Cell Phones. Some hotels offer a pager or cell phone to guests at check-in. In the case of cell phones, the hotel bills the guest for the number of minutes of recorded use, as indicated by the phone's internal usage meter. Calls placed through cell phones may not go through the hotel's CAS and therefore are priced outside the system and may require manual posting to the appropriate guest folios. Some hotels have begun experimenting with internal cell phones that allow only hotel-issued cell phones to work exclusively on the hotel's premises. When used, internal cell phones are issued to guests in lieu of in-room phones.

Related Technology. Often, hotels install telephone systems with sophisticated features for reasons other than just cost effectiveness. Examples include automatic call dispensing systems, telephone/room status systems, high-speed Internet access, and call detection software.

In many cases, *automatic call dispensing* is limited to wake-up services. In a staff-operated system, the staff member receiving the wake-up-call request enters the room number and time for each wake-up call into the call-dispensing system. Some self-service systems allow guests to place their own wake-up requests. At the scheduled time, a telephone call is automatically placed to the guest's room. Once the guest answers the call, the system may activate a synthesized voice that gives a greeting along with the current time, temperature, and weather conditions. Another variation on automatic call dispensing allows hotel staff to call all rooms simultaneously in case of an emergency or to call all guests associated with a specific group to remind them of a meeting, event, or function.

Telephone/room status systems can assist with rooms management and prohibit the unauthorized use of telephones in vacant rooms. Housekeeping or room service employees can use guestroom telephones to enter data concerning room service charges (for example, what was consumed from an in-room bar), maintenance information, or current room status information. These features not only improve communication, they also contribute to lower payroll costs and help ensure a more efficient in-room monitoring and restocking system for guestrooms.

An increasingly popular guestroom service is *high-speed Internet access (HSIA)*. Hotels may charge guests for HSIA service on a per-transaction, fixed-fee, or daily-fee basis. HSIA data services are brought to the hotel by an Internet service provider (ISP). Often there is a revenue-sharing agreement between the hotel and the ISP. HSIA systems may be wired or wireless.

A hotel may also rely on *call detection software,* a component of the hotel's call accounting system, to sense when a placed call is answered. Call detection equipment can pinpoint the exact moment a telephone call is connected, thereby improving billing accuracy and leading to a reduction in call accounting discrepancies, since only the charges associated with answered calls will appear on a guest's folio.

Property Management Systems

There are many automated hotel property management systems available. However, they do not all operate identically. Some generalizations about property management systems may illustrate the nature of front office applications. A property management system consists of sets of automated software packages (referred to as modules) that can support a variety of activities in front office and back office areas. Four common front office software modules are designed to help front office staff perform functions related to:

- Reservation management
- Rooms management
- Guest accounting management
- General management

Exhibit 6 summarizes front office property management system applications.

Reservation Management Software

An in-house reservation management software module enables a hotel to rapidly process room requests and generate timely and accurate room availability, room revenue, and reservation forecasting reports. Most lodging chains participate in remote reservation networks known as global distribution systems (GDSs), Internet distribution systems (IDSs), and central reservation systems (CRSs). GDSs capture, process, and forward reservation information generated mostly by travel agents and airline companies. The largest and best-known worldwide GDSs are Sabre, Galileo International, Amadeus, and Worldspan. IDSs are intermediary websites that represent hotel companies and offer overnight accommodations on a commission or mark-up fee basis. IDSs capture guest reservation data and may be automatically connected to the hotel's reservation management system through a GDS or CRS. Examples of Internet distribution sites include travelocity.com, travelweb.com, priceline.com, hotels.com, and orbitz.com. CRSs are often operated by the hotel company and typically communicate reservations data, track rooms reserved, control reservations by room type and room rate, and monitor the number of reservations received. Most reservation management applications create reservation records for seamless connectivity to a property management system.

A property relying on an in-house reservation module may be able to receive data sent directly from any or all remote reservations channels (GDS, IDS, or CRS).

Exhibit 6 Front Office Property Management System Applications

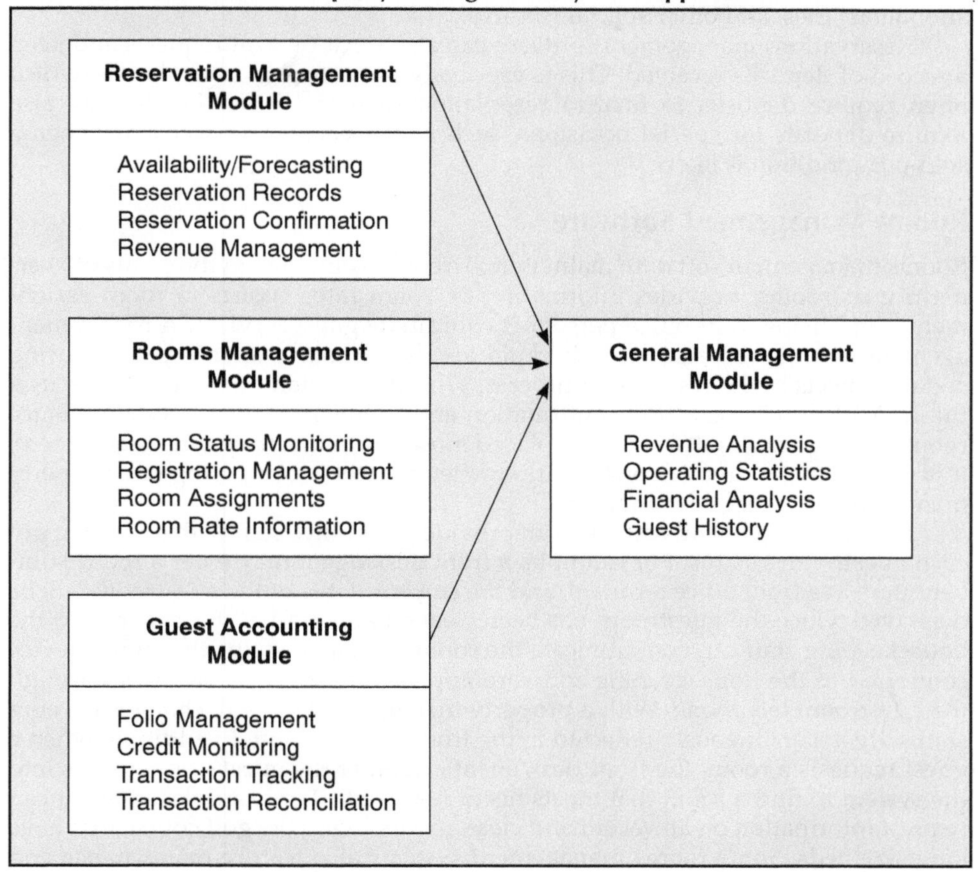

Automated in-house reservations records, files, and revenue forecasts are immediately updated as reservation data are confirmed. It is through electronic file updating that the system remains current and in control of reservations activities. Many systems allow real-time, two-way communication between remote reservations networks and property-level applications, thereby enabling instantaneous updates of inventory and guest information. With this approach, usually referred to as single image inventory, accurate guestroom availabilities and pricing are shared between systems through *seamless integration*.

In addition, previously received reservation data can be automatically reformatted into pre-registration applications, and a series of appropriate records and reports can be generated. Various reservation management reports summarize reservation data and guest account status information, as well as letters or e-mails of reservation confirmations sent to guests with processed reservations. Reservations management software also includes upgraded room rate control features, guest history referencing, and more detailed property information such as bed types, guestroom views, in-room amenities, convention space, public areas, recreational facilities, and other special features.

Reservations management software can also track deposit requests and keep a record of deposits received. This is especially important to resort hotels, which often require deposits to finalize reservation requests. Other hotels may also require deposits for special occasions, such as a special event weekend when a sold-out condition is likely.

Rooms Management Software

Rooms management software maintains current information on the status of overnight guestrooms, provides information on room rates, assists in room assignments, and helps front office personnel coordinate guest services. A rooms management module can also provide rapid access to room availability data during certain aspects of the reservation process. This information can be especially useful in short-term reservation confirmation and rooms revenue forecasting. Since rooms management software has replaced most traditional front office equipment, it is often a major area of consideration when a hotel is comparing one property management system over another.

Rooms management software can provide front office staff with a summary of each guestroom's status. For example, a front desk agent may enter a room number query at a front office terminal, and the current status of the guestroom will be displayed. Once the guestroom has been cleaned and readied for occupancy, the housekeeping staff can communicate the room's updated status through a device connected to the housekeeping software application, or, in some cases, through the guestroom telephone. With a property management system, changes in room status are instantaneously reflected in the front office system. In addition, when a guest requests a room, the front desk agent can enter the guest's preferences into the system to find a room that meets his or her needs. For example, an agent can request information on all vacant and clean rooms facing the golf course that have king-size beds. Some rooms management systems also feature maintenance and special-request dispatch capabilities. For example, a room with an air conditioning problem or needing extra towels can be registered and monitored through the property management system and a hotel engineer or housekeeper can subsequently be dispatched to fulfill the request.

Rooms management software also assists the reservations function. When rooms are temporarily taken out of inventory for maintenance or cleaning, the number of available rooms in the reservation office is automatically adjusted. This helps control future room inventory and ensure that all guests have rooms ready upon arrival.

Guest Accounting Management Software

Guest accounting management software increases the hotel's control over guest accounts and significantly modifies the front office audit routine. Guest accounts are maintained electronically, thereby eliminating the need for folio cards, folio trays, and account posting machines. The guest accounting module monitors predetermined guest credit limits and provides flexibility through multiple folio formats. At check-out, previously approved outstanding account balances may be automatically transferred to an appropriate back office accounts receivable file for subsequent billing and collection. Account management capabilities represent major benefits of a property management system. For example, a credit manager in a large convention hotel can automatically monitor the credit limits of all guests and receive a system-generated report for all accounts approaching or exceeding credit limits.

When the hotel's revenue outlets are connected to the front office system, remote point-of-sale terminals can seamlessly communicate guest charges to the property management system. These charges will be automatically posted to appropriate electronic guest folios. Automatic posting procedures are intended to improve accounting efficiency while reducing or eliminating late charges (charges posted to a guest account after the guest has checked out of the hotel).

General Management Software

General management software cannot operate independently of other front office software packages. General management applications tend to be report-generating packages that depend on data collected through reservations management, rooms management, and guest accounting management software modules. For example, general management software may be able to generate a report indicating the day's expected arrivals and the number of rooms remaining available for occupancy—a combination of reservation management and rooms management data. In addition to generating reports, the general management module serves as the internal link between front office and back office system interface applications.

Back Office Interfaces

A comprehensive property management system involves integrating the hotel's front office and back office areas. Although separate front office and back office software packages can operate independently of one another, integrated systems offer the hotel a full range of control over a variety of operational areas. Such areas include room sales, telephone call accounting, payroll, and account analysis. An integrated system cannot produce complete financial statements unless all the required data are stored in an accessible database. Many reports generated by the back office system depend on the accuracy of front office data collection. Most property management system vendors offer several back office application modules. Four popular back office applications are:

- *General ledger accounting software,* consisting primarily of accounts receivable and accounts payable application packages. Accounts receivable software monitors guest accounts and account billing and collection when integrated with the front office guest accounting module. Accounts payable software tracks hotel purchases and helps the hotel maintain sufficient cash flow to satisfy its debts.
- *Human resources software* may include payroll accounting, personnel recordkeeping, and labor scheduling. Payroll accounting includes time and attendance records, pay distribution, deductions, and withholdings. Personnel

records include personal profiles, labor history, and job performance evaluations. Labor scheduling involves tracking employee skills and availability in relation to the hotel's staffing requirements.

- *Financial reporting software* enables the hotel to develop a chart of accounts to help in producing balance sheets, income statements, and transaction analysis reports.
- *Inventory control software* monitors stocking levels, purchase ordering, and stock rotation. Additional computations include inventory usage, variance, valuation, and extensions.

System Interfaces

A variety of property management system interface applications are available in an automated environment.

Non-Guest-Operated Interfaces. Common interfaces that are initiated and directed by hotel staff include the following:

- A *point-of-sale (POS) system* allows guest account transactions to be quickly transmitted from remote revenue centers to the property management system for automatic posting to electronic folios.
- A *call accounting system (CAS)* directs, prices, and tracks guestroom telephone use for pricing and automatic posting to electronic folios.
- An *electronic locking system (ELS)* typically interfaces with the rooms management module to provide enhanced guest security and service.
- An *energy management system (EMS)* can be applied to automatically control the temperature, humidity, and air movement in public spaces and guestrooms through a rooms management interface.

An EMS is an automated control system designed to manage the operation of mechanical equipment in a lodging property. An EMS interfaced to a property management system offers a number of opportunities for energy control. For example, assume that 50 percent occupancy is forecasted for tonight at a 300-room hotel. Minimizing the hotel's energy consumption on this night becomes a factor in determining which rooms to sell. One approach would be to assign guests only to the lower floors and significantly reduce the energy demands of rooms on the upper floors. By interfacing an EMS with a front office rooms management system, it is possible to automatically control room assignments and achieve desired energy-cost savings.

Guest-Operated Interfaces. Hotels can provide automated conveniences and services by installing a variety of guest-operated devices. In some properties, guests may inquire about in-house events and local activities through automated information kiosks in public areas, or through the television or a portable communication device in their guestrooms. Connecting a printer to an information terminal enables guests to print desired information.

Through connected devices, guests can review their folios and complete the check-out process from remote locations as well as the comfort and privacy of their guestrooms. In-room televisions or other communication devices interfaced with a guest accounting module enable guests to simultaneously access folio data and to approve and settle their accounts by selecting a pre-approved method of settlement. Guestroom telephones interfaced with the property management system may also be used for this purpose. In-room specialty devices linked to external information services allow guests to access e-mail, websites, transportation schedules, local restaurant and entertainment guides, weather reports, news and sports updates, shopping catalogs, and video games.

An *in-room entertainment system* can be interfaced with a front office module or can function as a stand-alone application. In-room entertainment systems allow guests to access various forms of entertainment through the guestroom television or other connected device. If there is a charge for the service, such as a pay-per-view movie, a video game, or Internet access, the charge can be automatically calculated and posted to the guest's electronic folio. To keep guests from inadvertently tuning to a pay channel, the television is usually preset to a non-pay channel or preview channel. Incorporating a preview channel can significantly reduce the number of guest disputes about the validity of applied pay TV or movie charges. In-room entertainment systems may require the guest to contact someone in the front office to request that a pay channel be activated. In addition, a preview channel provides the hotel with advertising opportunities. The preview channel can display information about the hotel's facilities and special amenities. The hotel can also sell advertising for local attractions, thereby creating a modest revenue source.

There are two types of *in-room vending systems*. *Non-automated honor bars* consist of beverage and snack items in both dry and cold storage areas within a guestroom. The bar's beginning inventory level is recorded, and hotel employees on a daily basis note changes in inventory. Appropriate charges for missing or consumed items are noted for posting to the guest's folio. Since honor bars are available at all times, this system often results in an unusually high volume of late charge postings. *Automated honor bars* or *in-room vending equipment* may contain fiber-optic sensors that record the removal of stored products from designated compartments. When a sensor is triggered, these devices assume a sale has transpired and transmit point-of-purchase information to a POS microprocessor that, in turn, communicates to the front office accounting module for electronic folio posting.

Other technology-based guest amenities may include an in-room device connected to online resources. This amenity is popular in hotels serving meeting, convention, and business travelers, and may link with other hotel systems that automatically calculate the cost of the application and forward the charge for folio posting.

Automated Guest Services. Outstanding guest services can provide a competitive advantage in attracting potential guests. For example, in-room entertainment companies are developing systems to provide local information through guestroom software browsers, satellite television and radios, hand-held mapping devices, and mobile devices. Guests can locate restaurants, museums, shops, and other points of interest through access to websites, virtual shopping malls, e-mail, and other online resources and services. In a similar way, hotels can promote their own services or other hotels in the chain. If a guest is interested in a particular hotel or restaurant, for example, the system can automatically connect to the business site, way-finding application, or reservation application.

High-speed Internet access (HSIA) service has evolved from an upgrade amenity to a "must-have" for most hotels. HSIA service, whether wired or wireless, is usually provided in guestrooms as well as in public areas and meeting facilities. At resort locations, wireless HSIA may also be available at pools and recreational facilities, as well as on the beach. Hotels may also offer Internet access through guestroom televisions, the hotel business center, and informational kiosks located throughout the property. While guest Internet access often is complimentary, some hotel brands charge for the service, based on market conditions.

Internet service has also become a major requirement for hotels with meeting facilities. Meeting room Internet service usually requires higher speeds and greater bandwidth, so there may be higher costs the hotel must recover.

Many hotels now provide business centers featuring airline check-in, fax service, photocopiers, conference telephones, and Internet access. There may be charges for use of hardware and software as well as network access arranged through the business center.

Sales Automation Systems

Property management systems and sales automation systems are usually integrated. Once viewed merely as a way to coordinate and manage group reservations and meeting-room space availability, sales automation software now is considered a strategic tool that maximizes revenue while tracking the monetary value of group business relationships.

For front office management, this can be vitally important. By entering group guestroom allocations into a sales automation application, a hotel salesperson can evaluate the number of remaining available rooms on a continuous basis. As with a front office reservation module, in a sales automation system group allocations decrease with each group room reservation commitment. The group allocation will increase when groups give room reservations back to the hotel, or management allocates more rooms to a particular group.

Maintaining accurate and consistent information about the status of group guestroom reservations in both the property management and sales automation systems is critical. The hotel reservations staff may actually have rooms available to sell but be unaware of them, since they may incorrectly appear allocated to a group in the sales automation system even though the group has yet to commit to those rooms. Conversely, group salespersons may oversell group allocations, thereby resulting in no rooms in its block remaining available. To avoid conflicts between these two systems, the information must be properly balanced. Most property management systems directly interface the sales automation function. Interfacing gives group sales managers a clear view of rooms inventory in the property management system, since both systems rely on a single data source. In addition, when group room reservations are returned to the hotel, the rooms will be made immediately available for sale.

Sales automation systems collect sufficient data to identify booking trends, and are capable of tracking group histories. Most group tracking systems store actual group guestroom usage (called **group pickup**), room rates, and non-room (food and beverage, facilities, amenities, etc.) rates. The next time the group books space at the hotel or at an affiliated property in the hotel chain, the system will be capable of providing the group's history and thereby be better able to allocate a group block. Some chains provide affiliate properties access to centralized group history files through a specialized database system. This allows a hotel on the West Coast, for example, to research a group that stayed earlier at an affiliate hotel on the East Coast. Group history files store information on group sales and revenues and the number of rooms blocked (allocated) and booked (reserved). In addition, banquet menus, meeting space usage, VIPs, billing history, meeting planner, group coordinator, and many other pieces of important information may also be available. Such information can be important to front office management. For example, knowing the check-in and check-out pattern of group members may prove helpful for front office staffing. Knowing the group's history regarding its number of no-shows, early departures, suites reserved, and rooms with rollaway beds reserved may also be helpful.

Summary

The functions, activities, and areas of the front office are geared toward supporting guest transactions and services. To many guests, the front office represents the hotel. It is the main source for coordinating nearly every guest service the hotel provides. The financial transactions a guest makes while staying at a hotel determine the guest cycle of business through the property. Transaction flows can be divided into four stages: pre-arrival, arrival, occupancy, and departure. Within each stage, important front office tasks related to guest services and guest accounting can be identified and analyzed. Front office staff needs to be aware of guest services and guest accounting activities throughout the guest stay.

The guest chooses a hotel during the pre-arrival stage of the guest cycle. The arrival stage of the guest cycle includes registration and rooming functions. During the occupancy stage, the front office provides the guest with services, information, and supplies. Other guest services and guest accounting aspects of the guest cycle are completed during the cycle's departure stage. Since activities and functions tend to overlap between stages, some properties have revised the traditional guest cycle into a sequence of pre-sale, point-of-sale, and post-sale events. This sequence improves coordination among hotel operating departments.

Most front office functions are performed at the front desk. The front desk, prominently located in the lobby, is traditionally where guests register, request information and services, relate complaints, settle accounts, and check out. The functional efficiency of a front desk depends on its design and layout. The desk configuration should provide front desk staff with easy access to equipment, forms, and supplies necessary for performing assigned tasks. A property management system comprises software modules capable of supporting a variety of activities in front office and back office areas. In addition, guest- and non-guest-operated interfaces can be connected to the hotel's property management system for greater effectiveness and efficiency.

Key Terms

call accounting system (CAS)—A device linked to the hotel telephone system that accurately accounts for guest telephone calls by identifying each phone number dialed from guestroom telephones and tracking charges.

group pickup—The number of guestrooms a group actually uses.

guest cycle—A division of the flow of business through a hotel that identifies the contacts and financial exchanges between guests and hotel employees.

guest folio—A paper or electronic form front desk staff uses to chart transactions on an account assigned to an individual person or guestroom.

guest history file—A collection of guest history records containing information about interactions between the hotel and former guests.

house limit—A guest credit limit established by the hotel.

late charge—A transaction requiring posting to a guest account that does not reach the front office system until after the guest has checked out.

property management system (PMS)—A computer software package that supports a variety of applications related to front office and back office activities.

registration card—A printed form for a registration record.

reservation record—An electronic document storing such guest data as date of arrival, type and number of rooms requested, deposit, and number of persons in the party.

reservation file—A collection of reservation records.

voucher—A document detailing a transaction to be posted to an electronic folio; used to communicate information from an unconnected point of sale to the front office system.

Review Questions

1. What activities are involved in the four stages of the traditional guest cycle? Why have some properties replaced the traditional cycle with a three-stage sequence?
2. How does the departure stage of the guest cycle conclude both guest services and guest accounting activities? How can the front office use data about the guest stay?
3. How have front office recordkeeping systems evolved over the years?
4. What are some of the organizational concerns of front desk design? What criteria determine the appropriateness of a design?

5. What are some common telecommunications equipment items used in hotels? How do they work?
6. What are the four most common front office software modules? How do they streamline front office recordkeeping? How does a general management module depend on the other three modules?
7. How are newer technologies helping hotels offer more services?

Internet Sites

For more information, visit the following Internet sites. Remember that Internet addresses can change without notice. If the site is no longer there, you can use a search engine to look for additional sites.

Galaxy Hotel Systems
www.galaxyhotelsystems.com

MICROS
www.micros.com

Orbitz
www.orbitz.com

Pegasus Solutions
www.pegs.com

Priceline
www.priceline.com

Sabre Holdings
www.sabre-holdings.com

Travelocity
www.travelocity.com

Travelport
www.travelport.com

Travelweb
www.travelweb.com

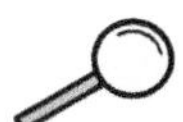

Case Studies

Making the Most of Moments of Truth

#1—Gordon Sumner's Food for Thought

Freelance writer Gordon Sumner stepped off the hotel elevator and glanced at his watch. It was 10:00 A.M. on a Thursday and he was grateful to have had the chance to sleep in late after his 11:30 P.M. arrival the night before. Now the only thing he needed to start the day off right was a hearty breakfast. He headed to the front desk for directions to the hotel restaurant.

"Good morning," the man behind the desk said. "How can I help you?"

"You have a restaurant here, don't you?"

"Yes, we do. In fact, it just received a Golden Palate award from our city magazine."

"Well, I don't know if I'd recognize award-winning food if I ate it, but I would like a good breakfast," Gordon said.

"Then we have just the place for you, sir."

Gordon got directions from the agent and within two minutes he was sitting at a table in a bright, well-decorated restaurant. Looking around, he noticed half-a-dozen other people lingering over breakfast and coffee at nearby tables. From what he could see, the food did look appetizing.

After several minutes passed without a visit from a server, Gordon finally noticed a server walking across the other side of the room. He caught her attention and asked to see a menu. Ten minutes later, he had to flag her down again. *Goodness,* he thought, *the food must be spectacular if this place can win awards despite such poor service.*

"Can I help you, sir?" she said as she approached his table.

"I'd like to order breakfast. Could I get a—"

"I'm sorry, sir, but we stopped serving breakfast at 9:45."

"Well, then, I guess an early lunch would be all right. I'm starving."

The waitress bit her lip. "Actually, we don't begin serving lunch until 11:15. That's about another hour from now."

It was frustrating to see people still enjoying their meals and to realize he wouldn't be able to join them. "All right," he said without enthusiasm, "could I get some coffee to go, then? Maybe I'll grab a newspaper from the gift shop and just—"

She was shaking her head. "I'm sorry, but the register is locked until lunch. We can't handle take-out orders."

"I see," he said, wondering why the man at the front desk hadn't bothered to explain any of this. "So tell me: where can a guy get something to eat around here?"

"You know, if I were you, I'd take the walkway over to the mall across the street. They have a pretty good food court."

Twenty minutes later, Gordon passed through the lobby on his way back from the mall and his fast-food meal.

The front desk agent called out to him, "And was your breakfast award-winning, sir?"

"No, I can't say that it was," Gordon replied icily as he walked by.

The agent looked stricken. "Oh! I'm sorry to hear that. I hope you'll give us the chance to serve you again."

"Not likely," Gordon said under his breath as he stepped into the elevator.

#2—Freddie Bulsara: Dancers, with Wolves

Reservations Manager Freddie Bulsara was looking forward to a glorious Sunday, thanks to his booking prowess. This weekend marked a double coup. On Saturday, the hotel had hosted 230 young ballet dancers and their adult chaperones who were in town for a Sunday morning dance competition. Today, they would check out, opening up a large block of rooms that would match—almost to the room—the needs of a 200-member contingent of conventioneers from the Royal Fraternal Order of Wolves.

Freddie marveled at the perfection of his plan. The dancers would check out by 9:00 A.M., before leaving for their competition; the Wolves were to begin arriving at exactly 1:00 P.M. *Groups like this are really going to put this property on the map,* Freddie told himself.

But something wasn't right. When Freddie stopped at the front desk to ask how things had gone with the dancers, LeighAnne Crenshaw looked up from her work and said, "I can't really say. I'll let you know once they leave."

Freddie felt his heart skip a beat. "It's 11:45, LeighAnne. What are you talking about?"

"When I came in this morning, I found a note here that says the dancers asked to be allowed a late check-out after their competition. I guess a lot of them wanted to be able to come back to their rooms and change their clothes before leaving. Their group leader had it all arranged."

"With *whom?*"

LeighAnne shrugged. "There's no name on the note, but it looks like Brian's handwriting. He would have been working the front desk when they all came in last night."

Brian. A new hire who hadn't been on the job for more than two months. *His misguided need to do anything a guest asks is going to ruin everything I've worked for,* Freddie thought. "Do you know when they'll actually be checking out, then?"

"Well, the competition started at 9:30, and they said it was about two hours long. With travel time, I'd guess they'll be coming back within the next thirty minutes, if that tells you anything."

It tells me we won't have time for housekeeping to finish with the rooms before the Wolves get here, Freddie thought. *We'll have to stall the conventioneers until their rooms are ready.*

"I take that back," LeighAnne said, nodding toward the front entrance. "That looks like their bus now."

"Thank goodness!" Freddie said. "The sooner they get back to their rooms, the sooner we can clear them out and get housekeeping started. It might be tight, but—"

Freddie stopped mid-sentence. His mouth dropped open as the bus doors sprang open and the passengers made their way across the sidewalk to the revolving doors. He expected a stream of little girls in pink tutus. What he saw was a huge pack of middle-aged men wearing wolf ears and shouting, laughing, and punching each other in the arm.

"Oh no," Freddie whispered. He glanced at the clock as the first members of the Royal Fraternal Order of Wolves crossed the lobby toward the front desk.

The man in front—a tall, barrel-chested individual—tugged off his wolf ears and stuck out his hand. "You must be Freddie!" he shouted with a grin. "Darrell Drucker. We spoke on the phone!"

Freddie tried to return the man's energetic handshake, but his heart wasn't in it. The Wolves were quickly filling up every available space in the lobby. "Hello, Mr. Drucker," he managed to say. "We weren't expecting you until one o'clock."

Mr. Drucker looked taken aback. "Why, it's one o'clock right smack on the dot!" Then surprise slowly spread across his face. "We musta forgot to turn our watches back when we crossed that time zone!" he said with a grin. "Well, Freddie, just point us to our rooms, and we'll get out of your hair."

"Actually, it's going to be—"

"Look at that!" one of the other Wolves shouted across the lobby. He was smiling and pointing at the entrance, where dozens of pre-teen girls in tutus and pink and white tights were pressing their way through the doors and into the packed lobby.

"They're ba-a-ack," LeighAnne said dryly, quoting a haunted-house movie from the 1980s.

Freddie just hoped there was a ghost of a chance he would be able to keep everyone happy until the situation was straightened out.

#3—Reg Dwight: A Night to Remember

It had been a quiet Monday night until front desk agent Reg Dwight picked up the telephone at 3 A.M. On the other end of the line was a representative from an international airline. "About half an hour ago, we received a bomb threat concerning a flight to London that already was fueled, filled with passengers, and preparing for take-off," the woman began. "For their own safety, we have had to deplane those passengers, and now we have 260 people who need rooms until we can clear the plane, scan the baggage, and arrange for alternate transportation. Can we send them your way for the duration?"

Although Reg had worked many nights alone at the front desk, this was the first time he had ever faced a situation like this. He took a deep breath. "How many rooms would be involved?"

"With all the families and couples, we would need only about 175 rooms. The airline will of course cover the lodging costs, as well as one meal for everyone at your restaurant."

Reg checked availability. The passengers would have to spread out over most of the hotel, but the rooms were there. He was just about to calculate the financial windfall of 175 rooms at a rack rate of $84 when the woman added, "At 'distressed passenger' rates, of course." *Oh,* Reg thought. *That's $35 per room.* Reg wasn't aware of any existing hotel policies for handling a situation like this. Although it definitely would not be a money-making proposition—it actually cost $40 to deliver a guestroom—Reg thought the value of providing a needed service would outweigh any financial drawbacks. He hoped his supervisor would think so, too.

He told the caller to send the passengers his way and he would take care of them. Reg then asked to be kept informed of the guests' new travel arrangements as soon as they were established. He figured the guests would arrive tired, anxious, and angry about having to get off a plane in the middle of the night and stay longer than expected. He hoped that, by being able to answer many of their questions, he could put them at ease.

"How soon will they arrive?" he asked.

"The buses should be leaving within fifteen minutes, so they will reach your hotel around four o'clock. Just one more thing. You may want to let passengers know that their carry-on and checked baggage will be sent over as soon as it is thoroughly scanned, but that may not be until six. We will send all the shoes over then too."

Did she say "shoes"?

"I'm sorry, I must go," she hurried on. "I will ring back as soon as we have any news to share. Thanks so much for working with us during this emergency."

As soon as she hung up, Reg dialed another call. He knew he was going to need much more help than was normally available at 4 A.M. He called his supervisor at home, waking her to find out who he should contact. In addition to saying that she would come to work herself, she recommended that he call in kitchen, dining room, housekeeping, and front desk staff. Since she had also faced a similar situation before, she explained about the shoes.

"Before passengers can deplane using the inflatable slides, they have to take their shoes off. They usually collect them later on the runway. But in situations like this, the airline will just dump them all in boxes and send them over—unsorted, unpaired—along with a jumble of unidentified carry-on bags and checked luggage. We can put all the baggage in the Heritage Room. The shoes can go in the Carlton Room if Lorenzo hasn't already set up the A-V equipment for the noon meeting that's scheduled there. Hopefully, the shoes will be out in time to allow A-V setup just before the group has to have it."

"I'll make sure that happens."

"Tell you what. I'll be there as soon as I can to help with checking everyone in and covering whatever else needs to be covered. I'll give this some thought myself, but I'd like you to have a list ready for me of all the things you can think of that might be affected by having 260 possibly upset and worried guests arriving—and what those guests might want or need. We're just lucky we had the rooms to give them."

Reg took a deep breath. "*Lucky* wasn't the first word that came to mind," he muttered.

Discussion Questions

1. What steps could the staff at Gordon Sumner's hotel have taken to improve their service?
2. What factors were out of Freddie Bulsara's control? How could he have prepared for problems?
3. What might Reg Dwight's list of affected areas and guest wants/needs include?

Case Number: 3323CA

The following industry experts helped generate and develop this case: Richard M. Brooks, CHA, Vice President, TWE Group; and S. Kenneth Hiller, CHA, General Manager, Holiday Inn, Beachwood, Ohio.

Family Reunions: Worth the Hassle?

Ten years ago, Mr. and Mrs. Johnson discovered the Boden Oceanside Resort and Lodge. Now they were checking in to the resort for the fourth time. But this time was special. They had planned a family reunion with their three children, their spouses, and five grandchildren—all of the grandchildren were under age six. Mr. and Mrs. Johnson were the first to arrive after the long drive from the city. Their check-in went smoothly and they made dinner reservations for thirteen people at 8 P.M. in the formal dining room.

What is the value of a customer? Ten years ago, who at the front desk could have predicted that the Johnsons would become frequent return guests and that this year they would have their small family reunion at the resort?

The week turned out to be a beautiful one for the Johnsons and their children's families. The front desk, on the other hand, was kept very busy by all of the requests. The staff wondered if they would survive the numerous families that had selected the resort for their reunions this summer. The many families were running the rooms division and restaurant staffs ragged. After the elder Johnsons checked in, the level of intensity seemed to take a quantum leap. The remaining Johnson family members arrived in separate vehicles, each having driven the six hours from the city where they had met the night before. The young children were full of energy and the parents were frazzled from being in the car for so long with the kids.

Two hours after check-in, the list of observations and special needs was growing. It included the following:

- Although it was in the high seventies, the night-time low was predicted to be in the mid-forties. One family from Florida requested a space heater because they were accustomed to sleeping in eighty-degree temperatures. The rooms in the lodge either have heat or no heat, with fans for moving the warm air rather than air conditioning. In the summer, the heat is turned off. However, even on cool nights, which most guests appreciate, the lodge stays warmer than the outside air. The space heater was placed in the room upon check-in.
- One of the Johnson children requested bumpers for the crib in her guestroom. Because the lodge had no bumpers ("bumpers" are padded pillows to keep children sleeping in cribs from hitting the side walls), the bell attendant took extra pillows to the room. They were placed in the crib with the child screaming all the while.
- By 8 P.M. it was obvious that the Johnson party would not be eating in the formal dining room. One of the couples came to the desk and canceled the reservation, stating that they would all eat on their own in the less formal lounge area.
- At 10 P.M., one of the families called down for room service. The kids had been too excited to sit in the lounge for their dinner and so didn't eat much. However, much to the family's disappointment, the lodge didn't have room service and didn't serve food after 9 P.M.
- One of the families walked through the lobby at least six times during their first three hours at the lodge. The mother was constantly saying "shhh" to the children while they ran around enjoying themselves.
- One of the families requested a room change to a smoking room. However, they would not accept a room on the ground floor. After a lengthy search, it was concluded that a room change would disrupt the expectations of many arriving guests over the next several days because the only available smoking room was on the ground floor of the lodge. The guests weren't moved after all.

At the front desk, Tabitha, the new front office manager, was shaking her head. This was only the first four hours of the Johnson family reunion at the lodge! What would the next four days be like? Was it worth it to attract families for reunions?

The Johnsons didn't even seem to want to be together. They had all requested rooms a good distance away from one another. How did the parents feel about this? What kind of psychological toll would this one family have on the staff of the lodge over the next four days?

But on the other hand, she considered, what would the revenue for the property be from this one family reunion? And what about future business? Could the staff continue to provide exceptional service to these guests even under the stressful circumstances?

Tabitha was out of the office for the next few days on a brief vacation. When she returned, she asked about the Johnson reunion. No one recalled any unusual occurrences. They remembered the name and a few members of the party. She called up the folio to see whether they had any unusual requests or had done many of the activities offered at the resort. What she found was a total bill of $8,900 with guest charges mainly for rooms and meals. She wondered how many other families would generate nearly $10,000 worth of business in just four days at the lodge. She closed the folio, taking note of the importance of frequent guests and their loyalty. When the next guests checked in for the first time, she couldn't help wondering whether they would someday be frequent guests.

Just a week later, she noticed that the lodge had sold six rooms for three nights to a family named Camper. When they checked in, it seemed like a small army had descended upon the resort. There were the grandmother and grandfather, their six grown children, and eighteen grandchildren, for a total guest count of twenty-six people. The average daily revenue for this small group was projected to be at least $3,000. Tabitha struck up a conversation with the grandfather, asking whether anyone from this party had stayed at the lodge in the past. He told her that no one had, but that they'd heard about the lodge from friends over the years.

As the front office manager, Tabitha thought about what she could be doing to be sure that more first-time guests would become frequent customers. What could they do, for example, to ensure that the twenty-six members of the Camper party would remember their visit and return again and again on their own or with the larger family group?

Discussion Questions

1. In order to make clear to your front office staff the value of an individual customer, how could you calculate the revenue a frequent customer may generate over a long period of time?
2. Family reunions are big business. As front office manager, how would you work with the sales department to ensure quality service for group business?

Case number: 608C17

This case also appears in Todd Comen, *Case Studies in Front Office Management* (Lansing, Mich.: American Hotel & Lodging Educational Institute, 2003).

Chapter 3 Outline

Competencies

1. Discuss the sales dimension of the reservations process, outline the different types of reservations, and describe reservation inquiries and their distribution channels. (pp. 85–98)
2. Describe the process of taking group reservations and discuss group reservation issues. (pp. 98–103)
3. Identify the tools managers use to track and control reservations availability, and discuss reservation records. (pp. 103–107)
4. Describe policies and procedures surrounding the confirmation, modification, and cancellation of different types of reservations. (pp. 107–110)
5. Explain the function of typical reservation reports, and summarize other reservation considerations. (pp. 110–120)

Taken from *Managing Front Office Operations,* Ninth Edition, by Michael L. Kasavana

Chapter 3
Reservations

FROM A GUEST'S POINT OF VIEW, the most important outcome of the reservations process is the hotel having a guestroom ready and waiting when the guest arrives. This guestroom should not be just *any* room, but *the* room that best meets the needs the guest expressed during the reservations process. At the same time, hotel managers have different objectives for the reservations process. They would like the reservations process to provide the highest occupancy and room revenue possible.

To achieve these outcomes, hospitality operations must have efficient reservations procedures in place. Finely tuned procedures allow reservations agents to perform many functions, including identifying what the guest requires and what rooms the hotel has available for the dates requested, recording and acting on reservation details, promoting hotel services, and ensuring accuracy. Reservations agents must be able to respond in a quick, accurate, and pleasant manner. The time an agent spends on researching rates and room package plans, creating records, filing, and other clerical tasks should be held to a minimum.

Processing reservations involves matching room requests with room availabilities and rates; recording, confirming, and maintaining reservations; and producing management reports. Reservation information is especially useful in other front office functions. For example, with the information gathered during the reservations process, front office personnel can use a property management system to finalize room assignments, initiate guest accounts, and track guests' special requests.

At the same time, achieving high occupancy and revenue takes considerable research, planning, and monitoring. In the past, the hotel reservations manager, the front office manager, the rooms division manager, and the general manager have been responsible for these duties. Since the duties associated with room sales have become more important and complex, many hotels have established the position of **revenue manager** to oversee them. A revenue manager is responsible for forecasting demand for each market segment the hotel seeks to attract—corporate transient, group, leisure transient, and others—as well as determining the guestroom rates that will provide sufficient room revenues and occupancies. The revenue manager must coordinate efforts with the reservations, front office, and sales departments to ensure a common base of operational information.

This chapter describes typical activities associated with the reservations process. These activities include:

- Formulating the reservation inquiry
- Determining room and rate availability

- Creating the reservation record
- Confirming the reservation record
- Maintaining the reservation record
- Producing reservation reports
- Researching, planning, and monitoring reservations

The nature of reservations is examined before these activities are addressed.

Reservations and Sales

Prior to automation, reservations agents focused primarily on basic room availability information; they did not have an effective way to identify available rooms by room type. When a guest requested a room, the reservations agent could confirm that a room was available. The agent, however, could not be sure that a particular type of room or that specific furnishings or features were available. Reservations agents would note special requests on the reservation record—such as a no-smoking room or a room with a scenic view or a certain type of bedding—but it was up to the front desk agent to fill such requests at the time of check-in. At the same time, the front desk agent was considered primarily responsible for maximizing hotel occupancy and room revenue. Front desk agents were often provided incentives to sell guests higher-priced rooms during check-in.

Automation of the reservations process provides accurate and current room and rate information. Since room features are normally categorized within the rooms management module, reservations agents can review room and rate information for a specific date. Requests for specific room types, location within the hotel, and special features can be immediately acknowledged and quickly confirmed as part of the reservations process. Many reservation systems automatically pre-assign specific rooms prior to the guest's arrival at the hotel. Pre-registration activities contribute to a more efficient check-in process for arriving guests.

Given the reservations department's increased role in the selling function, much of the responsibility associated with room revenue projections and profitability analyses has shifted to the reservations department. For this reason, many lodging companies currently view reservations as part of the sales department, even though the function has traditionally been part of the rooms division. Reservations agents are not merely order-takers; they are trained in sales techniques. Many hotel companies conduct extensive sales training programs with reservations agents, and use the position to identify staff members who would like to make sales their career. Many reservations offices have sales goals, including number of room nights, average room rate, and room revenue booked.

The ability of the reservations department to sell rooms, maximize revenue, enhance inventory control, and improve guest satisfaction is often cited as an important justification for investing in front office automation. With proper emphasis on sales and marketing techniques, properties can more accurately forecast and better react to business volumes. Gathering forecasted sales information and using it to determine pricing or room rate strategies is often referred to as *revenue management.*

As an increasing volume of reservations are completed online, without involvement of hotel personnel, there is greater reliance on designing intuitive websites that assist guests with self-reservations. When a web-based reservation application is connected to the hotel's property management system, reservation records can be seamlessly transmitted to the property level.

The Role of the Sales Department in Reservations

Since a great deal of the responsibility for achieving occupancy and revenue goals has shifted from the front desk to the reservations department, the sales department has taken a more important role in reservations. There are several reasons for this.

First, the sales department is a primary source of reservations for the hotel. Group sales managers or representatives create group reservations. These reservations are most commonly from corporations or trade associations holding important meetings. In addition, a sales representative may be assigned to attracting social, military, educational, religious, and fraternal groups, which together are usually referred to as the *SMERF market*. Although the actual guest reservations may go directly to the reservations office by telephone, central reservations office, group rooming list, group reservations mailer, or the hotel's website, the sales office typically originates the group sale. Therefore, management evaluates the sales department on how many group guestroom reservations it creates. Senior property managers frequently compare the number of rooms in a group's sales contract to the actual number of rooms the group reserves. In so doing, managers are able to verify that the sales department or the sales manager working with the group researched the group thoroughly before accepting the sales contract.

Second, the sales department is usually responsible for generating sales from other markets as well as the group market. The sales department may have a specialist assigned to corporations (to attract the business traveler market) and perhaps travel agencies as well (to pursue the travel agent market). In large or complex hotels, several managers may be assigned to these markets. The job of a sales agent is to familiarize local businesses and travel agencies with the features and benefits of the property. If the local company agrees to provide the hotel with a specific amount of business, it is often given discounted rates. Senior management must ensure that companies provided with discount plans are meeting their commitments.

Depending on the type of hotel, other sales managers may be assigned to work with online travel agencies (OTAs), Internet websites, and other reservation distribution channels. It is the responsibility of a specialized sales manager to familiarize distribution channels with the hotel's characteristics and its surrounding areas, in an effort to create a positive impression of the property and the travel destination. Distribution channels are regularly given current information regarding the property and the destination, and may also be offered special room rates and/or accommodation packages to help promote the property and attract guests.

Sales managers are often provided with financial or other incentives for meeting or exceeding their sales goals. In the past, goals were commonly established for room nights sold—that is, the total number of room nights the department and individual sales manager sold and the reservations office recorded. Unfortunately, this often led sales managers to significantly reduce room rates in order to close the sale. It is better for sales objectives and incentives (including promotions) to be related to the total revenue a sales manager generates, so that sales managers are not tempted to sell guestrooms at low rates just to meet room-nights-sold quotas.

The Reservation Sales Planning Process

The sales department can book business many months or years in advance. It is not uncommon to make group reservations five years in advance at large, group-oriented hotels. Some hotels have group contracts even further into the future, as the size of the group may limit the number of hotels that are able to accommodate the demand. Other hotels may have the majority of their group business booked no more than six months in advance. Either way, it is usually the sales department that initiates the reservation and revenue management processes, simply by focusing on committing rooms well into the future.

The reservations manager should be involved in every decision affecting the hotel's occupancy and revenue opportunities. In some cases, it is the reservations manager who monitors group and non-group business and informs the sales department of room availability. In other cases, the reservations manager may also be responsible for the hotel's revenue objectives. Every proposed group or corporate rate is evaluated, and the hotel's management team is notified when offering discounted rates jeopardizes revenue goals. Through this involvement, hotel managers can plan and control future business, rather than merely react to market conditions.

One example of planning and controlling group business is the mix of group and transient reservations a hotel accepts. This is generally decided in the annual budgeting process. The mix of business is very important, as it affects total room revenue. Since a hotel's sales department is generally focused on group sales, it is usually allocated a specific number of group rooms to sell. This is called a *group allocation*. The sales department is allowed to sell the rooms within the group allocation without additional approval. However, should sales managers desire to sell more rooms than have been set aside in the group allocation, they generally need the approval of the hotel's sales director or general manager. The reservations manager is usually the person who evaluates these requests and reports on their potential financial impact to room revenue forecasts.

Types of Reservations

The majority of hotel guests make reservations. Reservations may take many forms, but they can all be placed in one of two broad categories: guaranteed or non-guaranteed. It is important for hotel managers to know their state's law concerning guaranteed and non-guaranteed reservations. In some states, confirming a guaranteed reservation is considered a binding contract. If the hotel then fails to provide the room, legal penalties can be applied should the guest file a complaint with the proper state authority.

Guaranteed Reservations

A **guaranteed reservation** assures the guest that the hotel will hold a room until a specific time of the day following the guest's scheduled arrival date. This time may be check-out time of the following day or any other time the hotel chooses. The guest, in turn, guarantees to pay for the room, even if it is not used, unless the reservation is canceled according to the hotel's cancellation policies and procedures. Guaranteed reservations provide some protection for the hotel's revenues even in the case of a **no-show,** a situation in which a guest makes a reservation but does not register or cancel the reservation. Variations of guaranteed reservations are discussed in the following paragraphs.

Prepayment. A **prepayment guaranteed reservation** requires that a payment in full be received prior to the guest's day of arrival at the hotel. From the perspective of the front office, this is generally the most desirable form of guaranteed reservation. This type of guaranteed reservation is commonly used at resort hotels.

Payment Card. Major credit and debit card companies have developed systems to ensure that participating lodging properties receive payment for no-shows through **payment card guaranteed reservations.** Unless a credit or debit card guaranteed reservation is properly canceled before a stated **cancellation hour,** the lodging property will charge the guest's payment card account for one night's room rate plus tax; the card company will then bill the cardholder. Payment card guaranteed reservations are the most common form of guaranteed reservation. Resorts may charge a no-show guest for more than one room night, since the average length of stay at a resort is usually longer and it is more difficult for a resort to fill rooms that become available close to the day of arrival.

Advance Deposit. An **advance deposit guaranteed reservation** requires that the guest pay the hotel a specified amount of money prior to arrival. The amount of an advance deposit is typically large enough to cover one night's room rate and tax. (At resorts that traditionally have longer guest stays, advance deposits of several nights' room rate and tax are often required.) The pre-arrival amount will typically be larger if the reservation is for more than a one-night stay. If a guest holding an advance deposit guaranteed reservation fails to register or cancel, the hotel may retain the deposit and cancel the reservation for the remainder of the guest's stay. This type of guaranteed reservation is most common at destination resorts and convention center hotels. A variation on this type of deposit applies the deposit received to the last night of the stay. This is intended to ensure collection of room revenue should the guest depart earlier than scheduled.

Voucher or MCO. A type of travel agent guarantee is the travel agency voucher or miscellaneous charge order (MCO). The MCO is a voucher issued by the Airline Reporting Corporation (ARC) and is controlled by many of the same travel agency regulations that control airline tickets. Many resorts prefer MCOs if they must accept vouchers, because ARC guarantees payment if the travel agency defaults on the payment. With travel agency vouchers and MCOs, the guest has prepaid the amount of the deposit to the travel agent. The agent forwards a voucher or MCO to the hotel as proof of payment and a guarantee that the prepaid amount will be sent to the hotel when the voucher is returned to the travel agency for payment. Usually, with vouchers and MCOs, the travel agency deducts its commission before sending payment to the hotel.

Corporate. A **corporate guaranteed reservation** involves a corporation entering into an agreement with a hotel. A corporation may sign a contractual agreement with the hotel that states that the corporation will accept financial responsibility for any no-show business travelers the corporation sponsors. Such contracts are often popular in downtown or business center hotels catering to a large number of transient guests. The corporation, in turn, may receive a single comprehensive invoice from the hotel for several stays, thereby simplifying the billing process.

Non-Guaranteed Reservations

In the case of a **non-guaranteed reservation,** the hotel agrees to hold a room for the guest until a stated reservation cancellation hour (usually 4 P.M. or 6 P.M.) on the day of arrival. This type of reservation does not guarantee that the property will receive payment for no-shows. If the guest does not arrive by the cancellation hour, the hotel can release the room, meaning that it can add the room to the list of other rooms available for sale. If the guest arrives after the cancellation hour, the hotel will accommodate the guest only if a room is available.

It is common for hotels planning on full occupancy or nearing full occupancy to accept only guaranteed reservations. The goal behind this strategy is to maximize hotel revenue by reducing the number of potential no-shows. The efficiency and accuracy of a hotel's reservations process is especially critical in full or nearly full occupancy conditions.

Reservation Inquiries

A property receives reservation inquiries in a variety of ways. Regardless of the source, the reservations agent or website will collect information about the guest's stay through a process known as a *reservation inquiry.* The reservations agent or online process should collect such information as the guest's name, address, e-mail address, and telephone number; company or travel agency name (if applicable); date of arrival and date of departure; and the type and number of rooms requested. The reservations agent or online sequence should also try to establish the room rate, number of people in the party, method of payment or guarantee, and any special requests.

Distribution Channels

Hotel chains have come to realize that having multiple distribution channels for promoting their goods and services is critical to success. The more channels of distribution, the more opportunities guests will have to inquire about and book rooms. Reservation inquiries may come in through the property's reservations department (property direct), through a central reservations system, through a cluster reservations office, via a global distribution system (airline and travel agent network), via an intersell agency, or through Internet distribution systems

Exhibit 1 Sources of Reservations

Property Direct

Central Reservations System
- Affiliate Reservation Network (Hotel Chains)
- Non-Affiliate Reservation Network
  - Leading Hotels of the World
  - Preferred Hotels
  - Distinguished Hotels

Cluster Reservations Office

Global Distribution Systems
- SABRE
- Galileo International
- Amadeus
- WorldSpan

Intersell Agencies

Internet Distribution System

Third-Party Websites

(see Exhibit 1). Each of these distribution channels is discussed in the following sections.

Property Reservations Department. Hotels traditionally handled many of their reservation transactions directly. Depending on the volume of direct customer contact, a hotel may have a reservations department handle reservation inquiries rather than another department or online resource. A reservations department handles direct requests for accommodations, monitors any communication links with central reservations systems and intersell agencies, and maintains updated room availability information. Property-direct reservation requests can reach a hotel in several ways:

- *Telephone:* Prospective guests may telephone the hotel. For most hotels, this was one of the most common methods guests used to request a room reservation.
- *Mail:* Written requests for reservations are highly uncommon, except maybe for group, tour, and convention business. Generally, mail requests are sent directly to the reservations department.
- *Property website:* Hotel websites are among the most popular distribution channels today. A hotel's website handles reservation transactions through its automated links to the hotel's property management system.
- *Property-to-property:* Hotel chains typically encourage guests to plan their next hotel stay while in an affiliated property by offering direct communication

between properties. This approach can significantly increase the overall number of reservations handled among affiliated properties.

- *Faxes and text messaging:* Faxes and text messaging account for a small portion of reservation transactions. Another text option involves communicating reservations through TDD equipment. This equipment is a specially designed teletype machine that allows people with hearing disabilities to communicate by telephone.

Reservations agent sales process. Most hotels have specific sales procedures for reservations agents to use when taking a reservation from a caller. Common components of the reservations agents' sales process include the following:

1. *Greet the caller.* A warm greeting always sets the proper tone for the conversation. A greeting such as, "Thank you for calling the Casa Vana Inn. This is Holly speaking. How can I help you today?" is always more favorably accepted than a curt greeting such as, "Reservations."
2. *Identify the caller's needs.* It is appropriate to ask the caller about arrival and departure dates, the number of guests, bed preference (double, king, etc.), group or corporate affiliation, and other information that helps define the caller's needs. For example, if a caller states that he or she is traveling with children, the reservations agent should attempt to identify the number of children and their ages.
3. *Provide an overview of the hotel's features and benefits, based on the caller's needs.* Reservations agents should listen closely to what the caller has said in Step 2. Based on that discussion, the agent should highlight the hotel features and benefits that align with the caller's needs. For example, mentioning a year-round swimming pool might be a feature welcomed by families, but they probably would not be interested in the hotel's business center. On the other hand, the business center may be an attractive feature to business travelers.
4. *Propose a room recommendation, and adjust it according to the caller's response.* This step comes after the image of the property has been established (Step 3) and reassures the caller that the reservations agent has truly been listening. If the caller says the recommended room is too expensive or doesn't meet his or her needs, the agent should revise the recommendation as necessary.
5. *Close the sale.* Ask for the reservation; don't wait for the caller to make a decision. Such questions as, "Mr. Bradley, would you like me to reserve that room for you now?" may be appropriate after Mr. Bradley's needs have been addressed.
6. *Gather the reservation information.* Record all the reservation information necessary, according to hotel procedures. This process typically involves repeating the guest's name, arrival date, departure date, room type and rate, and special requests to the caller to confirm the information. This is also the time to secure the reservation guarantee and provide a reservation confirmation number.

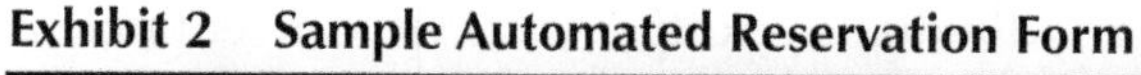

Exhibit 2 Sample Automated Reservation Form

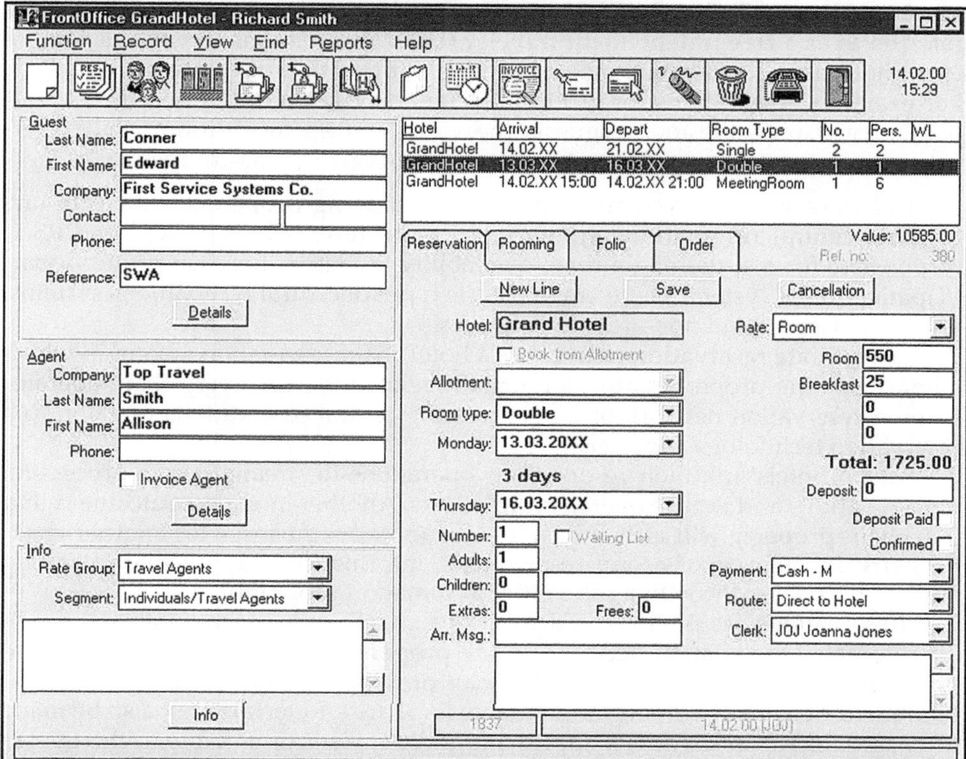

This electronic reservation record is from Hotellinx, a property management system offered by Hotellinx Systems Ltd., Turku, Finland. The company's Internet site (www.hotellinx.com) provides additional screen selections from its system.

7. *Thank the caller.* Closing a call as warmly as opening it leaves callers with a sense of confidence that they have selected the right hotel.

First and foremost, the reservations function is a sales process. One important quality of a successful reservations office is that the agents are trained to sell the hotel instead of being merely order-takers. They create a positive image of the property and instill a desire on the part of the caller to make a reservation. If the agents are excited about their work, their enthusiasm will carry over to callers. Conversely, if the reservations agent sounds unenthusiastic, the caller will not have a positive impression of the property and may decide to make a reservation elsewhere.

Most of the information gathered during the reservation inquiry will be used to create the **reservation record,** a process discussed later in the chapter. Exhibit 2 shows a sample reservation display screen used in an automated reservation system.

Reservations can be made for individuals, groups, tours, or conventions. A guest coming to the hotel as an individual and not part of a group is typically referred to as a **free independent traveler (FIT).** Reservations of persons coming to the hotel as part of a group may be handled differently from those of FIT guests. For example, reservations for group members may be recorded and filed under both the group's name and the guests' individual names. In addition, group reservations may receive special attention during pre-registration activities.

Central Reservations Systems. A majority of lodging properties belong to one or more **central reservations systems.** A central reservations system or CRS is responsible for maintaining a room availability inventory for each property participating in the system. There are two basic types of central reservations systems: affiliate networks and non-affiliate networks.

An **affiliate reservation network** is a hotel chain reservation system in which all participating properties are contractually related. Nearly every chain operates its own reservation network or outsources the central reservations function to a reservation technology supplier.

Chain hotels link their reservations operations to streamline the processing of reservations and reduce overall system costs. Another intended outcome is that one chain property will attract business for (or refer business to) another chain property. In the case of group reservations, information may be shared among affiliate properties through a sales office automation program.

Reservations are often passed from one chain property to another through an automated reservation network. If one property is fully booked, the reservations system handling the transaction may provide an online referral to accommodations at a chain property in the same local area. Referrals may also be made to properties whose locations appear more convenient or suitable to the guest's needs. Affiliate reservation networks that allow non-chain properties to participate in the reservation system are able to represent themselves to a broader market. Non-chain properties in an affiliate reservation system are referred to as **overflow facilities.** Reservation requests may be routed to overflow facilities only after all the available rooms in chain properties (within the targeted geographic area) have been booked. Overflow facilities typically pay a commission fee to the hotel or reservation network for these referrals.

A **non-affiliate reservation network** is a subscription system designed to connect independent or non-chain properties. Non-affiliate reservation networks enable independent hotel operators to enjoy many of the same CRS benefits as chain-affiliated operators. Like an affiliate reservation network, a non-affiliate network usually assumes responsibility for advertising its service and maintaining room availability data. Examples of non-affiliate reservation networks are The Leading Hotels of the World, Preferred Hotels & Resorts Worldwide, and Distinguished Hotels. In many cases, these non-affiliate networks accept only hotels of a certain quality or a limited number of hotels in any geographic area, to keep the value of their service high to participating members.

A central reservations office (CRO) typically deals directly with the public by means of a toll-free telephone number or online web address. Most large lodging chains support two or more reservation centers, with calls and contacts being directed to one of the centers. Reservation centers and websites operate twenty-four hours per day, most days of the year. At peak times, reservation centers will have a large number of agents and automated online servers available.

Central reservations offices typically exchange room availability information with member properties and communicate reservation transactions as they occur. This is normally accomplished through an online communications connection at the member hotel. In this way, reservations information is immediately transmitted between the central reservations entity and the hotel. Rapid-access reservation systems ensure that both the hotel and the central reservations system have accurate, up-to-date information on room availability and rates. Another approach is to have each hotel's property management system hold the master information for its room availability, rates, amenities, and so on; the central reservations system will then gain access when processing reservations. In either case, when a reservation is handled at a central reservations office, property-specific rate and availability data must be uploaded to the central reservation system, and completed reservation transactions processed by the central reservations office must be downloaded to the hotels' property management systems.

Central reservations systems normally provide participating properties with the communications equipment necessary for handling reservation transactions. Communication equipment may take the form of a desktop or notebook computer, an Internet website, an integrated network, a hand-held communication device, or a TDD (telecommunications device for the deaf). The central reservations system typically charges a fee to participating hotels for the services and support equipment it supplies. Hotels may pay a flat fee for the communication equipment and an additional fee for each reservation transaction processed through the system. Alternatively, some central reservations systems charge a flat percentage of room revenue to cover all CRO operational expenses. In turn, each property provides accurate and current room availability data to the central reservations office. Without such data, the central reservations office cannot effectively process reservation requests.

Affiliate and non-affiliate central reservations systems often provide a variety of services in addition to managing reservations processing and communications. A central reservations system may also serve as an inter-property communications network, an accounting transfer system, or a destination information center. For instance, a central reservations system may be used as an accounting transfer system when a chain hotel communicates operating data to company headquarters for processing. When a central reservations system communicates reports on local weather, special events, and seasonal room rates, it serves as a destination information center.

Cluster Reservations Office. Chains that have several properties in a geographic area may opt to establish a single reservation or "cluster" office or website. This satellite entity operates similarly to a hotel chain central reservations system, but serves one specific destination area instead of the entire company. Instead of a reservations agent at the hotel answering the telephone and processing reservation requests, all reservation transactions are channeled through the cluster reservation office or website. When a guest contacts one of the hotels directly for a reservation request, the hotel transfers the inquiry to the cluster entity. Similarly, the company's central reservations network is connected to the cluster network as well as the property itself.

There are several advantages to a cluster reservations office or website. First, there is usually a reduction in staffing; it takes fewer reservations agents or technology specialists to staff a central office than to staff separate reservations offices in every property. Since labor tends to be the highest expense at a hotel, any reduction in labor cost is generally welcome. Second, since reservations agents and websites are serving several hotels at the same time, cross-selling opportunities are created. For example, if Hotel A is full because of a convention, the cluster network can offer another company hotel nearby. This is a convenience for the guest and improves the occupancy of the alternative hotel. Finally, room rates and availability can be coordinated among properties, the brand's central reservations network, and the global distribution systems. This makes reservation processing even more efficient.

Cluster reservations offices and websites may operate centrally or remotely from hotel activities. This physical separation makes communication between the hotel reservation databases being served and the cluster network devices vitally important. Before clustering, general managers could easily review the work of their reservations agents by simply visiting the office within the hotel and observing them. With clustering, coordinating with remote offices and automated networks has its challenges. Perhaps the most important of these is accurate programming and facility descriptions, as there is less opportunity to become familiar with a hotel's rooms, convention services, and other amenities. It is essential, therefore, that the cluster office and website be current in regards to events, facilities, and services at all hotels.

Global Distribution Systems. Most central reservations systems, whether they are an affiliate or a non-affiliate network, connect with one of the **global distribution systems (GDSs).** Most airlines around the world are connected to one or more of these four GDSs: SABRE, Galileo International, Amadeus, and WorldSpan. Historically, GDSs have been owned by an airline or consortium of airlines, but that has changed, since airlines are no longer very involved in the lodging industry. GDSs provide worldwide distribution of hotel reservation information and provide a platform for selling hotel reservations worldwide. GDSs also support the distribution of airline tickets, automobile rentals, and other services required by travelers. By directly linking the reservation systems of hotels, airlines, car rental agencies, and travel agency companies on a global basis through the Internet or a private network, global distribution systems provide access to an extensive array of travel and tourism inventories around the world.

Selling hotel rooms is usually accomplished by connecting hotel companies' reservation systems with the GDSs. Most travel agents around the world have terminals connected to one or more of the many airline reservation systems to book airline travel. By having hotel accommodations and automobile rentals available in the automated system at the same time, most GDSs provide single-source access to most of a travel agent's selling requirements. In one transaction, a travel agent can sell an airline ticket, hotel room, and automobile rental.

Travel agents may be reluctant to book hotel rooms through GDSs, fearing that room availability and room rates are not current, and the confirmation process will not be efficient. Hotel companies have improved their service to guests and travel agents by linking their central reservations systems to GDSs, which allows travel agents to book reservations directly into hotel property management systems with immediate verification of room availability and rates. This linkage is called **seamless integration** or **seamless connectivity.**

Intersell Agencies. An intersell agency is a reservation system alternative to a GDS that contracts to handle reservations for more than one product line. Intersell agencies typically handle reservation services for airline companies, car rental companies, and lodging properties—a "one call does it all" type of approach. Although intersell agencies typically channel room reservation requests to a hotel central reservations system, they may also communicate directly with a destination hotel. The fact that a hotel participates in an intersell arrangement does not preclude its participation in other types of central reservations systems.

Internet Distribution Systems. Many hotel companies, airlines, and car rental firms offer online reservation services through an **Internet distribution system** or IDS. Examples of IDSs include Expedia, Hotels.com, Orbitz, Hotwire, Priceline, and Travelocity. IDSs enable travelers from many different market segments to use desktop and mobile devices to reserve hotel rooms, book flights, and select rental cars. Vacation travelers, business travelers, corporate travel offices, international visitors—all are able to use the World Wide Web to make travel and accommodation reservations. The variety of potential guests accessing reservation-capable websites to place reservations has prompted hospitality companies to develop user-friendly reservation search engine and booking procedures.

Large and small hotels alike have a presence on the Internet. Chains often have a website focusing first on the brand and its features, then on the individual properties within the chain. Most chain Internet sites allow visitors to book reservations. Independent hotels also support websites that, while they may not be as technically sophisticated as chain sites, provide similar information and allow visitors to complete a reservations process.

Some prospective hotel guests are concerned about the privacy and security of financial transactions over the Internet. However, hotel websites have adopted security procedures based on reliable encryption methods that protect against fraud. When users access online reservation systems, web browsers automatically engage a high-level security feature.

In addition to providing an effective reservations process and securing transactions, online systems are also capable of performing important marketing functions. Reservation features of many hotel websites enable users to participate in special events and rate promotions. Some enable users to access a multimedia presentation of the features and benefits of the hotel—complete with a "walk-through" of the property (a virtual tour of the various rooms and services offered). Others allow users to reserve golf tee-times, spa treatments, space on local tours, and other activities, as well as make dining room reservations.

Distribution Channel Revenues

Revenues derived by hotels (suppliers) and agents (sellers) forming distribution channels vary widely, depending on the channel or supplier/agent relationship. Central reservations offices typically charge affiliate properties either a fixed rate per night per room, regardless of reservation activity, or a transaction fee based on reservation activity, or both. The amount of revenue earned by the CRO depends on the financial arrangements contracted between the chain and its member properties. Global distribution systems and Internet distribution systems receive revenues from hotels through commissions, by levying transaction fees or transmission fees, and/or by selling hotel rooms that have been discounted.

To illustrate how revenues might be affected by various distribution channels, consider this sample transaction. Suppose a chain hotel is selling a guestroom for $100. If the sale came to the hotel directly, via its property reservations department, the hotel would receive $100. However, if a GDS agent sells the $100 room, the hotel receives less money. Why? Because there are multiple fees that reduce the net revenue to the hotel. The seller (a travel agency, for example) may earn a 10 percent commission ($10 in this case) and the GDS may charge a $3 transaction fee. In addition, the reservation transaction may be processed through the chain's CRS, which might charge $5 for its services. In this example, the hotel receives $82 for the sale, while paying out $18 in commissions and fees.

When hotels sell rooms via the various distribution channels discussed in this section, the objective is to offset associated commissions and other fees with an increase in occupancy and overall room revenue than would otherwise be realized.

Group Reservations

Group reservations can involve a variety of contacts: guests, meeting planners, convention and visitors bureaus, tour operators, and travel agents. Group reservations typically involve intermediary agents and require special handling. Usually, when a group selects a hotel, its representative deals with the hotel's sales or reservations department. If sufficient accommodations are available, an agreed-upon number of guestrooms, called a **block,** is set aside for the group's members. Group members may be given a special reservation identification code or reservation web address to use to reserve rooms within the group's assigned block. Reservations received from group members are applied against the rooms held in the group's block, thereby reducing the number of rooms available within the block. Rooms reserved for specific guests are referred to as **booked.** As group members reserve rooms, the room statuses change from *blocked* to *booked.* Normally, the hotel will establish progress dates to evaluate the degree of conversions from blocked to booked rooms. Unreserved rooms in the block may be released to the hotel's available room inventory at a predetermined date. This time frame is usually referred to as the group reservation **cut-off date.** Typically, the cut-off date is clearly stated in the contract the group's representative completes with the hotel. The hotel may honor reservation requests received after the cut-off date so long as rooms remain available.

Group Reservation Issues

Although group reservation procedures appear simple, a number of potential problems may develop. The following sections consider common group reservation participants and issues.

Creating a Group Block. Group business is often highly desired by hotels. Yet creating and controlling a group block has its pitfalls. When handling group blocks, the reservations manager should be aware of the following procedures:

- Group business demands that a contract be created specifying the exact number of rooms required and the quoted rates. The contract must also specify the main group arrival and departure dates, any special considerations such as suites or complimentary rooms, method of reservation, and the group and individual billing arrangements. Early arrival and late departure dates may also be included in the contract. The contract should also note the group cutoff date for room availability. This information should be applied to the front office system so that reservations can be automatically tracked.
- The reservations manager should verify the total number of rooms required for the group against what is available in the hotel. The sales department often has access to a front office terminal to verify general availability before booking the group. However, the group block should always be verified by the reservations manager to be sure the system inventory is accurate before confirming the room block to the group. If the group will take away rooms from transient (non-group) business, the reservations manager should notify the sales or general manager of the possible effect. This is called **non-group displacement.** Determining displacement is important, because the hotel may block rooms for group guests that it would normally sell to non-group guests, often at a higher rate. In addition, frequent guests of the hotel may have to be turned away and disappointed when a group takes these rooms. Transient guests may feel uncomfortable in a hotel dominated by group business, or will be forced to go elsewhere if they are not able to reserve rooms due to group blocks.
- Before blocking the rooms, the reservations manager should check the group's history with the hotel, if available. For example, if the group requests a fifty-room block and the record shows the group booked only forty rooms the year before, the reservations manager may wish to confer with the sales manager before finalizing the block. Reducing a block based on the group's history is called a **wash down** or a **wash.** If the group does not have a history at the hotel, it is sometimes possible to check with the hotel that last accommodated the group. By following these steps, the reservations manager helps control room inventories and ensures that as many rooms as possible are available for sale. It is important to note that the wash-down process must be handled very carefully. Contracts are legally binding and the hotel must provide the number of rooms specified in the contract. If a group leader finds out that a hotel does not have the number of available rooms specified in the contract, there can be significant legal consequences.

- As group reservations arrive, the reservations manager must monitor the room availability in the block. It is important for the reservations manager to notify the sales department when a block does not look like it will fill or if more rooms are needed in the block due to strong demand. The sales department can then contact the group and make adjustments to the room block. If more rooms are needed, there may be an impact on the group allocation and the hotel may have to choose between taking the additional group reservations or referring them to other hotels. If fewer rooms are needed than blocked, this can be an opportunity for the sales department to sell additional rooms.
- Group room sales programs are an important issue for the reservations manager to monitor. By definition, a *definite group* is a group that has signed a sales contract. All definite groups should be entered into the reservation system as soon as they have signed a contract, in order to maintain an accurate room inventory. A *tentative group* is a group that has had a contract sent to them, but has not signed or returned the contract to the hotel. Some hotels choose to enter tentative groups into their reservation system. In this way the hotels can keep track of what they believe they have sold of their group allocation. However, it is necessary to track tentative groups to be sure they are updated to definite status or removed from the reservation system. Holding tentative groups on the books for too long may prohibit the booking of a definite group and can cause confusion between the sales and reservation offices.
- The method of sending group reservations to the hotel is also important and often included in the sales contract. Attendees may be allowed to make reservations directly with the hotel and through the central reservations network or online. Direct registration activity may not always be desired. In other cases, the group sponsor may want to receive the reservation requests before they go to the hotel. Many corporate group reservations are provided to the hotel on a rooming list from the company; this may also apply to tour groups from travel agencies. Group leaders often prefer to closely control rooming and billing arrangements. Agents in the reservations office must be careful that they honor these arrangements and not accept reservations outside of the agreed-upon procedures.

Conventions and Conferences. Problems can occur during a convention or conference if a close working relationship is not established between the hotel's sales staff and the group's meeting planner. If good communication and a spirit of cooperation are established early on, many problems can be avoided. Suggestions for hotels dealing with convention groups include the following:

- Know the convention group's profile, including its cancellation, no-show, and last-minute reservation history.
- Review all relevant hotel reservation policies with the convention planner.
- Inform reservations agents that the convention has been scheduled, and go over the reservation process set up for the convention.
- Produce regularly scheduled reports to update the status of the convention block.

- Generate an up-to-date list of registrants at regular intervals.
- Correct errors found by the convention planner immediately.
- Confirm reservations from attendees as soon as they are received.
- Return rooms to the group's block when cancellations are received and inform the convention planner.
- Distribute a final rooming list to the convention planner and all hotel staff involved with the convention.

Convention and Visitors Bureaus. Large conventions sometimes require the use of rooms at more than one hotel to accommodate all the convention attendees. When conventions take rooms at many hotels in a city, they are often called city-wide conventions. Frequently, room requirements at several hotels are coordinated by a separate housing or convention bureau within the city. Special application software may be used to help monitor and coordinate this effort. Each hotel must determine the number and type of available rooms it is willing to set aside for convention use. The objective of the bureau is to accommodate all attendees by coordinating hotel availabilities with reservation requests. The convention and visitors bureau normally uses a communications network to notify participating hotels on a daily (or more frequent) basis. In return, each hotel informs the bureau of any requests or cancellations communicated directly to the hotel's reservation system. Through such an exchange of information, the bureau assists each hotel in effectively managing its convention block.

Tour Groups. Tour groups are groups of people who have had their accommodations, transportation, and related travel activities arranged for them by a professional tour operator. Hotels should be especially careful to research the reliability and past performance of tour operators and travel agents. Once acquainted with a tour operator's history, reservations managers may feel more secure when blocking and booking reservations for a tour group. Suggestions for dealing with tour group reservations include the following:

- Specify the number and types of rooms to be held in a group block, including rooms for drivers and guides.
- Clearly state a cut-off date, after which unused rooms in the block will be released for other hotel use. On or before the cut-off date, the tour operator should supply the hotel with a guarantee on the number of rooms the group will need (if the operator can't supply a final rooming list by this date).
- Specify a date by which the organizer will provide a final rooming list (if this date is different from the cut-off date).
- Monitor the amount of advance deposits required and their due date.
- Note on the reservation record any services and amenities the property will provide as part of the group package.
- Include on the reservation record the name and telephone number of the tour group's representative or agent.

- Note any special arrangements, such as early arrival, baggage handling, registration, and check-out procedures.

Attendee Management and Housing Systems Software. Attendee management and housing systems software is a supplemental reservation planning tool. Historically, group meeting planners and hotel reservation staffs had to coordinate group attendee reservation activities without the help of automated systems. Group reservations were once handled by telephone or via a printed reservation mailer. Group leaders would distribute mailers to potential attendees, who would complete the mailer and return it to the hotel. This was a time-consuming process that was often inaccurate, due to illegible guest handwriting or confusion over dates and rate plans or other issues. Hotels then had to report the reservations they received to group leaders, so they could keep track of group reservations on their end.

These problems were relieved when hotel companies allowed group reservations via their websites and call centers. Although a website can be helpful, the hotel staff must ensure that the site's group information is accurate. Group attendees using the website will receive the appropriate group rate for a guestroom allocated to the group only if the information is accessible at the time of the reservation.

Attendee management and housing systems software automates the group reservations and registration process. The software relies on the Internet to communicate with potential attendees. Attendee management applications focus only on meeting registration activities, while housing system applications are designed to handle guestroom reservations and meeting registration activities.

With an attendee management and housing registration system, the group leader creates a special website that provides information about the group event and reservation availability. The information is then linked to the group's main website, so people visiting the site can see the information. Some systems allow group leaders to load e-mail and postal addresses; the group leader can then send e-mail and printed messages via regular mail to prospective attendees. Attendees receiving the e-mail message can click on the Internet link contained in the message, then register for the meeting and reserve a room. Prospective attendees receiving the printed message are given the website address, so they can log on and make their reservations.

These systems capture guest information, including the guest's name, mailing address, e-mail address, payment card information, guestroom request, and much more. Guests can usually identify special needs; they may indicate that they plan to arrive early, for example, or request a no-smoking room. Group attendees can sign up for specific presentations, events, or recreational activities (they can reserve golf tee times or make spa reservations, for example).

Once the guest provides the information requested on the website, the information is sent to the group for processing. Simpler systems provide meeting planners with reports that are forwarded to the hosting hotel for manual processing. More sophisticated systems, like Passkey, actually interface with hotel reservation systems. When a reservation is made through a Passkey website to a "Passkey-enabled" hotel, the reservation is made, and confirmed to the guest, automatically. This eliminates the manual processing associated with transcribing printed reports into the hotel's reservation system. It also keeps the room inventories accurate between the group and the hotel. For large meetings, some systems combine the inventories of many hotels, thereby giving guests a choice of where to stay. This is especially important for meetings that use much of a city's guestroom inventory. Attendee management and housing system software can be very cost-effective because it simplifies the meeting registration and reservation processes. This is important to meeting planners and hotels alike, since it improves communications between them and reduces the amount of manual labor.

Reservation Availability

When a hotel or its website receives a reservation inquiry, it is important to compare the inquiry data with previously processed reservations. Processing a reservation request results in one of several responses. A hotel can:

- Accept the reservation as requested.
- Suggest alternative room types, dates, and/or rates.
- Suggest an alternative hotel.

In any **reservation system,** it is necessary to closely monitor the number of reservations in order to control **overbooking.** A hotel should use care when accepting reservations beyond its room capacity. Some states have laws concerning guests with guaranteed reservations who do not receive rooms when they arrive at a hotel. Reservation systems can be programmed to closely monitor overbooking.

Comparing historical reservation volumes against actual arrivals can produce an overbooking factor to serve as a booking guideline. Depending on the property's no-show reservation history, management may allow the reservations system to overbook. Overbooking is a strategy aimed at helping the hotel to achieve 100-percent occupancy by hedging against guests who do not arrive or cancel their reservations. Based on historical data and the experience of knowledgeable managers, reservation systems may be able to forecast cancellations, early check-outs, and no-shows with a high level of accuracy. Room reservation forecasts must be shared with the sales department and general manager, who may have additional information not entered in the reservation system, such as information about competitive pressures and other issues. By booking a hotel slightly beyond its available room capacity, the system attempts to ensure that as many rooms as possible are occupied.

Overbooking should be approached cautiously. If a reservation system is allowed to book too many rooms, guests with confirmed reservations may have to be turned away. This creates poor guest relations and discourages repeat business. To properly control overbooking, managers must monitor reservation system activity by controlling booking, blocking, and cancellation information.

Reservation Systems

An automated reservation management module in a property management system can keep close track of reservation activities. Such systems can tightly control room

Exhibit 3 Daily Arrival, Stayover, and Departure Report

ARRIVALS, STAYOVERS, DEPARTURES FOR KELLOGG CENTER
PAGE 001
01/19/XX 15:03

DATE	ARRIVE	STAYON	DEPART	GUESTS	SOLD	UNSOLD	REVENUE
01/19	19	83	4	135	102	43	5,185.00
01/20	34	57	45	131	91	54	4,604.00
01/21	37	55	36	130	92	53	4,495.50
01/22	15	6	86	29	21	124	1,116.00
01/23	12	14	7	36	26	127	1,252.00

Courtesy of Kellogg Hotel & Conference Center, Michigan State University, East Lansing, Michigan.

availability data and automatically generate many reservation-related reports. Exhibit 3, for example, shows a daily expected arrival, stayover, and departure report. It indicates that for January 19, nineteen arrivals, eighty-three stayovers, and four departures are expected. In addition, this report projects estimated room revenue based on reported reservation information. Automated systems can also generate reports summarizing reservations by room type, guest profile, and many other characteristics. The biggest advantage of an automated reservation system is the improved accuracy of room availability and rate information. As reservations agents input reservations and reservation modifications or cancellations into the system, the inventory of available rooms is immediately updated. In addition, front desk transactions involving no-shows, early departures, or walk-ins will immediately update the room availability. This is important, as it provides sales managers with the occupancy and room-rate information they need to help them achieve revenue objectives.

Exhibit 4 shows a guestroom control log from a hotel sales software package. For each day of the week, the screen shows the total number of rooms still available for sale, as well as the number of rooms allocated to definite and tentative group bookings and the number of rooms protected for front office sales to transient business. Room sales are coordinated in real time as salespeople, reservations agents, and the front office manager have instant access to the most current information.

Once all rooms in a specific category are sold, the reservation system can be programmed to refuse any further reservations in that category. When checking availability in a closed category, a reservations agent may receive a message such as the following displayed on the screen: *The category of rooms requested is not available.* Some reservation systems are programmed to automatically suggest alternative room types or rates, or even other nearby hotel properties. Systems can be programmed to itemize room availability for future periods and may display open, closed, and special event dates for an extended period of time. *Open dates* refer to available room days, while *closed dates* depict full-house forecasts. *Special*

Exhibit 4 Guestroom Control Log

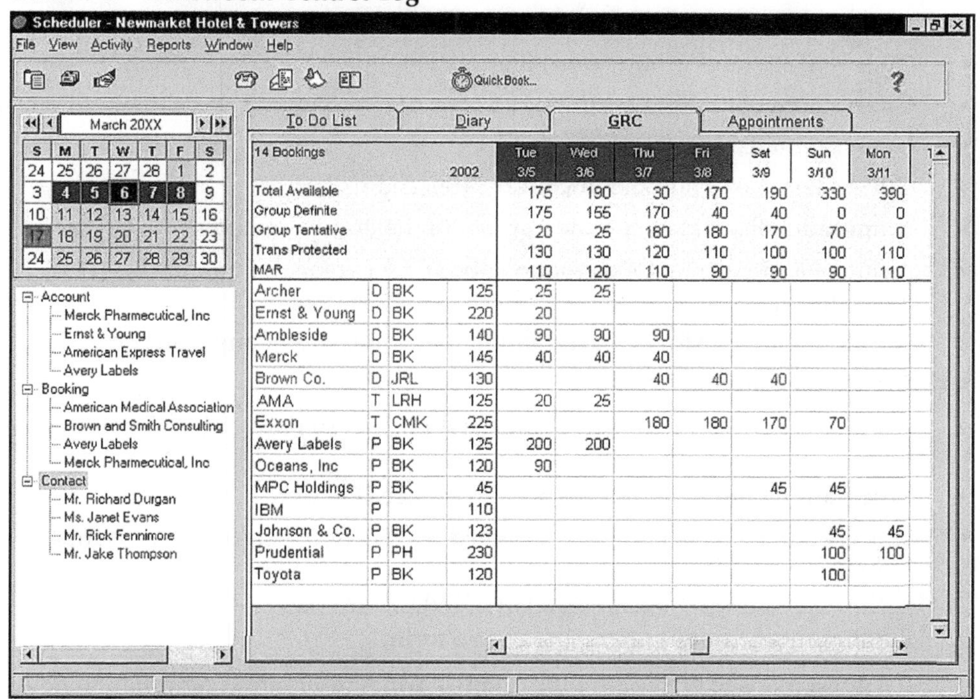

Source: Delphi for Windows/Newmarket International, Inc., Durham, New Hampshire. For more information, visit the company's Internet site at www.newmarketinc.com.

event dates can be programmed to alert reservations agents that a convention or large group is expected to occupy the hotel either before, during, or immediately following a caller's requested day of arrival. In addition, many reservation systems have a management override feature that enables overbooking. This override provision should be exercised with extreme care.

Reservation systems store reservation records electronically, thereby allowing the creation of waiting lists for high-demand periods. This feature contributes to the processing of group reservations and the implementation of revenue management strategies. The future time frame for tracking reservations is called the "reservation horizon"; most automated systems have horizons of two to five years.

Reservation Records

Reservation records identify guests and their occupancy needs before the guests' arrival. These records enable the hotel to personalize and/or customize guest service and schedule staff more accurately. Reservation records also contain a variety of data that the hotel can use to generate several important management reports.

Reservations agents or online hotel booking engines can create reservation records based on interactions with guests only after determining that a request for a reservation can be met. These electronic records initiate the guest cycle. To create a reservation record, the reservations system typically captures such guest data as:

- Guest's name (and group name, if applicable)
- Guest's home or billing address
- Guest's e-mail address
- Guest's telephone number, including area code
- Name, address, and telephone number of the guest's company, if appropriate
- Name of and pertinent information about the person making the reservation, if not the guest
- Number of people in the party, and perhaps the ages of any children
- Arrival date and time
- Number of nights required or expected departure date, depending on how the system is designed
- Reservation type (guaranteed, non-guaranteed)
- Special requirements (infant, disabled guest, or no-smoking accommodations, for example)
- Additional information as needed (method of transportation, late arrival, flight number, room preference, and so forth)

If a guest plans to arrive after the hotel's normal reservation cancellation hour, the guest should be informed of the property's policy for non-guaranteed reservations. Once the necessary information has been captured, the system may immediately assign a reservation confirmation number. Confirmation number assignment provides both the guest and the reservations department with a unique reference for the reservation record.

In the case of a guaranteed reservation, additional information is generally needed for the reservation record. Depending on the guest's method of guarantee, the following information may be required:

- *Payment card information:* This information consists of the payment card type, number, expiration date, security code number, and cardholder's name. Online reservation systems may be connected to a transaction processing service that allows for automatic verification of payment card information.
- *Prepayment or deposit information:* This information comes in the form of an agreement from the guest to submit a required deposit to the hotel before a specified date. A proposed advance deposit or prepayment guarantee should be closely monitored to ensure the correct amount is paid by the designated date; if it is not, the reservation may need to be canceled or reclassified as non-guaranteed. If the hotel's policy is to collect the deposit at the time of reservation, the guest should be notified. If a payment card is provided at the time the reservation is made, the transaction processing services will post the deposit to the hotel immediately.

- *Corporate or travel agency account information:* This information includes the name and address of the booking company, the name of the person making the reservation, and the client's corporate or travel agency direct billing account number (if previously assigned by the hotel). For efficiency, the hotel may preload an approved list of corporate and travel agency account numbers to expedite the verification process. Even if the corporation or travel agency does not require billing, a tracking account is usually set up in the reservation system to monitor the business the corporation or travel agency provides to the hotel. In this way the sales office will have the information necessary to negotiate or renegotiate contracts with such companies.

Reservations systems should disclose important aspects of guaranteeing a reservation. Guests must be aware that their accommodations will only be held until a specific time past their scheduled arrival time. Guests must also know that if they fail to cancel the reservation before a specified time, they may forfeit the deposit or the hotel may levy a charge against the guarantee.

Individual properties and chains may differ with respect to quoting and confirming room rates during the creation of a reservation record. Although published rates may be subject to change without notice, a rate quoted and confirmed during the reservations process must be honored. Reservation systems must be capable of modifying rates based on such factors as:

- Supplementary charges for extra services or amenities.
- Arrival or minimum stay requirements in effect for the dates requested (if any).
- Special promotions in effect for the dates requested (if any).
- Applicable currency exchange rates, which may alter final charges for international guests.
- Applicable room tax exemptions and percentages.
- Applicable service charges or gratuities.

Reservation Confirmation/Cancellation

A reservation confirmation means that the hotel acknowledged and verified a guest's room request and personal information. A written confirmation states the intent of both parties and confirms important points of agreement: names, dates, rate, type of accommodation, number of rooms, deposit required or received, and number of guests. *Confirmed reservations may be either guaranteed or non-guaranteed.*

Reservation systems normally generate a confirmation notice shortly after the reservation request is matched with availability. Information can be retrieved from the reservation record and automatically reformatted into a specially designed letter or e-mail format. While there are probably as many formats for confirmation letters and e-mails as there are hotels, all confirmation notices generally include:

- Name and address of guest
- Date and time of arrival

- Room type and rate
- Length of stay
- Number of persons in party
- Reservation classification (guaranteed or non-guaranteed)
- Reservation confirmation number
- Special requests, if any

Depending on the nature of the reservation, the confirmation notice may also include a request for a deposit or prepayment, or an update of the original reservation detailing reconfirmation, modification, or cancellation.

For guests requesting accommodations and services covered by the Americans with Disabilities Act, the confirmation notice is an important channel of communication. It assures these guests that their special needs are understood and the accommodations they need will be ready. Hotels often categorize guestrooms that are specially equipped for disabled guests in a separate inventory classification for improved control.

Confirmation/Cancellation Numbers

As part of the reservation confirmation process, systems may assign a reservation **confirmation number.** A confirmation number helps assure a guest that a reservation record exists. It can be especially useful to a hotel in referencing a specific reservation record requiring modification or cancellation. Similarly, reservation systems may issue a reservation **cancellation number** to guests properly canceling a reservation.

Issuing a reservation cancellation number protects both the guest and the hotel. In the event of any future misunderstanding, the assignment of a reservation cancellation number can prove that the hotel received the cancellation within policy guidelines. In the case of a canceled guaranteed reservation, a reservation cancellation number may relieve the guest of an obligation to pay any charges posted against the guarantee. Without a reservation cancellation number, a guest may have trouble disputing a no-show billing. Cancellation numbers are not normally assigned to guests who cancel their reservation after the hotel's stated cancellation hour. These reservations are considered canceled outside the available time frame. If the canceled reservation is non-guaranteed, the guest is not obligated to pay the hotel. Procedures for issuing cancellation numbers may be part of an established agreement between the hotel and a payment card company relative to no-show billing.

Each reservation system typically uses unique methods of generating confirmation and cancellation numbers. These numbers can include portions of the guest's scheduled arrival date, the reservations agent's initials, a property code, and other relevant information. For example, under one system, the cancellation number 36014MR563 represents these facts:

360 = guest's scheduled date of arrival (from consecutively numbered days of the year)

14	=	property code number
MR	=	initials of the reservations agent issuing the cancellation number
563	=	consecutive numbering of all cancellation numbers issued in the current year

Calendar dates can be expressed in three digits when the days of the year are numbered consecutively from 001 through 365 (366 in a leap year). These are often referred to as *Julian dates.* For example, the number 360 in the example corresponds to December 26 in a non-leap year.

Confirmation and cancellation numbers should be stored in separate files for quick referencing. Cross-referencing reservation cancellation numbers by scheduled date of arrival can help facilitate other related functions. For example, the cancellation of a reservation will result in updated reservation reports that assist management in staffing and facility planning.

No matter how thorough the reservations process, there is no way to avoid an occasional reservation change or cancellation. This fact does not make the proper creation of a reservation record any less important. A system's capabilities for storing and retrieving reservation records and related files are vital to the reservations process. If a person contacts the hotel or hotel website to change a reservation, for example, the reservations agent or automated filing system must be able to quickly access the correct record, verify its contents, and process the modification. The system must also be able to promptly re-file the reservation record and update pertinent reservation reports.

Modifying Non-Guaranteed Reservations

Guests sometimes make non-guaranteed rather than guaranteed reservations when they expect to arrive at the property before the hotel's reservation cancellation hour. However, situations can arise that make it impossible for a guest to arrive on time. For example, delayed airline flights, road-construction bottlenecks, or weather conditions may hinder travel. When delays are apparent, experienced travelers often contact the hotel and notify the staff of the delay, or change their reservations from non-guaranteed to guaranteed in order to avoid being canceled at the hotel's reservation cancellation hour. Reservations systems capable of processing reservation changes must closely adhere to hotel policies. Typically, a system would:

1. Access the correct non-guaranteed reservation record.
2. Capture the guest's payment card type, number, and expiration date.
3. Assign the guest a new reservation confirmation number, if it is hotel policy.
4. Complete the change from non-guaranteed to guaranteed reservation status according to additional system procedures, if any.

Canceling a Reservation

A prospective guest does the hotel a service when he or she takes the time to cancel a reservation. A reservation cancellation informs the hotel that a previously reserved room is once again available, and helps the front office more effectively manage its rooms inventory. Hotels should make processing reservation cancellations easy and efficient. Reservation cancellations, like any guest service, require the reservations website or front office staff to be as guest-friendly and effective as possible.

Non-Guaranteed Reservations. To cancel a non-guaranteed reservation, the reservation system may require the guest's name and address, number of reserved rooms, scheduled arrival and departure dates, and reservation confirmation number, if available. This information will ensure that the correct reservation is accessed and canceled. After recording the cancellation, the system should assign a cancellation number.

Payment Card Guaranteed Reservations. Most payment card companies will support no-show billings only if the reservation system issues cancellation numbers for properly canceled reservations. Reservations systems may follow a cancellation procedure for payment card guaranteed reservations that involves the following steps:

1. Access the correct reservation record.
2. Assign a reservation cancellation number.
3. Add the cancellation number to the reservation cancellation file.
4. Verify updated room availability information (room returned to available inventory).

Advance Deposit Reservations. Policies related to the cancellation of advance deposit reservations vary greatly among hotel companies and reservation systems. The reservation system should follow procedures similar to those it uses for processing reservation cancellations. Deposits are normally returned to guests who properly cancel reservations. While reservation systems must always be precise when assigning and recording reservation cancellation numbers, it is especially important when an advance deposit is involved.

Reservation Reports

An effective reservation system helps maximize room sales by accurately monitoring room availabilities and forecasting rooms revenue. The number and type of management reports available through a reservation system are functions of the hotel's needs and the system's capability and contents. Popular reservations management reports include the following:

- *Reservation transactions report:* This report summarizes daily reservations activity in terms of reservation record creation, modification, and cancellation. Other possible reports include specialized summaries such as cancellation reports, blocked room reports, and no-show reports.
- *Commission agent report:* Agents with contractual agreements may be owed commissions for business booked at the property. This report tracks the amounts the hotel owes to each agent.

- *Regrets and denials report:* Regrets and denials are ways of classifying lost business. Regrets are recorded when guests choose not to make a reservation. There may be several reasons for this, including room rate, room type availability, location, and other factors. Denials are recorded when the hotel is unable to accept a reservation request. This is most often due to room availability or restrictions put on new reservations. In many hotels, each of these situations is recorded for review by management. If the hotel is getting too many regrets due to rate, management may need to adjust the rate to be more competitive. Denials help management decide such things as group allocations, or whether more rooms of a certain type need to be added to the property. Some companies call this report the "turnaway report" or "lost business report."
- *Revenue forecast report:* This report projects future revenue by multiplying predicted occupancies by applicable room rates. This information can be especially important for the hotel's long-range planning and cash management strategies.

Expected Arrival and Departure Lists

Expected arrival and departure lists may be generated according to a predetermined schedule or on demand to indicate the number and names of guests expected to arrive, depart, or stay over.

A list of expected arrivals may be displayed or printed in the reservations department or via any connected device. Front desk agents depend on having expected arrival information to facilitate an efficient guest registration process. Similarly, expected departure information can be used to anticipate and expedite guest account settlement and check-out. Expected departure lists also help front desk staff members identify guests who may be staying beyond their expected departure date but have not told the hotel (overstays). This can be very important, especially when the hotel expects a high percentage of occupancy and may have already pre-assigned the occupied room for an incoming guest.

Reservation systems can also perform preregistration functions and provide other services for special guests, such as VIPs or those staying in specially prepared rooms. Depending on the amount of information collected during the reservations process, a guest may need only to sign a pre-arrival form or submit his or her payment card for processing to complete the registration process. By securing comprehensive information during the reservations process, a more efficient guest registration process may be possible.

Processing Deposits

Advance deposits for reservations should be processed by employees who do not have direct access to reservation records. Reservations personnel should not handle advance deposit payments, as a separation of duties provides a higher level of security for the hotel. Someone independent of the reservations process—the hotel's general cashier, for example—may be a good candidate as an independent reviewer. This employee should endorse and record deposit payments immediately after receiving them and record the following information in a deposits-received system file: form of payment, identifying payment number, amount of payment, date received, guest name, arrival date, and reservation confirmation number. The file should then be accessible by the reservations department. Each reservation record should be updated with the status of its deposit information. A transaction report should verify that the recorded deposits balance with the total reservation deposits entered for the day.

Generally speaking, advance deposits received from guests should be processed with a high level of security. Hotels should discourage guests from sending cash payments through the mail. Checks are better, but payment card deposits are almost always preferred.

Reservations Histories

Front office managers can develop an understanding of the hotel's reservations pattern by analyzing reservation information. The hotel's sales and marketing division can apply reservations data and assorted system reports to identify trends, review products and services, and assess the impact of marketing strategies. Reservations histories include statistics on all aspects of the reservations process, including the number of guests, occupied rooms, reservations (by distribution channel), no-shows, walk-ins, overstays, and understays (people who checked out before a stated departure date). *Overstays* differ from *stayovers* in that a stayover is simply a guest who *continues to occupy* a room between his or her day of arrival and expected departure date. Knowing overstay and understay percentages can help management devise a plan for accommodating walk-ins or guests who request reservations at the last minute. Histories are also very helpful to track individual groups. Knowing the group booking pattern (arrivals prior to the start of the group block and departures after the end of the group block, for example) may be important for more accurately projecting future bookings. Tracking group guests who depart before their expected departure date is important because it may indicate to the hotel reservations manager that additional reservations can be taken on dates held by the group, since a certain number of attendees tend to leave before their departure date.

Other Reservation Considerations

The topics covered in this section are not part of the typical reservations process. Nonetheless, it is important for front desk and reservations personnel to understand the legal implications of a reservation and be familiar with waiting lists, promotional packages, potential problems in the reservations process, and the impact of e-commerce and online reservations.

Legal Implications

The reservation agreement between the hotel and the guest begins at the time of guest contact. This agreement may be oral or written. Confirming a reservation to a prospective guest in language that states that the guest will be accommodated on a particular date may constitute a contract binding the hotel to provide accommodations on that date. If the confirmation is in response to a reservation request from the prospective guest, it may bind both the hotel and the prospective guest to fulfill the reservation.

Waiting Lists

Occasionally, a reservation request must be denied because the hotel is fully booked on the date in question. However, with sufficient lead time, interested guests may be put on a waiting list for the proposed date. Hotels experiencing high-volume reservations may satisfy excess demand through this technique. A waiting list might be developed and used according to these guidelines:

- Advise the guest that no rooms are currently available for the requested date(s).
- Offer to take the guest's name, telephone number, and e-mail address.
- Agree to notify the prospective guest immediately if a room becomes available due to a cancellation or change.
- Help the guest find alternative dates or accommodations if no rooms become available.

Having a waiting list, when properly implemented and managed, is a good business practice that provides a service to guests that helps foster good will.

Promotional Packages

Many hotels and resorts offer special promotional packages to potential guests. These packages always include the guestroom, plus optional features such as meals, golf, tennis, sports lessons, limousine service, and sight-seeing or other activities in or near the property. Generally, hotels and resorts provide guests with some sort of discount for purchasing a promotional package. Guests often consider promotional packages a bargain and a convenience, since they don't have to arrange to separately purchase the items and activities offered in the package.

Reservations personnel and website content must be very informative about all the packages a property offers. Before buying a package, guests will usually interact with a reservations agent or visit the property's website to learn more about the package in detail, including features and all related prices. If a guest wishes to stay at a resort for four nights, and the resort offers only a three-night package, the reservations agent or the website must be capable of pricing and applying an extra night's stay. Packages can be very effective for hotels and resorts, especially when they are well designed and properly sold.

Potential Reservation Problems

Some steps of the reservations process are more susceptible to error than others. If reservations agents are aware of these trouble spots and can successfully deal with them, mistakes will be less likely. The following sections discuss some common reservation problems.

Errors in the Reservation Record. Unfortunately, there are many opportunities for a reservations agent or a guest at a website to make an error when creating a reservation record. For example:

- The record may be created with an incorrect arrival or departure date, a misspelled guest name, or first and last names mistakenly reversed (for example, *Troy Thomas* might be recorded as *Thomas Troy).*
- The name of the person making a reservation on behalf of the guest may be accidentally entered as the guest's name on the reservation record.

To avoid such problems, the reservations system or agent should verify the information entered on the reservation record by displaying or reciting the information back to the person creating the reservation record. In addition, displaying or quoting the hotel's cancellation policy is appropriate as part of this process, as it can help avoid later problems related to no-show billings or non-return of deposits. Such communication can be especially important to hotels catering to international travelers. An error that prevents access to a reservation record can be disastrous to a hotel-guest relationship.

Misunderstandings Due to Industry Jargon. Sometimes reservations agents or web-based systems use industry jargon that is not always widely understood. This can lead to problems. For example:

- A family with a *confirmed reservation* may arrive two hours after the cancellation hour only to find that the hotel has no rooms available; the family thought a confirmed reservation was the same as a *guaranteed reservation.*
- Two business travelers book a *double room,* anticipating two beds; they are displeased to learn their room has only *one double bed.*
- Parents wishing to have their children stay in a *connecting room* mistakenly request an *adjacent room.* At check-in, the parents find that the children's room is across the hall or next door with no direct connection.

To avoid such problems, reservations agents or web-based systems should make every effort to minimize industry jargon and explain what various terms mean at a particular property. After accepting a reservation, the terms and conditions of reserved accommodations should be provided in addition to the hotel's general reservations policies and procedures.

Miscommunication with Central Reservations Systems. There are some unique possibilities for miscommunication between guests and reservations agents or online central reservations systems. For example:

- A central reservations system serving several hotels in the same city may confuse the guest, causing the guest to make a reservation at the wrong hotel, such as a chain's airport property rather than its mid-city property.
- A system that handles hotels in similarly named cities may book the guest into a hotel in the wrong city or state (for example, Charleston, West Virginia,

instead of Charleston, South Carolina; Pasadena, California, instead of Pasadena, Texas).

To avoid such problems, the hotel's reservations agents or website should furnish the guest with the full name and address of the property at which a reservation has been made. When a reservation system serves more than one hotel in the same city, a thorough description of the hotel's location is extremely helpful to guests. One feature of automated systems is a zip code check or a displayed map of the area. With this program, the reservations agent or guest enters the zip code of the hotel and the system identifies the city associated with the zip code, along with a map with directions to the property, thereby helping to minimize address errors.

Online Reservation System Failures. Unless a reliable communication linkage between the hotel and an online reservation application is maintained effectively, problems can occur. For example:

- The hotel may fail to update its online reservation system database with current room availabilities and rate changes.
- The online reservation system may be delinquent in communicating reservations it has booked to the property.
- Communications equipment, affecting either the online reservation system or the hotel, may become inoperable.
- The hotel may close reservations on a particular date with the online reservations system, but apply this change too late to be effective.
- The hotel may discover that it has rooms available on a certain date due to cancellations or early departures but fail to update the online reservation system in time to gain last-minute reservations.
- Global distribution systems and Internet distribution systems may present similar problems. Reservation systems without effective interfaces to GDSs and IDSs may have to constantly update room availability data through an off-line process. This can be time-consuming and error-prone.

To avoid such problems, hotel management must ensure accurate and timely communication between the hotel and the online reservation systems. This is typically a duty of the reservations manager. When closing reservations for a certain date, the hotel must check for any reservations an online reservation system may have confirmed but not yet communicated. Many companies have automated links between the hotel reservations system and central reservations network that eliminate the timing issues of opening and closing availability and changing rates (seamless integration). Faulty equipment at either end of the communication channel may impair the effectiveness of the reservations process. Attention must be paid to ensuring a sound working relationship between the online reservation system(s) and the hotel's reservation system.

In addition, it is appropriate to frequently double-check the global distribution systems and Internet distribution systems to be sure room availability and rates are correctly displayed. This can be done by reviewing the content of GDS and IDS online offerings on a regular basis.

E-Commerce

E-commerce is an important component in hotel reservations management. (The chapter introduced e-commerce earlier, but it is covered here in more detail because of its importance.) E-commerce extends the reach of hotels far beyond the traditional distribution channels of a hotel reservations office, call center, and global distribution system. Hotels have a presence in multiple distribution channels and direct access to the consumer through the Internet. Regardless of whether a hotel is part of a chain or is independent, it can participate in online commerce via the Internet. Linking with guests through the Internet is actually the easiest part of e-commerce. The more difficult part is knowing which sites provide the best distribution opportunities, which hotel features to present, and which room rates to display.

Initially, the Internet was recognized as an emerging force in hotel reservation distribution, and most hotel companies sought a web presence. At first, most hotels simply placed the content of their printed property brochures online. With first-generation websites, hotel guests desiring to make a reservation contacted the hotel's reservations office by phoning the number displayed on the website. The second generation of hotel website development offered guests the ability to book reservations online. Offering fully interactive reservation capabilities with multiple room types and rates and real-time confirmation quickly became the standard.

At first, many prospective guests checked the Internet to make a hotel selection, and then contacted the hotel directly to make their reservations. But, over time, "lookers" have become "bookers," as consumer confidence in online hotel reservation processing increased.

Hotel companies have expanded their website capabilities by adding specialized search engine capabilities, group sales, and advanced navigational features. Visitors to hotel websites typically can experience 360-degree panoramic tours of facilities, peruse restaurant and banquet menus, and many even receive hotel-generated web-cam streaming video. Searches can be conducted according to such parameters as city, number of guestrooms, types of guestrooms, brand of hotel, function room type, convention settings, nearby businesses, and local area points of interest. For example, potential guests can search for hotels with swimming pools, located near an airport, offering high-speed Internet access, and with twenty-four-hour room service. With some additional clicks, individual traveler and group reservations can be completed and confirmed. In the same transaction, guests may be able to reserve golf tee-times, spa treatments, dining room seating, and shuttle van arrangements.

E-commerce has become so important that a hotel may assign a manager to be responsible for overseeing online content and transactions (the revenue manager, for example). Some hotel companies assign corporate-level managers and implement elaborate technology to coordinate revenue management and e-commerce requirements company-wide.

Potential guests who search the Internet for overnight accommodations do so for convenience as well as price. Many websites offer air transportation and car rentals with hotel reservations through a comprehensive booking engine for the ease of bundled purchasing and potential pricing discounts.

The Internet provides many specialized travel-related sites for specific traveler profiles. For example, there are sites dedicated to:

- Brand-loyal travelers (for example, hilton.com, marriott.com, choicehotels.com, etc.)
- Meeting professionals (for example, mpoint.com, starcite.com, etc.)
- Bargain shoppers (priceline.com, site59.com, and so on)
- Cruise travelers (celebrity.com, cruise.com, cruisesonly.com, etc.)
- All-inclusive hotels (resortvacationstogo.com, for example)
- Interval-ownership vacations (rci.com, intervalworld.com, etc.)

There are many more travel-related websites, some general-purpose, others appealing to specific travel markets.

E-commerce is an effective and expanding distribution channel for potential guest reservations. However, e-commerce must be effectively managed on a daily basis, so management can be sure that hotel information and pricing are properly presented.

Single Image Inventory. In order for e-commerce to be effective, accurate and timely room rate and inventory data must be available to all hotel electronic distribution channels simultaneously. The best means to accomplish this is through single image inventory technology. Simply stated, *single image inventory* means that all reservation distribution channels draw from the same room availability, pricing, rate rules, services, and amenities information. Failure to have all online distributors working from the same data source can be chaotic and lead to unintentional overselling, availability shortages, and erratic levels of occupancy. When using single image inventory, all sellers base transactions against identical information.

E-Commerce Site Categories. E-commerce sites can be categorized as merchant-model or wholesaler sites, and as opaque or transparent sites. Each of these categories is examined in the following sections.

Merchant model. The merchant model, also called the *markup model,* is a hotel e-commerce strategy for an online intermediary, such as an IDS, negotiating room pricing with the hotel. The participating hotel is asked by the online seller (merchant) to provide rooms at a discount (for example, 20 to 30 percent) below the lowest published rate normally charged for the room type, or an alternate discounted rate (at the discretion of the hotel). This discounted rate is called the *net rate* and represents the amount paid to the hotel for each room sold at the agreed-upon discount by the merchant. In turn, the merchant or online seller takes on the responsibility for marketing the inventory allocated to it. The merchant will mark up the net rate to achieve the room rate charged to the guest. This is termed the gross rate.

For example, consider a standard room with a lowest published rate of $100. To determine the net rate, assume the merchant has negotiated a 25 percent discount with the hotel, thereby producing a net rate of $75. The merchant then determines the new selling price of the room (that is, the room's gross rate) by adding a set amount of dollar mark-up or by multiplying the net rate by a desired percentage. In the present example, using a 25 percent markup, this will generate a gross rate of $93.75 ($75 plus the 25 percent markup of $18.75). Therefore, the merchant earns a gross margin (gross rate minus net rate) of $18.75, the guest pays $6.25 less than the $100 rack rate, and the hotel earns $75.

Merchant-model sites tend to rank hotels based on their discounts; the more a hotel discounts its rooms, the more prominently the hotel is listed at a merchant website. Therefore, many hotel managers feel pressured to provide significant discounts to merchant-model websites, fearing that otherwise the hotel will not be promoted as well as its competition. Examples of merchant-model sites include Hotels.com (www.hotels.com), Lowestfare.com (www.lowestfare.com), Orbitz (www.orbitz.com), Lodging.com (www.lodging.com), and Travelocity (www.travelocity.com).

Wholesaler model. With the wholesaler model, the hotel tends to maintain greater control over its room price, as a commission is paid to the wholesaler based on a percentage of the hotel's net rate. Simply stated, the hotel sets the selling price and the wholesaler receives an agreed-upon sales commission (that is, percentage of the price). For example, consider a hotel company that offers a room with a rate of $100 to a wholesaler at a net rate of $80. In turn, the hotel agrees to allow the seller to add a 10 percent ($8) commission. In this example, the room will have a gross rate of $88 and the guest will pay $12 less than the hotel's $100 published rate. Some wholesalers, like Priceline and Hotwire, may negotiate a minimum margin (for example, $5 per room) to be added to the net rate rather than work on a percent commission.

Sellers using the wholesaler model tend to earn less than sellers using the merchant model. It is for this reason that online sellers tend to favor the merchant model; hotels, on the other hand, tend to favor the wholesaler model, because they maintain greater control over their rooms' final price to guests. Examples of wholesaler model sites include Expedia (www.expedia.com), Hotwire (www.hotwire.com), Priceline (www.priceline.com), Travelweb (www.travelweb.com), and Orbitz (www.orbitz.com). It is not uncommon for online reservation websites to work on both the merchant model and a wholesaler model platform.

Opaque sites. At an opaque website, a hotel room is marketed by a price and/or rating category. For example, a hotel may be described simply as a "three-star property" without any reference to brand or property specifics. At an opaque website, hotel rooms are treated as a commodity and are offered based on the action of the highest bidder. The services, amenities, and ambience of the property may not be considered in the hotel selection process. With opaque websites, the brand of the hotel and its features are hidden from the buyer until the transaction is completed. Only a quality rating and the room's general location are known to the buyer at the time of commitment to reserve, hence the use of the term *opaque.* Since neither the hotel's identity nor its brand is disclosed until after the sale is completed, defining whether the guest is a customer of the e-commerce site or the hotel can be challenging and confusing. Since both hotels and travel sites may offer loyalty club points or frequent shopper rewards, this can be important to determine.

Opaque sites often work on an auction basis. Potential guests may specify a rate they are willing to pay, and the site then works with available inventory within the guests' specified quality rating and/or price range. If it has no inventory to sell in the rating or price range specified, it may contact participating hotels to see if they will accept the guest's bid price. Since these rates may be significantly below the hotel's published or even usual discounted rates, profit margins are reduced. For this reason, many hotel companies do not offer loyalty club points or room upgrades for reservations made through opaque sites. Examples of opaque sites include Priceline (www.priceline.com) and Hotwire (www.hotwire.com). It is important to note that several opaque sites offer a transparency-site option as a special feature.

Transparent sites. As with opaque sites, rooms at transparent sites are classified or categorized based on room rate or star ranking. But, unlike opaque sites, transparent sites reveal the identity of hotels in the qualifying range before buyers make a purchase. Transparency allows the guest to select a preferred property among competing entities. Examples of transparent sites include Expedia (www.expedia.com), Hotels.com (www.hotels.com), lastminute.com (www.lastminute.com), and Travelocity.com (www.travelocity.com).

E-Commerce Trends. While most hotels rely on multiple e-commerce distribution channels simultaneously, the channels have become much more sophisticated in the hotel's overall selling strategy. For years, many hotels offered the same rooms on different channels at different rates, often underselling their own brand websites by offering special pricing to unbranded websites. This resulted in a significant erosion of the hotels' average room rates and therefore overall room revenue. Hotels have learned to exercise caution in selecting e-commerce sites, and have developed distinct strategies for each online partner. The majority of hotel branded sites offer a best rate guarantee, which assures the traveler that the lowest online rate appears on the hotel website; should a traveler find a lower rate for the same room on the same date, the hotel company will compensate the traveler (that is, refund the difference plus a premium). A guaranteed rate program normally applies to all distribution channels except opaque websites, since travelers do not learn the identity of the hotel property they are buying (until the transaction is completed), and therefore it is difficult to equate two quoted rates. An individual hotel that allows e-commerce sites to offer rates lower than the brand site may be penalized by its brand or chain.

As hotel e-commerce has evolved, its focus has shifted toward the processing of group room reservations and group meetings, embracing issues such as large room blocks, food and beverage catering menus, tradeshow space allocation, meeting room reservations, and audiovisual equipment scheduling. On some hotel websites, group leaders can use an online request for proposal (RFP) script to enter meeting dates, room and space requirements, and other meeting needs, to which the hotel can respond based on a database query. Catering considerations, the need to control meeting space, and the desire to maximize group revenues make an automated response beyond the capabilities of most hotel companies. The implementation of an automated group RFP response process, based upon sophisticated formulas that involve guestroom-to-meeting-space ratios and projected revenue ratios, has also helped coordinate group activities. Examples of online group search and RFP engines are PlanSoft (www.mpoint.com) and StarCite (www.starcite.com).

Another online booking trend involves the awarding of affinity or loyalty club points (generated by the online booking site) for hotel, auto, air, cruise, rail, and other travel services. In awarding points to guests, the online booking site becomes the featured product, not the destination hotel. Some hotel companies allow loyalty club members to redeem rewards in real time on an affiliated website as well. However, as hotels struggle to promote their unique identity online, such online booking agency practices may be considered confusing and harmful.

A popular online application is dynamic package pricing. Historically, online booking sites have offered only predetermined, rigidly defined (static) hotel packages—for example, "stay five nights and receive a sixth night at no charge, along with a discount on a rental car and airfare." As online booking engines evolve, websites are able to offer on-the-fly (dynamic) pricing of custom packages selected and assembled by the guest (for example, inclusive of accommodations, food service, recreational activities, holiday events, special occasions, etc.). E-commerce technology allows guests to build and bundle components to create a personalized package, generate a unique package price, and simultaneously make multiple reservations for the services placed in the custom package.

In addition, e-commerce capabilities can enable online booking sites to create virtual hotel brands by grouping a proprietary set of preferred hotel properties at a destination site (for example, Expedia's Bargain Hotels). This creates a more complex level of competition within the marketplace.

Summary

Effective hotel operations require an efficient reservations procedure. Reservation systems must be able to respond quickly, accurately, and pleasantly to requests for overnight accommodations. Reservations processing involves matching room requests with room availabilities; recording, confirming, and maintaining reservations; and producing management reports. Reservation information is especially useful in other front office functions.

The reservations office and hotel sales office must coordinate their activities and information regularly. The reservations manager participates in regular sales meetings and ensures that current reservation information is provided to the sales department. Successful reservations agents sell their hotel, creating positive images of the facilities and services. Hotels use specific sales processes to ensure that guests have the right information about the property, and the reservations agent collects all the guest information necessary to process a reservation. The reservation system should contain detailed and timely information covering room types and available rates. Given the capabilities of automation, much of the responsibility for room sales has shifted from the front office to the reservations department and associated websites. Requests for specific room types, locations, and special features can be acknowledged and confirmed as part of the reservations process.

The two major types of hotel reservations are guaranteed and nonguaranteed. Hotels can draw reservations from various market sources within the hospitality industry, including central reservations systems, intersell agencies, and property-direct reservations. There are two basic types of central reservations systems: affiliate networks and non-affiliate networks. In an affiliate network, all of the hotels participating in the network are contractually related (that is, part of a chain); in a non-affiliate network, participating properties are independent (non-chain). Global distribution systems connect central reservations systems with airline computer systems and terminals around the world. The term *intersell agency* describes a central reservations system that contracts to handle more than just hotel rooms. A property-direct system handles all requests for accommodations, monitors any communication links with central reservations systems and intersell agencies, and maintains updated room availability status reports for a single hotel.

Processing a reservation request can result in one of several responses: reservation acceptance; suggestion of alternative room types, dates, and/or rates; and suggestion of an alternative hotel property. In any reservation system, it is necessary to closely monitor the number of reservations accepted in order to avoid overbooking. A reliable reservation system can assist management in maintaining tight control over room availability data and can generate many reservation-related reports.

Reservation records identify guests and their occupancy needs prior to actual arrival. These records enable the hotel to personalize guest service and more accurately schedule staff. Reservation records are created based on interactions with potential guests. A reservation record initiates the hotel guest cycle. A reservation confirmation indicates the hotel's acknowledgment and verification of a guest's room request and personal information. A written confirmation states the intent of both parties and confirms important points of agreement, including the room type and rate for a specific date. Confirmed reservations may be guaranteed or non-guaranteed. As part of the reservation confirmation process, a reservation confirmation number may be assigned to each accepted reservation record. A confirmation number assures the guest that a reservation record exists. It can be especially useful to the hotel in retrieving a reservation record for updating, prior to guest registration. Similarly, hotels may issue a reservation cancellation number to guests properly canceling a reservation. Issuing a cancellation number to guests protects both the guest and hotel in the event of a no-show or a misunderstanding.

An effective reservation system helps maximize room sales by accurately monitoring room availabilities and forecasting rooms revenue. The number and type of management reports available through a reservation system are a function of the hotel's needs and the system's capability and contents. Typical reservations management reports include: reservation transactions report, commission agent report, regrets and denials report (or turnaway report), and a revenue forecast report.

Other reservation considerations include the legal ramifications of reservations, waiting lists, promotional packages, potential problems in the reservations process, and the impact of e-commerce on reservations.

Key Terms

advance deposit guaranteed reservation—A type of reservation guarantee that requires the guest to pay a specified amount of money to the hotel in advance of arrival.

affiliate reservation network—A hotel chain's reservation system in which all participating properties are contractually related.

block—An agreed-upon number of rooms set aside for members of a group planning to stay at a hotel.

book—To sell or reserve rooms ahead of time.

cancellation hour—The hour after which a property may release for sale all unclaimed non-guaranteed reservations, according to property policy.

cancellation number—A number issued to a guest who has properly canceled a reservation, proving that a cancellation request was received.

central reservations system—A network for communicating reservations in which each participating property is represented in an automated database and is required to provide room availability data to the central reservations center on a timely basis.

confirmation number—A code that provides a unique reference to a reservation record and assures the guest that the reservation record exists.

corporate guaranteed reservation—A type of reservation guarantee in which a corporation signs a contractual agreement with the hotel to accept financial responsibility for any no-show business travelers it sponsors.

cut-off date—The date agreed upon between a group and a hotel after which all unreserved rooms in the group's block will be given back to the general rooms inventory for sale.

free independent traveler (FIT)—A traveler who is not part of a group.

global distribution system (GDS)—A distribution channel for reservations that provides worldwide distribution of hotel reservation information and allows the selling of hotel reservations around the world; usually accomplished by connecting the hotel company reservation system with an airline reservation system.

guaranteed reservation—A reservation that assures the guest that a room will be held until a specific time of the day following the guest's scheduled arrival date. This time may be check-out time, the start of the hotel day, or any time the hotel chooses. The guest, in turn, guarantees to pay for the room, even if it is not used, unless the reservation is canceled according to the hotel's cancellation procedures.

Internet distribution system (IDS)—A direct-marketing distribution channel that provides property exposure and reservations management for independent hotels, chain hotels, and third-party intermediaries representing hotel companies.

non-affiliate reservation network—A central reservations system that connects independent (non-chain) lodging properties.

non-group displacement (or displacement)—The turning away of transient guests for lack of rooms due to the acceptance of group business.

non-guaranteed reservation—A reservation agreement in which the hotel holds a room for the guest until a stated reservation cancellation hour on the day of arrival; the property is not guaranteed payment in the case of a no-show.

no-show—A guest who made a room reservation but did not register or cancel.

overbooking—Accepting more reservations than there are available rooms.

overflow facility—A property selected to receive central system reservation requests after room availabilities in the system's participating properties within a geographic region have been exhausted.

payment card guaranteed reservation—A type of guarantee supported by payment card companies; these companies guarantee participating properties payment for reserved rooms that remain unoccupied.

prepayment guaranteed reservation—A type of reservation guarantee that requires a payment in full before the day of arrival.

revenue manager—The manager responsible for forecasting demand for each market segment the hotel seeks to attract—corporate transient, group, leisure transient, and others—as well as determining the guestroom rates that will provide sufficient room revenues and occupancies. Also typically manages e-commerce functions.

reservation record—A collection of data that identifies a guest and his or her anticipated occupancy needs before arrival at the property; enables the hotel to personalize guest service and accurately schedule staff.

reservation system—Software specifically designed to handle the creation, modification, confirmation, and/or cancellation of reservation records.

seamless connectivity/integration—The ability of travel agencies to book reservations directly into hotel reservation systems, as well as verify room availability and rates.

wash down (or wash)—Blocking fewer rooms than the number requested by a group, based on the group's history.

Review Questions

1. What role does a reservations manager or supervisor play in the sales department? What role does the reservations manager or supervisor play in forecasting occupancy and revenue?
2. What are the major types of reservations? What are the responsibilities of the guest and the hotel in each case?
3. What information does a reservations agent need to create a reservation record?
4. How do non-affiliate reservation networks differ from affiliate reservation networks? How do central reservations systems differ from intersell agencies?
5. What methods can be used to guarantee a reservation? What is the difference between them?
6. What are common reservation control devices used by hotels? How is each used to monitor room availabilities?

7. What guest information is necessary for a reservations agent to guarantee a reservation?
8. What is the main purpose of a confirmation letter or telephone call?
9. How does proper cancellation of a reservation benefit the hotel? How can hotels make cancellations as easy as possible for guests?
10. What is the purpose of a cancellation number? How might a cancellation number be generated?
11. What management reports can be generated from reservations data? What are the uses of expected arrival lists and reservations histories?
12. How can reservation procedures for conferences, conventions, and tour groups be made more efficient? What precautions should a reservations manager take before creating a group block?

Internet Sites

For more information, visit the following Internet sites. Remember that Internet addresses can change without notice. If the site is no longer there, you can use a search engine to look for additional sites.

Internet Reservation Sites

BizTravelBrokers.com
www.biztravelbrokers.com

Business Travel Net
www.business-travel-net.com

Hotels and Travel on the Net
www.hotelstravel.com

HotelsOnline
www.hotelsonline.com

Resorts Online
www.resortsonline.com

Travelocity
www.travelocity.com

TravelWeb
www.travelweb.com

Technology Sites

Agilysis Hospitality Solutions
http://hospitality.agilysys.com/index.aspx

Hospitality Industry Technology Exposition & Conference
www.hospitalityexpos.com

Hotel Electronic Distribution Network Association
www.hedna.org

Hotellinx Systems Ltd.
www.hotellinx.com

MICROS Systems, Inc.
www.micros.com

Newmarket International, Inc.
www.newmarketinc.com

Passkey
www.passkey.com

StarCite, Inc.
www2.starcite.com

Softbrands, Inc.
www.softbrands.com

Case Studies

Sarah's Serious Reservations—Working with the CRO

Sarah Shepherd was visiting her hotel chain's Midwest central reservations office in Des Moines, Iowa, wondering why her general manager had wanted her to spend a day touring the facilities with other reservations managers. She had a lot of work to do back in Bloomington, and she didn't understand what good it could do her to see how a roomful of reservations agents took orders over the telephone. "Frankly, I don't know either," her GM had told her. "I just have the suspicion that we could make a lot better use of our central reservations system. We're currently booking 30 percent of our rooms with them. Maybe we could do better. I'd like you to find out if that's true and bring back some recommendations."

Right now, I'd recommend catching an early flight home, she thought as the tour leaders began dividing the large group into smaller teams. Recognizing Gabe Culberson, the reservations manager from her sister property in Bloomington, she went to join his team. "At least I'll have a friend to commiserate with," she said under her breath. Sarah and Gabe were joined by Gwen Hsu, a reservations manager from one of the chain's St. Louis properties.

The tour began "on the floor," where Sarah, Gabe, and Gwen watched as 200 reservations agents answered an unending stream of telephone calls. "This is really the nerve center for the operation," their guide was telling them, trying hard to be heard without interrupting any of the ongoing phone conversations. "Every potential guest who picks up the phone and dials our toll-free number ends up talking to someone in this room. Using the information you've provided that appears on these monitors, agents answer guest questions about rates, availability, amenities, local attractions—the whole works. To the best of their ability, that is."

"What do you mean by that?" Gwen asked.

"Well, we can only pass along the information that managers like you provide. If it isn't in our reservations system, we don't know about it."

Gabe leaned toward Sarah. "That's for sure. You wouldn't believe the difference it made when we posted information about the new children's museum downtown." Then he chuckled. "What am I saying—you've probably noticed the healthy bump in family business, too, right?"

"What do you mean?" Sarah started to ask, but their tour guide was moving on.

The guide stopped behind a reservations agent who was telling a caller about one of the chain's downtown Chicago properties. "This is Michelle," the guide said, "and she's one of our most enthusiastic sales agents. I just wanted you to hear how she works her magic over the phone."

"—that's right, Mr. Davis," Michelle was telling the caller. "Now, I have you booked for a room with two double beds and a rollaway bed for five days. Since you mentioned that you and your wife will be traveling with three small children, though, I would personally encourage you to consider the benefits you would gain by staying in a suite instead. You're right. It is a more expensive room, but it will give your family substantially more room to spread out in during a long stay in the city. Plus, with the suite reservation I can also offer you a special family package price that includes reduced admission to the Field Museum of Natural History, the Museum of Science and Industry, and Shedd Aquarium. That will give your family something fun to do while you're at your conference." Michelle paused, scanning her terminal. "Yes, a hotel shuttle offers transportation to those attractions. Great, I'll reserve a suite in your name and make sure you get the family package price. You'll be able to pick up your museum and aquarium tickets at the concierge desk in the hotel lobby. Oh, and you might tell your wife that the hotel is just one block off of the Magnificent Mile, one of the best shopping districts in the nation. Thank you for calling, Mr. Davis. I hope you and your family will have a great stay."

Wow! Sarah thought with surprise. *She sounds just like one of my own sales agents. In fact, she might even be better than they are!*

The group started moving on when Michelle answered another call. Suddenly Sarah heard Michelle say the name of her own property in Bloomington.

"Wait a second," she called to their guide. "I'd love to hear this."

Michelle was studying her screen. "I'm sorry, sir. I do know that there's a new children's museum in Bloomington, but I don't have any information here about it. Other attractions? There is an annual Frontier Fest, but that's the only attraction I have a record of."

"What?" Sarah said, a bit too loudly. *The Frontier Fest died out two years ago. Why wasn't Michelle-the-Wonder-Agent telling this caller about the Worlds of Water Fun Park that opened less than a mile away last year or the new mall and movie theaters? And why didn't she know anything about the children's museum?*

"It's five minutes from the airport and shuttle service is provided. One moment while I check. I'm sorry, I don't have any information about fees or whether that's a hotel shuttle or an airport shuttle. There may be a charge."

But there isn't, Sarah thought, her heart sinking. *It's our own courtesy van. Why don't you know that?*

"I'm showing a rate of $105 for that room. Would you like me to reserve that for you, then, Ms. McQueen?" This time, Michelle paused for what felt like minutes to Sarah. "I understand. Well, thank you very much for your call. I hope we'll be able to serve you in the future."

Dejected, Sarah turned to her friend Gabe. "She just lost that sale for me."

Gabe peered at Michelle's monitor for a minute. "Actually, Sarah, I think *you* just lost that sale for your hotel." He explained what he meant over coffee during a break in their tour.

"Tell me how you work with central reservations," he said.

"I'm not sure I know what you mean. We tell them how many rooms they can sell, and usually they sell them. It's simple: people call in and the agents take orders."

"But it's not that simple—at least, it shouldn't be. You heard Michelle's conversation with that guy staying in Chicago. She definitely was not 'taking an order.' She was *selling*. She could do that because the Chicago property provided her with every piece of information she'd need in the selling process. That's what I try to do at our property. Anything that I'd normally tell our in-house sales staff I post to the central res system. If the pool is out for repair, if we've changed our menu, if we've added amenities or know of area attractions, if we offer special corporate discounts—all of that information gets added to the database here so it comes up on their screens when a guest calls in."

Sarah was suddenly thoughtful. "So you're saying Michelle didn't know about the children's museum or the defunct Frontier Fest or the courtesy van or our new rate structure because I didn't post the information."

Gabe nodded. "I also noticed that there wasn't any information about that renovation you guys did about a year and a half ago."

"Just rub it in, Gabe," Sarah said, starting to smile. "I admit I had no idea they could be such effective salespeople."

Just then Gwen Hsu walked up. "Oh, they're effective, all right. *Too* effective, if you ask me. My problem is that central res keeps overbooking my property, so I get a seemingly constant stream of guests—with confirmations—that I don't have any room for."

"So you walk them," Gabe said.

"Well, I sure don't walk the folks who've reserved with us directly. They're our regulars. The central res guests are usually one-timers who have to be in town for a meeting; odds are, I'll never see them again."

"Gwen, how often do you update your allocation of rooms with central reservations?" Sarah wondered.

"What do you mean?"

"Gabe's been telling me that central reservations can only work with the information we give them. I just wondered how often you changed their allocation or posted new occupancy information."

"I guess it's usually first-thing-in-the-morning, last-thing-at-night. In the morning, I post the allocation for the day; at night, I check in to see where they stand in relation to the reservations we've developed in-house. That's usually when I get the bad news."

"That may be the problem," Gabe interjected. "I'm on our system probably twelve times a day, updating information and adjusting the allocation. And we don't have a pattern of overbooking."

Gwen frowned, saying that sounded like a lot of work. She would have to evaluate it to decide whether the benefits warranted the extra effort. She then left to ask their guide a specific question before the second half of their tour began.

"That was a good question, Sarah," Gabe said. "You know, by the time the next trip to central res rolls around, I bet your property will be just as involved in and enthusiastic about the system as mine is."

"Actually, Gabe, I was thinking that, next time around, it'll be *your* property's turn to play catch-up," Sarah said, flashing a smile.

Discussion Questions

1. What kinds of information does Sarah need from other departments at her hotel that will enable her to work better with the central reservations office?
2. As the reservations manager, what might Sarah do to improve the effectiveness of her property's work with central reservations?

Case Number: 3324CA

The following industry experts helped generate and develop this case: Richard M. Brooks, CHA, Vice President, TWE Group; and S. Kenneth Hiller, CHA, General Manager, Holiday Inn, Beechwood, Ohio.

Booking Online

Most of the arrivals had checked in to the Boden by 5:00 P.M. on this beautiful late spring day. They seemed to want to get in their first swim of the season and maybe even a stroll on the beach before going to dinner. The computer showed that three more arrivals were expected, a party of three and two couples. Since it was going to be such a nice weekend, many of the guests had arrived without prior reservations, but, given the fact that the season was just getting underway, the resort was able to accommodate all of them. However, the last three parties would nearly fill the resort and lodge for the weekend. Rooms still available included a honeymoon suite, two mini-suites, and three double-double standard rooms. The front office supervisor, Sasha, was pleased with the results.

While Sasha reviewed the departure print-out for Saturday, a handsome tall couple and their daughter stepped from their vehicle under the porte cochere. The valet attended well to their needs, and before long the bell attendant had unloaded their luggage. Sasha assumed that this was the party who had reserved room 314, a room with two double beds and an ocean view, for the weekend. Indeed it was. She welcomed the party to the Boden Oceanside Resort and Lodge. The guest, Mr. Pardonme, said hello and handed Sasha a reservation confirmation. It was immediately obvious that the reservation had been made online by Mr. Pardonme.

Sasha brought up the reservation file on the computer screen and scanned the guest file to determine if the Pardonme party had been assigned a room comparable to the one specified on the reservation confirmation. She knew that sometimes guests who booked online were sold rooms that were not always available when they arrived at the resort. Her concerns were confirmed when she saw that they had been assigned room 314 when they had actually purchased a mini-suite. The price they were paying, however, was for a standard room like the one they had been assigned. Sasha wondered if the Pardonme party would even notice.

She checked them in to room 314 without mentioning the difference, hoping that the two double beds, the nice view, and a reasonably spacious bathroom would satisfy the guests. As it was, there weren't many choices left for them anyway! Sasha decided that if they were dissatisfied she would show them the last mini-suite available, but also let them know that it was usually sold for $145 rather than the $85 bargain online price they were paying per night. Moments later the Pardonmes returned to ask about the suite they were promised. Sasha asked the bell attendant to show them a suite that was usually saved for handicapped guests.

The bell attendant and the Pardonme party went to the suite and, upon entering, Mr. Pardonme thought that the hotel must have gone mad. "Where is the second bed?" he asked, looking a little perplexed.

"It's here on the wall," said the bell attendant. "It's a Murphy bed." Mr. Pardonme looked around the room, looked at his confirmation letter that described the room he had reserved, and shook his head.

Back at the front desk, Mr. Pardonme was a little upset. He told Sasha that the room he had reserved over the Internet was the one that he expected to sleep in for the next three nights. He purposely had phoned the Boden prior to reserving online to be sure that he could get the room of his choice. Whoever had been on reservations that day had told him not to worry because there were plenty of the mini-suites available for the nights he was booking for. She told him the rate that would guarantee him the room was $145 per night if he booked directly with the Boden through the reservations department. She wasn't sure why the online rate was so much lower, but she couldn't lower her rate. So Mr. Pardonme decided to try booking online, and now the room he had selected was not the one he had been assigned. He told Sasha that he wasn't interested in the alternative she had given him because the Murphy bed didn't give him and his wife any more privacy than the double-double that they had first been assigned.

Sasha didn't have any other rooms available that met his specific needs. She told Mr. Pardonme that the best she could do was either of the two rooms that they had been shown. The Pardonme party finally settled for the mini-suite with the Murphy bed. The room would be more comfortable than the first one they had been shown. Sasha did a room move on the computer and gave them the proper keys. She hoped they would enjoy that room. How much time would they spend in it anyway, she thought to herself. And they are getting a great price on the room anyway, so why were they being so picky?

Discussion Questions

1. What were the expectations of the guests?
2. What other options might Sasha have considered in this case?

Case number: 608C02

This case also appears in Todd Comen, *Case Studies in Front Office Management* (Lansing, Mich.: American Hotel & Lodging Educational Institute, 2003).

Overbooked at the Boden Oceanside Resort and Lodge

It was 9:30 P.M. and a couple was at the front desk insisting that they placed a reservation for three nights at the lodge over two months ago. The front desk agent, Rob, was unable to find their reservation anywhere. Rob had been with the hotel for two years and he knew his way around the front office. He had seen this trick before and didn't have much patience for it. As was the routine, however, he checked the reservation system, called the toll-free reservation service and thumbed through the manager's files trying to uncover anything that would suggest that the guests had a reservation for this evening. The guests' names were neither in the history file nor anywhere in the central reservation system.

The hotel was oversold and Rob was in no mood to work with the guests. He had already walked three other parties, two families with reservations and one couple from off the road who didn't have reservations for the evening. He had been taught to walk first-time guests or walk-ins with no reservations. Rob was always advised to hold rooms at whatever cost for those frequent guests who stayed at the resort for at least a week each year. These guests were sacred and never to be sacrificed, even if they didn't show up on the night they were expected. He told the couple politely that there were no rooms available and suggested they try another resort of similar quality down the road. The couple was getting quite belligerent by then and insisted on speaking with a manager.

Matt, the manager on duty, had been busy since coming on duty late that afternoon due to a fully booked house. As he approached the desk, he wondered why Rob couldn't deal with the situation. Matt listened to all of the details and noted that the guests claimed to have had a reservation for a couple of months. He checked the time, noting that it was relatively late, and also checked to see how many arrivals were expected. There were reservations that hadn't been claimed yet and they were all held with a credit card. He wondered if any of the late arrivals had phoned the hotel earlier to cancel their reservation and the message hadn't been entered into the system for some reason.

After pondering for a moment he made up his mind to check the couple in to a double-double that wasn't in the new section of the resort. He figured that they might complain that it wasn't their first choice, but at least it was a room. The couple was pleased when he told them that they could have a room for the night, but that the hotel was overbooked for the next three nights due to a number of small family reunions and that he couldn't guarantee them a room for the following evening. Rob was puzzled by Matt's quick decision, but graciously and smoothly checked the guests into the room that Matt had assigned them.

The remainder of the evening was quiet, with a couple of late arrivals. Rob had time to think over the events of the evening and wondered if he should stay with the resort or if he should apply at the new Four Winds resort that was advertising for an opening team just down the road.

The next day Rob called his manager and gave his two weeks' notice.

Discussion Questions

1. Which guests would you walk to another hotel?
2. What would be a guest-friendly way to walk guests?
3. What are the costs of walking a guest?

Case number: 608C05

This case also appears in Todd Comen, *Case Studies in Front Office Management* (Lansing, Mich.: American Hotel & Lodging Educational Institute, 2003).

Chapter 4 Outline

Competencies

1. List the seven steps of the registration process, explain the function of preregistration, and identify preregistration activities. (pp. 133–136)
2. Describe the function of registration records and registration cards, and identify factors that affect room and rate assignments during the registration process. (pp. 136–144)
3. Outline procedures for establishing the guest's method of payment at registration. (pp. 144–152)
4. Explain the importance of verifying the guest's identity, outline proper procedures for issuing guestroom keys or access codes to guests, and describe the front desk agent's role in addressing special requests from guests during registration. (pp. 152–154)
5. Discuss creative registration options, describe techniques used to upsell guests during registration, and explain how to handle situations in which guests cannot be accommodated by the hotel. (pp. 155–161)

Taken from *Managing Front Office Operations,* Ninth Edition, by Michael L. Kasavana

Chapter 4
Registration

ON-SITE REGISTRATION BEGINS when the front desk agent extends a sincere welcome to the arriving hotel guest. The front desk agent moves the guest into the registration process after determining the guest's **reservation status.** To a great degree, registration relies on the information recorded in the guest's reservation record. Front office personnel will find registration simpler and smoother when accurate and complete information has been captured during the reservations process.

This chapter examines the seven steps of the hotel registration process. The chapter also presents alternate registration options, discusses the front office sales role, and reviews potential strategies when guests cannot be accommodated.

The Registration Process

From a front desk agent's perspective, the registration process consists of seven steps:

1. Preregistration activities
2. Creating the registration record
3. Assigning the guestroom and room rate
4. Establishing the guest's method of payment
5. Verifying the guest's identity
6. Issuing the room key or access code
7. Responding to special requests

We will discuss each of these steps in the following sections.

Preregistration Activities

Preregistration activities (registration activities that occur before the guest arrives at the property) help accelerate the registration process. Guests can be preregistered using the information collected during the reservations process. Typically, preregistered guests need only verify information already entered onto a registration record and provide a valid signature in the appropriate place on a **registration form** or card.

Preregistration normally involves more than merely producing a registration document in advance of guest arrival. Room and rate assignment, creation of a guest folio, and other functions may also be part of the preregistration process.

However, some front office managers may be reluctant to assign a specific room to a guest in advance of check-in, since reservations are sometimes canceled or modified. Specific room assignments often become jumbled when last-minute changes in reservation status are made. In addition, assigning a large percentage of vacant rooms in advance of arrival may limit the number of rooms available to guests who are not preregistered. This imbalance can slow the registration process and create a negative impression of the hotel. Hotels will tend to develop pre-registration policies based on operational experience.

In some front office operations, preregistration services may be limited to specially designated or VIP guests or groups. However, most experienced front office managers prefer to preregister guests with reservation records because it shortens the check-in process and also helps them identify what rooms are available for those guests who do not have a reservation. Since data recorded during the reservations process serve as the basis for preregistration, front office systems will reformat data contained in a reservation record into a registration record. A sample system-generated preregistration card is shown in Exhibit 1. Although a hotel may have to void some pre-arrival room assignments due to last-minute changes, the registration time saved by guests who register without complications usually compensates for the inconvenience caused by the small percentage of cancellations or modifications.

Preregistration helps managers plan for the special requirements of guests as well as the hotel. For example, frequent guests may have a special room they enjoy at the hotel, and guests with disabilities may need rooms outfitted to their special needs. By preregistering these guests, the front desk agent can be sure to satisfy these guests or can notify the department responsible for satisfying the request. Consider the situation in which a room has been assigned to a family requesting an additional bed for an infant. The front desk can then notify the housekeeping department of the room assignment so that a crib can be delivered in advance of the family's arrival. In addition, preregistration helps managers when they anticipate the hotel will be at full occupancy over the next several days. In order to allocate guestrooms properly, it may be necessary to apply reservations management software that enables guest reservations of one or two nights to be preregistered into rooms that have been specially blocked beginning one or two nights in the future. In this way, rooms that are blocked will be available when the early arriving guests check in. In some hotels, this process may be closely monitored several days in advance to ensure that the required rooms remain available.

Preregistration lends itself to innovative registration options. For instance, a hotel courtesy van might pick up a guest arriving at the airport who has a hotel reservation. The driver of the van, equipped with a mobile device, could request the guest's signature on a pre-printed registration card, imprint the guest's payment card, and give the guest a pre-assigned room key—all before the guest arrives at the hotel.

Another variation on preregistration for air travelers involves actual services at the airport. Some luxury hotels have arrangements with nearby airports to provide guests with convenient check-in services. The guest may swipe or tap a major payment card at a remote kiosk interfaced to the hotel's property management system. This arrangement allows the front office to approve the guest's

Exhibit 1 Sample Computer-Generated Preregistration Card

Kellogg Hotel & Conference Center
at Michigan State University

Mike Kasavana
555 IT Lane
East Lansing, MI 48824
US

Arrival Date:	01-24-07	Confirmation #:	1067009
Departure Date:	01-25-07	Room Type:	SQN
No. of Nights:	1	Room:	703
Company:	Kasavana	Guests:	1 /0
Group:		Daily Rate:	$ 129.00
		Deposit:	$
Billing Info:	Direct Bill All Charges to MSU Account		

Please note that checkout time is 12:00 Noon.

If any of the above information is incorrect or incomplete, please use the section below.

Name: ______________________ Telephone: ______________________

Address: ______________________ City: ______________________

State/Prov: ______________ Zip Code: ____________ Country: ______________

The Kellogg Hotel & Conference Center is not responsible for, items in the vehicle, loss of property, including money and jewels, unless placed in a safe deposit box at the Front Desk. I agree that I am personally liable if my indicated company or group does not honor any charges billed to me. Such charges will include the cost of repairs to the guest room due to the damage other than normal wear and tear, and expenses incurred due to the extraordinary security measures undertaken due to bad behavior by me or my guests.

DEBIT CARD AUTHORIZATION WILL IMMEDIATELY BE DEDUCTED FROM YOUR CHECKING ACCOUNT

Credit Card: _____ **Debit Card:** _____ **Direct Billing:** _____ **Cash/Check:** _____

VA___ MC___ AX___ DS___ DC___

Signature: ______________________________________

55 S. Harrison Road, East Lansing, MI 48824 * Ph: 571-432-4000 * www.kelloggcenter.com

Courtesy of Kellogg Hotel & Conference Center, Michigan State University, East Lansing, Michigan.

credit, prepare guest registration records, prepare room keys, and print any waiting messages. When the guest arrives at the hotel front desk, the guest will experience an abbreviated check-in process.

A more sophisticated approach to preregistration involves registering guests designated for VIP service in a hotel area other than the front desk—for example, at a concierge desk. Some hotels arrange for VIP guests to be pre-processed and escorted directly to their guestrooms, thereby avoiding possible delays encountered at the front desk.

A hotel may take care to preregister guests who are members of the hotel's frequent traveler program, are part of an arriving group, or are travelers from a preferred corporate account. Preregistration ensures that these guests receive appropriate accommodations based on their level of loyalty or business affiliation. Some hotels make special provisions for reservations from e-commerce websites, as these reservations may be sold on a **run of the house** basis, meaning that the guest will be assigned whatever room is available at check-in time. Generally, a run-of-the-house guest does not benefit from preregistration activities.

Some hotel companies have centralized guest history systems. Guest reservations can be researched and compared to guest history files through advanced automation techniques. A guest history file will reveal guest preferences exhibited in prior stays that can be acted on as part of the current guest preregistration activity. For example, Wyndham Hotels & Resorts has a guest-loyalty program called "Wyndham ByRequest." Members of Wyndham ByRequest can enter certain personal preferences to create a guest profile or guest history file. This file contains such items as the type of pillow the guest prefers, or whether he or she would like complimentary bottled water placed in the guestroom prior to arrival. Through the preregistration process, the front office can notify housekeeping or room service about guest profile/history requests and preferences.

Creating the Registration Record

After a guest arrives at the hotel, the front desk agent verifies a preregistration record or creates a **registration record** containing important guest information.

Registration records facilitate the registration process. The registration record requires a guest to enter or verify his or her name, address, telephone number, e-mail address, company affiliation (if appropriate), and other personal data. Exhibit 2 shows a sample registration record. As this sample indicates, some registration records may include a statement about the hotel's responsibility for storing guest valuables, as state law may require such a statement. The registration record usually contains a space for the guest's signature to indicate acceptance of the room rate and date of departure. In some states, a guest's signature is a legal prerequisite to establishing an innkeeper/guest relationship. In many states, however, this requirement has been replaced by other provisions, such as the intentional establishment of credit by the guest at the time of registration.

Although a state or local municipality may require a signed registration form, an electronic record establishes the basis for registration processing. Guests arriving without reservations (walk-ins) normally will experience a different registration routine. Front desk agents will need to collect guest data and subsequently input that data into a front office system to create a registration record. Required registration information should be collected from guest responses during check-in.

Registration records require guests to indicate an intended method of payment for the guestroom and other hotel goods and services. In addition, front desk agents should confirm the guest's planned departure date and pre-assigned room rate. These elements are critical to rooms and revenue management. Clarifying the

Exhibit 2 Sample Registration Record

ROOM | NAME | RATE | RESV. ID

ADDRESS

GROUP

ARRIVAL | ETA | FLIGHT

DEPARTURE | RATE | PERS.

CLERK INITIALS

ADULT | CHDRN. | RESV. CLERK | RESV. DATE

REGISTRATION

FOR SAFE KEEPING OF MONEY, JEWELRY AND OTHER VALUABLES INDIVIDUAL SAFE DEPOSIT BOXES ARE PROVIDED AT THE FRONT DESK AT NO CHARGE. THE SHERATON INN-LANSING WILL NOT BE LIABLE FOR ANY ITEMS NOT SECURED IN THIS MANNER.

HOTEL | TYPE | NR-ROOM | NIGHTS

ROOM DESCRIPTION

GUEST'S SIGNATURE X

HOME ADDRESS

DEPOSIT

CITY | STATE | ZIP

SPECIAL SERVICES

DR. LIC. # | STATE

D.O.B.

METHOD OF PAYMENT

☐ AMERICAN EXPRESS ☐ CASH ☐ DINERS CLUB ☐ CHECK
☐ VISA ☐ CARTE BLANCHE ☐ MASTER CARD

Sheraton Inn Lansing

S. Creyts Rd. at I-496
Lansing, MI 48917

95093 (4-82)

Courtesy of The Sheraton Inn, Lansing, Michigan.

room rate at registration minimizes confusion and adjustments to the guest's folio at check-out. Many registration records also contain some form of acknowledgment on the part of the guest that he or she is responsible for payment in case the payment card or direct billing arrangement is not accepted for settlement.

Exhibit 3 diagrams the flow of guest registration information to electronic files and to other areas and functions of the hotel. The guest's intended method of payment may determine his or her point-of-sale charge status. For example, a guest paying one night's room rate by cash at registration is likely to have a *no-post status* in the hotel's revenue centers. In other words, the guest will not be allowed to charge purchases to a room account, as the guest did not provide a deferred payment method during registration. A guest presenting a valid payment card during registration may be allowed point-of-sale charge privileges, as the deferred payment for such items will eventually be charged to his or her room account. The decision to allocate charge privileges to a guest usually depends on the establishment of an acceptable method of credit at check-in.

At check-out, the information in a guest's registration record may be used as the primary source for creating a guest history file. This file may then become part of the hotel company's database to be used in the future by the hotel's sales and marketing staff. The information in a guest history database can be analyzed to assist management in developing contact strategies, marketing lists, and detailed reports.

Exhibit 3 Flow of Guest Registration Information

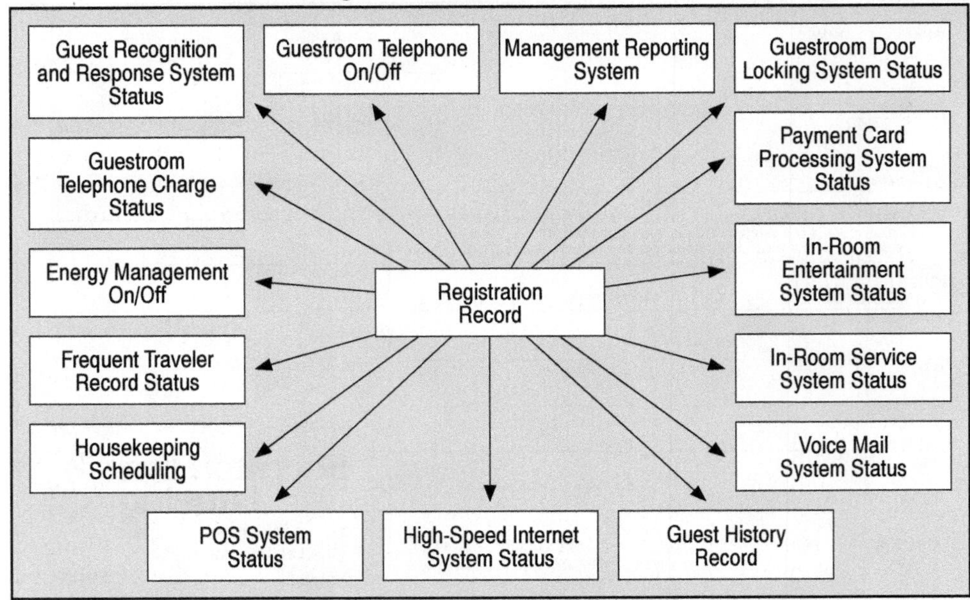

Assigning the Guestroom and Room Rate

Guestroom assignment is an important part of the registration process. Room assignment involves identifying and allocating an available room in a specific room category to a guest. When the guest request is ambiguous, or when a guestroom is unavailable in the guest's preferred category, a front desk agent may query the front office system to locate an acceptable available room.

On the basis of reservation information, specific rooms and rates may be pre-assigned (before the guest's arrival). Pre-assigning a specific room depends on the room's forecasted availability status and how appropriately the room meets the guest's needs. This requires the reservations system to interact with the rooms management module in the front office system. Guestroom assignments are finalized during the registration process.

Determining the guest's needs by room type alone is often insufficient. Hotels typically offer a variety of room rates for similar types of rooms. Room rates for rooms with identical bed configurations may vary based on room size, quality of furnishings, location, amenities, and other factors. Front desk agents must know the differences between the room types and be capable of querying the system to determine each room's rate category, current occupancy status, furnishings, location, and amenities to best satisfy guest requests. Future reservation commitments must also be considered during room assignment so that rooms are not assigned in conflict with near-future reservation needs.

The front desk agent's knowledge of the hotel and ability to use the system to determine room status and an appropriate room rate is critical to an effective registration process. The important topics of room status, room rates, room locations, and reservation blocks are addressed in the following sections.

Room Status. Effective room and rate assignment depends on accurate and timely guestroom status information. Room status information is usually discussed in terms of two timelines. In the long term (beyond the present night), a room's readiness is described by its reservation status. In the short term (tonight), a room's readiness is described by its housekeeping status, which refers to its availability for immediate assignment. Typical housekeeping status descriptions include:

- Occupied—the room has a registered guest or guests assigned to it.
- Vacant—the room is currently unoccupied.
- On-Change—the room is currently being cleaned for the next guest.
- Out-of-Order—the room has a condition that does not allow it to be rented.

An important aid to the registration of guests arriving early is the prompt relay of housekeeping information to the front desk. This is especially true during high-occupancy or full-occupancy (sold-out) periods. The more efficient the registration process, the more impressed an arriving guest is likely to be with the hotel's efficiency of operation. At most properties, the front desk agent is not authorized to assign a guestroom until the room has been cleaned, inspected, and released by the housekeeping department. Even though a guest arriving early may have to wait for a room, he or she will perceive the wait for a readied room as a better option than simply receiving a room key to a guestroom that has not been properly prepared.

Room status discrepancies can occur in front office systems for several reasons. First, there may be an actual variance, caused by incomplete or inaccurate recordkeeping. For example, a guest may settle his or her account for the nights the guestroom was originally reserved, but request to stay in the room for an additional night. While the front desk agent settles the account, the agent may accidentally indicate to the property management system that the guest has checked out, creating a room status discrepancy, since the front office will show the guest checked out, but the housekeeping department will indicate that someone continues to occupy the guestroom. (In this case, the guest is termed a **sleeper.**) Another room status discrepancy occurs when a guest leaves the hotel without settling his or her account; the front office still shows the room as occupied, but housekeeping lists the guestroom as vacant. (In this case, the guest is termed a **skipper.**) Room status discrepancies may also arise from delays in communicating housekeeping status updates from the housekeeping department to the front desk system.

In many properties, the property management system produces a daily front office report called the **occupancy report,** which lists rooms occupied for the current night and indicates those guests expected to check out the following day. The executive housekeeper typically receives a copy of this report on a daily basis and uses it to schedule housekeeping staff for the following day. A housekeeping staff scheduling report is created each morning, and the executive housekeeper uses it to assign staff members to specific floor sections. The rooms occupied by guests expected to check out are usually scheduled to be cleaned last, since many guests

Exhibit 4 Housekeeping Status Report

Housekeeper's Report

Date ____________, **20** ______ **A.M.** **P.M.**

ROOM NUMBER	STATUS	ROOM NUMBER	STATUS	ROOM NUMBER	STATUS	ROOM NUMBER	STATUS
101		126		151		176	
102		127		152		177	
103		128		153		178	
104		129		154		179	
105		130		155		180	
106		131		156		181	
107		132		157		182	
108		133		158		183	
120						195	
121		146		171		196	
122		147		172		197	
123		148		173		198	
124		149		174		199	
125		150		175		200	

Remarks: ______________________

____

____

____

Housekeeper's Signature

Legend:
- ✓ - Occupied
- 000 - Out-of-Order
- — - Vacant
- B - Slept Out (Baggage Still in Room)
- X - Occupied No Baggage
- C.O. - Slept In but Checked Out Early A.M.
- E.A. - Early Arrival

tend to occupy the guestroom until just prior to the hotel's departure time. Thus, if these rooms were assigned to be cleaned early, they might have to be cleaned again, should the guest use the room following its cleaning. Rooms of departed guests require more cleaning time than do rooms of guests who are staying over (making the room a stayover room). If a guest checks out before the stated departure date, the front desk must notify housekeeping that the room should no longer be classified as a stayover. A special housekeeping routine coordinated with the front desk is often needed for cleaning and inspecting early check-out rooms.

At the end of a work shift, the housekeeping department prepares a **housekeeping status report** (see Exhibit 4) based on a physical check of all guestrooms. This report indicates the current housekeeping status of each room. It should be compared with the front desk occupancy report, and any room status discrepancies should be brought to the attention of the front office manager. This process helps ensure that front desk agents work with accurate and timely room-availability information; this can be especially important when processing late check-ins.

Many front office systems define room status in more detail than just occupied or on-change. Typical status designations in front office systems include:

- V/O—vacant and on-change
- V/C—vacant and cleaned, but not yet inspected
- V/I—vacant and inspected
- O/C—occupied and cleaned

Room Rates. A **room rate** is the price a hotel charges for overnight accommodations. The cost structure of the hotel dictates the minimum rate for a room, and competition helps the hotel establish its maximum rate. The room rate range is the range of values between the minimum and maximum rates. A hotel will usually designate a standard rate for each room. This rate is typically called the **rack rate** because historically the standard rate was the one posted at the front desk in a device called a room rack. The rack rate is considered the retail rate for the room. In most cases, room rate discounts provided by the hotel are discounts to a room's rack rate.

In summary, the room rate is the actual price charged for a given room on a given night. The rack rate is the standard or non-discounted rate for a given room type (such as rooms with two double beds, rooms with one king-size bed, suites, and so forth). If a guest does not qualify for a discounted price, the guest is charged the rack rate. If the guest qualifies for a discount—for example, 10 percent off the rack rate as a result of membership in a qualifying group—the price charged for the room is 10 percent off the rack rate. Hence, when a guest is charged a non-discounted price, the rack rate is also the room rate, but when a discount is applied, the room rate is a percent of the rack rate.

Room rates are typically confirmed as part of the reservations process. Assigning rates for walk-in guests is usually the responsibility of the front desk agent, guided by the hotel's policies and sales guidelines. Front desk agents are often allowed to offer a room at a lower price than its rack rate. Normally, this occurs only with managerial approval. For example, hotel management may be expecting a low rate of occupancy. To attract as much business as possible to the hotel, walk-in guests may be offered a rate below the rack rate to entice them to register and stay at the hotel. Some hotels establish seasonal rate schedules in order to anticipate business fluctuations. The objective of room rate flexibility is to provide greater value during low-demand periods and to maximize room revenue during high-demand periods (a form of revenue management).

Other room rate schedules may reflect variations in the number of guests assigned to the room, service level, amenities, and room location. For example, room rates may include dining room meals. Under the **American Plan (AP),** room charges include the cost of the guestroom and may include three meals per day in the hotel's food service outlets. Under the **Modified American Plan (MAP),** the daily rate includes charges for the guestroom and two meals per day (typically breakfast and dinner). Sometimes, the phrase *full pension* is used in place of American Plan, and *semi-pension* in place of Modified American Plan. Some resorts use an **All Inclusive** rate that includes the cost of the guestroom plus meals, beverages, and hotel-supported activities. Under the **European Plan (EP)**, meals are priced separately from guestrooms. American resorts frequently use either the American Plan or the Modified American Plan. Most non-resort hotels in the United States set their rates according to the European Plan.

Room rates may also vary based on type of guest. If authorized, front desk agents should know how and when to apply a special room rate during the registration process. Special room rates may include:

- *Commercial* or *corporate rates* for companies that provide frequent business to the hotel.
- *Complimentary rates (no charge)* for business promotions to special guests and/or industry leaders, or for compensation to dissatisfied guests.
- *Group rates* for a pre-determined number of affiliated guests.
- *Family rates* for parents and children sharing the same guestroom.
- *Day rates* for less than an overnight stay (check-in and check-out on the same day).
- *Package-plan rates* for guestrooms sold in a bundled package that includes special events or activities.
- *Frequent traveler rates* for guests earning discounts through a loyalty or rewards program.

Eligibility for special rates is generally contingent on management policy and the guest's profile.

Room Locations. When assigning guestrooms, a front desk agent must be aware of the characteristics of each room type. In most hotels, guestrooms within specific room categories tend to be approximately the same size and offer similar furnishings and amenities. Some hotels, due to different construction techniques and materials, may have room types that vary significantly in size and configuration. Differences between guestrooms generally are attributable to their furnishings, amenities, and location. Front desk agents should be familiar with various guestroom configurations, as well as the hotel's floor plan, in order to satisfy guest rooming requests. Exhibit 5 provides an example of a simplified hotel floor plan. Note the connecting rooms and handicapper-accessible rooms depicted in the floor plan.

The front office system contains specific data about each room, such as its type, rate, floor, view, bedding, and other pertinent information. Front office systems can be programmed to provide other guestroom information, such as special room features and amenities, in an easy-to-reference format.

Individual guests or groups of guests may specify certain room locations in the hotel as part of a reservation request. Groups may be promised preferred rooms by the sales and marketing department or catering department. However, the department booking the rooms should be careful to check room availabilities with the reservations department before committing specific rooms or facilities

Exhibit 5 Simplified Hotel Floor Plan

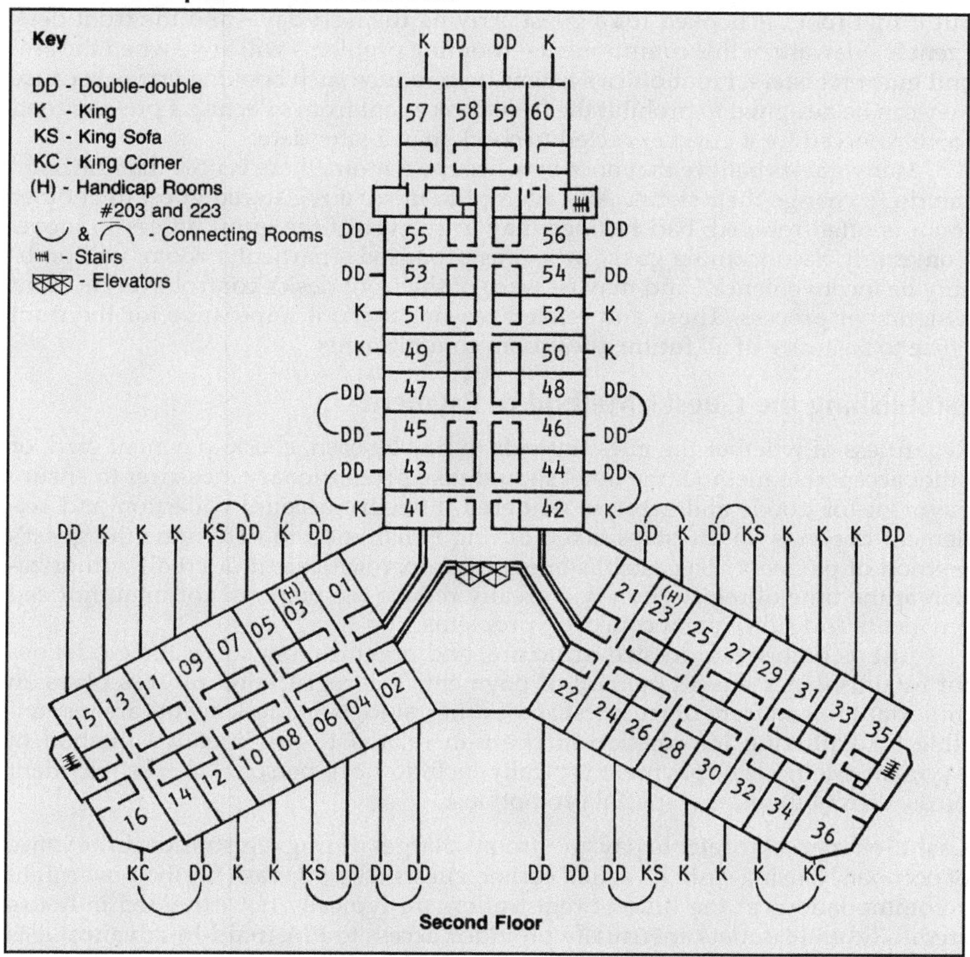

Courtesy of The Sheraton Inn, Lansing, Michigan.

to incoming guests or groups. Although the reservations department may block the desired rooms in advance, it is the responsibility of the front desk agents to assign guestrooms at registration to those group members not previously assigned a room from the preferred group block of rooms.

Reservation Blocks. A primary concern in the room assignment phase of registration concerns which rooms will be available in the near future, based on reservation blocks. Usually, a reservations agent or the front office supervisor blocks reserved rooms through an automated reservations file. If for any reason reserved rooms are incorrectly blocked or inadvertently overlooked, room assignment conflicts may result.

For instance, suppose a walk-in guest is assigned a room for a two-night stay. But if that room is booked for a guest arriving the next day—and the front desk agent is unaware of this commitment—rooming problems will arise when the second guest registers. Front office systems help reduce such booking errors because they can be designed to prohibit the front desk agent from selecting a pre-assigned room reserved for a guest expected to check in at a later date.

Many guests believe that once they occupy a room, there is little that the hotel can do to change their status. Any attempt to move a registered guest to another room is often resisted; bad feelings may arise even if the guest agrees to move. Conversely, the incoming guest, who was promised a particular room, will probably be inconvenienced and may be wary of the front desk's control over its room assignment process. These and related reasons make it imperative for the front office to be aware of all future guestroom commitments.

Establishing the Guest's Method of Payment

Regardless of whether the guest intends to pay by cash, check, payment card, or other acceptable method, the hotel should take precautionary measures to ensure payment for goods and services rendered. Effective account collection and settlement depends on the steps taken during registration to determine the guest's method of payment. The establishment of proper settlement or credit authorization at the time of registration will greatly reduce the potential for unauthorized payments and subsequent collection problems.

Just as hotels vary in size, structure, and organization, so do the guidelines for establishing a guest's method of payment. The registration process plays an important role in front office guest accounting, since front desk agents are responsible for gathering information at check-in related to the intended method of payment. Methods of payment typically include cash, personal checks, payment cards, direct billing, and special promotions.

Cash. Some guests prefer to pay guestroom charges during registration, in advance of occupancy, using cash. As stated earlier, guests who pay cash for their overnight accommodations at the time of registration are typically not extended in-house credit. Revenue outlets are usually provided access to **PIA (paid-in-advance)** lists of cash-paying guests who are thereby not authorized to have charge purchases posted to their guestroom accounts *(no-post status).*

In most properties, PIA lists are created automatically by a front office system that interfaces guest electronic folio files to the hotel's revenue outlets. Such systems will not allow outlet employees to post charges at the point of purchase to guest accounts that are not authorized for in-house charges. Guests without in-house charge privileges must settle their purchases at the point of sale with an acceptable form of payment. At some hotels, during check-in, front desk agents may require a cash-paying guest to leave an imprint of a payment card in order to extend in-house charge privileges to a cash-paying guest.

Hotels consider cashier's checks, traveler's checks, and money orders equivalent to cash. A hotel that accepts such forms of legal tender should require proper guest identification and treat such transactions as cash payments. Front desk agents should compare the picture and signature on the guest's identification with the appearance and signature of the person presenting the check or money order. When there is doubt, the check or money order should be verified with the issuing bank or agency.

Personal Checks. Some lodging properties allow transactions to be paid by personal check, while others have a strict policy against accepting personal checks. Although a hotel has no obligation to accept personal checks, it cannot refuse to accept a personal check on the basis of sex, race, or other grounds that would warrant illegal discrimination. Individual properties must establish policies for accepting personal checks. Hotels should also consider adopting policies relative to payroll checks, personal checks written on out-of-state and foreign bank accounts, government checks, and second- and third-party checks.

Some hotels allow guests to cash personal checks as long as they have a payment card on file that provides a check-cashing guarantee and the amount of the check is within the payment card company's established credit limit. When this is the case, front desk agents should imprint the payment card onto the back side of the guest's personal check or the guest's registration card. Some hotels accept personal checks only during standard banking hours; this provision often allows the daytime shift of the front office to obtain bank verification of the check, if necessary. Some hotels allow guests to write personal checks equivalent to the total amount of the guestroom rate and taxes only. When this is the case, cash or payment card payment will be required for all other purchases beyond this amount.

Hotels that accept personal checks should require proper identification. The guest's driver's license or passport number, address, telephone number, and e-mail address should be recorded on the *back* of a personal check as part of the hotel endorsement. Bank stamps and clearing house imprints will also be recorded on the *back* of the check. In some hotels, the amounts and dates of cashed personal checks are recorded on the guest's registration card. This procedure helps ensure that guests do not exceed the property's pre-established check-cashing limits (if any). If front office cashiers are not authorized to accept personal checks, they must be aware of what procedures to follow when a guest attempts to cash a personal check at the front desk.

Properties can also protect themselves against potential losses incurred through acceptance of fraudulent or bogus personal checks by following these basic guidelines:

- Do not refund cash if the original transaction was settled by personal check. If possible, return the guest's original personal check and, when appropriate, require an alternate form of payment. Some properties do not write a refund check, even if a refund is warranted, until the guest's bank verifies that the personal check in question was valid and has been cleared for payment.
- Accept personal checks written only on the current day. Do not accept undated or post-dated personal checks—that is, checks carrying no date or a future date instead of the current date. Such checks are not acceptable.
- Require that personal checks written to settle an account be made payable to the hotel, not to "Cash." Or, to put it another way, if guests want to write a check to "Cash," the guests should be given money in exchange for the check,

and not be allowed to use such a check to pay their hotel bills. Such a policy would undermine a non-paying guest's (skipper's) claim that a personal check made out to "Cash" was used to pay his or her hotel account when in fact it was used to gain spending money.

- Do not accept checks written on foreign banks unless the hotel's credit department has pre-approved acceptance of these types of checks.

Exhibit 6 shows some additional procedural steps for avoiding check fraud.

Second- and third-party checks. In general, hotels should not accept second- or third-party checks. A *second-party check* is one made out to the guest presenting the check. A *third-party check* is one made out to someone who has in turn signed the check over to the guest presenting it. When accepting such checks, hotels may experience collection problems, especially if the maker of the check has registered a "stop payment" order on the check. If the hotel accepts a second-party check, the front desk agent should require the guest to endorse the check at the front desk, in view of the front desk agent, even if the guest had previously endorsed the check. The front desk agent can then compare the guest's two signatures (previous and current endorsements) prior to accepting the check.

Check guarantee service. Some hotels use a check guarantee service to ensure that the checks guests present are valid. A check guarantee service relies on critical information appearing on the check, which the front desk agent can provide either by entering the information on a terminal keypad or by passing the check through a special magnetic ink reader. The check guarantee service, in turn, determines the check writer's credit history and either guarantees or denies payment support. If a supported check later is found to be invalid, the guarantee service is liable for the amount of the check, not the hotel.

Alternatively, some hotels use a system capable of providing immediate payment through electronic transfer, much like a debit card transaction. The equipment functions similarly to a payment card reader with an interconnected verification system. Valid checks have specially encoded bank identification and account numbers printed at the bottom front of the check. Check readers can capture and decipher the special numbering and use data transfer technology to contact the bank identified on the check and verify that the account has sufficient funds. Basically, the check is passed through the reader, which records the bank and account information and sends it forward through the system. If the information is valid, the funds are set aside and paid to the hotel through the same system. If the check is not valid, or the balance in the account is not sufficient to cover the amount of the check, the hotel is immediately notified and the check is declined.

Since check services typically charge a transaction fee, hotels use the services only for personal checks written to settle guest accounts. It is important to note that there are no service guarantees for checks drawn on foreign banks.

Payment Cards. There are two forms of payment (credit and debit) cards that can be used for payment of guest charges: contact cards that rely on a magnetic stripe being swiped for account access, and contactless cards that rely on wireless transmission for account exchange. Contact credit or debit cards are plastic cards with a magnetic stripe that are assigned a line of credit by the issuer of the card. When

Exhibit 6 Suggested Steps for Accepting Checks

Steps to Follow when Accepting Checks

1 Be cautious of new checking accounts

Of all the insufficient, "hot" checks, 90% are drawn on accounts less than a year old. The consecutive numbers in the upper right hand corner begin with 101 and you should be especially careful when taking low numbered checks. Because knowing the age of the account is so important, some banks now print a code of when the account was opened (for example, 0278 means February, 1978) on all checks.

2 Place all information on front of check

As described in Regulation CC, either write the information consecutively across the top of the front or use the cross method.

Driver's license number	Credit card number
Clerk's initials	Other ID or manager's approval

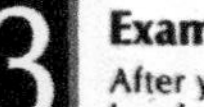

3 Examine driver's license carefully

After you have the license out of the customer's wallet and in your hand, quickly ask yourself the following questions: Is the person in the photo and in front of you the same person? Are the addresses on the check and license the same? When does the license expire? More than 60% of the forged checks last year were cashed with an expired driver's license. Also, the courts have ruled that licenses are legally worthless for identification as soon as they expire. Be sure you examine the driver's license carefully.

4 Other Negotiable Instrument Codes

On drafts issued by savings and loan institutions and mutual savings banks, magnetic bank routing numbers may start with the digit 2 or 3. Credit union drafts are honored by the bank on which they are drawn. International traveler's checks have routing numbers starting with 8000. U.S. Government checks contain the routing number 000000518.

5 Traveler's check identification

VISA—When held above eye level, a globe of the world will appear on the front left and a dove in the upper right.
MASTERCARD and THOMAS COOK—When held above eye level, on the right side of the check in a circle, a woman with short black hair will appear.
CITICORP—When held above eye level, a Greek god will appear on the right.
BANK OF AMERICA—No distinguishing watermarks.
AMERICAN EXPRESS—Turn check over. Moisten your finger tip and run it over the left denomination. If it smears it is good. Right side will not smear.

6 Be impressed with the check—not the person

Don't let a customer's appearance lull you into ignoring any of these steps. Frank Abagnale, the retired master forger, once cashed a $50 check written on a cocktail napkin, before a hidden camera for television, because the bank teller was more impressed by his appearance than by the item he presented. When you're in a hurry, or want to make an exception, think how you will defend your decision if the check is returned. Then, only the check will matter—not the circumstances in which you took it.

Developed by Frank W. Abagnale

Frank W. Abagnale & Associates/PO Box 701290, Tulsa, Oklahoma 74170/Telephone 918-492-6590

Courtesy of Frank W. Abagnale & Associates, Tulsa, Oklahoma.

a charge purchase is made against the card, it is applied to the cardholder's credit line. Statements are sent to cardholders every month. Some card accounts, called travel-and-entertainment (T&E) cards, are expected to be paid in full each month. American Express is an example of a T&E card. Cardholders of bank cards (Visa, MasterCard, and others) are typically provided an installment payment plan that applies a rate of interest on balances carried forward to the next payment cycle. Payment card purchases may be rejected by the issuing bank or agency if the account is over the pre-approved limit or if the purchase in question will take the account over the limit. Debit cards differ from credit cards in that a debit card is attached to a deposit account (that is, a savings or checking account). When a charge is incurred, it immediately reduces the balance in the debit cardholder's account; there is no credit extended. Debit card charges can be rejected if there are insufficient funds to cover the cost of the transaction, or if a charge will result in the account balance going below a predetermined minimum balance.

Careful authorization and verification of card payments are as important to front office cash flow as the precautions taken with any other method of payment. The front office usually compiles a set of steps for processing payment card transactions. In addition, payment card companies often require that front desk agents adhere to exact procedures in order to ensure transaction settlement. As shown in Exhibit 7, payment card companies also provide helpful tips for avoiding fraud and implementing sound processing procedures. Hotels should have an attorney review their payment card procedures to be sure the hotel adheres to state and federal laws, payment card industry (PCI) standards, and additional specifications contained in card company contracts. Local banks may also provide procedural guidelines. Front office management may also consider the following points when establishing a front desk policy for handling payment cards.

Expiration date and location validation. When a guest presents a payment card, the front desk agent handling the transaction should immediately check the card's expiration date. If the date shows that the card has expired, the front desk agent should bring this to the guest's attention and request an alternative method of payment. Since payment card companies are not required to honor transactions processed with an expired card, the acceptance of such a card places the hotel in an untenable position. If the hotel inadvertently accepts an expired or invalid card, it may not be able to collect payment for the guest's charged purchases. In addition, some banks issue cards that are good only in a specific country. The front desk agent must be especially careful when dealing with international travelers, as they may present payment cards that are clearly marked as being valid only in specific countries.

Online authorization. After checking a card's expiration date, the front desk agent should make sure the card is otherwise valid. Swiping or tapping a payment card will connect the card reader to an online clearinghouse service. Once a communication connection is established, the required card and transaction data are exchanged through an electronic-data-capture (EDC) process. On the basis of the captured data, the card verification service consults an account database and generates either an **authorization code** or a **denial code** for the transaction.

Invalid card. Front desk staff members should follow established front office and card-payment-company procedures when a card appears to be invalid, such

Exhibit 7 Tips from Payment Card Companies

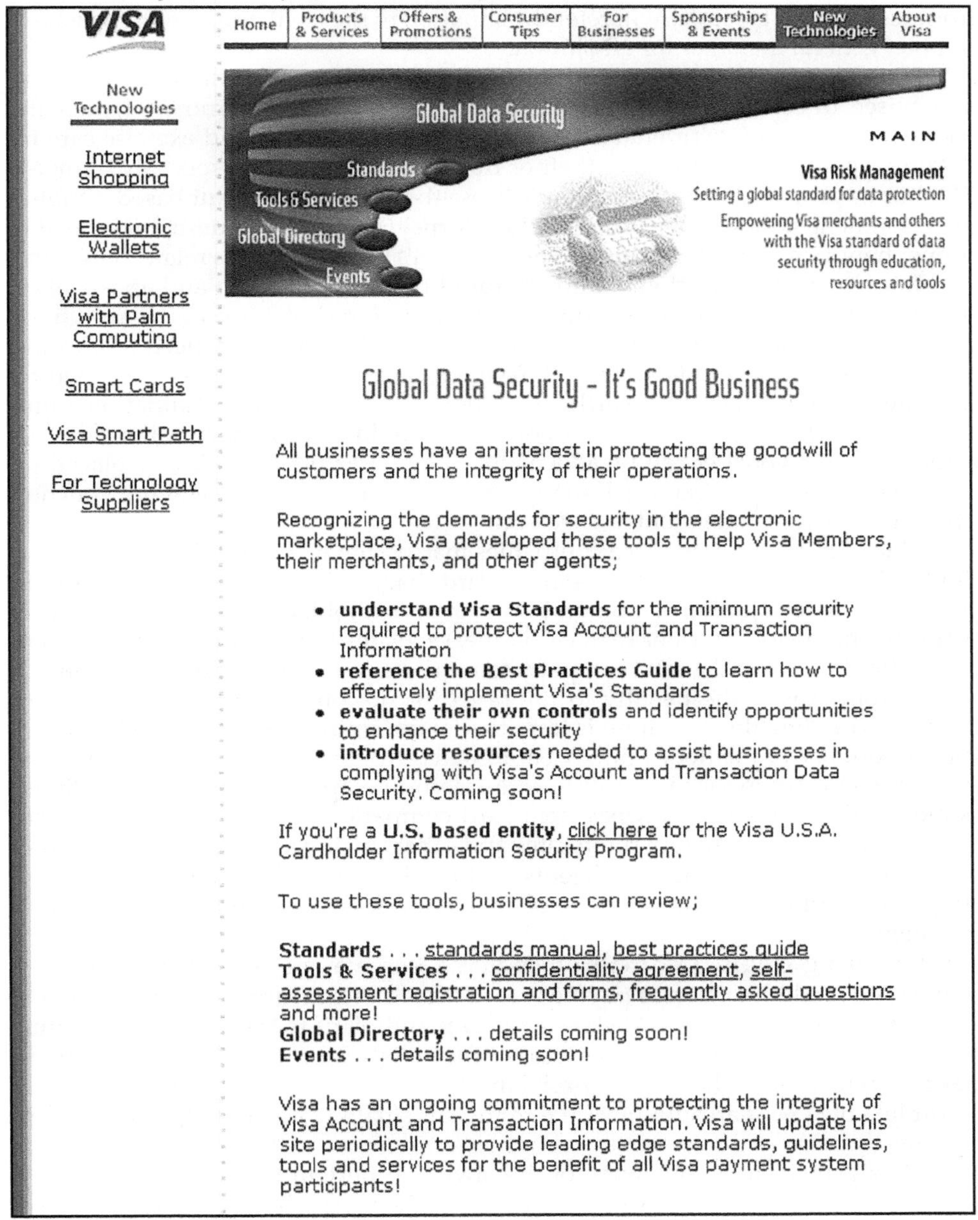

as when it has been tampered with, or the signature on the card does not match the signature on the hotel registration form. Normally, it is appropriate for staff members to politely request an alternate form of payment, without attracting attention or embarrassing the guest. If the guest has no other acceptable means of payment, front desk agents typically will refer the situation to the front office credit manager or hotel general manager for resolution.

If a guest presents a card that appears invalid, the front desk agent might be advised to contact hotel security. Although the federal government has made payment card fraud a criminal offense, lodging properties should exercise care in detaining guests they suspect of theft or fraud. Such detention, especially if unjustified or improperly instituted, might expose the hotel to a lawsuit based on false imprisonment and slander. The hotel's attorney should provide advice on the proper handling of invalid cards and on the hotel's vulnerability to related lawsuits.

Imprinting the voucher. Although rapid online verification and approval of payment cards has become the industry standard, some hotels may not have direct access to verification systems. In this case, front desk agents may need to imprint approved, valid cards onto approved payment card vouchers. Some hotels require front desk agents to circle the card's expiration date and initial the validation number on the imprinted voucher as proof that procedures have been followed. The imprinted card voucher can be attached to the guest's printed folio, or placed in a voucher file for safekeeping. Usually, the guest is not asked to sign the voucher until final account settlement at check-out.

Floor limits. Payment card companies may assign hotels a **floor limit.** A floor limit is the maximum amount in payment card charges the hotel can accept without requesting special authorization on behalf of a cardholder. If the amount a guest wants to charge to his or her card account exceeds the hotel's floor limit, the front office should contact the card company to request approval for the transaction.

In some cases, the penalty to the hotel for not obtaining authorization for charges exceeding the floor limit is forfeiture of the entire amount charged, not just the amount above the floor limit. An automated front office system that monitors guest account balances can identify guest accounts approaching the floor limit. Some lodging properties ask payment card companies to assign unusually high floor limits, given the hotel's room rates and other pricing structures. By receiving a higher floor limit, front desk agents will not have to inconvenience guests by frequently authorizing transactions or by having to secure alternate methods of payment.

Reserving credit. The front office may reserve a specified amount of preauthorized credit in a guest's payment card account to ensure payment for goods and services. For instance, a guest who arrives and plans to stay for several nights likely will incur room charges in excess of the hotel's floor limit. To avoid a potential payment card authorization problem, the front office may want to reserve a credit line of *at least* an amount equal to the anticipated charges to be incurred on the guest's folio.

Management must be aware of the laws that pertain to reserving credit, as well as related card policies. Consider the case of a guest who decides to leave earlier than planned, and tries to make a subsequent purchase elsewhere, only to discover that his or her credit is tied up in a reserve created by the hotel. Laws related to reserving credit vary by state. In some states, the hotel would be obligated to notify the payment card company to release the unused portion of the reserved line of credit when the guest checks out. Also, some states stipulate that a hotel

Exhibit 8 Suggestions for Resolving Credit Problems

When a payment card issuer refuses to authorize a transaction:

- Discuss the matter with the guest in private.
- Use care when describing the guest's unauthorized transaction (for example, do not call the guest's payment card "bad" or "worthless").
- Offer the use of a telephone to help resolve the matter with a payment card company representative.
- Allow the guest a chance to provide alternate, acceptable means of payment.

When a guest's personal check cannot be accepted:

- Explain the hotel's check cashing policy.
- Remain friendly and cooperative.
- Discuss alternative methods of payment with the guest.
- If local banks are open, direct the guest to a nearby branch, or offer the use of a telephone.

can reserve an anticipated amount of credit only if it informs the guest beforehand, and obtains the guest's consent. Hotels should consult legal counsel before establishing a front office policy for reserving credit against payment card accounts.

When a guest arrives to check in, the front desk agent should request a method of payment before retrieving the guest's registration information. The agent may then swipe or tap a payment card using the card reader attached to the front office system. The card reader processes the captured data and attempts to identify the arriving guest by displaying the registration record to the agent or by providing a list of possible matches. Once the agent has identified the proper guest, the system automatically calculates the amount of credit to be reserved and contacts the card company without intervention by the front desk agent. By the time registration is completed, the hotel should have an approval or denial code received from the payment card company displayed in the guest's electronic record.

Denying a credit request. When a front desk agent discovers that a guest's credit has been denied by the issuing card company, extreme care should be exercised in notifying the guest of the problem. In discussing problematic credit issues, the front desk agent must be as diplomatic as possible. The agent's tone of voice should remain friendly and subdued, no matter how belligerent the guest may become. While hotel staff members have certain rights to review and evaluate credit information, the guest also has the right to know why the front office will not accept his or her personal check, payment card, or direct-billing arrangement. Exhibit 8 suggests some procedures for resolving credit problems. These suggestions should be modified to fit the problem, the guest, and the hotel's policies.

Direct Billing. Some hotels extend credit to guests by agreeing to bill the guest or the guest's company for charges. **Direct billing** (also called "bill to") arrangements are normally established through communication between the front office and the guest or the guest's sponsoring company, and in advance of the guest's arrival. A potential guest or a sponsoring company representative may be asked to complete the hotel's application for credit. The front office manager normally reviews and is responsible for approving a guest's credit application. A list of approved direct billing accounts is usually maintained at the front desk for reference during registration. At check-out, a guest with approved credit simply signs his or her guest folio after approving its contents, and a statement is direct-billed to the third party for collection. In a direct billing arrangement, the hotel itself, not a payment card company or other agency, assumes full responsibility for account collection.

Special Promotions. During registration, guests may present vouchers, coupons, gift certificates, gift cards, or special incentive awards received from businesses, airlines, or other authorized agencies. Front desk agents must be aware of hotel agreements to honor such items and must know how to properly credit the bearer. Front desk agents must use care when handling special program vouchers because such documents tend to differ in value, conditions, or terms. Since program vouchers represent a form of payment and may be the actual documents the front office uses to reconcile the guest's folio, careful handling is warranted. Since vouchers and coupons represent pre-paid revenue to the hotel, the front desk should maintain a set of samples of all currently acceptable vouchers, coupons, gift cards, and certificates. This collection should be discussed with front desk staff in front desk training sessions and should be readily available to agents in case questions arise.

Payment Issues for Groups. Front desk agents must be careful when registering group guests and establishing the method of payment for them, because group members arriving at the hotel to attend a meeting or convention often have individual billing arrangements pre-established. In some cases, the guest's room and tax charges are direct-billed to a group master folio or account, while other charges, called **incidental charges** (such as Internet, food, beverage, and dry cleaning charges), may be the guest's personal responsibility. In such a case, credit for incidental charges will need to be established for each member of the group. However, when the group agrees to pay for all of the charges made by its members, it may not be necessary to establish individual guest lines of credit. Groups often pay guestroom, tax, and incidental charges for VIP guests or invited speakers, so these individuals may be asked to simply sign a registration form to verify date of departure before being issued a room key or guestroom access code.

Verifying the Guest's Identity

Many hotels require front desk agents to obtain positive guest identification before completing the registration process for any arriving guest. It is very common for front desk agents to ask for photo identification in the form of a driver's license or passport to ensure positive identification of the guest's name, address, signature, and photograph. Since the terrorist attacks of September 11, 2001, verifying the identity of guests has become common practice at nearly all hotels. For domestic guests, a driver's license or other form of photo identification is usually sufficient. International guests normally will need to present a passport. In both cases, the type of identification and identification number on the document should be recorded in the guest record. As an additional security measure, if the guest does not speak the local language, this fact should also be noted in the guest's record, as it can assist in identifying guests requiring foreign language translation, and is helpful in emergency situations.

Issuing the Room Key or Access Code

The front desk agent completes the guest registration process by issuing a room key. In some hotels, a newly registered guest is simply handed a guestroom key and directed to the guestroom by the front desk agent. In other hotels, the guest may be given a map showing guestroom location as well as the location of other hotel facilities such as the dining rooms, cocktail lounges, swimming pool, fitness center, meeting rooms, and parking facilities. For the security of both the guest and the property, room keys must be carefully controlled. The theft, loss, or unauthorized duplication and use of guestroom keys threaten hotel security.

Hotels should have written procedures governing guestroom key control. These procedures should state who is authorized to issue guestroom keys, who receives such keys, and where and how guestroom keys are created and/or stored at the front desk.

For security reasons, the front desk agent should never announce the room number of the guest when presenting the guestroom key to the guest. The front desk agent can, however, draw the guest's attention to the room number by writing it down or pointing to the room on the hotel map. Front offices that use a special code on guestroom keys instead of room numbers should have their front desk agents write the room number for the guest or discreetly explain to the guest how to interpret the room code on the key. Many hotels provide guestroom keys in envelopes, which gives front desk agents a convenient place to write the room number for guests.

If the hotel provides bell service, the front desk agent should ask whether the guest would like assistance from a bell attendant. If so, the front desk agent should introduce the bell attendant to the guest, hand the bell attendant the guest's room key, and ask the attendant to show the guest to the room. On the way to the room, the bell attendant should familiarize the guest with hotel information by explaining the special features of the hotel and such things as the locations of emergency exits, emergency procedures, restaurant locations, retail outlets' hours of operation, locations of ice and vending machines, and other appropriate information. Once inside the guestroom, the bell attendant can explain the features of the room, show the guest how the thermostat and in-room amenities work, answer any questions, and hand the room key to the guest. If the guest is displeased with the room or if the room is not prepared as the guest expected, the bell attendant should listen attentively and bring the matter to the attention of the front desk agent for corrective action. For example, if a family arrives at a hotel expecting a rollaway bed for a child to already be in the guestroom and it isn't there, the agent or bell attendant should make arrangements to ensure the bed is brought to the room.

Responding to Special Requests

Part of the guest registration process involves acknowledging and acting on special guest requests. For example, a guest may have requested two connecting rooms during the reservations process. These rooms should be blocked in advance of check-in to ensure availability when the guest arrives. If it appears that the guest's reservation requests were not properly handled, the front desk agent should strive to satisfy the guest's requests during the registration process, if possible.

Other special requests may involve guestroom:

- Location
- View
- Bed type
- Smoking/no-smoking status
- Amenities
- Special furnishings for disabled guests
- High-speed Internet access
- Entertainment systems, such as on-demand video systems and video game systems

A guest may request a room close to or far from an elevator; one that overlooks the ocean, pool, or city; one that has a king-size bed; or one that has a refreshment center or entertainment area. In addition, guests may ask for special furnishings in the guestroom. A couple arriving with a young child may request a crib. If the room was not pre-set with a crib, the front desk agent should contact housekeeping to arrange for prompt delivery of a crib. Special requests are best handled during preregistration. Some guests may ask for other special items, such as bed boards or ironing boards. Disabled guests may require rooms with certain design features—grab bars in the bathroom, for example, or special lights attached to smoke and fire detection systems. The Americans with Disabilities Act requires most lodging establishments to have special accommodations for disabled guests. These rooms should be specially reserved whenever possible and not sold to anyone who is not disabled unless there are no other rooms available in the hotel.

Sometimes special requests are made by another person on behalf of the guest. For example, the general manager may want to welcome a frequent guest by placing a fruit basket in the guest's room. Travel agents may order champagne to be delivered to a client's guestroom. Relatives of a honeymooning couple may request that champagne and flowers be placed in the room before the couple arrives.

While many of the details surrounding special requests can be handled during preregistration, it is important for the front office to follow up on each request. Guests are quickly disappointed if, upon arrival at the guestroom, they find that the hotel did not honor their requests. Front desk agents should mention the guest's special requests at check-in to ensure that the hotel has provided what the guest requested. In this way, guests are satisfied that their requests have been met.

Creative Registration Options

The registration process described in this chapter is typical of most hotels. Some hotels, however, have experimented with different techniques to make registration more efficient and effective. Registration techniques tried, with varying degrees of success, include the following:

- *Eliminating the front desk.* Instead of a front desk agent behind a front desk, a host waits in a reception area with a list of expected arriving guests and their pre-assigned guestrooms. The host identifies guests, completes an abbreviated registration process, and sometimes escorts guests to their rooms. The guest's credit is established when the reservation is made through a special interface between the central reservation software and the payment card company. With everything else in place, all the host or front desk agent has to do is preregister the guest and assign a room key. When the guest arrives, a simple verification of the information on the registration form completes the process. Sometimes this service is tied to the hotel's frequent traveler program or handled by the concierge staff.
- *Registering group guests at a special location.* An area separate from the front desk may be screened off and used only for managing guest services and/or providing check-in or check-out services for arriving group members at peak times.
- *Creating a unique, separate registration area for VIP guests.* This approach is similar to the hotel host or greeter concept just mentioned, but is available only to VIPs.
- *Combining hotel registration and meeting registration in a separate area for arriving group members.* Separating group guests from other guests enables the front office to offer specialized services to the group.
- *Registering guests off-site,* such as in airports, convention centers, and shuttle vans, allows guests to check in prior to arrival at the front desk.

The challenge is to make the hotel registration process innovative while treating guests with expediency and care.

Some front office registration services include temporary luggage storage for guests who arrive during busy periods. In addition, front desk agents may offer complimentary food or beverages to guests who may be inconvenienced during registration. Such guests may be directed to the hotel's lounge or restaurant to enjoy a more relaxed and leisurely wait while their guestrooms are being readied for occupancy.

Self-Registration

A guest registration concept that is becoming popular is **self-registration.** Self-registration terminals may be located on or off hotel grounds or made available through a mobile device or property website. Limited-service lodging brands as well as full-service brands are providing unattended terminals for guests who prefer to use self-service technology. Regardless of which guest-operated device is used, self-registration can significantly reduce guest registration time.

To use a self-registration option, a guest generally must have made a reservation that led to the creation of a reservation record. At the time of self-registration, the guest may need to enter a reservation confirmation number or swipe or tap a valid payment or guest-loyalty-program card. The terminal can capture and exchange data with the hotel's property management system to link to the reservation record. A self check-in terminal may also prompt the guest to enter additional registration data. Most terminals connect to a rooms management system, thereby enabling automatic room and rate assignment. Some terminals print or display registration materials (identifying the assigned room number) and a map (showing the location of the room). Customized greetings or messages about special hotel events or promotions can be displayed on the self-service device. The terminal may automatically dispense a guestroom key as a result of interaction with an electronic guestroom lock system.

Selling the Guestroom

Front desk agents will not have the chance to use efficient or innovative registration techniques if the guest is not convinced of the value of occupying a hotel room. Part of the front desk agent's job is to create consumer acceptance of the hotel's products: guestrooms, amenities, facilities, and services. Front desk agents can take several approaches to selling guests on the value of staying at the hotel.

Front desk agents should practice sales techniques specific to their work. The registration process, for example, must move through certain stages to ensure quick and careful registration. Within such stages, front office staff members have the opportunity to make individual sales presentations. Properly trained front office staff members can improve room revenue by applying front office sales techniques, especially the technique of upselling.

Upselling refers to the efforts of reservations and front desk agents to offer guests the opportunity to reserve rooms in categories above standard rate accommodations. Hotels normally have several rate categories based on such factors as room decor, size, location, view, amenities, and furnishings. Sometimes the rack rate differences among guestrooms are substantial. Exhibit 9 lists some general suggestions for upselling guestrooms.

To upsell, front office and reservations staff must be trained to be more than simply order-takers; they must be trained to be salespeople. Staff members should upsell rooms in much the same way that a food server in a restaurant sells an extra item such as an appetizer, beverage, or dessert. Reservations and front office staff should learn effective techniques for suggesting room upgrade options to guests. Upgrading involves knowing how and when to ask for a sale in a non-pressuring way and how to direct the sales effort toward a successful conclusion.

Offering guestroom options to an inquiring guest is the key to the reservations and registration sales process, and it requires thoughtful planning and practice. Although the majority of upselling is conducted during the reservations process, front desk agents will have similar sales opportunities with walk-in guests. Some hotels, as a matter of policy, offer registering guests more than one room option (when more than one option is available) and leave it to the guests to decide. To create guest acceptance, the front desk agent must know how to describe the

Exhibit 9 Suggestions for Upselling Guestrooms

- Always greet each guest with a smile in your voice as well as on your face. Be pleasant and businesslike. Remember: you are selling yourself as much as you are selling the hotel and its services.
- Establish and maintain eye contact with the guest.
- Find out the guest's name immediately and use it at least three times during the conversation. Always use courteous titles such as "Mr." or "Ms." when addressing the guest. Do not call a guest by his or her first name.
- Attempt to identify the needs of the guest, since these needs may not have been identified during the reservations process. Match the guest's needs to the furnishings and/or amenities from among available rooms. For example, a guest staying at the hotel for three or four nights may appreciate and be more willing to pay for a larger or more isolated room than a guest staying only one night. Guests on a honeymoon or special vacation may be willing to pay for a room with a scenic view.
- Upsell rooms when possible. Offer an upgraded room by pointing out its features and benefits first, then mention its rate. If the guest has a reservation, describe the differences between the reserved and the upgraded room. Walk-in guests provide the best opportunity for upselling. If two different types of rooms are available, mention the features, benefits, and rates of both. Do not risk losing the sale by mentioning only the higher-priced room.
- Complete the registration process.
- Thank the guest and wish him or her a pleasant stay.

hotel's facilities and services in an attractive and positive manner. It is not uncommon for hotels to offer incentive programs for reservations and front desk staff who successfully upsell guestrooms.

A guest will likely provide several clues about what is an acceptable accommodation to him or her; some information may even be available on the guest's reservation record. Front desk agents should mention the physical features as well as the benefits and conveniences of the various types of available rooms. A guest may select a room immediately after it is described, or may wait until the front desk agent describes all the options. In some cases, the only guestrooms available may be those in the higher-priced categories. Successful reservations and front desk agents can briefly and efficiently explain to the guest the value in a higher-priced room. However, if a guest has reserved a lower-priced room and does not want to pay the higher rate, a room should then be provided at the reserved (quoted) rate.

The front desk agent normally directs the guest through the remainder of the registration process after the guest has selected a room. As the guest is completing the registration, the front desk agent may reinforce the guest's choice by recapping the room's location and special features. As the registration process draws to a close, the front desk agent should inform the guest about the hotel's revenue outlets, services, and facilities. Most guests appreciate this information.

Before the guest leaves the front desk, the front desk agent should thank him or her for choosing the hotel and express a personal interest in making the stay pleasant. Some hotels require front desk agents to place a phone call to the guest's room shortly after registration, to ensure that the guest's accommodations are satisfactory.

Denying Accommodations

In general, a hotel is obligated to accommodate guests if rooms are available. Discrimination is prohibited in places of public accommodation on the basis of race, sex, sexual orientation, religion, or national origin. Legitimate reasons for refusing to accommodate a guest may include a lack of available rooms, the potential guest's disorderly conduct, or the guest's inability or unwillingness to pay for accommodations or services. In addition, state law may stipulate other reasons for denying accommodations. A front desk agent should not be the person who determines whether someone will be roomed or not; this is the responsibility of front office management. Management is also responsible for telling guests why they are being turned away. Management, with the advice of legal counsel and the state hotel association, should instruct front office staff on policies and procedures concerning the acceptance or rejection of potential guests.

Sometimes a hotel may be short of available rooms and may not be able to accommodate guests. It is imperative that the hotel set policies and procedures for handling these situations. Seldom, if ever, should a hotel be unable to accommodate a guest who has a reservation, especially a guaranteed reservation. When this happens, most hotels will make other arrangements for the guest. In the case of a guaranteed reservation, some hotels will arrange for and may pay for the guest's room at another property. It is important to remember that hotel policy may dictate no obligation to guests who do not hold guaranteed reservations. Generally speaking, guests with reservations who arrive before the hotel's reservation cancellation hour should be accommodated.

Walk-In Guests

A **walk-in** guest who has been traveling for an extended time may be disappointed to find that a hotel is fully occupied. Hotels have no obligation to accommodate guests who arrive without a reservation when no guestrooms are available. If a walk-in guest cannot be accommodated, front desk agents can assist the guest by providing directions to nearby hotels. The front desk agent might also offer to contact another hotel on behalf of the displaced guest.

Most of the time, guests who cannot be accommodated at the hotel would prefer to stay at a similar property. Hotels should keep a list, with contact information, of comparable properties in the local area. Hotels can benefit through mutual guest referrals in this way. Guest referrals allow one hotel to compare how well it is doing on a given night with other area hotels. Competing properties may reciprocate by sending overflow business to neighboring properties when the opportunity arises. Most importantly, however, referrals should be viewed as part of the hotel's guest relations program. The extra care paid to turned-away guests helps create an industry-wide atmosphere of caring and concern for all guests.

The situation may be more difficult when a walk-in guest incorrectly believes that he or she has a reservation. The hotel might take the following steps to clarify the situation:

- If the guest presents a letter of confirmation, verify the date and the name of the hotel; the guest may have arrived on a different date or at the wrong property. Most confirmation letters have a confirmation number that can help the front desk agent locate the reservation record in the hotel's system.
- Ask whether another person might have made the reservation for the guest; the reservation may be at another property, or it may be misfiled under the name of the person making the reservation, not the guest's name.
- Double-check reservations records for another spelling of the guest's last name. For instance, "B," "P," and "T" may have been confused when the reservation was made during a telephone conversation or entered incorrectly in a text document. Also, check to see if the guest's first and last names were inadvertently reversed in the reservation record.
- If the reservation was made through a travel agency or corporate representative, give the guest an opportunity to contact the originating source for clarification.
- Verify no-show registration information from the previous day, just in case the guest was mistakenly classified as a "no-show" because of an incorrect date of arrival.

If there seems to be no alternative to **walking** (turning away) the guest, a manager, not a front desk agent, should explain the matter to the guest in a private area away from the front desk. Registering one guest in view of another who cannot be accommodated can be extremely awkward and embarrassing to both the guest and the front office staff member.

Guests with Non-Guaranteed Reservations

A number of circumstances can delay a guest's scheduled arrival time or date. Guests frequently do not have the chance to change a non-guaranteed reservation to a guaranteed reservation by the time they realize they will arrive past the hotel's reservation cancellation hour. As a result, the hotel may not hold the reserved room for the guest and may not have a room available at the time the guest arrives. If the hotel cannot provide a guestroom, front office management must be extremely tactful when informing the guest. Blame should not be placed on either party, since the lack of accommodations may not be the fault of the guest or the front office staff.

Guests with Guaranteed Reservations

If reservations are carefully handled and sound forecasting procedures are followed, the hotel should not have to deny accommodations to a guest who has a guaranteed reservation. It is a serious matter to turn away a guest with a guaranteed reservation: some states have laws prohibiting hotels from doing so, and, should a hotel not be able to accommodate such a guest, penalties may be imposed upon the hotel by the state, at the guest's request. Even though hotels should do all they can to avoid turning away guests who have guaranteed reservations, they should have a policy for front desk staff members to follow if the situation occurs.

The front office manager should take charge and make the necessary decisions when it appears that the property does not have accommodations for a guest who has a guaranteed reservation. The manager may do the following:

- Review all room status reports and expected arrivals lists to ensure full occupancy is expected.
- Conduct an accurate count of rooms occupied, using all relevant data.
- Compare information in the rooms availability file, the housekeeper's report, and guest folios, looking for discrepancies in occupancy status.
- Contact in-house **due-outs** (guests expected to check out today) who have not yet checked out to confirm their departure times. Housekeeping staff can also visit select guestrooms to verify occupancy status. A guest may have left the hotel without properly completing check-out, and therefore the guestroom can be made available for an arriving guest. A departing guest may have left the hotel expecting to be billed, or may have paid in advance, or may simply have forgotten to check out. An early discovery of a room departure allows that room to be made available.
- Verify guestrooms with a status of "out-of-order" to ensure that they are not qualified to be occupied. Perhaps an out-of-order room might be readied for sale, if the room problems are minor—no bedspread, for example, or missing window drapes. If a guest is willing to occupy an out-of-order room, its rate could be appropriately adjusted. These decisions must be made by front office management. An out-of-order room should never be offered if the room has serious deficiencies, like no running water or telephone service. In addition, an out-of-order room should never be offered unless it is inspected first, and the department placing the room on out-of-order status is notified that it will be occupied. The front office manager should check the out-of-order report daily to ensure that all rooms are made available as quickly as possible.
- Identify rooms that have been pre-blocked for one or two days in the future. A guest can be assigned to one of these rooms, if the guest will depart early enough to not affect the room block.

Front desk staff should be consistent when discussing the lack of accommodations with arriving guests. Helpful suggestions include the following:

- Guests should be encouraged to return to the hotel at the earliest date of availability. Upon their return, they may be placed on a VIP list, provided a complimentary room upgrade, or presented with a small amenity as compensation for the inconvenience of having been turned away on their last visit.

- Management should prepare a follow-up letter to be sent to guests who arrived with a reservation but could not be accommodated, apologizing for the inconvenience and encouraging the guests to consider returning to the hotel (with appropriate incentives).
- If a member of a convention block cannot be accommodated, the group's meeting planner should be notified. The planner may be able to solve the problem by arranging for some attendees to alter their current rooming status. In such cases, it is important for the front office staff to have a positive working relationship with the group coordinator or meeting planner. This notification may better enable the coordinator or planner to properly deal with the problem and subsequent membership complaints.

Summary

Through the reservations process, a guest provides nearly all the information needed to complete registration. The focus of front office operations shifts to the registration process once the arriving guest's reservation status is known. Front office personnel will find registration smoother and simpler when the information in a reservation record is accurate and complete. The registration process can be divided into seven steps: preregistration activities, creating the registration record, assigning the room and rate, establishing the method of payment, verifying the guest's identity, issuing the room key or access code, and filling special requests.

Preregistration activities occur before guest arrival and are intended to accelerate the registration process. Guests can be preregistered when reservations agents or hotel websites with registration capabilities gather the proper information. Typically, preregistered guests need only verify registration information and provide a valid signature to complete the registration process. In addition, room and rate assignment, creation of a guest folio, and other functions may be part of a hotel's preregistration activities.

The registration record is a collection of important guest information, and is created at the time of check-in. Registration cards, or their computer-generated equivalent, should prompt front desk agents to inquire about the guest's intentions regarding method of payment and planned date of departure. Front desk agents should always confirm the guest's departure date and pre-assigned room rate.

Room assignment involves identifying and allocating an available room in a specific room category. Based on reservation information, specific rooms and rates may be assigned before the guest arrives. Pre-assigning a specific room depends on the room's forecasted availability status and how appropriately the room meets the guest's needs. Room assignments are finalized during the registration process. Effective room and rate assignment depends on accurate and timely room status information (long-term *reservation status* and short-term *housekeeping status*).

Effective account settlement depends on the steps taken during registration to determine the guest's method of payment. Proper settlement or credit authorization at the time of registration will greatly reduce the potential for subsequent collection problems. Just as hotels vary in size, structure, and organization, so do their guidelines for establishing the guest's method of payment. The registration process may also play an important role in guest accounting, since it deals directly with method of payment.

Many hotels require positive guest identification to complete the registration process. This has long been common practice in Europe, and has become common in the United States since 9/11. Hotel managers want to be sure they know who is staying at their property. For domestic guests, a driver's license or other form of photo identification is usually sufficient. International guests should be asked for their passports.

By issuing a room key, the front desk agent completes the registration process. Hotels should have written policies governing guestroom key control. If the hotel provides bell service, the front desk agent should ask whether the guest would like assistance from a bell attendant and then communicate specific room information to the bell attendant.

Part of registration is making sure that any special requests made by guests are acknowledged and dealt with. While many of the details surrounding special requests can be addressed during preregistration, it is important to follow up on each request. Guests will be disappointed if they arrive at their room and find that the hotel did not honor a request. Front desk agents should mention special guest requests during registration to assure the guest that the hotel will meet the guest's wants and needs.

Some hotels are trying creative registration options in an effort to better accommodate guests. A relatively new concept in front office registration is self-registration. Self-registration terminals can be located off-site (in airports, for example) or in the hotel lobby. These terminals vary in design and may resemble automated bank teller machines.

Upselling at the front desk is a common practice used to enhance the value of the guest's lodging experience while increasing hotel revenues. Front desk agents should identify opportunities for offering better accommodations to guests and selling their value. For example, guests who travel regularly as part of their work may appreciate rooms with special business amenities at a small increase in the room rate they confirmed. Many hotels provide incentive programs for agents making the most of such selling opportunities.

Relocating (or walking) guests must be done with great care and concern. Most guests who believe the hotel has not acted in their best interest will become upset; some may cause a disturbance or vow never to return. Further, they may criticize the hotel to friends and co-workers, creating an even larger negative image of the hotel. Walking a guest should be done by a manager, not a front desk agent. Hotels should attempt to bring the guest back as soon as possible. Front office managers must take care to minimize the number of guests who must be relocated, and be aware of any laws pertaining to guests who have guaranteed reservations. Upscale hotels usually pay for the guest's transportation to and from the hotel to which the guest is relocated (in addition to paying for the guestroom), and advise their telecommunications department to redirect incoming telephone calls and faxes to the other location.

Key Terms

All Inclusive—A billing arrangement under which room charges include the guestroom, meals, beverages, and activities.

American Plan (AP)—A billing arrangement under which room charges include the guestroom and three meals; also called "full pension."

authorization code—A code generated by an online payment card verification service, indicating that the requested transaction has been approved.

denial code—A code generated by an online payment card verification service, indicating that the requested transaction has not been approved.

direct billing—A credit arrangement, normally established through correspondence between a guest or a company and the hotel, in which the hotel agrees to bill the guest or the company for charges incurred.

due-outs—Guests expected to check out on a given day who have not yet done so.

European Plan (EP)—A billing arrangement under which meals are priced separately from rooms.

floor limit—A limit assigned to hotels by payment card companies indicating the maximum amount in payment card charges the hotel is permitted to accept from a card member without special authorization.

housekeeping status report—A report prepared by the housekeeping department indicating the current housekeeping status of each room, based on a physical check.

incidental charges—Charges made to a guest account other than the charges and tax for the guestroom.

Modified American Plan (MAP)—A billing arrangement under which the daily rate includes charges for the guestroom and two meals, typically breakfast and dinner.

occupancy report—A report prepared each night by a front desk agent that lists the rooms occupied that night and indicates those guests expected to check out the following day.

PIA (paid-in-advance)—A guest who pays his or her room charges in cash during registration; PIA guests are often denied in-house credit.

rack rate—The standard rate established by a hotel for a particular category of rooms.

registration form—A document used to help formulate a registration record; in many states, the guest's signature on a registration form is required by law.

registration record—A collection of important guest information created by the front desk agent following the guest's arrival; includes the guest's name, address, telephone number, and company affiliation; method of payment; and date of departure.

reservation status—An indicator of a room's long-term availability for assignment.

room rate—The price a hotel charges for overnight accommodations.

room status discrepancies—A situation in which the housekeeping department's description of a room's status differs from the room status information that guides front desk employees in assigning rooms to guests.

run of the house—Room assignment based on room availability at the time of check-in.

self-registration—A computerized system that automatically registers a guest and dispenses a guestroom key, based on the guest's reservation and payment card information.

skipper—A guest who leaves without paying for the room.

sleeper—An unoccupied guestroom wrongly shown as occupied on the property management system.

upselling—A sales technique whereby a guest is offered a more expensive room than what he or she reserved or originally requested, and is then persuaded to rent the room based on the room's features and benefits, and his or her needs.

walk-in—A guest who arrives at a hotel without a reservation.

walking—Turning away a guest who has a reservation, due to a lack of rooms.

Review Questions

1. What are the seven steps of the registration process?
2. What are the advantages of preregistering guests? What might limit the front office's ability to preregister guests?
3. What information is usually requested on a guest registration card? How is this information useful to the front office?
4. Why is current room status information essential to an effective guest registration process?
5. What are the advantages of a computerized room status system?
6. What are some examples of special room rates?
7. What major methods of payment do guests use? What forms of tender are generally considered equivalent to cash?
8. What procedures do front desk agents use for accepting a payment card as a method of payment during registration?
9. What are some creative registration options?
10. What is upselling? When is it appropriate? What are some things a hotel can do to upsell a guest?
11. What actions should the front office consider when a guest cannot be accommodated?

Internet Sites

For more information, visit the following Internet sites. Remember that Internet addresses can change without notice. If the site is no longer there, you can use a search engine to look for additional sites.

American Express Company
www.americanexpress.com

Diners Club International
www.dinersclub.com

Discover Card
www.discovercard.com

MasterCard Worldwide
www.mastercard.com

Visa Inc.
www.visa.com

Wyndham ByRequest
www.wyndham.com/wbr/main.wnt

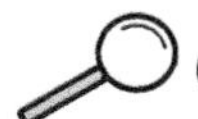

Case Studies

Checking In to the Boden Oceanside Resort and Lodge

Checking in to the Boden Oceanside Resort and Lodge should have taken John five minutes, even though the check-in line was three deep. However, there was only one front desk agent in sight and the people checking in seemed to have all kinds of questions. To complicate matters, their room keys couldn't be encoded for some reason, and the agent was trying to take a phone call from a guest at the same time.

When John finally reached the desk, the agent didn't make eye contact. John's name was on the reservation list and all of the details of his stay were in order. John was given a handful of brochures but the clerk didn't really explain any of them specifically. There was a map of the town, a brochure describing local events, and a brochure featuring various restaurants in the area. The map of the property was so small that it was difficult to make out exactly where one was on the property.

The best part of check-in was the 20 percent discount coupon for the Saturday brunch.

As John picked up his luggage, he looked around for a bell attendant. He wasn't quite sure where his room was, but knew its general direction. The desk clerk had not looked up at him while explaining where the room was on the map. He hoped that there would be signage to direct him once he got outside the main lobby.

After settling into his room, John noticed a constant humming sound coming from behind the wall. It sounded somewhat like a fan. John hated any extra noise and called the front desk to find out what the noise was.

The desk agent who had checked John in was on break and the new one informed him that the noise was indeed a fan from the kitchen that ran from 8 A.M. until 11 P.M. and that the room wasn't usually sold unless the hotel was sold out. John asked to be moved, since he would be in the hotel for five days. The agent told him it would be no problem and that he should come back to the front desk to get another room key. She asked whether he needed assistance with his luggage and then asked if he could hold the line for a second.

John waited on the phone for what seemed three or four minutes when the agent finally got back to him. She apologized and he said he would like help with his luggage.

After waiting for about ten minutes, John finally left his luggage in the room and went back to the front desk. The agent who had helped him was taking a phone reservation, but her assistant asked if he could help. John mentioned his desire to change rooms. The assistant leaned down to talk to the agent on the phone but was ignored momentarily. He told John he didn't know which room she had arranged for him and that she would be off the phone in a moment.

Twenty minutes later John was checked into a new room with an ocean view. He decided to go out for a walk and stopped first at the front desk to see if his luggage could be delivered to his new room. "Oh no!" said the agent. "I forgot to let the bell attendant know about the move and now he has gone home."

John found his way to his old room, picked up his luggage and took it to his new room.

As he lay on his bed substituting a rest for a walk, John couldn't help seeing a few cobwebs in the upper corners of the room, cracking wallpaper, and some dust on the ceiling trim.

After his nap, John had to call down to the front desk because there was no toilet paper in the bathroom. He was transferred to housekeeping, where the executive housekeeper answered cordially. She apologized and told him that she was severely understaffed due to budget freezes but would send someone up right away.

As John went for a walk later that afternoon, he was nearly knocked over in the hallway by a load of laundry being carried by a very small woman. She said something he couldn't understand in broken Spanish and English and hurried along on her errand.

As it turns out, John had been hired to inspect the property by the owners of the Boden Oceanside Resort and Lodge. He began to jot down some notes that he would use in his report to the owners.

Discussion Questions

1. What suggestions do you have for the front desk manager?
2. How many departments did John interact with during the arrival stage?
3. Why would the owners hire John to check out the property?

Case number: 608C04

This case also appears in Todd Comen, *Case Studies in Front Office Management* (Lansing, Mich.: American Hotel & Lodging Educational Institute, 2003).

Everybody Sells: Turning Front Desk Agents into Salespeople

"Come in, come in!"

Ben, a slim, gray-haired figure in a dark three-piece suit, rose from his leather desk chair and waved Keith into one of the two chairs on the other side of the massive oak desk. Keith said thank you and glanced around the general manager's office as Ben settled into the chair next to his. Keith had been in the office a few times before, but he was still impressed by the floor-to-ceiling bookshelves behind the desk, the lithographs of old hotels that lined the walls, the awards and testimonial plaques that were sprinkled throughout the room.

"The reason I wanted to talk with you today," Ben began, "is to discuss what we can do to bring up our average daily rate. You've been at the hotel a couple of weeks now and I assume you've learned your way around a bit."

"Yes sir."

Ben's eyes twinkled. "I've told you before, just because my hair is gray and I've been in the hotel business a hundred years, there's no need to call me 'sir.' 'Ben' will do."

Keith smiled and just stopped himself from saying "Yes sir" again.

"I've received word that corporate wants us to raise our ADR ten percent by the end of the quarter, and the front desk has got to do its part." Ben leaned back in his chair and clasped his hands over his vest. He reminded Keith of a kindly, longtime family lawyer getting set to dispense some grandfatherly advice. "I don't want to be insulting, but, since this is your first job as a front office manager—in fact, you're not that long out of college, is that correct?"

"That's right, just a few years," Keith said. "Still 'wet behind the ears,' you might say."

"Well, if you'll indulge me, I'd like to relate a little history of the relationship between the reservations department and the front desk; I think it will help you appreciate how we got to where we are today, and put into perspective what I'll be asking you to do to help us get that extra ten percent."

"Okay." Keith settled back for a long story.

"My first hotel job was in the reservations office. Back then there were no computers. We did have phones, however, in case you were wondering." Keith smiled as Ben chuckled. "People would call in requesting a room, and we would roll an index card into a typewriter and type out a reservation. The caller didn't make special requests, such as 'a room with a desk, please,' or 'a king-size bed, please,' and we didn't ask for any of that information, because we weren't sure what type of room would be available—back then inventory control was all done at the front desk. The card was simply a request that a room be held for the caller on a certain day. The cards would all be gathered up at the end of the shift and taken to the front desk, where they would be filed by the day the reservation was for.

"When the guest arrived at the hotel, the front desk agent would pull the card ('Yes, Mr. Whosis, we have a room for you') and then the selling would begin, based on what types of rooms the agent knew were still available: 'Would you like a king-size bed?' 'We have several rooms with a nice view of the park—would you care for one of those?' and so on. In other words, the front desk agents were the hotel's salespeople, because they had control of the guestroom inventory. They knew which rooms were available and which were not.

"Well, along came computers, and suddenly sales moved from the front desk to the reservations department. Why? Because computers allowed the reservations department to keep track of guestroom inventory. Now when a caller phoned the hotel, the reservationist could look at a computer screen and tell exactly what rooms were still available on the day the caller wanted to stay at the hotel. So the reservationist, instead of merely reserving 'a' room—the old card system could do that much—could now reserve a *particular* room. The reservationist could ask the caller all of the questions the front desk agent used to ask: 'What size bed would you like?' 'Would you like a room with a view?' 'For five dollars more I can reserve a room near the pool; would you like that?' and so on. Therefore, once computerized reservations systems arrived and guestroom inventory control shifted from the front desk to the reservations department, the sales function and all of the sales training shifted from the front desk to the reservations department, too."

Ben spread his hands in a gesture of regret. "Consequently, salesmanship was not emphasized at the front desk anymore. In fact, many agents saw no need to sell, because most guests had already told the reservationist exactly what types of rooms they wanted. Many front desk agents thought they would be 'bothering' a guest if they suggested a room other than the one called for by the reservation already entered into the computer.

"But—and this is something I could never get your predecessor to understand, or at least to act on," Ben frowned, "front desk agents can still have a tremendous impact on a hotel's bottom line, through upselling. For example, if a guest walks in with his wife, and the front desk agent sees that he has reserved a standard room, the agent should say something like the following: 'Sir, we have a room available that you might enjoy more than the one you've reserved. The room I'm thinking of is a corner room with a great view. It also has a whirlpool tub that's great for relaxing, a sitting area, and a king-size bed—which would be an upgrade from the two double beds in your present room—all for only $15 more. Would you like me to reserve this room for you?'

"Or, if an agent sees a guest come in lugging three sample cases, he can assume that this is a businessperson who probably would like enough space in his room to spread out business papers or samples or what have you. The agent should say something like this: 'Gee, it looks like you're really loaded down, sir. I see that you've reserved a standard guestroom, but I have a bigger room with plenty of desk space for only $10 more.' What's wrong with that?"

Ben stopped talking and looked at Keith expectantly.

"Nothing?" Keith ventured.

"That's right, there's nothing wrong with that!" Ben said enthusiastically. "The agent made a suggestion that might make the guest's stay more pleasant and also increase revenues for the hotel. That's all there is to upselling. But so few agents are trained to do that anymore. Like I said, computers changed everything. In the old days, reservationists were 'order-takers' and the front desk agents were the salespeople; now the roles are completely reversed. And it shouldn't be that way. Front desk agents still have a sales role to play."

Ben chuckled again. "Thank you for letting me climb up on my soapbox. You're probably wondering, 'What does all this have to do with me?' Well, what I want you to do is turn your front desk agents into salespeople again. We've got to teach them how to sell and give them the tools to sell so they'll have the confidence to sell."

"I hope this doesn't sound naive," Keith said, "but, can upselling really make that much difference? I mean, $5 here, $10 there, and not every guest is going to agree to an upgrade." Keith paused. "I guess I'm not sure how much that's really going to add to the bottom line."

"That's the beauty of upselling," Ben replied. "Every extra dollar you bring in through upselling falls to the bottom line. We've already spent the money to get the guest to the hotel—through advertising, the reservationist taking the call, and so on. Now that he's here, anything extra we can entice him into spending is pure gravy."

Ben smiled. "Now, don't get the wrong idea. I don't want to sound manipulative, because upselling—done properly—is not the art of tricking a guest into buying something he doesn't want. A front desk agent should never pressure a guest. However, there's nothing wrong with pointing out to a guest that, for a few dollars more, his or her experience at the hotel might be enhanced. Usually, guests are unaware that there are rooms available that might better fit their needs. Maybe the reservationist didn't do a great job of selling, who knows? So agents aren't trying to 'gouge' guests when they upsell—they are merely offering a guest some options that the guest might not have thought about, options that might make the guest's experience at the hotel more enjoyable. That's the way you should present upselling to your agents."

"I'll be glad to try," Keith said, "but I'm not sure how to go about it."

"Well, the first thing I'd do is assess the current sales skills of the staff," Ben said. "Is anyone selling right now? You've only been here a couple of weeks and I know you're not fully acquainted with your personnel, so I'd spend some time observing the agents. This might also give you ideas on what types of upselling opportunities the agents are missing. If you discover a pattern, that will give you a plan of attack on good ways to raise the ADR.

"What I suspect you're going to find," Ben continued, "is that few, if any, agents are upselling right now. But don't be discouraged. There are lots of techniques we can use in-house to train them; we may even send them to some outside seminars, or bring a trainer here if we have to. Also, you'll probably want to set up an incentive program to encourage the agents to sell."

Ben stood up to signal an end to the meeting and placed a hand on Keith's shoulder. "Don't worry, I'm confident you can do it. And you're not alone. All we need from the front desk area is an additional five percent; reservations and the sales department have targets to meet, too, and—working together—we'll make our numbers and corporate will be happy. If you run into trouble, don't hesitate to come see me."

"Thank you, Ben."

During the next week, Keith observed the front desk agents as they checked in guests. As Ben predicted, they didn't make any effort to upsell. They were polite and professional, but invariably they sent the guests to whatever room they had previously reserved. Even with walk-in guests there was no salesmanship. The agents always offered the walk-ins one of the hotel's standard guestrooms—the lowest-priced rooms in the house—and almost every walk-in simply accepted it. Keith observed only one walk-in guest who asked if there were better rooms available. The agent said yes, the hotel had some deluxe rooms available, and there was even one club room still available. (The hotel had three basic types of rooms: "standard" guestrooms with either two double beds, two queen-size beds, or one king-size bed; "deluxe" guestrooms with the same bed combinations but with slightly more floor space and better appointments; and "club" rooms that were really mini-suites with king-size beds, sitting areas, and special amenities such as thicker towels, upgraded toiletries, turn-down service, and so on.) When the guest asked the agent to describe the differences in the rooms, Keith was surprised to hear the agent do a terrible job of outlining the different features and amenities that accompanied each type of room. Later, Keith checked with some of the other agents and was shocked to learn that many of them had never seen any of the hotel's guestrooms.

As the week wore on, Keith noticed a pattern that concerned him: most of the hotel's club rooms were given away as upgrades to the hotel's business guests. Those rooms were supposed to be real money-makers for the hotel, because the hotel sold them at a higher rate than the standard and deluxe guestrooms, but that was precisely the problem—the rooms were rarely sold. As part of its special corporate rates, the hotel promised business travelers free upgrades to club rooms "subject to availability." And club rooms were always available, because front desk agents weren't selling them! If Keith did nothing more than get his agents to sell more club rooms, that would have a dramatic impact on ADR, because the rooms would be sold rather than given to guests who were already enjoying a discounted corporate rate.

At the end of the week, Keith met with his front desk agents at the beginning of their shifts and explained the situation. "The overall goal of the hotel is to raise ADR by ten percent; our contribution is to increase our numbers by five percent. We can do that by upselling—to all of our guests, but especially to our walk-ins. According to my research, about 12 percent of our guests are walk-ins, and since these guests have no prior reservations, they're not committed to a particular room and should be easier to upsell. If we start out by offering walk-ins our club rooms, rather than our standard rooms, then offer a deluxe room as a compromise if they don't want a club room, I think we can almost make our numbers right there, not even counting upselling to guests who already have reservations.

"Let me give you an example of how a little bit of upselling can make a big difference," Keith continued. "We sold about 1,000 rooms to walk-ins last month. All but fourteen of those guests were booked in standard rooms at around $55 per night. If we sell club rooms, which sell for $40 more, to 200 of those walk-ins—that's just one upgraded guest out of five—that brings in an additional $8,800 for the month. Project that over twelve months, and we're bringing in over $100,000 more revenue per year for the hotel. Just moving 200 walk-ins from a standard to a deluxe room at $75 a night would bring in $4,400 more a month. And those dollars fall right to the bottom line.

"If we sell out the club rooms—and that should be our goal every night—they are no longer available as free giveaways to businesspeople, which saves us money and gives us upselling opportunities: 'I'm sorry, Ms. Businessperson, but our club rooms are full tonight. I can go ahead and book you into your standard room, or I can upgrade you to a deluxe guestroom with lots of space and a king-size bed for just $20 more.' Don't save the club rooms so you are sure to have some available to give away as upgrades. What you want to do is sell them out, so we don't have to give them away."

"Isn't that unfair to the business travelers?" asked one agent.

"Not really," Keith replied. "Our deals with business travelers state that we will upgrade them to club rooms if any are available—but we certainly aren't obligated to deliberately not sell club rooms to make sure they're available. That's not good business, and businesspeople don't expect us to do that. The hotel put a lot of money into those club rooms, and it's entitled to try to recoup that investment if it can.

"I know the idea of upselling is a new one for many of you," Keith said in conclusion, "but it isn't that difficult, and I'm not going to just shove you out there unprepared. You're going to get some training, and I'm also going to come up with an incentive plan so you can share in the rewards of bringing more revenue to the hotel.

"Upselling can be enjoyable if you approach it the right way, so get ready to have some fun! And here's a slogan I want you to remember from now on: 'Everybody Sells!'"

Discussion Questions

1. What are some ways Keith can train his front desk agents to be salespeople?
2. What types of incentive plans might Keith put in place to encourage his front desk agents to sell?

Case Number: 3325CA

The following industry experts helped generate and develop this case: Richard M. Brooks, CHA, Vice President, TWE Group; and S. Kenneth Hiller, CHA, General Manager, Holiday Inn, Beachwood, Ohio.

Risking the Upgrade!

Things were hopping in the front office this Friday afternoon. Guests had been checking in for the Glamder wedding, which would last two days and was taking up a block of twenty rooms. It was a major wedding for the resort, and the sales department was very pleased. It was still the shoulder season, so an event such as this was welcome at this time of year. With the wedding room block, the resort was nearly fully occupied.

At 7:30, two men arrived at the front desk to check in a little late for the rehearsal dinner. The front desk agent, Clarice, greeted them cordially and requested their names. One introduced himself as John Jones. Clarice identified the correct guest record for John Jones, scanned it briefly to determine if indeed he was with the wedding party, how many days he would be staying, and the number of people in the room. She noticed that there was only one person booked for the room and asked whether he was traveling alone. He explained that his buddy had decided to attend the wedding at the last minute so they drove down together from Oregon.

Clarice reviewed the guest record again, taking notice of the room assignment and the price quoted for the room. Mr. Jones had been assigned to a small, less expensive room in the south wing of the resort for the low rate of $120. This room had only one queen size bed and a pull-out sofa. She took a look at the men and wondered who would get the pull-out sofa, since both of them were well over six feet tall.

While pondering what to do next, she asked whether they had ever stayed at the resort before. Mr. Jones said that he and his wife and two children had stayed at the resort just eight months ago and loved it. They had planned to go to Europe, but world circumstances influenced them to stay closer to home. They had stayed in a lovely suite and really enjoyed their time at the resort. The friend, however, had never stayed there.

Clarice then asked whether they would be comfortable in a room with a queen bed and a pull-out sofa. Mr. Jones quipped that since he was paying for the room, he would take dibs on the queen bed. The other gentleman didn't complain, but was a little disappointed. Clarice thought for a moment and asked whether they would like an upgrade to a more comfortable room. She couldn't guarantee one, but would see what she could do if they gave her a few moments. She asked them if they would like to have a refreshing drink in the lounge while she checked on room availability.

Since the men were late already, they decided a few more minutes wouldn't matter and that they would have a drink. After ten minutes and another check-in, the men were back wondering if anything had been found. Clarice said that the only thing she could find was a junior suite with two queen beds. It was a very comfortable room and would be the envy of the other wedding guests. She said it was $100 more per night. As the wedding party would last two nights, the total additional cost would be $200. Mr. Jones was quick to respond to the suggestion by saying he would be pleased to split the difference with the resort, meaning that the additional charge would be $50 per night.

Clarice pondered the offer. She cringed, wondering what her supervisor would have to say about upgrading guests from the lowest-cost room to one of the nicest the resort had to offer for only $50 per night. Her superiors had always pushed for getting top dollar for the suites.

On the other hand, Clarice had noticed that the suites hadn't been selling to walk-in customers. At this time of night, the room might not sell anyway, she thought to herself. And what were the chances of the room selling the following night when it wasn't reserved in advance? Clarice wondered whether to take the additional $50 per night and risk upsetting the supervisor whom she knew didn't like selling below rack rate, or just leave the two guys in the less expensive room. She thought for a moment and then decided to go with the upgrade. The two gentlemen were thrilled when they passed the front desk later that evening on their way to the rehearsal dinner. They had called their wives and told them of the warm reception and that they would have to plan a visit to the resort in the near future.

The following day the assistant front office manager asked to have a word with Clarice about the upgrade decision she'd made the previous afternoon. They had a brief discussion while Clarice answered phones for the PBX operator who was taking a dinner break. As expected, the assistant front office manager wasn't very pleased with the upgrade decision. Even though Clarice tried to explain her reasoning for the upgrade, the manager couldn't see her point and asked her never to do it again.

Discussion Questions

1. Did Clarice use good business sense or was she just being nice?
2. Should the manager have been called to help with this decision?

Case number: 608C07

This case also appears in Todd Comen, *Case Studies in Front Office Management* (Lansing, Mich.: American Hotel & Lodging Educational Institute, 2003).

Chapter 5 Outline

Competencies

1. Describe the role of the housekeeping department in communicating room status. (pp. 175–177)
2. Explain the relationship between the housekeeping and maintenance departments and identify typical cleaning responsibilities of the housekeeping department. (pp. 178–184)
3. Explain how executive housekeepers use such tools as area inventory lists, frequency schedules, performance standards, and productivity standards to plan the work of the housekeeping department. (pp. 184–188)
4. Discuss equipment and supply inventory issues, and distinguish between recycled and non-recycled inventories. (pp. 188–189)
5. Summarize the issues involved in a dilemma many hotels face: whether to cut back or eliminate housekeeping supervisors. (pp. 189–192)

Taken from *Managing Front Office Operations,* Ninth Edition, by Michael L. Kasavana

Chapter 5

The Role of Housekeeping in Hospitality Operations

This chapter has been excerpted from material in Chapters 1 and 2 of *Managing Housekeeping Operations*, Second Edition, by Margaret M. Kappa, Aleta Nitschke, and Patricia B. Schappert.

BECAUSE OF ITS IMPORTANCE to the efficient operation of the front office, in this chapter we will take a detailed look at the housekeeping department. The housekeeping department has frequent communication with the front office department, specifically with the front desk staff. Normally, front desk agents cannot assign guestrooms until the rooms have been cleaned, inspected, and released by the housekeeping department. In most properties, the housekeeping department is part of the rooms division along with the front office department, and the executive housekeeper works closely with the front office manager. In this chapter, we will look at the importance of communication between the front office and housekeeping departments, how housekeeping interacts with maintenance, the role of planning in the housekeeping department, and the changing involvement of housekeeping supervisors.

Communicating Room Status

Each night, a front desk agent or the property management system produces an **occupancy report.** The occupancy report lists rooms occupied that night and indicates guests who are expected to check out the following day. The executive housekeeper consults this list early the next morning and schedules occupied rooms for cleaning. As guests check out of the hotel, the front desk notifies housekeeping, either through the hotel's front office system, via telephone, or through some other room status update process. Housekeeping ensures that checked-out rooms are given top priority so that they can be cleaned and readied for arriving guests.

The executive housekeeper also uses the ten-day and three-day forecast reports prepared by the front office system. Forecast reports indicate how many rooms are projected to be occupied each day; this helps the executive housekeeper effectively prepare staff schedules to ensure that enough room attendants will be scheduled for each day's workload.

At the end of each work shift, the housekeeping department staff prepares a **housekeeping status report** (see Exhibit 1) based on a physical check of each room in the property. This report indicates the current housekeeping status of each room. It is compared to the front desk occupancy report, and any discrepancies are

Exhibit 1 Sample Housekeeping Status Report

Housekeeper's Report **A.M.**

Date ________________, **20** _____ **P.M.**

ROOM NUMBER	STATUS	ROOM NUMBER	STATUS	ROOM NUMBER	STATUS	ROOM NUMBER	STATUS
101		126		151		176	
102		127		152		177	
103		128		153		178	
104		129		154		179	
105		130		155		180	
106		131		156		181	
107		132		157		182	
108		133		158		183	
120		145		170		195	
121		146		171		196	
122		147		172		197	
123		148		173		198	
124		149		174		199	
125		150		175		200	

Remarks:

____

____

____

____

Housekeeper's Signature

Legend:

✓	-	Occupied
000	-	Out-of-Order
——	-	Vacant
B	-	Slept Out (Baggage Still in Room)
X	-	Occupied, No Baggage
C.O.	-	Slept In but Checked Out Early A.M.
E.A.	-	Early Arrival

brought to the attention of the front office manager. A **room status discrepancy** is the difference between the housekeeping department's description of a room's status and the room status information the front desk staff uses to assign guestrooms. Room status discrepancies can seriously affect a property's ability to accommodate guests and maximize rooms revenue.

Promptly notifying the front desk staff of the housekeeping status of rooms can be a tremendous asset in registering guests who arrive early, especially during high-occupancy or sold-out periods. Keeping room status information up to date requires close coordination and cooperation between the front desk and housekeeping department staffs.

In an automated room-status system, housekeeping staff and the front desk staff have instantaneous access to room status information. When a guest checks out, a front desk agent enters the departure into a front office terminal. Housekeeping is then automatically alerted that the room has been vacated and needs cleaning through a remote terminal located in the housekeeping department. Next, housekeeping attendants clean the room and notify the housekeeping supervisor when the room is ready for inspection. Once the room is inspected, the inspector enters this information into the room-status system. This housekeeping status update is then communicated to the front office system which, in turn, categorizes the room as clean, vacant, and available for sale.

While room occupancy status within an automated system is almost always current, reporting of each room's housekeeping status may lag behind. For example, the housekeeping supervisor may inspect several rooms in sequence but not update the room-status files until the end of a long inspection round. In a large hotel, contacting the housekeeping department after each room is inspected is generally inefficient, since answering a phone call or responding to a page leads to frequent interruptions. A delay in status reporting may also occur when a list of clean, inspected rooms is furnished to a staff member in the housekeeping department who does not immediately enter the data into the system.

The problems in promptly reporting each room's housekeeping status to the front office system can be reduced when the system is directly connected to the guestroom telephone system. With such a network, supervisors can inspect rooms, determine their readiness for sale, and then enter a code on the room telephone to change the room's status in the front office system. No one needs to answer the phone, since the computer automatically receives the relay, and there is minimal chance for error. Within seconds, the room's updated status can be displayed on the screen at the front office. This procedure can significantly reduce not only the number of guests forced to wait for room assignment but also the length of registration.

Teamwork between housekeeping and front office staffs is essential to daily hotel operations. The more familiar housekeeping and front office personnel are with each other's procedures, the smoother the relationship between the two departments.

Advanced housekeeping and front desk communication systems rely on wireless connectivity via a hand-held terminal carried by each housekeeper. The terminal may be a personal digital assistant (PDA) or similar device that resembles the mobile devices people carry with them to record appointments, telephone numbers, and personal notes. However, a housekeeping PDA is programmed for housekeeping purposes and uses the wireless connectivity for two-way communications between the housekeepers and other housekeeping department staff. With a PDA, a housekeeper's work schedule can be pre-loaded into his or her terminal before the beginning of the work shift. As the housekeeper's work is completed, the housekeeper records the information in the terminal and transmits it to the front office system so that the system's room status data is updated. If the housekeeping manager has an urgent request for a particular guestroom to be readied, the manager can use the terminal to communicate this information to the housekeeper working in that area. In addition, if a housekeeper needs additional supplies or identifies a maintenance problem, he or she can use the PDA to communicate such needs to the housekeeping or maintenance department. PDAs can also be used to dispatch housekeeping staff members in response to special guest requests—for more towels or for a crib, for example. The responding housekeeper can use the PDA to report when the request has been filled. In a large hotel with multiple buildings or a very large housekeeping department, the cost of PDA devices can be justified based on improved service to guests.

Housekeeping and Maintenance

In most non-lodging commercial buildings, housekeeping and maintenance personnel generally report to the same department manager. This makes sense, because these functional areas have similar goals and methods and operate most efficiently when they enjoy a close working relationship. In most midsize and large lodging operations, however, housekeeping personnel tend to report to the rooms division manager, while engineering and maintenance staff often constitute a separate division. Differing lines of accountability can become a barrier between these important support centers in a hotel.

It is unfortunate that support centers often seem to have an almost adversarial relationship. For example, housekeeping personnel sometimes resent having to clean up after various types of maintenance, while engineering personnel may be upset if the misuse of chemicals and equipment by housekeeping personnel results in additional work. To ensure the smooth operation of both departments, housekeeping and engineering managers need to devote attention to improving the working relationship between their departments. Teamwork is the key to successful hotel operations. Although the general manager is ultimately responsible for fostering a teamwork philosophy, each department and every employee can help.

Communicating Maintenance Work

Room attendants are the most logical and first line of offense in preparing the guestroom for an arriving guest. The housekeeping staff cleans the guestrooms and also is counted on to recognize guestroom deficiencies or malfunctions that can lead to guest dissatisfaction.

For instance, what happens if a room attendant does not recognize that a light bulb is burned out? Probably the guest will try to turn on the lamp, notice the burned-out bulb, become disgruntled, and call the front desk for assistance. Such an inconvenience is a strike against the hotel's image. The hotel can avoid this type of guest dissatisfaction by setting up a proactive system whereby housekeeping employees recognize deficiencies or malfunctions, report them, and ensure repair before guests occupy the guestroom. The following items are essential to a positive guest experience and can provide a starting point for training room attendants to understand their first-line responsibilities:

- *Sleep set:* Guests are uncomfortable when mattresses sag. A room attendant can tell when a mattress is sagging by inspecting it when the sheets are stripped away. Guest comfort can best be maintained by rotating mattresses periodically and replacing them when necessary. Most mattresses built for hotels have a convenient label identifying a rotation schedule, although housekeeping managers often create their own schedule. Whichever schedule is used, the goal is to make sure that every mattress is properly rotated in accordance with the manufacturer's recommendations.
- *Heating/air conditioning:* If a guestroom's temperature makes a room attendant feel uncomfortable while he or she is cleaning the room, chances are that guests who stay in that room will also be uncomfortable. For this reason,

housekeepers should be trained to recognize and report problems or potential problems with heating or air conditioning systems.

- *TV, radio, telephone:* Room attendants should test the radio and TV while cleaning the guestroom. When wiping off the telephone, they should make sure the phone is working properly.
- *Bedspreads:* One of the first things guests notice in a guestroom is the condition of the bedspread. Since a positive first impression is so important, room attendants should promptly report and replace worn bedspreads.
- *Lighting:* If the room attendant thinks the room seems dark, a guest may feel the same way. Housekeepers should check each lamp's placement and each bulb's wattage, and check whether the switch/fixture works.
- *Door:* Door hardware must work properly; if it doesn't, the guest will be irritated. In addition, faulty door hardware is a serious security issue. If a room attendant has difficulty entering the room to clean it, he or she should recognize and report this situation, and make sure the door is repaired before calling the room "vacant and ready."
- *Toilet:* If it takes more than one flush to get everything down the drain, or if the water continuously runs, the room attendant needs to report it to the maintenance staff immediately.
- *Vanity and tub:* Sparkling porcelain can make the guest feel the room is extra clean, especially if the faucets are shiny. Room attendants must be alert to stains, drips, or corroded hardware.
- *Towels:* "Soft" is the word most people use to describe how they want their towels. A soft towel that is clean and free of stains will feel new. If the linen is something less than soft and clean, it should be considered for replacement.
- *Bathroom walls and door:* Wall coverings become dated quickly. When coverings begin to peel or look worn, this should be reported. Privacy is important to many guests; room attendants should ensure that the bathroom door is working properly and report any problems to the maintenance staff.
- *Water temperature:* For safety's sake, room attendants need to evaluate the temperature of faucet water. How warm is it as it flows from the tap? How long does it take to get hot? Unusual extremes of cold or hot water should be recognized and reported.
- *Ventilation:* If a mirror fogs up while the bathroom is being cleaned, a similar fogging problem will probably frustrate the guest. The room attendant should check the bathroom fan and be sure it is clean and working properly.

Types of Maintenance

The housekeeping department is involved in many hotel maintenance activities and alerts the engineering department when serious maintenance problems are discovered. There are three kinds of maintenance activities: routine maintenance, preventive maintenance, and scheduled maintenance.

Routine maintenance activities are those that relate to the general upkeep of the property, occur on a regular (daily or weekly) basis, and require relatively minimal training or skills. These are maintenance activities that occur outside of a formal work order system and for which no specific maintenance records (time or materials) are kept. Examples include sweeping carpets, washing floors, cleaning readily accessible windows, cutting grass, cleaning guestrooms, shoveling snow, and replacing burned-out lightbulbs. The housekeeping department performs many of these routine maintenance activities. Proper care of many surfaces and materials by housekeeping personnel is the first step in the overall maintenance program for the property's furniture and fixtures.

Preventive maintenance consists of three parts: inspection, minor corrections, and work order initiation. For many areas within the hotel, housekeeping personnel perform inspections in the normal course of their duties. For example, room attendants and inspectors may regularly check guestrooms for leaking faucets, cracked caulking around bathroom fixtures, and other items that may call for action by engineering staff. Attending to leaking faucets and improper caulking around sinks and tubs can control maintenance costs by preventing greater problems, such as ceiling or wall damage in the bath below. Such maintenance protects the physical plant investment and contributes to guest satisfaction.

Communication between the housekeeping and engineering departments should be efficient so that most minor repairs can be handled while the room attendant is cleaning the guestroom. In some properties, a full-time maintenance employee may be assigned to inspect guestrooms and perform the necessary repairs, adjustments, or replacements.

Preventive maintenance sometimes identifies problems and needs beyond the scope of a minor correction. These problems are brought to the attention of engineering through the work order system and the building engineer then schedules the necessary work. This type of work is often referred to as **scheduled maintenance.**

Scheduled maintenance activities are initiated at the property based on a formal work order or similar document. Work orders are a key element in the communication between housekeeping and engineering. A sample work order is shown in Exhibit 2. In many properties, work orders are numbered, three-part forms. Each part of the form is color-coded for its recipient.

When a member of the housekeeping department fills out a work order form, one copy is sent to the executive housekeeper and two copies to engineering. The chief engineer gets one of these copies and gives the other to the tradesperson assigned to the repair. The individual completing the task indicates the number of hours required to complete the work, any parts or supplies required, and other relevant information. When the job is completed, a copy of the tradesperson's completed work order is sent to the executive housekeeper. If this copy is not returned to the executive housekeeper within an appropriate amount of time, housekeeping issues another work order, which signals engineering to provide a status report on the requested repair.

Engineering personnel generally keep data files and history records on all equipment. Equipment data files contain basic information about each piece of equipment. This information can include technical data, manufacturers'

Exhibit 2 Sample Maintenance Work Order

Maintenance/In-House Work Order

(Maintenance use)
Kellogg Center Maintenance Request Form

Kellogg Hotel & Conference Center at Michigan State University

Date__________

Location/Room Number______________________________

Contact Person______________________________

Requested Service/Nature of Problem ______________________________

____

____

____

____

____

____

____

Additional Comments ______________________________

____

____

____

Work Performed ______________________________

____

____

Person Completing Work______________________________

Date Performed ______________________________

Maintenance Supervisor Signature ______________________________

K7659

Courtesy of Kellogg Hotel & Conference Center, Michigan State University, East Lansing, Michigan.

Exhibit 3 Sample Equipment History Record

ACME VISIBLE CROZET VIRGINIA 60P01

HISTORY OF REPAIRS

DATE	W.O. NO.	DESCRIPTION OF REPAIRS	DOWN TIME	MAN HOURS	MATERIAL COST

TAG NO.	DESCRIPTION	WEEKLY CONTROL 1 2 3 4	MONTHLY INSPECTION CONTROL
			JAN FEB MAR APR MAY JUN JUL AUG SEP OCT NOV DEC

10 20 30 40 50 60 70 80

TYPIST PLEASE NOTE -- START ALL TYPING AT SAME POINT ON SCALE. THEN REMOVE THIS STUB. BE SURE YOU HAVE A WELL INKED RIBBON. CARE USED IN TYPING WILL IMPROVE REFERENCE DURING THE ENTIRE LIFE OF THE INDEX. TRY A FEW IN THE POCKETS TO SEE HOW THEY LOOK BEFORE TYPING THE ENTIRE LIST.

RE-ORDER FORM NO. 60P01

ACME VISIBLE RECORDS CROZET VIRGINIA

PRINTED IN U.S.A.

Courtesy of Acme Visible Records.

information, the item's cost, special instructions, warranty information, and references to other information as well (such as the storage location of manuals and drawings). Equipment history records (see Exhibit 3) are logs of the inspection and maintenance work performed on a given piece of equipment. History records may be on separate cards or may be incorporated into the equipment data files. The purpose of historical records is to provide documentation of the maintenance activities performed on a given piece of equipment. Many properties have automated these recordkeeping functions, thereby making it easier for the executive housekeeper to retrieve pertinent information when determining the need to request new equipment. Historical records also help the chief engineer determine how many and how often spare parts should be ordered.

Identifying Housekeeping's Responsibilities

Regardless of the size and structure of a housekeeping department, it is typically the responsibility of the hotel's general manager to identify which areas housekeeping will be responsible for cleaning. Most housekeeping departments are responsible for cleaning the following areas:

- Guestrooms
- Corridors

- Public areas, such as the lobby and public restrooms
- Pool and patio areas
- Management offices
- Storage areas
- Linen and sewing rooms
- Laundry room
- Back-of-the-house areas, such as employee locker rooms

Housekeeping departments of hotels offering mid-range and world-class service are generally responsible for additional areas, such as:

- Meeting rooms
- Dining rooms
- Banquet rooms
- Convention exhibit halls
- Hotel-operated shops
- Game rooms
- Exercise rooms

Housekeeping's cleaning responsibilities in the food and beverage areas vary from property to property. In most hotels, housekeeping has very limited responsibilities in relation to cleaning food preparation, production, and storage areas. The special cleaning and sanitation tasks required for maintaining these areas are usually carried out by kitchen staff under the supervision of the chief steward. In some properties, the dining room staff cleans service areas after breakfast and lunch periods; housekeeping's night cleaning crew does the in-depth cleaning after dinner service or early in the morning before the dining room opens for business. The executive housekeeper and the dining room managers must work closely together to ensure that quality standards are maintained in the guest service and server station areas.

The same cooperation is necessary between housekeeping and banquet or convention services. The banquet or convention staff generally sets up banquet and meeting rooms and is responsible for some cleaning after the rooms are used. The final in-depth cleaning is left to the housekeeping crew. This means that the final responsibility for the cleanliness and overall appearance of these areas falls squarely on the shoulders of the housekeeping staff.

As stated, the general manager typically designates which areas housekeeping will be responsible for cleaning. However, if areas of responsibility cross department lines, the managers of those departments must get together and settle among themselves any disputes about cleaning responsibilities. The agreement among the managers is then reported to the general manager for his or her approval. A good housekeeping manager can effectively solve problems with other managers, thereby relieving the general manager of day-to-day operational problems.

It is a good idea for the executive housekeeper to obtain a floor plan of the hotel and color in those areas for which housekeeping is responsible. Different colors can designate those areas for which other department managers are responsible. To ensure that all areas of the property have been covered—and to avoid future misunderstandings about responsibilities—copies of this color-coded floor plan should be distributed to the general manager and to all department managers. This way, everyone can see at a glance who is responsible for cleaning each area in the hotel. The color-coded floor plan also presents a clear and impressive picture of the housekeeping department's role in cleaning and maintaining the hotel.

Once housekeeping's areas of responsibility are identified, planning focuses on analyzing the work required for cleaning and maintaining each area.

Planning the Work of the Housekeeping Department

Planning is probably the executive housekeeper's most important management function. Without competent planning, every day may present one crisis after another. Constant crises lower morale, decrease productivity, and increase expenses within the department. Also, without the direction and focus that planning provides, the executive housekeeper can easily become sidetracked by tasks that are unimportant or unrelated to accomplishing the hotel's objectives.

Since the housekeeping department is responsible for cleaning and maintaining so many different areas of the hotel, planning the work of the department can seem like an enormous task. Without a systematic, step-by-step approach to planning, the executive housekeeper can easily become overwhelmed and frustrated by the hundreds of important details. These details must be addressed to ensure that the work is not only done, but done correctly, efficiently, on time, and with the least cost to the department.

Area Inventory Lists

Planning the work of the housekeeping department begins with creating inventory lists of all items within each area that will need housekeeping's attention. Preparing **area inventory lists** is the first planning activity, because the lists ensure that the rest of the planning activities address every item for which housekeeping is held accountable. Inventory lists are bound to be long and extremely detailed. Since most properties offer several different types of guestrooms, separate inventory lists may be necessary for each room type.

When preparing a guestroom area inventory list, it is a good idea to follow the sequence in which room attendants will clean items and in which supervisors will inspect items. This enables the executive housekeeper to use the inventory lists as the basis for developing cleaning procedures, training plans, and inspection checklists. For example, items within a guestroom may appear on an inventory list as they are placed from right to left and from top to bottom around the room. Other systematic techniques may be used, but the point is that *some* system should be followed—and this system should be the same one used by room attendants and inspectors in the daily course of their duties.

Exhibit 4 Sample Frequency Schedule

PUBLIC AREA #2—LIGHT FIXTURES			
LOCATION	TYPE	NO.	FREQ.
Entrance #1	Sconce	2	1/W
Lobby	Chandelier	3	1/M
Entrance #2	Crown Sconce	2	1/M
Behind Fountain	Sconce	3	1/W
Catwalk	Pole Light	32	1/M
Lower Level	Pole Light	16	1/M
Fountain Area	Pole Light	5	1/M
Restaurant Courtyard	Pole Light	10	1/M
Restaurant Courtyard	Wall Light	5	1/M
Restaurant Patio	Half-Pole Light	16	1/W
Restaurant Entrance	White Globe Pole Light	6	1/W
Crystal Gazebo	White Globe Pole Light	8	1/W
2nd Stairs to Catwalk	White Globe Pole Light	2	1/W
Fountain	White Globe Pole Light	4	1/W
Lounge Patio	Wall Light	4	1/W
Restaurant Entrance	Chandelier	1	1/W

Frequency Schedules

Tasks on an area's **frequency schedule** (see Exhibit 4) that are made part of housekeeping's deep cleaning program should be transferred to a calendar plan and scheduled as special cleaning projects. The calendar plan guides the executive housekeeper in scheduling the appropriate staff to perform the necessary work. The executive housekeeper must take into account a number of factors when scheduling **deep cleaning** of guestrooms or other special projects. For example, whenever possible, days marked for guestroom deep cleaning should coincide with low occupancy periods. Also, the deep cleaning program must be flexible in relation to the activities of other departments. For example, if the maintenance department schedules extensive repair work for several guestrooms, the executive housekeeper should make every effort to coordinate a deep cleaning of these rooms with maintenance's timetable. Careful planning will produce good results for the hotel with the least possible inconvenience to guests or to other departments.

Performance Standards

The executive housekeeper can begin to develop **performance standards** by answering the question, What must be done in order to clean or maintain the major items within this area? Standards are required quality levels of performance. Performance standards state not only *what* must be done, they also describe in detail *how* the job must be done.

One of the primary objectives of planning the work of the housekeeping department is to ensure that all employees carry out their cleaning tasks in a consistent manner. The keys to consistency are the performance standards that the executive housekeeper develops, communicates, and manages. Although these standards vary from one housekeeping department to another, executive housekeepers can ensure consistency of cleaning by demanding 100 percent conformity to the standards established for their departments. When performance standards are not properly developed, effectively communicated, and consistently managed, housekeeping department productivity suffers, because employees will not perform their tasks according to the necessary standards.

The most important aspect of developing standards is gaining consensus on how cleaning and other tasks are to be carried out. Consensus can be achieved by having individuals who actually perform the tasks contribute to the standards that the department eventually adopts.

Performance standards are communicated through ongoing training programs. Many properties have developed performance standards and have included them between the covers of impressive housekeeping procedure manuals. However, all too often, these manuals simply gather dust on shelves in the offices of executive housekeepers. Well-written standards are useless unless they are applied. The only way to implement standards in the workplace is through effective training programs.

After communicating performance standards through ongoing training activities, the executive housekeeper must manage those standards. Managing standards means ensuring conformity to standards by inspection. Experienced housekeepers know the truth of the adage, "You can't expect what you don't inspect." Daily inspections and periodic performance evaluations should be followed up with specific on-the-job coaching and retraining. This ensures that all employees consistently perform their tasks in the most efficient and effective manner. The executive housekeeper should review the department's performance standards at least once a year and make appropriate revisions as new work methods are implemented.

Productivity Standards

While performance standards establish the expected quality of the work to be done, **productivity standards** (see Exhibit 5) determine the acceptable quantity of work to be done by department employees. An executive housekeeper begins to establish productivity standards by answering the question, "How long should it take for a housekeeping employee to perform an assigned task according to the department's performance standard?" Productivity standards must be determined to properly staff the department within the limitations established by the hotel's operating budget.

Since performance standards vary in relation to the unique needs and requirements of each hotel, it is impossible to identify productivity standards that would apply across the board to every housekeeping department. Since the duties of room attendants vary widely among economy, mid-market, and luxury hotels, the productivity standards for room attendants will also vary.

Exhibit 5 Sample Productivity Standard Worksheet

Step 1

Determine how long it should take to clean one guestroom according to the department's performance standards.

Approximately 27 minutes*

Step 2

Determine the total shift time in minutes.

$8\frac{1}{2}$ hours × 60 minutes = 510 minutes

Step 3

Determine the time available for guestroom cleaning.

Total Shift Time	510 minutes
Less:	
Beginning-of-Shift Duties	20 minutes
Morning Break	15 minutes
Lunch	30 minutes
Afternoon Break	15 minutes
End-of-Shift Duties	20 minutes
Time Available for Guestroom Cleaning	410 minutes

Step 4

Determine the productivity standard by dividing the result of Step 3 by the result of Step 1.

$$\frac{410 \text{ minutes}}{27 \text{ minutes}} = 15.2 \text{ guestrooms per 8-hour shift}$$

*Since performance standards vary from property to property, this figure is used for illustrative purposes only. It is not a suggested time figure for cleaning guestrooms.

When determining realistic productivity standards, an executive housekeeper does not have to carry around a measuring tape, stopwatch, and clipboard and conduct time-and-motion studies on all the tasks necessary to clean and maintain each item on an area's inventory list. The labor of the executive housekeeper and other management staff is also a precious department resource. However, housekeeping managers must know how long it should take a housekeeping employee to perform the major tasks identified on the cleaning frequency schedules—such as guestroom cleaning. Once this information is known, the executive housekeeper can develop productivity standards.

Quality and quantity can be like two sides of a coin. On one side, if the quality expectations (performance standards) are set too high, the quantity of work that can be done accordingly may be unacceptably low. This forces the executive housekeeper to add more and more staff to ensure that all the work gets done. However, sooner or later (and probably sooner than expected), the general manager will cut the high labor expense of the housekeeping department. This action would force the executive housekeeper to reduce the staff size and realign quality and quantity by redefining performance standards in light of more realistic productivity standards.

On the other side, if performance standards are set too low, the quantity of work that can be done accordingly will be unexpectedly high. At first, the general manager may be delighted. However, as complaints from guests and staff increase and the property begins to look dingy because of neglect, the general manager may, once again, step in with a solution. This time, the general manager may choose to replace the executive housekeeper with someone who will establish higher performance standards and monitor department expenses more closely.

Actual productivity standards should be finalized after the hotel has been operating for a while. To determine the property's productivity standard for room cleaning, the housekeeping manager must take guestroom size, furnishings, bedding arrangement, bathroom design, and room configuration into consideration. If a housekeeper has to move from floor to floor or building to building, this travel time must be considered, since travel time takes away from cleaning time. In addition, the number of rooms in a suite must be considered. For example, a three-room suite with an elaborate living room, wet bar, and patio may be counted as four rooms to clean, given its complexity. As a result, housekeepers who clean suites may be assigned fewer rooms to clean.

The challenge is to effectively balance performance standards and productivity standards. Quality and quantity each can serve to check and balance the other. A concern for productivity need not necessarily lower performance standards—it can sharpen and refine current work methods and procedures. If room attendants constantly return to the housekeeping area for cleaning and guestroom supplies, something is wrong with the way they set up and stock their carts. Wasted motion is wasted time, and wasted time depletes the most important and most expensive resource of the housekeeping department: labor. The executive housekeeper must be constantly on the alert for new, more efficient work methods.

Remember, an executive housekeeper will rarely have all the resources necessary to do everything he or she may want to accomplish. Therefore, labor must be carefully allocated to achieve acceptable performance standards and realistic productivity standards.

Equipment and Supply Inventory Levels

After planning what must be done and how the tasks should be performed, the executive housekeeper must ensure that employees have the necessary equipment and supplies to get their jobs done. The executive housekeeper plans appropriate inventory levels by answering the following question: What amounts of equipment and supplies are necessary for the housekeeping staff to meet the performance and productivity standards of the department? The answer to this question ensures smooth daily housekeeping activities and forms the basis for planning an effective purchasing system. A purchasing system must consistently maintain the necessary amounts of items in housekeeping inventories.

Essentially, the executive housekeeper is responsible for two types of inventories: items that are recycled during the course of hotel operations, and non-recyclable items. Non-recyclable items are consumed or used up during routine activities of the housekeeping department. Due to limited storage facilities and management's desire not to tie up cash in overstocked inventories, the executive housekeeper must establish reasonable inventory levels for both recyclable and non-recyclable items.

Recycled Inventories. Recycled inventories include linens, most equipment items, and some guest supplies. Recycled equipment includes room attendant carts, vacuum cleaners, carpet shampooers, floor buffers, and many other items. Recycled guest supplies include such items as irons, ironing boards, cribs, and refrigerators, which guests may need during the course of their stay. Housekeeping is responsible for storing and maintaining these items as well as issuing them as guests request them.

The number of recycled items that must be on hand to ensure smooth operations is expressed as a **par number.** Par refers to the number of items that must be on hand to support daily, routine housekeeping operations. For example, one par of linens is the total number of items required to outfit all the hotel guestrooms once; two par of linens is the total number of items required to outfit all the hotel guestrooms twice; and so on.

Non-Recycled Inventories. Non-recycled inventories include cleaning supplies, guestroom supplies (such as bath soap), and guest amenities (which may range from toothbrushes and shampoos and conditioners to scented bath powders and colognes). Since non-recyclable items are used up in the course of operations, inventory levels are closely tied to the property's purchase ordering system. A purchase ordering system for non-recyclable inventory items establishes a par number that is based on two figures—a minimum quantity and a maximum quantity.

The **minimum quantity** is the fewest number of purchase units that should be in stock at any time. Purchase units are counted in terms of normal-size shipping containers, such as cases, drums, and so on. The inventory level should never fall below the minimum quantity. When the inventory level of a non-recyclable item reaches the minimum quantity, additional supplies must be ordered.

The actual number of additional supplies that must be ordered is determined by the **maximum quantity**. The maximum quantity is the greatest number of purchase units that should be in stock at any time. This maximum quantity must be consistent with available storage space and must not be so high that large amounts of the hotel's cash resources are tied up in an overstocked inventory. The shelf life of an item also affects the maximum quantity of purchase units that can be stored.

Supervisor Dilemma

The state of the economy has prompted a trend to eliminate middle managers. In the lodging industry, this trend has brought the position of housekeeping supervisor into question. General managers seem to be searching for more profit and, perhaps, a way to empower hourly employees. Is it possible to operate a clean and profitable hotel without housekeeping supervisors to inspect rooms?

Although the housekeeping supervisor position may have begun as a management extension of the executive housekeeper for larger properties, the job has centered on inspecting rooms in the past twenty years or so. Is it, then, an essential role? Does the hotel get its money's worth from this position?

Key issues hotels must consider are:

- Did the hotel hire the right people to be supervisors?
- Do the hotel's systems support the responsibilities of the supervisor?
- Is the hotel's mission enhanced as a direct result of the position?
- How would the "no supervisors" idea be introduced and then implemented?
- Would the number of room inspections be reduced or totally eliminated?
- Who would conduct room inspections if any are required?
- Who would conduct training?
- What changes would be made to job descriptions?
- How would quality standards be maintained or improved?
- What system would be used to ensure accurate room status updates?

The Rooms Chronicle surveyed some readers about housekeeping supervisors. Some managers eliminated supervisors, only to be disappointed by a gradual decline in the condition of guestrooms. Others, after making the change, saw guest comments and employee morale improve. One of the surveyed hotels reinstated inspections in 100 percent of the rooms after six months, while another did so after one year. Some have been successful at keeping 50 to 75 percent of their room attendants working independently.

How Is the Program Initiated? Most hotels based their decisions to eliminate supervisors on a desire to save payroll, although many were motivated by the total quality management philosophy of empowerment. At one hotel they eliminated supervisors because they wanted to speed up reporting of clean rooms to the front desk.

The hotels that successfully eliminated housekeeping supervisors gave advance, careful thought to all of the ramifications of this decision and involved the employees in planning. Some approached room attendants with the question, How does it make you feel to have someone check everything you do? When some frustration was expressed, they began to explore alternative ways to operate, incorporating room attendants' ideas for working independently.

Are Any Rooms Inspected? One of the properties surveyed operates without any room inspections. Management credits the work ethic of their room attendants for the attendants' ability to take full responsibility for the condition of their areas. Most hotels, however, inspect from one to five rooms per room attendant per week. As a rooms executive of a luxury hotel in the Midwest expressed it, "We conduct random verifications of our housekeepers' work. It should be like testing a pool for the level of chlorine—only a small sample is needed to know the condition of the entire pool."

Who Inspects if There Are No Supervisors? Most properties use housekeeping management to conduct random inspections, depending on the size of the hotel. Large hotels retain one or more supervisors for this purpose. The general manager of a resort hotel in Florida involves the entire hotel staff. "The use of supervisors does not have to be an all-or-nothing decision," says a general manager of a Midwestern resort. "We use supervisors only in the summer to work with our seasonal employees. During the rest of the year, our room attendants work independently. We've used this system for over a year and our comment card scores are still high, at 94 percent."

Are Job Descriptions Changed? If a hotel eliminates housekeeping supervisors, its room attendant job description is usually changed to make room attendants responsible for the cleanliness, readiness, and status updates for the rooms they clean. The room attendant must check equipment in the room to ensure that a guest will not find something in disrepair. Some hotels add responsibility for the hallway area around the guestroom and specify who will do the running if a bedspread or some other item needs to be replaced. The houseperson or porter job description usually is changed to complement the new structure.

How Do Pay Rates Change? Pay rates of room attendants are sometimes changed if supervisors are eliminated, with the majority of properties either setting rates according to quality of work or paying bonuses for exceeding quality standards. One hotel pays a $35 bonus biweekly if inspection scores are 90 percent or higher and if at least 1.9 rooms are cleaned per hour. The general manager of one all-suite hotel has a program in which room attendants earn the right to work without supervisors by achieving high scores on quality, attendance, and uniform care and are then paid 25 cents more per hour. At other hotels, pay rates are not increased.

Who Does the Training? Since most hotels use supervisors to train new housekeeping hires, who does the training if housekeeping supervisor positions are eliminated? Housekeeping managers could train, but, in these days of high turnover, the training function is often a full-time job. One option is to designate one or more room attendants as on-the-job trainers. In other hotels, at least one supervisor is retained who concentrates on training and retraining. "If I hire the right people and conduct ongoing training, my staff will be able to meet our standards," said one rooms executive.

What About Room Status? The morning check of vacant rooms is usually incorporated into the room attendant's job description by assigning him or her an area of responsibility rather than a list of dirty rooms. All rooms, hallways, vending areas, and elevator lobbies within this area are assigned. The room attendant will be the last person to see the rooms or area before the guest arrives or returns, so special care must be taken to ensure that the front desk always has the correct room status, whether occupied or vacant, clean or dirty.

Many property management systems are interfaced so a code can be entered on the guestroom phone or a mobile device to update a room's status. In other hotels, the room attendant must call either housekeeping or the front desk to change a room's status. When the front desk questions the status, someone is sent to double-check the room.

If a hotel eliminates its housekeeping supervisors, it should expect to spend more time checking room status discrepancies. Room attendants might clean a room, thinking it is a stayover, but while they are in another room, the first room's guest could check out. If the hotel has not adequately planned for this aspect, payroll saved on supervisors could easily be lost by poor room inventory management.

Tips for Success. A well-thought-out plan will provide for the cleanliness, maintenance, and status of every room. Since supervisors usually help prepare VIP rooms, do touch-ups on late check-outs, help with hurry-ups, assist with inventories, translate for room attendants who don't speak English, and clean rooms when there is a shortage of room attendants, all of these responsibilities must be reassigned elsewhere by hotels that wish to eliminate housekeeping supervisors.

If a hotel wishes to cut back or eliminate its housekeeping supervisory staff, it should involve its room attendants in the design of the new program, to help them have ownership of it. The new plan must be a win-win situation for the hotel and its room attendants, because employees are sensitive to management's efforts to save payroll at their expense. The program should be fine-tuned before implementation, because changes to pay rates or incentive plans after the fact serve as disincentives.

If the no- or fewer-supervisors concept is planned to suit the property's needs and implemented carefully, housekeeping employees and the hotel should make a successful transition.

Summary

The housekeeping department has frequent communication with the front office department, specifically with the front desk area. Normally, front desk agents cannot assign guestrooms until the rooms have been cleaned, inspected, and released by the housekeeping department. In most properties, the housekeeping department is part of the rooms division and the executive housekeeper works closely with the front office manager.

Each night, a front desk agent or the property management system produces an occupancy report, which lists rooms occupied that night and indicates guests who are expected to check out the following day. The executive housekeeper consults this list early the next morning and schedules occupied rooms for cleaning. The executive housekeeper also uses the ten-day and three-day forecast reports prepared by the front office system when creating staff schedules.

At the end of each work shift, the housekeeping staff prepares a housekeeping status report based on a physical check of each guestroom. This report is compared to the front desk occupancy report. A room status discrepancy is a situation in which the housekeeping department's description of a room's status differs from the room status information available at the front desk. Keeping room status information accurate and up to date requires close coordination and cooperation between the front desk and housekeeping departments.

In an automated room-status system, housekeeping staff and the front desk staff have instantaneous access to room status information. When a guest checks out, a front desk agent enters the departure into a front office terminal. Housekeeping is then automatically alerted that the room has been vacated and needs cleaning. Next, housekeeping attendants clean the room and notify the housekeeping supervisor when the room is ready for inspection. Once the room is inspected, the inspector enters this information into the room status system. This housekeeping status update is then communicated to the front office system. Advanced housekeeping and front desk communication systems rely on wireless connectivity via a hand-held terminal or some other mobile device carried by each housekeeper.

The housekeeping staff not only cleans guestrooms, it is also counted on to recognize guestroom maintenance needs that can lead to guest dissatisfaction. There are three kinds of maintenance activities: routine maintenance, preventive maintenance, and scheduled maintenance. Routine maintenance activities are those that relate to the general upkeep of the property, occur on a regular basis, and do not require a formal work order. Preventive maintenance consists of three parts: inspection, minor corrections, and work order initiation. Preventive maintenance sometimes identifies problems and needs beyond the scope of a minor correction. These problems are brought to the attention of engineering through the work order system. This type of work is often referred to as scheduled maintenance. Work orders are a key element in the communication between housekeeping and engineering.

Most housekeeping departments are responsible for cleaning the following areas: guestrooms; corridors; public areas, such as the lobby and public restrooms; pool and patio areas; management offices; storage areas; linen and sewing rooms; laundry room; and back-of-the-house areas, such as employee locker rooms. Housekeeping departments of hotels offering mid-range and world-class service are generally responsible for additional areas, such as meeting rooms, dining rooms, banquet rooms, convention exhibit halls, hotel-operated shops, game rooms, and exercise rooms. Housekeeping's cleaning responsibilities in the food and beverage areas vary from property to property. In most hotels, housekeeping has very limited responsibilities in relation to cleaning food preparation, production, and storage areas.

Planning the work of the housekeeping department begins with creating inventory lists of all items within each hotel area that require housekeeping's attention. Inventory lists ensure that the rest of the planning activities address every item for which housekeeping will be held accountable. When preparing a guestroom area inventory list, it is a good idea to follow the sequence in which room attendants will clean items and in which supervisors will inspect items. This enables the executive housekeeper to use the guestroom area inventory list as the basis for developing cleaning procedures, training plans, and inspection checklists.

The executive housekeeper can begin to develop performance standards by answering the question, What must be done in order to clean or maintain the major items within this area? Standards are required quality levels of performance. Performance standards state not only *what* must be done, they also describe in detail *how* the job must be done. While performance standards establish the expected quality of the work to be done, productivity standards determine the acceptable quantity of work to be done by department employees. An executive housekeeper begins to establish productivity standards by answering the question, How long should it take for a housekeeping employee to perform an assigned task according to the department's performance standard? To determine the property's productivity standard for guestroom cleaning, the housekeeping manager must consider room size, furnishings, bedding arrangement, bathroom design, and room configuration. If a housekeeper has to move from floor to floor or building to building, this travel time must be considered. In addition, the number of rooms in a suite must be considered. The challenge is to effectively balance performance standards and productivity standards.

After planning what must be done and how the tasks are to be performed, the executive housekeeper must ensure that employees have the necessary equipment and supplies to get their jobs done. Essentially, the executive housekeeper is responsible for two types of inventories: (1) recycled items, and (2) non-recyclable items. Recycled inventories include linens, most equipment items, and some guest supplies. Recycled equipment includes room attendant carts, vacuum cleaners, carpet shampooers, floor buffers, and many other items. Recycled guest supplies include such items as irons, ironing boards, cribs, and refrigerators, which guests may need during the course of their stay. Housekeeping is responsible for storing and maintaining these items as well as issuing them as guests request them. Non-recycled inventories include cleaning supplies, guestroom supplies (such as bath soap), and guest amenities (which may range from toothbrushes and shampoos and conditioners to scented bath powders and colognes).

The state of the economy has prompted a trend to eliminate middle managers, including housekeeping supervisors. Some hotel managers have eliminated these supervisors, only to be disappointed by a gradual decline in the condition of guestrooms; others have seen guest comments and employee morale improve after eliminating supervisors. Because hotels differ so widely, each hotel must decide this question based on its own needs and the expectations of its guests.

Key Terms

area inventory list—A list of all items within a particular area that need cleaning by or the attention of housekeeping personnel.

deep cleaning—Intensive or specialized cleaning undertaken in guestrooms or public areas. Often conducted according to a special schedule or on a special-project basis.

frequency schedule—A schedule that indicates how often each item on an area inventory list must be cleaned or maintained.

housekeeping status report—A report the housekeeping department prepares that indicates the current housekeeping status of each room, based on a physical check.

maximum quantity—The greatest number of purchase units that should be in stock at any given time.

minimum quantity—The fewest number of purchase units that should be in stock at any given time.

occupancy report—A report prepared each night by a front desk agent or the property management system that lists rooms occupied that night and indicates guests who are expected to check out the following day.

par number—A multiple of the standard quantity of a particular inventory item that must be on hand to support daily, routine housekeeping operations.

performance standards—A required level of performance that establishes the quality of work that must be done.

preventive maintenance—A systematic approach to maintenance in which situations are identified and corrected on a regular basis to control costs and keep larger problems from occurring.

productivity standards—An acceptable amount of work that must be done within a specific time frame according to an established performance standard.

room status discrepancy—A situation in which the housekeeping department's description of a room's status differs from the room status information at the front desk.

routine maintenance—Activities related to the general upkeep of the property that occur on a regular (daily or weekly) basis and require relatively minimal training or skills to perform.

scheduled maintenance—Activities related to the upkeep of the property that are initiated through a formal work order or similar document.

Review Questions

1. Why are two-way communications necessary between the front desk and housekeeping?
2. What are the systems the front desk and housekeeping use to track current room status?
3. What are the three kinds of maintenance activities?
4. What is the ideal relationship between housekeeping and maintenance? What is the actual situation in some properties?
5. What areas are most housekeeping departments responsible for cleaning in a hotel?
6. What additional areas may housekeeping be responsible for cleaning, depending on the property's service level?
7. What is the purpose of an area inventory list? What is an ideal way to sequence such a list?
8. What is a frequency schedule? How is it used in conjunction with a property's deep cleaning program?
9. What is the difference between a performance standard and a productivity standard?

Internet Sites

For more information, visit the following Internet sites. Remember that Internet addresses can change without notice. If the site is no longer there, you can use a search engine to look for additional sites.

Hotel Maintenance Management Software
www.attr.com

Resort Data Processing, Inc.
www.resortdata.com

The Rooms Chronicle...online
www.roomschronicle.com

Case Studies

VIP Gets Lost in the Service Shuffle, or How the ABC Hotel Dropped the Ball

Monday
10:00 A.M.

The eight o'clock Monday-morning sales meeting had been more tedious than most, Ms. Sarah Salesperson thought as she made her way back to her office. She poured herself a cup of coffee before sitting at her computer to compose a memo. The director of sales had hammered away at one of her pet themes that morning: "The secret to sales is, 'Don't drop the ball!'" I suppose she's right, Sarah mused as she began to type; dropping the ball is certainly easy enough to do at a 600-room hotel. In light of the morning meeting, she thought it might be wise to send a note about Mr. Bigbucks to Ray Smith, the front office manager. Mr. Bigbucks was a director at XYZ Corporation, an international firm that could mean $500,000 or more in room bookings in the next two years—if Mr. Bigbucks could be persuaded to place some of his group meetings and other business with the hotel. He was due to arrive at 1:30 P.M. today, and Sarah wanted everything to be perfect for him.

> Dear Ray:
>
> Just wanted to remind you that Mr. Bigbucks of the XYZ Corporation is arriving at 1:30 P.M. today for an overnight stay. *Please* make sure he gets the full VIP treatment. I've chatted with him on the phone a few times, and will meet with him in person next month about the possibility of booking some business with the hotel, but I won't be able to connect with him this visit—I'm flying to Dallas this morning.
>
> Don't worry—I remembered to fill out the VIP forms this time and everybody should have them by now!
>
> Sincerely,
> *Sarah*

10:30 A.M.

To make doubly sure Ray understood the importance of Mr. Bigbucks, Sarah walked down to the front office to deliver her memo in person, but Ray was not at his desk. Oh well, he'll probably be back in a minute, she thought. She left the memo on Ray's chair so he would notice it first thing.

11:10 A.M.

Ray finally escaped for a few minutes from a meeting the general manager called that morning, and went straight to his desk to check for messages. He read Sarah's memo and decided to drop it off at the front desk on his way back to the meeting.

11:20 A.M.

At the front desk, Evert was trying to stay calm and friendly despite the crowd milling in the lobby. He had been a front desk agent for only three weeks and still got nervous when tour buses pulled up outside the hotel. That morning two groups, the American Society of Poets and the Plate Glass Producers, were checking in; this afternoon the American Pharmaceutical Association would arrive for a four-day regional meeting. Evert didn't even notice Ray until Ray tapped him on the shoulder. "Make sure housekeeping knows about this," Ray said, and placed Sarah's memo beside Evert's computer keyboard. Evert half-turned and nodded while continuing to check in a guest.

11:45 A.M.

Evert took advantage of a lull to read what Ray had dropped off. He quickly picked up a walkie-talkie and called Gail, the executive housekeeper. "Hi Gail, it's Evert at the front desk. We've got a VIP, Mr. Bigbucks, arriving at 1:30 this afternoon. I'm changing room 816 from 'clean and ready' to 'out of order' until you can give it the VIP treatment, okay? Thanks."

11:50 A.M.

Why am I always at the other end of the hotel when I get a call like this? Gail thought as she hurried to the employee lunchroom. And why is it always when my staff is eating lunch or taking a break? She asked Mary and Teresa, two of her best room attendants, to interrupt their lunches and follow her to room 816. As the three of them were walking to the linen closet to get fresh bedspreads and blankets, she called Roger, the head of maintenance and engineering, and asked him to send someone to 816. Then she called George in the kitchen. "George, this is Gail. Are the amenities for 816 ready?" George said he was just finishing up and someone would drop them off soon.

1:20 P.M.

Gail stood in the doorway and cast a critical eye over room 816 one last time. The quiet and order she surveyed were in sharp contrast to the noise and bustle of the last hour and a half. A small army had descended on the suite and performed all the tasks needed to transform a guestroom from merely "excellent" to "perfect." As Mr. Thompson, the hotel general manager, had said to Gail on more than one occasion, "It's your job to put the 'wow factor' in every VIP room. When they open that guestroom door for the first time, that's what I want them to think: 'Wow!'"

Gail reviewed her informal "wow" checklist in her mind. The clean bed linen, blankets, and bedspread were upgraded to freshly ironed sheets, new blankets, and a new bedspread. Mary edged the carpet with a whisk broom to get every speck of dust, the furniture was pulled out and the carpet vacuumed underneath, and the chair and chair cushions were vacuumed. Then the carpet was spot-cleaned. All the drawers in the bedroom and bathroom were wiped out to make sure no dust or hair was hiding. As the drapes were taken down and replaced with freshly cleaned ones, Chris Jones arrived from maintenance and checked over all the room's mechanicals. While he was checking the bathroom, he noticed a small rust stain on the toilet seat. Teresa could not scrub it off, so Chris went off to find a new toilet seat to replace the old one. Nothing in the room made of wood escaped the polishing cloths. At around 1:00 P.M., Jessie arrived from the restaurant with the hotel's platinum amenities package: a miniature wicker chair about two feet high containing cheese, crackers, a bottle of wine, fruit, nuts, and bread sticks interlaced with packets of hard candy made by the hotel chef. Personalized matchbooks embossed with Mr. Bigbucks' initials, a vase of fresh-cut flowers, and a gilt-edged note signed by Mr. Thompson himself completed the amenities. The installation of the sparkling new toilet seat was completed just ten minutes before.

Gail gazed down at the undisturbed herringbone pattern in the carpeting, left by the vacuum Teresa ran as the last touch, and couldn't think of a thing she had missed. "Room 816's ready," she called in to the front desk, and went off to see if she could sneak in a few bites of lunch.

4:35 P.M.

Mr. Bigbucks arrived at the hotel looking a bit rumpled from the long plane trip and the taxi ride shared with four other people. The hotel lobby was crowded with pharmacists and late-arriving poets checking in at the conventions desk. He walked up to an unoccupied spot along the regular front desk area and waited until a front desk agent could break away from the group check-ins.

"Good afternoon, welcome to the ABC Hotel, my name is Joan. How can I help you?"

"Hi, my name is Bigbucks. I have a reservation for tonight."

"Let me check that for you." The computer keys ticked quickly. "Yes, you'll be staying for one night. Do you need help with your luggage?"

"No, I have just one small bag."

Joan finished the check-in process, smiling and remembering to make frequent eye contact, and gave Mr. Bigbucks the key packet to room 616.

4:40 P.M.

When Mr. Bigbucks opened the door to 616, he was mildly disappointed to find nothing waiting for him in the room. The room was spotless and fresh, but at most hotels he found flowers, chocolates, maybe a note to welcome him. Here...nothing. Maybe it's because I'm only staying one night, he thought, although he didn't know why that would make a difference. His flight had been delayed, so he had arrived at the hotel much later than he'd planned and had just enough time to unpack and take a quick shower before heading out to dinner at the home of XYZ's president.

5:15 P.M.

Dr. Lucky, a dentist from Omaha, walked up to the front desk with a suitcase in each hand. He was in town for a three-day meeting at the city's convention center near the hotel. "I'd like a suite please," he said.

Dr. Lucky put his bags down while the front desk agent scanned the computer terminal. "We have a suite on the eighth floor available." A bell attendant started to place Dr. Lucky's bags on a luggage cart but Dr. Lucky stopped him. He liked to save money on his business trips whenever he could. He collected his room key, rode the elevator to the eighth floor, and followed the arrows to 816. He set his suitcases down and fumbled briefly with the electronic door lock before swinging the door open. He bent to pick up his bags. When he caught sight of the suite, he straightened up slowly, the bags forgotten. "Wow!" he sighed reverently.

5:35 P.M.

After hesitating a moment over stepping on the perfectly groomed carpeting, Dr. Lucky walked into the suite. He paused a moment to take it all in—the shining surfaces, the hint of fragrance from the flowers, the wicker basket (was that a tiny chair?)—before bringing in his suitcases, shutting the door, and opening up the wine. He usually didn't stay at hotels as nice as the ABC Hotel, but he had decided to splurge a bit on this trip. I've got to do this more often, he thought, I had no idea ordinary guests were treated so well at these posh hotels. He was munching happily on the cheese and crackers and looking curiously at the candies—he'd never seen any quite like them before—when he noticed a note on the dresser:

> Dear Mr. Bigbucks:
>
> We hope you enjoy your stay with the ABC Hotel. If there is anything we can do to make your experience with us more pleasant, please let us know.
>
> *Jim Thompson, General Manager*

Dr. Lucky stopped in mid-chew. Oh, no, he thought, I've already eaten half the stuff in the basket. Will I have to pay extra for this?

5:40 P.M.

Mr. Bigbucks got in the elevator and pushed the button for the hotel lobby. At the third floor, the elevator stopped and the hotel's director of sales got in. The director and Mr. Bigbucks rode in silence to the lobby, where they both got off and headed in opposite directions.

6:00 P.M.

Dr. Lucky changed into more casual clothes and decided to spend the evening finding the convention center and exploring the city around the hotel. It was an easy decision to wait until tomorrow morning to call the front desk and straighten out the mix-up.

Tuesday
8:00 A.M.

Dr. Lucky went down to the hotel restaurant for breakfast. Since he planned to go back to his room before leaving for the convention center, he decided he would call the front desk later to discuss the wine-and-flowers mix-up. At the restaurant, he ran into a dentist he knew. They ate breakfast together and shared a cab ride directly to the convention center. Dr. Lucky promised himself he would stop at the front desk and get things straightened out when he got back.

8:30 A.M.

Mr. Bigbucks picked up his bag and pulled the door to room 616 closed behind him. He hadn't slept well. He was hoping the all-day meeting at corporate headquarters would end early so he could change his seven o'clock flight back home to something earlier. At the front desk, the agent was exceptionally friendly and efficient. On the way out to his cab Mr. Bigbucks passed Ray Smith. Ray was in a hurry; he had another meeting with the general manager about improving guest service.

Discussion Questions

1. What did the ABC Hotel do wrong?
2. How could the hotel have recovered with Mr. Bigbucks had it discovered its mistake while he was still at the hotel? How can the hotel recover with Mr. Bigbucks now?
3. What procedures should the hotel put in place to avoid such a mix-up in the future?

The following industry experts helped generate and develop this case: Gail Edwards, Director of Housekeeping, Regal Riverfront Hotel, St. Louis, Missouri; Mary Friedman, Director of Housekeeping, Radisson South, Bloomington, Minnesota; and Aleta Nitschke, Founder and Web Publisher of *The Rooms Chronicle*, Stratham, New Hampshire.

Tension in the Housekeeping Department

It was going to be a busy day at the Boden Oceanside Resort and Lodge. Today was Friday and 160 guests were checking out this morning. More than 200 rooms would be checked into by the end of the day for what was going to be a beautiful weekend. Maria, the front office manager, reviewed the arrival list and wondered if her counterpart in housekeeping would have the staff to ensure that all the rooms needed would be available by 3:00 P.M.

Staffing was still an issue for nearly all departments at the resort. Some of the larger resort operations in the state had trouble fully staffing for the busy seasons. The challenge for the front office manager and the director of housekeeping was to find qualified employees in a time of low unemployment for the local area. The executive housekeeper, Fran, was pleased because she had just hired a new room attendant, Adele. Fran had been in housekeeping for more than twenty years, and had been the executive housekeeper of the Boden for ten years.

Her problem this morning centered on a seasoned veteran, Mona, who had been with the hotel more than seven years. She had never moved up from room attendant, however, because her co-workers found her difficult to work with. The next step in her career would have been to move to supervisor, but that entailed inspecting rooms and giving direction. While she was not a team player, she did a great job on her own. Recently she had hurt her back for the third time and the doctor had ordered her not to do jobs that required repetitive motions. This restriction meant that she needed to work with another room attendant to get the job done.

Yesterday, Mona was teamed with Adele. The executive housekeeper thought that Mona could teach Adele the ropes, since the department trainer was off for a week. It seemed that the day went well for the two room attendants, so she assigned the two to work together again this morning. Since the resort was expecting a busy check-in, Fran had given the two the maximum number of rooms to clean for the day. Fran hoped that the two could work well as a team so that they could get their work done in a timely way.

At 10:00 A.M., Fran received a call from Maria. There were problems between two of Fran's room attendants. A guest had called in to the front desk exclaiming that two room attendants were screaming at each other in one of the rooms they were cleaning. Fran went immediately to the south wing of the resort. There she found Mona and Adele still arguing about a tip that had been left in room 309.

The guests had checked out by 8:30 A.M. after a four-night stay and left a $15 tip for the room attendants. Mona had pocketed the ten dollar bill and given the five to Adele. Although Adele had been on the job only a day, she knew that tips were to be split among the room attendants who had cleaned the room during the guest stay. In this case, not only was Adele entitled to two days of tips, but someone else would be expecting a portion of the tip as well.

Fran was furious because guests shouldn't be subjected to the sour energy of disgruntled room attendants. She quieted Adele and Mona down and asked them firmly to report to her office. She would be there in ten minutes after attending to the guest who had called the front office. Fran called the front office manager on the radio to ask if she would accompany her to the guest's room to be sure that the guest knew that her complaint was appreciated. Fran had never felt really comfortable interacting with guests. She still thought of housekeeping as being back of the house, and didn't expect her room attendants or supervisors to go out of their way to interact with resort guests.

Back in her office, Fran met with the two room attendants to work out the problem. Mona thought that, since she was the trainer, she was entitled to the majority of the tip. She believed that since Adele was only just learning, she should be prepared to assist wherever necessary. Adele said that Mona had made her clean all the bathrooms and that Mona wasn't even helping scrub the floor or toilet. Fran was very firm in her discussion with the two and told them that guests could be upset very easily when room attendants argued in public. "If there is a problem," she said, "come see me!"

"The mood was so tense you could cut it with a knife," said Fran later to her general manager, who stopped in to see how things were going. "I had to do something!"

Fran sent Adele and Mona home for the day to cool down. The following day, Mona was teamed with another room attendant, as was Adele. Fran figured that Mona was the problem and Adele just needed to work with someone with a different attitude.

Maria, the front office manager, caught up with Fran the next afternoon in the employee dining area and asked how things were going. Fran said that things seemed quiet, but she wasn't sure how the new room attendant would work out.

Discussion Questions

1. What are the advantages and disadvantages of the training that Adele received?
2. How could Fran have prevented some of the tension between the two room attendants?

Case number: 608C12

This case also appears in Todd Comen, *Case Studies in Front Office Management* (Lansing, Mich.: American Hotel & Lodging Educational Institute, 2003).

Filling the Shoes of a Veteran Executive Housekeeper

Mike wasn't a newcomer to housekeeping. He was most recently the assistant housekeeping manager at a hotel in Naples, Florida. Now he was walking into the shoes of a veteran of the housekeeping department at the Boden Oceanside Resort and Lodge. Mike had been hired to replace Fran, who had just retired after many years with the Boden. He was finding that Fran had run her operation almost flawlessly out of her head, rather than from written rules and guidelines.

Mike had met with numerous surprises during his first weeks at the Boden. Recently, housekeeping had been receiving low ratings from guests on the comment cards. The front office had been directing numerous guest complaints to the housekeeping department—mostly concerning towel shortages, stained sheets, and the need for new soap and shampoos. Mike understood that sometimes front desk agents misinterpreted complaints, but Mike knew better than to confront the front office manager about the possibility of her staff exaggerating the circumstances. He had learned long ago to take complaints as an opportunity for improvement.

This morning, shortly after Mike had arrived, the room attendants came to him to let him know that they were out of bathroom cleaning fluid. He wondered how this could be, as just last week he had requested an inventory of all housekeeping supplies and linens on hand. He had done so after noticing that linens were running low. In particular, frayed hand towels were being placed in bathrooms because good-quality ones were in short supply.

He assumed that, after the inventory, the assistant housekeeping manager would have ordered whatever was in low supply. Mike knew that the department had been understaffed for some time due to cost-cutting measures the hotel owners and general manager had instituted. He also knew that money hadn't been budgeted for new linens, even though the busy season would soon be upon them and the supply was inadequate for higher occupancy levels.

Now, as he entered the storage closet for the first time since his quick orientation tour (he always relied on his assistant to deal with inventory and stocking), Mike realized that he should have explored the purchasing process sooner.

Mike's strategy for moving into his new position was to let people continue to work at their jobs as before, observing and getting to know his staff, the guests, and the other department managers. He had enough on his plate just getting to know the culture of Boden's management, what was expected of him, and how the other managers worked to achieve the overall mission of the resort.

The storage room he now peered into was typical of many he had seen and worked in. Supplies were stocked by category, although there were no labels on the shelves. Linens were neatly folded and everything seemed to be in full view. It looked like most supplies were well stocked, so Mike wondered why the bathroom cleaner was out this morning. Mike looked around for an inventory sheet or anything that would tell him where the cleaner should have been stocked.

Just then Kit, his assistant manager, came down the corridor. Seeing Mike, she asked whether he needed anything. Mike told her that the front office manager was receiving complaints from guests about ragged hand towels and bath towels. Today, however, room attendants had informed him that they were out of bathroom cleaner. Kit was surprised that the cleaner was all gone because she always ordered a case every other week. Maybe someone stole some, she said.

Mike asked her what her ordering procedures were. Kit told him that she looks through the storeroom on a weekly basis and places an order every other week for cleaning supplies. She's been doing it for so long that she usually knows exactly what to order. She also told Mike that they don't run out of things very often, although they sometimes got down to the last unit. In those circumstances, she would run to the discount store to pick up some supplies if the order wasn't coming in for a few days.

After sending Kit out to the discount store for a case of bathroom cleaner, Mike sat down to figure out how to improve upon the system for purchasing housekeeping supplies. He also had to determine how he would ensure that guests would have acceptable linens for the upcoming season. He knew he couldn't order an entire new supply of linens and towels, so he had to develop a system to help him integrate new linens and towels into the system over a period of months.

Before putting pen to paper, Mike called the director of purchasing for the Boden to set up a meeting to discuss his needs.

Discussion Questions

1. What policies and procedures for inventory and purchasing would you put in place if you were Mike?
2. How does Mike's problem affect guest satisfaction?
3. What strategy should Mike use to convince the general manager to allocate more resources to the housekeeping department to meet his linen needs?

Case number: 608C13

This case also appears in Todd Comen, *Case Studies in Front Office Management* (Lansing, Mich.: American Hotel & Lodging Educational Institute, 2003).

Chapter 6 Outline

Competencies

1. Explain the concept of revenue management, and discuss how managers can maximize revenue by using forecast information in capacity management, discount allocation, and duration control. (pp. 205–210)
2. Discuss common formulas managers use to measure and manage revenue. (pp. 211–224)
3. Explain how revenue management decisions are affected by group room sales, transient room sales, other revenue opportunities, local and area-wide activities, special events, and fair market share forecasting. (pp. 224–234)
4. Discuss the revenue manager's role and position, summarize typical revenue meetings, outline potential tactics to use in periods of high and low demand, discuss revenue management tactics, and explain how revenue management software helps hotel managers. (pp. 234–247)

Taken from *Managing Front Office Operations,* Ninth Edition, by Michael L. Kasavana

Chapter 6
Revenue Management

HISTORICALLY, A HOTEL'S DAILY PERFORMANCE has been evaluated on either occupancy percentage or average daily rate (ADR). Unfortunately, such one-dimensional analyses fail to capture the relationship between these two factors. For example, hotel managers may decrease room rates, or ADR, in an effort to increase occupancy. This strategy, while helping to improve the occupancy percentage, may fail to offset the rooms revenue lost due to lower room rates. Unless occupancy increases can overcome the drop in rate, profits may actually decline. Similarly, increases in room rates, or ADR, may be accompanied by a decline in occupancy percentage. This means that some revenue will be lost because rooms that might have been sold at lower rates will remain unsold. Some hotel companies prefer to build occupancy percentage using low room rates to attract business, while others prefer to set a target average room rate and are willing to sacrifice occupancy to achieve it.

Revenue management presents a more precise measure of performance because it combines occupancy percentage and ADR into a single statistic: the *yield statistic.* Simply stated, revenue management is a technique used to maximize revenues. Revenue management, sometimes called yield management, takes into account as many of the factors influencing business trends as possible. It is also an evaluative tool that allows the front office manager to use potential revenue as the standard against which actual revenue can be compared.

There are various approaches to revenue management. Often, each approach is modeled to meet the needs of an individual hotel. This chapter presents many of the common elements and basic assumptions used in revenue management analysis. Although revenue management analysis can be performed manually, this approach is cumbersome, time-consuming, and prone to error. With the use of specialty application software, revenue management calculations can be automatically performed very quickly and accurately.

The Concept of Revenue Management

The concept of revenue management originated in the airline industry. Most travelers know that passengers on the same flight often pay different fares. Super-saver discounts, fourteen-day advance-purchase plans, non-refundable fares, and so forth have become the norm for airline pricing. What is not as widely known is the potential application of revenue management to other service industries. Revenue management has proven successful in the lodging, car rental, cruise line, railroad, and touring industries—basically, in situations where reservations are taken for a perishable commodity. The key to successful implementation appears to be an ability to monitor demand and to develop reliable forecasts.

When hotels first started using revenue management, they focused strictly on guestroom rates and the basic economic principles of supply and demand. If demand for room nights was projected to be low—that is, if the forecast was for low occupancy, the revenue management strategy would dictate keeping room rates low in an attempt to attract as much business as possible. The idea was to convert every room availability inquiry into a reservation, even at a low rate. As demand increased for the targeted time frame, the hotel would increase its room rates. Hotels tended to align rate strategies with market segmentations by offering select discounts to featured groups, such as American Automobile Association members and AARP members. In addition, hotels did some specialized forecasting. For example, the number of current reservations for a future date may be low, but, if a city-wide convention was coming to town at that time, a hotel manager might believe the hotel would actually have higher occupancy and would fine-tune room rates and project occupancy accordingly. As hotel managers became more comfortable with the concept and application of revenue management strategies, they realized there were more effective ways to adjust rates while maximizing occupancy. Hotel companies conducted extensive analyses of guests who stayed at their hotels as well as those who preferred to stay elsewhere. Managers realized that room rates could accurately be adjusted based upon the demand of specific market segments, such as the following:

- Business travelers booking less than seven days prior to arrival
- Leisure travelers booking three to six months in advance of arrival
- Members of the hotel's frequent guest program
- Travelers making reservations over the Internet
- Travelers making reservations at the hotel's website
- Travelers requiring car rentals, airline reservations, and other components of a complete travel package

Hotel managers focused on making the best of each selling opportunity. The key to successful revenue management is to sell the right product (guestrooms, banquets, ancillary services) to the right customer (business, leisure, convention, or government guest) on the right day (weekday, weekend), for the right price (rack rate, corporate rate, group rate, government rate, or discount rate).

Many hotels use revenue management techniques to evaluate the total revenue potential of a guest or group. This includes all of the potential guest revenue beyond the guestroom rental, such as revenue from the sale of food and beverages, telephone service, Internet access, spa services, fitness center services, business center services, and other hotel goods and services. However, this discussion will focus on guestroom revenue, since this is the most important revenue stream for most hotels and therefore should receive the most attention from hotel management.

Revenue management, in one form or another, is pervasive across the lodging industry. Major hotel companies have developed unique revenue management systems that provide data for balancing room rates and occupancy levels at the property level. Some hotel managers do not support decisions based on revenue management analysis, evaluation, and strategy. These managers believe revenue management is too quantitative in nature, or fail to see the potential benefits derived from the work necessary for revenue management.

Revenue management is based on supply and demand. Prices tend to rise when demand exceeds supply; conversely, prices tend to fall when supply exceeds demand. Proper pricing adjustments, which take existing demand into account and can even influence it, appear to be the key to increased profitability. To increase revenue, the hotel industry is attempting to develop new forecasting techniques that will enable it to respond to changes in supply and demand with optimal room rates. The hotel industry's focus is shifting from high-*volume* bookings to high-*profit* bookings. By increasing bookings on low-demand days and by selling rooms at higher room rates on high-demand days, the industry can improve its profitability. In general, room rates should be higher (in order to maximize rate) when demand exceeds supply, and lower (in order to increase occupancy) when supply exceeds demand.

Revenue management is about making predictions and decisions—predictions about how much and what type of business to expect, and the subsequent decisions a manager makes to get the most revenue from that business.

Hotel Industry Applications

All hotel companies have a common problem: they have a fixed inventory of perishable products that cannot be stored if unsold by a specific time. The *real* commodity that hotels sell is time in a given space. If a room goes unsold on a given night, there is no way to recover the time lost and therefore the revenue lost. Thus, these products are typically sold for varying prices that depend on the timing of the transaction and the proposed date of delivery.

To make predictions, called **forecasts,** managers need information. They have to understand the property and the competitive market in which the property operates. They also need to consider future events—or variables—that might affect business.

Forecasts help determine whether room rates should be raised or lowered, and whether a reservation request should be accepted or rejected to maximize revenue. Front office managers have successfully applied such demand-forecasting strategies to room reservation systems; management information systems; room and package pricing; rooms and revenue management; seasonal rate determination; pre-theater dinner specials; and special, group, tour operator, and travel agent rates.

Front office managers have identified several benefits of revenue management, including:

- Improved forecasting
- Improved seasonal pricing and inventory decisions

- Identification of new market segments
- Identification of market segment demands
- Enhanced coordination between the front office and sales divisions
- Determination of discounting activity
- Improved development of short-term and long-term business plans
- Establishment of a value-based rate structure
- Increased business and profits
- Savings in labor costs and other operating expenses
- Initiation of consistent guest-contact scripting (that is, planned responses to guest inquiries or requests regarding reservations)

Selecting revenue management strategies and tactics is really about picking and choosing the reservations that most closely match the guest mix that hotel management desires. Most hotel managers seek a mix of two or more guest segments. (Some common guest segments are group guests, business travelers, leisure guests, government travelers, or contract guests.) Having a guest mix ensures that the hotel's business will not be significantly affected if business from one of the guest segments goes into decline. For example, business travel significantly decreased in the United States and overseas after the terrorist attacks of September 11, 2001. Some hotels managed to maintain acceptable profitability because they had a diversified guest base; hotels that relied primarily on business guests had much more difficulty maintaining profitability. The goal is to identify high-yield guest segments—the ones with guests who will pay the most and stay the longest—so the highest possible profits can be realized. This is accomplished by controlling room rates and availability through rate and stay restrictions.

Different demand situations call for different tactics. The challenge is to view each day as a separate situation and implement tactics best suited to the property and its guests, market, and demand conditions. This is done through capacity management, discount allocation, and duration control.

Capacity Management. Capacity management involves various methods of controlling and limiting room supply. For example, hotels will typically accept a statistically supported number of reservations in excess of the actual number of rooms available in an attempt to offset the potential impact of early check-outs, cancellations, and no-shows. Capacity management (also called selective overbooking) balances the risk of overselling guestrooms against the potential loss of revenue arising from room spoilage (rooms going unoccupied after the hotel stops taking reservations for a given date).

Other forms of capacity management include determining how many walk-ins to accept on the day of arrival, given projected cancellations, no-shows, and early departures. Capacity management strategies usually vary by room type. That is, it might be economically advantageous to overbook more rooms in lower-priced categories, because upgrading to higher-priced rooms is an acceptable solution to an oversell problem. The amount of such overbooking depends, of course, on the level of demand for the higher-priced rooms. In sophisticated computerized revenue management systems, capacity management may also be influenced by the availability of rooms at neighboring hotels or other competing properties.

The risks in overbooking should be clearly understood. It is generally better to have some rooms vacant at the end of the hotel day than to walk guests to other hotels. Walking guests leads to guest dissatisfaction. Guests will change hotels or brands if overbooking relocates them too often. In addition, hotel management must be aware of how local laws interpret overbooking.

Between late 2001 and late 2003, one of the most critical issues U.S. hotel managers faced was **group attrition**. The traditional process of handling group reservations normally occurs in two phases. The first phase involves blocking a set of rooms that the group expects its attendees to occupy. The second phase occurs as attendees actually register for the event and book the blocked rooms.

The number of rooms a group requires for a specific number of nights is one of the factors the hotel may consider when determining whether to accept the group's business. Once the hotel accepts the group's reservation, it hopes the group can sell all of its blocked rooms. When a group fails to book its committed number of room nights, the resulting shortfall is termed *attrition*. Before late 2001, group attrition did not pose a serious problem for a majority of lodging properties, since hotels could compensate for it through sales efforts in a variety of other market segments (such as by accepting short-term reservations for business travelers). In fact, some hotels actually allowed for a small percentage of group attrition and accounted for it in comprehensive capacity management strategies. Since 2001, three factors have contributed to elevating the importance of group attrition: group history, online shopping, and business sourcing.

- *Group history:* Meeting planners who contract for a large number of guestrooms tend to base their projections on the group's attendance history. If the group is notorious for missing its targeted room nights, hotel management will make adjustments to the expected business at the front end rather than wait until late in the reservation cycle.
- *Online shopping:* Group attendees have Internet access and can make their own reservations online, often shopping for a lower room rate than the rate negotiated for the group at the host hotel(s). Alternately, attendees may opt to stay at a nearby property instead of at the host hotel if they discover a lower room rate.
- *Business sourcing:* The volume of occupancy generated by non-group segments, such as business and leisure travelers, has significantly decreased, thereby placing a heavier emphasis on successfully marketing to group and convention business.

Hotel managers and meeting planners have worked together to minimize group attrition problems. Meeting planners now use various techniques to ensure that their groups meet their room-night pickup commitments. For example, many groups restrict attendance at meetings to those who stay in approved hotels. Furthermore, some city-wide groups will not provide transportation to attendees who do not stay in the host hotels. And sometimes group registration fees are significantly higher for attendees who do not stay in the host hotels. For their part, hotel managers are doing a better job of managing their hotels' discount rates, to ensure that in-house groups receive the lowest published rate. In addition, some hotels do not offer loyalty-program rewards to guests who pay significantly discounted rates.

Discount Allocation. Discount allocation involves restricting the time period and product mix (rooms) available at reduced or discounted rates. For each discounted room type, reservations are requested at various available rates, each set below rack rate. The theory is that the sale of a perishable item (the guestroom) at a reduced room rate is often better than no sale at all. The primary objective of discount allocation is to protect enough remaining rooms at a higher rate to satisfy the projected demand for rooms at that rate, while at the same time filling rooms that would otherwise have remained unsold. This process is repeated for each rate level from rack rate on down as demand indicates. Implementing such a scheme requires a reliable mechanism for demand forecasting.

A second objective of limiting discounts by room type is to encourage upselling. In upselling, a reservation agent or front desk agent attempts to place a guest in a higher-rated room. This technique requires a reliable estimate of price elasticity and/or the probability of upgrading. (*Elasticity* refers to the relationship between price and demand. If a small increase in price produces a dramatic drop in demand, the market is said to be price *elastic.* If a small increase in price produces little or no effect on demand, the market is said to be price *inelastic.*)

Duration Control. Duration control places time constraints on accepting reservations to protect sufficient space for multi-day requests (representing higher levels of revenue). This means that, under revenue management, a reservation for a one-night stay may be rejected, even though space is available for that night.

For example, if Wednesday is close to selling out but adjacent nights are not, a hotel may want to optimize its revenue potential for the last few remaining rooms on Wednesday by requiring multi-day stays, even at a discounted rate, rather than accepting reservations for Wednesday only. Similarly, if the hotel is projected to be close to capacity Tuesday, Wednesday, and Thursday, accepting a one-night stay during any of those days may be detrimental to the hotel's overall room revenue, since it may block occupancy on the other days. Hotels facing such situations may require that guests wishing to reserve rooms during projected full-occupancy periods make reservations for more than one night. Duration control is a common technique that resorts use during peak periods like Christmas, New Year's, Easter, and the Fourth of July.

These strategies may be combined. For example, duration control may be combined with discount allocation. A three-night stay may be available for discount, while a one-night stay may require the rack rate. It must be cautioned, though, that using these strategies must not be apparent to the guest. A guest might not understand why he or she must stay three nights to get a discounted rate if he or she wants to stay only one night. Proper use of revenue management relies on selling; it never divulges the revenue management strategy being used.

Measuring Revenue

Revenue management is designed to measure revenue achievement. One of the principal computations involved in revenue management is the hotel's **yield statistic,** the ratio of actual room revenue to potential room revenue. Actual room revenue is the revenue generated by the number of rooms sold. Potential room revenue is the amount of money that would be received if all rooms were sold at their rack rates (or, as described below, at the hotel's *potential average rate*).

Potential revenue can be determined in more than one way. First, some resorts calculate their potential revenue as the amount the resort would earn if all rooms were sold at the double occupancy rate. Resorts generally have a high percentage of double occupancy. Commercial hotels often calculate their potential revenue by taking into account the percentage mix of rooms normally sold at both single and double occupancy. The second method results in a lower total potential revenue figure, since single rooms are assumed to sell at less than double rooms. In fact, while it is unlikely that a hotel will attain a potential that is based on 100 percent double occupancy (first method), a hotel using the second method may actually be able to exceed its "potential" if demand for double rooms exceeds sales mix projections.

The hotel's yield statistic will vary with the method it uses; therefore, once the hotel has chosen a preferred method, it should use that method consistently. The second method (using both single and double occupancy) is illustrated in the formulas that follow. For hotels using the first method (based on 100 percent double occupancy), formulas 1, 3, 4, and 5 are not applicable; for such hotels, the potential average double rate (formula 2) will be the same as the potential average rate (formula 5).

The mathematical computations required for revenue management are relatively simple, even though a series of formulas are usually involved. This section is intended to introduce the basic formulations of revenue management calculations.

For the following discussion, assume that the Casa Vana Inn has 300 guestrooms, has an ADR of $80 per room, and is currently operating at a 70 percent average occupancy. The hotel offers 100 one-bed and 200 two-bed guestrooms. Management has established single and double rack rates for each room type. Any one-bed room sold as a single is priced at $90; as a double, it sells for $110. Any two-bed room sold as a single is priced at $100; as a double, it sells for $120.

Formula 1: Potential Average Single Rate

If the Casa Vana Inn had not varied its single rate by room type (for example, if all singles were $90), the potential average single rate would equal its rack rate. When the single rate differs by room type, as in this case, the potential average single rate is computed as a weighted average. It is computed by multiplying the number of rooms in each room type category by its single room rack rate and dividing the sum total by the number of potential single rooms in the hotel. For the Casa Vana Inn, the potential average single rate is computed as follows:

Room Type	Number of Rooms	Single Rack Rate	Revenue at 100% Occupancy Singles
1 bed	100	$ 90	$ 9,000
2 beds	200	100	20,000
	300		$29,000

$$\text{Potential Average Single Rate} = \frac{\text{Single Room Revenues at Rack Rate}}{\text{Number of Rooms Sold as Singles}}$$

$$= \frac{\$29{,}000}{300}$$

$$= \$96.67$$

Formula 2: Potential Average Double Rate

If the hotel had not varied its double rate by room type, the potential average double rate would equal its rack rate. When the double rate differs by room type, as in this case, the potential average double rate is computed as a weighted average. It is calculated by multiplying the number of rooms in each room type category by its respective double-room rack rate and dividing the sum total by the number of potential double rooms in the hotel. For the Casa Vana Inn, this computation is as follows:

Room Type	Number of Rooms	Double Rack Rate	Revenue at 100% Occupancy Doubles
1 bed	100	$110	$11,000
2 beds	200	120	24,000
	300		$35,000

$$\text{Potential Average Double Rate} = \frac{\text{Double Room Revenues at Rack Rate}}{\text{Number of Rooms Sold as Doubles}}$$

$$= \frac{\$35{,}000}{300}$$

$$= \$116.67$$

Note: For lodging properties basing potential revenue on 100 percent double occupancy, this step is all that is necessary to determine potential average rate (see formula 5).

Formula 3: Multiple Occupancy Percentage

An important element in determining a hotel's yield statistic is the proportion of the hotel's rooms that are occupied by more than one person—that is, the multiple occupancy percentage. This information is important because it indicates sales mix and helps balance room rates with future occupancy demand. In the case of the Casa Vana Inn, if 105 of the 210 rooms sold (at 70-percent occupancy) are

6000
7200
9000
22,200

normally occupied by more than one person, the multiple occupancy percentage is computed as follows:

$$\text{Multiple Occupancy Percentage} = \frac{105}{210}$$

$$= 0.5 \text{ or } 50\%$$

Formula 4: Rate Spread

In addition to multiple occupancy percentage, another intermediate computation is important to yield statistics. The determination of a room **rate spread** among various room types can be essential to the use of yield decisions in targeting a hotel's specific market. The mathematical difference between the hotel's potential average single rate (formula 1) and potential average double rate (formula 2) is known as the rate spread. For the Casa Vana Inn, the rate spread is computed as follows:

$$\text{Rate Spread} = \text{Potential Average Double Rate} - \text{Potential Average Single Rate}$$

$$= \$116.67 - \$96.67$$

$$= \$\ 20.00$$

Formula 5: Potential Average Rate

A very important element in revenue management formulation is the **potential average rate.** A hotel's potential average rate is a collective statistic that effectively combines the potential average rate, multiple occupancy percentage, and rate spread. The potential average rate is determined in two steps. The first step involves multiplying the rate spread by the hotel's multiple occupancy percentage. The result is added to the hotel's potential average single rate to produce a potential average rate based on demand (sales mix) and room rate information. For the Casa Vana Inn, the potential average rate is computed as follows:

$$\text{Potential Average Rate} = \left(\text{Multiple Occupancy Percentage} \times \text{Rate Spread}\right) + \text{Potential Average Single Rate}$$

$$= (0.5 \times \$20) + \$96.67$$

$$= \$106.67$$

Formula 6: Room Rate Achievement Factor

The percentage of the rack rate that the hotel actually receives is expressed by the hotel's **achievement factor (AF),** also called the **rate potential percentage.** When revenue management software is not used, the achievement factor is generally calculated by dividing the actual average rate the hotel is currently collecting by the potential average rate.[1] The actual average rate equals total rooms revenue divided by either rooms sold or rooms occupied (depending on hotel policy). For the Casa Vana Inn, the room rate achievement factor is computed as follows:

$$\text{Achievement Factor} = \frac{\text{Actual Average Rate}}{\text{Potential Average Rate}}$$

$$= \frac{\$80.00}{\$106.67}$$

$$= 0.750 \text{ or } \underline{\underline{75.0\%}}$$

The achievement factor is also equal to 100 percent minus the discount percentage. By calculating its achievement factor, management discovers how much its actual room rates varied from established rack rates. In this case, the discount is 25 percent.

As shown below, the achievement factor can be used in one method of determining the yield statistic. It is not *necessary* to calculate the achievement factor, because the yield statistic can be determined without it. Nonetheless, the achievement factor is an important statistic in its own right because it allows management to monitor and therefore better control the hotel's use of discounting. For this reason, many hotels calculate the achievement factor as part of their revenue management efforts.

Formula 7: Yield Statistic

An important element in revenue management is the yield statistic. The yield statistic calculation incorporates several of the previous formulas into a critical index. There are various ways to express and calculate the yield statistic, all of which are equivalent:

1. $$\text{Yield} = \frac{\text{Actual Rooms Revenue}}{\text{Potential Rooms Revenue}}$$
2. $$\text{Yield} = \frac{\text{Room Nights Sold}}{\text{Rooms Nights Available}} \times \frac{\text{Actual Average Room Rate}}{\text{Potential Average Rate}}$$
3. $$\text{Yield} = \text{Occupancy Percentage} \times \text{Achievement Factor}$$

The first equation is used for a hotel that offers all its rooms at a single rack rate, regardless of occupancy. When (as is far more common) a hotel uses more than one rack rate for different room types and/or occupancies, potential rooms revenue equals total room nights available times the potential average rate.

The self-explanatory second equation is not demonstrated here. The third equation is illustrated below. For the Casa Vana Inn, the calculation is as follows:

$$\text{Yield} = \text{Occupancy Percentage} \times \text{Achievement Factor}$$

$$= 0.7 \times 0.75$$

$$= 0.525 \text{ or } \underline{\underline{52.5\%}}$$

Consider another example. Assume that the Cybex Hotel has 150 rooms and a rack rate of $70. On average, the hotel sells 120 rooms per night at an average room rate of $60. What is the yield for this property?

$$\text{Occupancy Percentage} = 120 \div 150 = 0.8 \text{ or } 80\%$$

$$\text{Rate Achievement Factor} = 60 \div 70 = 0.857 \text{ or } 85.7\%$$

$$\text{Yield} = 0.8 \times 0.857 = 0.686 \text{ or } \underline{\underline{68.6\%}}$$

When using this approach to determine the yield statistic, note that complimentary rooms must be treated in the achievement factor the same way that they are treated in the occupancy percentage. That is, if complimentary rooms are included in the occupancy percentage, the actual average room rate used to determine the achievement factor must equal room revenues divided by rooms *occupied,* not rooms *sold.* If complimentary rooms are ignored in the occupancy percentage, they should be ignored in calculating the actual average room rate as well.

Formula 8: RevPAR

Instead of computing yield as a percentage, some lodging operations prefer an alternate statistic that focuses on revenue per available room **(RevPAR)**. RevPAR can be calculated using either of the following equations:

$$\text{RevPAR} = \frac{\text{Actual Room Revenue}}{\text{Number of Available Rooms}}$$

$$\text{RevPAR} = \text{Occupancy Percentage} \times \text{ADR}$$

For example, suppose the 300-room Casa Vana Inn sells 180 rooms for a total of $11,520. What is this hotel's revenue per available room?

$$\text{RevPAR} = \frac{\text{Actual Room Revenue}}{\text{Number of Available Rooms}}$$

$$= \$11{,}520 \div 300 = \underline{\underline{\$38.40}}$$

or

$$\text{RevPAR} = \text{Occupancy Percentage} \times \text{ADR}$$

$$= 60\% \times \$64 = \underline{\underline{\$38.40}}$$

where occupancy percentage = 180 ÷ 300 = 0.6 or 60%
and ADR = $11,520 ÷ 180 = $64

Formula 9: Identical Yields

Calculations of different combinations of occupancy and actual average room rate may result in identical room revenue and yield statistics. Suppose the Casa Vana Inn is currently operating at 70-percent occupancy with an average rate of $80, but is considering strategies designed to raise its average rate to $100. What occupancy percentage must it achieve to match the yield it currently achieves? The formula for determining identical yield occupancy percentage is as follows:

$$\text{Identical Yield Occupancy Percentage} = \text{Current Occupancy Percentage} \times \frac{\text{Current Average Rate}}{\text{Proposed Average Rate}}$$

$$= 70\% \times \frac{\$80}{\$100}$$

$$= 0.560 \text{ or } \underline{\underline{56.0\%}}$$

Identical yields do not generally represent identical operating situations, however. Consider the following three levels of room sales for which the Casa Vana Inn derives identical yield statistics:

Case	Number of Rooms Sold	Occupancy Percentage	Average Room Rate	Room Revenue	Yield
1	190	63.3%	$88.42	$16,800	52.5%
2	200	66.7%	$84.00	$16,800	52.5%
3	210	70.0%	$80.00	$16,800	52.5%

Are these three yield cases identical? Even though all three cases produce identical levels of room revenue and yield statistics, there are some significant differences to note.

Case 1, which represents the smallest number of rooms sold, will most likely have the lowest associated operating costs. Case 1 also generates the highest average room rate, and may appear to be the most profitable of the three cases. Case 3 represents the largest number of rooms sold and hence most likely the highest associated operating costs. This case also presents the lowest average room rate. These facts may be somewhat misleading, however. Often, the more rooms that are sold, the more likely the hotel is to collect greater non-room revenue. In other words, a higher occupancy percentage may result in greater total (room and non-room) revenue. Case 2 represents a middle position in terms of both number of rooms sold and average room rate. Some hoteliers may favor this case, since an intermediate position is achieved regarding associated operating costs and total revenues collected.

Clearly, identical yields should not be assumed to reveal equivalent operating positions. When identical yields are computed, judging which scenario is best often requires property-specific criteria and management evaluation.

Formula 10: Equivalent Occupancy

Management can use the **equivalent occupancy** formula when it wants to know what other combinations of room rate and occupancy percentage provide equivalent *net* revenue.

The equivalent occupancy formula is very similar to the identical yield occupancy formula, but takes marginal costs into account by incorporating gross profit or contribution margin. The **cost per occupied room** (also called the **marginal cost**) of providing a room is the cost the hotel incurs by selling that room (for example, housekeeping expenses such as cleaning supplies); this cost would not be incurred if the room were not sold (as opposed to **fixed costs,** which are incurred whether the room is sold or not). The **contribution margin** is that portion of the room rate that is left over after the marginal cost of providing the room has been subtracted out.[2]

To find the equivalent occupancy, use either of the following formulas (which are equivalent versions of the same equation):

$$\text{Equivalent Occupancy} = \text{Current Occupancy Percentage} \times \frac{\text{Rack Rate} - \text{Marginal Cost}}{\text{Rack Rate} \times \left(1 - \text{Discount Percentage}\right) - \text{Marginal Cost}}$$

$$\text{Equivalent Occupancy} = \text{Current Occupancy Percentage} \times \frac{\text{Current Contribution Margin}}{\text{New Contribution Margin}}$$

Recall the example discussed under identical yield statistics. Now assume that the Casa Vana Inn is currently operating at 70-percent occupancy with an average rate of $80, and is considering strategies designed to raise its average rate to $100. Further assume that the marginal cost of providing a room is $12. What occupancy percentage must the Casa Vana Inn achieve to match the *net room revenue* it currently receives?

$$\text{Equivalent Occupancy} = \text{Current Occupancy Percentage} \times \frac{\text{Current Contribution Margin}}{\text{New Contribution Margin}}$$

$$= 70\% \times \frac{\$80 - \$12}{\$100 - \$12}$$

$$= 0.541 \text{ or } \underline{\underline{54.1\%}}$$

Recall from the discussion of identical yields that the Casa Vana Inn needs a 56-percent occupancy to produce an identical *yield statistic*—that is, equivalent gross revenue. However, the Casa Vana Inn does not need to match its gross revenue to achieve the same net revenue, since, by selling fewer rooms (at the higher price), it incurs fewer associated operating costs.

Although rack rates are raised relatively infrequently, discounting is a common practice in the lodging industry. What is the equivalent occupancy to 70 percent with an $80 average room rate if the average room rate is discounted by 20 percent (to $64)?

$$\text{Equivalent Occupancy} = 70\% \times \frac{\$80 - \$12}{\$64 - \$12}$$

$$= 0.915 \text{ or } \underline{\underline{91.5\%}}$$

A **discount grid** can help management to evaluate room rate discounting strategies. For example, if the average room rate of a hotel is $100 and its marginal cost (cost per occupied room) is $11, the grid in Exhibit 1 lists the occupancy percentages necessary to achieve equivalent net revenue, given different room rate discount levels. To prepare a discount grid, first calculate the marginal cost

73.6
76.6

Exhibit 1 Sample Discount Grid

Rack Rate $100.00
Marginal Cost $11.00

Current Occupancy	Equivalent Occupancy Percent Required to Maintain Profitability if Rates Are Discounted by:						
	5%	10%	15%	20%	25%	30%	35%
100%	106.0%	112.7%	120.3%	129.0%	139.1%	150.8%	164.8%
95%	100.7%	107.0%	114.3%	122.5%	132.1%	143.3%	156.6%
90%	95.4%	101.4%	108.2%	116.1%	125.2%	135.8%	148.3%
85%	90.1%	95.8%	102.2%	109.6%	118.2%	128.2%	140.1%
80%	84.8%	90.1%	96.2%	103.2%	111.3%	120.7%	131.9%
75%	79.5%	84.5%	90.2%	96.7%	104.3%	113.1%	123.6%
70%	74.2%	78.9%	84.2%	90.3%	97.3%	105.6%	115.4%
65%	68.9%	73.2%	78.2%	83.8%	90.4%	98.1%	107.1%
60%	63.6%	67.6%	72.2%	77.4%	83.4%	90.5%	98.9%
55%	58.3%	62.0%	66.1%	70.9%	76.5%	83.0%	90.6%
50%	53.0%	56.3%	60.1%	64.5%	69.5%	75.4%	82.4%
45%	47.7%	50.7%	54.1%	58.0%	62.6%	67.9%	74.2%
40%	42.4%	45.1%	48.1%	51.6%	55.6%	60.3%	65.9%
35%	37.1%	39.4%	42.1%	45.1%	48.7%	52.8%	57.7%
30%	31.8%	33.8%	36.1%	38.7%	41.7%	45.3%	49.4%
25%	26.5%	28.2%	30.1%	32.2%	34.8%	37.7%	41.2%

of providing a guestroom. Next, integrate this information into the equivalent occupancy formula and perform the calculations to fill in the grid. Completing a discount grid manually is quite time-consuming; spreadsheet programs greatly simplify the process.

Applying the yield and equivalent occupancy formulas to the same data will help illustrate their differences. Suppose once again that the Casa Vana Inn is currently operating at 70-percent occupancy with an average rate of $80 and a marginal cost of $12. Would the Inn be better off with an average rate of $100 and a 50-percent occupancy? What about $100 and 55-percent occupancy? Exhibit 2 presents these data and applies the yield statistic and equivalent occupancy formulas. Note that 50-percent occupancy falls below both the 56 percent necessary for identical yield and the 54.1 percent needed to produce equivalent net room revenue. Therefore, according to either approach, the Casa Vana Inn is worse off operating at a 50-percent occupancy and a $100 average room rate.

The second situation, however, finds the two approaches in conflict and illustrates the superiority of the equivalent occupancy formula. At 55-percent occupancy, the Casa Vana Inn falls short of the 56 percent needed to produce an identical yield statistic. When the yield statistic formula is used, the Inn appears to be worse off. However, the 55-percent occupancy level is higher than the 54.1

Exhibit 2 Application of Yield and Equivalent Occupancy Formulas

	Number of Rooms Sold	Occupancy Percentage	Average Room Rate	Gross Room Revenue	Total Contribution Margin*	Yield
Current	210	70.0%	$ 80	$16,800	$14,280	52.5%
Identical	168	56.0%	100	16,800	14,784	52.5%
Equivalent	162**	54.1%	100	16,200	14,280	50.6%
New	150	50.0%	100	15,000	13,200	46.9%
New	165	55.0%	100	16,500	14,520	51.6%

*Based on a marginal cost of $12. Since fixed costs are the same for all situations, the differences between total contribution margins will exactly equal the differences between net room revenues.

**Rounded down from 162.3. Based on this amount, net revenues would be $14,282.

percent required to produce equivalent net room revenue. With the equivalent occupancy formula, the Inn would be better off. A close look at the total contribution margin column—which shows that contribution (and therefore net room revenue) would rise—reveals that the equivalent occupancy formula provides more accurate and useful information.

Of course, the net gain in room revenue would have to be weighed against the potential loss of non-room revenue caused by a lower level of occupancy.

Formula 11: Required Non-Room Revenue per Guest

While equivalent occupancy accounts for marginal costs, unlike the yield statistic, both fail to account for changes in net non-room revenue due to changes in occupancy. A manager wanting some clear indication of whether a change in room rate will render more than an offsetting change in net non-room revenue may find an answer using **breakeven analysis.** This approach involves calculating or estimating a number of elements:

- The net change in room revenue due to room rate changes
- The amount of net non-room revenue needed to offset any reduction in net room revenue (when room rates are discounted) or the amount of net room revenue needed to offset any reduction in net non-room revenue (when room rates are increased)
- The average amount each guest spends in non-room revenue centers
- The change in occupancy likely to result from room rate changes

For example, a group may be negotiating for a lower room rate with a hotel. In order to make an appropriate group profit, the hotel may require some sort of additional food and beverage revenue, like a continental breakfast or group dinner. In other cases, the hotel may be unwilling to negotiate room rate but may add value to the group by hosting a complimentary cocktail reception or reducing parking fees. The same strategies apply to leisure guests coming to the hotel on a package plan. The package is priced competitively to attract guests, but the internal distribution of revenue should be designed to maximize profits.

The breakeven calculation is based on the **weighted average contribution margin ratio** (CMR_w) for all non-room revenue. While a detailed discussion of this topic is beyond the scope of this chapter, a simple formula for determining the CMR_w for all non-room revenue centers is as follows:[3]

$$CMR_w = \frac{\text{Total Non-Room Revenue} - \text{Total Non-Room Revenue Center Variable Costs}}{\text{Total Non-Room Revenue}}$$

Knowing the CMR_w and the average amount that guests spend in non-room revenue, and having estimated the probable change in occupancy (number of guests), the front office manager can then determine whether the net change caused by higher or lower room rates is likely to be more than offset by the net change in non-room revenue.

For example, suppose hotel management is considering room rate discounting in an attempt to increase occupancy and therefore net revenue. The formula used to determine the required non-room revenue per guest follows:

$$\text{Required Non-Room Revenue per Guest} = \frac{\text{Required Increase in Net Non-Room Revenue}}{\text{Number of Additional Guests}} \div CMR_w$$

The front office manager can compare the result of this equation with the actual average non-room spending per guest. If this number is higher than the actual average non-room spending per guest, the hotel is likely to lose net revenue by discounting its room rates; that is, the additional guests brought in through discounting will not spend enough to offset the net loss in room revenue. If the amount needed per additional guest is lower than the actual average amount spent, the hotel is likely to increase its net revenue through discounting.

As another example, assume that the 400-room Bradley Inn has a $144.75 potential average room rate (generating potential room revenue of $57,900) and a $12 marginal cost per room. The Inn currently operates at 60-percent occupancy (240 rooms sold per night) and an average room rate of $137.50. Management believes that it can raise occupancy to 75 percent (300 rooms sold per night) by lowering its average room rate to $110. It also believes it can raise occupancy to 90 percent (360 rooms sold per night) by lowering the average room rate to $91.67. Should management attempt either of these strategies?

It is important to note that since room revenue ($33,000) is the same for all three situations, looking simply at a yield statistic (57 percent) does not offer a solution. Equivalent occupancy calculations offer more useful information. A reduction in average room rate to $110 would require an equivalent occupancy of 76.8 percent (60 percent × $125.50 ÷ $98.00). A reduction to $91.67 would require an equivalent occupancy of 94.5 percent (60 percent × $125.50 ÷ $79.67). Based on management's forecasts of 75 percent and 90 percent occupancies, both average room rate reductions would result in a decrease in net room revenue.

Still, the average room rate reductions may be justifiable on the basis of increased *total* revenue. The first step in determining whether this is the case is calculating the total contribution margin (or, if fixed cost data are available, the net room revenue) of the three options:

Level of Occupancy		Number of Rooms		Room Contribution Margin		Total Revenue Contribution
60%	×	400	×	($137.50 − $12.00)	=	$30,120
75%	×	400	×	($110.00 − $12.00)	=	$29,400
90%	×	400	×	($91.67 − $12.00)	=	$28,681

An average room rate reduction to $110 brings in an additional 60 guests but results in a net room revenue loss of $720. A reduction in average room rate to $91.67 brings in an additional 120 guests but lowers net room revenue by $1,439. In either situation, to offset the loss, the Bradley Inn needs to earn an average net non-room revenue of $12 for each additional guest ($720 ÷ 60 extra guests; $1,439 ÷ 120 extra guests). If the non-room CMR_w is found to be 0.25, the required non-room spending for each additional guest is:

$$\text{Required Non-Room Spending} = \$12 \div 0.25 = \underline{\underline{\$48}}$$

In other words, if the Bradley Inn's guests typically spend an average of more than $48 per day in the Inn's non-room revenue centers, the Inn is likely to increase its total net revenue by offering either room rate discount.

Non-room revenue considerations can become critical factors in a revenue management analysis. Some hotels require that groups receiving discounted room rates contract for hotel food and beverage services to render the total revenue package attractive.

This discussion has thus far approached the breakeven analysis of required non-room revenue by examining a room rate *reduction* that decreases net room revenue and increases occupancy. Breakeven analysis can also be used to examine the net effects of a room rate *increase.* Consider the following situations.

When room rates are increased, occupancy percentage generally falls (unless demand is very inelastic). An increase in price may reduce room sales so much that net room revenue actually falls, despite the higher ADR. Because occupancy has declined, it is likely that non-room revenue will also decline. In this situation, it is clear that the price increase would hurt the hotel's financial position.

However, a room rate increase may in fact lead to higher net room revenue despite the decrease in occupancy it causes. Although higher net room revenue appears to be an outcome that management would desire, such a rate increase should not be implemented without careful analysis because, even if net room revenue goes up, *total* net revenue may still drop. This can occur when the occupancy decline reduces net non-room revenue by an amount greater than the net room revenue increase.

For example, assume that the 400-room Cybex Hotel is considering increasing its room rate from $80 to $90. Current occupancy is 80 percent. Forecasted occupancy after the price increase is estimated to be 75 percent. The marginal cost of selling a guestroom is $14. The average daily non-room spending per guest is

$75 and the weighted average contribution margin ratio for all non-room revenue centers is 0.30. Should management implement the rate increase? First, calculate the effect on net room revenue contribution:

Occupancy		Rooms		Room Contribution Margin		Total Contribution
80%	×	400	×	($80 − $14)	=	$21,120
75%	×	400	×	($90 − $14)	=	$22,800

Net room revenue would increase by $1,680 if the room rate were increased. The profit percentage per occupied room would increase from 82.5 percent ($66 ÷ $80) to 84.4 percent ($76 ÷ $90).

Next, calculate the effect on non-room net revenue:

Net Non-Room Revenue

At 80% occupancy: 320 guests × $75 × 0.30 = $7,200
At 75% occupancy: 300 guests × $75 × 0.30 = $6,750

Net non-room revenue would decrease by $450 if the room rate were increased.

Finally, subtract the net non-room revenue loss from the net room revenue gain. In this example, total daily net revenue would increase by $1,230 ($1,680 − $450) if the room rate is increased by $10. Given this net gain, management should implement the increase.

Now suppose that the front office manager had forecasted occupancy to be 71 percent after the rate increase rather than 75 percent. This change would lead to a different conclusion, as the following calculations demonstrate:

Occupancy		Rooms		Room Contribution Margin		Total Contribution
80%	×	400	×	($80 − $14)	=	$21,120
71%	×	400	×	($90 − $14)	=	$21,584

Net room revenue would increase by $464 if the room rate were increased. However, net non-room revenue would decrease by $810 if the room rate were increased:

Net Non-Room Revenue

At 80% occupancy: 320 guests × $75 × 0.30 = $7,200
At 71% occupancy: 284 guests × $75 × 0.30 = $6,390

In this revised example, total daily net revenue would decrease by $346 ($810 − $464). Given such circumstances, management should not implement the room rate increase.

RevPAG and GOPPAR

RevPAR is an established component of a revenue management analysis. Two additional measurements of hotel revenue and profitability have emerged as important considerations: RevPAG (revenue per available guest) and GOPPAR (gross operating profit per available room).

RevPAG is similar to RevPAR in that it measures total revenue; however, instead of reporting on a per-available-room basis, it uses the number of guests as a critical variable. The purpose of RevPAG is to determine the average revenue earned for each guest staying at a hotel. The RevPAG formula is:

$$\text{RevPAG} = \frac{\text{Total Revenue}}{\text{Number of Guests}}$$

RevPAG is most useful in hotels with multiple revenue outlets, such as restaurants, lounges, recreational activities, spa, and retail shops. It is a statistic that highlights the overall revenue derived per guest and is a more comprehensive measure than a per-room figure. Managers can also use RevPAG to identify areas in which the hotel is not capturing expected revenue. For example, a hotel may have a RevPAG of $110 per day, meaning that the average total revenue contributed by each guest (room revenue, food and beverage revenue, spa revenue, in-room entertainment revenue, etc.) is $110. However, if this average starts to decline, it indicates that the hotel is not earning as much revenue per guest as it did previously. Such a condition will lead hotel management to develop appropriate strategies and tactics to reverse the decline.

GOPPAR is a more sophisticated measurement than RevPAG, since it deals with gross operating profit. GOPPAR has the advantage of incorporating departmental expenses, not just revenue, resulting in a measure of gross operating profit, which is a number that represents the mathematical difference between departmental revenues and departmental expenses. By dividing the gross operating profit by the number of rooms available for sale, management can obtain a measure of profitability for the property. The purpose of GOPPAR is to quantify the hotel's profitability per available room. Industry analysts can also use GOPPAR to determine a hotel's financial value. Value can be especially important should the hotel's owner become interested in re-financing or selling the property. The GOPPAR formula is:

$$\text{GOPPAR} = \frac{\text{Departmental Revenues} - \text{Departmental Expenses}}{\text{Number of Available Rooms}}$$

Hotel management may do an adequate job generating revenue, but a less than satisfactory job controlling costs. If the hotel does not properly control expenses, all of its effort to maximize revenue will not produce an expected level of profitability. For example, a hotel may have a higher occupancy than expected, leading to a greater amount of revenue than initially projected. However, to accommodate the extra business, management may have scheduled more employees, leading to increased paid wages and possible overtime, and/or may have purchased more inventory (foods and beverages, etc.), thereby reducing eventual profitability of the unanticipated business increase.

While RevPAG and GOPPAR each have advantages, they also have potential shortcomings. For example, RevPAG may not be an effective measure for properties with limited revenue opportunities, such as budget or economy-service hotels. RevPAG may also produce somewhat distorted results for hotels with frequent short guest stays. In addition, since RevPAG is dependent upon the number of guests, it is difficult to use when making comparisons with other hotels, especially when double-occupancy percentages can vary significantly between similar properties.

GOPPAR has two major drawbacks. First, it is difficult to recognize as an industry-wide metric, since hotel profitability information tends to be proprietary and confidential. Whereas hotels are willing to provide average daily rate and occupancy statistics to neutral sources (such as Smith Travel Research), hotels consider operating profit data differently: usually only top-level managers and property owners are privy to profitability information. Second, GOPPAR is not timely; it may take up to one month after the close of business to calculate GOPPAR for an accounting period. Hotel management may prefer a metric that produces timelier results.

Elements of Revenue Management

The fact that flexible room rates affect both the number of guests and associated revenue transactions helps demonstrate the potential complexities of revenue management. Focusing attention only on room revenue potential may not present management with a comprehensive overview.

Revenue management becomes even more complex when room rate discounting is granted on a selective rather than general basis, and when it involves selling rooms for which there may be competing buyers. Hotels frequently offer discounts to certain categories of guests (for example, senior citizens and government employees). Hotels must also decide whether to accept or refuse group business at a discounted room rate. This section discusses various situations that can arise when hotels base their booking decisions on revenue management.

The following elements must be included in the development of a successful revenue management strategy:

- Group room sales
- Transient room sales
- Other revenue opportunities
- Local and area-wide activities
- Special events

One of the most important issues to understand about revenue management is that the practice changes from property to property. It may also change from season to season within a property, due to sources of business, competition, and other issues. However, there are certain elements important to developing basic revenue management skills.

Group Room Sales

In many hotels, groups form the nucleus of room revenue. It is common for hotels to receive reservations for group sales from three months to two years in advance of arrival. Some international business hotels and popular resorts commonly book groups more than two years in advance. Therefore, understanding group booking trends and requirements can be critical to the success of revenue management.

Sales and catering managers are in constant contact with new and existing clients. When a request comes in, the sales or catering manager must carefully research and document what the client is requesting. Then, the information is presented to the hotel's revenue meeting for consideration. Questions to be asked before a decision is made include:

- Does the group request fit into the hotel's strategy for the period? For example, the group requires 100 rooms, but that number will exceed the group allocation for the period.
- Are there other groups who are interested in the same period?
- What meeting space will the group require? Is it proportionate to the contracted number of guestrooms?
- What impact will this group have on booking additional group business for the same dates?
- What is the group willing to pay in room rate?
- Do the food and beverage functions include catered events or will the group use the hotel's restaurants?
- What revenue can the hotel plan to earn for rooms, food and beverage, and other sources?

To understand the potential impact of group sales on overall room revenue, the hotel should collect as much group profile information as possible, including:

- Group booking data
- Group booking pace
- Anticipated group business
- Group booking lead time
- Displacement of transient business

Group Booking Data. Management should determine whether the group blocks already recorded in the reservation file should be modified because of anticipated cancellations, historical overestimation of the number of rooms needed, or greater demand than originally anticipated by the group leader. If the group has a previous business profile, management can often adjust expectations by reviewing the group's booking history. Groups tend to block 5 to 10 percent more rooms than they are likely to need, in optimistic anticipation of the number of attendees. The hotel's deletion of unnecessary group rooms from a group block is called the **wash factor.** Management must be careful in estimating how many rooms should be "washed" from the block. If a group block is reduced by too many rooms, the hotel may find itself overbooked and unable to accommodate all of the members of the group.

Group Booking Pace. The rate at which group business is being booked is called the **group booking pace.** ("Booking" in this context refers to the initial agreement between the group and the hotel, not to the specific assignment of individual rooms in the block to group members.[4]) For example, suppose that in April of a given year, a hotel has 300 rooms in group blocks it is holding for scheduled functions in October of the same year. If the hotel had only 250 group rooms booked for October at the same time the year before, the booking pace would be 20 percent ahead of the previous year's pace. Once a hotel has accumulated several years of group booking data, it can often identify a historical trend that reveals a normal booking pace for each month of the year. Although this forecasting process appears simple, it can become very complicated due to unanticipated fluctuations, such as a one-time, city-wide convention. These variations should be noted so that they can be recognized in future booking pace forecasting. Management should strive to maintain a straightforward method for tracking group booking pace. Booking pace can be an invaluable forecasting variable.

Anticipated Group Business. Most national, regional, and state associations, as well as some corporations, have policies governing the locations of annual meetings. For example, a group may rotate its meeting location among three cities, returning to each every three years. Although a contract may not yet be signed, hotel management may be confident that the group will return according to the cycle. Of course, a group may not always return to the same hotel in the area. However, even when it goes to other hotels, the group may displace other group and non-group business that will need to find alternate accommodations in the area. The hotel analyzing these data can then forecast the "pressure" in the market and adjust its selling strategies accordingly. In addition, tentative bookings that await final contract negotiations should be included in the revenue management analysis.

Group Booking Lead Time. Booking lead time measures how far in advance of a stay bookings are made. Corporate group bookings tend to be smaller than association meetings and are often made within a year of the planned event. Larger association meetings may book two to five years in advance to ensure the availability of the required guestrooms and meeting space. Management should determine its hotel's lead time for group bookings so that booking trends can be charted. Booking trends can be combined with booking pace information to illustrate the rate at which the hotel is booking group business compared with historical trends (see Exhibit 3). This information can be very important when determining whether to accept an additional group and at what room rate to book the new group. If the current booking pace is lower than expected or lags behind the historical trend, it may be necessary to offer a lower room rate to stimulate increased occupancy. On the other hand, if demand is strong and the group booking pace is ahead of anticipated or historical trends, it may not be appropriate to discount room rates. Catering sales must also be taken into consideration when looking at booking lead times. For example, weddings are often planned a year or more in advance. If the catering department receives a request for the hotel ballroom a year in advance, management must decide to accept the catering request and potentially block group business, or hold out for the possibility that eventually a group will take guestrooms as well as the ballroom on the date in question. The group booking may never come, and, if the hotel turns down the catering business, the guestrooms and ballroom will be empty.

Displacement of Transient Business. Management should consult its demand forecast when determining whether or not to accept additional group business. **Displacement** occurs when a hotel accepts group business at the expense of transient guests. Since transient guests often pay higher room rates than group members and may be more likely to use hotel dining rooms, this situation warrants

Exhibit 3 Lead Time/Booking Pace for Sample Hotel

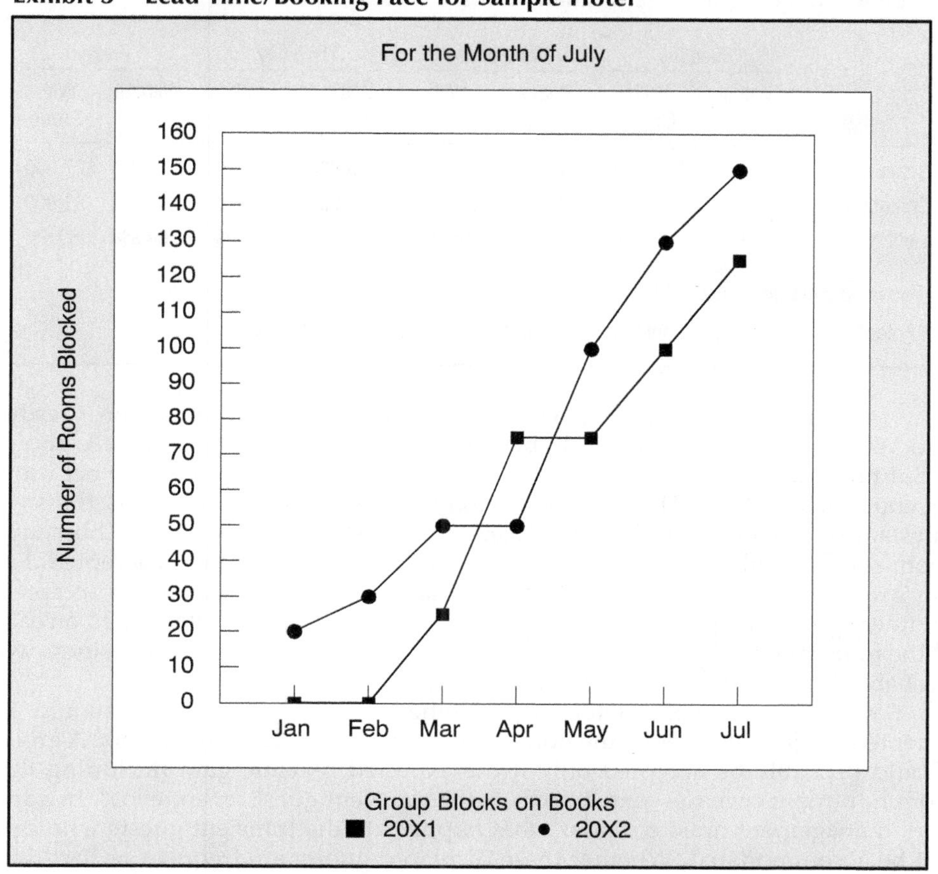

close scrutiny. Transient rooms are guestrooms sold to guests who are not affiliated with a group registered with the hotel. A non-group guest may also be called a free independent traveler, or FIT.

Assume that the 400-room Halbrook Lodge has a potential average rate of $100, an actual average transient rate of $80, an actual average group rate of $60, and a marginal cost of $15 per occupied room. Consider the impact of a proposed group block of sixty rooms during an upcoming four-day period:

	Tuesday	Wednesday	Thursday	Friday
Rooms Available	400	400	400	400
Definite Groups Booked	140	140	150	150
Expected Transient Demand	200	180	220	210
Available Rooms	60	80	30	40
Proposed Group Block	60	60	60	60
Transient Displacement	0	0	30	20

Exhibit 4 Revenue and Yield Calculations

	Tuesday		Wednesday		Thursday		Friday	
	Without Group	With Group	Without Group	With Group	Without Group	With Group	Without Group	With Group
Gross revenue	$24,400	$28,000	$22,800	$26,400	$26,600	$27,800	$25,800	$27,800
Contribution*	19,300	22,000	18,000	20,700	21,050	21,800	20,400	21,800
Yield**	61.0%	70.0%	57.0%	66.0%	66.5%	69.5%	64.5%	69.5%

*Based on a marginal cost of $15.

**Potential revenue = $100 potential average rate × 400 rooms = $40,000.

If the proposed group block is accepted, no displacement occurs on Tuesday and Wednesday; the hotel clearly benefits on these days because it sells rooms it did not expect to sell (earning an additional $3,600 gross and $2,700 net room revenue each day). On Thursday and Friday, however, thirty and twenty transient guests, respectively, would be displaced. Still, as shown in Exhibit 4, Thursday's room revenue will rise by $1,200 gross and $750 net if the group is accepted. Friday's room revenue will rise by $2,000 gross and $1,400 net if the group is accepted. In other words, accepting the group business will increase the hotel's yield on each of the four days. Since it also raises the hotel's occupancy, this group's business will probably increase non-room revenue as well.

Several factors help determine whether a group reservation should be accepted. As just illustrated, the hotel should first look at revenue factors. A group should probably be accepted only if the expected revenue gain (including that from non-room revenue centers) offsets the transient guest revenue loss. In addition, management must consider what happens to the transient guests who cannot be accommodated. Whether these displaced guests are frequent or first-time guests, they may decide not to return to a hotel that has turned them away. The transient revenue lost may not be confined simply to the nights in question, especially when frequent guests choose not to return. Of course, turning away potential group business may also reduce future business.

Another situation in which the transient revenue lost may not be confined simply to the nights in question occurs when a non-group guest wishing to come in on Tuesday for three nights will be turned away if the group is taken. Even though the group is displacing actual non-group rooms on Thursday because of lack of inventory, it is affecting Tuesday and Wednesday as well.

Deciding whether to accept a group that forces transient displacement is an issue that deserves careful consideration. Management must consider the long-term impact on future business.

Keeping track of a group's history can help re-allocate group rooms to transient when those rooms may not be needed. As mentioned earlier, most groups overestimate the number of rooms they need by about 5 to 10 percent. That percentage is called the wash factor. By knowing each group's wash factor, a manager can safely release the excess rooms from the block. If a group's block is reduced by too many rooms, the property may find itself oversold and unable to accommodate all of the guests. If the group doesn't have a history with the property, a manager might contact other hotels where the group has previously stayed to try to determine its wash factor.

Dynamic Packaging. One of the most creative aspects of revenue management is the customization of a travel package according to a specific guest's needs. This practice is termed **dynamic packaging.** Although hotel sales representatives have offered packages to travelers for years, through travel agents, the Internet, and direct selling, these efforts have simply involved the bundling of existing services into a single package. Such deals were considered static packaging, since no personalization or customization was involved, and the deals often failed to meet the traveler's specific needs. Static packages might include a basic guestroom, parking fee, and dinner certificate for the hotel's dining room. A golf package might include one or two rounds of golf. Static packages often came with many associated restrictions, such as limited length of stay and limited day of arrival. Perhaps most important, static packages allowed no substitutions. For example, all guests would receive a dining certificate even when they did not want to dine at the hotel restaurant, since the certificate was part of the bundled services offered for a package rate. Hence, the guests would have had to pay for something they did not intend to use.

Dynamic packaging addresses the issue of preferred contents. Guests can use an Internet booking engine such as a hotel brand website, property website, select airline website, or a third-party travel website to create a custom (dynamic) package. The custom package can include only those services and amenities the guest desires. Dynamic packaging has been shown to increase the perceived value of a hotel package and to be more satisfying for the traveler. Dynamic packages may include airline tickets, hotel guestrooms, car rental agreements, recreational activities, sporting events, dining certificates, spa offerings, entertainment tickets, and other hospitality-related components. Hotels participating in online dynamic packaging offer hotel rooms at specific rates for a series of dates to Internet website representatives. Hotels usually find dynamic packaging especially effective during anticipated periods of low occupancy. By offering special deals then, hotels have a better chance of promoting business, since a customized travel package will have components designed to simplify the booking process. Hotels typically control the number of guestrooms available for dynamic packaging, so that, as occupancy increases, the hotels can either increase the available room rates or withdraw rooms from remaining available inventory previously committed to the packaging program.

Dynamic packaging also offers the opportunity for upselling. For example, a hotel may offer a standard guestroom as part of a basic package. Upselling the guest to a deluxe guestroom may be one of the alternate components available to the traveler. Upselling can effectively produce additional revenue for the hotel without its incurring significant additional expense.

Transient Room Sales

As mentioned earlier, transient rooms are those rooms sold to non-group travelers. Transient business is usually booked closer to the date of arrival than group business. A commercial hotel may book a majority of its group business three to six months before arrival, but transient business only one to three weeks before arrival. At a resort hotel, group bookings may be established one to two years in advance, while transient business may be booked three months in advance. As with group business, management must monitor the booking pace and lead time of transient business to understand how current reservations compare with historical and anticipated rates. This leads to the more complex subject of transient room rate discounting.

In a previous example, room rates were set by bed type and number in inventory. However, in today's market there may be many other reasons to price rooms differently. To maximize room revenue, front office managers may decide to classify rooms by location, desirability, or size, and charge a premium for better rooms. For example, rooms that are smaller, near noisy corridors, or unrenovated, or that offer less desirable views are likely to be offered at lower rates. Therefore, these rooms may be classified as standard and be assigned a lower room rate. More desirable rooms may be classified as deluxe and be assigned higher room rates.

To build business, hotels may offer deluxe rooms at standard rates to attract guests. This is especially true in times of low demand. Then, as demand improves to a predetermined threshold, any remaining deluxe rooms can be offered at or near full rack rate. Under this strategy, management attempts to maximize room revenue, not just average room rate or occupancy percentage. The reasoning is that lower demand creates a more competitive situation for the hotel. Discounting may reduce the amount of business lost because of rate resistance and allows the hotel to sell rooms that might otherwise remain vacant. An astute manager must know when to eliminate room rate discounts. If room rates are increased too soon, occupancy may be lost. If room rates are increased too late, some rooms may be sold for less than they could have been sold for. When discounting a deluxe room to a standard rate, the reservation or front desk agent should tell the guest that he or she is being upgraded. This will add perceived value to the guest's stay. It also reduces the confusion on the part of the guest the next time he or she comes to the hotel and is quoted a higher rate.

Managers must also consider the ethics of revenue management when choosing strategies. If a guestroom is classified as standard, there is usually a very good reason for it. Therefore, it would appear unethical to sell the room at a rate higher than its rack rate just because someone may be willing to pay the higher rate. Even though demand may provide the opportunity for a higher rate, charging the rate just because the market will accept it for the period is not always a good business practice. Some hotels have done this and received criticism from the market for doing it. This is one reason many states require that room rates be posted in each room.

Another issue to consider in transient room sales is the discounting offered to certain sources of business. Discounts can be offered to corporate and government travelers, as well as senior citizens, military and airline personnel, travel agents, and others. Quite often, these discounts apply to a substantial portion of a hotel's business. Some hotel companies are following the lead of airlines by offering discounts to guests booking through the Internet. Their justification for these discounts is that there are lower costs associated with Internet reservations.

These savings are being passed along to the consumer. However, this practice is still maturing and it will take time for the traveling public and hotel management to understand the impact of this type of discounting. For example, several hotel brands offer a best-rate guarantee at their own website, thus reducing the impact of discount sites that book guestrooms at significant reductions. At least one hotel company has taken this issue very seriously. It has notified its franchisees that offering discount rates below the company's rate guidelines may jeopardize their franchise arrangement with the company.

Controlling discounts is crucial to producing an optimal yield. For example, if a hotel has very few rooms reserved over a holiday period, it may open all discounts to callers just to attract business. As demand builds over the period, the discounts may be selectively closed. When the front office manager believes that rooms can be sold at a higher rate without an offsetting loss in occupancy, the discount should be closed. Some discounts cannot be closed off. Whenever possible, contracts for discounts should provide for flexibility when business conditions warrant.

Other Revenue Opportunities

Revenue management decisions for hotels that offer additional revenue outlets (non-room revenues) involve more than what to charge as an appropriate room rate. A hotel that offers meeting and banquet space, recreational facilities, spas, and other revenue centers gives guests many more opportunities to consider and gives management more revenue opportunities to evaluate. Negotiations with meeting and wedding planners focus on the total package of meeting space, banquet service, audiovisual equipment rentals, and the like, not solely on guestroom rates. A revenue management analysis must consider all revenue opportunities affecting potential profitability to determine the economic value of the total business to the hotel. Only after such analysis can management calculate a meaningful room rate.

While banquet functions generate food and beverage revenues, they might also affect guestroom revenues. For example, if a banquet with no associated guestrooms is scheduled to occupy the hotel's grand ballroom on New Year's Eve, another group wishing to use fifty guestrooms *and* the grand ballroom may have to be turned away. In most instances, the group requiring both catering and guestroom space will produce more profit for the hotel; therefore, the hotel must view the group in light of its potential contribution to hotel operations. Cooperation and communication between hotel departments is important to effectively execute a revenue management program.

When considering what rates to charge people attending a meeting at the hotel, management should consider all revenue opportunities, as well as the profitability each of those opportunities would provide. For example, guestrooms may contribute a 75 percent departmental profit margin; banquet meals, a 30 percent profit margin; meeting room rental, a 90 percent profit margin; and audiovisual rentals, a 60 percent profit margin. To determine the price to charge attendees needing a guestroom, meeting space, banquet service, and audiovisual rentals, managers should determine the potential revenue (or profit margin) for each affected department. Managers can easily accomplish this with spreadsheet software or a revenue management software application. Once the potential revenue resulting from the business has been calculated, it should be compared to the hotel's budget for the time period. If the meeting's revenue (or profit margin) exceeds the budget amount, a favorable decision is appropriate, and managers should develop a written agreement with the meeting planners.

Meeting planners may request concessions from hotel management in consideration of the meeting. A concession is some sort of improved value for the meeting. Concessions include items that would lower the expense of the meeting from the planner's perspective. Concessions made in negotiations may include the cost of meeting space and/or reductions in all aspects of the meeting. Suppose a meeting planner requests a VIP suite for the meeting's leader at no cost to the leader or group; this concession reduces the cost of the meeting from the planner's perspective but ignores the reduction in revenues for the hotel. Other concession items may involve reduced guestroom rates, as well as discounts on meeting room rental, food and beverage pricing, and audiovisual rental. The meeting planner may also request that complimentary items, such as daily decorative flowers or a wine and cheese tray, be placed in the VIP suite.

Concessions represent a loss in revenue or an increase in expense to the hotel, thereby reducing the overall value of the meeting. All such low- or no-cost items must be individually negotiated before the hotel determines a fair value for the meeting.

Many hotels will not accept banquet-only business during a projected high-demand period until the group's banquet-only booking date draws near. However, if the hotel's room sales history indicates low occupancy demand for a date such as New Year's Eve, the hotel might allow the sales department to book the banquet-only business well in advance.

Local and Area-Wide Activities

Local and area-wide activities can have dramatic effects on a hotel's revenue management strategies. Even when a hotel is not in the immediate vicinity of a convention, transient guests and smaller groups displaced by the convention may be referred to the hotel (as an overflow facility). When this occurs, the front office manager should be aware of the convention and the demand for guestrooms it has created. (Most local convention and visitors bureaus regularly publish information about large groups who book in the area.) If the demand is substantial, transient and group rates may need to be adjusted.

Convention business may render a trend analysis of group and transient activity invalid. If the booking pace of either group or transient rooms sales is significantly altered, the front office manager should immediately investigate. An increase in demand could indicate a convention in the area or a large booking at another property. A decrease in demand could indicate a major group cancellation at a competing property, which is now reducing its regular pricing to fill its guestrooms.

Ethics and good business practice should play an integral part in a yield strategy or tactic. It is appropriate and legal for competitors to occasionally meet and discuss general business trends. However, it is *not* legal to discuss room rates or the establishment (fixing) of room rates. There may also be additional sources of information that identify what is affecting business in the area. For example, most visitor and convention bureaus publish a list of meetings in their areas. Under no circumstances should employees of two different hotels discuss rate structuring or any other hotel operating issue, since such activity might be considered a violation of anti-trust laws in the United States.

Special Events

Quite often, special events such as holiday celebrations, concerts, festivals, and sporting events are held in or near a hotel. The hotel may be able to take advantage of such demand-enhancing activities by restricting room rate discounts or requiring a minimum length of stay. This is a common practice—for example, during the Christmas holidays at many Southern resorts. Guests wishing to stay over Christmas may be required to guarantee a four- or five-night minimum stay. Similarly, room discounts were eliminated during the 1996 Summer Olympic Games in Atlanta, Georgia, due to high demand and limited availability. Minimum stays were also required. These are all sound revenue management tactics, but they must be managed carefully so the hotel does not alienate frequent travelers.

Fair Market Share Forecasting

One of the other important elements of revenue management is understanding how well the hotel is doing in relation to the competition. This is known as the **fair market share**. It is important to know whether the rates being quoted are competitive and whether the hotel is actually getting its fair share of the available business in a market.

A primary tool for this analysis is the Smith Travel Accommodations Report, or STAR report. The STAR report is historical, so the information it provides tells hotel management how well their revenue management strategies and tactics worked in the past. By reviewing the past, however, management can make key decisions on how the hotel should be positioned in the future. The key statistic in the STAR report is the RevPAR Index. This statistic tells hotel management whether the property received its fair share of the business for the period reported compared to its competition or competitive set. For example, if a property had a 100 percent RevPAR Index, it would have received its fair share of business for the market. Keep in mind that RevPAR takes both occupancy and average daily rate into consideration. If a hotel received a score of 105 percent, it would have actually achieved more than its fair market share for the period. A score of 90 percent, on the other hand, would indicate that the hotel's competitive set did better for the period. It is important to note that, since RevPAR takes both occupancy and rate into consideration, a hotel may have a lower rate of occupancy than its competition but still have a higher RevPAR Index, because it maintained a higher average daily rate.

This information should be analyzed whenever the STAR report arrives, but also used for forecasting the next several months and the same period next year. For example, most hotels have peak and off-peak seasons. Management usually finds it convenient to classify each month into a business season. The STAR report can be used to position rates for a coming month, or develop next year's budget, by season. It may show opportunities for rate improvement or provide an indication of necessary rate repositioning. For example, management may look at the STAR report for the last two years and identify that their RevPAR Index for June has been over 105 percent. That could be an indication that they can continue to command higher rates during the month because of high demand. However, the STAR report should not be the only source of information on which to base decisions. For example, if another 300-room hotel is expected to open before June of next year, it may be more difficult holding or increasing rates because there will be more competition in the market.

While the STAR report is very valuable, it relies on hotels themselves to convey important statistics to the report producer. Since the data collection necessary to generate a comprehensive report is time-consuming, the STAR report tends to be somewhat historical in nature. For this reason, it may not accurately reflect the success of a hotel's revenue strategies in the short term. Hotels may experience a one- to two-month delay in performance due to variable market factors. Many industry observers consider the STAR report a solid basis for trend analysis, since it normally aggregates three months or more for each reporting period. Longer-term reports tend to provide a better indication of revenue management successes. Other trade resources are available to managers formulating revenue management strategies and tactics. For example, TravelCLICK produces a series of reports, including Hotelligence, Internet Hotelligence, and RateVIEW/Phaser. These reports are based on information collected from a diverse set of sources, including global distribution systems and Internet booking engines, and are considered forward-looking, since they are built on actual reservation transaction data.

The Revenue Manager

The duties of the revenue manager make this position among the most important to the hotel's financial success. A revenue manager can often mean the difference between a struggling hotel and a profitable hotel. Although much of this chapter's discussion of revenue management has concentrated on guestroom revenues, most large hotels include non-room revenue opportunities in the analysis. For example, when considering what rates to apply to a group, the revenue manager typically considers the total revenue projection for the group (rooms, food and beverage, audiovisual rentals, and other ancillary revenue) in a final rate quotation. The revenue manager must have an overview of the entire hotel's revenue structure and the guests who make up the majority of the business.

When a hotel wishes to hire a revenue manager, it is best to start with a job description. Job descriptions vary among different types of hotels. For example, a limited-service downtown hotel would likely prepare a job description that is different from a similarly sized property located in a suburban area near an interstate highway.

A successful hotel revenue manager typically possesses many of the following skills:

- *Operational skills:* A revenue manager must have had experience in one or more revenue-generating hotel departments. He or she must understand sources of revenues and associated cost structures for each operating department, and must be aware of the interdependencies among departments to meet hotel goals.

- *Analytical skills:* A revenue manager must understand historical, current, and future revenue data. He or she must be able to evaluate hotel booking trends and to project occupancy demands when determining pricing strategies that ensure a balance between room rates and levels of occupancy.
- *Strategic skills:* The revenue manager must understand what is going on in the market and how market forces are likely to affect the hotel. The revenue manager must then apply those assessments to take advantage of favorable market conditions.
- *Organizing skills:* A revenue manager must maintain detailed records of current operations in order to develop a database of information for future application.
- *Communications skills:* A revenue manager must be able to explain revenue processes and decisions with respect to short-term and long-term business projections.
- *Good listening skills:* The revenue manager must be able to listen to revenue management team members, hotel department heads, and other staff. He or she needs to appreciate issues that others raise and suggestions they make.
- *Team-building skills:* A revenue manager must work to build consensus among the revenue management team and hotel department heads and staff. Effective revenue management strategies and tactics depend on the revenue manager's ability to build and maintain trust and confidence in working relationships.
- *Training skills:* Successful revenue management requires ongoing training of all those involved in the process. The revenue manager must be able to train staff at all levels of the organization, including the general manager, the front office manager, sales managers, the food and beverage manager, the reservations manager, the banquet manager, and others actively involved in the program.

In addition, the successful hotel revenue manager has the following personal qualities:

- *Patience:* He or she must make many revenue management decisions three, six, and twelve months or more before the dates they actually affect. A revenue manager must be patient and not change strategies too quickly in reaction to unforeseen changes in hotel or market conditions. The successful revenue manager will also be patient with staff members as they learn how revenue management works and the roles they play in successfully implementing revenue management programs.
- *Creativity:* A revenue manager always looks for new data sources and ways to implement revenue management techniques.
- *Cooperativeness:* The revenue manager must be insightful and able to solicit information from department heads and other staff. The department

managers who work most closely with the revenue manager are more likely to understand and support strategies and tactics they help create and implement.

- *Flexibility:* A revenue manager must be willing to change strategies and tactics as demand changes.

Using Revenue Management

The Revenue Meeting

Revenue management is an ongoing process. Whether the property is experiencing high demand or low demand, revenue management has a role and is part of the hotel's overall approach to business. Many hotels find it very useful to have a regular revenue meeting to share important business information and make appropriate revenue management decisions.

A common mistake is to consider revenue management a short-term process. Some managers try to make decisions within a few weeks of the arrival date. In fact, this is the opposite of what should be done. Successful revenue management looks months or years into the future, tracking business trends and guest demand. This is especially true of group-oriented hotels that have the majority of their rooms in their group allocation. These hotels usually book groups well into the future, so their revenue management decisions have impact well into the future as well. While changing rates within a few weeks of arrival in these hotels may improve ADR or RevPAR, the real impact is made when the group is booked and the rates are confirmed.

Because a property's staff members are essential to the success of revenue management efforts, they will want to meet as part of a revenue management team. This team usually includes representatives from key areas of the property. The general manager, all the sales managers and catering managers, and the reservations manager generally attend the revenue meeting as part of the revenue management team. If the hotel has a dedicated revenue manager, that person is also a regular attendee. Other managers may be invited to attend as needed. For example, the hotel controller may attend periodically to report on month-end results or special issues that the revenue meeting should address. The front office manager and food and beverage manager or catering manager may also be invited, as some decisions may need their involvement. Exhibit 5 lists ways that the revenue management team can encourage the entire staff to be involved in revenue management.

The team acts as satellite agents for implementing a revenue management plan. They can help a property determine whether past forecasts were accurate and may alert the revenue manager to significant patterns in group or transient behavior. The team can develop action plans for interdepartmental communication. With accurate forecasts in hand, all departments can prepare for the days ahead:

- Knowing how many guests are in-house can help food and beverage prepare
- Rate changes and adaptations in selling strategy affect the sales department

Exhibit 5 Getting the Staff Involved in Revenue Management

Here are some ideas for getting your staff involved in revenue management:

- Create a sense of competition. Show staff members the various forms and reports, such as TIMS or STAR. Let them know how your competition is doing and encourage them to exceed your biggest competitors.
- Post measurable, specific goals such as budgets or occupancy data. Staff members need to know exactly what is expected of them, so make sure the goals are challenging yet attainable.
- Show staff members how much they each affect the bottom line. Staff members who understand their role in the organization and the impact they have are more likely to support your efforts.
- Provide incentives or recognition for goal attainment. Seek and provide feedback on good work and follow up when goals aren't met. Coach staff members to correct problems.
- Train your staff. Simply telling them what you want them to do isn't enough. Take the time to show them *exactly* what you expect from them. Follow up continuously to make sure standards are being met.

- Occupancy percentages will affect housekeeping and uniformed services

The revenue management team may meet daily, weekly, and monthly. Daily meetings typically last only fifteen or so minutes. During the daily meeting, the team:

- Reviews the three-day forecast and makes sure that previously agreed-upon strategies and tactics are still in place. These strategies and tactics are then communicated to the staffs at the reservations office, central reservations office, and front desk.
- Reviews the previous day's (or weekend's) occupancy, room revenue, ADR, and yield statistic. These numbers are customarily available through night audit reporting. If there are variances from the forecast, they should be briefly discussed so that everyone understands what the differences are.
- Reviews the booking pace for near-term business (usually within three months). The revenue meeting attendees need to know whether the hotel is where it should be in the number of rooms and rooms revenue. The booking pace is compared to the day-to-day increase of business the hotel has planned. If the hotel is below the pace, there is a problem and action steps must be taken to build business. If the pace is above the plan, the hotel may have additional revenue opportunities to consider. Most commercial hotels do not have a lot of transient business on the books months in advance. In these properties, the booking pace is really concerned with group business. However, resorts may have strong transient demand months in advance. For instance, ski resorts and warm-weather resorts may track the booking pace of Christmas season packages sold to transient guests. The group booking pace may be checked weekly or less frequently for business further into the future.

- Reviews old business. In some cases, more research is necessary before a revenue decision can be made. For instance, group history may not be immediately available, the reservation pick-up of a city-wide convention may need to be checked, and a group's flexibility on meeting dates or its exact meeting room requirements may need to be checked before decisions can be made.
- Presents new business. There are two elements to new business: transient and group business. Transient business changes daily, especially within a week of arrival. This is true of all hotels. Because of this, the reservations manager must monitor transient demand closely and should present important changes during the revenue meeting. For instance, a hotel may expect to have 75-percent occupancy one week into the future, and transient demand has already driven occupancy above that forecast. The revenue meeting attendees need to know that, so they can review rates and other strategies. This should not be a reactive process. Plans should be set *in advance* for each day management believes an opportunity may arise to change rates. For example, suppose management believes that when a hotel reaches 90-percent occupancy, it should sell only rack rates. If a hotel is at 88-percent occupancy five days out, the reservations manager and front office manager should receive clear instructions at the revenue meeting about what to do when occupancy reaches 90 percent. The rate change should not have to wait for the revenue meeting the next day. At the same time, if last-minute cancellations take occupancy below 90 percent, the reservations manager should be able to offer selected discounts without having to wait for the next meeting.
- Discusses any last-minute adjustments that need to be made.
- Determines what information must be circulated as part of the interdepartmental communication plan.
- Reviews the 30–60 day outlook and communicates any updates in those forecasts.
- Reviews current channel distribution strategies.

At weekly meetings, the team might meet for an hour to:

- Review forecasts for 30, 60, 90, and 120 days out.
- Discuss strategies for upcoming critical periods.

At monthly meetings, members of the revenue management team discuss issues that affect the big picture. They might look specifically at slow months and determine what efforts might boost sales, such as additional marketing, appeals to locals, or special sales force deployment. They would also review the ongoing annual forecast. Some teams also use monthly meetings to provide any necessary training on revenue management skills.

All elements of revenue management should be viewed together when making a decision. While the process is potentially complex, a failure to include relevant factors may render revenue management efforts less than completely successful.

Yield statistics should be tracked daily. Tracking yield statistics for an extended period of time can help managers recognize trends. However, to use revenue management properly, management must track yield statistics for *future* days. Future period calculations must be done every business day, depending on how far in advance the hotel books its business. If a hotel is currently at 50-percent yield for a day three weeks away, there may be plenty of time to put strategies in place to increase the projected level of yield. Discounts may be opened to raise occupancy, or closed to raise average rate. If achieving full potential room revenue is not possible (and it usually is not), the front office manager must decide on the best combination of rate and occupancy.

Each sales contract for group business should be reviewed individually. Contracts should be compared with historical trends as well as with budgets. Sales managers are expected to make a group rate recommendation for each group proposal they bring to the meeting. This rate recommendation needs to be compared to the budget and perhaps forecast. If it meets or exceeds the hotel's objectives for the period, there is usually little discussion. However, if the proposed rates fall below expectations, there must be a good reason. A hotel usually has a group sales target or budgeted figure for each month. Each group should be examined to see if it will contribute to meeting the overall profit budget. For example, one group may have a guestroom rate that falls below the budgeted room rate, but its food and beverage functions will bring its total profitability in line with the budget. If current transient demand is strong and the group will produce only minimal revenue, the hotel might consider not booking it. If demand is weak, the hotel may decide to accept the group simply to create revenue by selling rooms that would not otherwise be sold. Using group booking pace analyses will help management determine whether the hotel is on track to reach its target.

Another factor is the actual group booking pattern already on the books. For example, a hotel may have two days between groups that are not busy. Management may solicit a lower-revenue-generating group to fill the gap. The opposite may also occur. A group may desire space during a period when the hotel is close to filling its group rooms goal. Adding the group may move group sales above the hotel's goal. While this appears to be favorable, it may displace higher-rated transient business. If the group wants the hotel, it may need to be quoted a higher-than-normal group rate to help make up for the revenue lost through the displacement of transient guests.

The same type of analysis is required for transient business. For example, due to the discounts the hotel offers, corporate and government business may be assigned the standard category of rooms. As these standard rooms fill, the hotel may have only deluxe rooms left to sell. If demand is not strong, management may decide to sell the deluxe rooms at the standard rack rate to remain competitive. It is best to look at a combination of group and transient business before making firm occupancy and rate decisions.

Since the objective of revenue management is to maximize revenue, tracking business by revenue source helps determine when to allow discounted room rates. As various sources of business are identified, each should be analyzed to understand its impact on total revenue. Quite often, front office managers will authorize discounted room rates for groups if the groups have the potential to generate repeat customers.

Potential High- and Low-Demand Tactics

Hotels need to determine revenue management strategies for both high- and low-demand periods. During times of high demand, the normal technique is to increase room revenue by maximizing average room rate. Transient and group business market segments may each require a unique, specific strategy.

The following are some transient business tactics used during high-demand periods:

- Try to determine the right mix of market segments in order to sell out at the highest possible room rates. This strategy is highly dependent upon accurate sales mix forecasting.
- Monitor new business bookings, and use these changed conditions to reassign room inventory. Certain inventory may be assigned to specific market segments. For example, standard rooms may be assigned to travelers who have reservations with deep rate discounts. As occupancy begins to climb, consider closing out low room rates and charging rack rates only for the remaining inventory of standard rooms. Management should be prepared to re-open lower room rates should demand begin to slack off. Management must closely monitor demand and be flexible in adjusting room rates. It is important to note here that rooms can always be sold for less than their posted rack rate. However, it is unethical to sell them for more than their posted rack rate.
- Consider establishing a minimum number of nights per stay. For example, a resort that always fills to capacity during a national holiday weekend may consider requiring a three-day minimum stay in order to better control occupancy fluctuation.

A number of group business tactics may be appropriate during high-demand periods. When deciding between two or more competing groups, for example, management should select the group that produces the highest total revenue. Management must rely on its experience with groups to develop sound revenue management policies.

Given the focus on total revenue, it may be wise to sell blocks of guestrooms to groups that also book meeting space, food and beverage service, and hospitality suites. A group that books ancillary space and services is likely to spend more time and money in the hotel. This tactic usually requires restricting the access of local patrons to function, meeting, and public spaces; if local patrons book these spaces, potentially more-profitable groups needing such space may be forced to go elsewhere. Another tactic is to offer price-sensitive groups dates when the hotel's occupancy is expected to be low. Most group contracts are written today so that group dates cannot be changed without the group leader's agreement. Exhibit 6 offers some additional high-demand tactics that a hotel can use, while Exhibit 7 lists tactics for excess-demand periods.

The underlying strategy for transient and group business during low-demand periods is to increase revenue by maximizing occupancy. Front office managers may find the following business tactics helpful:

Exhibit 6 High-Demand Tactics

1. **Close or restrict discounts.**
   Analyze discounts and restrict them as necessary to maximize the average rate. You may offer discounts for those who book longer stays, or restrict bookings to shorter stays.
2. **Apply minimum length of stay restrictions carefully.**
   A minimum length of stay restriction can help a property increase room nights. For groups, study the groups' patterns and decide how many days they are likely to add to their stay.
3. **Reduce group room allocations.**
   Communicate with group leaders on a regular basis. Make sure the group actually needs the number of rooms identified in its contract. If not, make adjustments.
4. **Reduce or eliminate 6 P.M. holds.**
   Reduce or eliminate the number of unpaid rooms that are being held until 6 P.M. When demand is high, you will need rooms to be available for sale.
5. **Tighten guarantee and cancellation policies.**
   Tightening guarantee and cancellation policies helps to ensure payment for room nights. Charge payment cards for the first night's stay on the day the reservation is made.
6. **Raise rates to be consistent with competitors.**
   Charge rates consistent with the competition, but limit rate increases to those rates published in the central reservations system and listed in brochures for the period.
7. **Consider a rate raise for packages.**
   If you're already offering a package discount, consider raising the rate for that package.
8. **Apply full price to suites and executive rooms.**
   In a high-demand situation, charge full price for suites and executive rooms.
9. **Select close to arrival dates.**
   By allowing reservations to be taken for a certain date as long as the guest arrives before that date, a property is able to control the volume of check-ins. It is important to track and monitor denials that occur due to this restriction.
10. **Evaluate the benefits of sell-throughs.**
    With a sell-through, the required stay can begin before the date the strategy is applied. This is often used when one day has a peak in occupancy and management does not want the peak to adversely affect reservations on either side of the peak day.
11. **Apply deposits and guarantees to the last night of stay.**
    For longer lengths of stay, make sure the deposits and guarantees apply to the last night of the stay, minimizing early departures.

- Carefully design a flexible rating system that permits sales agents to offer lower rates in certain situations. Such rates should be determined early in the planning process in anticipation of low-demand periods.
- Ensure that all Internet distribution channels have current rates and availability dates. In some cases, it may be beneficial to improve the listing in Internet

Exhibit 7 Excess Demand Tactics

Apply high-demand tactics.

In an excess demand situation, where demand may exceed availability, it is important to consider all restrictions normally employed during a high-demand situation.

Understand the cause of excess demand.

Find out exactly what is causing excess demand. Ask questions such as:

- Is it a one-day or multi-day event?
- What type of event is it? What is the guest make-up?
- What other properties are likely to sell out due to the event?
- Is the demand local or for a larger area?
- Are the potential guests likely to accept a minimum length of stay requirement or other stay restrictions?

Answers to these questions will help determine the best strategy to apply.

Examples:

- If you find out that the demand is due to a two-day event, you may consider a two-night stay requirement to weed out other transients who will stay only one night.
- If you find out that the guests are likely to cancel depending upon the specific circumstances of the event, you can require a 48- or 72-hour cancellation notice. *(For instance, your guests may be participating in a sporting tournament where certain teams may or may not advance to subsequent rounds. They may choose to return home once their participation in the event has ended.)* A more positive approach would be to make rooms available to the fans of the teams who advance to the next round.
- If the event is located close to your property, you may be able to close off discounts for this period.

distribution channels by paying for an improved search engine ranking or buying a banner advertisement.

- Strive to accurately project expected market mix. The precision of this projection will influence the eventual yield statistic.
- Closely monitor group bookings and trends in transient business. Do not close off lower rate categories and market segments arbitrarily.
- As low occupancy periods become inevitable, open lower rate categories, solicit price-sensitive groups, and promote corporate, government, and other special discounts. Consider developing new room rate packages and soliciting business from the local community (for example, weekend getaways for the local transient market).
- Consider maintaining high room rates for walk-in guests. Since these guests have not contacted the hotel prior to arrival, they typically present an opportunity to increase the average rate through top-down upselling techniques.

74%
$92
18.40

- A non-financial tactic involves upgrading guests to nicer accommodations than they are entitled to by virtue of their room rate. This technique may lead to increased guest satisfaction and enhanced guest loyalty. The implementation of this policy is strictly a management decision and has some risks. For example, the guest may expect the same upgrade on future stays. This may not be possible and the reservations or front desk staff should take extra care to explain that this is a special, one-time upgrade because the hotel appreciates the guest's business.

The preceding list of suggested tactics is not exhaustive, but it is representative of industry strategies. Some additional low-demand tactics are listed in Exhibit 8.

Implementing Revenue Strategies

Once all of this revenue management information has been organized and analyzed, the front office manager must determine what rates the hotel will use on any given day. Certain strategies and tactics come with warnings. Applying restrictions too rigidly can actually discourage business. Managers must constantly keep in mind that the ultimate goal is to meet guests' needs. Any tactic that fails to do so will not produce the desired effect. Too much revenue management can be just as ineffective as no revenue management at all. That being the case, there are four tactics that must be applied cautiously:

1. Hurdle rate
2. Minimum length of stay
3. Close to arrival
4. Sell-through

Hurdle Rate. Rack rates are always left open, whether demand is high or low. Then, the front office manager must set the lowest rate for a given date based upon anticipated demand. Rates that fall below this minimum will not be offered. This is sometimes called the **hurdle rate.** Any room rate that can be sold at a rate above the hurdle rate is acceptable for that date. Any rate below the hurdle rate should not be offered. Some automated revenue management systems will not even display rates below the hurdle rate, thus preventing their use. Hurdle rates can fluctuate from day to day, depending upon the hotel's desired yield and market conditions. The hurdle rate usually reflects the front office manager's pricing strategy to maximize revenue.

Sometimes incentives are offered to front desk and reservations agents for selling rooms above the hurdle rate. For example, if the hurdle rate for a given day is $80 and a reservations agent sells a room for $90, he or she might receive ten promotion points. At the end of the month, all promotion points are totaled. For every 100 points, the reservations agent might receive a monetary reward. Incentives of this kind must be applied carefully, however. Reservations and front desk agents may elect not to offer lower rates that provide fewer incentive points, even though they are above the hurdle rate. While they are building incentive points, they may actually be turning away business.

Incentives may also be provided for longer guest stays. For example, a guest staying three nights may qualify for a lower rate than a guest staying for one night.

Exhibit 8 Low-Demand Tactics

1. **Sell value and benefits.**
Rather than just quoting rates, make sure guests know you have the right product for them and the best value. Sell the various values and benefits of staying at your property versus others that guests may be considering.
2. **Offer packages.**
To increase room nights, one tactic is to combine accommodations with a number of desirable products and services into a single package with one price. Mention any additions, renovations, or new amenities. Non-room revenue can be included, for example: free movies, discounted attraction tickets, and shopping coupons.
3. **Keep discount categories open.**
Discounts are typically directed toward particular markets or are instituted during a particular time or season. During low-demand time it is important to accept discounts to encourage room nights.
4. **Encourage upgrades.**
Move guests to a better accommodation or class of service to enhance their experience and encourage them to come back to the property again and again.
5. **Offer stay-sensitive price incentives.**
A stay-sensitive price incentive provides a discount for guests who stay longer. For example, a guest staying three nights might get an additional $5-per-night discount, while a guest staying one night might not.
6. **Remove stay restrictions.**
Remove any stay restrictions so guests are not limited as to when they can arrive or depart. Guests who can only stay one night will be encouraged to stay as well as the guest who is staying for a week. This will help to maximize occupancy. It is extremely important to communicate this to staff as well as to the central reservations system staff.
7. **Involve your staff.**
Create an incentive contest to increase occupancy and room nights. Make sure to involve all members of your staff as well as central reservations staff.
8. **Establish relationships with competitors.**
Having a cordial relationship with competitors can help with referrals and can help to carry out cross-marketing efforts.
9. **Lower rates.**
There is great value in keeping guests at the property as long as you are at least covering the cost of occupancy. You may want to lower your rate as low as possible. Identify the hurdle rate, which is the lowest rate acceptable at that given moment.

This is a **stay-sensitive hurdle rate.** Reservations agents may receive incentives for booking a three-night stay, even if it is at a lower rate, because the total revenue generated from the reservation will be greater than the revenue of a one- or two-night stay.

Communicating hurdle rates can be done in various ways. Some hotels post the rate strategies in the reservations office and at the front desk where the agent can see them but the guest cannot. Some computer systems, as just stated, automatically display acceptable rates only. Whatever the communication method, it is essential that reservation information be kept current. Revenue strategies can change several times a day, and all front desk and reservations agents must know when a change occurs.

Minimum Length of Stay. A **minimum length of stay** strategy requires that a reservation must be made for at least a specified number of nights before it will be accepted. Examples of this were presented earlier in the chapter. The advantage of this strategy is that it allows the hotel to develop a relatively even occupancy pattern. It is common for resorts to use this approach during peak occupancy periods. Hotels may also use it during special events or high occupancy periods.

The use of minimum length of stay requirements is intended to keep an occupancy peak on one day from reducing occupancy on the days before and after the peak. This strategy should be applied with great care. With a strict minimum stay requirement, profitable guests who don't want to stay for the required time may choose to take their business elsewhere. This strategy should be applied only when it will encourage additional business rather than frustrate guests. To ensure that the strategy is working, managers can check denials and regrets on a daily basis.

Minimum lengths of stay can be applied with discount rates. For example, guests may have to pay rack rates for shorter stays, but be offered discounts for minimum lengths of stay.

Close to Arrival. A **close to arrival** strategy allows reservations to be taken for a certain date as long as the guest arrives before that date. For example, if the front office is expecting a 300-room check-in on a given date, the front office manager may decide that more than 300 rooms checking in may be too much of a strain on the front desk and its related departments. Therefore, guests arriving before that date and staying through the date will be accepted; however, additional arrivals on the peak arrival date will not be accepted. As with a minimum length of stay strategy, the reservations office should track the number of reservation requests denied due to this restriction.

Sell-Through. The **sell-through** strategy works like a minimum length of stay requirement except that the required stay can begin before the date the strategy is applied. For example, if a three-night sell-through is applied on Wednesday, the sell-through applies to arrivals on Monday, Tuesday, and Wednesday. Arrivals on each of those days must stay for three nights in order to be accepted.

A sell-through strategy is especially effective when one day has a peak in occupancy and management does not want the peak to adversely affect reservations on either side of the peak day. Hotels use a sell-through strategy as a technique to overbook the peak day. By properly forecasting no-shows, early departures, and reservation cancellations, management may be able to manage the peak day so that the overbooking is reduced and all guests with reservations are accommodated. Without such a strategy, the days before and after the peak may have reduced occupancy because the peak may block extended stays.

Room availability strategies can be used together with room rate strategies. For example, a three-night minimum length of stay can be used in conjunction with a hurdle rate of $90. If the guest desires only a two-night stay, the rack rate of $110 may be quoted to the guest or the reservation may not be accepted.

Revenue Management Software

Although the individual tasks of revenue management can be performed manually, the most efficient way to handle data and generate yield statistics is through revenue management software. This software can integrate room demand and room price statistics to simulate high-revenue–producing product scenarios.

Revenue management software does not make decisions for managers. It merely provides information and support for managerial decisions. Since revenue management is often quite complex, front office staff will not have the time to process the voluminous data manually. Fortunately, a computer can store, retrieve, and manipulate large amounts of data on a broad range of factors influencing room revenue. Over time, revenue management software can help management create models that show the probable results of decisions. Decision models are based on historical data, forecasts, and booked business.

Industries that have applied computer-based revenue management have observed the following results:

- *Continuous monitoring:* a computerized revenue management system can track and analyze business conditions twenty-four hours a day, seven days a week.
- *Consistency:* software can be programmed to respond to specific changes in the marketplace with specific corporate or local management rules resident in the software.
- *Information availability:* revenue management software can provide improved management information that, in turn, may help managers make better decisions more quickly.
- *Performance tracking:* a computer-based system can analyze sales and revenue transactions occurring within a business period to determine how well revenue management goals are being achieved.

Revenue management software can also generate an assortment of special reports:

- *Market segment report:* provides information regarding guest mix. This information is important for effective forecasting by market segment.
- *Calendar/booking graph:* presents room-night demands and volume of reservations on a daily basis.
- *Future arrival dates status report:* furnishes demand data for each day of the week. This report provides a variety of forecasting information that enables the discovery of occupancy trends by comparative analysis of weekdays. It can be designed to cover several future periods.
- *Single arrival date history report:* indicates the hotel's booking patterns (trends in reservations). This report relates to the booking graph by documenting how a specific day was constructed on the graph.
- *Weekly recap report:* indicates the sell rates for rooms, and the number of rooms authorized and sold in marketing programs with special and/or discounted rates.

- *Room statistics tracking sheet:* tracks no-shows, guaranteed no-shows, walk-ins, and turn-aways. This information can be instrumental in accurate forecasting.

Since management is interested in revenue enhancement, computer-based revenue management has become a popular hospitality industry software application.

Summary

Revenue management offers a more precise measure of room revenue and occupancy performance than other historical benchmarks. Revenue management is effective because it combines occupancy percentage and ADR into a single statistic. Revenue management focuses on maximizing room revenues while taking into account factors influencing business trends. It is an evaluative tool that allows front office management to use potential revenue as the standard against which actual revenue is compared.

Revenue management has proven successful in business environments in which reservations are taken for a perishable commodity. The key to successful revenue management appears to be reliable forecasting, since revenue management is based on conditions of supply and demand.

The key to successful revenue management is to sell the right product to the right customer on the right day for the right price. Major hotel companies have developed unique revenue management systems that provide data for balancing room rates and occupancy levels at the property level.

Between late 2001 and late 2003, one of the most critical issues U.S. hotel managers faced was group attrition. Since 2001, three factors have contributed to elevating the importance of group attrition: group history, online shopping, and business sourcing.

Because revenue management uses a set of demand-forecasting techniques to determine effective prices for a forecasted volume of business, it can be highly successful when applied to the rooms reservation process. Revenue management seeks to maximize revenue by controlling forecast information in three ways: capacity management, discount allocation, and duration control.

Capacity management involves a number of methods of controlling and limiting room supply. Capacity management may be influenced by the availability of rooms at neighboring hotels or competing properties. Group attrition affects capacity management by reducing the number of rooms actually occupied, even though the group committed to renting more rooms. Discounting involves restricting the time period and product mix (rooms) available at reduced prices. The primary objective of discount allocation is to protect enough remaining rooms at a higher rate to satisfy the projected demand for rooms at that rate, while at the same time filling rooms that would otherwise have remained unsold. Duration control places time constraints on accepting reservations in order to protect sufficient space for multi-day requests (representing higher levels of revenue).

The principal computation involved in revenue management is the yield statistic, which is the ratio of actual revenue to potential revenue. Actual revenue is the revenue generated by the number of rooms sold. Potential revenue is the amount of money the hotel would receive if all rooms were sold at full rack rate or potential average rate. The potential average rate is a collective statistic that combines the hotel's potential average single and double rates, multiple occupancy percentage, and rate spread into a single figure. The achievement factor is figured by dividing the hotel's actual average room rate by the potential average rate. Alternatively, some lodging operations prefer the statistic that focuses on revenue per available room (RevPAR).

The purpose of RevPAG is to measure the average revenue captured for each hotel guest. It is most useful in hotels that offer multiple revenue outlets. It can also help managers identify areas in which the hotel is not earning expected revenue. GOPPAR incorporates departmental expenses as well as revenue, resulting in a measure of gross operating profit.

Calculations of different combinations of occupancy and actual average room rate may result in identical room revenue and yields. Management must be careful not to assume that identical yields represent identical operating situations with respect to the number of rooms and number of guests in occupancy.

Dynamic packaging allows for the customization of a travel package to meet a specific guest's needs. It increases the perceived value of a hotel package and tends to be more satisfying for the traveler than static packaging. Hotels find dynamic packaging especially effective during periods of low occupancy.

A revenue management analysis must consider all revenue opportunities affecting potential profitability to determine the economic value of the total business to the hotel. Only after such analysis can management calculate a meaningful room rate.

The revenue manager's duties are among the most important to a hotel's financial success. A revenue manager can often mean the difference between a struggling hotel and a profitable one.

The revenue meeting is the forum that managers in most hotels use to make their important revenue management decisions. The revenue meeting is held as frequently as necessary. Both group and transient business issues are discussed and revenue strategies are implemented.

Revenue management becomes even more complex when discounting is granted on a selective rather than general basis, and when it involves selling rooms for which there may be competing buyers. Hotels frequently offer discounts to guests falling into certain categories (for example, senior citizens and government employees). Hotels must also decide whether to accept or refuse group business at a discounted rate. Understanding the impact of group business on the hotel's operating performance may be an important factor in how revenue management should be applied.

Since the objective of revenue management is to maximize revenue, tracking business by revenue source will also help determine when to allow discounted business. Some hotels may decide to allow specific types of discounted business, such as corporate business, because these markets are responsible for many repeat guests. As the various sources of business are determined, each should be analyzed to understand its impact on total revenue. Quite often, managers will take discounted business if it generates frequent customers, since the long-term impact is very positive.

Implementing yield strategies involves setting hurdle rates for rooms. The hurdle rate is the lowest rate that can be offered at a given time. The hurdle rate is sometimes stay-sensitive, meaning lower rates are available to guests who stay a minimum length of time. Sometimes incentives are used to encourage front desk and reservations agents to sell rooms at rates above the hurdle rate. Since hurdle rates change frequently, efficient communication of rates and changes is critical.

Revenue management often focuses on maximizing yield by controlling rates. Other strategies that focus on length of stay and arrival dates are also effective. These other strategies can be effectively combined with rate control to improve yield.

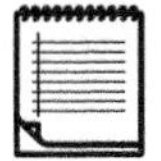

Endnotes

1. This method does not produce an achievement factor that is as precise as that which can be calculated by revenue management software. This is because the potential average rate is a weighted average of the rack rates of all rooms in the hotel. It is more accurate to use the weighted average of the rack rates of only the rooms that were actually sold (or occupied). Since the sales mix of rooms sold typically changes from day to day, so does the weighted average of those rooms' rack rates. Because it is impractical and cumbersome to manually calculate a weighted average of rack rates for rooms actually sold every day, the potential average rate of *all* rooms is generally used instead. The element of error this introduces may not be significant. Nonetheless, revenue management software is able to calculate the achievement factor more precisely because it can easily and automatically calculate the daily weighted average of the rack rates of rooms sold (or occupied).

2. In theory, and as used in our examples throughout the rest of the chapter, marginal costs are assumed to be constant at a given amount per room. In practice, this is not always the case. For example, certain labor costs may move incrementally; that is, as occupancy goes up, at some point management will have to add another front desk agent to help provide guest service. Also, room attendants are usually paid by the shift, not by the room; if a room attendant cleans twelve rooms one day and fifteen the next, the marginal cost per room will vary slightly. In addition, some properties are able to shut down wings not in use. If adding a guest means opening up an entire wing, the marginal cost of adding that guest will clearly be much higher than the marginal cost of simply adding a single room. For a more detailed discussion of these issues, see Raymond S. Schmidgall, *Hospitality Industry Managerial Accounting*, 7th ed. (Lansing, Mich.: American Hotel & Lodging Educational Institute, 2011).

3. For a more detailed discussion of breakeven analysis and contribution margin ratios, see Schmidgall.

4. Group business usually involves the hotel's sales division. The sales division typically *books* the group. It then turns the booking over to the reservations manager, who *blocks* the group. As individual group members contact the hotel, they are *booked* and the size of the block is reduced accordingly.

Key Terms

achievement factor—The percentage of the rack rate that a hotel actually receives; in hotels not using revenue management software, this factor is generally approximated by dividing the actual average room rate by the potential average rate.

booking lead time—A measurement of how far in advance bookings are made.

breakeven analysis—An analysis of the relationships among costs, revenue, and sales volume, allowing one to determine the revenue required to cover all costs; also called cost-volume-profit analysis.

close to arrival—A yield management availability strategy that allows reservations to be taken for a certain date as long as the guest arrives before that date; for example, a hotel may accept a reservation for a Wednesday night if the guest's actual stay begins on Tuesday night.

contribution margin—Sales less cost of sales for either an entire operating department or for a given product; represents the amount of sales revenue that is contributed toward fixed costs and/or profits.

cost per occupied room—The variable or added cost of selling a product that is incurred only if the room is sold; also called marginal cost.

discount grid—A chart indicating the occupancy percentage necessary to achieve equivalent net revenue, given different discount levels.

displacement—The turning away of transient guests for lack of rooms due to the acceptance of group business; also called non-group displacement.

dynamic packaging—The customization of a travel package according to a specific guest's needs. Hotels find dynamic packaging especially effective during expected periods of low occupancy.

equivalent occupancy—Given a contemplated or actual change in the average room rate, equivalent occupancy is the occupancy percentage required to produce the same net revenue as was produced by the old price and occupancy percentage.

fair market share—A comparison of a hotel's ADR and occupancy percentage, or RevPAR, against its competition to determine whether it is getting its share of business in the market.

fixed costs—Costs that remain constant in the short run even though sales volume varies.

forecast—A projection of estimated business volume.

GOPPAR—A revenue measurement that focuses on gross operating profit per available room.

group attrition—Under-consumption of, or failure to achieve, a committed number of group room nights.

group booking pace—The rate at which group business is being booked.

hurdle rate—In the context of revenue management, the lowest acceptable room rate for a given date.

marginal costs—The variable or added costs of selling a product, incurred only if the room is sold; also called cost per occupied room.

minimum length of stay—A revenue management availability strategy requiring that a reservation must be for at least a specified number of nights in order to be accepted.

potential average rate—A collective statistic that effectively combines the potential average single and double rates, multiple occupancy percentage, and rate spread to produce the average rate that would be achieved if all rooms were sold at their full rack rates.

rate potential percentage—The percentage of the rack rate that a hotel actually receives, computed by dividing the actual average room rate by the potential average rate; also called the achievement factor.

rate spread—The mathematical difference between the hotel's potential average single rate and potential average double rate.

revenue management—A technique based on supply and demand used to maximize revenues by lowering prices to increase sales during periods of low demand and raising prices during periods of high demand to increase revenue.

RevPAG—A revenue measurement that focuses on revenue earned per available guest.

RevPAR—A revenue measurement that focuses on revenue per available room.

sell-through—A revenue management availability strategy that works like a minimum length of stay requirement, except that the length of the required stay can begin before the date the strategy is applied.

stay-sensitive hurdle rate—In the context of revenue management, a hurdle rate (or minimum acceptable room rate) that varies with the length of the guest reservation.

wash factor—The deletion of unnecessary group rooms from a group block.

weighted average contribution margin ratio—In a multiple product situation, an average contribution margin for all operated departments that is weighted to reflect the relative contribution of each department to the establishment's ability to pay fixed costs and generate profits.

yield statistic—The ratio of actual rooms revenue to potential rooms revenue.

Review Questions

1. What is the goal of revenue management?
2. Why is communication between the various revenue centers important to the successful implementation of revenue management?
3. What are the importance and limitations of using historical data when planning revenue management strategies?
4. What might be the impact of closing discount rates when business is down?
5. What role does booking pace play in revenue management?
6. What is a wash factor? How does it affect revenue management?
7. Why is transient displacement analysis so important in determining whether to accept a group reservation?

8. What is the difference between marginal cost and fixed cost?
9. What does the equivalent occupancy equation consider that the identical yield equation does not? Why is the difference significant? What important question does neither equation address?
10. Should a group reservation be accepted or rejected solely on the basis of its effect on room revenue? Why or why not?
11. What are several tactics that may be appropriate to take when room demand is low? When room demand is high?
12. What is the hurdle rate? How is it used in revenue management? What availability strategies are used as part of revenue management?

Internet Sites

For more information, visit the following Internet sites. Remember that Internet addresses can change without notice. If the site is no longer there, you can use a search engine to look for additional sites.

Smith Travel Research
www.strglobal.com

TravelCLICK
www.travelclick.net

TIMS Reports
www.timsreports.com

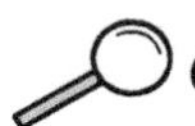

Case Study

Reviving Revenue Management

The Hearthstone Suites Hotel is an all-suite property with 250 rooms. A new property, the Fairmont Hotel, opened near Hearthstone Suites three months ago. Several months before the opening of the Fairmont, Laurie, the general manager at the Hearthstone Suites, pushed all her front office and reservations staff to sell as many rooms as possible. As she put it, "Whatever it takes, to stay competitive." The director of sales, Pat, supported the plan from day one, but Jodie, the front office manager, had misgivings from the start. Jodie was concerned that the revenue management program managers implemented a year and a half earlier would be totally useless because of the push for occupancy.

The most recent profit and loss statement indicates that Jodie's fears were realized. Though the occupancy is at budget year-to-date, the average daily rate (ADR) is down by $6. Also, the mix of commercial business is lower than planned—40 percent of guest mix instead of 50 percent. Also, the SMERF segment is higher than it should be—15 percent of guest mix instead of 5 percent. SMERF is a catch-all term for group business at substantially low rates—Social, Military, Educational, Religious, and Fraternal groups.

Jodie, Pat, and Laurie are in a meeting to discuss these latest figures. Laurie, the general manager, opens the meeting by saying, "Well, we've weathered the storm caused by the opening of the Fairmont. We managed to hold on to our occupancy level. But it looks like we have some regrouping to do. I trust you've each received the profit and loss statement I sent you. I'm concerned about the fact that we've lost so much of our share of the commercial business. And our ADR is much too low."

"I agree," says Jodie, "but I was just following orders when I had my staff focus on selling rooms. Our good occupancy rate has come at the cost of both revenue management and revenue. It will take quite a while to regain our former position."

"We all sat down and agreed months before the Fairmont opened that we should do our best to keep our occupancy numbers, and that's what we've done," says Pat. "You and your staff have worked hard and are to be commended, Jodie."

"Hear, hear," says Laurie, "and now we have some time to re-evaluate our position and start targeting that corporate segment again."

"I just hope it's not too late to win it back from Fairmont," sighs Jodie.

Later that day, Jodie gathers her front desk and reservations team to brief them about re-implementing the revenue management program. "I know you've all been putting a lot of extra effort into filling rooms over the past several months. I'm proud of you; the whole management team is. We've met our occupancy goals. The down side is that our guest mix is off. We've lost some of our commercial segment and gained too much of the SMERF segment. And our ADR is down a full $6. It's time we reviewed the revenue management program we use."

"The revenue what?" blurts Jack, a fairly new front desk agent. "You never told us about that."

"Now hold on a minute," counters Jodie, "some of you are so new that you haven't been fully trained in this program, but I know I've talked about it to some extent with all of you."

"Sure, you told me a little about it," offers Tracey, a reservationist. "I never have been comfortable with it, to tell the truth. One day I quote a guest $85 and he books a suite. A month later he calls back to book another and I quote $105. Then the guest asks why the rate went up—what am I supposed to say?"

"Well, there are things you can tell guests who ask that, but we're not going to get into that right now," says Jodie.

Bill, the most experienced front desk agent, speaks up. "I've been using the revenue management program all along, just like you showed me." He turns to his co-workers. "It's really not unreasonable when you look at the big picture of the hotel's revenue. I just tell inquisitive callers that our rates depend on their arrival dates. Some periods are busier for us than others, and that affects rates."

"Bill, it's good to hear that you continued using the revenue management program," Jodie says. "We can get into more detail on applying it in formal training. We've had a lot of changes since the push for volume began—changes in personnel, and even changes in the revenue management program itself. It's clearly time I evaluated the training needs in our department in the area of revenue management program execution. You can be confident, Tracey—and all of you—when you quote rates that they are competitive for what we offer. That reminds me," and here Jodie pauses a moment, "how many of you have actually been inside some of our suites?"

Three of the six employees raise their hands. "How many have seen rooms at the Fairmont or at any of our other competitors?" continues Jodie. Only Bill raises his hand. "So almost none of you have seen the difference between our suites and the single rooms other properties are offering?"

"There hasn't been time to look at what we're selling," protests Jack.

"Much less to look at what anyone else is selling," adds Linda, another reservationist.

"That's what I was afraid of," says Jodie. "In the next two weeks or so, as I'm re-evaluating training needs, I'm going to have each of you spend time gaining an appreciation of the value we offer—especially in comparison with the value of Fairmont's offerings and those of our other competition."

"Are we still going to be offering the $84 supersaver rate?" asks Tracey. "We've had a lot of repeat business because of that rate."

"I've had callers tell me we're the best deal in town," Linda says.

But Bill cautions, "We won't need to use it next week. The Home Builders convention is in and every room in town will be booked. We can afford to charge more next week."

"That's good thinking, Bill," says Jodie. "I know it's nice to be popular with guests and it's easy to use that discount whenever a potential guest shies away from a quoted rate, but the supersaver rate is intended to be used only as a last resort or in other special cases. We shouldn't be offering it too frequently. We also need to adjust our selling strategies when special events come along like this convention."

"Speaking of selling strategies, when are we going to get to go through that training module on selling skills you were talking about?" inquires Linda. "I've heard about it but I haven't gone through it yet."

Discussion Questions

1. How can the management team address the problem of low ADR?
2. What are some ways Jodie could make employees like Jack and Tracey more familiar and comfortable with the revenue management program?
3. What selling skills should training focus on for the Hearthstone Suites Hotel staff?
4. How can the Hearthstone Suites Hotel regain some of the commercial business it has lost?

Case Number: 370CF

This case was developed in cooperation with Lisa Richards of Hospitality Softnet, Inc., a marketing resources and support company (Sixty State Street, Suite 700, Boston, Massachusetts 02109; tel. 617-854-6554).

Chapter 7 Outline

- Sustainability and Green Philosophies
  - Good Earthkeeping and Going Green
  - Green Teams
  - Certification Programs
- Housekeeping's Role in a Green Property
  - Communication
  - Training
  - Purchasing
- Water Conservation
  - Linen Reuse Programs
  - Guestrooms
  - Laundry
  - Public Restrooms
- Energy Efficiency
  - Energy Management
  - Lighting
- Waste Management
  - Reduce
  - Recycle
  - Reuse
- Indoor Air Quality
  - Indoor Air Quality Programs
  - Fighting Mold
- Cleaning Chemicals

Competencies

1. Explain why it is important for hospitality properties to adopt environmentally friendly policies, and list "green" strategies and organizations that can help hospitality properties be good stewards of the environment. (pp. 257–265)
2. Describe the role that housekeeping plays in a "green" property. (pp. 265–268)
3. List ways that hospitality properties can conserve water. (pp. 268–272)
4. Explain the steps hospitality properties can take to become more energy efficient. (pp. 272–277)
5. List the three main components of a waste management program. (pp. 277–280)
6. Describe the importance of indoor air quality and how it can be safeguarded. (pp. 280–283)
7. Explain how executive housekeepers can safely manage cleaning chemicals. (pp. 283–284)

Taken from *Managing Housekeeping Operations*, Revised Third Edition, by Aleta A. Nitschke and William D. Frye

Chapter 7
Environmental and Energy Management

A majority of content in this chapter was contributed by Phil Sprague, President of PSA Energy Consultants, an energy consulting and hotel engineering audit company based in Mound, Minnesota.

ONE OF THE MOST DRAMATIC SHIFTS in the demands placed on executive housekeepers and other hospitality managers has been the increased need to know about energy management, sustainability, and environmentally responsible policies and procedures. Hospitality managers today must understand the role they play in ensuring their properties are wisely using resources, preventing waste, and contributing to an environment that is safe to reside in.

Why is there so much attention to "going green" in hotels lately? *Lodging Hospitality* says that environmentally friendly policies contribute to a **triple bottom line**: economic, environmental, and social.[1] Enacting environmentally sound policies increases the economic health of a property. The numbers are compelling and impossible to ignore. Properties that have instituted green policies have reaped millions of dollars in cost reductions. Economic benefits have included:

- Energy savings
- Waste reduction and lower disposal costs
- Eligibility for government incentives
- Reduced labor costs
- Reduced employee absenteeism
- Increased productivity

Environmental benefits include the conservation of limited resources. The actions that the hospitality industry takes to conserve water, save energy, reduce waste, and purify the air are making the world a healthier place to live. They reduce pollution and help preserve natural habitats. They ensure the long-term success of a property by helping to make tomorrow's world a sustainable environment.

The social benefits are also plentiful. Having environmentally sound management policies and initiatives—and publicizing those efforts—makes a property more attractive to its guests and to groups calling for environmental accountability. Green policies also can make the property more comfortable and healthy for guests. *Southern Hospitality* magazine cited the following ways hospitality properties can reap the benefits of environmentally friendly philosophies:

- Create a sense of pride in the community
- Increase the morale and health of employees
- Enhance a property's image
- Provide a competitive edge in the industry
- Establish a property as an environmental leader
- Create a deeper level of trust in guests, suppliers, and partners[2]

To explore the role that executive housekeepers and their departments play in a property's environmental policies, this chapter will examine sustainability initiatives and "green" philosophies, housekeeping's role in a green property, and specific policies that support water conservation, energy efficiency, waste reduction, clean air practices, and responsible cleaning chemical use.

Sustainability and Green Philosophies

The hospitality industry has been cited by the U.S. Environmental Protection Agency as a leader in environmentalism. Hospitality organizations have made an ever-growing commitment to the concept of **sustainability**—a way of doing business that says a company shouldn't take more than it gives back and should not sacrifice tomorrow for today's needs. Exhibit 1 tells the success stories of a few of the many hospitality properties that have made a commitment to sustainability.

A property's environmental policy must have commitment from not only the general manager, but from the owner(s) and central headquarters. The official sanction from top management will motivate employees and help them to realize that conservation is a part of their job responsibilities. They are also the ones who will conduct an environmental assessment, the first step to creating a property-wide environmental program. These assessments can establish baseline measurements and identify those areas in which the property can make the most improvement.

Good Earthkeeping and Going Green

The American Hotel & Lodging Association (AH&LA) has participated in several initiatives to help hoteliers demonstrate environmental leadership. The first initiative was launched in 2004—a partnership with the U.S. Environmental Protection Agency's (EPA) Energy Star. The program is called Good Earthkeeping, an educational program that provides resources and tools to help make hotels more profitable, competitive, and environmentally responsible through increased energy efficiency and ecological stewardship. The program helps hoteliers create a comprehensive strategic approach to energy management that assesses current energy performance, sets goals, tracks savings, and rewards improvements. It also makes available a series of Energy Star Webinars. Properties that participate in the Good Earthkeeping program become eligible for national recognition from the EPA.

A second initiative is Going Green, launched in July 2007 as part of a partnership with the International Tourism Partnership out of London, England. Going Green offers guidelines for hotels to set minimum standards to improve

Exhibit 1 Sustainability Success Stories

The Green Hotels Association and Energy Star, reported on several successful endeavors hospitality properties and organizations are making to help the environment:

- A lodge in Alberta, Canada, produces 50 to 90 percent of its electricity by solar and wind power, and 90 to 100 percent of its heat from solar energy and wood, resulting in a 90-percent reduction in fossil fuel use.
- Lodges in the Grand Canyon National Park compost more than 600 cubic yards of material each year; use non-toxic chemicals in transportation, cleaning, and food service; and encourage vendors to eliminate products that are harmful to the environment.
- The Columbus Hospitality Group reduced its energy bills and maintenance costs by $30,000 a year through a renovation that made its hotel more energy efficient. This included upgrading all lights; installing high-efficiency air conditioning units and pumps; installing occupancy sensors for lights and HVAC in offices and guestrooms; installing water-saving showerheads, toilets, and sinks; and installing energy-efficient TVs, VCRs, fax, and copy machines in rooms. Energy Star estimated that the property generated enough savings to increase its average daily revenue by $3.25.
- Marriott developed an auditing and inspection system for its properties to enhance their energy management systems and procedures. This resulted in a company-wide savings of $4.5 million annually.
- The Saunders Hotel Group began its environmental commitment in the 1980s when it pioneered ecotourism. It now involves staff members at all levels to conserve energy. The organization's most recent sustainability efforts included purchasing new energy efficient equipment for guestrooms and offices, and using energy management systems, motion sensors, fluorescent lighting, heat pumps, and ozone laundry systems in its properties.
- The Hyatt Regency Coconut Point Resort and Spa in Bonita Springs was the first Florida hotel to receive the state's two-palm certification in 2006. The property has reduced its water consumption by 28 percent, energy use by 1.8 percent, and waste disposal by 2.8 percent—after its initial one palm certification. The resort instituted a linen and towel reuse program and installed a laundry system that recycles water and steam and limits the water and detergent used. It donates leftover toiletries and used linens to charities.

Sources: Green Hotel Association, Energy Star, Florida Department of Environmental Protection.

sustainability and achieve goals for better environmental management. The Going Green program establishes six areas of focus for hospitality properties:

- *Policy and framework,* to develop a commitment from all employees
- *Staff training and awareness,* as a way to build a motivated staff
- *Environmental management,* aiming for the highest standards in terms of biodiversity protection, hygiene, safety, indoor air quality, and overall environmental management

the Rooms CHRONICLE®

States' Green Lodging Programs and Hotels' Eco-friendly Practices Plant the Seeds for Greener Bottom Lines

It has taken some time but the wait has been well worth it for hoteliers and current and future generations of guests. More and more states are following in the footsteps of California and are launching green lodging programs to preserve precious natural resources and recognize and reward hospitality businesses' eco-friendly practices.

In fact, the practice of eco-friendly practices has rippled from coast to coast to the point where states such as Florida, North Carolina, Pennsylvania, and Vermont also are getting green.

Pineapple Hospitality recently partnered with the Florida Department of Environmental Protection (DEP) to help the state's lodging industry create a healthier, safer indoor environment and reduce the generation of solid waste in hotels and motels. In the public-private partnership, Pineapple is providing hotels and motels with technical assistance on cost-saving green products and practices. Offering an arsenal of energy and water conservation, air quality improvement and waste reduction, recycling and reuse solutions, Pineapple is helping Florida DEP's nine certified Green Lodging facilities and 15 others currently enrolled and working toward the green designation to unearth a world of fresh ideas on how to help themselves while helping protect the environment.

Profits in the palm

Florida DEP'S Green Lodging Certification Program tiers its certified hotels into three levels:

One Palm Certification

To achieve this level of certification a hotel/motel must have completed the core activities representing a minimum set of best management practices in the areas of communication, water conservation, energy efficiency, waste reduction, and clean air. In addition, the property must obtain support from top management, form an active multi-disciplinary "green team," and operate in compliance with all applicable environmental laws and regulations.

Two Palm Certification

To achieve this level of certification a hotel/motel must have maintained the facility's one palm status for at least 12 consecutive months before applying for two palm certification. The hotel/motel had to have conducted an environmental baseline assessment, developed and enacted performance improvement goals, implemented at least one green project and evaluated its progress. If Two Palm certification status is not achieved within 24 months of obtaining the One Palm certification, the property may be moved to inactive status and will be removed from the Green Lodging Locator website: www.floridagreenlodging.com. A hotel in inactive status will no longer be able to consider itself a Florida Certified Green Lodge and will no longer be able to use the Florida Green Lodging Certification Program to promote the property.

the Rooms CHRONICLE®

(continued)

Three Palm Certification

To achieve this level of certification a hotel/motel must have maintained the facility's Two Palm certification and have demonstrated continual improvement for three consecutive years. To retain this certification level, the facility must continue to maintain or improve its high level of commitment to protecting the state's environment through the Florida Green Lodging program.

Who certifies these "Green Lodges"?

The Florida Department of Environmental Protection has trained Green Lodging Assessors (predominantly comprised of state and local government employees) throughout the state who visit the lodging facilities. The assessor verifies the facility's Green Lodging certification information via an onsite assessment. After a review by the DEP, the hotel or motel is certified if the lodge's information is complete, and correct, and the property meets all of the program requirements.

Green bandwagon

According to www.allstays.com, at least 35 states have documented lodging facilities that are "taking the right step forward for us and Earth one night at a time," including:

- Alaska
- Arizona
- Arkansas
- California
- Colorado
- Connecticut
- Florida
- Georgia
- Hawaii
- Indiana
- Iowa
- Kentucky
- Maine
- Maryland
- Massachusetts
- Michigan
- Montana
- New Hampshire
- New Jersey
- New Mexico
- New York
- North Carolina
- Ohio
- Oregon
- Pennsylvania
- South Carolina
- South Dakota
- Texas
- Utah
- Vermont
- Virginia
- Washington
- West Virginia
- Wisconsin
- Wyoming

As the Vermont Green Hotels Scorecard illustrates on the next page, Vermont's participating green hotels are using sound environmental management practices to reduce their impacts on the environment, improve their bottom lines, and satisfy customer demand for environmentally conscious lodging establishments.

Why get green?

The following are just a few reasons why hoteliers should consider adopting and implementing environmentally and ecologically friendly practices today:

- *Money Matters*—According to the U.S. Environmental Protection Agency (EPA), hotels and motels investing in energy-efficient lighting upgrades can expect to yield a profit of $6.27 on each dollar invested. Simple waste audits of lodging facilities can help one identify opportunities for reducing wastes, and recycling or reusing materials.

(continued)

the Rooms CHRONICLE® *(continued)*

Green Hotels: 30 VBEP partners: 18 Total participating properties: 48			
Environmental Policy & Mission	48	Towel/Linen Reuse Program	35
Energy Efficiency Upgrades	21	Composting	11
Using Recycled products	23	Using more enviro-friendly products	24
# of guest rooms for towel reuse	1758	Environmental Mgmt. Plan	30
Recycle & offer guests access & info	35	# of onsite assessments	11 in 0405

Saved Gallons of H_2O	Saved Gallons of Bleach	Saved Lbs. Detergent	Saved KWH	Saved Lbs. Recycled	Saved H_2O/gal. Propane
895,320	1,317	11,191.5	21,488	124,020	6,566

- *Win Customers*—According to the Travel Industry Association of America, within the United States alone 43 million people are self-proclaimed "eco-tourists" who are willing to pay 8.5 percent more to environmentally sensitive travel suppliers. A survey of U.S. travelers found 87 percent would be more likely to stay at "green" properties. By demonstrating that they care for the environment as well as their visitors' comfort, hoteliers can earn respect and customer loyalty and enhance their company's competitiveness.
- *Protect OUR Planet*—Lodging is the fourth most intensive user of energy in the United States' commercial sector. Improving energy efficiency in the hospitality industry will help reduce energy consumption, thereby reducing U.S. greenhouse emissions. Reductions in the use of hazardous cleaning materials, water consumption, and waste disposal will all contribute to protecting your state's land, air, and water resources.
- *Earn Recognition*—State DEPs and Pineapple can help green hotels and motels share their stories through positive public recognition. Green hotels and motels may be recognized through awards events, or in articles, news releases, newsletters, and other publications, both on the Internet and in print.

the Rooms CHRONICLE®

(continued)

Creating eco-friendly guestrooms

Hopefully, after reading this article and careful consideration, ownership and management will seek to realize the full potential of cost-effective, eco-friendly practices. Many resource agencies, consultants, and private companies, including Pineapple, stand ready to assist. One advantage is that these individuals and organizations have typically developed close relationships with leading green product providers to save hoteliers money and time while maximizing any potential rebates from utilities and local governments.

Perhaps Pineapple's Eco Rooms demonstrate the extent of its involvement the best. Typically providing a complete payback in 12 months or less, these Eco Rooms include several of the following:

- Energy-efficient lighting solutions such as GE fluorescent lamp bulbs and The WattStopper occupancy sensor nightlight;
- Bathroom amenity dispensers using biodegradable, hypoallergenic soaps, body wash, lotion, shampoo, and conditioner;
- Recyclable/biodegradable plastic bottles filled with all-natural bathroom amenities and hand soap packaged in recycled paper;
- Programmable digital thermostats to control guestroom energy consumption without compromising guest satisfaction;
- Patented low-flow/high-pressure showerheads and sink aerators;
- Early-closer toilet flappers and tank diverter valves;
- The Nature's Mist deodorization system, which helps hotels guarantee non-smoking rooms no matter what a property's guests' preference mix is;
- In-room air filters;
- A towel and linens reuse program;
- Non-toxic, non-allergenic, all-natural cleaning products;
- Facial and bathroom tissues made from 100-percent recycled materials and at least 30-percent post-consumer waste paper;
- Recycling receptacles for guestrooms, lobbies, meeting rooms, restaurants, kitchens, and offices.

Conclusion

The bottom line is that money talks and people walk. Chances are that many of your hotel's competitors already are undertaking some or most of these eco-initiatives and making more money and a better name for themselves in the process. More importantly, they are helping to preserve the environment in the process. Where will you stand on this issue?

Source: Ray Burger, *The Rooms Chronicle®*, Volume 13, Number 6, pp. 4–6.
For subscription information, please call 866-READ-TRC.

- *Purchasing,* to help properties work with suppliers for less wasteful practices
- *People and communities,* to encourage employees to look for environmental stewardship opportunities beyond the property
- *Destination protection,* to maintain a sense of place that supports the geographic character of a place—its environment, culture, heritage, aesthetics, and the well-being of its citizens[3]

Green Teams

Ensuring that a property follows environmentally sound policies means keeping track of a wealth of details that cross over many departments. Many hospitality properties have established committees or teams that work together to assess energy use, set goals, and monitor environmental activities.

The size of these "green teams" vary, but it is important that there is representation from top management and from those departments that have the greatest responsibility for resource management. These departments include:

- Housekeeping (and laundry).
- Engineering/ Maintenance.
- Kitchen.
- Front office.
- Purchasing.

In some properties, this team has a waste reduction subcommittee that establishes goals for reducing waste and training employees on the property's recycling program.

The green team is often responsible for establishing goals for the property and each department after an environmental assessment is conducted. It can also help increase staff awareness of goals by creating competitions, suggestion boxes, and reward programs.

Certification Programs

As the demand for greater environmental responsibility grows, regulatory and other bodies are beginning to place more demands on hospitality properties. For example, the Supreme Court recently strengthened the Clean Air Act, and Congress has increased demands that businesses behave responsibly. As a way of encouraging hospitality properties to enact environmentally sound policies, the EPA has announced that its $50 million earmarked for travel will go first to hotels and conference centers that self-certify on a 14-point environmental checklist.

Florida Green Lodging Certification Program. Some state environment departments are even offering certifications to properties that implement green strategies. One such state is Florida, which offers a Florida Green Lodging Certification Program through the Florida Department of Environmental Protection. Exhibit 2 lists the 10 steps in the department's certification program.

Exhibit 2 Florida Green Lodging Certification Program

1. Identify an environmental champion.
2. Obtain top management commitment and submit the admission application.
3. Create a Green Team.
4. Conduct an environmental assessment.
5. Establish goals and identify environmental improvement projects.
6. Submit your environmental baseline data to the FGLC Program Office.
7. Implement environmental improvement projects.
8. Evaluate and monitor the program.
9. Schedule on-site certifying visit.
10. Practice continual improvement.

Source: Florida Department of Environmental Protection

LEED Certification. The U.S. Green Building Council has established Leadership in Energy and Environmental Design (LEED) certification. The council promotes a comprehensive approach to sustainability that includes every element of a building's design and management. When new hotels are built, they can be awarded credits for such categories as sustainable sites, energy and atmosphere, water efficiency, indoor environmental quality, and materials and resources. This is a program that hotels have been slow to join until recent years.

Energy Star. The EPA rates energy efficiency in hotels. It scores hotels on how well they perform on a number of standards and provides those ratings to the public.

Green Leaf. Canada's Green Leaf and Audubon International have created the Audubon Green Leaf Eco-Rating Program that audits lodging facilities and awards them one to five Green Leaves, depending on whether they meet environmental best practices standards. The program began in 1998.

Housekeeping's Role in a Green Property

Given how much of the property housekeeping employees see and touch every day, they play a crucial role in identifying potential environmental opportunities throughout the hotel. The executive housekeeper in particular is responsible for a wide variety of environmental management duties, including:

- Communication.
- Training.
- Purchasing.

Communication

The housekeeping department's managers must determine how they are going to communicate the property's environmental initiatives to both staff and guests. To be most effective, multiple mediums can be used, such as newsletters, signs, websites, annual reports, placards in guestrooms, recorded messages on the television, and hint sheets that can be placed on guestroom carts. The executive housekeeper or another department representative can then be identified to communicate information to staff during pre-shift meetings, training sessions, and other staff meetings. It is also helpful to create a formal process for employees and guests to use for feedback on green practices. This could include an employee suggestion box or a guestroom survey form.

Bilingual Communication Issues. Housekeeping departments have always been among the most diverse departments in hotels and among the first to address multicultural issues. The hospitality industry as a whole employs a significant international population of employees.

The multiple languages spoken by employees can pose a unique challenge, since most of the training manuals, bulletin board material, and signs in the hotel are in a single language. The communication gap can result in situations where a significant amount of energy is wasted due to misunderstandings and ineffective communications. In a typical U.S. lodging property, the three key areas affected the most by this issue are housekeeping, laundry, and the kitchen.

Housekeeping employees visit every room of the hotel on a daily basis and have the responsibility for taking corrective action and reporting problems. There are specific procedures that room attendants follow to provide a quality product and conserve energy. They must be able to communicate these things no matter what language they speak.

The temperature setting on thermostats is the most common challenge for U.S. housekeeping departments with non-English-speaking workers. With most of the rest of the world on the Metric system, non-U.S. employees typically think in terms of Centigrade rather than Fahrenheit. This can cause difficulty in setting thermostats to the proper temperature. One solution has been to issue each room attendant a placard with a sketch showing a typical guestroom thermostat setting.

Room attendants are also responsible for turning off all lights and appliances, and closing the draperies after cleaning a guestroom. They should also report any potential plumbing problems that are noticed while cleaning the room.

Another housekeeping area where language can be an issue is in the on-premises laundry. Washing, drying, and ironing must be done properly to maintain the quality, comfort, and life of linens and to conserve energy, water, and chemicals. The executive housekeeper needs to find a way to communicate the preventive maintenance plan as well as develop checklists that can be used by employees regardless of the language they speak.

Training

Some estimates say that the annual cost of energy and water for a hotel can be reduced by as much as 10 percent by training employees to operate the hotel efficiently. Training can help a property reduce energy consumption without any capital investment.

Each hotel has its own personality and methods for conducting employee training. Executive housekeepers should design programs appropriate to the property's culture.

Housekeeping. Housekeeping staff members typically work throughout 80 percent of the hotel on a daily basis. Therefore, housekeeping training can be critical to the efficient operation of the guestroom block. Some "green" skills that training should cover include the following:

- Control of the heating, ventilation, and air conditioning, (HVAC) system of guestrooms is essential. Temperatures in vacant guestrooms should be set back according to season and geographical location parameters. Typically, HVAC settings should be 74 degrees Fahrenheit during the cooling season and 68 degrees Fahrenheit during the heating season. One important tool of housekeeping management is a weather-board to visually post for room attendants the HVAC settings for the day.
- Room attendants should turn off all exhaust fans and close all windows in vacant guestrooms. Entry of outside air during heating/cooling seasons causes a huge waste of energy.
- Room attendants should open the drapes to use free light while cleaning but close the blackout drapes to within six inches before leaving the room.
- Coffee pots, hair dryers, and irons should be unplugged before room attendants leave the guestroom. Disconnecting these items is a safety issue as well as an energy saver. Room attendants should also turn off all lights in every room and ceiling fans and whirlpool tubs (when present) when they exit.
- Room attendants should clean all light fixtures in guestrooms on a regular basis. They should especially ensure bathroom fluorescent fixtures with lenses are cleaned at least twice per year. This action will increase light output by approximately 25 percent.
- For hotels with through-the-wall heating/cooling units, room attendants should ensure all discharge air grills are clean and that drapes do not obstruct the flow of air from the unit.

Laundry. The laundry area (along with the kitchen) is one of the most intensive energy users in the hotel. The laundry and kitchen use about five times more energy per square foot than the rest of the property. The managers of these areas must be very conscious of training employees in the following basic energy-conservation strategies:

- Process full loads as recommended for both washers and dryers. If smaller loads are necessary, consider installing a residential-style washer and dryer.

- Lint screens and dryer exhausts must be cleaned on a frequent basis. Verifying that proper air flow is passing through the dryers will preserve the life of the burners.
- The flames on gas dryers should be checked regularly to ensure efficient burning. In conjunction, verify that the proper amount of combustion air is provided to the dryer to ensure a complete combustion of natural gas.
- Clean light fixtures and discharge air grills throughout the laundry on a regular basis. Lint buildup in the laundry area can reduce the efficiency of the equipment and present a fire hazard.
- Verify that the domestic hot water temperature for the wash wheel is set correctly and in accordance with detergent requirements.

Purchasing

Purchasing plays a major role in a property's environmental plan. **Eco-purchasing** involves evaluating purchasing practices and products on durability, reusability, recyclability, and content as well as the traditional price and quality standards. Packaging and delivery methods should also be evaluated.

Some experts suggest that **just-in-time buying** will reduce waste. Just-in-time buying is the practice of buying products just before they run out. Experts have said that employees will use more of a product if there is a large quantity of it on the shelf, while they will be more conservative with it if there is a small amount.

Things that an executive housekeeper can do to make the purchasing process more "green" include:

- Purchasing in bulk and concentrate.
- Requiring vendors to take back pallets and non-recyclable boxes and crates.
- Using local suppliers.
- Looking for simplicity in products and minimal packaging of items.
- Purchasing and maintaining more durable supplies that won't have to be replaced as often.
- Purchasing sheets with higher thread counts for longer wear.

Energy Star rates equipment based on its energy efficiency. The Energy Star website (www.energystar.gov) provides a calculator that can help housekeeping managers calculate how much energy savings a given piece of equipment can provide.

Water Conservation

Water conservation is one of the most cost-effective programs a hotel can implement. Not only does a property save water and reduce its water expense, but it also saves money in decreased electricity costs, sewage bills, and decreased chemical costs.

Hotels use a large volume of water, detergent, and cleansers every day. One AH&LA study found that, on average, each occupied room uses 209 gallons of water daily. Such high water use has made the issue of conservation increasingly important, especially in communities that have been hit heavily by drought.

In 2007, the South experienced heavy drought conditions that drained reservoirs to dangerously low levels. The Hyatt Regency Atlanta, a 1,260-room property that uses tens of millions of gallons of water each year, found itself searching for extra water conservation measures in addition to those it already had in place. It already outsourced its laundry to a facility outside of metro Atlanta (where the worse drought conditions were in effect), had a linen reuse policy, and guestrooms with low-flow fixtures. As the drought deepened, it began to irrigate its green plants with condensation from the cooling system and started putting fewer water pitchers in meeting rooms.

In 1992, the Environmental Protection Agency launched the Water Alliances for Voluntary Efficiency (WAVE). Endorsed by AH&LA, it's a country-wide program to promote efficient water use that initially focused on the lodging industry. WAVE encourages lodging properties to reduce water consumption by pointing out the economic and competitive benefits of doing so. Many of the WAVE partners—who include Westin, Hyatt, Sheraton, and LaQuinta—have reduced their water consumption by 30 percent annually.

Properties, especially resort properties with extensive landscaping demands, have also begun to use **effluent** or **reclaimed water**. Effluent water is water that is partially treated wastewater from community sewage or industry. It is usually cleansed of major pollutants, but still contains enough trace amounts of salt, minerals, and bacteria to render it undrinkable. This water can be used for irrigation, toilets, decorative fountains, and cooling towers.

Other common water conservation efforts include:

- Towel and linen reuse program in guestrooms.
- Low-flow faucets and showerheads in guestrooms.
- Low-flow toilets in guestrooms.
- Automatic faucets or toilets in public restrooms.
- Water-efficient clothes washing machines.

Linen Reuse Programs

Linen reuse programs are one of the most obvious and popular forms of water conservation. People at home rarely change their sheets and towels daily. Linen reuse programs remind guests of this and invite them to reuse their guestroom linens and towels rather than have them removed for washing. Since the early 1990s, hotels across the country have adopted various forms of reuse programs. They have been extremely popular with guests who appreciate that hotels are being environmentally conscious. Some hotels have reported 70 to 90 percent guest participation.

Exhibit 3 Linen Reuse Card

Help Us
Help the Environment

In our sincerest efforts to serve our guests, we also wish to pursue initiatives and policies that better serve the environment.

Upon check in, your room has been thoroughly cleaned and supplied with fresh linens. To contribute to the environment through the reduced usage of water, energy and potentially harmful detergents, please place this card on your pillow if:

Fresh Linens
are Not Necessary Today

Most estimates say that properties can save up to 13.5 gallons of fresh water and $6.50 a day per room with a linen reuse program. Such programs not only save water, but also electricity, gas, detergents, toweling, sheets, and labor.

Properties can create their own informational cards for guests or use one that is pre-designed by organizations such as AH&LA or the Green Hotels Association. These cards can be hung on a towel rack or placed on the bed. See Exhibit 3. They explain why the hotel has implemented a linen reuse program and how it works. Most hotels with linen reuse programs will not change sheets in occupied rooms unless a guest requests it or until three or four days have passed. Towels that are hanging on the rack will be left in the room while ones left on the floor will be changed. Sheets and towels are always changed upon check-out.

Guestrooms

The guestroom is one of the highest water-consuming areas of a hotel, primarily because of the bathrooms, which have a shower, toilet, and sink. The guestroom is also the place where the most inexpensive water conservation efforts can be made.

National standards now require that all showerheads in hotels consume no more than 1.75 gallons of water per minute. This can be tested by placing a bucket under the shower, running it for one minute, and then measuring the output. Unlike the old-style water conservation showerheads, the new ones provide a comfortable shower with an adequate supply of water. They typically pay for themselves in less than six months in saved water and the energy required to heat it.

Whoever is testing the showerheads should also look to see whether any water is also pouring out of the spigot into the tub when the shower diverter is turned on. If this is occurring, this is an indication that the diverter needs to be repaired immediately.

Older toilets consume as much as three to four gallons of water per flush. Water standards now require that toilets consume no more than 1.6 gallons per flush. This can be accomplished by installing new toilets or by installing a new flapper valve kit that will reduce the water consumed by an older toilet.

Flapper valves in guestroom toilets are the most notorious water wasters in hotels. A leaking flapper valve can cause numerous guest complaints because of the noise from constantly running water. All flapper valves in toilet tanks should be replaced at least every two to three years with a high-quality natural rubber flapper valve. The watertight seal of the flapper valve can be checked by placing food coloring in the tank and observing the bowl. If the coloring seeps through to the bowl, the flapper valve should be replaced immediately. Leaking flapper valves can cost about $150 per year per room in wasted water.

The flow rate at bathroom sinks should not exceed one gallon per minute. Flow rates can be reduced by installing an aerator that injects air into the water, causing an illusion of more water flowing. A simpler method is to turn down the hand valves under the sink to a minimal, but acceptable, level. This will conserve water and the energy to heat it.

Laundry

The largest consumers of water in an on-premises hotel laundry are the wash wheels (extractors). Here again, it is extremely important that employees wash only full loads. The wash wheels also have automatic fill valves that have a propensity to stick and waste a considerable amount of water. Laundry employees can listen for the continuous sound of water running and request that engineering repair any faulty valves immediately.

Water usage can also be drastically curtailed by decreasing the number of daily loads that are washed. This will require either the implementation of a voluntary linen reuse program in guestrooms or a change in standard operating procedures.

Laundry managers can work with appliance vendors to adjust washing machines to ensure the greatest overall energy efficiency. Increasing the spin cycle on the wash, for example, can decrease drying time by as much as one half.

Another way to save water is through major renovations. Many laundries are switching to an ozone-type washing system that uses less than half the amount of water of a traditional wash wheel.

Public Restrooms

Most public restroom toilets and urinals use a flush-valve type of flushing system. These toilets and urinals do not have water tanks, but flush by simply releasing water into the appliance to allow thorough flushing. It is now becoming standard

Exhibit 4 Energy Resource Demands

Market trends suggest that the demand for energy resources will rise dramatically over the next 25 years:

- Global demand for all energy sources is forecast to grow by 57 percent over the next 25 years.
- U.S. demand for all types of energy is expected to increase by 31 percent within 25 years.
- By 2030, 56 percent of the world's energy use will be in Asia.
- Electricity demand in the United States will grow by at least 40 percent by 2032.
- Currently, 50 percent of U.S. electrical generation relies on coal, a fossil fuel, while 85 percent of U.S. greenhouse gas emissions result from energy-consuming activities supported by fossil fuels.

Sources: Annual Energy Outlook (DOE/EIA-0383(2007)), International Energy Outlook 2007 (DOE/EIA-0484(2007), Inventory of U.S. Greenhouse Gas Emissions and Sinks: 1990–2005 (April 2007) (EPA 430-R-07-002)

practice for many hotels to install ultrasonic motion sensors on these appliances that will automatically flush them with the proper amount of water each time they are used. While these devices do not necessarily save a lot of water, they do ensure that your facilities are flushed every time they are used and, therefore, help eliminate plugged lines.

Energy Efficiency

According to the American Hotel & Lodging Association, the hospitality industry spends $3.7 billion a year on energy. AH&LA estimates that reducing energy use by 10 percent across the hospitality industry would save the industry $285 million each year while increasing guest satisfaction. Exhibit 4 shows predicted demands for energy resources during the next 25 years.

Properties that are committed to energy efficiency not only decrease their consumption of natural resources, they also can save a great deal of money and improve their bottom line. Energy savings is a way of reducing costs without reducing guest service or satisfaction.

The Environmental Protection Agency estimates that every $1 in energy savings is the equivalent of increasing operating margins by $2 to $3. When Starwood Hotels & Resorts Worldwide implemented an energy management program, it was able to save $3.4 million in energy costs—the equivalent of renting 9,370 additional rooms.

When Hilton Hotels implemented an energy management plan, it saved nearly 43 million kilowatt-hours of electricity per year and prevented 65 million pounds of carbon dioxide emissions—the equivalent of removing 6,450 cars from the road for a year.

Energy Management

As mentioned earlier, Energy Star is an EPA program that helps to identify energy-efficient products. Hospitality managers can go online to consult the Energy Star rating of products before purchasing them. Energy Star also provides calculators that help determine the savings each item can provide to a property.

Computerized energy management systems have grown in popularity. These software programs help hotel managers collect and analyze data collected from major energy-consuming appliances. Such systems can help a property determine when a piece of equipment should be run, what its maintenance needs are, and whether it would be cost-effective to modify or replace it.

Common activities to ensure more efficient use of energy include:

- Using equipment rated as energy efficient by Energy Star.
- Using programmable thermostats.
- Using sensor lighting indoors and outdoors.
- Using energy-efficient lighting in both the front and the back of the house.
- Using a computerized energy management system.
- Installing renewable energy generating equipment (such as solar power).
- Purchasing green power through a local utility.
- Installing tinted or double-paned windows.

Exhibit 5 shows a list of ways housekeepers can affect the amount of energy a hotel consumes.

Sometimes energy efficiency is as simple as turning things off. When PSA Energy Consultants conducts full-service energy audits (see Exhibit 6 for the steps the company takes), it almost always identifies many energy-consuming items that can be turned off at key points during the day and night. The chief engineer or facilities services manager can identify air handling units, exhaust fans, lighting, air conditioners, and other items that can be turned off.

After these items are identified, the hotel can consider installing a seven-day or 24-hour time clock to control them automatically. If the hotel has a centralized energy control system, it may be cost-effective to add a time clock to the scheduling feature of this system. This is the single largest energy-saving idea that can be implemented in a hotel and can provide significant savings with very little capital expenditure.

Guestroom energy controls are becoming more reliable, easier to use, and less expensive. These energy controls typically turn off or set back heating and cooling levels during unoccupied periods. New wireless models are less expensive to install and provide additional technical features.

Public-space global controls for the entire property are also becoming less expensive, more effective, and easier to use. This is typically a capital expenditure; control systems vary considerably in size and may cost in the range of $50,000 to $150,000. The hotel will likely see a three- to five-year return on investment, depending on the application and the identified opportunities to save energy.

Exhibit 5 Housekeeping Activities that Promote Energy Efficiency

The following housekeeping procedures can save energy:

	Procedure	Explanation
1.	Turn off or reset heating and cooling systems in unoccupied rooms.	Turning off heating and cooling systems in unoccupied rooms will help reduce costs without affecting the comfort of guests and staff.
2.	Close draperies and shades when leaving guestrooms.	This will reduce heat loss in winter and heat gain in summer.
3.	Turn off guestroom lights, televisions, and radios in unoccupied rooms.	Create reminder cards to remind guests to turn off lights, televisions, and radios when they leave the room.
4.	Use natural lighting when cleaning guestrooms.	Remind housekeeping to close draperies when leaving guestrooms.
5.	Clean lighting fixtures.	Bulbs will produce more light after cleaning.
6.	Limit the amount of hot water used for cleaning.	Limiting the amount of hot water used for cleaning will save water heating costs.
7.	Report any necessary equipment repairs.	Regular equipment maintenance will increase performance and decrease energy consumption.
8.	Install Energy Star clothes washers.	Energy Star clothes washers use 50 percent less energy. They also use 40 to 50 percent less water, which means less water to heat and shorter drying times.
9.	Capture and reuse waste heat from laundry operations.	Capturing and reusing emitted heat will decrease energy expenses.

Source: Florida Green Lodging Certification Program, Florida Energy Extension Service.

Lighting

Compact Fluorescent Lamps. Compact fluorescent lamps are the backbone of high-efficiency lighting. They are more energy efficient than incandescent bulbs, last about ten times longer, and do not emit lost energy through heat. Compact fluorescent lighting products continue to improve in terms of longer lamp life, better color, and a variety of sizes. The most common application for compact fluorescent lamps in hotels is in the guestroom. There are usually three to five table and floor lamps in a guestroom. A 20-watt spiral-type compact fluorescent lamp typically will provide higher light levels than 75-watt or 100-watt incandescent lamps.

To illustrate the energy expense savings, take a 300-room hotel with four 100-watt lamps per room and compare the energy cost for the old incandescent lamps to the new compact fluorescents. Assuming the lights operate about four hours per day, they will run a total of 1,460 hours per year. At $.08 per kilowatt-hour, the

Exhibit 6 Six Steps to Successful Energy Management

1. **Energy accounting.** Create a baseline and track the hotel's progress.
2. **Full-service energy audit**. Inventory every conceivable piece of energy-consuming equipment and then set priorities for projects that can help save energy.
3. **Implement.** Train employees, particularly in housekeeping and engineering, on procedures that will improve guest comfort and save energy.
4. **High-payback capital retrofit projects.** Implement capital projects such as lighting retrofits, lighting controls, energy efficient motors, time clocks, and adjustable speed drives.
5. **Capital projects specific to hotel.** These might include larger projects such as co-generation, free cooling, mechanical system upgrades, and computerized controls for all equipment in the hotel. Some of these may not be cost-effective, however.
6. **Ongoing security program.** Verify that savings have been made and then continue to upgrade the ideas in the full-service energy audit as technology improves.

Source: PSA Energy Consultants

annual cost of operating the old system is $14,016. But by converting all of the guestroom lamps in this 300-room hotel to 20-watt compact fluorescents, the hotel will save approximately $11,212 per year. Such a conversion program will also reduce labor costs associated with replacing burned-out lights by about 90 percent.

The cost to purchase the new energy-efficient compact fluorescents is estimated to be about $5 each, for a total conversion cost of $6,000. The project will, therefore, provide about a six-month return on investment. Many utilities will pay up to 50 percent of the cost of installing compact fluorescents. In that case, the project would have a three-month return on investment. This is a significant opportunity for hotels to reduce their electrical consumption and energy expense without affecting guest comfort.

Compact fluorescent lighting technology is also available in specialty lamps for decorative fixtures. These include flame, candle, and globe-type lamps that are available in wattages as low as 15 watts.

The majority of all public spaces in hotels, including ballrooms, corridors, lobbies, meeting rooms, and game rooms, are lighted with fixtures that are referred to as "recessed can down lights." These fixtures typically use a wide variety of incandescent lamps that range from 75 to 150 watts each. A large portion of these fixtures, especially those in meeting rooms, restaurants, and bars, are on dimmable switches known as rheostats. Dimmable compact fluorescent reflector lamps are evolving slowly, but product quality and reliability have been questionable thus far. Some of these lamps do not dim to required levels, and the purchase cost has been somewhat high. When they do become viable, dimmable compact fluorescent lamps will represent a major development and an opportunity to reduce energy use throughout a property's public space. Not only will these lamps save on direct energy costs (it will take less money to keep them burning), they will

the Rooms CHRONICLE®

Straight Talk about Hotel Energy Myths

Fluorescent lights

Many people believe that turning fluorescent lights on and off consumes more energy than simply leaving them on continuously. This is absolutely not true. There is no greater energy savings than one hundred percent, which occurs whenever lights are turned off. Turning lights off and on frequently, however, will slightly shorten the life of the lamp.

Magnets and ozone

There are many vendors with some unusual products and concepts for saving energy. One vendor recommended putting magnets in the basin of a cooling tower as a form of water treatment, for example. He also recommended wrapping magnets around water supply pipes to swimming pools. The vendor touted the idea that the polarity of the magnets would perform some magic treatment to the water, therefore eliminating the cost of adding water treatment to the various water systems throughout the hotel such as pool water, laundry water, and chilled water for air conditioning.

Be very suspicious of vendors selling products to eliminate the need to treat water. Water treatment performed incorrectly can cost a substantial amount of money if equipment becomes corroded or if health problems result from improperly treated waters.

Over the years, there have been numerous ozone-related products introduced to the market whose worthiness could not be substantiated. Here again, water treatment was the most common application of ozone devices. Years ago, the Massachusetts Institute of Technology conducted extensive testing on many of these products and energy-enhancing concepts. They concluded that, in general, most ozone products did not work.

Today, ozone products have been developed to replace laundry detergent and to provide fresh air to guestrooms and public spaces. Some of these products are much improved over the older varieties. It is recommended, however, that whenever you are approached by a vendor offering any product that uses ozone to save money and purify air, you should thoroughly examine the product, research the purported technology, and obtain references from reliable people who are using it.

Light bulb buttons

Light bulb buttons are tiny disks that stick to the end of a light bulb before it is screwed into the socket. A light bulb button can reduce energy consumption in an incandescent light by 30 to 50 percent. Unfortunately, the light bulb button causes a corresponding reduction in light output.

Over-exaggerated savings

Vendors are known to either slightly or extremely exaggerate the savings of the products they were selling. This is why it is useful to consult an independent energy advisor when making capital expenditures on energy-saving devices.

The proper investment of time, research, and expertise early on can pay handsome dividends in the form of energy savings. Thorough testing and common the Rooms CHRONICLE® *(continued)*

sense should prevail when determining true energy savings. Keep in mind that the savings realized are not just based on the quality of the product or the source and type of energy consumed; they are also determined by the utility rates in each hotel's given area, which can vary substantially.

Source: *The Rooms Chronicle®*, Volume 14, Number 2, pp. 1–3.
For subscription information, please call 866-READ-TRC.

also provide indirect savings because they can significantly reduce the air conditioning load required in a hotel's public spaces.

Motion Sensors. One of the most abused energy wasters in hotels is lighting that is left on in unoccupied areas. To correct this, properties are installing light-switch motion sensors in areas such as room attendant closets, storerooms, and offices. These light-switch motion sensors typically cost less than $25, and can be installed by a maintenance engineer in minutes. Depending on the nature of the application, the typical return on investment by using these devices is less than six months. Ceiling motion sensors can also be used in areas such as meeting rooms, conference rooms, and public restrooms. These devices are more expensive and cost in the range of $200, but control a larger lighting load. Audits have revealed that lights are frequently left on in these areas when they are unoccupied.

Waste Management

The three R's of waste reduction—reduce, recycle, and reuse—are quickly becoming as well-known as their academic predecessors. Waste reduction programs that incorporate all three can help a property make a real difference in the world around it. According to the Florida Energy Extension Service, a large lodging property can generate as much as eight tons of waste per day—and up to 60 percent of this is recyclable. The most common source of waste is the kitchen.

To determine what and how to reduce, reuse, and recycle, many lodging managers begin by conducting a waste audit of each operational area. The executive housekeeper may be asked to conduct the audit in the housekeeping department and for guestrooms. This audit begins with a walk-through of every area to identify recyclable materials, the source of material, and the quantity of recyclable materials being collected or thrown away. The analysis should determine who collects waste, what type of waste is generated, when it is collected, where it is stored, and how the waste is collected at the source and diverted to recycling.

The waste reduction team can then create a plan from the audit and other information it collects. Each area of the property may be given its own waste reduction plan. There may be separate ones for the guestrooms, swimming pool and spa areas, public spaces, and the laundry.

Common waste reduction activities include the following:

- Recycling such materials as office paper, newspaper, aluminum cans, magazines, steel cans, and cardboard
- Purchasing products with recycled content, such as office paper, toilet tissues, paper towels, and paper napkins
- Purchasing in bulk
- Purchasing items that use reduced packaging or for which the supplier takes the packaging back and reuses it
- Using a trash compactor
- Composting yard trash and food waste

Reduce

Reducing waste is an area in which the housekeeping department can take an active role. As properties have looked for ways to reduce waste, the ideas have been as varied as the types of waste themselves.

One initiative that has been growing in popularity after initial resistance is the idea of shampoo and conditioner dispensers in bathrooms rather than the small bottles which create a great deal of waste and have to be thrown out after one use. Companies have developed tamper-proof models that protect the guests. Properties that use them have found that the cost savings means that they can purchase name-brand hair products that appeal to guests, thus making the program a popular one.

Bottled water, for all its popularity, also represents a source of potential waste because of the use of plastic bottles. Four Seasons Hotel in Jackson Hole, Wyoming, chose to start replacing the bottled water they put in guestrooms during turndown service with pitchers of local tap water.

Other amenities are also under examination. Many properties have removed underused amenities from guestrooms and offer them by request only. These include such things as shower caps, shoeshine cloths, sewing kits, and mouthwash. Some will also reuse items if the seal is not broken.

Tissues, toilet paper, and paper towels are also areas where many hotels have successfully reduced waste. In guestrooms, room attendants can be taught to not replace toilet paper until it is nearly gone. Instead, they can leave a second roll of toilet paper in the room for guests, ensuring that they will not run out. In public restrooms, some properties replace paper towels with electric hand dryers that are designed to minimize paper waste.

Environmental groups have encouraged properties to replace disposable glasses in guestrooms with reusable glasses. Properties that do this must ensure that they follow health and sanitation rules by removing these glasses from the room every day and washing and sanitizing them through the dishwasher. They should not be rinsed out or washed in the room.

Some properties that offer dry cleaning service have found ways to reduce the waste associated with this service. They return laundered clothes to guests in reusable garment bags or baskets, offering plastic wrap for dry cleaned clothing only upon request, and have eliminated the cardboard backing for laundered shirts.

Savings can also be found in the handling of chemicals. The executive housekeeper can set up mixing stations to reduce chemical spillage. The staff can be trained in how to mix liquid concentrates to ensure safety and save money. Along

Exhibit 7 Items for a Hotel Recycling Program

The following items are commonly included in a hotel recycling program:

Aluminum cans	Fluorescent bulbs	Paint
Antifreeze	Food waste	Plastic bottles
Appliances	Freon	Plastic buckets
Batteries	Furniture	Radios
Building materials	Glass jars	Scrap metal
Cardboard	Landscape waste	Steel containers
Carpet	Magazines	Telephone books
Cell phones	Motor oil	Televisions
Cooking grease	Newspapers	Wood
Computers	Office supplies	

these same lines, housekeeping can use refillable pump spray bottles instead of aerosol cans.

Recycle

The second component in a waste management program is recycling and using recycled materials. (Exhibit 7 lists some of the items typically included in a hotel recycling program.) There are many ways a hospitality organization can participate in recycling. The Warwick Hotel in Seattle, Washington found that it saved a substantial amount of money by creating a recycling program. Thanks to recycling, it reduced the number of pickups for its five garbage containers from four times a week to two times a week, thus saving $730 a month in waste disposal bills.

Room attendants collect waste from guestrooms every day. Most commonly, this waste includes paper products, food-related wastes, and bathroom wastes. When first setting up a recycling program, the executive housekeeper (or some other housekeeping manager) will need to conduct a waste audit by selecting three random rooms and collecting garbage from them daily for seven days to determine the quantity and type of waste generated. This will let the manager know what type of volume of recyclables to plan for. Housekeeping management will have to decide where to store recyclables and how to train employees to collect and sort them.

Some properties now provide two trash cans in each guestroom—a recycling can or receptacle and a regular trash can. This helps save time for room attendants who won't have to sift through the waste. Room attendants can collect and sort recyclables as the room is cleaned. A housekeeping cart can be arranged to have separate bags on the side for trash and recycling.

In addition to recycling waste found in guestrooms, the housekeeping department can also recycle waste that it generates in its back-of-the-house areas. Cardboard boxes can be recycled, as can clothing hangers, plastic containers, and tissues.

The executive housekeeper can also evaluate the housekeeping products that the property is currently using and determine whether recycled products or products with recycled content can be purchased instead.

Exhibit 8 Take the Soap Home!

Bar soap is one amenity offered by all hotels. It's something that travel associations such as AAA and Mobil have as requirements for their ratings. Unused bars of soap are usually discarded by the housekeeper. Several reuse ideas have been attempted for used bars of soap, such as:

- Making it into liquid soap by chopping it or flaking it and soaking it in water
- Giving it to homeless shelters
- Using them in crafts projects to make carvings

However, these ideas save only a tiny percentage of the tons of bar soap discarded every day. Green Hotels Association suggests a simpler answer: Ask guests to take their partially used soap home. It recommends posting a sign in the bathroom that says "Save the Wrapper." The sign can explain the waste issue and encourage guests to save the wrapper they take off the new bar of soap so that they can take the soap home in the wrapper at the end of their stay and use the soap at home.

Newspaper Recycling Programs. Many properties—especially those serving a large number of business travelers—have begun newspaper recycling programs. Programs vary from property to property and range from simply recycling papers to reducing the number of newspapers provided. At some properties, guests are asked at check-in whether they would like to receive a complimentary newspaper. If they do not, then newspapers aren't delivered. Some properties also provide a door hanger in each guestroom that guests can put out if they do not want to receive a newspaper. Other properties put complimentary newspapers in a central location (such as on tables near elevators, in the breakfast lounge, at the front desk, etc.) rather than deliver them to every room. Properties doing this often find that they use fewer newspapers. Unread newspapers can sometimes be returned to the newspaper vendor. Newspapers can be donated to such places as animal shelters, pet stores, fish markets, mailing companies, moving companies, and paint shops. The hotel itself might be able to use old newspapers.

Reuse

Much of the waste generated by a hotel can be reused—by the property, by another organization, and even by guests (see Exhibit 8). Linens are a popular item for reuse. Stained tablecloths can be turned into napkins, room service tray placemats, chef's aprons, or uniform ties. Retired sheets can be made into laundry bags. Retired terry can be made into hot pads or kitchen urn covers. Retired linens and towels as well as leftover bottles of shampoo, lotions, bar soap, and toilet paper can also be donated to schools, homeless shelters, humane societies, veterinarian offices, pet boarding houses, etc. Other items that can be donated include excess clothing hangers (or those left by guests in the room); these can be given to a local dry cleaner or thrift shop.

Indoor Air Quality

Lodging properties have been focusing on clean air concerns for decades. In 1995, AH&LA's Educational Institute published a manual on hotel air quality management—an action guide for engineers and managers. In it, R.A. Riedel wrote that the EPA says air inside buildings is sometimes as much as 100 times more polluted than the air outside. It's considered one of the most severe environmental risks to health in the United States.

Common clean air practices include:

- Using environmentally preferred cleaners.
- Using environmentally preferred High Efficiency Particulate Air (HEPA) filters.
- Cleaning all air handler units and coils at least annually.
- Venting exhaust fans to the outside.
- Running a dehumidifier.
- Making sure that rooms where smoking is permitted are well-ventilated or properly filtered.

A healthy indoor environment is one in which the surroundings contribute to productivity, comfort, and a sense of health and well-being. The indoor air is free of significant levels of odors, dust, and contaminants, and is circulated to prevent stuffiness without creating drafts. Temperature and humidity are appropriate to the season and the clothing and activities of the occupants.

Indoor air contaminants come from a number of sources. They can include contaminated outdoor air (pollen, dust, industrial pollutants, vehicle exhaust fumes), emissions from nearby sources (loading docks, dumpster odors, exhaust from the building, unsanitary debris near the outdoor air intake), soil gas (radon, underground fuel tank leakage, pesticides), moisture or standing water that promotes microbial growth (rooftops after rainfall, crawlspaces, air and moisture flow through the wall system, condensation within a wall, water-damaged furnishings, standing water from clogged or poorly designed drains), HVAC system, personal activities (smoking, cooking, body odors, cosmetic odors), housekeeping activities (cleaning materials and procedures, deodorizers and fragrances, airborne dust or dirt circulated by sweeping or vacuuming), chemicals and off-gassing from furnishings (carpets, wall coverings, ceiling tiles, interior paints and coatings), and redecorating/remodeling/repair activities (emissions from new furnishings, dust and fibers from demolition).

Indoor Air Quality Programs

Because there are plenty of potential indoor air contaminates to deal with, properties need to establish programs to manage their indoor air. Engineers and other property managers are often charged with creating an indoor air quality preventive maintenance program. Doing so will benefit guests and save unnecessary costs in the long run. **Indoor air quality** can be defined as:

- The introduction and distribution of adequate ventilation air.
- The control of airborne contaminants.
- The maintenance of acceptable temperature and relative humidity.

One challenge that hoteliers face is that some efforts to reduce energy costs contribute to poor indoor air quality. Hotel managers must make sure that adjusting one area doesn't cost the property in the other area.

Poor housekeeping practices that fail to remove dust and other dirt can cause indoor air quality complaints. On the other hand, some cleaning materials can produce odors and emit a variety of chemicals. Housekeeping staff may be the first to recognize and respond to potential air quality control problems as they work throughout the property. Housekeeping department managers should consider the following topics:

- *The importance of clean air.* Managers should understand both the financial factors and the human factors.
- *Cleaning schedules.* Managers should consider how cleaning activities are scheduled, particularly for public areas. Housekeeping managers may want to schedule the use of some cleaning agents during low occupancy periods, because they introduce strong odors or contaminants into the atmosphere.
- *Purchasing.* Housekeeping managers should become familiar with the chemicals in cleaning and other maintenance products and their potential toxicity, and make sure they select the safest available products. Much of the information needed for this type of research is provided by product labels and the products' material safety data sheets.
- *Materials handling and storage.* Managers should make certain that cleaning materials are used and stored properly by staff members.
- *Trash disposal.* Managers should make sure that staff members follow proper trash disposal procedures. If there is a restaurant at the property, perishable refuse should be disposed of daily. Managers should ensure that trash containers are covered, pest control is effective, and the trash collection area is cleaned at least daily.

All personnel should be trained on the importance of clean air practices. Housekeeping employees in particular should be familiar with and able to recognize crucial air quality factors such as gas leaks and improper exhaust emissions. When housekeeping employees are able to identify and properly report problems, the problems can be addressed as small concerns before they turn into larger, expensive problems.

Fighting Mold

Mold and mildew have become increasingly alarming problems for hotels, especially newer ones built in high-humidity climates. Several hotels that were either brand new or which added on major wings ended up closing their doors after only a few years because they became so infested with mold that the buildings were unlivable. It took years and millions of dollars in renovations before they could reopen.

Mold and mildew can lead to serious indoor air quality problems. Hotels, in particular their engineering departments, must take aggressive action to prevent mold growth. According to the Environmental Protection Agency, the following actions can help control moisture, which can help prevent mold:

- Fix leaks as soon as possible.
- Watch for condensation and wet spots and respond to them rapidly.
- Prevent moisture buildup in contained areas.
- Keep heating, ventilation, and air conditioning drip pans clean.
- Vent moisture-generating appliances.
- Maintain low indoor humidity.
- Perform regular inspections and maintain documentation logs.

Properties are also increasingly turning to low-moisture extractors when cleaning guestrooms as a way of preventing mold. Hotels do deep cleaning on guestroom carpets throughout the year. Typically, guestroom carpets took a long time to dry when the hotels used wet-extraction cleaning methods, because the rooms were in an enclosed space. The EPA advises that carpets need to dry within 48 hours to prevent mold and mildew; groups such as LEED say that carpets should dry in 24 hours or less. Low-moisture extractors reduce carpet-drying times to as little as 30 minutes while using fewer chemicals. Tankless low-moisture machines have the greatest efficiency, and carpets cleaned with them need the least amount of time to dry.

Cleaning Chemicals

A hotel's housekeeping and laundry personnel use more cleaning chemicals during the course of their daily tasks than any other staff members in a hospitality organization. This puts the responsibility for the care and proper use of these chemicals firmly on the shoulders of the executive housekeeper. The executive housekeeper must carefully manage chemicals from purchasing through use and disposal.

Executive housekeepers are increasingly choosing environmentally sound chemicals that are safer for employees and guests. Product labels provide information about how biodegradable the cleaning chemicals are, and suppliers should be able to provide cost information regarding environmentally responsible chemical choices.

Executive housekeepers should choose cleaning products with low levels of **volatile organic compounds**. They also want to look for cleaners that are non-toxic, biodegradable, and non-corrosive. Housekeeping employees must follow label instructions carefully. The executive housekeeper may want to conduct experiments by incrementally increasing or decreasing product use to calculate maximum efficiency in the use of the product. The rule of thumb is to use as little chemical as possible to get the job done.

The amount of hazardous chemicals stored at a property can be reduced by smart inventory practices. Just-in-time inventory can reduce the amount of time that cleaning chemicals and other potentially hazardous products have to be stored at the property.

Housekeeping employees need to clean up chemical spills, excesses, and run-offs quickly before the chemical soaks into carpets or other materials or gets trapped in the ventilation system. If the use of strong cleaning chemicals in a particular area will significantly affect that area's air quality, housekeeping should post warning notices for guests and others.

Finally, executive housekeepers need to make sure that when chemicals are disposed of that they go into the waste management system and not the storm sewer system.

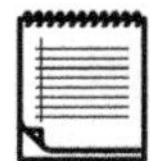

Endnotes

1. Patricia Sheehan, "Seeing Green," *Lodging Hospitality*, July 1, 2007, pp. 22–24.
2. Shelli Johannes-Wells, "Moving Hospitality into 'Greener Pastures,'" *Southern Hospitality*, Summer 2007, Volume 30, Issue 2, pp. 14–16.
3. Kevin Maher, "Gone Green: The AH&LA's Environmental Partnership," *Lodging*, July 2007, p. 24.

Acknowledgments

Much of the information in this chapter was adopted from the following articles in *The Rooms Chronicle®*.

In particular, these issues provided a great deal of information:

- Volume 10, No. 3 Energy savings comes from employee training.
- Volume 11, No. 4 Water conversation can be invisible to the guest.
- Volume 11, No. 5 The top 10 energy-saving projects for a hotel.
- Volume 12, No. 2 2004 Lighting technology update.
- Volume 12, No. 3 Finding ways to minimize energy expense as gas costs keep rising.
- Volume 13, No. 4 It's time to reexamine energy saving capital projects.
- Volume 15, No. 4 Time to get serious about water conservation—Here are several steps to get started.

For information on subscribing to *The Rooms Chronicle®*, please call 866-READ-TRC.

Key Terms

eco-purchasing—Purchasing policies that evaluate products for durability, reusability, recyclability, content, packaging, and delivery methods.

effluent water—Partially treated wastewater from community sewage or industry.

just-in-time buying—The practice of buying products just before current inventory runs out.

reclaimed water—Partially treated wastewater from community sewage or industry.

sustainability—Reducing one's ecological footprint so that resources are not irresponsibly depleted.

triple bottom line—A three-pronged approach to sustainability that includes economic, social, and environmental management.

volatile organic compounds—Also known as VOCs, they emit gasses which can have short- and long-term adverse health effects. Examples include paint strippers, permanent markers, disinfectants, degreasers, and other cleaning supplies.

Review Questions

1. What types of programs exist to help hospitality properties become better environmental stewards?
2. What role does the housekeeping department play in a property's environmental program?
3. How have linen reuse programs contributed to water conservation?
4. What is the most energy efficient form of lighting?
5. What are the three elements of a waste management program?
6. What are some important elements of indoor air quality programs?
7. What factors should an executive housekeeper consider when choosing cleaning chemicals?

Internet Sites

For more information, visit the following Internet sites. Remember that Internet addresses can change without notice. If the site is no longer there, you can use a search engine to look for additional sites.

AH&LA's Good Earthkeeping Program
www.ei-ahla.org/content.asp?ID=146

Earth 911
www.earth911.com

EC3 Global
www.ec3global.com

Energy Star
www.energystar.gov

Florida Green Lodging
www.FloridaGreenLodging.org

Green Lodging News
www.greenlodgingnews.com

WasteWise
www.epa.gov/wastewise

Chapter 8 Outline

Competencies

1. Describe the management process in terms of the functions front office managers perform to achieve organizational objectives. (pp. 287–290)
2. Identify room rate categories and explain how managers establish room rates. (pp. 290–301)
3. Discuss issues involved with forecasting room availability and apply the ratios and formulas managers use. (pp. 301–312)
4. Explain how front office managers forecast rooms revenue and estimate expenses when budgeting for operations. (pp. 312–316)
5. Describe how managers use various reports and ratios to evaluate front office operations. (pp. 316–331)
6. Explain what front office managers can do to plan for disasters. (pp. 331–332)

Taken from *Managing Front Office Operations,* Ninth Edition, by Michael L. Kasavana

Chapter 8

Planning and Evaluating Operations

MOST FRONT OFFICE MANAGERS will readily admit that they rarely have all the resources necessary to accurately monitor the guest cycle. Resources available to managers include staff members, budgeted funds, work shifts, materials, and equipment. All are in limited supply. An important part of a front office manager's job involves planning how to apply limited resources to attain the department's objectives. An equally important function is evaluating the success of front office activities in meeting the department's objectives.

Management Functions

The process of front office management can be divided into specific management activities. Exhibit 1 illustrates how management functions fit into the overall front office management process. Although specific front office management tasks vary among hotels, fundamental management functions remain similar in scope.

Planning

Planning is probably the most important management function in any business, yet managers may fail to provide the attention it requires, and may overlook it entirely. Without competent planning, front office work would be chaotic. Without the direction and focus planning provides, the front office manager may become overly involved with tasks that are unrelated to or inconsistent with accomplishing the department's goals. A front office manager's first step in planning should involve determining the department's goals.

Managers should identify both near-term goals and long-term goals, and develop a plan for achieving them. An example of a near-term goal might be to increase next month's occupancy from 82 to 85 percent. A long-term goal might be to improve guest satisfaction scores well beyond the current level. The front office manager should use these general goals as a guide to planning more specific, measurable objectives. Planning also includes determining the strategies and tactics the department will use to attain the objectives.

An important component of planning is communication, which is essential for success. An effective front office manager will communicate the plans under development with supervisors to ensure that departmental activities are consistent with overall hotel planning. At the same time, it is a good idea to share tentative or preliminary plans with department members likely to be affected by the plan and

Exhibit 1 Overview of the Management Process

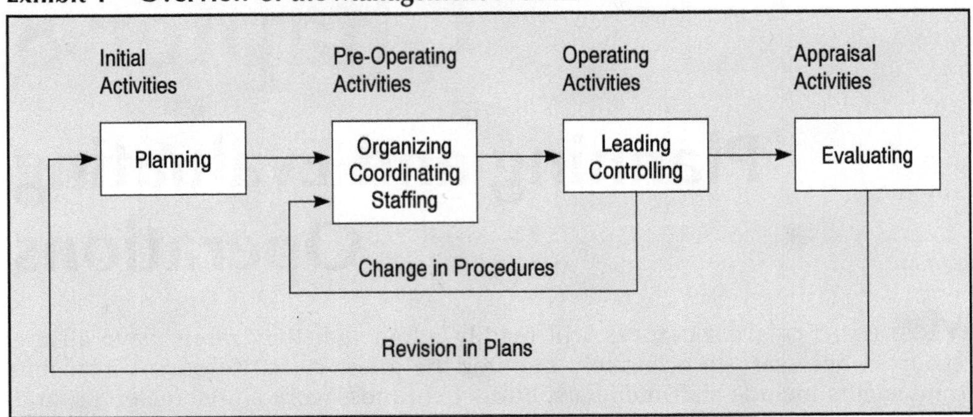

seek their input and feedback. Communication is most effective in written form so that ideas are documented and clearly illustrated for reviewers.

There are several benefits to communication and idea-sharing. First, department staff members can contribute to the planning process and thereby gain ownership of the plan (or portions of the plan). Staff members who are included in the planning process typically are more willing to accept and support the overall plan. Second, staff members involved in the planning process have the opportunity to provide constructive comments before the department manager finalizes the plan. If staff members have concerns about the plan, the department manager is able to address these issues during the planning phase. Third, once the plan is finalized, everyone involved will have a more comprehensive understanding of the goal or objective. If several different competing perspectives emerge during the planning process, compromises may be required. Staff members tend to develop a better understanding of the compromises that are made when they are part of the planning process.

Organizing

Using the planned goals as a guide, a front office manager organizes the department by dividing the work among front office staff. The manager should distribute work so that everyone participates and the work can be completed in a timely manner. Organizing includes determining the order in which tasks should be performed and establishing completion deadlines for each group and subgroup of tasks.

Coordinating

Coordinating involves bringing together and using available resources to attain planned goals. A front office manager must be able to coordinate the efforts of many individuals to ensure that work is performed efficiently, effectively, and on time. Coordinating front office procedures may involve engaging with other departments, such as sales, housekeeping, food and beverage, and accounting.

Many front office goals depend on other departments for achievement. For example, the goal of improving guest satisfaction scores may partially depend on the housekeeping staff's promptly notifying the front desk staff when a clean and vacant room has been readied for the next arriving guest. The front office manager's ability to coordinate with various department managers is closely related to his or her other management skills, such as planning and organizing.

Staffing

Staffing involves recruiting applicants and selecting those best qualified to fill available positions. To properly recruit employees, it is essential to develop job descriptions that thoroughly describe the position and that clearly identify the skills and qualities applicants must possess to satisfactorily fill it. The front office manager will work with the human resources department to develop job descriptions for front office positions. At most hotels, the human resources department is usually involved in the first level of qualifying and interviewing job applicants. Human resources staff members are also relied upon to resolve issues that may arise regarding whether a job description properly represents the position. The staffing process also involves scheduling employees. Most front office managers develop staffing guidelines based on formulas for calculating the number of employees required to meet guest and operational needs under specific conditions.

Leading

Leading is a complicated management skill that is exercised in a wide variety of situations, and is closely related to other management skills such as organizing, coordinating, and staffing. For a front office manager, leadership involves overseeing, motivating, training, disciplining, and setting an example for the front office staff. For example, to direct the work of others, a front office manager must first analyze the work to be done, organize the tasks in a logical order, and consider the environment in which staff will perform the tasks. In addition, if the department is behind in getting the work done, the front office manager steps in and assists until the workload is under control again.

A front office manager's leadership impact often extends beyond the front office. With so much of the hotel's business activity flowing through the front desk, other department heads count on the front office manager to provide direction. Senior managers at a hotel often depend on the front office manager's strong leadership skills to ensure that assignments are completed successfully.

One of the best ways to lead a department is by example. It is often necessary for department managers to participate in the department's day-to-day operations to demonstrate job knowledge and skills mastery. For instance, working at the front desk may involve greeting guests, checking guests in and out, pre-blocking rooms, working with housekeeping staff, charting room status, and more. When a manager leads effectively, this behavior demonstrates what is expected of all department employees. A manager must be available to department employees and will earn their respect as the unit leader if he or she leads by example. This often means working varying shifts to be available to all front desk staff, not just to the workers on one particular shift.

Controlling

Every front office department has a system of internal controls to protect the hotel's assets. For example, one form of internal control is requiring a witness's signature when a cashier makes a cash deposit at the end of the shift. Internal control systems work only when managers believe in the systems' importance and follow established procedures. The control process ensures that the actual results of business operations closely match planned results. The front office manager also exercises a control function when keeping front office operations on course in attaining planned goals.

Evaluating

Proper methods of evaluation determine the extent to which planned goals are, in fact, attained. The task of evaluating is frequently overlooked in many front office operations, or is performed haphazardly. Evaluating also involves reviewing and, when necessary, revising or helping to revise front office goals.

This chapter focuses on elements of two front office management functions: planning and evaluating front office operations. It begins by examining three important front office planning functions:

- Establishing room rates
- Forecasting room availability
- Budgeting for operations

It concludes by examining various methods a front office manager may use to evaluate the effectiveness of front office operations.

Establishing Room Rates

A front office revenue management system will almost always have more than one room rate category for each guestroom. Room rate categories generally correspond to types of rooms (suites, two beds, one bed, etc.) that are comparable in square footage and furnishings. Differences are based on criteria such as room size, location within the hotel, view, furnishings, and amenities.

The **rack rate** is the price for an overnight accommodation, as determined by front office management, for a particular room or room type. The rack rate is posted on the room rate schedule to inform front desk agents of the standard selling price of each guestroom in the hotel. Unless the guest qualifies for an authorized room rate discount, the rack rate will apply. The term *rack rate* predates front office automation and references the process by which an employee would identify the retail room rate from a manual filing system located at the front desk, called a *room rack,* hence the name *rack rate*. With front office automation, an electronic file replaces the rack. Electronically stored room rate data is accessed by front office staff members, as well as reservation agents, at the time of reservation or registration. Often, operational policies mandate that rack rates be reported to local and state authorities, and posted in public areas or inside the guestroom. Rack rates must be kept current and accurately reflect the appropriate accommodation charge for each room and room rate category.

Room rates are normally assigned by room type category. For example, a standard room with two double beds and no special amenities may be assigned the hotel's lowest rack rate. Larger rooms, with different sleeping accommodations and amenities, will be assigned a higher rack rate. Concierge floor rooms with more amenities and perhaps better outdoor views will likely be assigned an even higher rack rate. Suites usually command the highest rack rate because of size, number of beds, quality of furnishings, and other amenities.

When a resort property includes a meal plan in its room pricing (for example, Bed and Breakfast, Modified American, or Full American Plan), the rack rate is usually based on the room characteristics as well as the number of people expected to occupy the room. In this case, a resort's pricing for a single room rate may be greater than the value of the property's double occupancy rate divided by two, since the hotel incurs certain fixed costs no matter how many guests occupy the room.

Front office employees are expected to sell rooms at the rack rate unless a guest qualifies for a discounted room rate. Although rack rates are important, more often than not, guests may ask for and qualify for discount rates. For example, special rates are often quoted to groups and certain guests for promotional purposes, especially during low occupancy periods. Special room rate categories include:

- *Corporate or commercial rate:* the rate offered to companies that provide frequent business for an individual hotel or hotel chain.
- *Group rate:* the rate offered to group, meeting, and convention attendees staying at the hotel.
- *Promotional rate:* the rate offered to individuals who may belong to an affinity group such as the American Automobile Association or American Association of Retired Persons, to promote their patronage. The rate may also be extended during special low occupancy periods to other guests to promote occupancy.
- *Incentive rate:* the rate offered to guests in affiliated organizations such as travel agencies and airlines because of potential referral business. The rate may also be offered to promote future business; it is often extended to group leaders, meeting planners, tour operators, and other decision-makers capable of providing the hotel with additional room sales.
- *Family rate:* a rate reserved for families with children.
- *Package plan rate:* a rate that includes a guestroom in combination with other events, activities, or services, such as meals, golf, tennis, or parking.
- *Internet rate:* a special discounted rate that many hotel companies offer through an Internet website. A web rate is usually classified as the "best available rate" and is available to guests making an online reservation. Many hotel companies guarantee that the best available rate is at their own website and often offer a bonus plan for guests who find lower rates elsewhere. During projected lower occupancy business cycles, web rates tend to be discounted rates. Since a hotel company incurs less expense selling a guestroom through a private website, its rates will naturally be lower. Comparatively,

global distribution systems, travel agency sites, corporate call centers, and other distribution channels may offer higher room rates.

- *Distressed-inventory rate:* a special room rate offered when a hotel projects or experiences low occupancy. This rate usually represents a significant discount off the rack rate and is implemented to help build occupancy. The idea behind distressed-inventory rates is that the discount will be sufficient to attract consumers who seek lower rates. Distressed-inventory rates are usually found on Internet websites that offer hotel rooms based on targeted price and not on a specific hotel property; in fact, online shoppers may need to commit to the room rate even before learning the identity of the hotel property or brand. Most hotels restrict the use of distressed-inventory rates to only those times when extremely low occupancy is predicted.
- *Complimentary rate:* a room rate provided to special guests, important industry leaders as a sales incentive, and those guests who have experienced a problem at the hotel to the point where management wishes to give them a complimentary rate as compensation. The term *complimentary rate* usually means that the guest will not be charged for the guestroom during the stay. However, the guest may still be charged for incidental items such as food and beverages, Internet access, etc.

The front office manager must be sure that the sale of rooms at special rates is rigidly controlled. Special rates represent discounts from the rack rate and therefore may adversely affect the average room rate and room revenue. The front office manager should examine the circumstances under which special rates are granted to ensure that front office staff members are adhering to prescribed policies. All policies should be clearly explained to front office staff, who should obtain proper approval when applying a special room rate. For example, a complimentary room (provided at no charge) does not increase room revenue, but it may or may not decrease the average room rate, depending on the front office accounting system. Most hotels require the general manager or another senior member of the management team to approve complimentary rates before guests arrive.

Establishing rack rates for room types, and determining discount categories and special rates, are some of the major duties of the hotel's revenue manager. The revenue manager recommends rack rates to senior hotel management after analyzing forecasted occupancy and business conditions in the marketplace. Rack rates are usually determined on a yearly basis (subject to frequent revision review) and are a major decision factor in the annual hotel budgeting process. Determining discounted rates is more tactical and is a decision the revenue manager, or possibly a revenue committee, must make. When determining rack rates or discounted rates, management should consider such factors as operating expenses, guest demand, market conditions, inflationary factors, and related business issues.

Room rates often serve as a market positioning statement, since they directly reflect service expectations to the hotel's target market. Room rate positioning can be critical to a hotel's success. For example, a property offering economy facilities and limited guest services will most likely not succeed if its rates are positioned in the mid-price or upscale levels.

The following sections examine three popular approaches to pricing rooms: the **market condition approach,** the **rule-of-thumb approach,** and the **Hubbart Formula.**

Market Condition Approach

The market condition approach reflects a relatively commonsense strategy. Managers identify comparable hotels in their geographic market and research their room rates. These comparable properties compose what is often referred to as the **competitive set,** which is usually made up of six to ten properties in a market area. The competition can be based on location, property ratings, property type, brand identification, or other factors. Not every lodging property in a particular location is a direct competitor. Guests who look for moderately priced lodging will generally limit their research to properties in that price range.

The thought behind this approach is that the hotel can charge only what the market will accept, and this is usually dictated by the competition. This information is available through various public domain sources. Hotels may also periodically make *blind calls* to competing hotels. Staff members making blind calls do not identify their hotel; they simply ask for availability and rates on specific dates at nearby hotels. (Note that, with caller ID, "blind" calls may not truly be blind unless the hotel takes steps to hide its identity within the caller ID system.)

A competitive analysis usually focuses on these questions:

- How do our hotel's room rates compare to those of our competition?
- Are our rates much lower or higher than those of the competition? How are our rates affecting our revenue and market share?
- What is our current occupancy percentage? What is the occupancy percentage of the competitive set? Will our total revenue improve if we increase (or decrease) our rates?
- Have any industry trends emerged during the past six months?

Most of the answers to these questions cannot be determined through simple phone calls to hotels or reviews of competitors' websites. Three well-known commercially available reports from neutral sources that provide this information are the TIMS, Phaser, and RateVIEW reports. Future occupancy and rate trends can be determined by studying the quoted rates and availability for the competitive set. The TIMS Report lists one month's rate information for a property and five local competitors. The rates are broken down daily and include information on sold-out nights, low rate, low rate variance from the subscribing property, low corporate rate, low corporate rate variance, special rates availability, high-low comparisons, and an index of room types and rates for the period. Exhibit 2 shows a sample TIMS report. A Phaser Report is a comparative analysis of room rates, including information from internal distribution channels (such as central reservations offices) and external distribution channels (such as global distribution systems) for a property and its competitive set. RateVIEW is a series of reports providing details on how a property compares with its competitive set for future dates, looking at many distribution channels.

Exhibit 2 Sample TIMS Report

TIMS Competitive Rate Analysis Report for the
***Sample* TIMS Report**

TIMS Code: Sample **Reporting Period: Nov 10,'00 thru Dec 7,'00** **Data Captured: Nov 8,'00**

High - Low Rate Comparison

		Fri 11/10	Sat 11/11	Sun 11/12	Mon 11/13	Tue 11/14	Wed 11/15	Thu 11/16	Fri 11/17	Sat 11/18	Sun 11/19	Mon 11/20	Tue 11/21	Wed 11/22	Thu 11/23
SHERATON	High Rate	209	209	209	209	209	MLS	209	209	209	209	209	209	209	209
	Low Rate	135	135	125	169	169	MLS	155	89	125	89	125	125	125	79
	Variance	74	74	84	40	40		54	120	84	120	84	84	84	130
EMBASSY SUITES	High Rate	129	129	169	169	XXX	169	169	169	XXX	169	169	169	99	99
	Low Rate	89	89	89	169	XXX	169	169	169	XXX	169	169	169	99	99
	Variance	40	40	80	0		0	0	0		0	0	0	0	0
HILTON	High Rate	104	104	184	184	194	XXX	184	164	214	184	184	184	184	184
	Low Rate	69	69	69	139	139	XXX	139	79	189	59	69	69	59	59
	Variance	35	35	115	45	55		45	85	25	125	115	115	125	125
MARRIOTT	High Rate	172	172	172	XXX	XXX	172	172	172	172	172	172	172	172	172
	Low Rate	84	84	159	XXX	XXX	172	169	84	159	159	159	159	69	69
	Variance	88	88	13			0	3	88	13	13	13	13	103	103
RADISSON	High Rate	139	139	139	139	139	139	139	XXX	XXX	XXX	XXX	139	139	139
	Low Rate	89	89	89	99	99	99	99	XXX	XXX	XXX	XXX	99	99	99
	Variance	50	50	50	40	40	40	40					40	40	40
WESTIN	High Rate	XXX	XXX	255	255	255	XXX	XXX	255	255	255	255	255	255	255
	Low Rate	XXX	XXX	169	189	179	XXX	XXX	119	159	129	169	169	119	79
	Variance			86	66	76			136	96	126	86	86	136	176

		Fri 11/24	Sat 11/25	Sun 11/26	Mon 11/27	Tue 11/28	Wed 11/29	Thu 11/30	Fri 12/01	Sat 12/02	Sun 12/03	Mon 12/04	Tue 12/05	Wed 12/06	Thu 12/07
SHERATON	High Rate	209	209	209	209	209	209	209	209	209	209	209	MLS	209	209
	Low Rate	79	79	89	129	129	129	89	89	89	89	129	MLS	129	89
	Variance	130	130	120	80	80	80	120	120	120	120	80		80	120
EMBASSY SUITES	High Rate	129	129	149	149	149	149	149	129	129	149	149	149	149	XXX
	Low Rate	89	89	89	149	149	149	149	89	89	89	149	149	149	XXX
	Variance	40	40	60	0	0	0	0	40	40	60	0	0	0	
HILTON	High Rate	104	164	184	184	184	184	184	164	224	184	194	194	194	194
	Low Rate	59	59	59	139	139	139	139	89	184	139	139	139	139	139
	Variance	45	105	125	45	45	45	45	75	40	45	55	55	55	55
MARRIOTT	High Rate	172	172	172	172	172	172	172	172	172	172	172	172	172	172
	Low Rate	69	69	159	159	129	129	129	84	84	129	129	129	129	129
	Variance	103	103	13	13	43	43	43	88	88	43	43	43	43	43
RADISSON	High Rate	139	139	139	139	139	139	139	139	139	139	139	139	139	139
	Low Rate	89	89	89	99	99	99	99	89	89	89	99	99	99	99
	Variance	50	50	50	40	40	40	40	50	50	50	40	40	40	40
WESTIN	High Rate	255	255	255	255	255	255	255	255	255	255	255	255	255	255
	Low Rate	79	79	79	169	169	169	169	85	85	179	179	230	179	179
	Variance	176	176	176	86	86	86	86	170	170	76	76	25	76	76

Another, more reliable way to determine historical market conditions is to subscribe to industry reports that provide this information from neutral sources. The best-known historical report is the Smith Travel Accommodations Research (STAR) Report. The STAR Report provides historical information on occupancy, average room rate, RevPAR, and market share. Exhibit 3 shows a portion of a sample STAR trend report, and Exhibit 4 shows a portion of a sample STAR summary report. By tracking this information over a period of months and years, the rates and occupancy of the competitive set can be well established.

There are many problems with this approach, although it remains popular. First, if a hotel is new, construction costs will most likely be higher than those of the competition. Therefore, a new hotel is not likely to have an identical cost structure or be as profitable as the competition initially. Second, this approach does not take the value of the hotel into consideration. Since the property is new, and perhaps offers newer amenities, the value of the property to guests can be greater. The market condition approach is really a marketing approach that allows the local market to determine the rate. It may not take into account what a strong sales effort may accomplish. It can, in effect, allow the competition to determine the rates, and this could significantly affect the profitability of a hotel's operation. Third, a drastic and uncharacteristic downturn of business (such as the Great Recession in the late 2000s) has the potential to render many historical views of rates less useful.

In the United States, hotel managers must not base their rates on the rates of other hotels through direct discussions with competitors. Such discussions would be considered violations of U.S. antitrust laws. This is one reason some hotels use a

Exhibit 3 Sample STAR Trend Report

Sample - STAR Trend Report

	Occupancy						Average Room Rate						REVI		
Year Month	Prop	% CHG	Comp Set	% CHG	OCC Index	% CHG	Prop	% CHG	Comp Set	% CHG	ADR Index	% CHG	Prop	% CHG	Comp Set
20X1 May	62.4	2.0	60.2	8.5	103.7	11.5	90.89	18.3	104.40	4.6	87.1	14.4	56.74	16.6	62.87
20X1 June	72.5	20.4	68.2	8.3	106.3	11.2	94.69	3.3	105.97	4.4	89.4	1.0	68.67	24.4	72.24
20X1 July	71.7	5.4	64.9	3.6	110.5	9.4	93.82	.3	96.50	7.2	97.2	7.0	67.27	5.1	62.67
20X1 August	65.8	1.5	60.3	2.6	109.1	4.2	92.34	.8	94.52	3.7	97.7	2.8	60.80	2.4	56.99
20X1 September	68.2	4.4	64.9	5.7	105.1	10.7	110.07	1.6	116.46	5.6	94.5	6.8	75.07	2.8	75.57
20X1 October	83.3	4.9	80.7	6.0	103.2	1.1	128.09	22.3	131.06	20.6	97.7	1.5	106.69	28.4	105.71
20X1 November	67.6	3.0	64.6	2.4	104.6	.7	116.17	7.6	116.95	9.1	99.3	1.4	78.52	4.3	75.58
20X1 December	44.6	2.0	43.1	6.1	103.5	4.4	95.48	9.8	96.04	6.7	99.4	2.9	42.59	7.7	41.35
20X2 January	70.7	3.5	68.5	2.0	103.2	1.6	114.20	9.8	112.13	7.3	101.8	2.2	80.71	5.9	76.83
20X2 February	84.1	14.1	83.1	10.9	101.2	2.8	129.90	21.0	134.90	25.2	96.3	3.4	109.22	38.1	112.09
20X2 March	81.1	4.7	74.9	3.1	108.3	1.6	118.20	5.6	126.53	13.7	93.4	7.1	95.90	.7	94.75
20X2 April	67.7	1.6	65.1	.5	104.0	2.1	106.50	7.2	117.00	.8	91.0	7.9	72.11	8.7	76.12
20X2 May	69.5	11.4	64.3	6.8	108.1	4.2	106.07	16.7	118.23	13.2	89.7	3.0	73.68	29.9	76.06
20X2 June	73.6	1.5	59.8	12.3	123.1	15.8	111.34	17.6	112.26	5.9	99.2	11.0	81.93	19.3	67.19

Exhibit 4 Sample STAR Summary Report

Sample Inns & Suites Executive Summary Report July

July Monthly	Operating Performance Sample Inns & Suites												Oper
	Occupancy Percent			Average Room Rate			Room Revenue	Rooms Avail	Rooms Sold	Occupancy Percent			A
Segment	1996	1995	% CHG	1996	1995	% CHG	% CHG	% CHG	% CHG	1996	1995	% CHG	199
United States	81.8	83.3	1.8	69.53	63.90	8.8	16.0	8.5	6.6	73.9	74.3	.5	70
Region													
New England	82.7	84.3	1.9	69.79	67.86	2.8	14.3	13.3	11.1	75.1	74.3	1.1	83
Middle Atlantic	84.4	85.0	.7	69.23	64.82	6.8	7.3	1.2	.4	75.7	74.3	1.9	87
South Atlantic	82.1	84.3	2.6	69.17	58.88	17.5	25.9	10.1	7.2	73.1	73.2	.1	70
East North Central	85.1	85.2	.1	62.39	58.80	6.1	9.3	3.1	3.0	73.4	75.1	2.3	67
East South Central	84.8	87.3	2.9	60.76	55.20	10.1	16.4	8.9	5.7	74.4	75.2	1.1	57
West North Central	83.4	83.9	.6	64.84	61.85	4.8	3.9	.4	.9	73.5	76.2	3.5	57
West South Central	75.0	81.7	8.2	64.79	61.80	4.8	34.0	39.1	27.8	69.9	71.3	2.0	59
Mountain	81.5	81.2	.4	76.19	71.37	6.8	14.6	6.9	7.3	75.0	76.1	1.4	61
Pacific	79.6	79.5	.1	79.35	74.44	6.6	13.0	5.9	6.0	75.9	75.1	1.1	80
Price													
Luxury	81.0	80.5	.6	97.65	84.71	15.3	21.2	4.4	5.1	75.2	74.9	.4	117
Upscale	81.7	83.3	1.9	80.09	74.67	7.3	14.5	8.8	6.8	76.0	76.8	1.0	87

blind-call approach to rate assessment among their competitive set. As previously mentioned, in a blind-call survey, staff at the researching property phone competitors pretending to be potential guests. During the calls, staff members inquire about room rates for select future dates. Rates may also be available from many public sources, such as the Internet, global distribution systems, published rate brochures, directories from the American Automobile Association, and many others.

Rule-of-Thumb Approach

The rule-of-thumb approach establishes the minimum average room rate at $1 for each $1,000 of construction and furnishings cost per room (and assumes the hotel maintains a 70 percent average occupancy). For example, assume that for a given hotel the average construction and furnishings cost for its guestrooms is $80,000 per room. Using the $1 per $1,000 approach results in an average minimum room rate of $80 per room for that hotel. Singles, doubles, suites, and other room types would be priced differently, but the minimum average room rate would be $80.

The emphasis placed on the hotel's construction and furnishings cost limits the applicability of using this approach, as it fails to consider the effects of inflation over time. For example, a well-maintained hotel costing $100,000 per room today may have been constructed at $20,000 per room forty years ago. The $1 per $1,000 approach would suggest an average selling price of $20 per room; however, a much higher rate would appear to be appropriate. The suggested rate of $20 per room does not take into account inflation and increased costs of labor, furnishings, and supplies. In these cases, management might consider the current replacement cost of the hotel, rather than its original construction and furnishings cost, as a basis for the rule-of-thumb application. Another way of accounting for inflation would be to index current costs against original costs. For example, if a hotel was built five years ago and inflation has increased at an annual rate of 3 percent, the $1 per $1,000 five years ago would require $1.16 per $1,000 now.

The rule-of-thumb approach to pricing rooms also fails to consider the contribution of other facilities and services toward the hotel's desired profitability. In most hotels, guests pay extra for goods and services such as food, beverages, Internet access, and dry cleaning. If these services contribute to profitability, hotel management may have less pressure to charge higher room rates.

The rule-of-thumb approach should also consider the hotel's occupancy level. As pointed out, the rule-of-thumb approach assumes 70 percent occupancy when determining the appropriate average room rate. However, if a lower occupancy percentage is expected, the hotel will have to capture a higher average rate to generate the same amount of room revenue. Hotels tend to have a very high level of fixed expenses (especially depreciation and mortgage expenses). For instance, a mortgage payment does not fluctuate and remains the same every month, regardless of the hotel's percentage of occupancy. The front office manager must understand the relationship between room rate and room occupancy on room revenue to ensure that revenue goals and financial obligations are met.

Hubbart Formula Approach

Another approach to average room rate determination is the Hubbart Formula. To determine the minimum average room rate, this approach considers operating costs, desired profits, and expected number of rooms to be sold. In other words, this approach starts with desired profitability, adds income taxes, then adds fixed charges and management fees, followed by overhead expenses and direct operating expenses. The Hubbart Formula is considered a *bottom-up* approach to pricing rooms because its initial item—net income (profit)—comes from the bottom line of a standard income statement. The second item needed for this formula—income taxes—is the second item from the bottom of the income statement, and so on. The Hubbart Formula approach involves the following eight steps:

1. Calculate the hotel's desired profit by multiplying the desired rate of return (ROI) by the owners' investment.
2. Calculate pretax profits by dividing desired profit (Step 1) by 1 minus the hotel's tax rate.
3. Calculate fixed charges and management fees. This calculation includes estimating depreciation, interest expense, property taxes, insurance, amortization, building mortgage, land, rent, and management fees.
4. Calculate undistributed operating expenses. This calculation includes estimating expenses for the following categories: administrative and general, information technology, human resources, transportation, marketing, property operation and maintenance, and energy costs.
5. Estimate non-room operated department income or loss—that is, food and beverage department income or loss, telecommunications department income or loss, and so forth.
6. Calculate the required rooms department income. The sum of pretax profits (Step 2), fixed charges and management fees (Step 3), undistributed operating expenses (Step 4), and other operated department losses less other operated department income (Step 5) equals the required rooms department income. The Hubbart Formula, in essence, places the overall financial burden of the hotel on the rooms department.
7. Determine the rooms department revenue. The required rooms department income (Step 6), plus rooms department direct expenses of payroll and related expenses, plus other direct operating expenses, equals the required rooms department revenue.
8. Calculate the average room rate by dividing rooms department revenue (Step 7) by the expected number of rooms to be sold.

Illustration of the Hubbart Formula. The Casa Vana Inn, a 200-room property, is projected to cost $9,900,000 inclusive of land, building, equipment, and furniture. An additional $100,000 is needed for working capital, bringing the total cost of construction and opening expenses to $10,000,000. The hotel is financed with a loan of $7,500,000 at 12 percent annual interest and cash of $2,500,000 provided by the owners. The owners desire a 15 percent annual return on their investment. A 75 percent occupancy is estimated; thus, 54,750 rooms are projected to be sold during the calendar year (200 × .75 × 365). The hotel's income tax rate is 40 percent, and additional expenses are estimated as follows:

Property tax expenses	$250,000
Insurance expenses	50,000
Depreciation expenses	300,000

Administrative and general expenses	300,000
Data processing expenses	120,000
Human resources expenses	80,000
Transportation expenses	40,000
Marketing expenses	200,000
Property operation and maintenance expenses	200,000
Energy and related expenses	300,000

Non-room revenue center income (loss) is estimated as follows :

Food and beverage department	$150,000
Telecommunications department	(50,000)
Rentals and other departments	100,000

The rooms department estimates direct operating expenses to be $10 per occupied room.

Exhibit 5 contains the calculations used in the Hubbart Formula and reveals a minimum average room rate of $67.81.

Exhibit 6 contains the formula for calculating room rates for single rooms (x) and double rooms ($x + y$), where the price differential between single and double room rates is represented by the variable y. Assume that the Casa Vana Inn has a double occupancy rate of 40 percent (that is, two out of every five rooms sold are sold at the double rate) and a room rate differential of $10. Applying the formula from Exhibit 6, single and double rates would be calculated as follows:

$$\text{Doubles Sold Daily} = \text{Doubles Occupancy Rate} \times \text{Numbers of Rooms} \times \text{Occupancy Percentage}$$

$$= .4(200)(.75)$$

$$= \underline{\underline{60}}$$

$$\text{Singles Sold Daily} = \text{Rooms Sold Daily} - \text{Doubles Sold Daily}$$

$$= (200 \times .75) - 60$$

$$= \underline{\underline{90}}$$

Using the minimum average rate of $67.81 calculated in Exhibit 5, the required single and double rates can be determined as follows:

$$\text{Singles Sold } (x) + \left[\begin{array}{c}\text{Doubles Sold} \times \\ (x + \text{Rate Differential})\end{array}\right] = \text{Average Room Rate} \times \text{Daily Number of Rooms Sold}$$

$$90x + 60(x + \$10) = (\$67.81)(150)$$

$$90x + 60x + \$600 = \$10{,}171.50$$

$$150x = \$9{,}571.50$$

$$x = \frac{\$9{,}571.50}{150}$$

$$x = \$63.81$$

$$\underline{\text{Single Rate}} = \underline{\underline{\$63.81}}$$

$$\underline{\text{Double Rate}} = \$63.81 + \$10.00$$

$$= \underline{\underline{\$73.81}}$$

Exhibit 5 Calculating Average Room Rate: Hubbart Formula

Item	Calculation	Amount
Desired net income	Owners' Investment ROI $2,500,000 × .15 = $375,000	
	Pretax income $= \frac{\text{net income}}{1 - t}$	
	Pretax income $= \frac{\$375{,}000}{1 - .4}$	
	Pretax income =	$625,000
Plus: Interest expense	Principal × interest rate = interest expense $7,500,000 × .12 =	+ 900,000
Income needed before interest expense and taxes		1,525,000
Plus: Estimated depreciation, property taxes, and insurance		+ 600,000
Income before fixed charges		2,125,000
Plus: Undistributed operating expense		1,240,000
Required operated departments income		$3,365,000
Departmental results excluding rooms		
Less: Food and beverage department income		(150,000)
Rentals and other department income		(100,000)
Plus: Telephone department loss		50,000
Rooms department income		3,165,000
Plus: Rooms department direct expense	54,750 × $10 = $547,500	547,500
Rooms revenue		3,712,500
Number of rooms sold		÷ 54,750
Required average room rate		$ 67.81

Exhibit 6 Determining Single and Double Room Rates from an Average Room Rate

Singles sold (x) + Doubles Sold (x + y) = (Average Rate) (Rooms Sold)

where:		
x	=	Price of singles
y	=	Price differential between singles and doubles
x + y	=	Price of doubles

Alternatively, the double rate could be set as a percentage of the single rate. When this is the case, the formula is slightly altered:

$$\text{Singles Sold }(x) + \left[\begin{array}{c}\text{Doubles Sold }(x) \times \\ (1 + \text{Percentage Differential})\end{array}\right] = \begin{array}{c}\text{Average} \\ \text{Room Rate}\end{array} \times \begin{array}{c}\text{Daily Number} \\ \text{of Rooms Sold}\end{array}$$

The percentage differential is simply the percentage difference of the double rate over the single rate. To understand this approach, consider the Casa Vana Inn again. Assume a 40 percent double occupancy and a price differential of 15 percent:

$$\text{Singles Sold }(x) + \left[\begin{array}{c}\text{Doubles Sold }(x) \times \\ (1 + \text{Percentage Differential})\end{array}\right] = \begin{array}{c}\text{Average} \\ \text{Room Rate}\end{array} \times \begin{array}{c}\text{Daily Number} \\ \text{of Rooms Sold}\end{array}$$

$$\begin{aligned}
90x + 60(x)(1.15) &= (\$67.81)(150) \\
90x + 69x &= \$10{,}171.50 \\
159x &= \$10{,}171.50 \\
x &= \frac{\$10{,}171.50}{159} \\
x &= \$63.97 \\
\underline{\text{Single Rate}} &= \underline{\underline{\$63.97}} \\
\underline{\text{Double Rate}} &= \$63.97(1.15) \\
&= \underline{\underline{\$73.57}}
\end{aligned}$$

The Hubbart Formula is most useful in setting *target* minimum average room rates as opposed to *actual* average room rates. It is important to note that the Hubbart Formula generates an average room rate as a target price at the hotel's point of profitability. It relies on management's accurate estimates of total rooms occupied and the single/double occupancy mix to determine target rates. If these estimates are incorrect, the targets will be incorrect.

Suppose a hotel company is planning to build a new property. Using the Hubbart Formula, management computes an average target room rate of $75. Knowing the current average rate for competing hotels in the area is only $50, management must consider whether the proposed hotel, projected to open in two years, has too high a targeted room rate.

To evaluate its potential, management assumes the competitor's average price will increase at 5 percent per year over the next two years, to $55.13 (that is, $50 × 1.05 × 1.05). Since the proposed hotel would be new construction, management reasons that a price premium may be acceptable in the marketplace. A projected average room rate difference of nearly $20, however, appears to be too large. A more reasonable initial average room rate might be $65; after three years of successive five percent price increases, the new hotel's daily average room rate would increase to just over $75, as follows:

	Annual increase at 5%	Selling Price
Initial room rate (new hotel)		$65.00
At the end of year 1	$3.25	$68.25
At the end of year 2	$3.41	$71.66
At the end of year 3	$3.58	$75.24

Considering this situation, hotel developers will have to finance the additional deficit in the first year ($75 for the targeted average rate versus $65 expected average rate when the hotel opens). In order to operate effectively, the hotel will need to devise some method of financing the projected room revenue shortfall. Unfortunately, hotels do not typically generate profits during the first few years of operation. When this is the case, operating deficits should be included in the hotel's financing plan.

Planned Rate Changes

Room rack rates are likely to change during a calendar year, depending on market factors such as location, seasonality, or major events in the area. Knowing this, hotels may publish a rack rate range instead of a specific room rack rate. For example, resorts may have several different rack rates for the same room types during a year, reflecting peak (high demand), shoulder, and off-peak (low demand) seasons. Room rack rates will tend to vary widely between these seasonal periods. Major events also can have a big impact on rates. For example, consider a planned rate change when a geographic area hosts the NFL Super Bowl. Hotels in the area may plan special (higher) room rates, given the expected high demand associated with upcoming Super Bowl events.

Forecasting Room Availability

The most important short-term planning that front office managers engage in is **forecasting** the number of rooms available for future reservations. *Room availability forecasts* are used to help manage the reservations process and guide front office staff in effective rooms management. Forecasting may be especially important on nights when a full house (100 percent occupancy) is likely.

A room availability forecast can also be used as an *occupancy forecast*. Since there is a fixed number of rooms available on any given night, forecasting the number of rooms available for sale and the number of rooms expected to be occupied can be useful in computing an expected occupancy percentage. The forecasted availability and occupancy numbers are very important to daily front office operations. Occupancy forecasts may be an important consideration for making room rate pricing decisions. This information can also influence when rooms can be placed on out-of-order status for maintenance or repair work. Without an accurate forecast, rooms may go unsold or be sold at less-than-optimal rates. Room occupancy forecasts can be useful to the front office manager attempting to schedule an optimal number of employees for an expected volume of business. These forecasts may be helpful to other hotel department managers as well. For example, the housekeeping department manager needs to know how many rooms the front office expects to be occupied to properly schedule room attendants. Restaurant managers must know the occupancy forecast to better schedule service staff, while the chef can use this information to determine how much food to purchase for the restaurant.

Obviously, a forecast is only as reliable as the information on which it is based. Since forecasts can serve as a guide in determining operating costs, every effort should be made to ensure forecasting accuracy.

Forecasting is a difficult skill to develop. The skill is acquired through experience, effective recordkeeping, and accurate counting methods. Experienced front office managers have found that several types of information can be helpful in room availability forecasting:

- A thorough knowledge of the hotel and surrounding attractions
- Market profiles of the targeted guests
- Occupancy data for the past several months and for the same calendar period of the previous year
- Reservation trends and a history of reservation lead times (how far in advance reservations are made)
- A listing of special events scheduled in the surrounding geographic area
- Business and historical profiles of specific groups booked for future dates
- The number of non-guaranteed and guaranteed reservations and an estimate of the number of reservations expected to be no-shows
- The cut-off date for group room reservation blocks being held for forecasted dates
- Estimated room availability of competing hotels for the forecast dates (which might be calculated based on information revealed through blind calls or website activity)
- The impact of citywide events or conferences on forecasted dates
- Plans for remodeling or renovating the hotel property that would change the number of available rooms
- Construction or renovation plans of competing hotels in the local area

Forecasting Data

The process of forecasting room availability generally relies on historical occupancy data as well as future reserved rooms already committed. Historical data is used to take part of the guesswork out of forecasting. To facilitate projections, the following daily occupancy data should be collected:

- Number of expected room arrivals: based on existing reservations and historical trends for projected reservations and cancellations prior to the arrival date.
- Number of expected room walk-ins: based on historical records of transient guests.
- Number of expected room stayovers (rooms occupied on the prior night that will continue to be occupied for the night in question): based on existing reservations.
- Number of expected reservation room no-shows: based on historical records.
- Number of expected room understays (check-outs occurring before expected departure date): based on historical data.
- Number of expected room check-outs: based on existing departure dates.

Exhibit 7 Occupancy History of the Holly Hotel

Occupancy History
First Week of March

Day	Date	Guests	Room Arrivals	Room Walk-Ins	Room Reservations	Room No-Shows
Mon	3/1	118	70	13	63	6
Tues	3/2	145	55	15	48	8
Wed	3/3	176	68	16	56	4
Thurs	3/4	117	53	22	48	17
Fri	3/5	75	35	8	35	8
Sat	3/6	86	28	6	26	4
Sun	3/7	49	17	10	12	5
Totals		766	326	90	288	52

Occupied Rooms	Overstay Rooms	Understay Rooms	Room Check-Outs
90	6	0	30
115	10	3	30
120	12	6	63
95	3	18	78
50	7	0	80
58	6	3	20
30	3	3	45
558	47	33	346

- Number of expected room overstays (check-outs occurring after the originally reserved departure date): based on historical records.

Hotels with a projected high double occupancy percentage may be as concerned with guest counts as room counts. For example, an all-inclusive resort with a large amount of business from vacationing couples may want to forecast the number of guests as well as room count activity. Convention hotels often have the same concerns.

Management often discovers that much of the data used in forecasting is contained in reports, documents, and other data sources at the property. Daily reports, for example, will likely be invaluable in forecasting work. Specialty reports can be summarized and stored in a way that is easily accessible to online applications.

Overall, these data are important to room availability forecasting, since they are used in calculating various daily operating ratios to help determine the number of available rooms for sale. Ratios are a mathematical expression of a relationship between two numbers that is determined by dividing one by the other. Most statistical ratios that apply to front office operations are expressed as percentages. The ratios examined in the following sections are percentage of no-shows, walk-ins, overstays, and understays. Occupancy history data shown in Exhibit 7 for a fictitious property (the Holly Hotel) are used to illustrate the calculation of each front office ratio. Managers should look for consistency in ratio values. Consistency may be finding identifiable patterns among ratio outcomes. Without consistency, forecasting ratios and projecting operating performance may be complex and more difficult.

Percentage of No-Shows. The percentage of no-shows indicates the proportion of reserved rooms in which the expected guests did not arrive to occupy (and did not cancel) on the expected arrival date. This ratio helps the front office manager decide when (and if) to sell already committed rooms to walk-in guests.

The percentage of no-shows is calculated by dividing the number of room no-shows for a specific period of time (day, week, month, or year) by the total number of room reservations for the same period. Using figures from Exhibit 7, the percentage of no-shows for the Holly Hotel during the first week of March can be calculated as follows:

$$\text{Percentage of No-Shows} = \frac{\text{Number of Room No-Shows}}{\text{Number of Room Reservations}}$$

$$= \frac{52}{288}$$

$$= .1806 \text{ or } \underline{\underline{18.06\%}} \text{ of Reserved Rooms}$$

Some properties track no-show statistics in relation to guaranteed and non-guaranteed reservations. Non-guaranteed reservations typically have a higher no-show percentage than guaranteed reservations, since the potential guest with a non-guaranteed reservation has no obligation to pay for the accommodations despite not arriving and registering at the property. Properly incorporating no-show allowances into room availability forecasts also depends on the hotel's mix of business; for example, corporate groups generally have a much lower no-show percentage than do other types of groups or individual guests. A hotel that works with a large corporate meetings market will most likely have a low no-show percentage. Conversely, a hotel with very little corporate group business, such as a hotel located in a suburban area alongside an interstate highway, is likely to have a much higher percentage of no-show reservations, since most guests desire flexibility in their travel plans. Hotels and resorts strive to control no-shows through a number of policies and procedures, such as requiring an advanced deposit and/or contacting the guest before arrival to confirm that travel and room arrangements remain as planned.

Percentage of Walk-Ins. The percentage of walk-ins is calculated by dividing the number of rooms occupied by walk-ins by the total number of room arrivals for the same period. Using figures from Exhibit 7, the percentage of walk-ins for the Holly Hotel during the first week of March can be calculated as follows:

$$\text{Percentage of Walk-Ins} = \frac{\text{Number of Room Walk-Ins}}{\text{Total Number of Room Arrivals}}$$

$$= \frac{90}{326}$$

$$= .2761 \text{ or } \underline{\underline{27.61\%}} \text{ of Room Arrivals}$$

Walk-in guests occupy available rooms that are not held for guests with reservations. Hotels may be able to sell rooms to walk-in guests at a higher room rate, since these guests usually have less opportunity to consider alternate properties. Front desk agents are sometimes asked to escort a walk-in guest to a guestroom under consideration. This tends to be a more effective method to sell rooms than online virtual tours or using descriptive adjectives when selling to people over the telephone. Walk-in guestroom sales help improve both occupancy and room revenues. However, from a planning perspective, it is generally preferred to have committed reservations in advance than to count on walk-in traffic.

Note that other ratios can dramatically affect the walk-in ratio. For example, if a hotel has ten no-shows beyond forecast, it may accept more walk-ins than usual to make up for the lost business. When this information is tracked for historical purposes, it is essential that the other ratios also be tracked to understand the interactivity between them. There will be a better opportunity for walk-ins (and possibly a higher room rate) if competing hotels are experiencing high demand.

Percentage of Overstays. Overstays represent rooms occupied by guests who stay beyond their originally scheduled departure dates. Overstay guests may have arrived with reservations or as walk-in guests. Overstays should not be confused with **stayovers.** Stayover rooms are rooms occupied by guests who arrived to occupy a room before the day in question and whose *scheduled* departure date isn't until after the day in question.

Using historical data, the percentage of overstays is calculated by dividing the actual number of overstay rooms by the total number of *expected* room check-outs for the same day or period. The number of expected room check-outs is the number of rooms shown by the front office system as due for departure. Stated another way, the number of expected room check-outs can be calculated from historical data as the number of actual departures minus understays plus overstays. Note that in this case, the term *understays* refers to guests checking out prior to the day in question, *not* to those guests who were *originally scheduled* to depart on that day but chose to check out a day early. For purposes of room availability forecasting, a guest is considered an understay if he or she checks out of the hotel before the stated date of departure.

Overstays and understays can be determined for periods beyond one day by summing the actual overstay and understay counts calculated separately for each day within the longer period. Using figures from Exhibit 7, the percentage of overstays for the Holly Hotel during the first week of March can be calculated as follows:

$$\text{Percentage of Overstays} = \frac{\text{Number of Overstay Rooms}}{\text{Number of Expected Check-Outs}}$$

$$= \frac{47}{346 - 33 + 47}$$

$$= .1306 \text{ or } \underline{\underline{13.06\%}} \text{ of Expected Check-Outs}$$

To help regulate room overstays, front office agents are trained to verify an arriving guest's departure date at the time of check-in. Such verification can be critical, especially when the hotel is at or near full occupancy and there are no provisions for overstay guests. Overstays may also prove problematic when specific rooms have been blocked for arriving guests. This is especially important for a specific room that may have special importance to an incoming guest.

Percentage of Understays. Understays represent rooms occupied by guests who check out before their originally scheduled departure dates. Understay guests may have arrived at the hotel with reservations or as walk-ins.

The percentage of understays is calculated by dividing the number of understay rooms by the total number of expected room check-outs for the same day or period. Using a similar approach to that just described for determining the percentage of overstays, the understays are counted as understays only on the day of their early check-out, and understay counts should be determined separately and summed for each day in a multi-day period. Using figures from Exhibit 7, the percentage of understays for the Holly Hotel during the first week of March can be calculated as follows:

$$\text{Percentage of Understays} = \frac{\text{Number of Understay Rooms}}{\text{Number of Expected Check-Outs}}$$

$$= \frac{33}{346 - 33 + 47}$$

$$= .0917 \text{ or } \underline{\underline{9.17\%}} \text{ of Expected Check-Outs}$$

Guests leaving before their stated departure date create empty rooms that typically are difficult to fill. Thus, understay rooms potentially represent lost room revenue. Overstays, on the other hand, are guests staying beyond their planned departure date and may represent a potential increase in room revenue. When a hotel is not operating at full occupancy, overstay guests often result in additional, unexpected room revenue. In an attempt to regulate understay and overstay rooms, front office staff should:

- Confirm or reconfirm each guest's departure date at registration. Some guests may already know of a change in plans that will affect their reservation, or a mistake may have been made in the original processing of the reservation. The sooner erroneous data are corrected, the greater the chance for improved room availability planning.
- Present an alternate guestroom suggestion to an overstay guest, explaining that an arriving guest holds a reservation for his or her assigned room.
- Review group history. Many groups hold large closing events on the last day of their meetings, and group members may even make reservations to attend. However, changes in plans or other priorities may require some guests to leave the hotel before the event. Front office managers may be better able to plan for these early departures, based on the group's departure history.

- Contact potential overstay guests about their scheduled departure date to confirm their intention to check out. Room occupancy data should be examined each day; rooms with guests expected to check out should be flagged. Guests who have not departed by the hotel's posted check-out time should be contacted and asked about their departure intentions. This procedure permits a revised count of overstays and allows sufficient time to modify previous room availability planning, if necessary.

Forecast Formula

Once relevant occupancy statistics have been gathered, the number of rooms available on any given date can be determined by the following formula:

	Total Number of Guestrooms
−	Number of Out-of-Order Rooms
−	Number of Room Stayovers
−	Number of Room Reservations
+	Number of Room Reservations × Percentage of No-Shows
+	Number of Room Understays
−	Number of Room Overstays
	Number of Rooms Available for Sale

Note that this formula does not include expected walk-in guests. Walk-in guests are not included in the formula since the number of walk-ins to be accommodated is determined by the number of rooms that remain available for sale. If a hotel is full due to existing reservations, stayovers, and other factors, it cannot accept walk-ins.

As an example, consider the Holly House, a 120-room property, where on April 1 there are three out-of-order rooms and fifty-five stayovers. On that day, there are forty-two guests with reservations scheduled to arrive. Since the percentage of no-shows has been recently calculated at 18.06 percent, the front office manager calculates that as many as eight guests with reservations may not arrive (42 × .1806 = 7.59, rounded to 8). Based on historical data, six understays and fifteen overstays are also expected. The number of rooms projected to be available for sale on April 1 can be determined as follows:

	Total Number of Guestrooms	120
−	Number of Out-of-Order Rooms	− 3
−	Number of Room Stayovers	− 55
−	Number of Room Reservations	− 42
+	Number of Room Reservations × No-Show Percentage	+ 8
+	Number of Room Understays	+ 6
−	Number of Room Overstays	− 15
	Number of Rooms Available for Sale	19

Therefore, the Holly House is considered to have nineteen rooms available for sale on April 1. Once this figure is determined, front office management can decide whether to accept more reservations and can determine a reasonable level of staffing. Front office planning decisions must remain flexible; they are subject to change as the front office learns of reservation cancellations and modifications. Note also that room availability forecasts are based on assumptions whose validity may vary on any given day.

Sample Forecast Forms

Front office managers may prepare several different room availability forecasts, depending on their needs and the needs of other managers in the hotel. For example, occupancy forecasts are typically developed on a monthly basis and reviewed by food and beverage and rooms division managers to forecast revenues, project expenses, and develop labor schedules. A ten-day forecast may be used to update labor scheduling and cost projections and may later be supplemented by a more current and accurate three-day forecast. Together, these forecasts help many hotel departments maintain appropriate staffing levels for expected business volumes and thereby help contain costs.

Ten-Day Forecast. At most lodging properties, the ten-day forecast is developed jointly by the front office manager and the reservations manager, possibly in conjunction with a room availability forecast committee. Many properties develop a ten-day forecast as an extension of the yearly forecast. A ten-day forecast usually consists of:

- Daily forecasted occupancy figures, including room arrivals, room departures, rooms occupied, and number of guests.
- The number of group commitments, with a listing of each group's name, arrival and departure dates, number of rooms reserved, number of guests, and perhaps quoted room rates.
- A comparison of the previous period's forecasted and actual room counts and occupancy percentages.

A special ten-day forecast may also be prepared for food and beverage, banquet, and catering operations. This forecast usually includes the expected number of guests, which is often referred to as the **house count.** Sometimes the house count is divided into group and non-group categories so that the hotel's dining room managers can better understand the nature of the business and their staffing needs.

To help various hotel departments plan their staffing and payroll levels for the upcoming period, the ten-day forecast should be completed and distributed to all department offices in advance of the coming period. This forecast can be especially helpful to the housekeeping department. A ten-day forecast form, as shown in Exhibit 8, is typically developed from data collected through several front office sources. (The occupancy multiplier mentioned in section 10 of the exhibit is discussed later in the chapter.) An equivalent report can be automatically generated by the hotel's property management system.

Exhibit 8 Sample Ten-Day Forecast Form

Ten-Day Occupancy Forecast

Location: ______________ #: ______________ Week Ending: ______________

Date Prepared: ______________ Prepared By: ______________

To be submitted to all department heads at least one week before the first day listed on forecast.

	Fri.	Sat.	Sun.	Mon.	Tues.	Wed.	Thur.	Fri.	Sat.	Sun.
1. Date and Day (start week and end week the same as the payroll schedule)										
2. Estimated Departures										
3. Reservation Arrivals—Group (taken from log book)										
4. Reservation Arrivals—Individual (taken from log book)										
5. Future Reservations (estimated reservations received after forecast is completed)										
6. Expected Walk-Ins (% of walk-ins based on reservations received and actual occupancy for past two weeks)										
7. Total Arrivals										
8. Stayovers										
9. TOTAL FORECASTED ROOMS										
10. Occupancy Multiplier (based on number of guests per occupied room for average of the same day for last three weeks)										
11. FORECASTED NUMBER OF GUESTS										
12. Actual Rooms Occupied (taken from daily report for actual date to be completed by front office supervisor)										
13. Forecasted Variance (difference between forecast and rooms occupied on daily report)										

14. Explanation (to be completed by front office supervisor and submitted to general manager; attach additional memo if necessary)

APPROVED: ______________ DATE: ______________
General Manager's Signature

First, the current number of occupied rooms is reviewed. The estimated numbers of overstays and expected departures are noted. Next, relevant reservation information is evaluated for each room (and guest) by date of arrival, length of stay, and date of departure. These counts are then reconciled with reservation control data. Then, the actual counts are adjusted to reflect the projected percentage

Exhibit 9 Refining a Forecast

A yearly forecast provides an excellent starting point for developing shorter-term, more accurate forecasts. Managers can better assess business by reviewing current reservations and booking pace. The closer the forecast is, the more accurate it will be.

Here is a checklist for revising forecasts:

- List all group bookings and transient reservations on the books.
- Examine arrivals, departures, and group information for the given period.
- Determine if demand for this particular period of time is high or low.
- Chart the peaks and valleys on a graph to better identify high/low demand.
- Have sales agents call competing properties for rates and consider adjusting your rates.
- Make decisions to maximize revenue during each time period.

of no-shows, anticipated understays, and expected walk-ins. These projections are based on the hotel's recent history, the seasonality of business, and the known history of specific groups scheduled to arrive. Finally, conventions and other groups are listed on the forecast to alert various department managers to possible periods of heavy, or light, check-ins and check-outs. The number of rooms assigned each day to each group may also be noted on the report.

Most automated systems provide a summary of recorded data in a report format for the front office manager to use. This is a key feature in revenue management systems that are programmed to forecast business. These revenue management systems possess special trend analysis and regression analysis applications. Starting with the revenue management system's forecast, the front office manager applies knowledge and skill to ultimately determine the accuracy of the forecast. Exhibit 9 presents a checklist that some revenue managers use when revising room availability forecasts.

Three-Day Forecast. A three-day forecast is an updated report that reflects a more current estimate of room availability. It details significant changes or events not highlighted on the ten-day forecast. The three-day forecast is intended to guide management in fine-tuning labor schedules and adjusting room availability information. Exhibit 10 shows a sample three-day forecast form. In some hotels, a daily revenue meeting is held to focus on occupancy and rate changes for the next several days. The results of this meeting are often reflected in the three-day forecast.

Room Count Considerations. Control books, charts, software applications, projections, ratios, and formulas can be essential in short- and long-range room availability planning. Each day, front office management performs several physical counts of rooms occupied, vacant, reserved, and expected to check out, to complete the occupancy statistics for that day. An automated system may reduce the need for most final counts, since the system can be programmed to continually update room availability information.

Exhibit 10 Sample Three-Day Forecast Form

Three-Day Forecast

Date of Forecast: ____________________ Forecast Completed By: ____________________

Total Rooms in Hotel: ____________________

	Tonight	Tomorrow	3rd Night
Day			
Date			

	Tonight	Tomorrow	3rd Night
Previous Night Occupied Rooms[1]			
− Expected Departures			
− Early Departures			
+ Unexpected Stayovers			
+ Unoccupied Rooms[2]			
= Rooms Available For Sale			
+ Expected Arrivals			
+ Walk-ins & Same Day Reservations			
− No-Shows			
= Occupied Rooms			
= Occupancy %			
= Expected House Count[3]			

1 Previous night occupied rooms is determined from either the actual number of rooms occupied last night or the forecasted number of rooms from the previous night.
2 Unoccupied rooms equals the total number of rooms in the hotel less the number of rooms occupied.
3 Expected house count equals the forecasted occupied rooms times the multiple occupancy percentage for the day (found on the computer report).

Distribution: General Manager, Front Desk, Housekeeping, All Food and Beverage, Accounting, Sales, Banquets, Security

It is important for front desk agents to know *exactly* how many rooms are available, especially if the hotel is expected to operate at nearly 100 percent occupancy. Once procedures for gathering room count information are established, planning procedures can be extended to longer periods of time to form a more reliable basis for revenue, expense, and labor forecasting. The checklist in Exhibit 11 may be applicable to non-automated and semi-automated operations alike.

Exhibit 11 Sample Daily Checklist for Accurate Room Counts

- Make counts of the rack and reservations. On tight days, a count should be made at 7:00 A.M., noon, 3:00 P.M., and 6:00 P.M. On normal days, a 7:00 A.M. and 6:00 P.M. count will suffice.
- Check room rack against the folio bucket to catch sleepers and skippers.
- Check housekeeping reports against the room rack to catch sleepers and skippers.
- Check for rooms that are due out, but still have balances on their folios, especially where payment cards are the indicated source of payment.
- Check reservations for any duplications.
- Call the reservations system to make sure all cancellations were transmitted.
- Check the switchboard, telephone rack, and/or alphabetical room rack to make sure that the guest is not already registered.
- Call the local airport for a report on canceled flights.
- Check the weather reports for cities from which a number of guests are expected.
- Check reservations against convention blocks to catch duplications.
- Check with other hotels for duplicate reservations if a housing or convention bureau indicated the reservation was a second choice.
- Check arrival dates on all reservation forms to be sure none were misfiled.
- Check the rooms cancellation list.
- If a reservation was made through the reservations manager, sales manager, or someone in the executive office and the property is close to full, call that staff person. Often, such guests are personal friends and are willing to help out by staying somewhere else.
- Close to the property's cut-off time, consider placing a person-to-person phone call to any guest with a nonguaranteed reservation who hasn't arrived. If the person accepts the call, confirm whether or not he or she will arrive yet that night.
- After the property's cut-off time, if it becomes necessary, pull any reservations that were not guaranteed or prepaid.
- If any rooms are out-of-order or not presently in use, check to see if they can be made up. Let housekeeping know when a tight day is expected, so that all possible rooms are made up.
- Before leaving work, convey in writing all pertinent information to the oncoming staff. Good communication is essential.

Budgeting for Operations

The most important long-term planning function that front office managers perform is budgeting for front office operations. The hotel's annual operations budget is a profit plan that addresses all revenue sources and expense items. Annual

Exhibit 12 Rooms Revenue Summary for the Emily Hotel

Year	Rooms Revenue	Increase in Dollars	Percentage Increase Over Prior Year
20X1	$1,000,000	—	—
20X2	1,100,000	$100,000	10%
20X3	1,210,000	110,000	10%
20X4	1,331,000	121,000	10%

budgets are commonly divided into monthly plans that, in turn, are divided into weekly (and sometimes daily) plans. These budget plans become standards against which management can evaluate the actual results of operations. In most hotels, room revenues are greater than food, beverage, banquet, or any other revenues. In addition, rooms division profits are usually greater than those of any other division. Therefore, an accurate rooms division budget is vital to creating the hotel's overall budget.

The budget planning process requires the closely coordinated efforts of all management personnel. While the front office manager is responsible for rooms revenue forecasts, the accounting division staff will be relied on to supply department managers with statistical information essential to the budget preparation process. The accounting division staff may also be responsible for coordinating the budget plans of individual department managers into a comprehensive property-wide operations budget for top management's review. The general manager and controller typically review departmental budget plans and may prepare a comprehensive hotel budget report for approval by the hotel's owners. If the budget is not satisfactory, elements requiring change may be returned to the appropriate division managers for review and revision.

The front office manager's primary responsibilities in budget planning are forecasting rooms revenue and estimating related expenses. Rooms revenue is forecasted with input from the reservations manager, while expenses are estimated with input from all department managers in the rooms division.

Forecasting Rooms Revenue

Historical financial information often serves as the foundation on which front office managers build rooms revenue forecasts. One method of rooms revenue forecasting involves an analysis of rooms revenue from past periods. Dollar and percentage differences are noted and the amount of rooms revenue for the budget year is predicted.

For example, Exhibit 12 shows yearly increases in net rooms revenue for the Emily Hotel. For the years 20X1 to 20X4, the amount of rooms revenue increased from $1,000,000 to $1,331,000, reflecting a 10 percent yearly increase. If future conditions appear to be similar to those of the past, the rooms revenue for 20X5 would be budgeted at $1,464,100—a 10 percent increase over the 20X4 amount.

Another approach to forecasting rooms revenue bases the revenue projection on past room sales and average daily room rates. Exhibit 13 presents rooms revenue statistics for the 120-room Bradley Hotel from 20X1 to 20X4. An analysis of

Exhibit 13 Rooms Revenue Statistics for the Bradley Hotel

Year	Rooms Sold	Average Daily Rate	Net Rooms Revenue	Occupancy Percentage
20X1	30,660	$50	$1,533,000	70%
20X2	31,974	52	1,662,648	73%
20X3	32,412	54	1,750,248	74%
20X4	32,850	57	1,872,450	75%

these statistics shows that occupancy percentage increased three percentage points from 20X1 to 20X2, one percentage point from 20X2 to 20X3, and one percentage point from 20X3 to 20X4. Average daily room rates increased by $2, $2, and $3 respectively over the same periods. If future conditions are assumed to be similar to those of the past, a rooms revenue forecast for 20X5 may be based on a one percent increase in occupancy percentage (to 76 percent) and a $3 increase in the average daily room rate (to $60). Given these projections, the following formula can be used to forecast rooms revenue for the year 20X5 for the Bradley Hotel:

$$\text{Forecasted Rooms Revenue} = \text{Rooms Available} \times \text{Occupancy Percentage} \times \text{Average Daily Rate}$$

$$= 43{,}800 \times .76 \times \$60$$

$$= \underline{\underline{\$1{,}997{,}280}}$$

The number of rooms available is calculated by multiplying the 120 rooms of the Bradley Hotel by the 365 days of the year. This calculation assumes that all rooms will be available for sale each day of the year. This will probably not be the case, but it is a reasonable starting point for projection. Note also that at some point occupancy will not be able to grow any further, and may actually decline. For example, new competitors may enter the market, taking occupancy away from the hotel. Management needs to anticipate this shift and adjust its forecasts to take into account the increased competition. The same logic applies to projecting rate growth. Hotel management may decide to hold or even reduce rates to maintain or improve occupancy when new competitors enter the market.

This simplified approach to forecasting rooms revenue is intended to illustrate the use of trend data in forecasting. A more detailed approach would consider the variety of different rates corresponding to room types, guest profiles, days of the week, and seasonality of business. These are just a few of the factors that may affect rooms revenue forecasting.

Estimating Expenses

Most expenses for front office operations are *variable expenses* in that they vary in direct proportion to rooms revenue. Historical data can be used to calculate an approximate percentage of rooms revenue that each expense item may represent. These percentage figures can then be applied to the total amount of forecasted rooms revenue, resulting in dollar estimates for each expense category for the budget year.

Exhibit 14 Expense Categories as Percentages of Rooms Revenue for the Bradley Hotel

Year	Payroll and Related Expenses	Laundry, Linen, and Guest Supplies	Commissions and Reservation Expenses	Other Expenses
20X1	16.5%	2.6%	2.3%	4.2%
20X2	16.9%	2.8%	2.5%	4.5%
20X3	17.2%	3.0%	2.6%	4.5%
20X4	17.4%	3.1%	2.7%	4.6%

Typical rooms division expenses are payroll and related expenses; guestroom laundry (terry and linen); guest supplies (bath amenities, toilet tissue); hotel merchandising (in-room guest directory and promotional brochures); travel agent commissions and direct reservation expenses; and other expenses. When these costs are totaled and divided by the number of occupied rooms, the cost per occupied room is determined. The cost per occupied room is often expressed in dollars and as a percentage. Exhibit 14 presents expense category statistics of the Bradley Hotel from 20X1 to 20X4, expressed as percentages of each year's rooms revenue. Based on this historical information and management's current objectives for the budget year 20X5, the percentage of rooms revenue for each expense category may be projected as follows: payroll and related expenses, 17.6 percent; laundry, linen and terry, and guest supplies, 3.2 percent; commissions and reservation expenses, 2.8 percent; and other expenses, 4.7 percent.

Using these percentage figures and the expected rooms revenue calculated previously, the Bradley Hotel's rooms division expenses for the budgeted year are estimated as follows:

- Payroll and related expenses
  $1,997,280 × .176 = $351,521.28
- Laundry, linen, terry, and guest supplies
  $1,997,280 × .032 = $ 63,912.96
- Commissions and reservation expenses
  $1,997,280 × .028 = $ 55,923.84
- Other expenses
  $1,997,280 × .047 = $ 93,872.16

In this example, management should question why costs continue to rise as a percentage of revenue. If costs continue to rise (as a percentage, not in real dollars), profitability likely will be affected. Therefore, one of the outcomes of the budget process will be to identify where costs are increasing as a percentage of revenue. Then, management can analyze why these costs are increasing disproportionately with revenue and develop a plan to address the issue.

Since most front office expenses vary proportionately with rooms revenue (and therefore occupancy), another method of estimating these expenses is to estimate variable costs per room sold and then multiply these costs by the number of rooms expected to be sold.

Refining Budget Plans

Departmental budget plans are commonly supported by detailed information gathered in the budget preparation process and recorded on worksheets and summary files. These documents should be saved to provide an explanation of the reasoning behind the decisions made while preparing departmental budget plans. Such records may help resolve issues that arise during the budget review. These support documents may also provide valuable assistance in the preparation of future budget plans.

If no historical data are available for budget planning, other sources of information can be used to develop a budget. For example, corporate headquarters can often supply comparable budget information to its chain-affiliated properties. Also, national accounting and consulting firms can usually provide supplemental data for the budget development process.

Many hotels refine expected results of operations and revise operations budgets as they progress through the budget year. Reforecasting is normally suggested when actual operating results start to vary significantly from the operations budget. Such variance may indicate that conditions have changed since the budget was first prepared. While operating budgets are seldom changed once the hotel's management and owners approve them, reforecasting provides a more realistic picture of current operating conditions.

Evaluating Front Office Operations

Evaluating the results of front office operations is an important management function. Without thoroughly evaluating the results of operations, managers will not know whether the front office is attaining planned goals. Successful front office managers evaluate the results of department activities on a daily, monthly, quarterly, and yearly basis. The following sections examine important tools that front office managers can use to evaluate the success of front office operations. These tools include:

- Daily report of operations
- Occupancy ratios
- Rooms revenue analysis
- Income statement
- Rooms schedule
- Rooms division budget reports
- Operating ratios
- Ratio standards

Daily Report of Operations

The **daily report of operations,** also known as the *manager's report,* the *daily report,* and the *daily revenue report,* summarizes the hotel's financial activities during a twenty-four-hour period. The daily report of operations provides a means of reconciling cash, bank accounts, revenue, and accounts receivable. The report also serves as a posting reference for various accounting journals and provides important data that must be input to link front and back office automated functions. Daily reports of operations are often uniquely structured to meet the needs of individual hotel properties.

Exhibit 15 presents a sample daily report of operations for a hotel with food and beverage service. Rooms statistics and occupancy ratios form an entire section of a typical daily report of operations. Enriched by comments and observations from the accounting staff, statistics shown on the daily report of operations may take on more significance. For example, statistics about the number of guests using the hotel's valet parking services take on added meaning when remarks indicate that valet sales are down while occupancy is up. The front office manager may presume that the front office staff is not properly promoting available guest valet parking services.

The information provided by the daily report of operations is not restricted to the front office manager or hotel general manager. Copies of the daily report of operations are generally distributed to all department and division managers in the hotel.

Occupancy Ratios

Occupancy ratios measure the effectiveness of the front office and reservations sales staffs in selling the hotel's primary product: guestrooms. The following rooms statistics must be gathered to calculate basic occupancy ratios:

- Number of rooms available for sale
- Number of rooms sold
- Number of guests
- Number of guests per room
- Net rooms revenue

Generally, these data are presented on the daily report of operations. Occupancy ratios that can be computed from these data include occupancy percentage, multiple (or double) occupancy ratio, average daily rate, revenue per available room (RevPAR), revenue per available customer (RevPAC), and average rate per guest. Computed occupancy percentage and average daily rate may also appear on a hotel's daily report of operations. These ratios typically are extensive and are usually calculated on a daily, weekly, monthly, and yearly basis.

The front office system typically generates occupied rooms data and calculates occupancy ratios for the front office manager, who analyzes the information to identify trends, patterns, or problems. (The front office system may be programmed to do much of this analysis.) When analyzing the information, there should be consideration of how a particular condition may produce varying effects on occupancy. For example, as multiple occupancy increases, the average daily room rate may also increase. This is because when a room is sold to more than one guest, the room rate may be greater than when the room is sold as a single. However, since the room rate for two guests sharing a room is usually not twice the rate for one person, the average room rate *per guest* decreases.

Exhibit 15 Sample Daily Report of Operations

DAILY REVENUE REPORT

Day ______ Of ______ Day ______ Date ______ Year: ______

Hotel ______________________ Completed By: ______________________

OCCUPANCY SUMMARY	ACTUAL TODAY	%	MONTH TO-DATE	%
SGL Rooms Occupied				
DBL Rooms Occupied				
COMP Rooms Occupied				
TOTAL Rooms Occupied				
O.O.O Rooms				
Vacant				
TOTAL Available Rooms		100%		100%
House Use				
TOTAL Hotel Rooms				
AVG House Rate (Inc Comps & Perms)	$		$	
AVG Trans Rate (Excl. Comp & Perms)	$		$	
TOTAL # GUESTS				
Relocated				
Room Sales Efficiency				
TOTAL ROOMS OCCUPIED				
Forecast / Frecast				
Budget				

REVENUE SUMMARY	TODAY	MTD	BUDGET MONTH END
Net Rooms			
Food			
Beverage			
Banquet Other			
Long Distance			
Local			
Laundry / Valet			
Garage			
Gift Shop			
Health Club			
Pro Shop (Merchandise)			
Golf Fees			
Tennis Fees			
TOTAL HOTEL			

ROOMS REVENUE ANALYSIS

Type	TODAY # Rooms	%	Ave. Rate	Revenue	MONTH-TO-DATE # Rooms	%	Ave. Rate	Revenue
Rack								
Corporate								
Guaranteed Corporate								
Preferred								
Weekend Rate								
Packages								
Government / Military								
Other								
Total Non Group								
Group								
Total Transient								
Permanents								
Complimentary								
Total		100%				100%		
Club Floor								
Frequent Guest								
RSVP								
Breakations								

COMPLIMENTARY ROOMS

Guest Name	Room No	Company	Check In Date	Check Out Date	Authorized By

REORDER FROM STANDARD REGISTER FORMS SELECTOR R0750

PRINTED BY THE STANDARD REGISTER COMPANY U.S.A.

Exhibit 15 *(continued)*

FOOD & BEVERAGE ANALYSIS

Outlet		TODAY Revenue	# Covers	Ave. Check	MONTH-TO-DATE Revenue	# Covers	Ave. Check
Room Service	Food						
	Food						
	Food						
	Food						
	Food						
	Food						
	Food						
Banquet	Food						
	Total Food						
Room Service	Bev.						
	Bev.						
	Bev.						
	Bev.						
	Bev.						
	Bev.						
	Bev.						
	Bev.						
	Bev.						
Banquet	Bev.						
	Total Bev.						
Total Food & Bev.							
Room Rental							
Customer Sev. Inc.							
Miscellaneous							
Total Food & Bev. Dept.							

GROUP ANALYSIS

Group	# Rooms	# Guests	Avg. Rate	Revenue
TOTAL				

MARKET SEGMENTS MONTH-TO-DATE

Group	# Rooms	Avg. Rate	Revenue
National Assoc.			
Reg & State Assoc.			
Corporate			
Incentive			
SMERFE			
Tour & Travel			
Frequent Guest			
Total Group			

ARRIVALS	YESTER-DAY	TODAY	ACTUAL MTD
6 PM Resv.			
Guaranteed Resv.			
Walk-ins			
Same Day Cancellations			
6 PM No Show			
Guaranteed No Show			
Relocated			
Total Actual Arrivals			

DEPARTURES	YESTER-DAY	TODAY	ACTUAL MTD
Expected			
Unexpected			
Stayovers			
Total Actual Departures			

Anticipated Occupancy Tonight ______ %

OUT OF ORDER ROOMS

Room No.	Reason	Number of Nights O.O.O.

The following sections examine how daily occupancy ratios are calculated for the Gregory Hotel. Rooms division data needed for the calculations are as follows:

- The Gregory Hotel has 120 rooms and a rack rate of $98. (For simplicity's sake, assume that this rack rate is applicable to both single and double room occupancies.)
- Eighty-three rooms were sold at varying rates.
- Eighty-five rooms were occupied by guests. (Rooms sold does not equal rooms occupied by guests because, on this particular day, single guests occupied two rooms at a complimentary room rate, thereby generating no rooms revenue. Note that the handling of complimentary rooms may differ among hotel properties.)
- Ten rooms were occupied by two guests; therefore, a total of 95 guests were in occupancy.
- $6,960 in rooms revenue was generated.
- $7,363.75 in total revenue was generated, including rooms, food, beverage, telecommunications, and other.

Occupancy Percentage. The most commonly used operating ratio in the front office is occupancy percentage. **Occupancy percentage** relates the number of rooms either sold or occupied to the number of rooms available during a specific period of time. It is important to note that some hotels use the number of rooms *sold* to calculate this percentage, while other hotels use the number of rooms *occupied* to calculate the statistic. Including complimentary rooms in the calculation can change certain operating statistics, such as average room rate. Using rooms sold, rooms occupied, or both is valid, depending upon the property's needs and history. This discussion will use rooms occupied to illustrate the occupancy percentage calculation.

Sometimes out-of-order rooms may be included in the number of rooms available. At properties that evaluate management performance partly on the basis of occupancy percentage, including out-of-order rooms in the number of rooms available provides the manager with incentive to get those rooms fixed and recycled more quickly. Including all rooms also provides a consistent base on which to measure occupancy. Conversely, not including out-of-order rooms may allow managers to artificially increase the calculated occupancy percentage simply by improperly classifying unsold rooms as out-of-order. Some properties do not include out-of-order rooms because the rooms are not available for sale. Also, to the extent that the occupancy percentage is used to evaluate the performance of front office staff having no control over out-of-order rooms, including those rooms may unfairly penalize the front office staff. Regardless of the approach chosen, it should be used consistently.

The occupancy percentage for the Gregory Hotel is calculated as follows:

$$\text{Occupancy Percentage} = \frac{\text{Number of Rooms Occupied}}{\text{Number of Rooms Available}}$$

$$= \frac{85}{120}$$

$$= .708 \text{ or } \underline{\underline{70.8\%}}$$

Multiple Occupancy Ratio. The **multiple occupancy ratio** (frequently called the double occupancy ratio, although this phrasing may not always be accurate) is used to forecast food and beverage revenue, indicate clean linen requirements, and analyze average daily room rates. Multiple occupancy can be calculated by determining a **multiple occupancy percentage** or by determining the average number of guests per room sold or occupied (also called the *occupancy multiplier* or the *multiple occupancy factor*).

The multiple occupancy percentage for the Gregory Hotel is calculated as follows:

$$\text{Multiple Occupancy Percentage} = \frac{\text{Number of Rooms Occupied by More Than One Guest}}{\text{Number of Rooms Occupied}}$$

$$= \frac{10}{85}$$

$$= .118 \text{ or } \underline{\underline{11.8\%}}$$

The average number of guests per room sold for the Gregory Hotel is calculated as follows:

$$\text{Average Guests per Room Sold} = \frac{\text{Number of Guests}}{\text{Number of Rooms Sold}}$$

$$= \frac{95}{83}$$

$$= \underline{\underline{1.14}}$$

Average Daily Rate. Most front office managers calculate an **average daily rate** (ADR) even though room rates within a property vary significantly from single rooms to suites, from individual guests to groups and conventions, from weekdays to weekends, and from high- to low-demand periods.

The average daily rate for the Gregory Hotel is calculated as follows:

$$\text{Average Daily Rate} = \frac{\text{Total Room Revenue}}{\text{Number of Rooms Sold}}$$

$$= \frac{\$6,960}{83}$$

$$= \underline{\underline{\$83.86}}$$

Some hotels include complimentary rooms in the denominator to show the true effect of complimentary rooms on the average daily rate. This statistic may also be referred to as the *average house rate*.

Revenue per Available Room (RevPAR). Revenue per available room or **RevPAR** is one of the most important hotel statistics, because it provides a statistical benchmark for comparison with similar hotels. RevPAR divides the total room revenue of the hotel by the number of available rooms.

The RevPAR for the Gregory Hotel is calculated as follows:

$$\text{RevPAR} = \frac{\text{Total Room Revenue}}{\text{Number of Available Rooms}}$$

$$= \frac{\$6{,}960}{120}$$

$$= \$58$$

Revenue per Available Customer (RevPAC). Revenue per available customer or **RevPAC,** while not as popular a statistic as RevPAR, can be an important industry statistic. RevPAC divides the total revenue generation of the hotel by the number of guests staying overnight, thereby showing the average revenue generated by each guest. For hotels with high volumes of multiple occupancy, this figure is especially important, since it provides an average room rate spending figure per guest. In most hotels, the higher the multiple occupancy, the greater the total revenue.

The RevPAC for the Gregory Hotel is calculated as follows:

$$\text{RevPAC} = \frac{\text{Total Revenue}}{\text{Number of Guests}}$$

$$= \frac{\$7{,}363.75}{95}$$

$$= \$77.51$$

Average Rate per Guest. Resort hotels, in particular, are often interested in knowing the **average rate per guest** (ARG). This rate is computed inclusive of every guest in the hotel. Some hotel companies include children in the number of guests.

The average rate per guest for the Gregory Hotel is calculated as follows:

$$\text{Average Rate per Guest} = \frac{\text{Total Room Revenue}}{\text{Number of Guests}}$$

$$= \frac{\$6{,}960}{95}$$

$$= \$73.26$$

Rooms Revenue Analysis

Front office staff members are expected to sell rooms at the rack rate unless a guest qualifies for an authorized discounted room rate. A **room rate variance report** lists those rooms that have been sold at other than their rack rates. With this report, front office management can review the use of various special rates to determine whether staff has followed all appropriate front office policies and procedures. Automated front office systems can be programmed to routinely generate a room rate variance report.

One way for front office managers to evaluate the sales effectiveness of the front office staff is to generate a **yield statistic,** which is actual rooms revenue as a percentage of potential rooms revenue.

Yield Statistic. Potential rooms revenue is the amount of rooms revenue that can be generated if all the rooms in the hotel are sold at rack rate on a given day, week, month, or year. The ratio of actual to potential rooms revenue is known as the achievement factor in a yield statistic. The potential revenue for the Gregory Hotel is $11,760 (all 120 rooms sold at the rack rate of $98). Given actual rooms revenue of $6,960, the yield statistic for the Gregory Hotel can be calculated as follows:

$$\text{Yield Statistic} = \frac{\text{Actual Rooms Revenue}}{\text{Potential Rooms Revenue}}$$

$$= \frac{\$6{,}960}{\$11{,}760}$$

$$= .5918 \text{ or } 59.18\%$$

This result reveals that, for the day in question, actual rooms revenue was 59.18 percent of the amount that could have been generated if all 120 rooms had been sold at the full rack rate of $98. This achievement statistic reveals that a significant amount of room rate discounting occurred.

Income Statement

The hotel's **income statement** or statement of income provides important financial information about the results of hotel operations for a given period of time. The period may be one month or longer, but should not exceed one business year. Since a statement of income reveals the amount of net income for a given period, it is one of the most important financial statements management uses to evaluate the overall success of operations. Although front office managers may not directly rely on the hotel's statement of income, it is an important financial indicator of operational success and profitability. The hotel income statement relies in part on detailed front office information that is supplied through the rooms schedule. The rooms schedule is discussed in the next section.

The hotel's statement of income is often called a consolidated income statement because it presents a composite picture of all the hotel's financial operations. Rooms division information appears on the first line, under the category of operated departments. The amount of income generated by the rooms division is determined by subtracting payroll and related expenses and other expenses from the amount of net revenue produced by the rooms division over the period covered by the income statement. Payroll expenses charged to the rooms division may include those associated with the front office manager, front desk agents, reservations agents, housekeepers, and uniformed service staff. Since the rooms division

Exhibit 16 Sample Consolidated Statement of Income

Eatonwood Hotel
Summary Statement of Income
For the year ended 12/31/20XX

	Schedule	Net Revenue	Cost of Sales	Payroll & Related Expenses	Other Expenses	Income (Loss)
Operated Departments						
Rooms	1	$ 6,070,356		$ 1,068,383	$ 473,487	$ 4,528,486
Food	2	2,017,928	$ 733,057	617,705	168,794	498,372
Beverage	3	778,971	162,258	205,897	78,783	332,033
Telecommunications	4	213,744	167,298	31,421	17,309	-2,284
Rentals and Other Income	5	188,092				188,092
Total Operated Departments		9,269,091	1,062,613	1,923,406	738,373	5,544,699
Undistributed Operating Expenses						
Administrative and General	6			227,635	331,546	559,181
Marketing	7			116,001	422,295	538,296
Property Operation and Maintenance	8			204,569	163,880	368,449
Utility Costs	9				546,331	546,331
Total Undistributed Operating Expenses				548,205	1,464,052	2,012,257
Totals		$ 9,269,091	$ 1,062,613	$ 2,471,611	$2,202,425	
Income After Undistributed Operating Expenses						3,532,442
Rent, Property Taxes, and Insurance						641,029
Income Before Interest, Depreciation and Amortization, and Income Taxes						2,891,413
Interest Expense						461,347
Income Before Depreciation Amortization, and Income Taxes						2,430,066
Depreciation and Amortization						552,401
Gain on Sale of Property						1,574
Income Before Income Taxes						1,879,239
Income Taxes						469,810
Net Income						$ 1,409,429

is not a merchandising facility, there is no cost of sales to subtract from the net revenue amount.

Revenue generated by the rooms division is usually the largest single amount produced by revenue centers within a hotel. Based on the figures in Exhibit 16, the amount of income earned by the Eatonwood Hotel's rooms division during the year was $4,528,486—or 81.7 percent of the total operated department income of $5,544,699.

Rooms Schedule

The hotel's income statement primarily contains summary information. The separate departmental income statements prepared by each revenue center provide

Exhibit 17 Sample Rooms Division Income Statement

Rooms—Schedule #1
Eatonwood Hotel
For the year ended 12/31/20XX

	Current Period
Revenue	$6,124,991
Allowances	54,635
Net Revenue	6,070,356
Expenses	
Salaries and Wages	855,919
Employee Benefits	212,464
Total Payroll and Related Expenses	1,068,383
Other Expenses	
Internet/Satellite Television	20,100
Commissions	66,775
Complimentary Guest Services	2,420
Contract Services	30,874
Guest Relocation	1,241
Guest Transportation	48,565
Laundry and Dry Cleaning	42,495
Linen	12,140
Operating Supplies	122,600
Reservations	40,908
Telecommunications	12,442
Training	7,122
Uniforms	60,705
Other	5,100
Total Other Expenses	473,487
Total Expenses	1,541,870
Departmental Income (Loss)	$4,528,486

more detail. Departmental income statements are called "schedules" and are referenced on the hotel's statement of income.

Exhibit 16 references the rooms schedule as *1*. The rooms schedule appears in Exhibit 17. The figures shown in Exhibit 17 for the rooms division revenue, payroll and related expenses, other expenses, and departmental income are the same amounts that appear for the rooms division under the category of operated departments in Exhibit 16.

The hotel accounting division, not the front office accounting staff, generally prepares the rooms schedule. The figures are derived from several sources, as follows:

Rooms Division Entry	Source Documents
Salaries and wages	Time cards, payroll records
Employee benefits	Payroll records
Commissions	Travel agency billings
Contract cleaning	Supplier invoices
Guest transportation	Invoices
Laundry and dry cleaning	Housekeeping and outside laundry/ valet charges for employee uniforms
Linen	Supplier invoices
Operating supplies	Supplier invoices
Reservation expenses (if any)	Reservation system invoices
Other operating expenses	Supplier invoices (such as from equipment rentals, etc.)

(Reservation expenses are fees the hotel pays for central reservation services and reservations made through global distribution and Internet distribution systems.)

By carefully reviewing the rooms schedule, the front office manager may be able to develop action plans to improve the division's financial condition and services. For example, the income statement may indicate that the hotel's telecommunications revenue is down, due to the application of a long-distance surcharge. This analysis reveals that guests are choosing to make fewer telephone calls using the hotel's telecommunications system, because the cost per call was increased by the surcharge. Therefore, even though the revenue *per call* may have increased, overall telecommunications revenues have decreased.

Housekeeping provides another example. If the housekeeping department manager increases the number of rooms a room attendant is assigned to clean per day from fourteen to fifteen, the department will likely need to schedule fewer attendants. This can produce savings in wages, benefits, and possibly cleaning supplies. However, front office managers should be aware that taking measures to reduce costs may result in reduced guest services.

Rooms Division Budget Reports

Generally, the hotel's accounting division also prepares monthly budget reports that compare actual revenue and expense figures with budgeted amounts. These reports can provide timely information for evaluating front office operations. Front office performance is often judged according to how favorably the rooms division's monthly income and expense figures compare with budgeted amounts.

A typical budget report format should include both monthly variances and year-to-date variances for all budget items. Front office managers are more likely to focus on the monthly variances, since year-to-date variances merely represent the accumulation of monthly variances. Exhibit 18 presents a rooms division budget report for the Gregory Hotel for the month of January. This budget report does not yet contain year-to-date figures, since January is the first month of the business year for this particular hotel.

It is important to note that Exhibit 18 presents both dollar and percentage variances. The dollar variances indicate the difference between actual results and

Exhibit 18 Sample Monthly Rooms Division Budget Report

Gregory Hotel
Budget Report—Rooms Division
For January 20XX

	Actual	Budget	Variances $	Variances %
Revenue				
Room Sales	$156,240	$145,080	$11,160	7.69%
Allowances	437	300	(137)	(45.67)
Net Revenue	155,803	144,780	11,023	7.61
Expenses				
Salaries and Wages	20,826	18,821	(2,005)	(10.65)
Employee Benefits	4,015	5,791	1,776	30.67
Total Payroll and Related Expenses	24,841	24,612	(229)	(0.93)
Other Expenses				
Commissions	437	752	315	41.89
Contract Cleaning	921	873	(48)	(5.50)
Guest Transportation	1,750	1,200	(550)	(45.83)
Laundry and Dry Cleaning	1,218	975	(243)	(24.92)
Linen	1,906	1,875	(31)	(1.65)
Operating Supplies	1,937	1,348	(589)	(43.69)
Reservation Expenses	1,734	2,012	278	13.82
Uniforms	374	292	(82)	(28.08)
Other Operating Expenses	515	672	157	23.36
Total Other Expenses	10,792	9,999	(793)	(7.93)
Total Expenses	35,633	34,611	(1,022)	(2.95)
Departmental Income	$120,170	$110,169	$10,001	9.08%

budgeted amounts. Dollar variances are generally considered either favorable or unfavorable as follows:

	Favorable Variance	Unfavorable Variance
Revenue	Actual exceeds budget	Budget exceeds actual
Expenses	Budget exceeds actual	Actual exceeds budget

For example, the actual amount of salaries and wages for rooms division personnel in the month of January was $20,826, while the budgeted amount for salaries and wages was $18,821, resulting in an unfavorable variance of $2,005. This dollar variance is bracketed to indicate that it is unfavorable. However, if the revenue variance is highly favorable, an unfavorable variance in expenses (such as in payroll) is not necessarily negative. The comparative variance may merely indicate the greater expense associated with serving more guests than were anticipated when the budget was created. One way to verify whether a variance is really unfavorable or favorable is to divide the actual rooms occupied for the period into the actual cost and the budgeted cost. If the actual cost is at or below the budgeted cost per room, the variance is actually positive, even though there was more expense.

Percentage variances are determined by dividing the dollar variance by the budgeted amount. For example, the 7.61 percent variance for net revenue shown in Exhibit 18 is the result of dividing the dollar variance figure of $11,023 by the budgeted net revenue amount of $144,780.

The budget report shows both dollar and percentage variances because either dollar variances alone or percentage variances alone may not indicate the significance of the variances reported. For example, dollar variances fail to indicate the magnitude of change from the budgeted base. The monthly budget report for the front office of a large hotel may show that actual net revenue varied from the budgeted amount by $1,000. This may seem to be a significant variance, but if the $1,000 variance is based on a budgeted amount of $500,000, it represents a percentage difference of only 0.2 percent. Most front office managers would not consider this a significant variance. However, if the budget amount for the period was $10,000, a $1,000 variance would represent a percentage variance of 10 percent, a percentage variance most front office managers would consider significant.

Percentage variances alone can also be deceiving. For example, assume that the budgeted amount for an expense item is $10, and the actual expense was $12. The dollar variance of $2 represents a percentage variance of 20 percent. While this percentage difference appears significant, it probably would not be worth a front office manager's time to investigate a $2 variance.

The fact that actual results of front office operations differ from budgeted amounts on a budget report shouldn't be surprising. Any budgeting process, no matter how sophisticated, is unlikely to be perfect. Front office managers should not analyze every variance. Only significant variances require management analysis and action. The hotel general manager and controller can provide criteria by which the front office manager can determine which variances are significant.

Operating Ratios

Operating ratios assist managers in evaluating the success of front office operations. Exhibit 19 suggests more than twenty ratios that may be useful to managers in evaluating the success of front office operations.

Payroll and related expenses tends to be the largest single expense item for the rooms division as well as the entire hotel. For control purposes, labor costs are analyzed on a departmental basis. Dividing the payroll and related expenses of the rooms division by the division's net room revenue yields one of the most frequently analyzed areas of front office operations—labor cost.

Operating ratios should be compared against proper standards—budgeted percentages, for example. Any significant differences between actual and budgeted

Exhibit 19 Useful Rooms Division Operating Ratios

	Net Revenue	Payroll and Related Expenses	Other Expenses	Departmental Income
% of total hotel revenue	X			
% of departmental revenue		X	X	X
% of departmental total expenses		X	X	
% of total hotel payroll and related expenses		X		
% change from prior period	X	X	X	X
% change from budget	X	X	X	X
per available room	X	X	X	X
per occupied room	X	X	X	X

labor cost percentages must be carefully investigated, since payroll and related expenses represent the largest single expense category.

One method for analyzing payroll and related expenses involves a form similar to the one shown in Exhibit 20. Actual figures for the current and previous periods, as well as budgeted amounts, are itemized for comparative analysis. Any significant differences should be highlighted and explained in the remarks section. By conducting a payroll and related expenses analysis, the front office manager demonstrates to general management that he or she attends to the most important controllable expense in the rooms division. Careful attention to staffing as the number of rooms sold fluctuates can guarantee that the percentage of payroll and related expenses to total revenue remains relatively constant from month to month.

Ratio Standards

Operating ratios are meaningful only when compared against useful criteria such as:

- Planned ratio goals
- Corresponding historical ratios
- Industry averages

Ratios are best compared against planned ratio goals. For example, a front office manager may more effectively control labor and related expenses by projecting a goal for the current month's labor cost percentage that is slightly lower than the previous month's. The expectation of a lower labor cost percentage may reflect

Exhibit 20 Sample Payroll Analysis Form

Front Office Payroll Analysis

Hotel: ______________________ Period Ending: ______________________

JOB CATEGORY	Amount Last Year	Amount This Year	Amount Budgeted
Front Office	______	______	______
PBX	______	______	______
Head Housekeeper	______	______	______
Asst. Housekeeper, Housekeeping Staff	______	______	______
Housepersons & Porters	______	______	______
Linen Staff	______	______	______
Laundry Staff	______	______	______
Reservations Staff	______	______	______
Maintenance, Gardener, & Asst. Maintenance	______	______	______
Security, Life Guard, & Uniform Service Staff	______	______	______

	(Last Year)	(This Year)
Payroll and Related Expenses	______	______
Net Revenue	______	______
Labor Cost Percentage	______	______
STATISTICS		
Rooms Rented	______	______
Rooms Cleaned	______	______
Housekeepers Hours Paid	______	______
Number of Rooms Per Housekeeper	______	______
Cost Per Room (Housekeepers)	______	______

REMARKS:

____

____

the front office manager's efforts to improve scheduling procedures and other factors related to the cost of labor. By comparing the actual labor cost percentage with the planned goal, the manager can measure the success of his or her efforts to control labor costs.

Industry averages may also provide a useful standard against which to compare operating ratios. These industry averages can be found in publications prepared by the national accounting firms and trade associations serving the hospitality industry.

Experienced front office managers realize that operating ratios are only indicators; they do not solve problems or necessarily reveal the source of a problem. At best, when ratios vary significantly from planned goals, previous results, or industry averages, they indicate that problems *may* exist. Considerably more analysis and investigation are usually necessary to determine appropriate corrective actions.

Planning for Disasters

Disaster planning is an area that front office managers, and even some senior hotel managers, often overlook. While this is not a day-to-day operating issue, it is important that front office managers have a disaster action and recovery plan in place and make sure that the front office staff is familiar with it.

There are various types of disasters to consider, ranging from power failures and automated systems failures to criminal activities, severe weather, floods, fires, and terrorism. While it is unrealistic to think that every conceivable disaster can be anticipated, many can, and plans should be in place to deal with them. If the hotel has a security department, its director should be involved in the design, documentation, implementation, and ongoing revision of front office disaster plans. If the hotel has no security department, various other sources from which to draw expertise include the American Hotel & Lodging Association (AH&LA) and the American Hotel & Lodging Educational Institute.

Given today's level of hotel automation, disaster plans must state which supplemental or corrective actions front office personnel need to take if essential technology applications fail. Training front office staff in what to do if the property management system, telecommunications system, electronic locking system, and other important automated systems fail is of critical importance. While most system outages are often relatively short-term and minor in scope, they definitely undermine the hotel's ability to serve its guests.

Unfortunately, one of the most common issues a hotel business experiences is criminal activity, whether it is at the front desk, in a revenue outlet, in a guestroom, or elsewhere. Front office managers should prepare for possible criminal activity affecting the front office by creating procedures for dealing effectively and safely with it. Front office staff should know whom to contact if they become aware of or witness criminal activity, and what additional procedures to follow. For example, hotel staff should know that it is unwise to touch or move anything in a guestroom if an incident has occurred that requires police investigation.

Severe weather, floods, and other natural disasters often require special planning to deal with them successfully. Hotel management's plans for coping with natural disasters should be coordinated with local and regional disaster planning agencies. In addition, these plans should consider the possible loss of utilities or the isolation of the property. For example, a snowstorm may prevent employees from reporting for a work shift or may prevent employees from departing the property at the end of a work shift.

A fire, terrorism attack, or other disaster may require a complete hotel evacuation and shutdown of operations. Front office staff must know how to conduct themselves, remembering at all times that they are representatives of the hotel.

They must know what documentation to remove from the property, what to secure by locks, and what to do with hotel assets like cash and cashier banks. Some front office staff members may be called upon to assist with evacuating guests, which might include directing them to various safe locations away from the property, as spelled out in the front office disaster plan.

Foreseeable disasters require planning and training so the front office department and the hotel as a whole can successfully deal with them should they occur. Management should periodically review and update disaster plans; plans should not be drawn up and then placed on a shelf to gather dust. Training, which can range from a simple fire drill to more elaborate instruction involving a simulated robbery or bomb threat, should not be a one-time event; it must be ongoing to be effective, with refresher sessions regularly scheduled.

Summary

Resources available to front office managers include staff members, budgeted funds, work shifts, materials, and equipment, each of which is in limited supply. The front office manager's job involves planning and evaluating the use of such limited resources in meeting the organization's objectives. The process of management can be divided into specific management functions: planning, organizing, coordinating, staffing, leading, controlling, and evaluating. Although specific front office management tasks vary from hotel to hotel, fundamental management functions are similar in scope.

Planning is probably the most important management function. Without competent planning, productivity may be extremely low. Without the direction and focus planning provides, the front office manager may become overly involved with tasks that are unrelated to or inconsistent with accomplishing the hotel's objectives. Communication is an important component of planning. An effective manager communicates department planning activities to managers he or she reports to, as well as to staff members likely to be affected. Using the planned goals as a guide, a front office manager performs an organizing function when dividing the work fairly among front office staff. Organizing includes determining the order in which tasks are to be performed and when each group of tasks should be completed.

The management function of coordinating involves using resources to attain planned goals. A front office manager must be able to coordinate the efforts of many individuals who are all doing different sets of tasks at the same time. The management function of staffing involves recruiting and selecting applicants and scheduling employees. Staffing guidelines are usually based on formulas for calculating the number of employees required to meet guest and operational needs under specified conditions.

Leading is a complicated management skill that is exercised in a variety of situations and is related to other management skills. For a front office manager, leading involves overseeing, motivating, training, and disciplining employees and making decisions. One of the best ways to lead a department is by example. Every hotel has a system of internal controls for protecting the assets of the business. The control process ensures that the actual results of operations closely match planned results. The management function of evaluating determines the extent to which planned goals are attained. Evaluating also involves reviewing and revising front office goals.

Three important front office planning functions are establishing room rates, forecasting room availability, and budgeting for operations. Hotels will normally have several different room rates. The rack rate is listed on the room rate schedule to inform front desk agents of the standard selling price of each guestroom in the hotel. Front office employees are expected to sell rooms at the rack rate unless a guest qualifies for an authorized room rate discount. Establishing rack rates for room types and determining discount categories and special rates are some of a revenue manager's major duties. When determining rack rates or discounted rates, management should consider such factors as operating expenses, guest demand, market conditions, inflationary factors, and related business issues.

Setting room rates through the market condition approach is the simplest and most commonly used. In this approach, the hotel's rates are set to be competitive with similar hotels in the market. The rule-of-thumb approach to setting room rates sets the rate at $1 for each $1,000 of construction and furnishings cost per room, assuming a 70 percent occupancy. The Hubbart Formula for determining the average price per room considers costs, desired profits, and expected number of rooms sold. The front office manager must understand the effects of rate and occupancy on room revenue to ensure that the hotel meets its revenue goals.

The most important short-term planning statistic is forecasting the number of rooms available for sale on any future date. Room availability forecasts are used to help manage the reservations process, guide room sales efforts, and plan staffing requirements. The process of forecasting room availability generally relies on historical occupancy data. Such statistics as the percentage of no-shows, walk-ins, overstays, and understays can be critical factors in effective forecasting.

The most important long-term planning function that front office managers perform is budgeting. The annual operations budget is a profit plan that addresses revenue sources and expense items. It is divided into monthly plans which, in turn, are divided into weekly (and sometimes daily) plans. Budget plans become standards against which management can evaluate operational results. The front office manager's primary responsibilities in budget planning are forecasting rooms revenue and estimating related expenses. The process requires the front office manager and accounting division personnel to coordinate their efforts.

Evaluating the results of front office operations is an important management function. Tools used in this function include the daily report of operations, occupancy ratios, rooms revenue analysis, the hotel income statement, the rooms schedule, rooms division budget reports, operating ratios, and ratio standards.

Operations planning must also include disaster planning. Disasters can include weather and other natural disasters, fires, criminal activities, terrorist acts, and automated systems failures. Front office management must create disaster action and recovery plans, often coordinating them with other hotel departments, as well as local and regional disaster planning agencies. Plans should be thoroughly documented, and front office staff members must be trained. This may involve simulation activities like fire drills or mock hotel evacuations.

Key Terms

average daily rate—An occupancy ratio derived by dividing net rooms revenue by the number of rooms sold.

average rate per guest—An occupancy ratio derived by dividing net rooms revenue by the number of guests.

competitive set—The group of hotels in a market that provides the most important competition for a hotel.

daily report of operations—A report that summarizes the hotel's financial activities during a twenty-four-hour period and provides insight into revenues, receivables, operating statistics, and cash transactions related to the front office; also known as the manager's report, daily report, and daily revenue report.

forecasting—The process of predicting events and trends in business; typical forecasting for the rooms division includes room availability and occupancy.

house count—The forecasted or expected number of guests for a particular period, sometimes broken down into group and non-group business.

Hubbart Formula—A bottom-up approach to pricing rooms; in determining the average price per room, this approach considers costs, desired profits, and expected rooms sold.

income statement—A financial statement that provides important information about the results of hotel operations for a given period of time.

market condition approach—An approach to pricing that bases prices on what comparable hotels in the hotel's competitive set are charging for a similar product.

multiple occupancy percentage—The number of rooms occupied by more than one guest divided by the number of rooms occupied by guests.

multiple occupancy ratio—A measurement used to forecast food and beverage revenue, indicate clean linen requirements, and analyze daily revenue rate; derived from the multiple occupancy percentage or by determining the average number of guests per rooms sold; also called the double occupancy ratio.

occupancy percentage—An occupancy ratio that relates the number of rooms sold to rooms available for sale during a specific period of time.

occupancy ratios—A measurement of the hotel's success in selling rooms; typical occupancy ratios include occupancy percentage, multiple occupancy ratio, average daily rate, revenue per available room, revenue per available customer, and average rate per guest.

operating ratios—A group of ratios that assist in the analysis of hospitality operations.

overstay—A guest who stays after his or her stated departure date.

rack rate—The standard rate the property establishes for a particular category of guestrooms.

revenue per available customer (RevPAC)—A revenue management measurement that focuses on revenue per actual guest.

revenue per available room (RevPAR)—A revenue management measurement that focuses on revenue per available room.

room rate variance report—A report listing rooms that have not been sold at rack rates.

rule-of-thumb approach—A cost approach to pricing rooms in which the room rate is set at $1 for each $1,000 of construction and furnishings cost per room, assuming an occupancy of 70 percent.

stayover—A room status term indicating that the guest is not checking out today and will remain at least one more night; a guest who continues to occupy a room from the time of arrival to the stated date of departure.

understay—A guest who checks out before his or her stated departure date.

yield statistic—The ratio of actual rooms revenue to potential rooms revenue.

Review Questions

1. How do the seven functions of management fit into the overall management process? How do these functions apply to the front office manager's position?
2. What kinds of special room rates might a hotel offer? What are the three common methods of establishing room rates?
3. What information do front office managers require to develop room availability forecasts? Why are these forecasts important? How reliable are such forecasts?
4. What steps can front office employees take to control understays and unwanted overstays?
5. What are the differences between RevPAR and RevPAC? How can the front office manager use each ratio?
6. How do ten-day and three-day forecasts help ensure efficiency in front office operations? What is the relationship between these forecasts? What departments in the hotel rely on these forecasts, other than the front office?
7. What are the front office manager's primary responsibilities in budget planning? How are they performed?
8. What occupancy ratios are commonly calculated by the front office? What is the significance of occupancy ratios?
9. What methods can a front office manager use to evaluate how effectively the front office is selling rooms?
10. How can front office managers use budget reports to analyze operations? Why is reporting both dollar and percentage variances valuable?
11. What are some useful standards against which front office managers should compare operating ratios? What is the significance of a variance from standards?
12. What can a front office manager do to prepare his or her staff to deal with disasters?

Internet Sites

For more information, visit the following Internet sites. Remember that Internet addresses can change without notice. If the site is no longer there, you can use a search engine to look for additional sites.

American Hotel & Lodging Association
www.ahla.com

American Hotel & Lodging Educational Institute
www.ahlei.org

Smith Travel Research
www.smithtravelresearch.com

TIMS Reports.com
www.TIMSreports.com

TravelCLICK
www.travelclick.net

Chapter Appendix

Manual Operations Plans

The following plans and procedures are suggested as an outline for use whenever a disaster or something else causes the property management system to go down for a significant amount of time. (Illustration 1 outlines some immediate actions that can be taken.) The objective is to establish clear control and coordination responsibilities. Each property should prepare its own version based on its own operational needs and should prepare similar documents for all other critical systems (POS, sales and catering, etc.). All of these plans should be reviewed periodically to ensure that they stay current.

The key to running a hotel manually is good, organized communication between management and all operationally focused departments within the hotel, especially the front desk, reservations, and housekeeping. Most employees will never have worked in a manual environment and will be used to relying exclusively on the front office computer system. Consequently, all instructions to employees should be clear and precise, and the plans should be practiced regularly. Maintaining guest service is of utmost importance during this period.

Management/Staff Roles

The following roles are suggested for the key management and operations staff. The task assignments should be customized to the nature of each hotel's operations. For example, while many properties may not have a systems manager, they should have one person who has responsibility for coordinating all support activity on the automated systems. It is most important that the responsibility for performing each task be clearly understood by all.

General Manager/Hotel Manager

- Authorizes notification of all management personnel.
- Receives status reports from systems personnel.
- Makes/approves operational decisions regarding system downtime.

Systems Manager

- Determines magnitude of problem; estimates system downtime. Determines status of all correction activities in progress.
- Notifies response team on severity of problem and recommends degree of contingency to implement.
- Ensures that all necessary functions and personnel are prepared to begin manual operations, if necessary, and notifies appropriate service/vendor personnel.
- Keeps management updated regarding contingency status.
- Supervises repair, restoration, and replacement of data, components, systems, or entire computer room as needed.

Illustration 1 Downtime Quick Response Checklist

Quick Response Checklist

1. Alert managers.
2. If the system is down because of a power failure, *turn off all equipment immediately*. Failure to do so could result in further hardware damage. If the critical items are on uninterruptible power supplies (UPSs) with automated shutdown routines, monitor these to ensure that they are in fact closing down correctly.
3. Distribute the most recent downtime reports and destroy prior lists.
4. Designate a rack clerk, responsible for maintaining the room inventory and status, to begin to record all check-ins, check-outs, etc.
5. Designate a posting clerk, responsible for writing all charges on the guest folios.
6. Alert retail outlets that the system is inoperable and that they must close checks to the manual key. All room charges must be taken to the front desk for manual posting.
7. Alert the audit staff members no later than four hours before their shifts that the system is down and that they should report early to begin a manual audit.
8. Alert the central reservation help desk of the situation and estimated downtime, and arrange an alternative for continued delivery of reservations and feedback of hotel availability status.
9. The rooms division manager should write a letter to all in-house guests and arrivals notifying them of the situation.
10. Issue battery-operated radios to all key personnel, including the PBX operator.

- Prepares report for hotel management that details problems, causes, and solutions; plan performance; and suggestions for modifications as necessary.

Reception Manager

- Coordinates front office activity with the systems manager and reservations manager.
- Supervises the front office activity during downtime.
- Monitors controls and audit trails during downtime.
- Supervises in-house runners.
- Supplies food and beverage outlets with current guest list, no-post list, and cash guest list.
- Documents observed or perceived problems in plan operation for review and/or revision.
- Coordinates reconstruction of data, once system is restored.

Front Desk Supervisor

- Monitors and controls registration functions.
- Maintains room status control sheet.
- Maintains walk-in list.
- Communicates status changes to housekeeping.
- Maintains status change log.
- Supervises bucket clerk.
- Supervises re-entry of check-ins, check-outs, and moves once the system is restored.

Reception Agents

- Controls filing of guest charges and maintenance of current balances. Supervises generation of source documents, vouchers/receipts, etc.
- Assists cashiers in balancing shift.
- Assists with posting of charges/payments once the system is restored.

Reservation Manager

- Distributes thirty-day and one-year room availability reports to all reservation agents.
- Supervises manual booking of reservations.
- Maintains manual reservations file.
- Maintains a manual room availability control chart.
- Supervises re-entry of reservations once the system is restored.

PBX Operator

- Notifies computer staff when the system is down.
- Maintains and updates telephone reference list with assistance of front office.

All Outlet Managers

- Coordinates food and beverage contingency plan with systems manager.
- Supervises execution of contingency plan in all food and beverage outlets.
- Supervises manual operation of outlets, including ordering, service, payment, and posting of all checks.
- Supervises entering of all information once system is restored.
- Assists in balancing process during downtime.

Cashiers

- Responsible for three-part check and check control sheet distribution to outlet cashiers.
- Monitors the manual tip control sheet and disbursement of charge tips.

Assistant Controller

- Coordinates accounting department activity with the systems manager.
- Supervises execution of the contingency plan in the accounting office.
- Supervises data reconstruction after the system is restored.

Accounts Receivable Manager

- Works with the front desk supervisor and bucket clerk on maintaining the manual guest ledger.
- Maintains manual banquet billings.
- Coordinates advance deposit refunds with accounts payable during extended downtime.
- Maintains manual payment card account balances.
- Monitors advance deposit activity.
- Supervises restoration of data.

Housekeeping

- Supervises manual room status controls.
- Establishes initial room status sheet (P.M.) housekeeping report.
- Supervises vacant room inspection.
- Supervises distribution of updated room status lists to front desk.
- Supervises manual assignment of room attendants.
- Maintains room status change log.

Night Reception Manager

- Performs regular audit functions when and where necessary.
- Helps generate manual reports during extended downtime.
- Supervises the night clerks during downtime.
- Assists in the restoration of data.
- Performs update and distribution of reports.
- Balances hotel accounts at the end of the day.

Manual Front Desk Overview

Illustration 2 lists items and staff required to manually operate the front desk. Make sure that the room rack report (see Illustration 3) and any other standard forms are already filled out with the room numbers and other data that do not change. Prepare "crash kits" stocked with all necessary office supplies (pens, cards, pads, tape, etc.) and keep them in an area that is convenient to the front desk.

Illustration 2 Items and Staff Needed for Manual Front Desk Operations

Forms:	Manual Room Rack	
	Cash Guest Report	
	House Count Sheet	
	Registration Cards (handwritten or pre-printed)	
	Guest Folios (handwritten or pre-printed)	
	Reservations Forms (handwritten or pre-printed)	
	Most recent downtime reports from system	
Miscellaneous:	Index cards and alphabetical file	
	Calculator with tape (battery operated)	
	Pencils with erasers	
	Payment card imprinters	
Personnel:	Posting Clerk:	Responsible for posting all charges to guest folios
	Rack Clerk:	Responsible for maintaining room inventory and current status
	Runners:	Responsible for communications between departments, ensuring that departments are passing information correctly and that everyone is following the manual operating procedures

Returning to Automated Operations

When the system is fully operational again, it won't know that anything has happened since it went down, and it must be brought up-to-date through the manual entering of all transactions that occurred in the interim. This requires an organized effort on the part of all members of management to keep all users posting on the correct day. If all night audit work is organized into batches, all staff can concentrate on one day's activity at a time. A night audit must be run for each day that the system was down in order to bring the system up to the current date. Manual downtime procedures must be maintained until the system is running and its data has been verified as fully up-to-date. General steps in bringing the system up-to-date are:

1. Process the first day's work. Process all activity that was not posted on the day that the system went down, including check-ins, check-outs, all transactions, and room status changes.
2. Some systems (PBX, call accounting, mini bars, pay movies, etc.) that use an interface to post charges to guest folios may hold charges in a buffer. If these systems were operating during the time that the property management system was not, charges may post automatically when the interface is restored. This could result in charges being posted to the wrong accounts, double posting of charges, phones or mini bars being turned off or on inappropriately, and so on. Each of these systems should have a backup printer to report charges (including date, time, and room number) it was unable to send to the property management system. This is the information needed to post charges manually to the correct guests' folios, but the reports do not imply that charges are not still being held in a buffer. Check with the vendor for each of these systems to

Illustration 3 Sample Manual Room Rack Report

Manual Room Rack

Floor Number ________ **Section Number** ________

Room #:	________	Room Type:	________
Status:	________	Guest Name:	________
Room Features:	________	Check-Out:	________
Room #:	________	Room Type:	________
Status:	________	Guest Name:	________
Room Features:	________	Check-Out:	________
Room #:	________	Room Type:	________
Status:	________	Guest Name:	________
Room Features:	________	Check-Out:	________
Room #:	________	Room Type:	________
Status:	________	Guest Name:	________
Room Features:	________	Check-Out:	________
Room #:	________	Room Type:	________
Status:	________	Guest Name:	________
Room Features:	________	Check-Out:	________
Room #:	________	Room Type:	________
Status:	________	Guest Name:	________
Room Features:	________	Check-Out:	________
Room #:	________	Room Type:	________
Status:	________	Guest Name:	________
Room Features:	________	Check-Out:	________
Room #:	________	Room Type:	________
Status:	________	Guest Name:	________
Room Features:	________	Check-Out:	________
Room #:	________	Room Type:	________
Status:	________	Guest Name:	________
Room Features:	________	Check-Out:	________
Room #:	________	Room Type:	________
Status:	________	Guest Name:	________
Room Features:	________	Check-Out:	________

discuss how their systems work and how best to handle a situation where the property management system, the interface, or even the system in question is down. Add this information to the disaster action and recovery plan.

3. Perform a full rooms and financial audit for that day.
4. Run a night audit process on the computer system.
5. Once the above procedures are complete and the system is on the next day, process the remaining days' transactions in the same manner. Perform night audit and run a close-of-day for each day until the current day and time are reached.

Chapter 9 Outline

Competencies

1. Identify typical cleaning responsibilities of the housekeeping department. (pp. 345–349)
2. Describe the tools the housekeeping department uses to plan its work. (pp. 349–361)
3. Explain the executive housekeeper's role in organizing the housekeeping department. (pp. 361–367)
4. Identify basic management functions of the executive housekeeper. (pp. 367–379)

Taken from *Managing Housekeeping Operations*, Revised Third Edition, by Aleta A. Nitschke and William D. Frye

Chapter 9

Planning and Organizing the Housekeeping Department

LIKE ALL OTHER MANAGERS in a hotel, the executive housekeeper uses available resources to attain objectives set by top management executives. Resources include people, money, time, work methods, materials, energy, and equipment. These resources are in limited supply, and most executive housekeepers will readily admit that they rarely have all the resources they would like. Therefore, an important part of the executive housekeeper's job is planning how to use the limited resources available to attain the hotel's objectives.

The executive housekeeper uses objectives set by the general manager as a guide in planning more specific, measurable goals for the housekeeping department. For example, one of the executive housekeeper's first planning activities is to clarify the department's cleaning responsibilities and to map strategies for carrying out these responsibilities effectively. Strategies will identify the types of cleaning tasks and indicate how frequently the tasks must be performed.

This chapter begins by identifying some of the executive housekeeper's most important planning functions. The major cleaning responsibilities of the housekeeping department are identified, and suggestions for planning work within the department are presented. In addition, the chapter examines the organizational structure of several housekeeping departments and presents sample job descriptions for executive housekeeper positions. Job descriptions are also presented for typical housekeeping positions in a mid-market hotel. The chapter closes by showing how other important management functions of the executive housekeeper fit into the overall process of management.

Identifying Housekeeping's Responsibilities

Regardless of the size and structure of a housekeeping department, it is typically the responsibility of the hotel's general manager to identify which areas housekeeping will be responsible for cleaning. Most housekeeping departments are responsible for cleaning the following areas:

- Guestrooms
- Corridors
- Public areas, such as the lobby and public restrooms
- Pool and patio areas
- Management offices

- Storage areas
- Linen and sewing rooms
- Laundry room
- Back-of-the-house areas, such as employee locker rooms

Housekeeping departments of hotels offering mid-range and world-class service are generally responsible for additional areas, such as:

- Meeting rooms
- Dining rooms
- Banquet rooms
- Convention exhibit halls
- Hotel-operated shops
- Game rooms
- Exercise rooms

Housekeeping's cleaning responsibilities in the food & beverage areas vary from property to property. In most hotels, housekeeping has very limited responsibilities in relation to cleaning food preparation, production, and storage areas. The special cleaning and sanitation tasks required for maintaining these areas are usually carried out by kitchen staff under the supervision of the chief steward. In some properties, the dining room staff cleans service areas after breakfast and lunch periods; housekeeping's night cleaning crew does the in-depth cleaning after dinner service or early in the morning before the dining room opens for business. The executive housekeeper and the dining room managers must work closely together to ensure that quality standards are maintained in the guest service and server station areas.

The same cooperation is necessary between housekeeping and banquet or meeting services. The banquet or meeting services staff generally sets up banquet and meeting rooms and is responsible for some cleaning after the rooms are used. The final in-depth cleaning is left to the housekeeping department. This means that the final responsibility for the cleanliness and overall appearance of these areas falls squarely on the shoulders of the housekeeping staff.

The general manager typically designates which areas housekeeping will be responsible for cleaning. However, if areas of responsibility cross department lines, the managers of those departments must get together and settle among themselves any disputes about cleaning responsibilities. The agreement among the managers is then reported to the general manager for his or her approval. A good housekeeping manager can effectively solve problems with other managers, thereby relieving the general manager of day-to-day, operational problems.

It is a good idea for the executive housekeeper to obtain a floor plan of the hotel (either paper or digital) and "color in" those areas for which housekeeping is responsible. Different colors can be used to designate those areas for which other department managers are responsible. To ensure that all areas of the property have been covered—and to avoid future misunderstandings about responsibilities—copies of this color-coded floor plan should be distributed to the general

the Rooms CHRONICLE®

Executive Housekeeper IS the Driving Force

Say it's Monday and the day is well under way. The roomkeepers are off doing their assignments, the laundry is humming, and the public space cleaners are started on their chores. The executive housekeeper decides the time is right for a walkdown. After all, it was a busy weekend, lots of guests in the house, and the executive housekeeper wants to review the property's condition.

This walkdown is one of the most important functions of the executive housekeeper. Undeniably, the executive housekeeper's number one job is to ensure a clean hotel, and inspections are the key to this goal. But exactly what is an executive housekeeper looking for during a walkdown? Clean hallways? Public space furniture arranged neatly? Litter-free grounds? Employees doing the right things in the right places? Yes. All of this and more. The executive housekeeper must look at the big picture.

For instance, when a public space cleaner patrols the hotel hallways, he concentrates on picking up litter and emptying ashurns. When an executive housekeeper walks the building, he or she is reviewing the physical state of the building.

It is big picture things like the condition of the upholstery on the lobby sofa or the scratches in the chair rail along the hallway that the executive housekeeper must notice. It is the role of the executive housekeeper to identify trends of decline in the state of the property and gather the resources necessary to make things right. Whether correcting the problem means coordination of efforts between other departments or preparation of a capital budget for money allocation, the executive housekeeper must be responsible for initiating activity.

Public areas

One maintenance item that can easily get out of control is nicks in doors and hallways. The best executive housekeepers trace the source of the nicks in order to eliminate the cause. Perhaps there's a sharp corner on one or more roomkeeper carts? A bellman's cart? Rollaway beds? Room service carts? The executive housekeeper surveys the hotel, decides the magnitude of the problem, and arranges with engineering to have the situation corrected. Redirecting painters, closing down sections of rooms, and communicating with various departments are actions that must be arranged in order to eliminate the shoddy-looking nicks.

The executive housekeeper worries about the general appearance of the building—what might be guests' first impressions? The condition of lobby furniture, the appearance of vending areas, the orderliness of roomkeeper carts—things that guests see before getting inside their rooms.

An executive housekeeper would notice that a vending machine is again out of a certain item(s) and would take responsibility for correcting the situation. An executive housekeeper would notice that the plant service has not been making regular visits as contracted. An executive housekeeper would notice that longer walk-off mats are needed at certain entrances.

Guestrooms

Within guestrooms, an executive housekeeper would be concerned not just with cleaning but with the general condition of the rooms. For instance:

(continued)

the Rooms CHRONICLE® *(continued)*

- Are mattresses, pillows, and bedspreads beginning to show wear and tear?
- Are the case goods holding up according to manufacturers' expectations?
- If air vents are collecting dust, an executive housekeeper asks "why?" Is the room attendant not performing cleaning tasks as assigned? Or is there a more serious problem within the air handling system?
- Are guestroom windows fogged? What is engineering's position on replacing them?
- Are balcony railings deteriorating? Do they need replacement, paint, or welding?
- What is the condition of draperies? What cleaning program should be employed? Vacuuming the drapes? Remove them to process through the dryer? Contract with an outside vendor to dry clean the drapes?
- What is the quality of bedmaking throughout the hotel? An executive housekeeper will tear apart a freshly made bed to inspect the condition of all components and the technique of the room attendant.
- Are the bathroom fixtures intact? No cracks or stains or leaks? Have room attendants been reporting problems? Has engineering been responding to the reports?
- Is the room overloaded with promotional materials? Pizza promotions, long distance dialing instructions, the latest frequent guest program—each flier takes up space in the guestroom and impacts the guest's impression of the room. It is an executive housekeeper's role to review the room, ensure that materials are current and necessary, and put a stop to clutter.
- Does the television work? The remote control? The telephone speed buttons? Are directions current and easy to follow?

Many of the items that an executive housekeeper must inspect require remedies that involve other hotel managers. Engineering, for example, must work hand in hand with housekeeping toward the general upkeep of the property. Accounting must be supportive in conducting inventories and preparing paperwork for building capital expenditure budgets. Purchasing must assist in gathering bids for replacement of inventory. And general managers must be involved in endorsing the improvements.

The condition of the property is the most valuable asset of the hotel. The executive housekeeper must be the driving force toward achieving perfection. In fact, the responsibility for getting things to happen must rest with the executive housekeeper.

In the real world the executive housekeeper often feels powerless to get other managers to help solve hotel problems. But the executive housekeeper is dependent upon others for cooperation. For instance, the front office must agree to close a section of rooms for deep cleaning. So, the executive housekeeper must continually work to gain commitment from all parties. It is the role of the executive housekeeper to not only see the big picture, but to enhance it at every opportunity.

Source: Mary Friedman, *The Rooms Chronicle®*, Volume 8, Number 3, pp. 4–5.
For subscription information, please call 866-READ-TRC.

manager and to all department managers. This way, everyone can see at a glance who is responsible for cleaning each area in the hotel. The color-coded floor plan also presents a clear and impressive picture of the housekeeping department's role in cleaning and maintaining the hotel.

Contemporary lodging properties are often attempting to "go green" in almost all aspects of their operations, including housekeeping. This may add another arc of responsibility for executive housekeepers. From encouraging guests to reuse linens to more comprehensive sustainability mandates, most hotels are or will likely move to adopt more environmentally friendly housekeeping standards.

Once housekeeping's areas of responsibility have been identified, planning focuses on analyzing the work required for cleaning and maintaining each area.

Planning the Work of the Housekeeping Department

Planning is probably the executive housekeeper's most important management function. Without competent planning, every day may present one crisis after another. Constant crises lower morale, decrease productivity, and increase expenses within the department. Also, without the direction and focus that planning provides, the executive housekeeper can easily become sidetracked by tasks which are unimportant or unrelated to accomplishing the hotel's objectives.

Since the housekeeping department is responsible for cleaning and maintaining so many different areas of the hotel, planning the work of the department can seem like an enormous task. Without a systematic, step-by-step approach to planning, the executive housekeeper can easily become overwhelmed and frustrated by the hundreds of important details. These details must be addressed in order to ensure that the work is not only done—but done correctly, efficiently, on time, and with the least cost to the department.

Exhibit 1 shows how the executive housekeeper can plan the work of the department. The exhibit lists the initial questions that focus the planning activities of the executive housekeeper and identifies the end result of each step in the planning process. The resulting documents form the plans that must be in place for the housekeeping department to run smoothly. The following sections examine each step in the planning process.

Area Inventory Lists

Planning the work of the housekeeping department begins with creating **area inventory lists** of all items within each area that will need housekeeping's attention. Preparing area inventory lists is the first planning activity because the lists ensure that the rest of the planning activities address every item for which housekeeping will be held accountable. Area inventory lists are bound to be long and extremely detailed. Since most properties offer several different types of guestrooms, separate inventory lists may be needed for each room type.

When preparing a guestroom area inventory list, it is a good idea to follow the sequence in which room attendants will clean items and in which supervisors will inspect items. This enables the executive housekeeper to use the inventory lists as the basis for developing cleaning procedures, training plans, and inspection

Exhibit 1 Basic Planning Activities

INITIAL PLANNING QUESTIONS	RESULTING DOCUMENTS
1. What items within this area must be cleaned or maintained?	Area Inventory Lists
2. How often must the items within this area be cleaned or maintained?	Frequency Schedules
3. What must be done in order to clean or maintain the major items within this area?	Performance Standards
4. How long should it take an employee to perform an assigned task according to the department's performance standards?	Productivity Standards
5. What amounts of equipment and supplies will be needed in order for the housekeeping staff to meet performance and productivity standards?	Inventory Levels

checklists. For example, items within a guestroom may appear on an area inventory list as they are found from right to left and from top to bottom around the room. Other systematic techniques may be used, but the point is that *some* system should be followed—and this system should be the same one used by room attendants and inspectors in the daily course of their duties.

Frequency Schedules

Frequency schedules indicate how often items on area inventory lists are to be cleaned or maintained. Items that must be cleaned on a daily or weekly basis become part of a routine cleaning cycle and are incorporated into standard work procedures. Other items (that must be cleaned or maintained biweekly, monthly, bimonthly, or according to some other cycle) are inspected on a daily or weekly basis, but they become part of a **deep cleaning** program and are scheduled as special cleaning projects. Exhibit 2 presents a sample frequency schedule for light fixtures found in a public area of a large convention hotel. Exhibit 3 presents a sample frequency list for special project duties carried out by housekeeping's night cleaning crew.

Tasks on an area's frequency schedule that are made part of housekeeping's deep cleaning program should be transferred to a calendar plan (whether computer- or paper-based) and scheduled as special cleaning projects. The calendar program guides the executive housekeeper in scheduling the appropriate staff to perform the necessary work. The executive housekeeper must take into account a number of factors when scheduling deep cleaning of guestrooms or other special projects. For example, whenever possible, days marked for guestroom deep cleaning should

Exhibit 2 Sample Frequency Schedule

PUBLIC AREA #2—LIGHT FIXTURES

LOCATION	TYPE	NO.	FREQ.
Entrance #1	Sconce	2	1/W
Lobby	Chandelier	3	1/M
Entrance #2	Crown Sconce	2	1/M
Behind Fountain	Sconce	3	1/W
Catwalk	Pole Light	32	1/M
Lower Level	Pole Light	16	1/M
Fountain Area	Pole Light	5	1/M
Restaurant Courtyard	Pole Light	10	1/M
Restaurant Courtyard	Wall Light	5	1/M
Restaurant Patio	Half-Pole Light	16	1/W
Restaurant Entrance	White Globe Pole Light	6	1/W
Crystal Gazebo	White Globe Pole Light	8	1/W
2nd Stairs to Catwalk	White Globe Pole Light	2	1/W
Fountain	White Globe Pole Light	4	1/W
Lounge Patio	Wall Light	4	1/W
Restaurant Entrance	Chandelier	1	1/W

coincide with low occupancy periods. Also, the deep cleaning program must be flexible in relation to the activities of other departments. For example, if the engineering department schedules extensive repair work for several guestrooms, the executive housekeeper should make every effort to coordinate a deep cleaning of these rooms with engineering's timetable. Careful planning will produce good results for the hotel with the least possible inconvenience to guests or to other departments.

Performance Standards

The executive housekeeper can begin to develop **performance standards** by answering the question, "What must be done in order to clean or maintain the major items within this area?" Standards are required quality levels of performance. Performance standards state not only *what* must be done, they also describe in detail *how* the job must be done.

One of the primary objectives of planning the work of the housekeeping department is to ensure that all employees carry out their cleaning tasks in a consistent manner. A 2006 study indicated there may be large differences in the amount of cleaning products used by room attendants at the same hotel (or the same shift), reinforcing the importance of establishing, communicating, and measuring performance standards.[1] The keys to consistency are the performance standards which the executive housekeeper develops, communicates, and manages. Although these standards will vary from one housekeeping department to another, executive

Exhibit 3 Sample Frequency List for Night Cleaning Projects

Special Projects	Frequency Per Week	Frequency Per Month
1. Wash down tile walls in restrooms	1	
2. Strip and wax the following:		
Restrooms (as necessary)		1
Basement hallway	1	
Lounge, lobby, and stairs		1
3. Shampoo the following:		
Registration area		1
Stairs		1
Restrooms		1
All dining rooms		2
All lounges		1
Coffee shop		1
Meeting rooms		1
Guest elevators		1
Employee cafeteria (as needed)		2
4. Spot shampoo the following:		
Front entrance		2
Side entrance		2
Front desk area		2
5. Wash windows in pool area		1
6. Dust louvers in pool area		1
7. Clean guest and service elevator tracks	1	
8. Polish kitchen equipment		1
9. Polish drinking fountains	1	
10. Clean outside of guest elevators	2	

housekeepers can ensure consistency of cleaning by demanding 100 percent conformity to the standards established by their departments. When performance standards are not properly developed, effectively communicated, and consistently managed, the productivity of the housekeeping department suffers because employees will not be performing their tasks in the most efficient and effective manner.

The most important aspect of developing standards is gaining consensus on how cleaning and other tasks are to be carried out. Consensus can be achieved by having individuals who actually perform the tasks contribute to the standards that are eventually adopted by the department.

Performance standards are communicated through ongoing training programs. Many properties have developed performance standards and have included them between the covers of impressive housekeeping procedure manuals. However, all too often, these manuals simply gather dust on shelves in the offices of executive housekeepers. Well-written standards are useless unless they

the Rooms CHRONICLE®

To Give a 100-Percent Clean Appearance, Rotate Guestroom Tasks and Projects

Can a room cleaner clean 100 percent of every assigned room every day? Probably not! Shortage of supplies, time, or equipment may prohibit the room cleaner from doing perfect work in every room. But with a good daily job description and proper organization of tasks and projects, a room cleaner can consistently produce a high quality room.

The housekeeping manager should begin with a good room cleaner daily job description. Go to the guestroom and write all areas that need cleaning. Room cleaners should then test the items on the cleaning list with a time clock. With this information, a manager can decide what tasks will be included in the daily routine and which will be completed some other way.

The areas that don't need attention every day, such as changing bedspreads, washing walls, or shampooing carpets, become either special projects or deep cleaning items. Since guests do have expectations of a completely clean room when they arrive, room cleaners must be organized in a way that results in a room that appears as if it has been thoroughly cleaned that same day. To accomplish this, managers must have a frequency list for special cleaning tasks.

Many tasks fall into the category of deep cleaning. For instance, changing the sheer drapes is a deep cleaning task that may need to be done only biannually. An easy way to complete projects that fall into this category is to close down a block of rooms for deep cleaning. Thorough cleaning of a series of rooms is easily accomplished by having a cleaning team, supply inventory, and cleaning equipment ready. This is also a good time for engineering to review the rooms for preventive maintenance items.

There are various other ways to organize the completion of deep cleaning rooms. For instance, a deep cleaning team might be given a short schedule of check-out rooms. A hotel in downtown Minneapolis hires a group of workers with disabilities as their special clean team. They are assigned approximately six rooms per day to deep clean and are paid by the room.

Another deep cleaning method is to schedule every room cleaner with one room per day as a deep clean room. When the room cleaner accepts responsibility for deep cleaning one room per day, management may choose to institute a "perfect room" incentive to keep the quality high.

But there are other tasks that need to be done less often than every day but more often that deep cleaning: for instance, washing door frames, light switch plates, or bathroom air vents. One method of accomplishing these tasks is to highlight each as a special daily project that is announced at the morning meeting. Monday might be "wash the door frame" day so that each room cleaner will wash the door frame in every assigned room.

The difficulty of managing special cleaning tasks is tracking which rooms have been completed. For example, if on Monday the hotel is only 75 percent occupied, then 25 percent of the rooms did not get the door frames washed.

(continued)

the Rooms CHRONICLE® *(continued)*

To overcome this dilemma, many housekeepers post a projects chart in the room cleaner closet on each floor. Room cleaners simply mark off which tasks have been accomplished in each room. With this system, relief room cleaners can easily see the status of the floor and participate in the project cleaning.

Although there are many variations on the rotation systems described above, all share the same goal—to present a thoroughly clean room to each arriving guest.

Source: Mary Friedman, *The Rooms Chronicle®*, Volume 5, Number 5, p. 4.
For subscription information, please call 866-READ-TRC.

are applied. The only way to implement standards in the workplace is through effective training programs.

After communicating performance standards through ongoing training activities, the executive housekeeper must manage those standards. Managing standards means ensuring conformity to standards by inspection. Experienced housekeepers know the truth of the adage, "You can't expect what you don't inspect." Daily inspections and periodic performance evaluations should be followed up with specific on-the-job coaching and retraining. This ensures that all employees are consistently performing their tasks in the most efficient and effective manner. The executive housekeeper should review the department's performance standards at least once a year and make appropriate revisions as new work methods are implemented.

Productivity Standards

While performance standards establish the expected quality of the work to be done, **productivity standards** determine the acceptable quantity of work to be done by department employees. An executive housekeeper begins to establish productivity standards by answering the question, "How long should it take for a housekeeping employee to perform an assigned task according to the department's performance standard?" Productivity standards must be determined in order to properly staff the department within the limitations established by the hotel's operating budget.

Since performance standards vary in relation to the unique needs and requirements of each hotel, it is impossible to identify productivity standards that would apply across the board to every housekeeping department. Since the duties of room attendants vary widely among economy, mid-market, and luxury hotels, the productivity standards for room attendants will also vary.

When determining realistic productivity standards, an executive housekeeper does not have to carry around a measuring tape, stopwatch, and clipboard and conduct time and motion studies on all the tasks necessary to clean and maintain each item on an area's inventory list. The labor of the executive housekeeper and other management staff is also a precious department resource. However, housekeeping

Exhibit 4 Sample Productivity Standards Worksheet

Step 1

Determine how long it should take to clean one guestroom according to the department's performance standards.

Approximately 27 minutes*

Step 2

Determine the total shift time in minutes.

8 hours × 60 minutes = 480 minutes

Step 3

Determine the time available for guestroom cleaning.

Total Shift Time	480 minutes
Less:	
Beginning-of-Shift Duties	20 minutes
Morning Break	15 minutes
Afternoon Break	15 minutes
End-of-Shift Duties	20 minutes
Time Available for Guestroom Cleaning	410 minutes

Step 4

Determine the productivity standard by dividing the result of Step 3 by the result of Step 1.

$$\frac{410 \text{ minutes}}{27 \text{ minutes}} = 15.2 \text{ guestrooms per 8-hour shift}$$

*Since performance standards vary from property to property, this figure is used for illustrative purposes only. It is not a suggested time figure for cleaning guestrooms.

managers must know how long it should take a housekeeping employee to perform the major tasks identified on the cleaning frequency schedules—such as guestroom cleaning. Once this information is known, productivity standards can be developed.

Let's assume that, at a mid-market hotel, the executive housekeeper determines that a room attendant can meet performance standards and clean a typical guestroom in approximately 27 minutes. Exhibit 4 presents a sample productivity standards worksheet and shows how a productivity standard can be calculated for room attendants working 8-hour shifts. Calculations within the exhibit assume that room attendants take a half-hour, unpaid lunch period. The exhibit shows that the productivity standard for room attendants should be to clean 15 guestrooms per 8-hour shift.

Quality and quantity can be like two sides of a coin. On one side, if the quality expectations (performance standards) are set too high, the quantity of work that can be done accordingly may be unacceptably low. This forces the executive housekeeper to add more and more staff to ensure that all the work gets done.

the Rooms CHRONICLE®

Experiment with Piece Rate Proves Positive for Northern Michigan Resort

With more and more employers competing for a shrinking work force, it has become difficult for housekeeping managers to find and retain top-notch staff, much less motivate them to do their work efficiently. But are external factors to blame? Or can something be done from within to attract and keep good staff?

Crystal Mountain Resort is a family-owned resort located in the smallest of Michigan's 83 counties. The four-season resort employs anywhere from 250 to 480 people (a large percentage of which are housekeepers) year-round. Even as the largest employer in the area, though, Crystal Mountain is not immune to the same problems encountered by housekeeping managers nationwide: retaining good help.

When Sharlene Thomas, director of facilities services at Crystal Mountain, took a look at their lodging forecast for the upcoming summer, she knew she had to make a few changes. She faced a record summer of overnight guests attributable to the resort's addition of a second golf course and booming conference business. Thomas knew that she needed to somehow motivate her staff to work efficiently and compensate them well enough to retain them, even when they were turning a record number of rooms. And she also knew that Crystal Mountain's current system, where her staff was paid an hourly rate, was not as powerful a tool as it should be to entice and retain quality staff; nor did it set her apart from other area employers who were competing for the same work force.

Having heard of the success that a nearby Michigan resort, The Homestead, had in its implementation of "piece rate" compensation for its staff, Thomas called the resort to inquire further. The Homestead's executive housekeeper came to meet with Thomas, as well as Crystal Mountain's executive housekeeper and personnel services director. All loved the idea of paying by the room.

The idea behind piece rate is that room attendants are paid for work based on the quantity of units cleaned. In Crystal Mountain's particular case, where they have many different types and sizes of lodging units, each unit is assigned a different value and time standard, and housekeepers' wages are determined not only by the number of units cleaned, but by the type as well.

Crystal Mountain started experimenting with piece work in March of 1998 with the Resort's spring cleaning. Prior to that, room attendants were paid an average of $6.95 an hour using the hourly pay rate. With the piece rate method of compensation, housekeepers have earned an average rate as high as $9.95 an hour.

"It was scary at first," admitted Thomas. "It was a big change for many people and at first we had to have several meetings and pow-wows to sort out the little details." Thomas noted that the housekeepers were concerned especially about the time they spent not actually cleaning units, i.e., stocking storerooms, making deliveries, and hauling linen. "We had to assure them that these rates included these little extras."

Crystal Mountain also took this time to make a few changes within the department to eliminate as many non-cleaning activities for the housekeepers as possible.

the Rooms CHRONICLE®

(continued)

In explaining the new system to her staff, Thomas stressed that piece rate would be much more beneficial to them. "Our housekeepers are able to make more money than they did with the hourly rate, providing they work hard and efficiently," she pointed out. "Piece rate also allows us to be more flexible in our scheduling. Several housekeepers have dropped to four days a week because they can now make the same amount of money in four days that they used to make in five. Yet we still schedule based on occupancy and demand.

"The piece rate system has allowed two room attendants to earn between $15 to $16 an hour, which allowed them to cut down to just four days a week of work," Thomas added.

And the benefits to Crystal Mountain? "Our people are more productive," said Thomas. "Productivity has increased 30 percent. There is no way that we could have turned over the volume we saw this summer without piece rate."

Quality is also a key element of piece work at Crystal Mountain, as credit is not given for work performed until quality standards have been met. Thomas or another supervisor checks every guest departure and any rework is performed by the person(s) who cleaned the unit.

New hires start at $6 an hour. After a week of training, they begin to be paid according to piece work standards. And should a room attendant work overtime, their overtime wage is calculated at time-and-a-half of their average hourly wage for that week.

Piece rate has not completely solved the problem of finding good room attendants. Crystal Mountain was still understaffed most of the summer, and during extremely busy times they contracted out for extra help. However, Thomas is convinced that piece rate has allowed her to retain her high-quality employees by keeping them happier. "In time, once the word spreads, I'm sure we'll entice more staff.

"Our housekeepers have a huge responsibility," Thomas says. "We demand high quality; however, it was hard to expect this when we were paying only $6 an hour." According to Thomas, roughly 99 percent of the room attendants love the new method of compensation. "We're still playing with it," she says. "It will take about a year to make it win-win."

(Authors' Note: The pay rates presented in this article were the prevailing wage scale when the article was published.)

Source: *The Rooms Chronicle®*, Volume 7, Number 1, p. 13.
For subscription information, call 866-READ-TRC.

However, sooner or later (and probably sooner than expected), the general manager will cut the high labor expense of the housekeeping department. This action would force the executive housekeeper to reduce the staff size and to realign quality and quantity by redefining performance standards in light of more realistic productivity standards.

On the other side, if performance standards are set too low, the quantity of work that can be done accordingly will be unexpectedly high. At first, the general manager may be delighted. However, as complaints from guests and staff increase and the property begins to reflect dingy neglect, the general manager may, once again, step in with a solution. This time, the general manager may choose to replace the executive housekeeper with a person who will establish higher performance standards and monitor department expenses more closely.

The challenge is to effectively balance performance standards and productivity standards. Quality and quantity each can serve to check and balance the other. For example, at some properties, eliminating redundant tasks from checkout and stayover rooms and training room attendants to concentrate on areas that guests really notice has helped reduce cleaning times in stayover rooms by eight to nine minutes while maintaining positive guest perceptions.[2] A concern for productivity need not necessarily lower performance standards—it can sharpen and refine current work methods and procedures. If room attendants are constantly returning to the housekeeping area for cleaning and guestroom supplies, there is something wrong with the way they set up and stock their carts. Wasted motion is wasted time, and wasted time depletes the most important and most expensive resource of the housekeeping department: labor. The executive housekeeper must be constantly on the alert for new and more efficient work methods.

Remember, an executive housekeeper will rarely have all the resources necessary to do everything he or she may want to accomplish. Therefore, labor must be carefully allocated to achieve acceptable performance standards and realistic productivity standards.

Inventory Levels

After planning what must be done and how the tasks are to be performed, the executive housekeeper must ensure that employees have the necessary equipment and supplies to get their jobs done. The executive housekeeper plans appropriate inventory levels by answering the following question: "What amounts of equipment and supplies will be needed for the housekeeping staff to meet the performance and productivity standards of the department?" The answer to this question ensures smooth daily housekeeping activities and forms the basis for planning an effective purchasing system. A purchasing system must consistently maintain the needed amounts of items in housekeeping inventories.

Essentially, the executive housekeeper is responsible for two types of inventories. One type stores items which are recycled during the course of hotel operations; the other type stores non-recyclable items. Non-recyclable items are consumed or used up during routine activities of the housekeeping department. Due to limited storage facilities and management's desire not to tie up cash in overstocked inventories, the executive housekeeper must establish reasonable inventory levels for both recyclable and non-recyclable items.

Recycled Inventories. Recycled inventories include linens, most equipment items, and some guest supplies. Recycled equipment includes room attendant carts, vacuum cleaners, carpet shampooers, floor buffers, and many other items. Recycled guest supplies include such items as irons, ironing boards, cribs, and refrigerators, which guests may need during the course of their stay. Housekeeping is responsible for storing and maintaining these items as well as issuing them as they are requested by guests.

the Rooms CHRONICLE®

And the Standard Is Still 30 Minutes?

Recently the TRC staff visited with an executive housekeeper of a typical business hotel. Sitting in a guestroom, they glanced around at the amenities of the room. Amazing things have been incorporated into hotel rooms in the last decade. Consider the additional supply and labor costs of these items.

Comforters and duvets

Comforters and their covers, commonly known as duvets, are only part of the recent posh bed ingredients. Previously, hotel beds included only a mattress pad, two sheets, a blanket, and a bedspread. Consider the time necessary to change a posh bed versus a standard bed. Cah-ching.

Bed skirts

In recent years hotel owners have chosen the comforter/dust ruffle combination over the previously accepted bedspread. Sometimes called bed skirts, this move away from bedspreads adds difficulty and time to the bed-making process. Cah-ching.

Double pillows

Many hotels have increased guest comfort by providing twice the number of pillows. Double beds have four pillows, kings have six. This practice, well-appreciated by guests, doubles the time required to change the pillowcases while making the bed. Cah-ching.

Coffeemakers

Another guest convenience, coffeemakers, silently steals away precious room attendant minutes. Washing the pots, cleaning the baskets, wiping up the spills, restocking the accessories—adding a coffeemaker to the guestroom adds to the work load of the staff. Cah-ching.

China cups

Use of glass glasses was one upgrade requiring careful room attendant procedures. Adding china cups for the coffeemaker is another. Cups must be sanitized by washing in the kitchen's dishwashing machine and must be carefully carted to and from the guestrooms. Cah-ching.

Ironing boards and irons

Now that hotels have figured out how to hang ironing boards and irons in the guestroom closet; have identified cord-retracting, self-turn-off, self-cleaning irons; and have found a source for replacement ironing-board covers—now the guests are complaining that there is no place to plug in the iron. And managers are still working on ways of protecting the iron from theft. Cah-ching.

Mini kitchens

A set of four dishes, pots and pans, utensils, and refrigerators to clean, microwaves to wipe out, dishwashers to load and unload, more wastebaskets, more trash (read "yucky food trash"), more bug and rodent problems—and yes, guests are booking suite hotels and extended-stay facilities with more fervor every year. Cah-ching.

(continued)

the Rooms CHRONICLE®

(continued)

Pullout sofas

In previous times, guests who needed extra accommodations within their rooms requested a roll-away bed. Bingo, extra revenue for the hotel. Today, owners provide sofa beds in many rooms. Extra linen. Extra labor. No extra revenue. Cah-ching.

Bathrobes

When rates are high, amenities should be plentiful. And the addition of bathrobes is a wonderfully accepted guest treat. Managers just have to ensure the rate does actually withstand the cost of purchase, upkeep, handling, and replacement for the luxurious robes. Cah-ching.

Electronic equipment

Somewhere a few years ago when the fax machine was the hottest craze, many business hotels decided to place machines in guestrooms. Now, with technology advances, room attendants must not only dust the fax machines and provide supplies, they must also clean computer screens and keyboards/controls, organize electrical cords, and sanitize remote controls. Cah-ching.

Live plants

As hotel designers move the guestroom more to a residential look, live plants become a helpful corner filler. Sometimes rented and cared for by plant maintenance firms, most hotels have resorted to purchasing plants directly and assigning room attendant staff to care for them. Cah-ching.

Guest safes

Though guest safes do not require a lot of room attendant attention, staff training must still include the details of safe operation and staff must be vigilant about inspecting the safes in check-out rooms. Cah-ching.

Closet hangers

When hotels originally provided coat hangers for guest use, they were very basic, ball-top hangers. Now there are pant hangers, skirt hangers, and satin-padded hangers to straighten. And it's classy to use open-top hangers that are frequently taken home by guests. Cah-ching.

Summary

Isn't it interesting how the guestroom has evolved? Generally, items have been added to guestrooms to improve guest comfort. Or sometimes they were added to keep pace with the competition. In some cases, as with coffeemakers and irons, offering items free in the guestroom might actually have eliminated previously profitable services. Cah-ching.

How is the hotel compensated for the increased luxury of the guestroom? The remuneration for these amenities is received from increased room rates. Have room rates gone up over the last decade? Definitely, yes. But isn't it interesting that the accepted standard amount of time for cleaning a standard guestroom has remained at 30 minutes?

Source: *The Rooms Chronicle®*, Volume 10, Number 6, pp. 8–9.
For subscription information, call 866-READ-TRC.

The number of recycled items that must be on hand to ensure smooth operations is expressed as a **par number.** Par refers to the number of items that must be on hand to support daily, routine housekeeping operations. For example, one par of linens is the total number of items needed to outfit all the hotel guestrooms once; two par of linens is the total number of items needed to outfit all the hotel guestrooms twice; and so on.

Non-Recycled Inventories. Non-recycled inventories include cleaning supplies, guestroom supplies (such as bath soap), and guest amenities (which may range from toothbrushes and shampoos and conditioners to scented bath powders and colognes). Since non-recyclable items are used up in the course of operations, inventory levels are closely tied to the purchase ordering system used at the property. A purchase ordering system for non-recyclable inventory items establishes a par number that is based on two figures—a minimum quantity and a maximum quantity.

The **minimum quantity** is the fewest number of purchase units that should be in stock at any time. Purchase units are counted in terms of normal-size shipping containers, such as cases, drums, and so on. The inventory level should never fall below the minimum quantity. When the inventory level of a non-recyclable item reaches the minimum quantity, additional supplies must be ordered.

The actual number of additional supplies that must be ordered is determined by the **maximum quantity.** The maximum quantity is the greatest number of purchase units that should be in stock at any time. This maximum quantity must be consistent with available storage space and must not be so high that large amounts of the hotel's cash resources are tied up in an overstocked inventory. The shelf life of an item also affects the maximum quantity of purchase units that can be stored.

Organizing the Housekeeping Department

Organizing refers to the executive housekeeper's responsibility to structure the department's staff and to divide the work so that everyone gets a fair assignment and all the work can be finished on time.

Structuring the department's staff means establishing the lines of authority and the flow of communication within the department. Two important principles that should guide the organization of a department are:

- Each employee should have only one supervisor.
- Supervisors should have the authority and information necessary to guide the efforts of employees under their direction.

The executive housekeeper delegates authority to supervisors and must ensure that each employee recognizes the authority structure of the department. While the executive housekeeper may delegate authority, he or she cannot delegate responsibility. The executive housekeeper is ultimately responsible for the actions of department supervisors. Therefore, it is important that supervisors be well informed about hotel policies, procedures, and the limits of their authority.

Exhibit 5 Organization Chart for a Small Economy Hotel

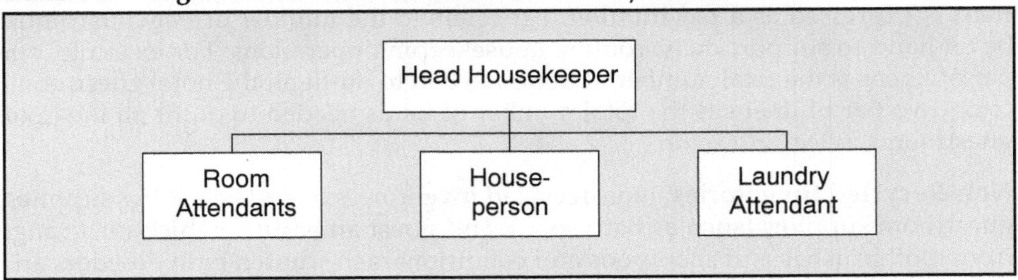

Exhibit 6 Organization Chart for a Large Mid-Market Hotel

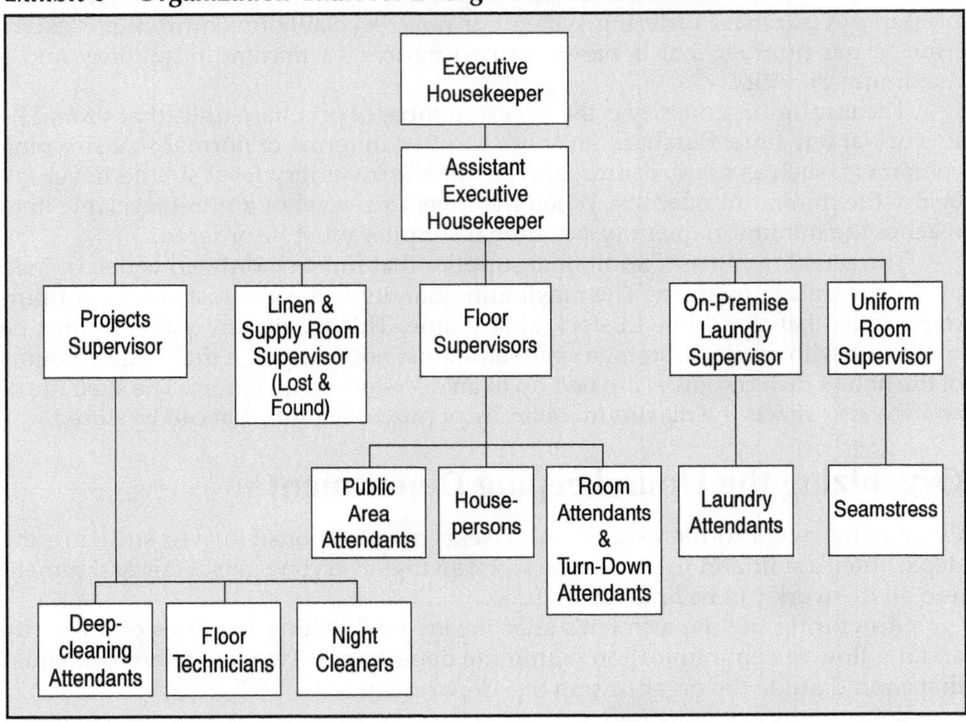

The Department Organization Chart

An **organization chart** provides a clear picture of the lines of authority and the channels of communication within the department. Exhibits 5 through 7 present sample organization charts for housekeeping departments of different sizes and service levels. At small economy properties, the title of the housekeeping department manager depends on the specific duties and responsibilities of the position. The position title is often "head housekeeper," or simply "housekeeper." When compared to the housekeeping departments of other types of hotels, the housekeeping staff of the economy property seems small. However, within the economy

Exhibit 7 Organization Chart for a Large Luxury Hotel

Director of Housekeeping
Asst. Director of Housekeeping
Secretary
Payroll Clerk
Administrative Asst.
Executive Housekeeper Rooms
Asst. Executive Housekeeper Rooms
Executive Housekeeper Public Space
Asst. Executive Housekeeper Public Space
Administrative Asst.
First Shift Asst. Housekeeper
Second Shift Asst. Housekeeper
Third Shift Asst. Housekeeper
Administrative Asst. Housekeeper
Projects Asst. Housekeeper
Uniforms-Banquet Linens Asst. Housekeeper
Building Supervisors
Houseman Supervisor
Second Shift Rooms Supervisor
Second Shift Public Space Supervisor
First Shift Area Supervisors
Third Shift Area Supervisor
Third Shift Area Supervisor
Administrative Supervisor
Projects Supervisor
Uniforms Banquet Linens Supervisor
Floor Super-visors
Trainers
Floor Super-visor
Public Space Asst. Supervisor
Lost and Found Asst. Supervisor
Inventory and Supply Asst. Supervisor
First Shift Asst. Supervisor
Second Shift Asst. Supervisor
Third Shift Asst. Supervisor
Head House-man
Asst. Head Houseman Trainer
First Shift Asst. Supervisors
First and Third Shift Trainers
Third Shift Asst. Supervisor
Third Shift Asst. Supervisor PAC Team
Projects Asst. Supervisor
House-keepers
House-keepers
Housemen
Lobby Attendants
A.M. PAC Team
Third Shift Lost and Found Clerks
Project Persons
Uniform Clerks
Seam-stresses
Valet Inventory Cleaner
Uniform Clerks
Restaurant Linen Clerks
Linen Distributor
Housemen
Project Housemen
Lobby Attendants
Office Cleaners
Night Cleaners
PAC Team
Rooms Control
Rooms Rags/Linen Rejects
First Shift Inventory Supply
Second Shift Inventory Supply
Third Shift Inventory Supply
Uniform Clerks
Seam-stresses
Valet Inventory Clerks

Positions shown in the bottom two rows are all on the same organizational level, as are those on the third and fourth rows from the bottom. They have been separated to meet space constraints.

Courtesy of Opryland Hotel, Nashville, Tennessee

property, the housekeeping staff may account for nearly half of the total number of employees at the hotel. Exhibit 6 suggests that properties offering mid-market service generally have large housekeeping staffs supervised by executive housekeepers. Exhibit 7 shows that very large properties offering world-class service may have a separate housekeeping division with several managers who are led by a director of housekeeping.

The organization chart of the department not only provides for a systematic direction of orders, but also protects employees from being overdirected. The chart shows that each employee takes direction only from the person who is directly above him or her in the department's organization. An organization chart also shows how grievances or other communications are channeled through the department.

A copy of the chart should be posted in an area so that all housekeeping employees can see where they fit into the overall organization of the department. Some housekeeping departments post organization charts that show employees at the top and the executive housekeeper at the bottom. Posting this type of chart emphasizes the importance of the work performed by the majority of employees; it conveys that employees are "at the top of the chart." Such a chart also illustrates how the entire department balances on the managerial talents of the executive housekeeper and other department managers.

Task Lists and Job Descriptions

If the executive housekeeper has planned the work of the housekeeping department properly, organizing the department staff becomes a relatively straightforward matter. Executive housekeepers use information gathered from earlier planning activities to identify the number and types of positions that are needed and to develop task lists and job descriptions for each of these positions.

A task list identifies the tasks that must be performed by an individual occupying a specific position within the department. The tasks on the list should reflect the total job responsibilities of the employee. However, the list should not be a detailed breakdown of the procedures that the employee will follow in carrying out each task. The task list should simply state what the employee must be able to do in order to perform the job.

Some types of **job descriptions** simply add information to the appropriate task lists. This information may include reporting relationships, additional responsibilities, and working conditions, as well as equipment and materials to be used in the course of the job. Exhibit 8 presents sample job descriptions for typical housekeeping positions found at medium-size mid-market properties.

To be most effective, job descriptions must be tailored to the specific operational needs of individual properties. Therefore, the form and content of job descriptions will vary among housekeeping departments. Exhibit 9 presents a sample job description for the position of executive housekeeper at a medium-size mid-market hotel.

The range of duties and responsibilities of executive housekeepers at various sizes and types of properties varies enormously. This is because many of the housekeeping management functions at small, independent economy hotels may

Exhibit 8 Sample Job Descriptions for Typical Housekeeping Positions

ROOM ATTENDANT

Basic Function

Performs routine duties in the cleaning and servicing of guestrooms and baths under supervision of a floor supervisor.

Duties and Responsibilities

1. Enters and prepares the room for cleaning.
2. Makes the bed.
3. Dusts the room and furniture.
4. Replenishes guestroom and bath supplies.
5. Cleans the bathroom.
6. Cleans the closet.
7. Vacuums the carpet.
8. Checks and secures the room.

Relationships

Reports directly to the floor supervisor.

HOUSEPERSON

Basic Function

Performs any combination of the following tasks to maintain guestrooms, working areas, and the hotel premises in general in a clean and orderly manner.

Duties and Responsibilities

1. Cleans rugs, carpets, and upholstered furniture using a vacuum cleaner, broom, and shampoo machine.
2. Cleans rooms, hallways, and restrooms.
3. Washes walls and ceilings, moves and arranges furniture, and turns mattresses.
4. Sweeps, mops, scrubs, waxes, and polishes floors.
5. Dusts and polishes metalwork.
6. Collects soiled linen for laundering.
7. Receives linen supplies.
8. Stores linen supplies in floor linen closets.
9. Maintains housekeeping carts.
10. Removes trash collected by room attendants.

Relationships

Reports to the head houseperson.

LOBBY ATTENDANT

Basic Function

Keeps all lobbies and public facilities (such as lobby restrooms, telephone areas, the front desk, and offices) in a neat and clean condition.

Duties and Responsibilities

1. Cleans and maintains all lobbies and public restrooms.
2. Sweeps carpets.
3. Empties ashtrays and urns.
4. Polishes furniture and fixtures.
5. Vacuums and polishes elevators.
6. Keeps the front of the hotel free from trash.

Relationships

Reports to the floor supervisor.

LINEN AND UNIFORM ATTENDANT

Basic Function

Stores and issues uniforms, bed linen, and table linen; also takes inventory and maintains linen room supplies.

Duties and Responsibilities

1. Sorts items and counts and records number of items soiled.
2. Places linen and uniforms in containers for transport to laundry.
3. Examines laundered items to ensure cleanliness and serviceability.
4. Sends torn articles to the seamstress for repair.
5. Stores laundered linen and uniforms on shelves after verifying numbers and types of articles.
6. Issues linen and uniforms, which are both to be exchanged on a clean-for-soiled basis only.
7. Counts and records linen to fill requisitions.

Relationships

Reports to the linen room supervisor.

be carried out by the general manager. In the case of chain-affiliated properties, many housekeeping management functions are performed by staff at corporate headquarters. This leaves the task of implementing standardized procedures to the general managers and head housekeepers at individual properties.

Since job descriptions may become outdated as work assignments change, they should be reviewed at least once a year for possible revision. Properly written job descriptions can ease employee anxiety by specifying responsibilities,

Exhibit 9 Sample Job Description for the Executive Housekeeper at a Medium-Size Mid-Market Hotel

Executive Housekeeper

Job Description: The Executive Housekeeper is responsible for ensuring efficient operations of the Housekeeping Department, as well as supervising the entire Housekeeping Department including rooms, front/back of house, public areas, and laundry.

JOB DUTIES

- Establish and maintain a key control system for the department.
- Monitor and direct all Housekeeping and Laundry personnel.
- Inspect rooms daily
- Review Housekeeping staff's worked hours for payroll compilation.
- Prepare employee schedule according to the business forecast, payroll budget guidelines and productivity requirements.
- Maintain required pars of all Housekeeping and Laundry supplies by ordering all needed supplies and amenities on a monthly/quarterly basis.
- Conduct monthly and quarterly Housekeeping inventories on a timely basis.
- Ensure guest privacy and security
- Motivate, coach, counsel and discipline all Housekeeping personnel.
- Maintain a professional working relationship and promote open lines of communication with other managers, employees and all other departments.
- Coordinates availability of rooms with Front Office Manager
- Monitors the responses on customer comment cards, identifies problem areas and formulates solutions.
- Conducts continual inspections to determine hotel's overall level of cleanliness; performs follow-up.
- Strives to reduce accidents within the department
- Schedules and supervises all rotational and special cleaning programs as required
- Monitors quality of rooms by conducting and documenting inspections of cleaned room
- Prepares maintenance work orders in regard to replacement or repair of furniture, fixtures, etc
- Insures completion by following through on orders, ensures compliance with accident/loss prevention programs, and health/sanitation standards.

Job Requirements:

- At least 1 year of progressive experience in a hotel or a related field.
- Supervisory experience required.
- Long hours sometimes required.
- Must be able to convey information and ideas clearly.
- Must maintain composure and objectivity under pressure.
- Must be effective in handling problems in the workplace, including anticipating, preventing, identifying and solving problems as necessary.
- Must be effective at listening to, understanding, clarifying and resolving the concerns and issues raised by coworkers and guests.
- Must be able to work with and understand financial information and data, and basic arithmetic functions.
- Adhere to all Hotel policies and practices.
- Report to work punctually and regularly.
- Work safely and successfully, including meeting productivity standards.
- Adhere to established grooming standards.
- Practice the Open Door Policy.
- Provide a picture perfect environment that encourages high standards and enthusiasm.
- Greet all Team Members and thank them for a job well done.

Management Position: Yes

Exhibit 10 Overview of the Management Process

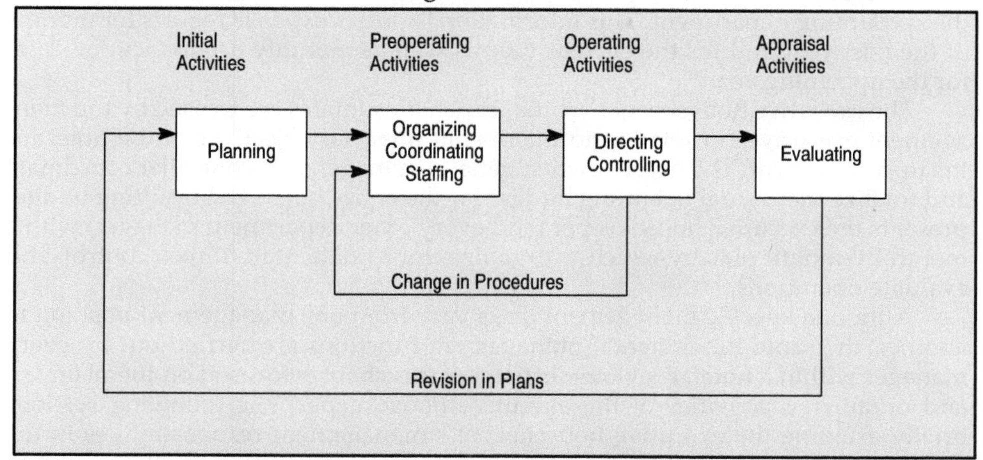

Source: Jack D. Ninemeier, *Planning and Control for Food and Beverage Operations*, 6th ed. (Lansing, Mich.: American Hotel & Lodging Educational Institute, 2004), p. 16.

requirements, and peculiarities of their jobs. Employees should be involved in writing and revising job descriptions for their positions.

Each employee of the housekeeping department should be given a copy of the job description for his or her position. A job description may also be given to all final job candidates before an employment offer is made. This is preferable to having someone accept the job and then decide the job is unsuitable because he or she was unaware of all of its requirements.

Other Management Functions of the Executive Housekeeper

Exhibit 10 presents an overview of the management process and shows how each management function contributes to the overall success of a hotel or, for that matter, any sort of business. Top executives must plan what the hotel is to accomplish by defining its objectives. The desire to attain these objectives leads to organizing, coordinating, and staffing activities. Once members of the hotel staff are selected, management can direct the course of their work and implement control systems to protect the hotel's assets and to ensure smooth, efficient operating activities. Finally, management must evaluate the extent to which the objectives of the organization have been attained. An analysis of actual operating results may lead to changes in organizing, coordinating, or staffing procedures. Also, as a result of evaluating all planning and operating activities, management may find that revisions to the organization's plans or objectives are needed.

An important planning activity of the executive housekeeper is drafting the housekeeping department's operating budget. The housekeeping operating budget estimates expenses of the department for the upcoming year. Expenses include labor, linens, laundry operation, cleaning compounds, some types of equipment, and other supplies. Initial expense estimates are based on information supplied by the accounting department. This information includes expense reports for months of the past year and for the current year as well as monthly occupancy forecasts for the upcoming year.

The executive housekeeper's initial expense estimates are revised by top management executives in relation to the overall financial objectives of the hotel for the upcoming year. The hotel's owner, general manager, and controller coordinate and finalize the annual operating budget for the entire hotel. The resulting budget presents the executive housekeeper (and every other department manager) with a month-by-month plan by which to organize, coordinate, staff, direct, control, and evaluate operations.

Although specific management tasks vary from one management position to another, the same fundamental management functions are carried out by every manager within a hotel. Previous sections of this chapter focused on the planning and organizing activities of the executive housekeeper. The following sections briefly examine the executive housekeeper's management responsibilities in the areas of coordinating, staffing, directing, controlling, and evaluating the operation of the housekeeping department.

Coordinating and Staffing

Coordinating is the management function of implementing the results of planning and organizing at the level of daily housekeeping activities. Each day, the executive housekeeper must coordinate schedules and work assignments and ensure that the proper equipment, cleaning supplies, linens, and other supplies are on hand for employees to carry out their assignments.

Staffing involves recruiting applicants, selecting those best qualified to fill open positions, and scheduling employees to work. Since labor is housekeeping's largest expense item, properly scheduling employees is one of the most important management responsibilities of the executive housekeeper.

Most housekeeping departments use some type of staffing guidelines. These guidelines are usually based on formulas that are used to calculate the number of employees required to meet operational needs at specific occupancy levels. The use of labor forecasting software has gained favor among lodging managers, with some evidence that it can help reduce the time that department managers spend scheduling employees.[3] However, the management function of staffing goes beyond simply applying a formula. Staffing must be adequate to meet the deep cleaning schedules for various areas of the hotel and to meet the needs of other special cleaning projects. Therefore, the executive housekeeper must be flexible and creative, establishing staffing patterns that permit the department to reach its goals within the limits of the budget plan.

Team Cleaning. Many years ago, team cleaning guestrooms was a hot new procedure in the hotel industry. But for many reasons, including lack of accountability of individual room attendants, enthusiasm for the procedure cooled, and it did not become standard practice. But now, it seems team cleaning guestrooms could be the solution to some of today's housekeeping challenges. With increasing concern for safety and security, assigning two people to clean a room could save many dollars in liabilities and lawsuits. Additionally, team cleaning might be a way to put some fun into a relatively mundane task.

Here's how it is being done. Teams of two people are usually assigned 30 to 35 rooms. Individuals rotate duties of bedroom and bathroom cleaning. Room attendants pick their own partners, and new employees become alternates until a new team is formed.

One hotel uses teams of three people and incorporates responsibility for the honor bar. The first person strips the soiled linens and restocks the in-room bar. Before going on to the next room, he or she helps the second person make the beds. The second person then finishes the bedroom while the third person cleans the bathroom. This technique is very fast-paced with approximately eight minutes being spent in each room.

Hotels that presently use team cleaning suggest that you let the idea come from the employees and that you give them ownership in the implementation process. Start with only one team and gradually, as systems are ironed out, add more teams. Keep a list of alternates in case team members are sick. Also, monitor the teams to ensure that partners work at the same speed. Advantages of team cleaning include the following:

- Fewer tools are needed; for example, one vacuum, one cart, and one caddy of cleaning supplies equip one team.
- Morale is higher. On days when someone doesn't feel 100 percent, having a teammate eases the stress.
- Attendance improves, as room attendants are less likely to let their partners down by calling in sick.
- Some special cleaning tasks are accomplished more easily with two people (for example, moving beds or pulling out credenzas).
- Very importantly, safety is improved with two people in the room.
- Getting new employees up to speed seems to be easier with teams because they have buddies to coach them along.
- Room attendants seem to like having more rooms in their "sections." A variety of room types breaks the monotony.

Careful planning is the key to success. Some of the considerations that executive housekeepers need to address include:

- Have linen and chemical inventories equally distributed so that teams are not fighting for supplies.
- If something stops a team, two or three people are stopped, as opposed to only one in traditional guestroom cleaning. Having supplies available is critical, as is giving teams an accurate list of room assignments.
- Some hotels save on labor costs due to team cleaners completing rooms faster than individuals. However, primary savings result from better attendance, less equipment, fewer accidents, and more employee interest in improving the process.

- Scheduling may require special effort to accommodate getting teams the same days off.

At a riverfront hotel, the executive housekeeper was able to give each team a separate locked cage with supplies, a cart, and a vacuum cleaner so that other employees would not disturb their things.

Another manager, at a northeastern inn, found that potential workers who were very nervous about their new jobs were comforted by working together. They were able to talk to each other and help each other become efficient. This manager has instituted team cleaning in other hotels. Incidentally, believing four eyes are better than two, he operates his hotels without supervisors, relying on the team members to check their own work. He credits team cleaning as contributing to longevity of service and high morale of housekeeping employees at his hotels.

One property has used team cleaning for more than 25 years and finds it contributes to low turnover of the housekeeping staff, better morale, and better speed. With two room attendants to a room, attendants are not working alone and feel safer. The room attendants also watch less TV in a room when there is someone to talk with. They vary the tasks—one dusts and vacuums while the other does the bathroom—and in the next room they switch. Four eyes are better than two for seeing items left behind or something not right in a room. An experienced worker may be paired with a new worker for training. Most of the room attendants change teams each day. The manager says the housekeeping staff is a happy group of workers, and many have been with the property for ten years or more.

Team cleaning works in hotels that are willing to make a change. Their key to success is involving the employees in the planning and giving room attendants the flexibility to get the work done.[4]

Directing and Controlling

Many people confuse the two very different management functions of directing and controlling. The easiest way to distinguish them is to remember that managers direct people and control things.

Directing is focusing employee activity on the goals established in the planning phase, using the strategies and organization established in the organizing, coordinating, and staffing phase. For an executive housekeeper, directing involves supervising, motivating, training, and disciplining employees. Motivating the housekeeping staff is a particularly important skill and is closely connected with the executive housekeeper's ability to lead the department. Motivation (or the lack of it) is contagious. Attitudes and work habits filter down to employees from their supervisors. The attitudes and work habits of supervisors are usually a reflection of the leadership provided by the executive housekeeper. A strong executive housekeeper personally expresses a genuine interest in everyone's performance and, thereby, creates an atmosphere in which motivation can thrive. On the other hand, an executive housekeeper who plays favorites with supervisors will find discontent everywhere as supervisors, in turn, play favorites with employees under their direction.

Controlling refers to the executive housekeeper's responsibility to devise and implement procedures that protect the hotel's assets. Assets are anything the hotel owns that has commercial or exchange value. An executive housekeeper helps safeguard the hotel's assets by implementing control procedures for keys, linens, supplies, equipment, and other items.

Evaluating

Evaluating is the management function of assessing the extent to which planned goals are, in fact, attained. Monthly budget reports prepared by the hotel's accounting staff are important evaluation tools for all managers in a hotel. These reports provide timely information for evaluating housekeeping operations, especially the department's monthly labor expense. The executive housekeeper uses these reports to compare actual departmental expenses to amounts estimated in the budget. Significant differences between actual amounts and budgeted amounts are called variances. Significant variances may require further analysis and action by the executive housekeeper.

In addition, the executive housekeeper needs information on a daily and weekly basis in order to closely evaluate the performance of the staff and the overall productivity of the department. Evaluation in these areas begins with performance and productivity standards developed by earlier plans. Daily inspection reports and quarterly performance evaluations are used to monitor how well the actual performance of employees compares with performance and productivity standards.

Supervisor Dilemma

The state of the economy has prompted a trend to eliminate middle managers. In the lodging industry, this trend has brought the position of housekeeping supervisor into question. General managers seem to be searching for more profit and, perhaps, a way to empower hourly employees. Is it possible to operate a clean and profitable hotel without housekeeping supervisors to inspect rooms?

Although the housekeeping supervisor position may have begun as a management extension of the executive housekeeper for larger properties, in the past twenty years, the job has centered on inspecting rooms. Is it, then, an essential role? Does the hotel get its money's worth from this position?

Key issues hotels must consider are:

- Did the hotel hire the right people to be supervisors?
- Do the hotel's systems support the responsibilities of the supervisor?
- Is the hotel's mission enhanced as a direct result of the position?
- How would the idea be introduced and then implemented?

the Rooms CHRONICLE®

Team Cleaning Gets High Scores at Maine Hotel

To design a more efficient method of thoroughly cleaning guestrooms and to develop a new procedure for training new room attendants, all old standards and traditional taboos for the housekeeping department were set aside. For instance, the staff decided to:

- Focus on the room being cleaned to standards, not on the amount of time required
- Require room attendants to inspect their own rooms
- Eliminate section assignments based on seniority
- Assign two room attendants to work as a team

Implementation of these decisions was difficult. In fact, the new standards were perceived as radical. But the staff persevered. Two room attendants were chosen (not the best cleaners, but the best leaders) to try team cleaning. For one week they received double pay while they cleaned rooms together to smooth out the details of the procedures. They then were paired with other room attendants until all had been trained. Some employees were not able to adapt to team cleaning and found it better to resign.

With 117 rooms on two floors, six team setups were created, including three complete cart/vacuum sets on each floor. Sets were numbered one through six and contained most of the materials necessary to clean a room. Room attendants were instructed to stay within their stations, calling upon a runner to keep the cart supplied and remove soiled linen. Requests for more hangers or bedspreads or telephone books were to be called to the voice mail of the runner.

It has been three years since this system was put into place at the Ramada Conference Center in Lewiston, Missouri. The average room time, including lunch breaks and cart stocking time for room attendants and one floor runner, is approximately sixteen minutes.

Each morning the head housekeeper prepares room assignments using a base of twenty rooms or less per team. When room attendants arrive, they draw chits like in a lottery to determine their teammate and cart for the day (i.e., 1-A, 1-B, 2-A, etc.). The duties for cleaning a room are written step-by-step as "A" tasks and "B" tasks, with making the bed(s) as the only joint assignment. The task list includes follow-up inspections of their rooms, noting maintenance items, and moving an air-cleaning machine from room to room.

Not only has the quality and consistency of room cleaning improved, the staff has also been able to eliminate half of the necessary equipment, such as carts and vacuums. In addition, training of new room attendants has been cut to two days, throughout which they are totally productive. During the last Ramada quality inspection report, the housekeeping department lost only one point from a perfect score. Not only does management like the team system, but by now even the room attendants are believers.

Source: Gary Adams, *The Rooms Chronicle®*, Volume 7, Number 3, p. 4.
For subscription information, call 866-READ-TRC.

- Would the number of room inspections be reduced or would they be totally eliminated?
- Who would do room inspections if any are required?
- Who would conduct training?
- What changes would be made to job descriptions?
- How would quality standards be maintained or improved?
- What system would be used to ensure accurate room status updates?

The Rooms Chronicle® surveyed some of its readers on the topic of housekeeping supervisors. Some managers eliminated supervisors, only to be disappointed by a gradual decline in the condition of guestrooms. Others, after making the change, saw guest comments and employee morale improve.

One of the surveyed hotels reinstated inspections in 100 percent of the rooms after six months, another did so after one year. While some have been successful at keeping 50 to 75 percent of their room attendants working independently, others operate entirely without supervisors.

How Is the Program Initiated? Most hotels based their decisions to eliminate supervisors on a desire to save payroll, although many were motivated by the total quality management philosophy of empowerment. One hotel eliminated supervisors because it wanted to speed up reporting of clean rooms to the front desk.

The hotels that successfully eliminated housekeeping supervisors gave advance, careful thought to all ramifications and involved the employees in planning. Some approached room attendants with the question, How does it make you feel to have someone check everything you do? When some frustration was expressed, they began to explore alternative ways to operate, incorporating room attendants' ideas for working independently.

Are Any Rooms Inspected? One property surveyed operates without any room inspections. Management credits the work ethic of their room attendants for the attendants' ability to take full responsibility for the condition of their areas. Most hotels, however, inspect from one to five rooms per room attendant per week. As a rooms executive of a luxury hotel in the Midwest expresses it, "We conduct random verifications of our housekeepers' work. It should be like testing a pool for the level of chlorine—only a small sample is needed to know the condition of the entire pool."

Who Inspects If There Are No Supervisors? Most properties use housekeeping management to conduct random inspections, depending on the size of the hotel. Larger hotels retain one or more supervisors for this purpose. The general manager of a resort hotel in Florida involves the entire hotel staff. The general manager, sales department, bell staff, front desk agents (A.M. and P.M. shifts), guest service agent, housekeeping secretary—each inspects two rooms a day.

"I'm fortunate that in my present position we use supervisors," says an executive housekeeper of another resort, "but based on my experience at other hotels, there are many ways this concept can fail. If the room attendant base is not stable (for example, due to high turnover, or if many temporary employees are used), room quality can suffer." She added, "If unqualified room attendants are forced to work independently, an executive housekeeper may spend long hours trying to inspect all the rooms, and manager burnout or failure of the department in other areas may occur."

"The use of supervisors does not have to be an all-or-nothing decision," says a general manager of a midwestern resort. "We use supervisors only in the summer to work with our seasonal employees. During the rest of the year, our room attendants work independently. We've used this system for over a year and our comment card scores are still high, at 94 percent."

Are Job Descriptions Changed? The room attendant job description is usually changed to include final responsibility for cleanliness, readiness, and status updates for each room. The room attendant must check equipment in the room to ensure that a guest will not find something in disrepair. Some hotels add responsibility for the hallway area around the guestroom and specify who will do the running if a bedspread or some other supply item needs to be replaced. The houseperson or porter job description usually is changed to complement the new structure.

The executive housekeeper at a southern hotel instituted an "excellence team" on which room attendants earn a position through performance, attendance, and attitude. The job description includes all of the above, and team members sign a contract for performance.

How Do Pay Rates Change? Pay rates of room attendants are sometimes changed, with the majority of properties either setting rates according to quality of work or paying bonuses for exceeding quality standards. One hotel pays a $35 bonus biweekly if inspection scores are 90 percent or higher and if at least 1.9 rooms are cleaned per hour.

The general manager of one suites hotel has a program in which room attendants earn the right to work without supervisors by achieving high scores on quality, attendance, and uniform care and are then paid 25 cents more per hour. The "excellence team" members at the property mentioned earlier earn one dollar more per hour if they maintain the standards of their increased responsibility. At other hotels, in instances where the entire staff is structured to work independently, pay rates are not increased.

Who Does the Training? Since most hotels use supervisors to train new hires, who does the training if those jobs are eliminated? Housekeeping managers could be used, but in these days of high turnover, the training function is often a full-time job. One option is to designate one or more room attendants as on-the-job trainers. In other hotels, at least one supervisor is retained who concentrates on training and retraining. Because room attendants assume final responsibility for the condition of the room, an excellent training program is essential.

"If I hire the right people and conduct ongoing training, my staff will be able to meet our standards," says a rooms executive. "We rely on support and positive reinforcement to keep our housekeepers excited."

In all the surveyed hotels, if the quality of a room attendant's work declines, he or she goes through a retraining program in order to attain the improvements needed, and if standards are not met, routine disciplinary procedures are used.

What about Room Status? The morning check of vacant rooms is usually incorporated into the room attendant's job description by assigning him or her an area of responsibility rather than a list of dirty rooms. All rooms, hallways, vending areas, and elevator lobbies within this area are assigned. The room attendant will be the last person to see the rooms or area before the guest arrives or returns, so special care must be taken to ensure that the front desk always has the correct room status, whether occupied or vacant, clean or dirty.

Many property management systems are interfaced so a code can be entered on the guestroom phone to update the status. In other hotels, the room attendant must call either housekeeping or the front desk to change room status. When the front desk questions the status, someone is sent to double-check the room.

Without supervisors, expect to spend more time checking discrepancies. Room attendants might clean a room, thinking it is a stayover, but while they are in another room, the first room's guest could check out. If the hotel has not adequately planned for this aspect, payroll saved on supervisors could easily be lost by poor room inventory management.

Tips for Success. A well-thought-out plan will provide for the cleanliness, maintenance, and status reporting of every room. Since supervisors usually help prepare VIP rooms, do touch-ups on late check-outs, help with hurry-ups, assist with inventories, translate for room attendants who don't speak English, and clean rooms when there is a shortage of room attendants, all of these things must be accounted for in a successful plan.

Involve room attendants in the design of the program to help them have ownership. The plan must be a win-win situation, because employees are sensitive to management's efforts to save payroll at their expense. The program should be fine-tuned before implementation, because changes to pay rates or incentive plans after the fact serve as disincentives.

If the concept is planned to suit the property's needs and implemented carefully, the employees and the hotel will prosper.

How Can the Department Improve? IYADWYADYAGWYAG: "If you always do what you always did, you'll always get what you always got." If you have supervisors, but you are not satisfied with the results, step back to analyze what you've always done. If you have supervisors but are thinking of eliminating the positions, clarify the end results you want and think creatively about how to get where you want to be.

the Rooms CHRONICLE®

Hotel Wisdom: A Baker's Dozen Strategies for Directors of Housekeeping

1. **Learn to look at your hotel from an operational perspective as if you owned it.** The most successful housekeepers are those who take ownership of their property. Directors of housekeeping are critical to making the first impressions positive, whether it is in public space, the guestroom, or bathroom. Housekeeping has responsibility for corridors, pool and patio areas, management offices, storage and linen areas, the laundry, and many related areas. Strong and successful housekeepers plan the work of the department effectively, using inventory control, setting standards, and maintaining schedules.

2. **Honor the idea that the hotel guest is your guest, as if in your own home.** It is the sense of pride and hosting that makes a huge difference in whether someone has a *job* or a *career*. To do this:

   - Maintain your awareness over the entire property, even if it is outside of your particular direct area of responsibility. This includes parking areas, public areas, access points to the hotel, and the all-important curb appeal.
   - Work with the other property managers (as opposed to "hiding" in the office) because it takes the entire team to create a great experience for guests.
   - Effective directors of housekeeping show their pride by offering to assist senior management in other areas of discussion, even in sales, as appropriate. Remember, "everyone sells" should be a hotel's mantra for success; and housekeepers regularly come in contact with vendors and others who need hotel services.

3. **Know about the condition of the property from firsthand experience.** Personally and regularly inspect every type of accommodation in your hotel. Being aware of changes in the hotel can also help management to be better aware of potential problems. One executive housekeeper said she "always imagined that somewhere in the hotel there was a dirty washcloth hanging on the back of a bathroom door, on a wall hook or over a shower curtain rod." And she didn't want someone else to find it first.

4. **When recruiting people, pay attention to the "human" resource role. Balance "high touch" and "high tech."** Recruit and select people wisely. Encourage your general manager to pay competitively or better, and lead in incentives. As director of housekeeping, recognize your team regularly with "thank you's" and expressions of appreciation. Retain the champions by whatever it takes to keep them. Give them the training to succeed and then share in their successes with incentives and the chance to be part of a very cohesive and proud team. The greatest reward is recognition by others for a job well done.

the Rooms CHRONICLE©

(continued)

5. **Maintain and increase training.** This element is crucial in housekeeping. The development of the staff to the point where guestroom attendants can be completely trusted to finish their jobs with "pizzazz" because they take pride/ownership in their rooms should be a goal for everyone. Allow guestroom attendants who pass and maintain cleaning inspections at the highest levels the privilege of self-inspection. A few other thoughts:
   - There is no excuse today for inadequately prepared or untrained housekeeping and laundry staff. There is enormous training support available at very low cost online from the major brands and a wealth of support from CDs, books, newsletters, and the Internet. When running high-occupancy, many mangers claim to be too busy to train. When occupancy is flat or declining, cutting ongoing training to save money will really cost more, as it will drive the best employees to consider leaving and the loyal customers to the competition because it appears you don't care. Remember, "the only thing worse than an untrained staff that leaves is an untrained staff that stays to service your customers."
   - Today's successful and confident director of housekeeping will also embrace technology in training. Use of computers, training DVDs, and even language-free videos should be the norm.
   - If appropriate to your market, recognize and address the language challenge that some housekeeping personnel face. This may include getting the hotel to pay for your learning of a new language to improve your effectiveness, offering an English as a Second Language course for employees, and/or investing in alternative language training materials.
6. **Clearly share with all staff members the expectations and goals provided by ownership and/or management.** Newcomers to the industry sometimes imagine huge profits when they compare their hourly wage with the room rates paid by guests. Those who have been in the industry for more than just a few years quickly realize that profits and losses go in cycles. The expenses of operating a successful hotel can be enormous. Therefore, it is important to share the realities of the cost of doing business with staff at all levels. All employees should understand the total costs of ownership, including payroll benefits, franchise or royalty fees, management company fees, the concepts of debt service, and more. Make those expectations understood, explain the value and rationale to all staff, and be certain these expectations can be measured fairly.
7. **Hold regular one-on-one sessions with all direct reports in housekeeping and laundry.** These sessions should not be formal reviews, but guideposts to reinforce positive actions or to correct a potentially dangerous course of action. When I first started doing these more than 20 years ago, the first time was awkward because people were gun-shy or afraid of hidden agendas. When it became apparent that these were honest dialogues, the sessions evolved into opportunities to address potential problems and to form plans for improved performance in a non-threatening manner.

(continued)

the Rooms CHRONICLE®

(continued)

8. **Constantly assess time management.** The 80-20 rule of priorities and value remains true much of the time. Eighty percent of our problems often come from the same 20 percent of guestrooms or staff members. To fix the 20 percent is the problem. Research why things go smoothly with the remaining 80 percent, and then replicate that success. The question needs to be not, "Are we doing things right," but, "Are we doing the right things correctly?"
9. **Work with front office management to capitalize on forecasts for long-term efficiencies.** Operating budgets are usually approved by hotel ownership or its management company in a remote location. And typically, the housekeeping budget is tied to forecasted occupancy. Working with the front office allows an effective director of housekeeping to plan for deep-cleaning during slower periods and to replace capital items on a pre-planned schedule that does not interfere with periods of high activity.
10. **Master the art of inventory controls.** There are many inventories to attend to, including but not limited to:
    - Linens
    - F&B materials
    - Pillows and furniture
    - Uniforms
    - Cleaning equipment
    - Cleaning supplies
    - Guest amenity supplies
    - Guest loan items

Properly addressing the ordering, receipt, use, storage, and security of these (and other) items is a financial necessity.

11. **Study, embrace, and insist on proper safety and security.** Room and laundry attendants regularly deal with an array of chemicals. While most chemicals may initially be in the proper containers and concentrations, maintain care to continue to use them accurately and safely. Give training and provide follow-up checklists for linen rooms, on-premise laundry, housekeeping carts, and using equipment. Post and follow government regulations, such as OSHA and state/provincial guidelines. Specific security practices should be considered, reviewed, discussed, and constantly monitored. Housekeeping staff may be working in isolated areas and should be trained in the best ways to provide cleaning services safely.
12. **Embrace the brand standards and suppliers.** A majority of hotels in the U.S. today are part of a brand, and the trend is growing globally. The director of housekeeping should learn what the brand's requirements and expectations are as they pertain to housekeeping services and programs. Convey to your staff the brand's expectations and maintain its standards for all housekeeping services. After all, aside from the human capital aspect, the greatest asset any

the Rooms CHRONICLE® *(continued)*

branded hotel has is its brand name recognition by guests and their expectations that accompany it. With regards to suppliers, do you take the time to work with your general manager or purchasing manager to understand the brand's supply programs? If there is a better local price or distribution, have you made certain those products effectively do the job? For hotels that are affiliated with a brand, your local hotel association will likely know of qualified vendors, programs, or products to assist you in maintaining high standard levels.

13. **Know your budgets, costs, and results.** The housekeeping department usually employs the largest number of people in a hotel. The outstanding housekeeping managers are those who are often able to obtain higher compensation for their staff by effectively reducing turnover and managing their total budgets while exceeding guest expectations. Budgets need not be a mystery, and most caring general managers should be pleased to share information pertaining to operating budgets with applicable personnel because it helps everyone understand the bigger picture.

Source: John Hogan, Ph.D., CHA, MHS, CHE, *The Rooms Chronicle®*, Volume 14, Number 5, pp. 4–5. For subscription information, call 866-READ-TRC.

How can you improve hiring processes for both supervisors and room attendants so that their qualifications will strengthen the team? Single out the winning characteristics of your best employees and hire people who have the same traits.

How can you enhance room attendant training so that quality is not dependent on inspections? Manufacturing businesses usually cannot make a profit while performing quality inspections on 100 percent of their product. Systems are established to produce the product correctly the *first* time so that it is not necessary to spend hours and money checking, reworking, or scrapping product. Inspections are used only as random checks to ensure that systems are working properly. Should hotels operate any differently?

How can you revise the hotel's systems so that the entire team of supervisors and room attendants feels enthusiastic and responsible for promoting the hotel's mission of pleasing the guest? Find ways to allow the supervisor to be proactive as a teacher and communicator rather than negative as a police officer. Can a room attendant's pride be increased by having direct responsibility to the guest?

If there is room for improvement, it may be time to rethink the entire department and restructure job responsibilities appropriately. Short-term profit improvements gained by position eliminations may be insignificant compared to the results of creatively working toward the long-term goals of the hotel.[5]

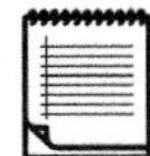

Endnotes

1. Michael C. Sturman, "A New Method for Measuring Housekeeping Performance Consistency," *The Center for Hospitality Research Reports*, Cornell University, September 2006, pp. 6–13.

2. Rob Heyman, "Shaping up Hotel Housekeeping Programs, *Lodging Management*, October, 2006, www.lodgingmagazine.com.

3. Adam Kirby, "Spare the Spreadsheets," *Hotels Magazine*, May 2007. www.hotelsmag.com/article/CA6485309.html.

4 The section on team cleaning was adapted from Mary Friedman, *The Rooms Chronicle®*, Volume 2, Number 6, p. 4; and Marilyn Faulkner, *The Rooms Chronicle®*, Volume 2, Number 4, p. 13. For subscription information, call 866-READ-TRC.

5. The section on supervisors was adapted from *The Rooms Chronicle®*, Volume 2, Number 3, p. 5; and Mary Friedman, *The Rooms Chronicle®*, Volume 2, Number 5, pp. 4–5. For subscription information, call 866-READ-TRC.

Key Terms

area inventory list—A list of all items within a particular area that need cleaning by or the attention of housekeeping personnel.

deep cleaning—Intensive or specialized cleaning undertaken in guestrooms or public areas. Often conducted according to a special schedule or on a special-project basis.

frequency schedule—A schedule that indicates how often each item on an area inventory list needs to be cleaned or maintained.

job description—A detailed list identifying all the key duties of a job as well as reporting relationships, additional responsibilities, working conditions, and any necessary equipment and materials.

maximum quantity—The greatest number of purchase units that should be in stock at any given time.

minimum quantity—The fewest number of purchase units that should be in stock at any given time.

non-recycled inventories—Those items in stock that are consumed or used up during the course of routine housekeeping operations. Non-recycled inventories include cleaning supplies, small equipment items, guest supplies, and amenities.

organization chart—A schematic representation of the relationships between positions within an organization, showing where each position fits into the overall organization and illustrating the divisions of responsibility and lines of authority.

par number—A multiple of the standard quantity of a particular inventory item that represents the quantity of the item that must be on hand to support daily, routine housekeeping operations.

performance standard—A required level of performance that establishes the quality of work that must be done.

productivity standard—An acceptable amount of work that must be done within a specific time frame according to an established performance standard.

recycled inventories—Those items in stock that have relatively limited useful lives but are used over and over in housekeeping operations. Recycled inventories include linens, uniforms, major machines and equipment, and guest loan items.

Review Questions

1. What resources can the executive housekeeper use to attain the objectives set by top executives in a hospitality operation?
2. What areas are most housekeeping departments responsible for cleaning in a hotel?
3. What additional areas may housekeeping be responsible for cleaning, depending on the property's service level?
4. Why is it important for an executive housekeeper to take a systematic, step-by-step approach to planning?
5. What is the purpose of an area inventory list? What is an ideal way to sequence such a list?
6. What is a frequency schedule? How is it used in conjunction with a property's deep cleaning program?
7. What is the difference between a performance standard and a productivity standard?
8. What is the most important aspect of developing performance standards? How are standards best communicated once they are developed?
9. What two important principles should guide the organization of the housekeeping department?
10. What are the fundamental management functions that should be carried out by every hotel manager?

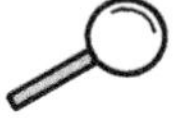

Case Study

Under Pressure

Philip knocked tentatively on his general manager's office door. "You wanted to see me, Mrs. Smith?"

"Yes, Philip, please sit down." The general manager shifted some papers on her desk and handed Philip Stone, the executive housekeeper, a copy of the labor-cost budget. "Take a look at last month's report. Notice which direction the labor costs are going."

Philip quickly scanned the report he had previously studied in detail. "They're rising by about two percent, almost the same as the previous months of this quarter. In fact, they've been rising at about that monthly rate for the past year."

"Yes, Philip, I'm well aware of that. But that's why we hired you. You are supposed to turn these numbers around, and now—90 days after you started—there's no change in direction at all. I need you to do something about this immediately. I can't have this creeping overhead! Get back to me tomorrow with your action plan for how you're going to make sure labor costs are reduced next month."

Mrs. Smith then stood up and opened the door for Philip to leave.

Walking back to his office, Philip considered implementing a quick job-saving solution such as giving each room attendant an extra room to clean. As he mentally rehearsed breaking this news to the room attendant staff, Philip noticed his office was occupied.

"Betty! Jane! What can I do for you?" Philip asked, entering his office.

"Mr. Stone, we've been meaning to talk to you for a couple weeks," Jane said, "but we didn't want you to think we were a bunch of complainers, being as this job is new to you and all."

"Why, of course not, Jane. You two are some of the hardest-working room attendants in the department. You have the best productivity and set a wonderful example for all our other employees."

"Well, it's that productivity thing we want to talk to you about. We want to help make sure the rooms are done and done right, but you've been asking too much of us lately. We're burning out. And it's not just Betty and me. There are other employees who've been around a long time like us, and we can't keep up anymore. If you don't find a way to lighten the workload a little, you're going to kill us."

Betty chimed in, "I remember when we were expected to do only 17 rooms a shift. Now we're up to 22 rooms on a regular basis. I promise, Mr. Stone, we weren't slacking before. If we have to do more than 22 rooms, they're just not going to be clean, and I don't want a guest checking into any one of *my* rooms that isn't clean."

Philip felt a first-class headache coming on as he realized this would be a poor time to suggest room attendants take on extra rooms or spend less time per room. "Is there something specific that you think would help?"

"Yeah," said Jane. "Give us fewer rooms to clean so we don't all get ulcers!"

"Well, ladies, your break is over, you'd better get back to work. I appreciate your coming to talk to me. I'll let you know in a couple days what I decide to do," Philip said, looking at his watch in hopes of speeding the two women out.

The two room attendants exchanged disappointed glances. Betty shrugged and said, "OK, but you will get back to us, won't you? You're not just trying to get rid of us?"

"No. I'll get back to you by the day after tomorrow. Would that be OK?" Philip asked.

"If we don't have heart attacks first," Jane muttered as she and Betty left.

Philip sat at his desk with a sigh and pulled out his department's productivity standards. According to the information left him by the previous executive housekeeper, each room should take 26 minutes to clean. He decided to analyze how many rooms each room attendant was actually cleaning.

After a half-hour of analyzing productivity data, Philip identified the following problems:

- Forty percent of his room attendants were performing at the hotel's productivity standards or better
- Sixty percent of his room attendants were each cleaning fewer than 17 rooms a day and averaging longer than 26 minutes to clean a room
- The 60 percent performing below standards were all either new hires or still in training
- The housekeeping department has had 60 percent of its personnel in training or at new-hire status for the past ten months, due to high turnover

Philip then began to outline presentations for the general manager and for his own employees. First, he decided, he would explain the cause of rising labor costs to his general manager. "I'll have to tell her that turnover and poor training are causing lower productivity. We're not hiring the right people for the right positions, and then we're not bringing their productivity levels up to standards."

Philip determined he would tell Mrs. Smith she has to spend money to bring the labor-costs curve down. His suggestions included:

- Update job descriptions so new hires have more realistic expectations
- Provide more resources to the training department
- Organize training better so room attendants come up to speed within 30 days
- Terminate new hires if they do not meet productivity standards after 30 days
- Hold weekly recruitment meetings with human resources

He hoped that, although his suggestions wouldn't please Mrs. Smith, they would illustrate that the resources needed for the short term would be less costly than steadily increasing labor costs.

Philip struggled a little more over what to tell his room attendants. Ideally, he thought, he could encourage the more experienced 40 percent to pitch in and help bring the 60 percent up to speed. By doing just a little more now, they could reduce stress and tension in the long run. All he had to do, he thought, was convince them to give a little more a little bit longer. "At least I'm not giving them more rooms to clean," he decided.

As Philip set his presentation plans aside to go back to his daily work, he stopped and took one more look at them. "Hmmm," he thought. "Perhaps I should ask a few of my colleagues at other hotels how they would handle this."

Discussion Question

1. What feedback would executive housekeepers give Philip?

Case Study

Teams Can Triumph over Trials

Joanne Sommer has just been hired as the Ascot Hotel's executive housekeeper. The hotel's general manager, Jack Robbins, told Joanne he wants to maintain and improve the team cleaning system he had the previous executive housekeeper implement three months earlier for all housekeeping employees.

Mr. Robbins hadn't used team cleaning in the past and, as a "big picture" person who focuses on results, he shows little interest in the details of implementation. He was attracted to team cleaning by a management article that claimed team cleaning would cut costs, reduce turnover, improve attendance, and clean rooms faster. These are the results he wants.

Unfortunately, the initial implementation had not gone smoothly. The previous executive housekeeper switched the entire department over to teams at the same time, and immediately found herself with a scheduling nightmare. The goal of assembly-line efficiency was impossible to achieve because support systems were not effective. For example, when the laundry allowed torn or stained linens to be stocked on carts, team members often did not discover the problem until they put the sheets on a bed. Valuable time was lost as replacement linens were fetched, especially when the runners replenishing carts were also behind schedule, which seemed to happen frequently. Before, this situation would have put one employee behind schedule. Now, it puts two people behind schedule, costing the hotel more time and labor.

Teams find that they run out of supplies more quickly now and have to take extra trips to the housekeeping storage area to restock. Teams also lose time when they have to wait for a room to be vacated by a guest. While this was always an issue, now it holds up two people instead of one.

To make matters worse, some of the teams initially assigned are now experiencing personality conflicts. Several employees enjoyed working alone and resent being paired with other people. As a result of these and other problems, most housekeeping employees dislike the new system.

Joanne believes that the team cleaning concept could work at the Ascot Hotel if properly implemented. She recognizes that it was not properly implemented at the outset, and that mistakes have increased employee resistance and made successful implementation even more difficult.

Discussion Questions

1. What are some signs that, initially, the team cleaning system was implemented poorly?
2. What could Joanne do to gain employee buy-in and support? How might she be able to make working on teams attractive to housekeeping employees?
3. What issues must Joanne clarify with Mr. Robbins if team cleaning is to succeed at the Ascot Hotel? What kind of detail information would encourage Mr. Robbins to maintain a commitment to team cleaning?

The following industry experts helped generate and develop these cases: Gail Edwards, CHHE, St. Louis, Missouri; Mary Friedman, Edina, Minnesota; and Aleta Nitschke, CHA, founder of *The Rooms Chronicle*®, Garfield, Minnesota.

Chapter 10 Outline

Competencies

1. Identify the executive housekeeper's responsibilities in relation to the budget planning process. (pp. 387–389)
2. Explain how the executive housekeeper uses the operating budget as a control tool. (pp. 389–390)
3. Describe hotel income statements and rooms division income statements, and identify the line items on a rooms division income statement that are affected by expenses incurred by the housekeeping department. (pp. 390–396)
4. Explain how the executive housekeeper estimates department expenses during the budget planning process. (pp. 396–404)
5. Identify four actions that an executive housekeeper can take to control expenses. (p. 404)
6. Describe purchasing responsibilities of the executive housekeeper, identify factors to consider when determining the size of an annual linen purchase, and discuss capital budgets. (pp. 405–413)
7. Identify issues that an executive housekeeper should address when considering the use of outside contractors to perform cleaning services. (pp. 413–416)

Taken from *Managing Housekeeping Operations*, Revised Third Edition, by Aleta A. Nitschke and William D. Frye

Chapter 10
Controlling Expenses

SINCE HOUSEKEEPING IS NOT A REVENUE-GENERATING DEPARTMENT, the executive housekeeper's primary responsibility for achieving the property's financial goals is to control the department's expenses. In addition to salaries and wages, inventoried items are a key area for the executive housekeeper's exercise of cost control measures.

This chapter describes the budgetary process and explains how budgets are determined for the operational expenses that fall within the executive housekeeper's responsibility. The chapter also examines the executive housekeeper's responsibility for controlling the costs associated with housekeeping operations. The role of the executive housekeeper in formulating capital budgets will also be discussed.

The Budget Process

The operating budget outlines the financial goals of a hotel. The purpose of the operating budget is to relate operational costs to the year's expected revenues. The yearly operating budget is broken down into budgets for each month of the fiscal year. In addition, each department prepares its own monthly budget. These budgets cover individual areas of responsibility and serve as a guide for how the department will achieve its expected contribution to the property's financial goals.

Essentially, a budget is a plan. It projects both the revenues the hotel anticipates during the period covered by the budget and the expenses required to generate the anticipated revenues. The executive housekeeper's responsibility in the budgetary process is twofold. First, the executive housekeeper is involved in the planning process that leads to the formulation of the budget. This entails informing the rooms division manager and general manager what expenses the housekeeping department will incur in light of forecasted room sales. Second, since the budget represents an operational plan for the year, the executive housekeeper ensures that the department's actual expenses are in line with budgeted costs and with the actual occupancy levels.

As a plan, a budget is not "set in stone." It may need to be adjusted in light of unforeseen or changing circumstances. If anticipated room sales do not materialize, then expenses allocated to different departments will need to be adjusted accordingly. If occupancy levels exceed expectations, then increased expenses need to be planned for and incorporated into a revised budget. If unexpected expenditures are required, their effect on the overall plan needs to be assessed. New ways may need to be determined for the property to meet its financial goals and objectives.

As a plan, a budget is also a guide. It provides managers with the standards by which they can measure the success of operations. By comparing actual expenses with allocated amounts, the executive housekeeper can track the efficiency of housekeeping operations and monitor the department's ability to keep its expenses within the prescribed limits.

Types of Budgets

Two types of budgets are used in managing a hotel's financial resources: capital and operating budgets. The difference between the two essentially lies in the types of expenditures involved.

Usually, a **capital budget** plans for the expenditure of company assets for items costing $1,500 or more. Typically, these items are not used up in the normal course of operations; instead, they have a life span that exceeds a single year. Furniture, fixtures, and equipment are typical examples of **capital expenditures**. Capital expenditures in equipment for the housekeeping department may include room attendant carts, vacuum cleaners, carpet shampooers, pile lifters, rotary floor scrubbers, laundry equipment, sewing machines, and trash-handling equipment. In addition, major initial purchases of recycled inventory items—such as linen, towels, blankets, and uniforms—are capital budget items since they have a relatively long useful life and are not used up in the course of normal operations.

An **operating budget** forecasts revenues and expenses associated with the routine operations of the hotel during a certain period. **Operating expenditures** are those costs the hotel incurs in order to generate revenue in the normal course of doing business. In the housekeeping department, the most expensive operational cost is salaries and wages. The costs of non-recycled inventory items, such as cleaning and guest supplies, are also considered operational costs.

Planning the Operating Budget

The budgeting process begins far in advance of the start of the period for which the budget is planned. The process of planning an annual operating budget generally takes several months. It involves gathering information, formulating initial plans, reconsidering goals and objectives, and making final adjustments. The budget-planning process requires a closely coordinated effort of all management personnel.

Operating budgets are typically prepared for each fiscal year; the annual operating budget summarizes the anticipated year-end results. Monthly operating budgets are also prepared for the property's fiscal year. This enables managers to clearly outline seasonal variations in expected revenues and corresponding expenses. It also provides managers and department heads with valuable tools to monitor actual results.

In budget planning, the first step is always to forecast room sales. The reason for this is twofold. First, room sales generate the revenue for operating various departments. Second, and more important, most of the expenses that each department can expect—and the ones that departments are most able to control—are most directly related to room occupancy levels. This is especially true of the housekeeping department where salaries and wages and the usage rates for both recycled and non-recycled inventory items are direct functions of the number of occupied rooms. The concept of "cost per occupied room" is the major tool the executive housekeeper uses to determine the levels of expense in the various categories. Once the executive housekeeper knows predicted occupancy levels, expected expenses for salaries and wages, cleaning supplies, guest supplies, laundry, and other areas can be determined on the basis of formulas that express costs in terms of cost per occupied room.

Occupancy forecasts are generally developed by the front office manager, who works closely with the property's general manager. The forecast is based not only on past levels of occupancy (and their distribution among the budget periods), but also on information supplied by the marketing department concerning the anticipated effect on room sales of special events, advertising, and promotions. Some hotels generate forecasts for room sales that predict the level of occupancy for each day of the coming year.

Once occupancy levels are predicted, the departments whose costs fluctuate with occupancy levels can forecast expected costs and submit prepared budgets to the general manager and controller for review. Upper management analyzes and adjusts the departmental budget plans so they reflect the property's goals and objectives. Often, budgets are returned to department heads with comments and recommended adjustments. Such feedback primarily reflects the concern of upper management to maximize profits and control expenses while maintaining appropriate levels of service.

By specifying expense levels in relation to room sales, the budget actually expresses the level of service the hotel will be able to provide. In this regard, it is important for department heads to report how service levels will be affected by budget adjustments. This is especially important for the executive housekeeper. If upper management tones down the operating budget submitted by the executive housekeeper, the executive housekeeper should clearly indicate what services will be eliminated or downgraded in order to achieve the specified reductions.

The cycle of feedback and discussion continues as department heads revise their budgetary plans and provide additional input in response to recommended adjustments. It is through this back-and-forth process that agreement is ultimately reached. The final budget represents the forecasts, goals, and constraints that everyone adopts. Each department is then committed to operating under the limits expressed in the budget and achieving its contribution to the overall plan. Once approved, the operating budgets set a standard by which departmental performance can—and will—be evaluated.

Using the Operating Budget as a Control Tool

An operating budget is a valuable control tool with which to monitor the course of operations during a specified period. Each month, the hotel's accounting department produces statements reporting actual costs in each of the expense categories. The form of these statements is nearly identical to that of the operating budget; actual costs are listed alongside budgeted costs. Such reports enable the executive housekeeper to monitor how well the housekeeping department is doing in relation to the budgeted goals and constraints.

Controlling expenses in the housekeeping department means comparing actual costs with budgeted amounts and assessing the variances. When comparing actual and budgeted expenses, the executive housekeeper should first determine whether the forecasted occupancy levels were actually achieved. If the number of occupied rooms is lower than anticipated, a corresponding decrease in the department's actual expenses should be expected. Similarly, if occupancy levels are higher than forecasted, the executive housekeeper can expect a corresponding increase in housekeeping expenses. In either case, the adjustment in expenses should be proportional to the variation in occupancy levels. The executive housekeeper's ability to control housekeeping expenses will be evaluated in terms of his or her ability to maintain the cost per occupied room expected for each category.

Small deviations between actual and budgeted expenses can be expected and are not a cause for alarm. Serious deviations from the budgeted plan require investigation and explanation. If the actual costs far exceed the budgeted amounts while the predicted occupancy level remains the same, the executive housekeeper needs to find the source of the deviation. In addition to discovering why the department is "behind budget," the executive housekeeper needs to formulate a plan to correct the deviation and get the department back "on budget." For example, a re-examination of staff scheduling procedures or closer supervision of standard practices and procedures may be necessary. Other steps might include evaluating the efficiency and cost of products being used in the housekeeping department, and exploring the alternatives.

Even if the executive housekeeper finds that the department is far "ahead of budget," it is not necessarily a cause for celebration. It may indicate a deterioration of the service levels that were built into the original budget plan. *Any* serious deviation from the plan is a cause for concern and requires explanation. Identifying and investigating such deviations on a timely basis is one of the most valuable functions an executive housekeeper can perform in terms of the operating budget.

Operating Budgets and Income Statements

An operating budget is identical in form to an **income statement**. An income statement—or statement of income—expresses the actual results of operations during an accounting period, identifying revenues earned and itemizing expenses incurred during that period. The difference between an income statement and an operating budget is that the first expresses the actual results of operations for a period that has ended, while the second expresses the expected results of operations for a current or coming period. The one is a report of what actually occurred, while the other is a forecast or plan for what is to come. The operating budget is a plan for the period in the sense that it predicts or anticipates what the income statement will actually show at the end of that period. The success of the hotel's plan as expressed in the budget is determined by how closely its forecasted numbers match the numbers on the end-of-the-period income statement.

In the budget-planning process, upper management collects information from the various department heads to prepare a budget for the entire property. This budget takes the form of an income statement for the coming period. Income statements that predict the results of current or future operations, as opposed to reporting actual results, are often referred to as **pro forma income statements**.

The Hotel Income Statement

The statement of income provides important financial information about the results of hotel operations for a given period. The period may be one month or longer, but cannot exceed one business year. Since a statement of income reveals

Exhibit 1 Summary Income Statement—Vacation Inn

Vacation Inn
Summary Income Statement
For the year ended December 31, 20XX

	Schedule	Net Revenue	Cost of Sales	Payroll and Related Expenses	Other Expense	Income (Loss)
Operated Departments						
Rooms	1	$1,041,200	$ 0	$ 185,334	$ 79,080	$ 776,786
Food	2	420,100	160,048	160,500	44,013	55,539
Beverage	3	206,065	48,400	58,032	22,500	77,133
Telephone	4	52,028	46,505	14,317	6,816	(15,610)
Total Operated Departments		1,719,393	254,953	418,183	152,409	893,848
Undistributed Operating Expenses						
Administrative and General	5			104,244	48,209	152,453
Sales and Marketing	6			33,231	33,585	66,816
Property Operation and Maintenance	7			31,652	49,312	80,964
Utilities	8			0	88,752	88,752
Total Undistributed Operating Expenses				169,127	219,858	388,985
Gross Operating Profit		$1,719,393	$254,953	$ 587,310	$372,267	504,863
Rent, Property Taxes, and Insurance	9					200,861
Depreciation and Amortization	10					115,860
Net Operating Income						188,142
Interest Expense	11					52,148
Income Before Income Taxes						135,994
Income Tax	12					48,707
Net Income						$ 87,287

Source: Raymond S. Schmidgall, *Hospitality Industry Managerial Accounting*, 6th ed. (Lansing, Mich.: American Hotel & Lodging Educational Institute, 2006), p. 100.

the bottom line—the net income for a given period—it is one of the most important financial statements used by top management to evaluate the success of operations. Although the executive housekeeper may never directly use the hotel's statement of income, this statement relies in part on detailed information supplied by the housekeeping department.

The sample statement of income shown in Exhibit 1 is often called a summary statement because it presents a composite picture of all the financial operations of the hotel. Rooms division information appears on the first line, under the category of operated departments. The amount of income generated by the rooms division is determined by subtracting payroll and related expenses and other expenses from the amount of net revenue produced by the rooms division over the period covered by the income statement. Payroll and related expenses charged to the rooms division include the wages, salaries, and benefits paid to housekeeping *and* front office staff, reservation agents, and uniformed service staff. Since the rooms division is not a merchandising facility, there is no cost of sales to subtract from the net revenue amount.

The revenue generated by the rooms division is often the largest single amount produced by revenue centers within a hotel. Using the figures shown in Exhibit 1, the amount of income earned by the rooms division during the year was $776,786, or 86.9 percent of the total income of $893,848. Since the rooms division is generally the hotel's major source of income, and since housekeeping is a major source of expense incurred by the rooms division, the executive housekeeper plays an important role in the hotel's overall financial performance.

The Rooms Division Income Statement

The hotel's statement of income shows only summary information. More detailed information is presented by the separate departmental income statements prepared by each revenue center. These departmental income statements are called **schedules** and are referenced on the hotel's statement of income.

Exhibit 1 references the rooms division as Schedule 1. This rooms division income statement appears in Exhibit 2. The figures shown in Exhibit 2 for rooms division Net Revenue, Payroll and Related Expenses, Other Expenses, and Departmental Income are the same amounts that appear on Exhibit 1 for the rooms division under the category of operated departments.

The format and specific line items used by the rooms division for its departmental income statement will vary with the needs and requirements of individual properties. The following sections briefly describe typical line items found on a rooms division income statement.

The first heading on the rooms division income statement records revenue from room sales during the period. The second heading, Allowances, identifies rebates, refunds, and overcharges of revenue. These are generally not known at the time that room sales are recorded. Instead, allowances are adjusted at a later date and may not appear as a budgeted line item on a pro forma income statement.

Net Revenue is arrived at by subtracting Allowances from Total Revenue. It is the Net Revenue figure that is transferred to the hotel's income statement as sales derived from the hotel's lodging operation.

The executive housekeeper is directly concerned with many of the line items listed in the expense sections of the rooms division's income statement. The largest single expense category listed is Salaries and Wages. The personnel costs associated with the housekeeping department are incorporated into this total, which also includes payroll costs for all rooms division employees. Regular pay, overtime pay, vacation pay, severance pay, incentive pay, holiday pay, and employee bonuses are included in this expense category.

The expense item referred to as Employee Benefits is generally calculated by the personnel or accounting departments. It includes payroll-related insurance expense, pension, and other related personnel costs. The share of Employee Benefit expense that belongs to the housekeeping department is included in this line item.

Many of the expense items listed under the heading Other Expenses fall under the direct responsibility of the executive housekeeper. These include the following:

- Contract Services
- Laundry and Dry Cleaning
- Linen
- Operating Supplies
- Uniforms

Exhibit 2 Sample Rooms Department Schedule

Vacation Inn **Rooms** **For the year ended December 31, 20XX**	Schedule 1
Revenue	
Transient—Regular	$ 543,900
Transient—Group	450,000
Permanent	48,000
Other	2,000
Allowances	(2,700)
Net Revenue	1,041,200
Expenses	
Salaries and Wages	159,304
Payroll Taxes	10,420
Employee Benefits	15,610
Total Payroll and Related Expenses	185,334
Other Expenses	
Cable/Satellite Television	4,900
Cleaning Supplies	3,200
Commissions	5,124
Contract Services	3,100
Guest Supplies	5,126
Laundry and Dry Cleaning	12,706
Linen	9,494
Miscellaneous	3,000
Operating Supplies	12,742
Reservations	9,288
Telecommunications	4,685
Training	4,315
Uniforms	1,400
Total Other Expenses	79,080
Total Expenses	264,414
Departmental Income	$ 776,786

Source: Raymond S. Schmidgall, *Hospitality Industry Managerial Accounting*, 6th ed. (Lansing, Mich.: American Hotel & Lodging Educational Institute, 2006), p. 99.

Contract Services includes the cost of contracting outside companies to clean lobbies and public areas, wash windows, and exterminate and disinfect areas of the rooms division. The pros and cons involved in the executive housekeeper's decision to employ contract cleaning services will be discussed at the end of this chapter.

The Laundry and Dry Cleaning expense item refers to the cost of both outside and in-house laundry and dry-cleaning services. It includes the cost of dry cleaning curtains and draperies as well as washing or cleaning awnings, carpets, and rugs in areas of the rooms division. All the expenses incurred by the property's in-house laundry facility (except salaries, wages, and benefits) are reflected in this expense item. The costs of supplies used to keep the house laundry in a clean and sanitary condition are included—plus the costs of all supplies used in the laundry operation itself. In addition, printing and stationery costs associated with laundry lists, printed forms, service manuals, and office supplies used by in-house laundry personnel are included. Finally, the cost of purchasing or renting uniforms for in-house laundry employees, along with the costs of uniform cleaning or repair, are incorporated in the total expense recorded in this category. Many hotels use a separate schedule to itemize all the costs within this expense category.

The Linen expense item includes the replacement costs or rental fees for sheets, pillowcases, towels, facecloths, bath mats, blankets, and other items included in the linen inventory.

The Operating Supplies expense item includes the cost of guest supplies, cleaning supplies, and printing and stationery items. All guest and cleaning supplies fall within the executive housekeeper's area of responsibility, and their inventories are maintained in the housekeeping department.

The Uniforms expense item includes the cost of purchasing or renting uniforms for all employees of the rooms division as well as other related costs.

Some of the expense categories listed under the heading Other Expenses fall outside the executive housekeeper's areas of responsibility. The Commissions expense refers to remunerations paid to outside sources, such as travel agents and online distribution channels such as Orbitz®, Expedia®, Travelocity® and Priceline.com® who market and secure rooms business for the hotel. Reservations includes the cost of a reservations service and a central reservation system involving telephone, fax, and Internet expenses. Fairly common Other Expenses line items not shown in the sample statement include Cable/Satellite Television, Telecommunications, Training, and Guest Transportation.

In the budget-planning process, the rooms manager will solicit information from the executive housekeeper concerning the expense categories that fall under the housekeeping department's areas of responsibility. In particular, the rooms manager will be interested in assessing expected expenses as a percentage of the revenue forecasted for room sales. Every controllable cost can be expressed as a percentage of revenue. For each expense category, the rooms manager will have a standard percentage that is considered to be an appropriate level of expense in relation to generated revenues. The rooms manager will expect that all projected expenses fall within an acceptable range of standard cost percentages for each category. The rooms manager may also build improvements on past cost percentages into selected expense categories, assuming that greater efficiencies will be achieved through better training, closer supervision, and tighter controls. The rooms manager's goal is to maximize the department's income by minimizing its expenses while still preserving or enhancing the service levels. Crucial to achieving this goal are the executive housekeeper's calculations of anticipated expenses and comments on how budget adjustments may affect the quality of service.

The operating budgets under which the executive housekeeper operates take the form of monthly income statements for the rooms division. Projected revenues and expenses for each month of the budgeted period will represent the rooms division's operational plan. The executive housekeeper will be held accountable for controlling the expense areas that fall within the housekeeping department's areas of responsibility. As the budgeted period progresses, monthly

Exhibit 3 Sample Monthly Rooms Division Budget Report

Vacation Inn
Budget Report Rooms Division
For January 20XX

	Actual	Budget	Variances $	Variances %
Revenue				
Room Sales	$156,240	$145,080	$11,160	7.69%
Allowances	437	300	(137)	(45.67)
Net Revenue	155,803	144,780	11,023	7.61
Expenses				
Salaries and Wages	20,826	18,821	(2,005)	(10.65)
Employee Benefits	4,015	5,791	1,776	30.67
Total Payroll and Related Expenses	24,841	24,612	(229)	(0.93)
Other Expenses				
Commissions	437	752	315	41.89
Contract Services	921	873	(48)	(5.50)
Guest Supplies	1,750	1,200	(550)	(45.83)
Laundry and Dry Cleaning	1,218	975	(243)	(24.92)
Linen	1,906	1,875	(31)	(1.65)
Operating Supplies	1,937	1,348	(589)	(43.69)
Reservations	1,734	2,012	278	13.82
Uniforms	374	292	(82)	(28.08)
Other	515	672	157	23.36
Total Other Expenses	10,792	9,999	(793)	(7.93)
Total Expenses	35,633	34,611	(1,022)	(2.95)
Departmental Income (Loss)	$120,170	$110,169	$10,001	9.08%

income statements will be produced that show the actual amounts alongside the amounts originally budgeted.

Exhibit 3 shows a monthly budget report for rooms that indicates both budgeted forecasts and actual results. The last two columns in Exhibit 3 show dollar and percentage variances. The dollar variances indicate the differences between actual results and budgeted amounts. Dollar variances are considered either favorable or unfavorable based on the following situations:

	Favorable Variance	Unfavorable Variance
Revenue	Actual exceeds budget	Budget exceeds actual
Expense	Budget exceeds actual	Actual exceeds budget

For example, the actual amount of salaries and wages for rooms division personnel in the month of January was $20,826, while the budgeted amount for salaries and wages was $18,821, resulting in a variance of $2,005. The variance is bracketed to indicate an unfavorable variance. However, if the revenue variance is favorable, an unfavorable variance in expenses (such as in payroll) is not necessarily negative. Rather, it may merely indicate the greater expense of serving more guests than were anticipated when the budget was created.

Percentage variances are determined by dividing the dollar variance by the budgeted amount. For example, the 7.61 percent variance for net revenue shown in Exhibit 3 is the result of dividing the dollar variance figure of $11,023 by the budgeted net revenue amount of $144,780—and then multiplying by 100.

Virtually all actual results of rooms division operations will differ from budgeted amounts for revenue and expense items on a budget report. This is only to be expected because any budgeting process, no matter how sophisticated, is not perfect. Executive housekeepers should not analyze every variance. Only significant variances require management analysis and action. The general manager and controller should provide the executive housekeeper with criteria for determining which variances are significant.

Budgeting Expenses

The budgeting process begins with a forecast of room sales. Since expense levels in all the expense categories on the departmental income statement vary with occupancy, everything in the operating budget depends upon how accurately occupancy levels are forecasted.

Early in the budget-planning process, the rooms manager will give the executive housekeeper the yearly forecast of occupancy levels, broken down into monthly budget periods. This information may be delivered on a form such as the one in Exhibit 4. Using historical data, along with input from the hotel's marketing department, the rooms manager will predict the occupancy percentage for each budgeted period. The second column of the form translates the anticipated occupancy percentage into the actual number of rooms expected to be occupied. By multiplying the number of expected occupied rooms by the average rate per room, the rooms manager can forecast the amount of revenue anticipated from room sales. For the rooms manager, this projection of revenue is the most important part of the operating budget. The appropriateness of all expenses expected will be measured in terms of the percentage of revenue represented by each expense category.

For the executive housekeeper, the most important information in the rooms manager's forecast is not so much the total expected sales dollars, but the projected number of occupied rooms for each budget period. This is because nearly all the expense levels for which the executive housekeeper is responsible are directly dependent upon the number of occupied rooms the housekeeping department will have to service.

The executive housekeeper can predict a certain level of expense for each expense category when he or she knows: (1) the cost per occupied room for each category of expense and (2) the number of occupied rooms forecasted for each budget period. At this point, the budgeting process simply involves relating costs per occupied room to the forecasted occupancy levels.

Exhibit 4 Summary of Forecasted Rooms Sales

Months of the Year	Budget Period	Occupancy Percentage	Number of Occupied Rooms	Average Price per Room	Total Rooms Sales
	1.				
	2.				
	3.				
	4.				
	5.				
	6.				
	7.				
	8.				
	9.				
	10.				
	11.				
	12.				

Salaries and Wages

Salaries and Wages expense for the housekeeping department is related to such positions as executive housekeeper, assistant housekeeping managers, supervisors, linen room attendants, room attendants, housepersons, lobby attendants, and others employed in the housekeeping operation.

By using a staffing guide, the executive housekeeper can determine how many labor hours in each job classification are needed to ensure smooth operations at varying levels of occupancy. When planning the Salaries and Wages expense for the operating budget, the executive housekeeper can use the staffing guide in conjunction with the occupancy forecasts to determine staffing needs for each budget period. After determining the number of labor hours needed for each job category, the executive housekeeper can multiply the number of hours by the position's average per-hour wage to calculate the expected cost for that job category. By summing the calculations for all positions, a total wage cost can be determined for each budget period. Costs associated with salaried positions in the housekeeping department can be averaged into each monthly budget period. In forecasting salary and wage costs, the executive housekeeper will need to account for any scheduled salary and wage increases as well as any cost-of-living adjustments planned by the property.

the Rooms
CHRONICLE®

Tips for Keeping Housekeeping Productivity in Line With Budgeted Expectations

Late check-outs, trashed rooms, trainees, temporary workers. There is no end to the drain on room attendant productivity. Considering all the issues that affect housekeeping's efficiency, is it still possible for a good manager to maintain budgeted productivity? Absolutely. Here are some of the tricks:

"No show" rooms. The front office staff will check-in guaranteed reservations before the date rolls on the property management system. But, before the audit shift ends in the morning, they will check the rooms out. These rooms are included in the total number of rooms occupied, but they do not require cleaning. These are bonuses for housekeeping, and in larger hotels can often account for a full person's load.

Supervisors, public space, and other housekeeping staff. In case of emergency, there are a number of people who can clean rooms yet who are not included in budgeted productivity. Using supervisors, public space, or laundry workers can help a housekeeping manager in critical times, but because those people have other responsibilities, if this trick is over-used, the other areas will suffer.

"No service" rooms or Do Not Disturbs. When a room attendant encounters a guest who does not desire service, the room is a bonus for productivity. Room attendants should be given incentives to request another room assignment, to go home early, or to help in another area of the hotel where their wages can be transferred.

Selling rooms. In some hotels, selling rooms to room attendants is a very common practice. In other words, room attendants are paid a predetermined flat amount per room to pick up extra rooms beyond their assignment. Since employees are eager to earn the additional money, if the rooms are cleaned within their eight-hour day, this system will improve productivity. However, keep in mind that the extra wage will negatively affect housekeeping (when the total room revenue is flat) if the department is measured by percent of sales.

Assign extra rooms daily. One of the easiest ways to maintain budgeted productivity is to assign an extra room. For instance, if the budget is for 15 rooms per eight hour shift, establish 16 as the standard assignment. The one extra room will cover the time used by trainees, meetings, suites, and so on.

In the same way, when productivity is in line, find times to assign one less room. Room attendants will appreciate the occasional lighter load.

Another option is to assign one extra room mid-week and one less on weekends. This works well in hotels that have messy weekend guests and neat weekday business travelers.

Communicate with other departments. Housekeeping managers are obligated to maintain excellent communication with all other departments. Too often it is the impact of other departments that causes a drop in room attendant productivity. Establish solid working relationships with other managers. For instance, the sales department may require that all the poolside guestrooms be converted to exhibit space. The housekeeping manager should reply that this can be accomplished—if sales will pick up the cost of the labor.

the Rooms CHRONICLE®

(continued)

Or, perhaps the housekeeper discovers a large number of discrepant rooms each day. (Discrepant rooms are those that are marked clean, but are found to be dirty or vice versa.) Meet with the front office manager to explain the actual cost of the errors made by his or her staff. To help the front office manager resolve the problems, offer to give immediate feedback on room status conflicts. And suggest that someone on the front office staff payroll be sent to check every discrepant room and update the status appropriately.

Or, perhaps it is unclear how accounting is charging various payroll items. Meet with the controller to analyze every line of the previous month's budget and to check the coding on each employee. Often a room attendant is assigned to clean offices or public bathrooms and is not re-coded for such work. Make sure to have a crystal-clear understanding of how accounting assigns the costs of housekeeping.

Or, it could be that if engineers were given access to rags and cleaning spray bottles, they might give a quick wipe-up of their mess when making repairs in guestrooms. Often, (especially when housekeeping makes an extra effort to keep the engineers' office or shop clean) maintenance workers will clean behind themselves totally without bothering housekeeping.

Analyze Daily Routines

In analyzing room attendant productivity, perhaps the review of their daily routines is most important. For example, one hotel found that the slowness of their service elevators accounted for one hour of lost productivity for each room attendant each day. (Fifteen minutes to get to their stations in the morning, fifteen to go to lunch, fifteen to return, and fifteen at the end of the day.) Another hotel found that room attendants were making at least two trips per day to the laundry for linen that should have been delivered to their cart by linen runners. Another found that room attendants were sharing vacuum cleaners and constantly running between sections. Another found that they were paying for lunch breaks.

After these operational issues are discovered, solutions can be instituted. For instance, the elevator problem was resolved by staggering the start/break times of room attendants, by keeping the carts on the guestroom floors and by adding a person in the evening to restock the carts and closets.

In one hotel, it was the daily soap operas that were costing productivity. Room attendants were sneaking a half-hour break in an empty room to watch their favorite television show. They rushed to complete their rooms in the morning (but did not mark on their sheets that the rooms had been cleaned) and then relaxed in the afternoon. This problem was remedied in part by temporarily adding muscle to the inspection process with management checking almost immediately behind each room attendant. A notation was made on each room attendant's assignment sheet of the time each room was inspected. The natural "pace" of each room attendant soon became clear and productivity measures were revised accordingly. (Of course, there were disciplinary measures also taken.)

It is the responsibility of the executive housekeeper to know exactly how each employee's time is allocated. Only with this knowledge can the manager truly control productivity.

Source: Mary Friedman, *The Rooms Chronicle®*, Volume 6, Number 5, pp. 4–5.
For subscription information, please call 866-READ-TRC.

Employee Benefits

Calculations related to employee benefits depend on the number of labor hours expected to be scheduled, the types of job classifications involved, and the property's policies regarding employee benefits. The kinds of benefits in this expense category may include charges for the cost of holiday or vacation pay, employee meals, payroll taxes, medical expenses or insurance, social insurance such as pensions, and staff parties or social events. With the help of human resources or accounting staff, the executive housekeeper can determine what levels of expense to budget for employee benefits.

Outside Services

If the hotel employs any outside contractors for major cleaning projects or for laundry and dry-cleaning services, then the costs of these services are averaged throughout the budget periods. The executive housekeeper can consult current contracts or past invoices to determine the expense levels to budget.

In-House Laundry

The executive housekeeper needs to work closely with the laundry supervisor to budget laundry expenses. The forecasts of occupancy levels provided by the rooms division, along with the property's staffing guide, will be the basis for determining all expenses related to salaries, wages, and benefits for laundry personnel.

The cost of operating the hotel's on-premises laundry is directly related to the volume of soiled items to be processed. This, in turn, is a direct function of the hotel's occupancy levels. Therefore, the cost of laundering room linens and uniforms can be budgeted on the basis of historical information that shows the cost per occupied room of laundry operations. Multiplying the cost per occupied room for laundry operations by the number of occupied rooms forecast for each budget period will provide a figure for the expected laundry expense during the budget period.

Linens

Although linen supplies in the housekeeping department are a recycled inventory item, their life spans are ultimately limited. New linens must be purchased throughout the year as older linens are removed from service due to loss, damage, or wear. Replacement cost for new linens is an expense that needs to be worked into the budget-planning process.

Monthly physical inventories of linens show the executive housekeeper how long the existing stock of linens lasts and how much of each type of linen needs to be reordered to maintain appropriate par levels. The results of physical inventories of linens are submitted to the hotel's general manager, who routinely transfers the information to the hotel's accounting department. In turn, the accounting department regularly processes the information and provides valuable statistical information related to usage rates, losses, and expenses per occupied room. The executive housekeeper can use the cost per occupied room for replacement linen to forecast linen expense for the periods covered by the operating budget. Multiplying

the Rooms CHRONICLE®

Payroll Dollars: Where Do They Go?

Two frequent causes of wasted payroll dollars in housekeeping are employee time spent traveling and time spent searching for supplies. These can be remedied by better department organization.

Travel time is defined as the amount of time an employee spends on his or her way somewhere, as opposed to time spent accomplishing a task. For instance, a room attendant may have to rotate between room assignments on various floors or in various buildings. Perhaps slow elevators mean long waits to get to work areas. Or it may be a long walk from the work area to the break room or cafeteria. Other causes of excessive travel time are a late check-out, which requires going back to an area already completed, and a supervisor sending a room attendant back to a room that was improperly made up.

Travel time is also a factor with public space cleaners, for whom the order of task assignments may mean excessive travel time.

Employees must have proper tools to effectively complete their tasks. When time is spent in search of supplies, payroll dollars are being wasted. For instance:

- Does a room attendant have to rummage through a pile of pillowcases to find one without stains?
- Does he or she have to seek out a vacuum cleaner that works?
- Does it take a half hour for the employee to load the cart with amenities and supplies?
- Does the room attendant stand in the laundry area, waiting for towels to dry?
- Is the room attendant returning to housekeeping for toilet paper, matchbooks, soap, etc.?

In the case of public space cleaners, time is often wasted when they have to change equipment between tasks. For instance, does the cleaner leave the department with a vacuum, return 10 minutes later for a broom and dustpan, return again for the buffer, and so on?

- Explain to the front desk how randomly assigning guests to rooms throughout the property during low occupancy periods can mean that payroll dollars are needlessly spent on travel time. Devise a system to restrict available rooms to certain predetermined areas as much as possible, while still making different types of rooms available for guests.
- In times of low occupancy, do not assign stray rooms in a particular section for cleaning. After a day or two, there may be enough dirty rooms in that area to warrant sending a room attendant.
- Instruct all room attendants to stay in their sections and use the telephone to call in their supply needs. Items not needed urgently can be picked up at break time. Urgently needed items should be delivered to the room attendants by a designated "on call" person (a laundry worker, public cleaner, or someone on a beeper for easy contact.)

(continued)

the Rooms CHRONICLE®

(continued)

- Stagger the start times and breaks of room attendants. This can help if slow elevators delay room attendants getting to work areas. Staggering starts also allows for coverage of early cleaning requests or late checkouts.
- Ensure that the room attendant training programs are minimizing the need to send cleaners back into a room that has been improperly done.
- Install quality control programs in the laundry to eliminate the possibility of stained linen being sent to the floors.
- Begin a preventive maintenance program on vacuum cleaners to keep them operational. Buy new equipment on a regular basis to replace worn-out vacuums.
- Maintain adequate linen pars. It is often the case that the labor dollars spent due to shortages of linen exceed the dollars necessary to purchase an additional par. Present a proposal to the management team to demonstrate this.
- Assign one evening houseperson to restock the room attendant carts with linens, toilet paper, tissues, and glasses.
- Prepare supply or amenity baskets in your central storage area to be issued each morning to room attendants. They carry these to their carts and are immediately ready to begin cleaning rooms. Replenish the baskets at lunchtime, if necessary.
- Organize public space carts so they carry the most frequently used items.
- Organize public space equipment in storage locations that make the most efficient use of the cleaners' time.
- Organize public space assignments in a way that makes sense not only by location, but also by task.
- Be on the lookout for things that steal your employees' time, and find solutions to correct those situations.

Source: Gail Edwards, CHHE, *The Rooms Chronicle®*, Volume 1, Number 3, p. 5.
For subscription information, please call 866-READ-TRC.

the cost per occupied room for linen replacement by the number of occupied rooms forecasted for the budget period will yield the linen expense to be built into the operating budget.

Operating Supplies

The operating supplies expense category for the housekeeping department includes non-recycled inventory items, such as guest supplies and amenities, cleaning supplies, and small equipment. As with the other housekeeping expense categories, the executive housekeeper can budget for the costs of these items on the basis of cost per occupied room.

Guest supplies include pens, stationery, matches, soap, shampoo, toilet and facial tissue, garment bags, and other amenities the hotel provides in each room for the convenience and use of its guests. The cost per occupied room for guest supplies is the same as the cost of one room par for these items. Budget amounts for guest supplies are determined by multiplying their cost per occupied room by the number of occupied rooms in the budget's forecast.

Cleaning supplies include not only chemical cleaners, polishes, and detergents, but also small equipment needed on a daily basis such as applicators, brooms, brushes, mops, buckets, spray bottles, and a variety of cleaning cloths. By following inventory control procedures, the executive housekeeper has an effective system for tracking the usage rates for the various cleaning supply items at different levels of occupancy. By dividing the cost of the number of purchase units used each month by the number of occupied rooms that month, a cost per occupied room can be established for each item in the cleaning supply inventory. Summing the results for all inventoried items yields a cost per occupied room for cleaning supplies. Multiplying this figure by the number of occupied rooms forecasted for the budget period provides the cleaning supply expense for the operating budget.

Uniforms

Provisions must be made in the operating budget for the cost of new and replacement uniforms. In addition, the cost of washing or dry-cleaning uniforms, as well as costs associated with repairing damaged uniforms, may need to be reflected in the operating budget.

Like linens, uniforms are a recycled inventory item. But unlike linens—whose usage rates and replacement needs are very predictable—the need for new uniforms during the budget period depends on factors such as personnel turnover and new hirings. To help organize information for the operating budget and for future purchasing, the executive housekeeper should maintain an itemized list of all types of uniforms maintained in the department's inventory. The cost information should be itemized for each part (for example, shirt, blouse, pants, skirt) of each type of uniform. The number of people working in each uniformed position may be obtained from human resources. Since men and women in the same position may require different uniforms—sometimes at different costs—the executive housekeeper also needs to consider the number of men and women occupying each uniformed position.

There are some rules of thumb that the executive housekeeper can use when budgeting for uniform purchases. While these rules of thumb may be helpful, executive housekeepers should keep in mind that uniform par levels vary from property to property.

The executive housekeeper should start by budgeting for one complete uniform for each person. Next, for uniforms that are dry-cleaned, the executive housekeeper should budget for one additional uniform per person. For uniforms that are washed, the executive housekeeper should budget for two additional uniforms per person, since laundering greatly reduces a uniform's useful life span. As a final rule of thumb, the executive housekeeper should budget three additional sets of uniforms for cooks. Taking into consideration an annual plan for replacing uniforms, the executive housekeeper should divide the cost of new uniforms into those months during the budget period in which they will be purchased.

In determining the cost of repairing uniforms, the executive housekeeper needs to consider not only the materials needed for repairs, but also the cost of the time spent by the supervisor or seamstress to repair the uniforms. Records of past repairs and productivity standards for repair can provide information relevant to the executive housekeeper's estimate for budgeting the cost of repairs.

Controlling Expenses

Controlling housekeeping expenses means ensuring that actual expenses are consistent with the expected expenses forecast by the operating budget. There are basically four methods the executive housekeeper can use to control housekeeping expenses: accurate recordkeeping, effective scheduling, careful training and supervision, and efficient purchasing.

Maintaining accurate records is the first step in controlling expenses and identifying problems in relation to managing inventories. Accurate recordkeeping enables the executive housekeeper to monitor usage rates, inventory costs, and variances in relation to standard cleaning procedures.

Effective scheduling permits the executive housekeeper to control salaries and wages and the costs related to employee benefits. It is important to schedule all housekeeping employees according to the guidelines in the property's staffing guide. Since the staffing guide bases its guidelines on the level of room occupancy, it ensures that personnel costs stay in line with occupancy rates. At the same time, the need for adequate staffing to maintain the desired level of service leaves the executive housekeeper little room to "cut corners" by scheduling fewer employees than the staffing guide recommends. The executive housekeeper can ensure that the approved guidelines expressed in the property's staffing guide are consistently followed in all employee scheduling decisions. Adjusting weekly work schedules in light of anticipated occupancy levels is an ongoing responsibility of the executive housekeeper.

Training and supervision should not be overlooked as a cost control measure. The recommendations in the property's staffing guide are based on the assumption that certain performance and productivity standards are consistently achieved. Effective training programs that quickly bring new hires "up to speed" can significantly reduce the time during which productivity is lower than the standards set for more experienced personnel. Close and diligent supervision, as well as refresher training, can ensure that performance and productivity standards are met—and may even bring about improvements. Finally, effective training and supervision are an important part of controlling the cost of inventoried items. For example, training employees in the proper use of cleaning supplies can improve usage rates and, over time, lower the cost of cleaning supplies per occupied room.

Efficient purchasing practices afford the executive housekeeper the greatest opportunity to control department expenses. The executive housekeeper bears an important responsibility to make sure that the hotel's money is well spent and the maximum value is received from products purchased for use.

Purchasing Systems

Efficient purchasing practices can make a significant contribution to the executive housekeeper's role in controlling housekeeping expenses. In fact, the most controllable expenses under the executive housekeeper's responsibility involve the various items whose inventories are maintained by the housekeeping department. Inventory control procedures enable the executive housekeeper to know when to buy and how much to buy for each inventoried item. Deciding what to buy, whom to buy it from, and exactly how to purchase it requires careful consideration on the part of the executive housekeeper.

Although the actual purchasing may be done by the hotel's purchasing department, quantities and specifications are submitted to the purchasing department by department heads. When ordering items for the housekeeping department, the executive housekeeper will need to fill out and sign a purchase order such as that shown in Exhibit 5. This order form then has to be approved by the controller and general manager. For all items purchased for the housekeeping department, the recommendation of the content, quantities, and source of a purchase is made by the executive housekeeper. Although various properties have various procedures for processing and approving purchases, the evaluation of what's needed, when it's needed, how much is needed, and from whom it is needed fall under the responsibility of department heads. The executive housekeeper needs to know how to obtain the best value when purchasing the items needed by the housekeeping department.

Linen Replacement

Next to salaries and wages, linens are the highest expense item in the housekeeping budget. The initial purchase of linens for the hotel will greatly influence the costs of replacing linens that become lost or are taken out of service due to damage or excessive wear. The fabric type, size, and color will influence both initial purchases and replacement costs. Colored items are usually more expensive and have shorter life spans than white ones since the colors fade through repeated washings.

The physical inventory records show the executive housekeeper how long the existing stock of linens will last and how much of each type of linen needs to be reordered to maintain par levels. Typically, linen purchases are made annually with deliveries scheduled to be drop-shipped on a quarterly basis. This arrangement enables the executive housekeeper to conserve available storage space by using a supplier's warehouse facilities while periodically receiving replacement stock.

Planning linen purchases on a yearly basis can also result in considerable savings. Linen brokers provide a convenient and quick way to purchase linens, but they are expensive. Ordering larger quantities in bulk can often win lower per-unit prices. Planned annual linen purchases also enable large hospitality chains to order linen supplies directly from linen mills. Although these orders require considerable lead time to prepare, a property saves on the premiums charged by linen brokers to process orders and arrange deliveries. Unforeseen emergency needs could then be filled through a linen broker.

Exhibit 5 Sample Purchase Order

Purchase Order

Purchase Order Number: ____________ Order Date: ____________

Payment Terms: ____________

To: ____________ (supplier) From/ Ship to: ____________ (name of operation)

____________ ____________

____________ (address) ____________ (address)

Delivery Date: ____________

Please Ship:

Quantity Ordered	Description	✔	Units Shipped	Unit Cost	Total Cost

Total Cost ____________

Important: This purchase order expressly limits acceptance to the terms and conditions stated above, noted on the reverse side hereof, and any additional terms and conditions affixed hereto or otherwise referenced. Any additional terms and conditions proposed by seller are objected to and rejected.

____
Authorized Signature

The quantity of linen to purchase is determined by assessing the hotel's quarterly requirements to maintain linen at the proper par level. Physical inventories of linens can be used to calculate an annual consumption rate that shows how much linen is "used up" either by normal wear and tear, damage, loss, or theft. With this information, the executive housekeeper can use the following formula to determine the size of annual linen purchases:

$$\text{Annual Order} = \text{Par Stock Level} - \text{Linen on Hand}$$

the Rooms
CHRONICLE®

Tips to Remember, Mistakes to Avoid When Purchasing

Whether it is for a 60-room limited-service property or a 1,500-room, full service resort, all managers inevitably face the challenge of procuring goods. As an agent dedicated to protecting the financial interests of the owner or operator, it is essential to produce the greatest output or service and to reduce costs to achieve a healthy bottom line. A strong purchasing program can effectively save money for the hotel and accomplish this goal.

Size Does Matter

The size of the hotel, either as a stand-alone property or collectively as part of a larger ownership or management portfolio, is the starting point for effective purchasing decisions. Remember that many pricing structures are based on volume.

Be realistic when negotiating prices for anything from bedding to linens and carpets to curtains. A 2,000-room resort will have a much higher usage rate and will be able to command much lower prices than the 300-room hotel just down the street. Realistically estimating one's buying leverage will save the buyer and the seller time and negotiation troubles as well as lost goodwill or good faith.

If intent on saving money on linens for example, the prudent manager should consider purchasing twice the supply now to obtain a lower price today, as opposed to purchasing two orders six months apart and paying a higher price. This could save a large amount of money, but there are drawbacks. A larger sum of capital is required to buy linens, and if it is tied up in linen inventory on the shelf, the hotel may not be able to commit the money to other needs or projects. The ultimate decision depends on what management values most: the savings derived from one large order or realizing the benefits of other investments that can be made with the funds.

Credibility Counts

During the bidding process, be truthful about the hotel's estimated usage. If the property is expecting to replace 100 mattresses in the next year do not tell suppliers that the estimated usage will be 125 or 150 mattresses. The deceiving hotel manager may find himself enjoying a large savings today but the long-term consequences will eventually bring a greater negative impact than the short-term economic benefit. The manager's credibility will likely become questionable and his hotel's purchasing reputation could be tarnished with that supplier.

Keep in mind that there are only a relatively small handful of hotel suppliers and institutional vendors in each market. And contrary to the assumed laws of competition, suppliers *do* talk to each other and share feedback regarding questionable accounts. Yes, the first year will be good while the hotel revels in its purchasing prowess. However, the vendor who feels that he or she was taken advantage of by an unscrupulous client will quietly increase that hotel's prices for supplies in the future, thus decreasing their bank account.

Rebates and Purchasing Promotions

If a purchasing manager is able to negotiate a custom price for a product, such as in-room coffee makers, he should not assume that the hotel will also be able to

(continued)

the Rooms
CHRONICLE®

(continued)

collect manufacturer's rebates and thus make the final acquisition price even lower. Many times, by buying certain products at the right time, a hotel can collect points towards future purchases. These points may not be available on already low negotiated prices. When faced with this situation, the manager must determine what is most important to the hotel: a lower price now or a greater discount later. The price will only go so low; it may go low in different promotions, but there is a bottom price.

Communicate Clearly

Effective communication is a key to success in every aspect of business and can be especially helpful in purchasing. Consider purchasing custom printed letterhead as well as purchase specification forms and bid request fax sheets. Make sure the hotel's purchasing policies, payment terms, and receiving hours are clearly outlined on the forms used during the bid process. This is important for several reasons.

First, exact purchase specifications and purchase quantity are necessary to enable competing suppliers to fairly and accurately bid on the exact same product. Also, this information will assist each vendor in determining whether they can fulfill the order according to the terms dictated. Without this information, problems invariably arise as one vendor may be bidding to supply the hotel with high-grade paper while another may be submitting a bid to supply lower-grade paper.

More significant than the probable price spread, the hotel may actually receive a different product than which it intended to acquire. This will require additional time, labor, and expense by both the hotel and the vendor to handle the refused goods, process the credit for refused merchandise, and to fulfill the original order as intended. More than likely, the vendor may actually lose money on the transaction to keep the hotel satisfied by providing the higher quality goods. A pattern of refusals by the hotel or misfulfillment by the vendor will inevitably lead to harsh feelings by both parties.

It's About Business

Finally, remember why the hotel is in business. The basic purpose of any business, including the hotel, is to make money by earning a profit through transactions. Now, remember why the hotel's suppliers are in business: to make money and earn a profit. Both parties need each other to survive; and both need strong communication and understanding from each other to grow their company.

The hotel and its vendors are not competitors; so work together, be honest, and communicate effectively, and both sides will be stronger in the end.

Source: Louis A. Quagliana, *The Rooms Chronicle®*, Volume 12, Number 2, p. 14.
For subscription information, please call 866-READ-TRC.

The executive housekeeper is expected to carefully select suppliers and linen products to ensure that the hotel receives good value for money spent. The most important considerations are the suitability of the products for their intended uses and whether the products are economical. Regarding linen, the expected useful life of the linen is often more important than purchase price in determining whether alternative products are economical or not. The cost of laundering linens over their useful life is usually much greater and more important than their initial price.

The life span of linen is measured in terms of how many times it can be laundered before becoming too worn to be suitable for guestroom use. Linen that is purchased at bargain prices but that wears out after only moderate laundering will damage guests' perceptions of quality, increase annual linen usage rates, and increase costs in the long run. Durability, laundry considerations, and purchase price are the main criteria to use in selecting linen. A cost per use can be calculated in order to evaluate alternative linen purchases using the following formula:

$$\text{Cost per use} = \frac{\text{Purchase Cost} + \text{Life span Laundering Costs}}{\text{Number of Life span Launderings}}$$

The laundering costs over the life span of a linen product can be determined by multiplying the item's weight by the hotel's laundering cost per pound—and then multiplying again by the number of launderings the item can withstand before showing excessive wear.

When orders of new linens are received, shipments should be checked against purchase orders and inspected to ensure that the linens meet all quality and quantity specifications. Newly received linen orders should be immediately moved to the main linen room for storage. In the main linen room, new linens that have not yet been put into service should be stored separately from linens that are already in use.

Inventories for all new linen received and issued at the hotel should be kept on a perpetual basis. This means that a running count should be kept for on-hand quantities of every type of new linen stored in the main linen room. The inventory record should show the linen type, specific item, price, storage location, and dates of ordering and receiving. As linen items are put into service to replace worn, damaged, lost, or stolen linen, the quantity recorded on the perpetual inventory record should be adjusted accordingly.

The executive housekeeper is responsible for placing new linen in use on an as-needed basis to maintain the par level for each linen item. Issuing new linen to be used in daily operations typically occurs each month on the basis of shortages revealed by a physical inventory. New linen may also be issued between physical inventories to replace discarded linens. Some hotels inject a predetermined quantity of new linen into circulation at preestablished intervals based on past usage rates. New linens should be placed into service on a "first-in, first-out" basis. New linen not in service should be under the control of the executive housekeeper or laundry supervisor in the main linen room or another secure place.

Uniform Replacement

Uniforms need to be replaced when they become damaged or worn. The executive housekeeper needs to establish a procedure for issuing new or replacement uniforms. A notation could be made on the employee's uniform card that a damaged uniform was received and discarded, and that a new uniform was issued. The date and the employee's signature should be recorded on the inventory card.

The executive housekeeper is generally responsible for receiving, storing, and controlling all new uniforms held in the hotel's custody but not placed into service. The executive housekeeper is also responsible for placing new uniforms into service to ensure that all uniform requirements are met, clean uniform replacements are available, and the laundry is not unduly burdened with clean uniform processing.

As with linens, the main criteria for purchasing replacement uniforms are durability, life span, and the quality of materials. The purchase price of uniforms is a secondary consideration. Comfort, practicality, and ease of maintenance are also important considerations. New uniforms should be purchased to maintain the par levels established for uniforms. Comparing the on-hand quantities with the established par levels will show the executive housekeeper how many replacement uniforms should be ordered.

Purchasing Operating Supplies

Some hotel chains have centralized, national purchasing systems for major housekeeping items in order to achieve quantity discounts. Other hotels may join together in purchasing groups to achieve savings on bulk purchases of commonly used items. But, for the most part, operating supplies are purchased by the individual property and with the direct involvement of the executive housekeeper.

Inventory tracking forms can be used to create an exhaustive list of operating supplies that the executive housekeeper will need to purchase on a regular basis. Inventory control procedures will show how often and in what quantities supply items will need to be purchased to maintain par levels. Usage rates and cost-per-occupied-room figures can be determined from the inventory records. This information can form the basis for an effective purchasing system. By following careful purchasing procedures, the executive housekeeper can help the hotel control costs while ensuring that adequate supply levels are maintained.

Before buying any product, the executive housekeeper should obtain samples in order to test the product and determine whether it meets specifications. Suitability for the intended task, quality, ease of handling, and storage requirements are just as important as the price in determining whether a product is economical.

Value—not price—should be the leading consideration in making purchase decisions. An inexpensive cleaning agent that has to be used in much larger quantities than a more expensive one may actually cost more in the long run. The crucial concern is to obtain the best value for the money.

Selecting the right vendors can often make the executive housekeeper's purchasing systems more efficient. The executive housekeeper needs to competitively shop suppliers and vendors for the products to be purchased on a regular basis. When asking for price quotations, the executive housekeeper needs to be as precise as possible regarding such specifications as weight, quality, packaging, size, concentration, quantities, and delivery times.

In evaluating alternative suppliers, the executive housekeeper needs to be concerned with how well the supplier will service the hotel's account. It is important that the vendors selected appreciate the operations of a hotel's housekeeping department, fully understand the products they sell, and be able to provide demonstrations and even training in how to use the products. It is not unusual for the executive housekeeper to select one vendor for all guest supply items, another for cleaning products, and still another for all paper products. By limiting the number of suppliers with whom the housekeeping department has to deal, the executive housekeeper can streamline the purchasing process, reduce paperwork, and use time more efficiently. In addition, concentrating business with a limited number of suppliers often achieves greater purchasing—and thereby bargaining—power, resulting in improved quantity discounts and better service.

Another consideration in selecting vendors is whether they will be able to stock the products the hotel purchases at their own warehouse facilities and drop-ship the products to the hotel on an as-needed basis. This enables the executive housekeeper to achieve savings by purchasing products in bulk whenever possible and, at the same time, solve the problem of limited storage space.

In the process of reordering operating supplies, the executive housekeeper needs to periodically reevaluate the suitability of existing products for their intended purposes. Meeting with housekeeping staff who use the product can help determine any problems that may lead to a reconsideration of quality or functionality. The functionality of the product should be tested, and the executive housekeeper should determine whether the existing specifications for the product should remain the same. Alternative products should be investigated and compared to existing products in terms of performance, durability, price, and value.

Worksheets can be used to monitor usage rates and costs for the various types of operating supplies kept in inventory. Exhibit 6 illustrates one such worksheet for tracking the use of various chemical cleaners. For each product, the Monthly Chemical Use Report identifies the vendor, the product name, and its intended use. Each month, physical inventories provide the executive housekeeper with information concerning how many purchase units of each chemical cleaner have been used. Multiplying the number of units used by the cost per unit yields the total cost of the product used during the month. Dividing the total cost by the number of occupied rooms yields a cost per occupied room figure for each product. By reducing the size of each purchase unit (e.g., gallons, cans, pints, quarts) to a common-sized unit (e.g., ounces) and multiplying the number of purchase units used by the common-sized amounts, the total amount used for each product can be determined in terms that render the different-sized products comparable. After using a common measure to calculate the actual amounts used, the executive housekeeper can divide by the number of occupied rooms to determine the usage of each product per occupied room. In this way, the Monthly Chemical Use Report enables the executive housekeeper to compare the relative efficiency of using various products for similar tasks. By comparing the costs per occupied room and the usage per occupied room achieved by alternative products, the executive housekeeper can evaluate which products yield greater cost savings and make purchasing decisions accordingly.

Capital Budgets

Purchases of most inventoried items in the housekeeping department occur monthly. These costs appear in the operating budget as expenses against the revenue

Exhibit 6 Monthly Chemical Use Report

For April, 20XX Number of Occupied Rooms 25,410									
VENDOR	PRODUCT	INTENDED USE	UNITS USED	COST PER UNIT	TOTAL COST	COST PER OCC. ROOM	AMOUNT PER UNIT	TOTAL UNITS	USAGE PER OCC. ROOM
Johnson	G.P. Forward	All-purpose cleaner	108 gal.	$15.48	$1,671.84	$.066	128 oz.	13,824	.544
Johnson	Spartan	Degreaser	39 gal.	17.02	663.78	.026	128 oz.	4,992	.196
Johnson	Brady	Floor stripper	48 gal.	25.28	1,213.44	.048	128 oz.	6,144	.242
Armstrong	S-490	Special area stripper	5 gal.	25.88	129.40	.005	23 oz.	115	.005
Johnson	Complete	Composition floor wax	142 gal.	26.32	3,737.44	.147	128 oz.	18,176	.715
Johnson	Fortify	Porous floor seal	67 gal.	34.20	2,291.40	.090	128 oz.	8,576	.338
Johnson	Snap Back	Spray buff	.5 gal.	40.00	20.00	.001	128 oz.	64	.003
Johnson	Conq-R-Dust	Dust mop treatment	10 can	4.58	45.80	.002	128 oz.	1,280	.050
Dillon Chem	Waterless Cleaner	Wood floor stripper	35 gal.	12.80	448.00	.018	128 oz.	4,480	.176
Ecolab	Revitalize	Carpet shampoo	17 gal.	26.01	442.17	.017	128 oz.	2,176	.086
Amrep	Misty	Steam cleaner	6 gal.	11.61	69.66	.003	128 oz.	768	.030
Johnson	Carpet Odor Eliminator	Powdered deodorant	3 can	3.65	10.95	.001	24 oz.	120	.005
Core	Unbelievable	Carpet spotter	70 pints	6.72	470.40	.019	16 oz.	1,120	.044
SSS	Gum Remover	Tar & gum remover	61 can	4.86	296.46	.012	12 oz.	732	.029
Dumond C	Lift Away	Graffiti remover	3 can	14.95	44.85	.002	15 oz.	45	.002
Zep	Once Over	Wall & vinyl cleaner	27 can	5.95	160.65	.006	22.5 oz.	608	.024
Ecover	Ecological	Bathroom bowl cleaner	3 quart	4.69	14.07	.001	32 oz.	96	.004
P-G	Safeguard Dispenser	Dispenser soap	12 gal.	15.31	183.72	.007	128 oz.	1,536	.060
Johnson	Lemon Shine Up	Furniture polish	35 can	11.04	386.40	.015	15 oz.	525	.021
3M	Stainless Steel Polish	Metal cleaner	52 can	11.04	574.08	.023	21.5 oz.	1,118	.044
3M	Tarni-Shield	Brass cleaner	43 bottle	9.42	405.06	.016	10 oz.	430	.017
	Vinegar	Neutralizer	26 gal.	1.59	41.34	.002	128 oz.	3,328	.131

generated over the same period. Major purchases of machines and equipment in the housekeeping department are not included on operating budgets. Instead, purchases for items with relatively high costs and long life spans are planned as part of capital budgets because they involve additional capital investments by the hotel.

Capital budgets are prepared annually. The executive housekeeper will be asked to specify the need for funds to purchase machines and equipment for the housekeeping department. It is crucial that the executive housekeeper be prepared to justify any requests for capital expenditures. Although such requests may be part of an overall modernization or renovation program, they more typically involve a need to replace existing machines or equipment.

Typically, the need to replace major machines and equipment is discovered when a particular item cannot be repaired. However, the executive housekeeper can effectively predict the useful life of each machine in the housekeeping department based on how often it is used and its estimated number of working hours, provided by the machine's manufacturer and supplier. Executive housekeepers should be aware, however, that machines and equipment that receive high usage will not live up to the guarantees and estimates of useful life provided by suppliers.

When purchasing housekeeping equipment, executive housekeepers need to focus on long-range considerations. Major purchases of machines and equipment represent a capital expense for the hotel, and planning is required. Whenever possible, it is important to choose a supplier who can service the machines in a quick and efficient manner. If such a supplier cannot be found, the executive housekeeper will need to order an adequate number of replacement parts so that the hotel itself will be able to service the machines.

The executive housekeeper is expected to be able to recommend the proper type, quality, and quantity of equipment needed to keep guestrooms and public areas clean and attractive. The housekeeping department needs equipment that will last through continuous use with a minimum of maintenance. Cost effectiveness is the most important consideration. As always, purchase price needs to be considered along with the quality and durability of the product.

Contract vs. In-House Cleaning

A number of outside contractors offer a variety of cleaning services to hotels. Outside contractors are available for nearly any cleaning task that needs to be done, including outside laundry and dry-cleaning services, floor cleaning and care, outside window cleaning, overhead cleaning, masonry cleaning, and descaling and scouring of restroom fixture traps. Given these services, a hotel could even use outside contractors for its entire housekeeping operation.

An important decision that arises in an increasing number of contexts is whether to contract outside services for cleaning tasks or undertake them as in-house operations. The issue is often approached in terms of how to best control costs while ensuring that necessary tasks are accomplished and quality standards are maintained. In many situations, the issue is one that involves both capital budget and operating budget considerations.

While wages and materials are monthly expenses that can be budgeted, the equipment needed to start an in-house cleaning program is a capital expense that occurs all at once. Often, after the initial start-up cost for machines and equipment, the monthly expense that the hotel will incur with an in-house cleaning program is less than the monthly expense it would incur with an outside contractor. In addition, many executive housekeepers believe that an in-house staff will perform higher-quality work than an outside contractor because of the opportunity for increased control.

The executive housekeeper may be asked to demonstrate how long it would take to recover the initial start-up costs for machines and equipment through the monthly savings achieved by an in-house cleaning program. By dividing the savings achieved each month into the total amount of capital expenditure for the needed equipment, the executive housekeeper can calculate how many months it would take to pay back the initial investment. In determining monthly expenses that an in-house operation would incur, the executive housekeeper needs to consider the costs of salaries and wages, employee benefits, materials and supplies, training, and supervision. The decision as to whether the initial investment is possible and worth the monthly savings is one that belongs to the hotel's upper management and ultimately to the owners.

In some situations, the initial start-up costs are deemed too high for the monthly savings achieved. In other cases, the nature of the cleaning task may be so specialized or infrequent that initiating an in-house cleaning program is not reasonable or cost-efficient. In still other situations, the monthly expense for outside contractors is lower than the monthly expenses an in-house operation would incur in performing the same tasks. There are always pros and cons to consider when assessing the need for contracted cleaning services.

For whatever reason, the executive housekeeper will sometimes be charged with the task of arranging for outside contractors to perform some cleaning service. The initial problem is choosing the appropriate contractor. The executive housekeeper should request cost estimates from at least three different contractors. For area cleaning tasks, contractors base quotations on the exact size of the area to be cleaned; the executive housekeeper cannot collect comparable cost quotations until exact measurements are obtained. For laundering tasks, quotations are based on dry weight or on a per-piece basis. Quotations also specify the frequency of the service desired as well as collection and delivery times. For any kind of contract cleaning, the executive housekeeper should obtain cost quotations on the basis of carefully defined needs, precise descriptions of work, and clear indications of the frequency of service. The same specifications should be submitted to each contractor to ensure that cost estimates are fully comparable.

Both previous and current clients of each contractor should be checked for reports on the quality and efficiency of the services. The reputation and ability of the contractor's local organization, as opposed to the credentials of the home office, should be assessed. Visiting the contractor's place of business may provide insights into the kind of operation the contractor runs.

After selecting an appropriate contractor, it is important to establish the precise nature and frequency of the services desired in the written contract. The terminology describing the task, frequency, and expected performance needs to be as clear and precise as possible. All contracts should incorporate a cancellation clause. Certain contracts should also have penalty clauses to ensure compliance with all specifications.

After contracting an outside cleaning service, it is essential to monitor the quality of the contractor's work. Routine inspections and regular meetings with the contractor will enable the executive housekeeper to identify and discuss any problems or concerns in a timely manner. Assigned tasks and completion dates should be discussed clearly and documented in writing. It is also important to monitor invoices received from outside contractors; invoices should be checked for accuracy before being submitted to the accounting department for payment.

While the use of outside contractors for cleaning services appears to be increasing in the hospitality industry, the executive housekeeper should periodically assess whether replacing outside services with in-house operations can be justified as a cost control measure. After the initial capital investment in machines

Can Contract Cleaning Save the Day? Or Should the Hotel Save Its Money?

Whether the hotel is large or small, sometimes there are cleaning jobs that require outside help. It may be that the staff does not have the equipment, supplies, time, or personnel to perform the job.

That's when contract cleaners are called. Love them or hate them, contract cleaners play an important role in the hotel industry. Some of the more common jobs contracted are window washing, carpet shampooing, kitchen cleaning, third-shift public space cleaning, and renovation cleanup. Here are some things to consider before signing an agreement.

Advantages of Using Contract Cleaners

- They provide generally skilled laborers, well trained in their areas of expertise.
- They provide all supplies and equipment.
- They provide uniformed workers and have responsibility for all wages and benefits.
- Their workers stay on the job until it is done.
- They are accountable for the results.

Disadvantages of Using Contract Cleaners

- Workers are not representatives of the hotel and may not have skills for guest interaction.
- Workers may not show up within the time frame designated.
- Contract cleaners may not meet the hotel's standards for quality.

Tips for Making It Work

1. Obtain at least three bids for the job. Make sure a representative of each company visits the property to review the project before bidding. Ask the companies to list the equipment and supplies that will be used.
2. Work only with companies that are well established and recommended. A minimum of five years in the business should be required.
3. Check references thoroughly, and visit other job sites.
4. Inquire about the training provided to each company's workers.
5. Write time expectations for the job into the contract.
6. Write the hotel's quality expectations into the contract.
7. Verify insurance coverage for workers, guests, hotel employees, and assets.

(continued)

the Rooms CHRONICLE® *(continued)*

8. Greet the cleaners when they arrive, and review the job parameters.
9. Visit the job site shortly after work has begun to ensure that the hotel's expectations are being met.
10. Give the project a walk-down at completion to review the contractor's work.
11. Never pay in advance.

Source: Mary Friedman, *The Rooms Chronicle®*, Volume 3, Number 5, p. 4.
For subscription information, please call 866-READ-TRC.

and equipment is recovered through monthly savings in operating expenses, the reduced costs and increased control that often accompanies in-house operations can be of significant value to the property.

Key Terms

capital budget—A detailed plan for the acquisition of equipment, land, buildings, and other fixed assets.

capital expenditures—Items costing $1,500 or more that are not used up in the normal course of operations, and that have a life span that exceeds a single year.

income statement—A report on the profitability of operations, including revenues earned and expenses incurred in generating the revenues for the period covered by the statement.

operating budget—A detailed plan for generating revenue and incurring expenses for each department within the hospitality operation.

operating expenditures—Costs incurred in order to generate revenue in the normal course of doing business.

pro forma income statement—A report that predicts the results of current or future operations, including revenues earned and expenses incurred in generating the revenues for the period covered by the statement.

schedule—A report which gives supporting detail to a property's financial statements.

Review Questions

1. What are the basic responsibilities of the executive housekeeper in the budget process?
2. What is the difference between a capital budget and an operating budget?

3. Why is forecasting occupancy levels such a critical part of the budget-planning process?
4. How can the operating budget be used as a tool to control expenses?
5. What is the relationship of an operating budget to an income statement?
6. What are some of the typical expenses (or line items) an executive housekeeper might encounter when preparing the department's budget?
7. What two factors can help the executive housekeeper predict a certain level of expense for each expense category?
8. What are the four basic methods an executive housekeeper can use to control expenses?
9. What basic responsibilities does the executive housekeeper have in terms of purchasing operating supplies?
10. What types of situations should be assessed when deciding whether to use outside contractors for cleaning services?

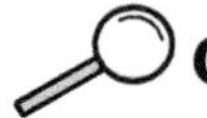

Case Study

Dangerous Discrepancies

Herbert McMurtry, the general manager of the Hotel Commodore, convened a 10:00 A.M. meeting with the hotel's front office manager, executive housekeeper, and chief engineer. Mr. McMurtry was frustrated because that morning's report revealed six vacant rooms charged to guests who had already left a day or two earlier, an error that has become too common.

As his imposing figure entered the small meeting room, Mr. McMurtry opened the meeting: "I want to thank you all for meeting with me this morning because I have a number of things to cover and I don't want to hold you up from your jobs...Oh," he paused, furrowing his brow, "Where's Todd?"

Just as Mr. McMurtry finished his question, Todd, the front desk manager, burst into the room, "I'm so sorry to be late, Mr. McMurtry," Todd said. "I had another darn discrepant room to deal with."

"That's just why I wanted to speak with all of you." Mr. McMurtry continued. "I'm getting pretty upset because the property has been losing revenue due to chargebacks. To make matters worse, last week I had to deal with a very angry Ms. Spencer, of the Spencer Spinet Company, who flew here all the way from New York just to check into a dirty room. She is a regular, high-paying customer of our hotel and now she'll probably take her business elsewhere. And this wasn't the first time I had to face this sort of complaint. I'd like to find out what's going on here. I have a feeling your departments aren't communicating. If this keeps up, it's going to affect our bottom line *and* your bonuses."

Todd quickly spoke up, "Well, most of the time we get a chargeback because a guest neglects to notify the front desk upon checking out, sometimes days before the expected check-out time. We bill guests as originally booked but, if they claim that they checked out earlier, we have to reimburse them, their room is never rented, and we lose out. I think we should physically check all the rooms for occupancy each afternoon."

Isabel, the executive housekeeper, immediately responded, "I don't know, Todd, you have to consider the increased labor costs and the demands on my staff. Room checks are just Band-Aids to cover up bigger problems. There must be a better way to handle it. Let's think of ways to encourage guests to let us know when they've checked out. Perhaps the housekeeping staff can help."

"I don't know about chargebacks," Tomas, the hotel's chief engineer said, "but I think if everyone just followed our established procedures for out-of-order rooms, we wouldn't have problems with guests checking into unready rooms."

"Oh, c'mon Tom," Todd chimed in. "I'm under pressure to fill rooms. Frankly, maintenance can be too slow for me. If I have a potential sell-out, my staff checks the out-of-order rooms. If one looks good, I sell it."

Mr. McMurtry cast Todd an irritated glance. "While we can't afford to have rooms sitting vacant, giving someone an out-of-order room is just plain bad for business, Todd," he stressed. "There's no guarantee that your staff will know what's wrong with the room from a brief visual check. We need a more experienced eye than yours."

Tomas agreed, "Remember when the Paper Clip Manufacturers Association was in town for a convention and we checked someone into a room with a plumbing leak? The room was out-of-order when he checked in but, because we were at full capacity, we used the room anyway. We had to move him to another hotel because he wound up with two inches of standing water in the bathroom!"

"There's also the problem with discrepant rooms you faced before coming to this meeting, Todd," Isabel added, "My staff cleans rooms by noon and then an hour later the rooms are listed as dirty. How does that happen?"

"If guests check into rooms and then aren't satisfied," replied Todd, trying not to get defensive, "I move them to other rooms. The computer is programmed to default their original rooms as dirty."

"But I know that some of those guests never even *see* the room," Isabel replied. "They just change their minds right at the front desk. It would be better for all of us if the front desk would automatically redesignate those rooms as clean and vacant."

"I see your point," Todd said, trying to be patient, "but my staff is really busy too and it interferes with our other work if we are constantly switching back and forth on our computer screens. The worst thing I can do is keep guests waiting while I fiddle with the computer."

Mr. McMurtry quickly responded to Todd's last point, "Yes, but there's also no sense in hurrying guests to unprepared rooms or making them wait for rooms that are ready."

The conversation was heating up and Mr. McMurtry could see that they might be sitting there for the rest of the day if he didn't cut it short. "We've talked about a lot here. Now I want you all to agree on at least three solutions to these problems and come back to me with an action plan by the end of the day." With that he excused his managers and waited for the good news to roll his way.

Discussion Questions

1. What solutions would you suggest for reducing chargebacks within the hotel?
2. How can the different divisions within the Hotel Commodore cooperate to resolve conflicts over room status?
3. What are some ways in which the front office could eliminate room discrepancies?

Case Study

Lean Profits in a Land of Plenty

The 600-room Knightsrest Hotel, a property catering largely to business travelers, is in a good location near an airport and a busy government facility. Though the hotel seldom reaches full occupancy, it does good business. Still, the owners have been disappointed by the profit margins. The general manager, Nancy Wood, has determined that one element contributing to the hotel's unacceptable financial performance is that housekeeping expenses are way out of line. When she mentioned this to Sue Miller, the executive housekeeper, they agreed to hire Bonnie Hansen, a housekeeping consultant, to come in and look at the Knightsrest's housekeeping operations.

Bonnie begins her consultation by asking Sue how supplies are ordered. Sue explains that the hotel has a standing order placed every two weeks to replace supplies "assumed" to have been used.

As Bonnie walks around the property, she notes a number of things. All room attendants have access to the main storeroom, which is left open, and are expected to stock their own carts. Throughout the hotel, most housekeeper caddies are stocked with the same brand name cleaning supplies (purchased, as Sue explains to Bonnie, at great savings from a discount house), although the amount of supplies on each cart varies widely. Bonnie hears some room attendants explain that they occasionally stock their carts with extra supplies because the main storeroom too frequently runs out of certain items. Some carts have brand name items Bonnie did not see in the main storeroom. Bonnie also notes that the linen closets on each floor are filled with housekeeping supplies; in fact, housekeeping supplies seem to be stored in just about every nook and cranny available, including telephone equipment rooms. Some supplies are crammed so tightly into spaces that they are damaged. This is particularly true of guest stationery items imprinted with the hotel's logo.

As Bonnie looks through the guestrooms, she notes that the same high-quality amenities are used in all rooms. In stayover rooms, new soap and shampoo are left every day. She sees a room attendant using furniture polish on Formica™ surfaces. The room attendant tells her that this is her own personal touch. "They want us to use just water," explains the room attendant, "but this smells nice." This room attendant also explains to Bonnie that the cleaning chemical provided by the hotel for use on bathtubs refuses to suds up, so she and many other room attendants add the hotel guestroom shampoo to improve the chemical's effectiveness.

Throughout the day, Bonnie observes housekeeping staff using only large 3.0 mil garbage bags, many only half-filled when discarded. Walking through the kitchens, she notes employees wearing shower caps with hotel logos over their hair. She watches as the public space cleaner, Tom Harper, runs back and forth for supplies. First, Tom notices a bit of mud on the floor, so he leaves to get a mop and bucket. After cleaning up the mud, he notices some smudged windows, so he returns the mop and bucket and eventually returns with window cleaning supplies. Finally, he leaves once more and returns a few minutes later with a vacuum cleaner. The vacuum's suction is weak; apparently the bag is full.

On her rounds, Bonnie sees several employees reading *USA Today* during their breaks. Sue explains to her that the hotel orders one copy per room. Bonnie also notes that virtually all employees—including managers—use the hotel's logo notepads, ordered as guestroom amenities.

On her way to the general manager's office to talk with Ms. Wood and Sue, Bonnie sees that each of the executive offices has its own coffee maker and everyone seems to use the single-serving coffee supplies that are charged to housekeeping for guestroom use. Bonnie sees guestroom hand lotion bottles sitting on many desks as well as tissue boxes, pens, and desk organizers like those she saw stocked in the main housekeeping storeroom.

Discussion Questions

1. What problems and weaknesses is Bonnie likely to identify in her discussion with Ms. Wood and Sue?
2. What suggestions might she make to address these problems and weaknesses?

The following industry experts helped generate and develop these cases: Gail Edwards, CHHE, St. Louis, Missouri; Mary Friedman, Edina, Minnesota; and Aleta Nitschke, CHA, founder of *The Rooms Chronicle*®, Garfield, Minnesota.

Chapter

11

Safety and Security

Chapter Outline

Chapter Overview

Hotel guests depend upon the hotel to maintain an environment in which they will be as safe as possible. Guests, however, are not the only people concerned about safety. Employees count on the hotel to provide working conditions that allow them to do their jobs free from concerns about unnecessary risks. The owners of a hotel want its managers to develop practices and procedures that will safeguard the hotel's assets and minimize the owner's legal liability. In addition, there are governmental agencies at all levels that are charged with monitoring the safety-related efforts of hotels.

The hotel industry is committed to safety. To achieve this goal, it relies upon a variety of internal security–oriented tools, including recodable locks, alarm systems, surveillance systems, and emergency plans that can be used to reduce safety and security risks. In this chapter, you will learn about all of these. You will also learn how external resources, such as local law enforcement personnel and the hotel's insurers, help properties to be safe and secure.

Depending on their location and the services offered, some hotels have unique safety and security issues. These include protecting guests in swimming pool areas, spas, exercise areas, and, in many cases, parking lots. While hoteliers cannot guarantee their guests' safety, they have a responsibility to exercise reasonable care in protecting the welfare of guests. In this chapter, you will learn how hotels can meet the reasonable-care standard.

Threats to the security of hotel assets can come from both internal and external sources. To protect assets adequately, programs must be in place to guard against threats of both types. In this chapter, you will learn about ways to reduce the chances of incurring losses due to dishonest guests and employees. In some cases, safety and security threats are unique to specific hotel departments. For example, in the front office, cash is routinely kept on hand and must be safeguarded while the housekeeping department must control theft of room supplies and furnishings by both employees and guests. This chapter examines in detail the important and specific security concerns of the front office, housekeeping, food and beverage, sales and marketing, and maintenance and engineering departments.

Taken from Foundations of Lodging Management, Second Edition, by David K. Hayes, Jack D. Ninemeier and Allisha A. Miller

Even in the best managed properties, the risk of a safety- or security-related crisis is real, and all hotel employees must know how to respond. In this chapter, you will learn how a hotel's crisis management plan can help address the many concerns that can arise when a hotel faces or experiences a severe safety or security threat.

Chapter Objectives

1. To stress the importance of keeping hotel guests and employees safe.
2. To identify a variety of internal and external resources available to help hoteliers meet their safety and security goals.
3. To describe to you safety threats that are unique to the hotel industry.
4. To stress the importance of property security.
5. To identify internal, external, and area-specific threats to hotel security.

THE IMPORTANCE OF SAFETY

Regardless of the size of the hotel, all of its employees must be concerned about **safety** and **security**.

LODGING LANGUAGE

Safety: Protection of an individual's physical well-being and health.

Security: Protection of an individual's or business's property and other assets.

Concern for the safety of guests and the security of their possessions is not merely good business; it is also a legal responsibility of the hotel's ownership and becomes an important responsibility of each hotel staff member. Employees and other non-guests visiting the hotel also have a legal right to expect their health and well-being to be protected by management.

Legal Liability for Guest and Employee Safety

Since the earliest days of travel, hotel guests have been rightfully concerned about their safety, especially when they were sleeping. Innkeepers and hoteliers responded to these concerns by striving to provide a safe haven for travelers. In addition to the good intentions of hotel managers, however, there are specific laws that require those who operate hotels to provide the traveling public with a safe and secure environment. These laws, however, do not hold hotels directly responsible for everything that could happen to guests during their stay.

For example, a guest may slip and fall in a bathtub. The hotel will not be held responsible for any resulting injuries if it is determined that it has exercised **reasonable care** in the manner in which it provides and maintains its bathtubs.

LODGING LANGUAGE

Reasonable care: A legal concept identifying the amount of care a reasonably prudent person would exercise in a specific situation.

Assume, however, that the hotel had purchased bathtubs with surfaces that were well-known to become extraordinarily slippery when wet. Assume also that many guests had slipped and fallen in the tubs and that management knew about these instances. In addition, assume that the hotel's franchisor, on several occasions when the hotel was inspected, had advised the hotel's owners to install slip-resistant materials on the floor of the tubs to reduce the chances of injury. If, in the face of this information, the hotel's

Correctly programmed key cards and properly working door locks are a few examples of important safety and security controls.

owners refused to install the non-slip surfaces, they would, in all likelihood, be held liable, to some degree for the guest's fall if a lawsuit was filed.

As an hotelier, it is important to remember that the legal standard of reasonable care means that you must operate your hotel with a degree of care equal to that of other reasonable persons (i.e., reasonable hoteliers). For example, if you know, or should have known, about a threat to the safety of your guests, it is reasonable to assume that you would either immediately eliminate the threat or clearly inform your guests of it. Not doing so would indicate that you exhibited an absence of reasonable care for the safety of your guests.

If a threat to guest safety results in loss or injury, and it is determined that the hotel did not exercise reasonable care in regard to that threat, the hotel may be held wholly or partially liable for the resulting loss or injury. If a hotel is found to be liable for injuries to a guest or employee, it will likely have to bear the cost of that liability. For example, assume that a hotel manager knew about a defective lock on a guest room door but did not authorize an immediate repair. Subsequently a guest rented the room with the defective lock and was robbed and assaulted by an assailant who obtained unlawful entry to the room through the door with the defective lock. In this case, it is highly likely that an attorney hired by the guest to seek **damages** against the hotel would be successful. In this hypothetical case, the damages could include **compensatory damages** and possibly even **punitive damages**.

LODGING LANGUAGE

Damages: The actual amount of losses or costs incurred due to the wrongful act of a liable party.

Compensatory damages: A monetary amount intended to compensate injured parties for actual losses or damage they have incurred. This typically includes such items as medical bills and lost wages. Also known as "actual damages."

Punitive damages: A monetary amount assessed to punish liable parties and to serve as an example to the liable party as well as others not to commit the wrongful act in the future.

These damages could result in extremely large amounts of money the hotel would be required to pay the injured guest—costs that could have been avoided had the guest room lock been repaired, as it should have been, in a timely manner.

It is important to note that hoteliers do not do their job of maintaining a safe property properly simply to avoid paying damages. A demonstrated concern for guest safety is

LODGING ONLINE

Some hoteliers take the issues of guest safety and security so seriously that they have established separate trade associations designed to assist one another's safety efforts. Canadian hoteliers are leaders in this area. To view the Web site of the Alberta Hotel Safety Association (AHSA), go to:

www.albertahotelsafety.com

How important to you is safety when you choose a hotel?

not merely a good business practice; it is also the right thing to do. Guest safety is an important part of every hotel employee's job, and it is the job of the hotel's managers to make sure that employees, as well as guests, are safe while on the property.

Hotel Responsibility for Guest Safety

You have learned that a hotel can be held legally responsible for the results of injury to guests (and employees) if it does not exercise reasonable care. To demonstrate reasonable care, a hotel must address three main issues. These are:

1. The hotel's facility
2. The hotel's staff
3. Policies and procedures implemented by the hotel

Each of these plays an important part in the safety and security of overnight guests and those who work in or visit a hotel.

FACILITY

Every hotel offers different products and services to guests in a variety of different locations and settings. Each hotel, however, should be as safe as possible. This is not to imply that accidents cannot happen, but rather that the management and staff of the hotel should develop and maintain an active **threat analysis** program.

LODGING LANGUAGE

Threat analysis: A systematic procedure designed to identify and eliminate identifiable safety risks.

A threat analysis program is an organized procedure by which a hotel facility is assessed for possible hazards. For example, in a hotel with a parking lot, the lights in the parking area should be periodically checked to see if they are functioning properly. If it is discovered that they are not working properly, they pose a potential safety hazard and that hazard must be eliminated by repairing the lights.

In some cases, it may not be possible to completely eliminate a safety risk. When this is the case, reasonable care demands that guests *must* be informed of the risk. For example, most observers would agree that entering a hotel's swimming pool without a lifeguard present presents a risk to safety. However, most hotels with swimming pools do not employ a full-time lifeguard during the time the pool is open for use by guests.

In this case, the known risk (absence of a life guard) must be communicated to guests. Signage can be developed to communicate the risk. Possible wording alternatives, posted in the pool area in the language(s) of guests, and in a highly visible location, might include:

- Swim At Your Own Risk
- No Lifeguard On Duty
- Adult Swimmers Only

- Children Must Be Supervised By An Adult
- Children Under the Age of 16 Must Be Supervised by an Adult
- No Running or Diving

Note that each of these statements seeks to inform swimmers about risks related to swimming in an area without a lifeguard present. In most cases, if no lifeguard is present during most of the time a hotel's pool is open, the hotel's **insurer** would provide or suggest the actual language to be used to inform swimmers of their safety risk.

LODGING LANGUAGE

Insurer: The entity providing insurance coverage to a business.

Additional steps that can be taken in a threat analysis program are to prohibit behavior by guests and others that could pose a threat to safety. For example, a hotel might establish and enforce a policy prohibiting the use of glassware (glass bottles or drinking glasses) in a pool area. It would do so to eliminate the threat to safety that could come from broken, and thus nearly invisible, glass fragments in a pool area where people are likely to be bare-footed.

Each hotel facility will have its own safety issues; however, three steps are important parts of an effective threat analysis program and can help to demonstrate a hotel's commitment to using reasonable care to protect guests from harm. These three steps include:

Identifying and removing known threats to safety

Informing guests about any remaining safety threats

Prohibiting behavior that is known to create safety threats

STAFF TRAINING

It takes the effort of every employee in the hotel to eliminate, to the greatest degree possible, threats to the safety and security of guests and their property. In larger hotels, there may be a full-time director of safety and security and a staff of departmental employees who routinely patrol the hotel's grounds, make safety and security checks, and direct the hotel's safety programs. In other cases, the hotel may contract with a private security firm to provide security services. In still other cases, off-duty police may be hired to assist with the hotel's security efforts. However, even in the smallest of limited-service hotels, all employees need to be trained in security and safety methods.

Training employees to protect guests and themselves and to assist with the hotel's security efforts is an ongoing process. One way to view the safety-training needs of employees is to think about the training required by all employees and the training essential only to members of a specific department. For example, teaching all employees to promptly report any unauthorized or suspicious person found loitering in the hotel's parking lot is appropriate, whereas training about the safe handling of food would be appropriate only for those employed in the food and beverage department.

Specific hotels or hotel companies develop and implement many detailed safety-training programs. In addition, excellent training materials related to safety and security are developed and continually updated by the Educational Institute of the American Hotel & Lodging Association (E.I.). These materials are made available to hotels at a very reasonable cost.

In most limited-service hotels, safety and security is not a completely separate department. Instead, safety and security programs are administered within each hotel department and are overseen by the general manager or a designated **safety and security committee**.

LODGING LANGUAGE

Safety and Security committee: An interdepartmental task force consisting of hotel managers, supervisors, and hourly-paid employees responsible for monitoring and refining a hotel's safety and security efforts.

LODGING ONLINE

The Educational Institute (E.I.) offers a variety of safety- and security-related training products suitable for all of a hotel's employees and other programs that are departmental-specific. In addition, E.I. offers a self-paced training program leading to the Certified Lodging Security Officer designation (CLSO). To learn about that program and others, go to:

www.ei-ahla.org/

When you arrive, enter "Safety and Security" in the search field.

Do you think every hotel should have a CLSO on its staff?

Many hotels find that maintaining an effective safety and security committee is preferable to a separate safety and security department because the very operation of interdepartmental committee reinforces the message that guest safety and hotel security is the responsibility of every one of its managers, supervisors, and employees.

Regardless of the size or organizational structure of the hotel's safety and security efforts, the training of employees is a key component of any effective program.

Managers are not the only persons interested in the safety of a hotel's employees. In 1970, the federal government passed the Occupational Safety and Health Act, which created, within the Department of Labor, the Occupational Safety and Health Administration **(OSHA)**.

LODGING LANGUAGE

Occupational Safety and Health Administration (OSHA): A federal agency established in 1970 that is responsible for developing and enforcing regulations to help ensure safe and healthful working conditions.

The purpose of the Occupational Safety and Health Act is to bring about safe and healthful working conditions. OSHA has been very aggressive in enforcing the rights of workers. Together with its state-level partners, OSHA has more than 2,000 inspectors and additional complaint-discrimination investigators, engineers, physicians, educators, standards writers, and other technical and support personnel located in over 200 offices throughout the country. This staff establishes and enforces protective standards, and assists employers and employees through technical assistance and consultation programs.

All hotels are legally required to comply with the extensive safety practices, equipment specifications, and employee communication procedures mandated by OSHA. Among other mandates, the OSHA requirements call upon employers to:

- Provide a safe workplace for employees by complying with OSHA safety and health standards
- Provide workers with needed tools and equipment that meet OSHA specifications for health and safety
- Establish training programs for employees who operate potentially dangerous equipment
- Report to OSHA immediately (within 8 hours) any worksite accident that results in a fatality or requires the hospitalization of three or more employees
- Maintain the "OSHA 300" form (an on-site record of work-related injuries or illnesses) and keep it available for inspection for a period of five years
- Display OSHA notices about employee rights and safety in prominent places within the hotel
- Provide all employees access to the Material Safety Data Sheets (MSDS) that provide information about the dangerous chemicals they may be handling during work
- Offer no-cost hepatitis-B vaccinations for employees who may have come in contact with blood or other body fluids

LODGING ONLINE

OSHA maintains an active Web site with valuable information that can be easily accessed. To stay current on OSHA regulations and enforcement programs, visit and bookmark:

www.osha.gov/

How do you think hotel managers can best keep up with changing OSHA requirements?

OSHA inspectors have the legal authority to inspect a hotel to see whether it is in compliance with their regulations. When OSHA was established, few businesses viewed it as a partner in their worker-safety efforts. Today, astute hoteliers recognize that compliance with OSHA standards results in fewer accidents, lower insurance costs, and a healthier workforce.

In addition to OSHA, hotel operators may find that there are state and local laws regarding employee safety that also must be followed. In some cases, a state or local governmental agency may share responsibility for enforcing employee and guest safety-related issues. For example, in most cities, the local fire department will be responsible for ensuring that locally required fire-suppression systems are in place and operational.

POLICIES AND PROCEDURES

The specific safety and security policies and procedures that are best for an individual hotel will vary based upon its size, location, physical layout, and the guest amenities offered. In all cases, however, written policies and procedures help inform all hotel employees of what is expected when responding to safety and security threats. While a text or a legal manual can identify the importance of standardized policies and procedures, each hotel must consider its own property-specific threats, concerns, and solutions. These solutions, formalized in writing and consistently followed by every employee, will go a long way toward confirming that the hotel consistently demonstrates reasonable care.

SAFETY RESOURCES

Fortunately, hoteliers have a number of resources at their disposal as they seek to create lodging environments that are safe and secure. In this section, we will examine some of the most important of these.

Internal Resources

Internal safety and security systems have advanced rapidly in the lodging industry. Among the most important internal tools available to hoteliers are:

- Recodable locks
- Alarm systems
- Surveillance systems
- Emergency plans

The appropriate selection and use of these tools depends upon the safety and security needs of the individual hotel.

RECODABLE LOCKS

The purchase and use of a **recodable locking system** by a hotel was once such a significant event that the hotel could actually market its use of such locks to potential guests. Today, recodable locks are the industry standard, and no hotel should operate without them.

The effective use of industry standard safety resources can greatly reduce the likelihood of legal action taken against a hotel.

ALL IN A DAY'S WORK 11.1

THE SITUATION

J.D. Ojisima, the general manager of the hotel, walked quickly to the hotel's pool area.

"There are an awful lot of kids and only one adult down at the pool," was the statement made a few minutes earlier to the front office manager by a housekeeper, who had gone to the pool area to replenish the towel supply. All housekeepers in the hotel had been trained to report any activity that could possibly be considered dangerous, and this housekeeper had performed well.

Because she could not leave the front office area unattended, the front office manager had called J.D. to ask for assistance.

"What's the problem?" stated the guest when J.D. arrived at the pool. "I rented a room at this hotel to hold my son's eleventh birthday party. These are his friends. Are you saying we are not allowed to invite friends to visit when we are registered guests in your hotel?"

J.D. quickly counted more than 25 children attending the swim party at the pool and only one adult: the father who had rented the single sleeping room for the party.

A RESPONSE

Here is a case where facilities, staff, policies, and procedures must all play a part in how the hotel responds to a safety threat. Children should be able to use a hotel's pool with adult supervision. In this case, however, most reasonable people would doubt whether one adult can effectively supervise 25 young children. Generally, J.D.'s first responsibility would be to satisfy the guest. In this case, however, the greater responsibility is to safeguard the children and the hotel. As a result, J.D. must act decisively to remove this safety threat, even if it means upsetting the guest. If no additional adults are present to help with supervision, J.D. should act to remove enough of the young swimmers from the water to ensure the safety of all.

In the future, J.D. should address and formulate a written policy (if one does not currently exist) regarding the issue of the friends of registered guests and their permitted use (or nonuse) of hotel swim facilities as well as a reasonable adult/ child supervision ratio that can be consistently enforced by all hotel employees.

LODGING LANGUAGE

Recodable locking system: A hotel guest room locking system designed so that when guests insert their "key" (typically an electromagnetic card, but increasingly an electronic chip or password) into the guest room locking device for the first time, the lock is immediately recoded, canceling entry authorization from the previous guest's key.

Most recodable locking systems in use today are independent and stand-alone; that is, no wiring to a central computer or PMS is required. Except in life-threatening emergencies, only standard magnetic strip cards issued to guests or hotel staff will open the lock. This means that the hotel's entire room security system is controlled by software programmed into the individual locks, which are activated by **keycards** coded by a card-issuing computer.

LODGING LANGUAGE

Keycard: The electromagnetic card used in a recodable locking system.

Keycards are time-sensitive and can typically be issued up to 12 months in advance. Thus, individuals or groups can be sent room keys to speed registration when reservations are confirmed.

In a recodable locking system, each lock contains a card reader and electronic lock control module connected to a motor-actuated lock mechanism. Standard AA alkaline batteries or a wireless signal activate the lock. A warning light, visible only to staff, warns when the batteries are in need of replacement. When a guest inserts the keycard (or in a radio frequency-based or wireless system types in a password) for the first time, the lock is immediately recoded, thereby canceling entry authorization for the previous

LODGING ONLINE

To view the operational features of two of the lodging industry's most popular recodable locking systems, go to:

www.onity.com/ or:

www.saflok.com/

How important do you think room security is to the average hotel guest? Is anything more important?

guest. Multiple keycards can be issued to the same guest. In addition to guest rooms and exterior doors, recodable locks can be used to limit guest access to designated areas, such as special elevator floors, swimming pools, spas, exercise rooms, and reserved breakfast or bar areas. They can also limit employee access to specified storage areas within the hotel.

The safety and security challenge for the individuals managing a recodable lock system is to ensure that front office agents do not issue keys to individuals not properly registered in the guest room. For example, assume the (very common) situation where a guest approaches a front office agent and states, "I have misplaced my room key. Can you please give me another?" In a hotel that is exercising reasonable care in its issuance of duplicate room keys, the hotel staff member responding to the guest must:

- Be trained to issue duplicate keys only to confirmed registered guests.
- Maintain an accurate data system that identifies registered guests and their assigned room numbers.

Because guest rooms must be regularly cleaned and maintained, management issues master keycards to hotel employees who need them. With today's recodable lock systems, an electronic record is kept of all keycards used in the lock for a specific period of time. As a result, should the need arise, management can determine whose keycard was used to open a lock and at what day and time the key was used. The use of recodable locks not only reduces the possibility that guests can be victimized in their room by someone who had rented the same room on a previous night, they also help reduce the incidence of employee theft from rooms.

ALARM SYSTEMS

Alarms of many types are used in the hotel industry. They can be either audible or silent. Audible alarms typically consist of high-pitched buzzers, bells, or other noises. Alarm devices, whether audible or silent, normally consist of electrical connections, photoelectric light beams, seismic detectors, infrared beams, magnetic contacts, or radio frequency (RF) fields that, when activated, create the alarm.

Alarms many be classified as either an **internal alarm** or a **contact alarm**.

LODGING LANGUAGE

Internal alarm: A warning system that notifies an area within the hotel if the alarm is activated.

Contact alarm: A warning system that notifies (contacts) an external entity, such as the fire or police department, if the alarm is activated.

Internal alarms generally are designed to serve as a deterrent to criminal or mischievous activity. For example, a warning buzzer on a hotel's fire exit door would typically be wired only to notify hotel personnel if the door was used. In a like manner, an alarm on a liquor storeroom door might serve to notify a manager or the food and beverage director. Conversely, an alarm activated by a front office agent during or after an armed robbery would most likely be wired directly to the local police department for the purpose of contacting them immediately.

Some important areas that may be protected by internal alarms include:

- Storage areas
- Hotel facilities such as pools, spa, and exercise areas
- Hotel grounds and the property perimeter

Some important areas that are more likely to be protected by contact alarms include:

- The front office
- Food and beverage cashier stations
- The controller's office

Hotel fire alarms are so important that they are mandated by federal law and local building codes. Good hotels have these devices wired as both internal and contact alarms. Remember that in case of a fire, hotel employees, guests, and the fire department would all need to be made aware of the danger. Thus, heat or smoke detectors in a guest room should set off an internal alarm that would be heard by the guest in the room as well as by the staff at the front office and should be checked immediately by the appropriate hotel employee. By contrast, a fire alarm activated in a public area may result in an automatic contact and summons of firefighters because the alarm was wired directly to the local fire department.

The hotel staff responsible for doing so should periodically and frequently check all alarms for proper operation. This is necessary because a hotel with a non-functioning alarm system will have great difficulty demonstrating that it exercised reasonable care toward employee and guest safety should the need ever arise. An effective and comprehensive alarm system is an invaluable tool in every hotel's complete safety and security efforts.

SURVEILLANCE SYSTEMS

Properly implemented, electronic surveillance can play a major role in a hotel's safety and security programs. Surveillance is generally done in one of two ways. The first involves simply recording the activity within an area of the hotel. Thus, for example, a hotel could set up a digital camera that records the activity outside a liquor storeroom. Then, if the storeroom was broken into on a given night, a record of the break-in would exist that could be useful in identifying the thieves. Surveillance systems are most frequently used to record activity at the front office, near entrances and exits, in parking areas, and near cashiers.

Some hotels use **closed-circuit television (CCTV)** as a tool in their safety and security programs.

LODGING LANGUAGE

Closed-circuit television (CCTV): A camera and monitor system that displays, in real time, the activity within the camera's field of vision. A CCTV consisting of several cameras and screens showing the camera's fields of vision may be monitored in a single location.

The potential uses of CCTV in a hotel are many. CCTV can be used, for example, in a multiple-entry property where management desires to monitor activity outside each entrance. To be most effective, a CCTV system must be monitored. Viewing monitors are typically placed in a central location and viewed by an assigned employee who is trained to respond appropriately to activities seen on the monitor. For example, if an outside entrance is being monitored, and the monitor shows that a break-in is being attempted, the employee may be trained to summon the local police. Some hotels that use CCTV also have an intercom in the area being monitored, thus extending the effectiveness of the employee monitoring the system by making it possible to talk with anyone observed in the monitored area. States generally mandate the use of CCTV to improve security in casino hotels.

Some hotel managers attempt to create the illusion of having a CCTV system in place, when, in fact, the cameras are not operating as cameras or the monitors are not constantly monitored. This is typically done in an effort to save money on the cost of operating the

CCTV system. The rationale is that the mere presence of the cameras will deter criminals since they will not realize that they are not actually being observed. The courts and juries have found, however, that this approach does not establish reasonable security care by a hotel because victims may mistakenly think that help is on the way (because they believe their situation is being monitored) and base their behavior on that belief. No help is likely to arrive if the monitors are not being viewed. Hotel managers who wish to operate an unmonitored CCTV should consult with both their insurers and their legal counsel before implementing such an approach.

EMERGENCY PLANS

Despite a hotel staff's best efforts, safety and security emergencies will occur. When they do, the hotel must be ready to respond appropriately. Pre-planning is the very best tool available to managers concerned with safety and security. In unforeseen emergencies, it may not be possible to determine the proper response until the actual event occurs. But in the case of crises that are foreseeable (such as severe weather storms or power outages), some of the actions a hotel must be prepared to take will be quite similar, if not the same, in each crisis.

LODGING LANGUAGE

Emergency plan: A document describing a hotel's predetermined, intended response to a safety/security threat it may encounter.

An emergency plan is, quite simply, the identification of a potential threat to the safety and/or security of the hotel as well as the hotel's planned response to the threat. For example, an emergency plan for a hotel near a heavily wooded area might include an evacuation plan to be implemented in case of a forest fire. A hotel on a Florida coast might include in its emergency plan a method of evacuating the hotel in the event of an impending hurricane.

Responses to events such as the following are included in most hotels' emergency plans:

- Fire
- Flood
- Power outages
- Severely inclement weather (e.g., hurricane, snow storm, tornado)
- Robbery
- Death or injury to a guest or employee
- Intense negative publicity by the media

In all of the above cases, the hotel's management and employees may be called upon to react quickly. The emergency plan prepares them to do so. This can be accomplished because many crises share similar characteristics that can, to some degree, be controlled by pre-planning: These characteristics include:

- Extreme importance
- Disruption of normal business
- Potential for human suffering
- Property damage
- Financial loss
- Potential scrutiny by the media
- Threat to the reputation or health of the business

An emergency plan must be a written document. This is important because it must identify precisely what is expected of management and employees in times of crisis. In addition, if the hotel becomes subject to a lawsuit as a result of the crisis, a written emergency plan can help show that it exercised reasonable care in preparing for the crisis.

An emergency plan should be kept simple because it will likely be implemented only in a time of heightened stress. A clearly developed emergency plan should include, for each crisis identified:

- The type of crisis
- Who should be told when the crisis occurs (include telephone or pager numbers)
- What should be done (and who should do it) in the event the crisis occurs
- Who should be informed of the results or impact of the crisis when it is over

Plans for managing an emergency should be developed by the hotel's top-level managers with input from other staff members as applicable. Representatives of insurance companies and local fire/police departments can also provide useful information. Large hotels typically have a security department whose personnel would be involved in implementing emergency plans. Managers of small, limited-service properties must include these responsibilities as an integral part of their jobs. Regardless of hotel size, however, plans must be in place that indicate, for every emergency that can reasonably be anticipated, what exactly must be done and who exactly is responsible for doing it.

The actual plan should be reviewed frequently by management and should be shared with employees so that they know what to do during the emergency. Where practical, hotels should practice the implementation of their plan. By doing so, they demonstrate strongly their commitment to ensuring the safety and security of the hotel and everyone in it.

External Resources

Hoteliers are not alone in their efforts to provide for guest safety. Local law enforcement officials also are charged with maintaining individual safety and community security. They are natural allies of hoteliers. In addition, the hotel's insurers have a deep-seated interest in the safety and security efforts of the hotel's owner and staff. These two resources are readily available to hoteliers and should be utilized to the greatest extent possible.

LOCAL LAW ENFORCEMENT

Hotel employees can and should be well-trained, but their safety and security efforts will be improved tremendously when the hotel's managers establish and maintain an excellent relationship with local law enforcement professionals. Hotel general managers should personally know the individual(s) responsible for law enforcement in the area where their hotel is located. Local law enforcement officials can advise and assist managers and, in many cases, provide no-cost safety and security training for the hotel's employees. In addition, they can advise hoteliers about the best procedures and processes to be used in working together to remove unruly guests from the hotel, an event that, unfortunately, does occur in even the best managed properties.

In many communities, a general manager can request a property safety and security review from the local police. This will likely result in the identification of specific steps the hotel can take to reduce safety and security threats as well as actions it can take to make improvements. Good managers make it a point to meet frequently with local police because they are an important source of information and assistance.

PROPERTY INSURERS

Risk is inherent in running any business, and hotels are no exception. Hotels seek protection from risk by purchasing insurance. Doing so makes good financial sense. Some types of insurance coverage may be required by law (such as **workers' compensation**). Other insurance is required by the hotel's lenders (when the hotel has been purchased with borrowed money) to protect their financial interest in the property.

LODGING LANGUAGE

Workers' Compensation: An insurance program designed to assist individuals who are victims of a work-related injury or illness.

When assessing risk, and before selling insurance to a business, an insurance company predicts the average number of times the risk is likely to result in actual loss or damage. The average monetary value of the loss is then established. The **premiums** (fees) for the insurance to protect against the loss are then determined.

LODGING LANGUAGE

Premiums: The fees paid for insurance.

These fees must be low enough to attract those who want to buy the insurance, but high enough to support the number of losses that is likely to be incurred by the insurer.

The fewer the number of **claims** (potential losses), workers injured, and lawsuits that result from safety- and security-related incidents, the lower the risk that the insurance company will have to compensate those who are insured for their losses.

LODGING LANGUAGE

Claim (insurance): A demand for compensation as the result of loss, injury, or damage.

When there are few claims, the premiums charged for insurance are lower. As a result, it is in the best interest of hotels (because they want to minimize the insurance premiums they pay) and of their insurers (because they want to avoid paying claims) to minimize the number of losses incurred. Because this is so, insurers should partner with hoteliers in finding ways to reduce accidents and other sources of potential loss or damage. Just as a hotel's managers should know and work cooperatively with local law enforcement officers, the hotel's insurance companies should be consulted on a regular basis to identify policies, procedures, and actions that can be taken to reduce potential claims by improving the property's safety and security.

SPECIAL SAFETY–RELATED THREATS

Every business has unique threats to safety and security, and hotels are no exception. These unique threats often require extra caution or effort on the part of the hotel's staff. For many hotels, four of the most important of these areas of special concern are swimming pools, spas, exercise facilities, and parking lots.

Swimming Pools

Hotel swimming pools are exceptionally popular although they are typically used by only a small percentage of hotel guests. Consistently, in opinion polls regarding desirable services, travelers rank the presence of a swimming pool near the top of the list of hotel amenities that influence their hotel selection. The potential legal liability resulting from accidental slipping, diving, or even drowning, however, requires that the individual(s) responsible for taking care of the pool area be extraordinarily vigilant in enforcing pool safety procedures.

It is not possible to avoid every possible accident in a pool area. It is possible, however, to minimize the chances for accidents. Figure 11.1 lists 10 key practices that affect swimming pool safety and legal liability. They should be reviewed on a monthly basis with affected employees to ensure consistent compliance.

Most hotels do not employ full-time lifeguards at their pools. If lifeguards are provided, they must know effective surveillance, rescue procedures, and techniques specific to the facility they are protecting. When groups (especially children) are using a pool, it is the responsibility of the group leaders to provide supervision, regardless of whether lifeguards are provided.

Swimming pools pose a significant safety threat, and managers should take every precaution available to minimize those threats.

1. Post the pool's operating hours and open the pool to guests only during those hours.
2. Clearly mark the depths of pools accurately the on sides and ends and in both metric measure and feet/inches.
3. Ensure that the pool and pool area are properly illuminated and that any electrical components are regularly inspected and maintained to comply with local electrical codes.
4. Install self-closing and self-latching and/or locking gates to prevent unauthorized access to the pool area. If possible, lock the entrance to the pool with a recodable lock.
5. Have appropriate life-saving equipment on hand and easily accessible as well as at least one cardiopulmonary resuscitation (CPR) certified employee on duty at all times the pool is opened.
6. Allow pool use only by registered guests and specifically authorized others.
7. Contact the hotel's insurer to determine the number, placement, and content of necessary pool warning signs.
8. Post all pool policy and information signs in the language(s) of guests. Enforce the policies at all times.
9. Provide an emergency telephone in the pool area that rings directly either to the front desk or to 911 depending on the preference of the hotel's insurer.
10. Carefully document all activities related to pool maintenance, local ordinance compliance, and operating policy enforcement.

FIGURE 11.1 Swimming Pool Safety

When lifeguard services are not provided, the group should be advised that there are no lifeguards on duty and that its leaders must provide stringent and effective surveillance and supervision while the participants are in, on, and around the water. The hotel should provide the group leaders with specific supervisory and safety guidelines to be followed while the pool is in use. This can be done verbally or by use of a written "Pool Rules" fact sheet. The hotel's staff should continuously assess the numbers of guests in, on, and around the water to determine how many adults are needed to ensure the safety of the group members.

Spas

Hotels that have common area spas, whirlpools, or hot tubs face special safety and liability concerns. While spas are popular, they can be dangerous to young children, the elderly, intoxicated individuals, and people taking special medications. As with pools, it may be impossible to prevent all possible accidents, but the practices listed in Figure 11.2 can go a long way toward improving guest safety and minimizing the legal liability of the hotel. Management should review these practices with staff on a monthly basis to ensure compliance.

1. Inspect and document the inspection of spa drain covers on a daily basis.
2. Post all spa policies signs in the language(s) of guests.
3. Install a thermometer and check the spa temperature frequently; recording your readings. A range not to exceed 102–105 degrees Fahrenheit (38.9–40.6 degrees Celsius) is recommended.
4. Display spa temperatures in a manner that is easily readable by guests.
5. Clearly mark the depths of the spa in both metric measures and feet/inches.
6. Do not allow the consumption of alcohol while using the spa.
7. Install non-slip flooring surfaces around the spa and provide stairs/ladders for entry and exit.
8. Prohibit spa use by children and non-guests.
9. Provide an emergency telephone in the spa area that rings directly either to the front desk or to 911 depending on the preference of the hotel's insurer.
10. Carefully document all activities related to spa maintenance, local ordinance compliance, and operating policy enforcement.

FIGURE 11.2 Spa Safety

Exercise Facilities

Many hotels offer their guests the use of a fitness center or exercise room. These areas typically contain a variety of types and kinds of exercise equipment. In most cases, these rooms are not staffed by the hotel on a full-time basis. The rooms do, however, require regular attention. Hotel staff should pick up hazardous items (e.g., towels and weights) that might litter the floor and cause falls, and they should monitor exercise equipment for malfunctions or breakage and remove or immediately repair any machine that is broken or unsafe.

Statistics provided by insurers indicate that treadmills are, by far, the most dangerous apparatus in an exercise room. Even an experienced user can slip, trip, or lose balance on a treadmill. Falls from treadmills can cause serious physical harm, including broken limbs, concussions, and other serious injuries. Accidents are not the only safety risk. Equipment can easily transmit bacteria and other germs. Hoteliers operating exercise facilities must do their best to create a safe and secure exercise environment. One way to do so is by the use of posted signs.

Signs act as a constant reminder of the dangers inherent to exercise facilities. In general, signs can be classified into four types:

Policy Signs. Signs stating rules and regulations involving the use of the facility.

Warning Signs. Signs stating specific risks in an area of the facility or with a particular piece of equipment.

Directional Signs. Signs indicating entrances, exits, fire evacuation plans, and other safety information.

Emergency Signs. Signs indicating where various emergency items are stationed, such as fire extinguishers, first aid kits, and telephones.

Signs in the exercise room (as well as in other areas where safety communications are important) should be made of durable material that will hold up well. They should be made using letters of a size that is easy to read from at least 5 to 10 feet away. Signs should be printed in bright colors that will attract the reader's attention (signs with a white background and colored letters are the best) and should be placed from four feet to six feet from the floor for easy viewing. Computer printouts and handwritten signs can act as temporary or emergency communication devices but should be avoided in most cases.

Parking Areas

Many hotels have parking areas for guest vehicles. While hotels do not insure the vehicles parked in their lots, they are responsible for providing reasonable care in the protection of vehicles and guests using the lots. Figure 11.3 lists 10 key practices that affect the safety of parking areas. They should be reviewed on a monthly basis to ensure compliance.

1. Inspect parking lot lighting on a daily basis. Arrange for replacement of burned-out lights immediately.
2. Inspect parking lot surfaces daily and arrange for pavement patches immediately if they threaten guest safety. Keep surfaces free of ice and snow in inclement weather.
3. Ensure that parking lot stripes and directional signs are easily seen to avoid pedestrian/vehicle accidents.
4. Post easily readable signs in the parking lot reminding guests not to leave valuables in their vehicles.
5. If valet parking is provided, document the training of all drivers employed.
6. Require guests to identify their vehicles by license number or make/color upon check-in.
7. Keep landscaping around parking lots well trimmed to avoid dangerous areas that may provide hiding places for individuals who could threaten guest safety or property security.
8. If possible, arrange for regular and frequent parking lot drive-through patrols by local law enforcement officials.
9. Arrange for daily daytime and nighttime walk-through patrols by hotel staff.
10. Use a manager's daily log to document parking lot maintenance procedures.

FIGURE 11.3 Parking Lot Safety

Best Sleep Hotel

Performed by: ____________________

Date of Inspection: __________ Time of Inspection: __________

To ensure the integrity of your walk-through, this checklist should be completed in sequence as it appears.

As appropriate, a check must be placed in the "yes" or "no" column to the right of this paper. If "no" is required, please indicate the problem in the "comments" section. If a work order is submitted, note the work order number in the "comments" section.

ITEM	*YES*	*NO*	*COMMENTS*
Outdoor parking lot is well-lighted.	❑	❑	
Outdoor parking lot is free of trash and debris.	❑	❑	
Painted stripes are easily seen and in good condition.	❑	❑	
Directional signs are posted in conspicuous locations.	❑	❑	
Lot is patrolled at irregular intervals.	❑	❑	
All entrance gates are locked after 8:00 p.m. with the exception of the main entrance.	❑	❑	
Emergency call boxes are located throughout the parking lot and are functioning properly.	❑	❑	
Closed circuit cameras function properly and send clear images to security.	❑	❑	
Gangs or vagrants are noticed and reported to police.	❑	❑	
Cars are checked for length of stay; (note cars that are covered with tarp or excessive dirt).	❑	❑	
Security is aware of long-term stay automobiles.	❑	❑	
Correct percentage of Americans with Disabilities Act (ADA) parking is available and well-marked.	❑	❑	
Grass areas and bushes are well-maintained.	❑	❑	
Bushes and plants are trimmed and away from entrance doors.	❑	❑	
Walkways are well-lighted.	❑	❑	
Walkways are free of trip hazards	❑	❑	
Outside entrances are free of trash and debris	❑	❑	
All external doors leading to the inside are closed, locked and card accessible.	❑	❑	
Key card readers work properly at each entrance.	❑	❑	
All entrances are well-lighted.	❑	❑	
All entrances are secured.	❑	❑	
Directional signage at each entrance is compatible with ADA requirements.	❑	❑	
Outdoor ADA requirements are met regarding wheelchair ramps.	❑	❑	
Other:	❑	❑	
Other:	❑	❑	
Other:	❑	❑	

FIGURE 11.4 MOD Checklist for Parking Areas

The hotel's manager on duty (MOD) should be assigned, as part of his or her daily responsibilities, to conduct a walk-around of the parking area as part of the hotel's overall safety and security program. This walk-around also should be documented. Figure 11.4 is an example of a manager on duty checklist related to parking areas in a hotel.

Despite a hotel's best safety-related efforts, accidents can and will happen. When they do, an **incident report** must be prepared to document the "who, what, when, where, how" as well as the hotel's response to the accident or injury. Figure 11.5 is an example of an incident report used in a hotel.

LODGING LANGUAGE

Incident report: A document prepared to record the details of an accident, injury, or disturbance and the hotel's response to it.

Incident Report

Hutchinson Hotel and Ocean Suites
Sweet Water, FL 10065

Complainant

Last Name ____________ First Name ____________ Initial ________
Address ____________ City ________ State ________ Zip ________
Home Telephone ____________ Business Telephone ____________ E-mail: ________

Type of Incident

Injury _____ Theft _____ Accident _____ Property Damage _____ Other _____

Injury

First aid given? Yes _____ No _____ First aid refused? Yes _____ No _____
EMS called? Yes _____ No _____ Taken to emergency? Yes _____ No _____
Type of injury ________________________________

Detail of Incident

____
____
(Write on back if necessary)

Property and Value

Damaged/Missing Item(s) Estimated Value
________________________________ ________________
________________________________ ________________
(Write on back if necessary)

Room Entry (only if applicable)

Room Number: ________ Entered by: ____________ Witnessed by: ____________
Room entered? Y ____ N ____ Time ____ Door locked? Y ____ N ____ Door chained? Y ____ N ____

Police Response to the Incident

Police Officer: ____________ Shield # ____________ Report # ____________
Arrest made? Y _____ N _____ Citation issued? Y _____ N _____ Warning issued Y _____ N _____

Witnesses to the Incident

1. Name: ________________________ Telephone: ____________
   Address: ____________ City ____________ State ____________
2. Name: ________________________ Telephone: ____________
   Address: ____________ City ____________ State ____________
   Comments: ________________________________
   ____
   ____
   Report Prepared by ________________________ Date ____________

FIGURE 11.5 Hotel Incident Report

An incident record should be prepared whenever a guest or employee suffers an accident or injury (a safety-related event) as well as when there has been a loss or damage to property (a security-related event). Other examples of safety-related documentation that should be maintained by the hotel include minutes from safety and security committee meetings, general staff meeting notes relevant to safety issues, records of employee training related to safety and security, and safety seminars attended or certifications acquired by employees.

PROTECTING PROPERTY FROM SECURITY THREATS

As you learned earlier in this chapter, safety-related programs are designed to keep people safe from harm, and security-related efforts are directed toward the protection of property from the threat of theft or damage. The safety of people is always more important than the security of property. Good hoteliers know, however, that they must use sound judgment and establish effective programs to protect the personal assets of guests as well as the assets of the hotel itself. Not to do so would be a disservice to the traveler and the hotel's owners.

Threats to the security of assets can come from individuals inside the hotel (internal threats) or outside the hotel (external threats). In both cases, these individuals seek to steal or damage property that rightfully belongs to the hotel's guests, employees, or owners. Effective hoteliers design, implement, and monitor security programs that reduce, to the greatest extent possible, the internal and external threats to asset security. In addition, hoteliers must know about the unique and specific threats to asset security that exist in individual hotel departments. It is not possible to eliminate all potential for property loss or damage. However, knowledge of specific lodging industry threats to security, as well as implementation of activities developed to minimize the impact of these threats, can help hoteliers show evidence of the reasonable care the law requires them to demonstrate.

Internal Threats

Sometimes employees steal assets owned by guests or by the hotel. When it is clear that an employee is involved in such activity, the response of management should be appropriate and, above all else, consistent. Some hotels include a phrase in their employee handbook warning that theft will be grounds for dismissal. When the theft or loss of property involves significant amounts of money, the hotel may pursue the filing of criminal charges against the employee. Regardless of the approach used, it should be applied equally to all employees and at all levels.

Consider what happens, for example, when a supervisor or manager involved in criminal activity is caught but then allowed to resign while in the same hotel, an hourly employee caught in the same activity is fired and/or prosecuted. This would leave the hotel open to charges of discrimination or unfair labor practices against which it may be difficult to defend. It also sends the hotel's employees a mixed message about management's view of theft.

Towels are one of the most common targets for guest pilferage.

ALL IN A DAY'S WORK 11.2

THE SITUATION

RING!!!!!!! RING!!!!!!! RING!!!!!!! RING!!!!!!!

The telephone woke Dale Parrot, the front office manager at the Better Inn and Suites hotel, from a deep sleep. It was 3:00 a.m. on Sunday morning.

"Mr. Parrot," said Shingi Rukuni, the night auditor and only employee on duty at the hotel, "Room 219 is having a really loud party. I'm getting lots of guest complaints from rooms located near theirs."

"Did you call the room and ask them to hold it down?" asked Dale.

"Yes, I did," replied Shingi. "I called them at 10:00 p.m., when the party started, then again at 1:30 a.m., 2:15, and 2:45, when the complaints really started coming in. They just stop for a couple minutes, then start right up again. I think they're drunk. I don't know what to do next!"

A RESPONSE

Surprisingly, the real problem in this case is not *the noise coming from room 219. Unruly guests are a fact of life in most hotels. The auditor's uncertainty about what to do about it indicates a lack of training by the front office management staff or a lack of direction from the hotel's general manager and suggests that a training deficiency is this hotel's larger problem. Whatever the hotel's policy toward unruly guests (number of specific warnings before the guest is asked to leave or is escorted off the property by local law enforcement officials), it should be documented, clearly communicated, and then followed. The comfort and safety of all the hotel's guests must be considered as should the latitude allowed for "partiers" before the hotel's forced-removal policy is established.*

If the hotel wishes to communicate to employees that theft of all types will be dealt with swiftly and consistently, it must treat internal threats to property security just as seriously as the threats posed by non-employees. A hotel faces two basic types of internal asset threats: those related to cash and those related to other assets.

THREATS TO CASH

In many cases, when hoteliers consider employee theft, they think of employees stealing money. **Embezzlement** is a potential problem in hotels, but using procedures and policies designed to prevent it can minimize its likelihood.

LODGING LANGUAGE

Embezzlement: The theft of a company's financial assets by an employee.

Some hotels are so concerned about employee theft that they **bond** employees who are in a position to embezzle funds.

LODGING LANGUAGE

Bond(ing): Purchasing an insurance policy to protect against the possibility that an employee will steal.

There are many ways that employees can defraud their employers of cash, and managers must stay current in the areas of cost- and revenue-control systems. Good financial controls based on solid control principles go a long way toward reducing employee theft. Of particular importance are controls related to cashiering positions because cashiers can commit fraud in a variety of ways. Typical methods of **fraud** related to cashiering include:

- Charging guests for items not purchased, then keeping the overcharge
- Changing the totals on credit card charges after the guest has left or imprinting additional credit card charges and pocketing the cash difference
- Misadding legitimate charges to create a higher-than-appropriate total with the intent of keeping the overcharge

- Purposely short-changing guests when giving back change and then removing the extra change from the cash drawer
- Voiding legitimate sales as mistakes and keeping the cash amount of the legitimate sale
- Charging higher-than-appropriate prices for hotel goods or services and then recording the sale at the proper price while keeping the overcharge

LODGING LANGUAGE

Fraud: The intentional use of deceit, trickery, or other dishonest methods to take another's money or property.

In addition to cashier theft that can affect the hotel or hotel guests, employees can steal cash in the accounts-payable area by paying the hotel's bills in such a way as to funnel money to the embezzling employee or in the accounts-receivable area by fraudulently diverting funds intended for the hotel to the embezzling employee. The responsibility for preventing the theft of hotel funds falls to the controller (or general manager) and each hotel department head involved in the handling of cash.

THREATS TO OTHER ASSETS

Cash is not the only hotel asset that can be stolen by employees. In fact, the number and type of assets that can be unlawfully taken by employees is large. Those responsible for a hotel's asset security often find it helpful to create programs designed to protect the three non-cash assets most subject to employee theft. These three loss areas involve the stealing of time, company property, and services.

It may seem strange to consider time a hotel asset, yet it is the asset most easily taken by employees. In nearly all cases, employees are paid for their work by the hour or, as in the case of salaried individuals, by the week or month. In effect, the hotel is exchanging one asset (cash), for another (employee time). When an employee takes a hotel's money but does not respond by giving the hotel the time agreed upon, the hotel loses. The theft of time can consist of employees fraudulently filling out time sheets or punching time cards. In some large hotels, particularly those with weak supervision programs, theft of time may result from employees simply disappearing for some time with the result that work they should have performed is not completed.

The best way to prevent theft of time by employees is to have strong controls in place with regard to time cards. To help in this area, hotels are increasingly issuing individual employee swipe cards to reduce the chances of "buddy punching," the practice of one employee fraudulently checking (punching) another employee in or out.

Managers must be vigilant when considering plans to reduce employee theft that involves lack of productivity. This can be challenging, especially in large properties. Good supervision, however, and a realistic workload for each employee on a work schedule that is reviewed daily will help to improve the hotel's ability to detect such theft.

Company property can disappear through the actions of employees as easily as through those of guests. In fact, employees usually know which assets management has neglected to protect as well as it should. From food in a food storage area to zippered laundry bags in housekeeping, employees often find that the physical assets of a hotel are of a type they could use personally. That makes these items very susceptible to employee theft. The best approach to preventing the theft of company property involves:

- Carefully screening employees prior to hiring them
- Reducing the chances for theft through the use of effective recodable locks, inventory systems, and other security measures
- Informing managers and employees of the penalty for theft
- Treating all proven cases of similar theft in a similar manner

It is unlikely, even with the best controls, that all employee theft in a hotel can be eliminated. There are simply too many opportunities for dishonest employees to take advantage of their access to the hotel's physical resources. Effective employee screening, however, and the creation of an environment that discourages stealing and consistently disciplines, terminates, or prosecutes employees for known cases of theft will help reduce the problem.

Some employees steal company property, and others steal services provided by the hotel. In many ways, this type of theft is harder to detect than the theft of company property. For example, assume that a front office supervisor, working late at night, spends an hour or more per day making a long-distance call to his girlfriend who lives several states away. This inappropriate use of hotel assets will result in the hotel's incurring a larger-than-necessary long-distance telephone bill for the month as well as experiencing the theft of time discussed earlier. This theft of services may go undetected unless someone at the property is monitoring the long-distance telephone bills generated by each administrative telephone extension number. In-room movies and games, telephone tolls, printing, copy, and faxing services are among the services susceptible to employee theft. Proper managerial controls must be in place to minimize, to the greatest degree possible, the chances for loss of hotel services.

External Threats

Since hotels are open 24/7, they are susceptible to asset threats any time of the day or night. Guests or non-guests can pose these threats. As is the case when protecting assets from threats posed by employees, hoteliers protecting hotel assets from the illegal activities of non-employees must be aware of, and guard against, threats to cash and non-cash assets.

THREATS TO CASH

Nearly all hotels keep some money on the property at all times. Because that is true, and because many hotels are laid out in a way that offers thieves the chance to make a rapid getaway by automobile, hotel staff members can sometimes be confronted by armed or unarmed robbers. Preventing such robberies is best achieved by management working with the hotel staff and local law enforcement officials to identify and minimize the opportunities for thieves to rob the hotel.

It is important for hoteliers to understand that a robbery is *not* an occasion to protect cash assets. A robbery is a time to protect staff! In the event of a robbery, the hotel staff member(s) involved should obey the robber's demands and make no movements that might be perceived by the robber as an attempt to stop the crime. Employees should do *nothing* that could risk or jeopardize their lives. Employees can, of course, be trained to observe the robber carefully for the purpose of later recalling physical characteristics, such as height, weight, color and length of hair, color of eyes, mustaches or beards, tattoos, accents, or other identifying characteristics. During a robbery, complying with the robber's demands and observation of the robber should be the employee's only concern.

To help apprehend robbers, many managers install a contact alarm system in their cashier's cash drawers. This alarm is activated when a predetermined bill or packet of bills is removed from the cash drawer. The alarm is wired to summon local law enforcement officers trained to deal with robbery-in-progress situations. If no such alarm is in place, an employee who is robbed should, at the earliest safe opportunity, contact local law enforcement officials as well as others indicated in the robbery section of the hotel's emergency plan.

THREATS TO OTHER ASSETS

Robbers steal from hotels, but so do guests. In fact, guests are much greater threats than robbers to the non-cash assets of hotels. Most often, the targets of guests are not cash but the products and services the hotel sells. Every experienced hotel manager has a "you won't believe this one" story about a guest who removed (or tried to remove!) a significant asset from a hotel illegally. From furniture, television sets, and artwork to minor items such as towels, robes, bed linens, and in-room clock radios, guest theft costs hotels millions of dollars annually in lost assets.

The reality for most guest theft, however, is that it is simply recognized as a cost of doing business. It makes little sense, for example, to accuse a guest of stealing a wooden clothes hanger (even if the hanger was, in fact, stolen by the guest) and then attempt to charge the guest for the item.

Some hotel managers place small signs in guest rooms offering to sell guests those items that frequently disappear. Other managers, in an effort to deter theft, word guest room signs in such a way as to imply that a room attendant will be held financially responsible for any loss of guest room items. Whether managers use these in-room signs (neither of which is recommended by the authors) or other less obtrusive approaches, guests and visitors to a hotel represent a significant threat to asset security. Therefore, it is good business practice to take precautions designed to reduce theft. To that end, security-conscious hoteliers:

- Hang all artwork in lobbies and guest rooms with lockdown-style hangers
- Avoid placing valuable decorations and décor pieces in areas where guests can easily take them
- Train room attendants to alert management if excessive amounts of terry cloth products or in-room items are missing from stay-over rooms
- Bolt televisions and in-room computers securely to guest room furniture
- Train all employees to be alert regarding the loss of hotel property and to report any suspicious activity they encounter

It is important to remember that theft of services by guests can happen just as easily as the theft of physical assets, and proper controls must be in place to prevent these occurrences. Just as nearly all retail stores endure losses from shoplifters, hotels lose items to guest pilferage. However, retail stores and their hotel counterparts must diligently seek to limit the losses caused by theft through the implementation of policies and procedures designed to reduce such losses.

Area-Specific Threats

Threats to a hotel's assets can occur at any time and in any department. Some departments, however, by the nature of their operation, are subject to specific security threats of which hoteliers should be especially aware. These include the front office, housekeeping, food and beverage, sales and marketing, and maintenance departments.

FRONT OFFICE

In addition to the threats to cash posed by employee theft or robbery, the largest area of concern at the front desk is the fraudulent selling of rooms. Consider, for example, the night auditor who checks a guest into the hotel very late at night. The guest states that he or she only needs the room for a few hours to get some sleep before continuing on their travel. The auditor collects the guest's payment in cash at the time of arrival, but later reduces the day's room revenue by the same amount, stating that the guest was unhappy with the room, left early, and the guest's cash was refunded. Obviously, this could have happened. On the other hand, it is also possible that the guest stayed for the short time indicated at arrival and the auditor has defrauded the hotel of one night's room revenue.

Alternatively, assume that a front office agent simply gives the key to a vacant guest room to a friend or relative and collects no room revenue from that individual. The room, of course, must be cleaned the next day by the housekeeping staff. Again in this case, the hotel has been defrauded of its rightful room revenue. The hotel's managers must have systems in place that daily compare rooms cleaned with rooms actually sold to minimize the chances for employee fraud at the front desk.

HOUSEKEEPING

Managers in the housekeeping department must be aware of two distinctly different security issues. The first is the theft of housekeeping supplies, such as in-room amenities, towels, and sheets. Thefts such as these can, of course, be committed either by guests or by employees. While it is virtually impossible to stop all theft of minor amenities and in-room items, proper controls and systems should be in place to detect and respond to significant thefts of this type.

The second and much more sensitive housekeeping issue involves theft from guest rooms by room attendants or other employees. When guests travel, they often keep valuables in their rooms. This is true despite the recommended use of safety-deposit boxes for such items.

If a guest claims that there has been a theft from his or her room, managers must consider four possible scenarios:

1. The guest has made an honest mistake and the item(s) reported stolen has simply been misplaced by the guest
2. The guest is attempting to defraud the hotel because the item was not stolen
3. The theft was committed, but by another hotel guest
4. A hotel employee committed the theft

Obviously, the management of the hotel must be very careful in such situations. If, upon inquiry, management believes that a theft has in fact occurred, it is the best policy to report the incident to local law enforcement officials who are trained to investigate the crime.

FOOD AND BEVERAGE

Because food and beverage items can be used by virtually everyone, they are a common target for theft. Guests may take silverware and glassware as mementos of their stay, and employees may pilfer the same items for their own homes. More significantly, however, employees who purchase products for the food and beverage department may defraud the hotel by accepting kickbacks from vendors or by purchasing and then stealing food and beverage items intended for the hotel. It is in the development of systems and procedures to reduce the threat of this type of fraud about which hotel managers must be extremely vigilant.

SALES AND MARKETING

Sales and marketing staff are frequently responsible for preventing fraudulent behavior directed at the hotel by unscrupulous individuals. Very often, this takes the form of outside parties billing the hotel for marketing services that were not rendered or were not requested. Typically, this scam takes the form of an official-looking invoice arriving in the sales and marketing department by mail or fax. The invoice states that the hotel owes money for its listing in a published directory of hotels targeted toward a specific group, such as government employees. The invoice will also likely state that the hotel must pay promptly to avoid being dropped from the directory. In fact, however, the directory does not even exist. Those responsible for sending the invoice hope that the hotel will pay the invoice without investigation. This scam and others of a similar nature are common, and hotels that do not have sufficient control of their accounts-payable system may fall prey to them.

It may seem unusual to consider sales and marketing employees themselves as a source of fraud; however, due to the nature of their interaction with clients, threats to asset security do exist. Some of these threats take the form of irregularities with expense accounts. Misstating mileage traveled, clients entertained, or sales trips taken can cause the expense account expenditures of sales staff to be overstated, and as a result their reimbursements will be too high. To combat such potential problems, the hotel must have a good check-and-balance system that requires documentation of sales expenses and routine audits of reimbursements.

MAINTENANCE

A unique problem in the maintenance department relates to the loss of small but sometimes expensive hand tools and supplies. It is important to remember that the types of items typically used in a hotel's repair shop are the same items employees and guests would use to do repairs in their own homes. Thus, portable hand drills, electric saws, wrenches, and the like can easily turn up missing if they are not carefully controlled.

It might seem as if this would be an easy problem to alleviate. In fact, taking an inventory of small hand tools like pliers or screwdrivers on a monthly basis is time-consuming and is often not done. When this is the case, dishonest employees know that they can take small items without much fear of detection. In addition, tools left at a worksite in the hotel during meals or other breaks can, if unsecured, be stolen by guests or others in the hotel. To prevent either of these problems, small hand tools should always be inventoried monthly to determine losses, if any. In addition, hand tools should never be left unattended

LODGING GOES GREEN!

The world's largest hotel chains have been meeting regularly to discuss international guiding principles for sustainable tourism, safety, hotel design, and development. Accor, Carlson, Four Seasons, Hilton, InterContinental, Marriott, Rezidor SAS, Starwood Hotels & Resorts Worldwide Inc. and TAJ Hotels, Resorts and Palaces have actively supported the development of these guiding principles.

There is an increasing realization that the hospitality industry should be leaders in the effort. In fact, there is an overwhelming case for hotels to be designed and operated according to sustainable principles. As well as the need to preserve the environment and avoid wastage of resources, businesses are increasingly realizing that a more sustainable approach means a longer-term and more profitable business environment.

The London-based International Tourism Partnership (ITP) (www.tourismpartnership.org) is a membership organization of leading companies from the travel and tourism industry. Its aim is to provide the hotel, travel and tourism industry with the knowledge and ability to develop practical solutions for more responsible business.

in a public area of the hotel. The temptation for theft and potential for loss are too great. While it may inconvenience the department, the head of the maintenance department may consider requiring a **sign-in/sign-out program** for all tools if regular inventories indicate that theft is a significant problem.

LODGING LANGUAGE

Sign-in/Sign-out Program: A system in which employees taking responsibility for hotel assets (such as hand tools, power equipment, or keys to secured areas) must document their responsibility by placing their signature and the date on a form recording their possession (sign-out) and return (sign-in) of the item.

HOTELS AND GLOBAL TERRORISM

The events of September 11, 2001, brought home to hoteliers and to all Americans the very real threat of terrorist attacks. Globally, hotels have increasingly become a target of terrorist attacks. The reasons why hotels are targeted are varied but include the fact that they are often considered by terrorists as symbols of the affluence and influence of Western-culture. Hotel guests usually represent precisely the kind of people terrorist seeks to eliminate, including foreign diplomats, businesspeople, wealthy tourists, and local elites.

Unlike many other potential attack sites (such as foreign embassies or military instillations), hotels generally are unguarded; have multiple points of entry; and have a constant flow of traffic, including hotel guests, employees, and delivery personnel. As a result, hotels are relatively easy to enter without attracting undue attention.

Because hotels are often pictured on the Internet, their physical layout (including precise locations of entrances, exits, and atriums) is easy to determine prior to an attack. As well, because of their high visibility, terrorists can be assured of a great deal of international media attention when hotels are targeted.

The likelihood that a single hotel will be terrorism target is small, but it increases with its size, location, ownership, and symbolic importance. Because the threat of a terrorist attack is real, managers in all properties should be concerned and assess their security procedures so as to take practical steps to protect lives in the event of an intentional explosion, fire, or other disaster, possibly even including the use of biological or chemical weapons. Hoteliers whose properties are at a high risk of terrorist attack must exercise special vigilance. While it may not be possible to prevent all possible attacks, hoteliers can take positive steps to minimize their risk. These include:

- The proper maintenance of existing security and safety equipment/procedures. For example, if surveillance equipment is in current use, it should be properly maintained, and information about building-evacuation procedures should be an integral part of new employee training.
- Careful consideration of potential vulnerability. As the possibility of a terrorist attack increases, so should the precautions taken to address it.
- Controlled access to nonpublic areas of the property.
- The screening (background checks) of employee applicants in accordance with applicable laws.
- Management training that addresses information to yield an awareness of the terrorist threat, the importance of remaining diligent, and the need to be prepared and to keep emergency plans current.
- Regular participation in "best practices" discussions with hoteliers who face similar threats and with local law enforcement officials who can provide guidance.

Since September 2001, the U.S. Congress has enacted many bills related to homeland security. In many cases, these bills affect the hotel industry. It is likely that more hotel-related legislation involving fire safety, emergency/crisis planning, and the prevention of terrorist acts will be passed at the federal or even state level. As a result, professionals in the hotel industry should carefully monitor developments in these important areas.

Lodging Language

Safety
Security
Reasonable Care
Damages
Compensatory Damages
Punitive Damages
Threat Analysis
Insurer
Safety and Security Committee
Occupational Safety and Health Administration (OSHA)
Recodable Locking System
Keycard
Internal Alarm
Contact Alarm
Closed-Circuit Television (CCTV)
Emergency Plan
Workers' Compensation
Premiums
Claim (Insurance)
Incident Report
Embezzlement
Bond(ing)
Fraud
Sign-in/Sign-out Program

For Discussion

1. As you have learned, safety and security are the responsibility of all hotel employees. In some hotels, however, there is a security department with its own full- and part-time employees. List three factors that might cause the management of a hotel to employ designated security staff on a regular basis.
2. Guest safety is a primary concern of all effective hotel managers. What steps can you take to ensure that all of the hotel's employees share your concern for guest safety? Identify at least three specific activities.
3. Material Safety Data Sheets are a valuable source of safety-related information for workers. In most cases, however, these documents are provided only in English and Spanish. Increasingly, the hotel industry employs individuals whose native language is neither of these. Assume that your hotel employs 25 such individuals speaking five different languages. How would you help ensure the safety of these workers with regard to handling chemicals and other toxic materials?
4. Good relations with local law enforcement officials are extremely helpful to a hotel. What are two specific activities the managers of a hotel can undertake to build positive relations with the local police?
5. Some hotel managers believe that uniformed security personnel in the hotel increase the comfort level of guests in the same manner as would uniformed police officers. Other managers feel that uniformed security personnel increase guests' concern about security and their own safety and thus have a negative effect. If it were your decision, would you put your security force in police-style uniforms or uniforms that blend with your clientele? What factors would influence your decision-making?
6. Swimming pool safety is always a concern for hoteliers. Do you believe that there should be a hotel policy limiting the number of additional guests that a registered hotel guest can invite to swim at a hotel pool, or should pools be reserved for registered guests only? What factors would influence your decision?
7. Good recordkeeping is an important part of a hotel's safety and security efforts. Identify three reasons why this is so.
8. Guests with physical limitations related to their movement, hearing, or sight present special safety concerns for a hotel. This is especially true in times of emergency. What are some steps hoteliers can take to ensure that such guests receive needed assistance in case of a hotel emergency, such as a fire or other situation requiring a forced evacuation?

9. Assume that your hotel's housekeeping department is experiencing periodic losses of products that you believe are due to employee theft. As a general manager, what specific steps would you suggest be taken to address this issue?

10. Pilferage of hotel assets by employees is common in the hotel industry. Would you recommend terminating a good hotel employee proven to have pilfered a bar of soap from a room attendant's cart? Why or why not?

Team Activities

TEAM ACTIVITY 1

The text indicated that the three major areas of concern for hoteliers seeking to demonstrate that they exercise reasonable care are related to:

- The hotel's physical facilities
- The hotel's staff
- Policies and procedures implemented by the hotel

While all of these are important, which does your team believe is *most* important? Why?

TEAM ACTIVITY 2

On Thanksgiving Day 2008, the world looked on in horror as terrorists armed with assault rifles, submachine guns, and hand grenades attacked Mumbai, India's financial and entertainment capital for nearly three days (November 26–29). The final result was 166 people killed. Among the direct targets were two of the city's most famous 5-star hotels: the Taj Mahal Palace and Tower and the Oberoi Trident complex. Western tourists and businesspeople especially were singled out for attack. The final death toll included 28 foreign nationals from 10 countries, 6 of which were Americans.

Use the Internet (Wikipedia.org) to familiarize your team with the November 28, 2008, attack on Mumbai. Next, assume that your team is operating a large hotel in a major metropolitan area such as New York, London, Paris or Mumbai. What are three concrete actions you could employ to reduce the threat to your guests and property that could result from your hotel being targeted by terrorists?

Chapter

12 The Maintenance Department

Chapter Outline

Chapter Overview

Hotel guests have expectations about their hotel stays that simply must be met. These include such basic items as ample hot water for baths and showers, guest room lights that work, and comfortable temperatures in the hotel's public spaces and guest rooms. Employees working in a hotel expect that the tools and equipment they need to do their jobs will be safe and in good condition. In addition, the owners of a hotel have expectations. Among other things they expect that the building and its contents will be correctly repaired and maintained to protect the value of their investments in them. The hotel's maintenance department meets and fulfills all of these expectations and more.

In some hotels, the maintenance department is known as the maintenance and engineering department or as the engineering and maintenance department. For that reason, the head of the maintenance department is commonly referred to as the chief engineer. Regardless of the name used to identify the department, the chief engineer and the department's staff are responsible for properly maintaining the hotel's building and grounds.

A well-run maintenance department assists the hotel's sales effort by providing guests with the very best experience possible as it relates to the appearance and functioning of the building's exterior and interior. This makes it easier for the sales and marketing team to sell rooms in the hotel. In this chapter, you will learn about the major areas of responsibility of the maintenance department and how it interacts with the hotel's front office, housekeeping, and food and beverage departments.

Chief engineers and their staff members are responsible for the routine maintenance of the hotel. This includes such tasks as lawn care and adding appropriate chemicals to the hotel's swimming pool. In addition to routine maintenance, every chief engineer or manager in charge of maintenance should develop an effective preventive maintenance program. These are implemented to prolong the life of a hotel's facilities and equipment and to ensure their peak operating efficiency. It is also important that the department be ready for any emergency maintenance that may be required. In this chapter, you will learn about routine, preventive, and emergency maintenance.

In most cases, a hotel's chief engineer will also have responsibility for helping the hotel's general manager monitor and manage utility usage. When utilities such as water, gas, and electricity are not well managed, and the equipment that utilizes these resources is not well maintained, the hotel's operating costs will be higher than necessary. As a result, profits will be lower than they should be. In this chapter, you will also learn how the maintenance department can effectively oversee this important concern.

Taken from *Foundations of Lodging Management,* Second Edition, by David K. Hayes, Jack D. Ninemeier and Allisha A. Miller

Chapter Objectives

1. To identify the areas of responsibility assigned to the maintenance department of a lodging facility.
2. To explain to you the importance of routine maintenance in a professionally managed hotel.
3. To explain the importance of preventive maintenance in a professionally managed hotel.
4. To explain to you the importance of emergency maintenance in a professionally managed hotel.
5. To describe the processes required to properly manage and control utility consumption in a lodging facility.

THE ROLE OF MAINTENANCE

Every hotel has a variety of valuable **assets**.

LODGING LANGUAGE

Asset: The resources owned by an organization. These include cash, accounts receivable, inventories, goodwill, furniture, fixtures, equipment, buildings, and real estate.

Assets include the hotel's staff, its cash in the bank, its customer base, and its reputation. The hotel's grounds, buildings, and equipment comprise the hotel's most visible and usually the most expensive asset, and they directly affect the value of the hotel's other assets. How guests perceive the hotel's facilities impacts its profitability. It is important, then, for the hotel's managers to develop systems to protect its physical assets by performing essential maintenance on the hotel's facilities.

When a hotel's building, equipment, and grounds are properly maintained, guests will be more likely to perceive a positive experience during their stay, and the hotel's ability to increase sales is enhanced. This is the primary job of the maintenance department. When guests experience poor facilities such as potholes in parking areas, leaking faucets, burned-out light bulbs, poor heating/cooling capacities, or insufficient hot water, their dissatisfaction increases, and the hotel's sales potential is diminished. In addition to guest satisfaction, however, an effective maintenance department will achieve many other important goals, including:

- Protecting and enhancing the financial value of the building and grounds
- Supporting the efforts of other hotel departments
- Ensuring maintenance-related adherence to brand standards
- Controlling maintenance and repair costs
- Controlling energy usage
- Minimizing guests' facility-related complaints
- Increasing the pride and morale of the hotel's staff

These goals can be achieved if the maintenance department effectively performs **preventive maintenance**, **routine maintenance**, and **emergency maintenance**, and if it properly manages the hotel's utility usage.

LODGING LANGUAGE

Preventive maintenance: Maintenance activities designed to minimize maintenance costs and prolong the life of equipment.

Routine maintenance: Maintenance activities that must be performed on a continual (ongoing) basis.

Emergency maintenance: Maintenance activities performed in response to an urgent situation.

The main role of the maintenance department is to ensure that the property is properly functioning so that guests will enjoy their stay.

Areas of Responsibility

The staff in the maintenance department of a hotel is fully responsible for the facility's upkeep (its maintenance), but it is also responsible for selected **engineering** tasks and, when necessary, specific renovation tasks.

LODGING LANGUAGE

Engineering: Designing and operating a building to ensure a safe and comfortable atmosphere.

These three distinct areas sometimes overlap. To understand the complete role of the maintenance department, we will examine its engineering, maintenance, and renovation activities separately.

ENGINEERING

Some hoteliers use the terms "engineering" and "maintenance" interchangeably. Thus, in some hotel companies, the department responsible for the care of the hotel is just as likely to be called "engineering" as "maintenance," and in some cases, its name will be a combination of both terms (maintenance and engineering). Engineering, as a building specialty, however, is different from maintenance.

The engineering of a building refers to the application of physics, chemistry, and mathematics to design and operate a building that provides a comfortable atmosphere for guests and employees. For example, in a hotel lobby area that must be air-conditioned, the building's engineer calculates the amount of air-conditioned air required to cool it properly. Factors that are considered include the temperature and humidity of the outside air, the desired lobby temperature, the temperature at which air-conditioned air enters the lobby, and the movement of the air once it is inside the lobby. Based on these calculations, the size of the air-conditioning unit required to cool the lobby is determined, as are the optimum number and location of air vents and fans delivering the cold air to the area. The engineering knowledge required to balance these features and make the right decision about air conditioner or heating capacity is significant.

Improperly engineered facilities can result in underpowered or overpowered equipment, increased building deterioration, excessive energy usage, and higher-than-necessary operating costs. In most cases the head of the maintenance department in a hotel will not

LODGING ONLINE

Engineering a building's heating, refrigeration, ventilation, and air-conditioning systems is quite complex, and special knowledge is required to manage it. To familiarize yourself with an organization whose members specialize in this field, review the Web site of the American Society of Heating, Refrigerating, and Air Conditioning Engineers at:

www.ashrae.com/

How important to you is your ability to control the temperature of a room in which you are trying to sleep?

have actually designed the building's **HVAC** systems, but he or she must be thoroughly familiar with them as well as with the engineering of the building's electrical, water, and waste systems.

LODGING LANGUAGE

HVAC: Industry shorthand term for "heating, ventilating, and air-conditioning."

In very small hotels, the entire maintenance department may consist of only one full-time (or even part-time) maintenance staff member. Larger properties employ dozens of maintenance and engineering staff. Whatever a hotel's size, however, there are engineering issues to be addressed because providing a safe and comfortable environment is an ongoing process that must be continually administered.

MAINTENANCE

Maintenance, as the term implies, refers to "maintaining" the hotel's physical property. It has been said that maintenance costs are like taxes; if they are not paid one year, they will be paid the next year—and with a penalty!

The maintenance-related costs of a hotel are often related to the hotel's age. As a building ages, its maintenance costs generally increase. Even brand-new hotels, however, require **POM**-related expenditures. These costs include staff wages and benefits, replacement parts, contract services, and energy costs.

LODGING LANGUAGE

POM: Short for "property operation and maintenance." The term is taken from the Uniform System of Accounts for Hotels and refers to the segment of the income statement that details the costs of operating the maintenance department.

The maintenance department should maintain the property in the most effective manner possible given the budget assigned it. To do so, hotel maintenance must be:

Planned. From routinely changing air filters in heating and cooling units to awarding a contract for tree trimming, the maintenance department performs too many tasks to leave these activities to chance. An effective maintenance manager is a careful administrator who reviews every piece of equipment and required activity in the hotel and then plans what should be done, when it should be done, and who should do it.

Implemented. Some maintenance managers know what *should* be done in their properties and have good intentions of completing all the required tasks, yet do not do them. Shortages of properly trained staff, insufficient budgets, lack of supervisory skills, inadequate tools, and/or underestimation of the time required to perform a given task can all adversely impact the ability of the department to achieve its goals.

Many excellent checklists and suggested activities have been developed for maintenance departments. Virtually every franchisor offers such checklists free of charge to its franchisees because it is in the best interests of the franchisor for every hotel in the system to represent the brand as well as possible.

Checklists and suggested activities that are not properly implemented, however, will not result in an acceptable maintenance program. Thus, when evaluating a maintenance department, the important factor is not whether it has planned an acceptable maintenance program for the hotel, but the degree to which it has effectively implemented or performed the planned program.

Recorded. Record-keeping is an immensely important maintenance function. Routine, scheduled maintenance tasks cannot be properly planned unless maintenance personnel know when these tasks were last performed. For example, if the plan calls for lubricating hot water pumps every six months, a written record must be kept of the last time the pumps were lubricated. Similarly, if a faucet in a guest room is replaced, a record should be kept of when the replacement was made. This will enable the maintenance department to evaluate the quality (length-of-life) of the faucets used and to take advantage of any warranty programs that apply to the replacement parts.

In many cases such as fire-suppression systems, elevators, and other safety-related equipment, local ordinances or laws may require that records documenting the performance of system maintenance be kept on file or displayed publicly. Even when it is not mandated by local ordinance, however, excellent record-keeping in all areas of the maintenance department is a good indicator of overall departmental effectiveness.

The cost of maintaining a building is very closely related to its original design and size as well as to the facilities it includes. Hotels with food service and banquet facilities, swimming pools, and exercise rooms, for example, will experience greater maintenance costs than limited-service hotels that do not have these facilities. High-rise buildings will have elevator systems that must be maintained, while one-story hotels will not. Resort facilities spread over any acres will need more landscape care than those located on smaller parcels of ground.

The materials and construction techniques used in building the hotel will also affect its POM costs. A hotel with an exterior that must be painted will experience exterior painting costs, while a hotel made of masonry will not. Energy costs will also be affected by construction. Hotels built with good insulation and well-made windows will naturally experience lower energy costs than those that are not built this way.

The finishes and interior equipment specified for installation by the hotel's builders have a tremendous impact on long-term POM costs. Durable finishes and high-quality, long-life equipment may initially be more expensive but will generally reduce operating and maintenance costs.

RENOVATION

Even with the very best of maintenance programs, hotel buildings wear out with use and must be renovated to compete well against newer properties. Hotel buildings have a predictable life span that directly affects their maintenance and renovation needs.

Figure 12.1 details the typical life span of a hotel building. As can be seen, the challenges of maintaining a building increase as it ages.

Building Age	Building Characteristics and Requirements
1–3 years	Low maintenance costs incurred
3–6 years	Maintenance costs increase
6–8 years	Refurbishment required; average maintenance costs incurred
8–15 years	Minor renovation and refurbishment required
15–20 years	Major renovation and refurbishment required
20+ years	Restoration required; high maintenance costs incurred

FIGURE 12.1 Hotel Life Span

Because every hotel will at some point need renovation and refurbishment, its owners must take steps to reserve funds for the time when renovation is undertaken. Owners do this by establishing an **FF&E reserve**.

LODGING LANGUAGE

FF&E Reserve: Funds set aside by ownership today for the future "furniture, fixture, and equipment" replacement needs of a hotel.

Generally, FF&E reserves are funded by setting aside 1–5 percent of a hotel's gross sales revenue. If designated funds such as these are not reserved, the hotel may not be able to undertake minor renovations, major renovations, or **restoration** when needed.

LODGING LANGUAGE

Restoration: Returning an older hotel building to its original, or better than original, condition.

Figure 12.2 lists specific items that must be considered when planning a hotel's short- and long-term renovation program.

LODGING LANGUAGE

Case Goods: Non-upholstered furniture such as guest room dressers, tables, end tables, and desks.

Refurbishment and minor renovation is actually an ongoing process in most hotels. Major refurbishment should take place every 6 to 10 years, and the costs associated with doing so are often very high. Extra cleaning costs are likely to be incurred during construction. Moreover, it is almost inevitable that guest services will be disrupted, resulting in unhappy guests who must be satisfied, and in lost revenue from out-of-service areas that normally generate revenue.

Restoration takes place when a hotel undergoes a renovation so extensive that walls are frequently relocated, guest rooms and public space are totally reconfigured, and mechanical systems are replaced with more modern ones. The typical hotel undergoes a restoration every 20 to 25 years. Restorations are a challenging time for management, the maintenance department, and guests. If restoration is not undertaken when needed, however, the revenue-producing potential of the hotel will decline.

	Minor Renovation	**Major Renovation**
Guest Rooms	Drapes, bedspreads Lamps, shades Carpets Upholstered furniture Faucets Mattresses	Bed frames, mattresses Wall lights Wall vinyl **Case goods** Sinks, countertops Televisions
Food and Beverage	Carpets, chairs, reupholster booths Table top décor Dishes, flatware	Decorative lighting Tables Serving equipment Wall coverings
Public Space	Table lamps, lobby furniture Lobby carpet Lobby wall coverings Meeting rooms	Overhead lighting Corridor carpet Corridor vinyl Restrooms

FIGURE 12.2 Selected Hotel Renovation and Replacement Considerations

Interactions

The efforts of the maintenance department affect the guests, the hotel's managers, and even the hotel's line employees. On a departmental basis, maintenance has the most interaction with the front office and housekeeping. In full-service hotels, the food and beverage department will also regularly interact with maintenance.

FRONT OFFICE

The maintenance department interacts with the front office in many ways. Among the most important of these are:

Providing room-status updates. When a room or its contents are damaged and cannot be rented to another guest, the maintenance department will place it in an OOO (out-of-order) status. Front office staff must then be informed about the room's status, including how long it will be unrentable and the date when it is most likely to return to service.

Responding to guest service requests. Guests occupying hotel rooms generate a variety of requests for assistance from the maintenance department. Such requests can include, for example, adjustment of the reception on televisions, replacement of light bulbs, adjustment of in-room heating or cooling (HVAC) units, and the resolution of plumbing complaints. Guests with such needs or concerns will typically call the front office, whose staff must then relay the request for service to a member of the maintenance staff.

Communicating information about specific hotel conditions. The normal maintenance performed in a hotel can result in disruption to regular building functions and/or guest services. When, for example, a swimming pool must be closed for resurfacing, or when water must be temporarily shut off to make plumbing repairs, or when a power outage disrupts electrical service to the entire hotel, the maintenance department must keep the front office well-informed of the status of the repairs or disruption and how these will affect the hotel's guests and employees.

Additional interactions between the maintenance department and the front office can include assisting with guests' needs in meeting rooms, the servicing or repairing of front office equipment and furniture, and carefully coordinating the scheduled maintenance of rooms with the front office manager to minimize disruption to guests and any negative impact on hotel revenues.

Housekeeping: Making minor repairs in guest rooms is a major responsibility of all maintenance departments. Because the housekeeping department cleans the rooms, its staff members play a critical role in identifying major and minor repair issues and reporting them to maintenance. When these two departments work well together, minor issues such as loose handles on dressers and drawers, torn wall vinyl, and leaky faucets can all be quickly identified and repaired.

Food and Beverage: The food and beverage department of a hotel may be very small, as in many limited-service properties, or extremely large, as in a convention or resort hotel. In both cases, however, the normal repair and maintenance on items such as kitchen cooking equipment, refrigerators and freezers, dishwashing equipment, and ice makers may be performed by the maintenance department's staff. Repairs to frequently used items such as dining and meeting room tables and chairs may also be completed by maintenance staff.

MANAGING MAINTENANCE

The job of maintaining a building begins immediately after it is designed, engineered, and built. With a properly trained staff, maintenance tasks can be planned and implemented to maximize the life of the property while minimizing the cost of operating the building. Managing maintenance in a hotel is a process that can be examined in a variety of ways. One helpful way is to consider maintenance as either routine, preventive, or emergency.

In each of these approaches, staffing the department with properly skilled employees is critically important.

Staffing

The talents of the maintenance staff crucially affect a hotel's profitable operation. This is true because so much of a guest's impression of the quality of a hotel is dependent on the work of the maintenance department. The quality of the maintenance staff and the quality of their work will, in the guest's eyes, represent the quality of the entire hotel. When maintenance work is performed poorly or is not undertaken at all, it quickly shows. The solution to this potential problem lies in the selection of an excellent manager to head the maintenance department. In most hotels, there will also be a need for appropriately trained maintenance assistants.

CHIEF ENGINEER

In the hotel industry, the head of maintenance may hold a variety of titles. The most widely used titles are **chief engineer** and **maintenance chief**. Whatever the title, the person with this role is the head of one of the hotel's most important departments.

LODGING LANGUAGE

Chief engineer: The employee responsible for the management of a hotel's maintenance department. Sometimes referred to as "maintenance chief."

Maintenance chief: The employee responsible for the management of a hotel's maintenance department. Sometimes referred to as "chief engineer."

In smaller hotels, the chief engineer may take a very hands-on role in the maintenance effort. This could involve actually performing maintenance and repair tasks. In larger hotels, with a larger staff, the chief engineer serves in an administrative role that consists of planning work, organizing staff, directing and evaluating employee efforts, and controlling the POM budget. Regardless of a hotel's size, the chief engineer must be well-organized, attentive to detail, and a cooperative member of the management team.

MAINTENANCE ASSISTANTS

In addition to the chief engineer, the maintenance department may employ one or more individuals with varying degrees of skill in the areas of:

- Engineering
- Mechanics
- Plumbing
- Electricity
- Carpentry
- Water treatment (for pools and spas)
- Landscaping
- Grounds maintenance

The needs of each specific hotel dictate the actual skills, make-up, and number of maintenance staff required. It would be difficult to find one person skilled in all of the technical maintenance areas needed in a hotel. When the necessary skills or manpower needs exceed the capabilities of the in-house staff, the chief engineer,sometimes in consultation with the general manager, must decide to **outsource** the work. The ability to effectively determine which tasks are best performed by in-house or outsourced staff is a characteristic of an excellent chief engineer.

LODGING LANGUAGE

Outsource: To obtain labor or parts from an outside provider. Typically done to reduce costs or obtain specialized expertise.

ALL IN A DAY'S WORK 12.1

THE SITUATION

"The telephone is ringing off the hook!" Dani Pelley, the front office manager, told Lindsey Noel, the hotel's general manager. "I called maintenance and Ted said they were looking into it."

"It" was a complete outage of the satellite system used to deliver television reception to the hotel. The hotel's pay-per-view features were down and the free-to-guests channels were unavailable. Guests were calling the front desk to complain or to request a repair on their television sets.

"What do we do now?" asked Dani.

Lindsey picked up the walkie-talkie, radioed Ted, the chief engineer, and got the bad news: Satellite reception was indeed down. The hotel's equipment was not at fault, but the satellite service provider was experiencing equipment difficulty due to a heavy rainstorm in the area. The chief had just gotten off the telephone with them to report the problem, and they estimated a repair time of between 2 and 24 hours. Until the problem was fixed, there would simply be no TV reception in the guest rooms.

A RESPONSE

Sometimes hotels experience maintenance or facility problems that are simply beyond their control. In this situation, the most important thing for management to do is inform guests and appropriate hotel employees about the problem, keep them updated as to any changes in the estimated repair time, and be prepared to make room-rate adjustments or provide other compensation as approved by management.

In smaller hotels, calling each room may be appropriate. In larger properties that are so equipped, activating the telephone message light in each room and recording a message explaining the problem may be a good solution.

Routine Maintenance

When managing a hotel's routine maintenance tasks, the chief engineer is simply directing the customary care of the facility. For example, in hotels with lawns and plant beds around entrances or parking areas, it is customary to periodically cut and edge the grass and to maintain the visual integrity of the plant bed by pulling weeds and replacing foliage as needed. If this work is not done, the curb appeal of the hotel suffers. Cleaning interior windows, picking up trash in the parking lot, and shoveling snow in climates that require it are additional examples of routine maintenance. Often, only limited employee training is required to adequately complete routine maintenance tasks.

The chief engineer is generally the person who decides whether to perform routine maintenance work in-house or to pay an outside vendor to perform it. Regardless of the decision, an effective chief engineer must be concerned with both the exterior and interior of the hotel.

EXTERIOR

On the outside of the hotel, tasks such as lawn care, landscaping maintenance, grounds care, and leaf and snow removal are important issues. Just as important is attention to the details required for the care of the hotel building itself. This includes such tasks as routine roof inspection and repair, window cleaning and window seals inspection, and the care and painting, if required, of the building's exterior finishes.

The location of a hotel will dictate, to a large degree, the items that must be considered for routine exterior maintenance. A resort hotel in the Miami, Florida, area will have exterior maintenance needs that are different from those of a downtown high-rise hotel in Chicago, Illinois. Regardless of the setting, however, properly maintaining the outside of the hotel improves curb appeal, decreases operational costs, and ultimately increases the building's value. The maintenance department must ensure that routine exterior maintenance is performed correctly and in a timely manner.

INTERIOR

The chief engineer must also supervise routine maintenance inside the hotel. Some examples of routine interior maintenance tasks include the care of indoor plants, the washing of interior windows (if not assigned to housekeeping), and, in some cases, the care and cleaning of floors and carpets.

One significant task nearly always assigned to the maintenance department is the changing of light bulbs. Regardless of their type, light bulbs will burn out and then must be replaced. In some instances, individual light bulbs are immediately replaced when they burn out. That is, the maintenance department implements a **replace as needed** program for bulbs.

LODGING LANGUAGE

Replace as needed: A parts or equipment replacement plan that delays installing a new part until the original part fails or is near failure. For example, most chief engineers would use a replace-as-needed plan in the maintenance of refrigeration compressors or water pumps.

The cost to a hotel of replacing a light bulb consists of two components. These are the price of the bulb itself and the labor dollars required to change the bulb. Therefore, in special cases, such as the light bulbs in a hotel with high ceilings that require special lifts or ladders for access, the hotel may implement a **total replacement** program that involves changing all bulbs, including those that have not burned out, on a regularly predetermined schedule.

LODGING LANGUAGE

Total replacement: A parts or equipment replacement plan that involves installing new or substitute parts based on a predetermined schedule. For example, most chief engineers would use a total replacement approach to the maintenance of light bulbs in high-rise exterior highway signs.

Using this approach, while it involves discarding some bulbs or lamps with life remaining, may significantly reduce bulb-replacement labor costs and make the hotel's total bulb-replacement costs lower.

Another form of routine interior maintenance involves items related to guest rooms and public spaces. These items must be attended to on a regular basis when they malfunction, wear out, or break and need repair or replacement. For example, a room attendant in a guest room may notice and report that a chair leg is broken or that the tub in the room drains slowly. Similarly, a front office agent may report that a guest has complained about poor television reception or reported a toilet that does not flush properly. When events such as these occur, the maintenance department is notified with a **work order**, or maintenance request. Figure 12.3 shows a sample work order.

LODGING LANGUAGE

Work order: A form used to initiate and document a request for maintenance. Also referred to as a "maintenance request."

In a well-managed hotel, any staff member who sees an area of concern can initiate a work order. Work orders are prenumbered, multicopy forms that, depending on the number of copies preferred by the general manager, are used to notify maintenance, the front office, housekeeping, and others who may need to know when a maintenance request is initiated or completed. In some hotels, blank work order forms are placed in the guest room for guests to initiate. In some cases, these requests can be initiated using the hotel's in-room television system.

Regardless of their original source, the work orders, once received by the maintenance department, are reviewed and prioritized. For example, a work order indicating an inoperable guest room lock would take priority over one addressing a crooked picture in another guest room. A maintenance employee completes the task(s) called for on the

Best Sleep Hotel Work Order

Work Order Number: ______ (Preassigned) ______ Initiated By: ______

Date: ______ Time: ______ Room or Location: ______

Problem Observed: ______

Received On: ______ Assigned To: ______

Date Corrected: ______ Time Spent: ______

M&E Employee Comments: ______

Chief Engineer Comments: ______

FIGURE 12.3 Work Order

work order and informs the proper departments, and the information related to the work performed is carefully retained. In a well-run department, the chief engineer keeps a room-by-room record of replacements and repairs that have been made.

Some general managers evaluate the effectiveness of their maintenance department based on the rapidity with which maintenance work orders are completed. While the timely completion of maintenance requests should not be the only factor for judging a maintenance department, it is an important indicator of effectiveness and efficiency. When work orders are not completed promptly (or at all), the maintenance department loses credibility in the eyes of the hotel's staff and guests. An effective chief engineer monitors the speed at which work orders are prioritized and completed and then, if needed, takes corrective action.

Preventive Maintenance

When not performing routine maintenance or responding to work orders, the maintenance department has a good many other maintenance-related tasks to perform. In fact, many hoteliers believe that the most important maintenance performed in a hotel is its **PM (preventive maintenance) program**.

LODGING LANGUAGE

PM (preventive maintenance) program: A specific inspection and activities schedule designed to minimize maintenance-related costs and to prolong the life of equipment by preventing small problems before they become larger ones.

An effective PM program saves money for a hotel by reducing:

- Long-term repair costs (because equipment life is prolonged)
- Replacement parts costs (because purchases of parts can be planned)
- Labor costs (because PM can be performed during otherwise slow periods)
- The dollar amount of adjustments and allowances due to guest dissatisfaction (because guest inconvenience is reduced)
- The costs of emergency repairs (because they will occur less frequently)

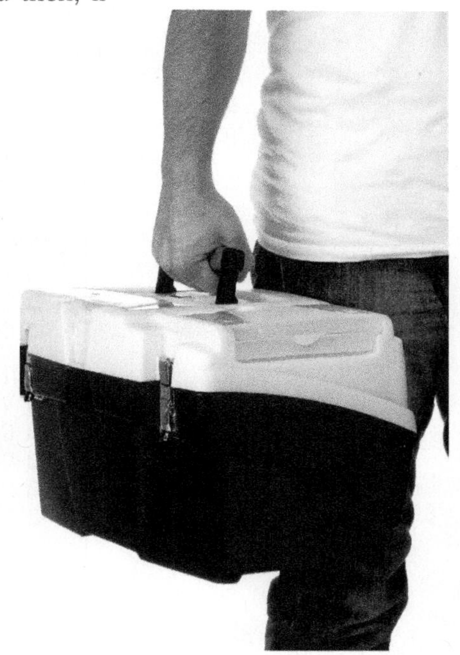

A well-managed maintenance program performs routine and preventive maintenance tasks.

LODGING GOES GREEN!

Like the Housekeeping department, the maintenance department in a hotel will purchase and use a variety of chemicals to do its job. This includes products such as general-purpose cleaners, industrial degreasers, carpet cleaners, floor finishes/sealers, and floor finish strippers. Handled improperly, these chemicals can pose a significant threat to the environment and to employees using them. In many cases, these chemicals are sold in concentrated form and thus must be dispensed. As a result, the dispensing equipment used must be carefully maintained and calibrated to ensure the safety of maintenance workers and to minimize the environmental impact of the cleaning product.

The maintenance department in a hotel illustrates the fact that a truly green orientation entails more than the purchase of environmentally friendly products. It requires the right employee practices as well. As a result, those hoteliers who are committed to environmentally friendly operation must also be committed to aggressive "green-practices" employee training programs. This is especially important in a hotel's maintenance department, but it is also true in every department within the hotel.

In addition to saving money, a good PM program reduces guest complaints, eases the job of the sales staff, enhances the eye appeal and functionality of the hotel, and improves employee morale.

Schedules for PM programs can come from a variety of sources. Equipment suppliers often suggest maintenance activities for their products, franchisors may mandate PM schedules, and local ordinances may require specific PM activities (such as boiler equipment or water heater inspection). Most important of all, the chief engineer's skill and experience and knowledge of the hotel's needs dictate PM schedules.

Most PM activities involve basic inspection, replacement, cleaning, and lubrication. PM is not generally considered to be a repair program, nor should it be viewed as one. Repairs must be completed when they are needed, while PM activities should be performed on a scheduled basis.

Some chief engineers design PM programs that are segmented into activities to be performed daily, weekly, monthly, semi-annually, and annually. Others segment the hotel into major areas (e.g., food service and laundry) and then develop area-specific PM schedules. In both cases, the PM program should identify what is to be done, when it is to be done, and how it is to be done. It should also provide an easy method to document the completion of the activity.

Figure 12.4 is a sample of a daily, monthly, and annual PM task list for a dryer in a hotel's laundry area.

PM ACTIVITY: LAUNDRY AREA DRYER

DAILY
- ❑ Clean lint trap
- ❑ Wipe down inside chamber with mild detergent
- ❑ Clean and wipe dry the outside dryer shell

MONTHLY
- ❑ Vacuum the inside of dryer (upper and lower chambers)
- ❑ Check and tighten, if needed, the bolts holding dryer to floor
- ❑ Check all electrical connections
- ❑ Check fan belt for wear; replace if needed
- ❑ Lubricate moving parts

ANNUALLY
- ❑ Check pulley alignment
- ❑ Adjust rotating basket if needed
- ❑ Lubricate motor bearings
- ❑ Lubricate drum bearings if needed

FIGURE 12.4 Sample PM Task List for Laundry Area Dryer

LODGING ONLINE

Carpet and area rug care can be complex, but a variety of resources are available to help determine how to best care for these items. To view one such free resource, go to the Web site of the Carpet and Rug Institute at:

www.carpet-rug.org/

How much do you think hotel managers should know about the proper care and cleaning of commercial carpets? Where should they learn about it?

The chief engineer of a hotel must have a written and complete PM program in place. All of the hotel's equipment, including furnaces, air conditioners, water-heating equipment, and elevators, must have individual PM programs. In addition, the maintenance department must create specific PM programs for the following areas:

- Public space
- Guest rooms
- Food service
- Laundry
- Other equipment

PUBLIC SPACE

Public space PM programs are vitally important but relatively simple to develop. In public spaces such as lobbies, corridors, and meeting areas, PM programs should include such items as windows, HVAC units, furniture, lights, elevators, and carpets. In fact, carpet care is one of the most challenging PM activities of all. Carpet care duties are often shared between housekeeping and maintenance, with housekeeping taking responsibility for minor (spot) cleaning issues, and the maintenance department responsible for long-term carpet PM.

It is important for public space appearances to be well maintained because they significantly influence guest opinions about the entire hotel. Professional hoteliers know that a good first impression goes a long way toward ensuring a satisfactory guest stay.

GUEST ROOMS

The hotel's guest rooms are perhaps the most important and certainly the most extensive area for PM. Despite that, some chief engineers do not implement aggressive guest room PM programs. The guest room PM program is critical to the hotel's sales efforts, to its ability to retain guests, and to the maintenance of the asset's monetary value. In fact, there are few things a chief engineer should pay more attention to than the PM program used for guestrooms.

An effective PM program requires a quarterly, or more frequent, inspection of guest rooms with a careful examination of each item on the guest room **PM Checklist**.

LODGING LANGUAGE

PM Checklist: A tool developed to identify all the critical areas that should be inspected during a PM review of a room, area, or piece of equipment.

The checklist for any PM area is developed to help maintenance staff with their inspections. Figure 12.5 is an example of a PM checklist that can be used for guest rooms.

Note that the extensive checklist in Figure 12.5 can be tailored for each individual property. For example, hotels that have in-room microwaves and refrigerators could add these items to the guest room PM checklist. If some guest rooms contain whirlpool-type tubs, these could be included. It is the responsibility of the chief engineer to develop a custom PM checklist and inspection schedule for guest rooms and then to see that the

	The Best Sleep Hotel Guest Room PM Checklist										
	Place an "x" by any item not meeting hotel standards										
Year______________		Room Number______________									
Area	Item	Quarter				Area	Item	Quarter			
Inspected	Inspected	1	2	3	4	Inspected	Inspected	1	2	3	4
Entrance	Number sign					Bathroom	Floor tile/grouting				
Door	Exterior Finish					continued	Telephone				
	Interior Finish						Blow Dryer				
	Peep hole						GFI plug operational				
	Door closer					Drapes	Drape Hooks				
	Deadbolt						Drape wand				
	Lock/lock plate						Valance				
	Evacuation/fire safety plan						Drape rods and brackets				
	Innkeeper's laws frame					Bedroom	Entrance ceiling				
	Hinges						Room ceiling				
Closet	Shelf Stable						Night Stand				
	Clothes Hooks						Night stand drawers				
	Clothes Rod						Dresser				
	Carpet/Covebase						Dresser drawers				
	Luggage Rack						Headboard				
	Vinyl/Walls						Desk				
	Closet door finish						Desk chair				
	Closet door operation						Upholstered chairs				
	Closet door mirror						Bed frames				
Fixtures,	Entry light						Mattress (condition)				
lights and	Closet light						Mattress (turned)				
bulbs	Swing lamps						Mirrors				
	Dresser lamps						Art work				
	Desk lamp						Wall vinyl				
	Pole lamp						Electrical switches				
	Bathroom					HVAC	Filters changed				
	Smoke Detector						Fan				
	Sprinkler head						Motor				
Bathroom	Door Finish						Controls				
	Door lock						Condensate pan				
	Ceiling condition						Wiring				
	Overhead Fan					TV/Radio	Picture quality				
	Toilet operation						Swivel				
	Toilet caulking						Lock down				
	Tub diverter spout						Volume				
	Tub tile/grouting						Remote control				
	Tub stopper						Cabinet condition				
	Shower head						Connections				
	Curtain rod secure						Video game controls				
	Safety bar secure					Telephone	Line 1				
	Non-skid surface						Line 2				
	Sink Faucet						Jacks secure				
	Sink stopper					Connecting	Interior Finish				
	Piping					Door	Exterior Finish				
	Aerator						Frame				
	Toilet Paper holder						Door Stop				
	Towel rack						Lock(s) operation				
	Mirrors						Door knob				
	Vinyl Walls						Hinges				
						Other					
Inspector initials											
The Best Sleep Hotel, 20XX											

FIGURE 12.5 Guest Room PM Checklist File location

inspections are performed when scheduled. When they are, guest room quality complaints will be minimized and long-term repair costs will be reduced because small problems will be uncovered and attended to before they become big ones.

FOOD SERVICE

There are three major PM concerns in the food service area. The first is back-of-the-house equipment. The ovens, ranges, griddles, fryers, and other production equipment in the kitchen are heavily used and, of course, must be properly maintained. Specialty equipment such as dishwashers, fryers, and convection ovens may require the PM expertise of specifically trained technicians. If so, these outsourced vendors should be selected and their work scheduled by the chief engineer or by the food and beverage director. In all cases, every piece of kitchen equipment as well as all mechanical bar equipment should be included in the PM program.

A second area of PM concern in the food services area is the dining and lounge space used by guests. Included in this program are chairs, tabletops, and bases. An especially annoying PM issue for guests involves table leveling. In a professionally managed hotel, there is simply no excuse for wobbly tables or for foreign objects (such as folded paper napkins and match books) to be placed under tables to make them level. In addition, PM must include all fixed seating, booths, self-serve salad or buffet areas, lighting fixtures, and guest-check processing equipment.

A third area of PM concern in food and beverages, and one that is sometimes overlooked, includes meeting and conference rooms and equipment. Included in this PM program are light fixtures, tables, chairs, and wall coverings within the hotel's meeting rooms. In addition, the PM program must include transport carts and any audiovisual-elated items owned by the hotel. These may include flip chart stands, TVs, overhead projectors, computer projection units, and speaker telephones. In those hotels that have determined that audiovisual-related equipment will be the responsibility of the maintenance department (instead of the banquet area of the food and beverage department), equipment in this area must also be maintained.

LAUNDRY

In the laundry, the washers, dryers, folding equipment, water supply lines, drains, lighting fixtures, and temperature-control units require PM programs. The clothes dryer is an especially important concern because of the potential for fire. Dryer drum temperatures can be very high, and the lint build-up during the natural drying process requires vigilance on the part of the maintenance department as well as housekeeping personnel. Lint traps should be cleaned at least once per day (or more often) and should be thoroughly inspected weekly.

In many cases, the company supplying laundry chemicals to the hotel maintains the equipment used to dispense chemicals into the washers. This does not relieve the maintenance department of that type of responsibility. If chemical usage is too high, this may be because the chemical supplier has adjusted equipment to overdispense chemicals in an effort to sell more products. For this reason and because improperly maintained chemical-dispensing units may result in substandard laundry quality and even cause damage to linen and terry, the maintenance department should make chemical dispenser maintenance an important part of the laundry PM program even if it is performed in conjunction with the dispensing equipment supplier.

LODGING ONLINE

Diversey Inc. is a company that supplies chemicals to hotel laundries. It does an excellent job of PM on its own dispensing equipment. To view the company's Web site, go to:

www.johnsondiversey.com

When you arrive, click "Lodging" under the "Industries" tab.

How important do you think clean sheets and towels are to guests' satisfaction when staying in a hotel?

LODGING ONLINE

A comprehensive PM program for hotels is sometimes easier to maintain than to begin because there are so many pieces of equipment to be included. Today, software exists to help a chief engineer decide what must be maintained and how frequently to schedule PM. To view one software company's hotel-oriented PM program, go to:

www.attr.com/

What are some reasons why it is better to do PM on a piece of equipment rather than repair it when it breaks down?

OTHER AREAS AND EQUIPMENT

Additional areas of concern when developing a PM program can include pools and spas, front office equipment, electronic guest room locks, exterior door locks, motor vehicles such as courtesy vans, and in-hotel transportation equipment including housekeeper's carts and luggage carts, just to name but a few.

A quality PM maintenance program involves a vast number of pieces of equipment and areas of the hotel. An effective chief engineer develops, maintains, and documents an effective and comprehensive PM program that both reduces repair costs and enhances the image of the hotel.

Emergency Maintenance

The strongest rationale for implementing well-designed and aggressive routine and PM programs is the ability to manage and minimize repair costs. Despite the very best routine and PM efforts of the chief engineer and the maintenance staff, however, a hotel sometimes requires emergency maintenance. Emergency maintenance occurrences are generally defined as those that:

- Are unexpected
- Threaten to negatively impact hotel revenue
- Require immediate attention to minimize danger or damage
- Require labor and parts that must be purchased at a premium price

For example, assume that a water pipe bursts in one of the hotel's unoccupied guest rooms in the middle of the night. A short time later, the guests in the room one floor below the room with the broken pipe call the front desk to complain about water coming into their room from the ceiling. Clearly, this situation requires emergency maintenance. If not attended to immediately, extensive repair work to the pipe as well as to the ceilings and walls around the leak may be required.

Hotel managers can encounter a variety of situations that require immediate attention from the maintenance department. Some of these include:

No heat or air-conditioning in room. This is especially an emergency during extremely cold or hot weather, and when the HVAC unit controlling air temperature is not working due to mechanical malfunction.

No electricity in room. Blown electrcial fuses in a hotel are fairly common. Even more common is a blown **GFI outlet**. While these are easy to reset, many guests will not know how to do so. The result can be frequent emergency power outage calls to the front desk, followed by the need for maintenance staff to reset the outlets.

LODGING LANGUAGE

GFI outlet: Short for "Ground Fault Interrupter" outlet. This special electrical outlet is designed to interrupt power (by "tripping" or "blowing") before significant damage can be done to a building's wiring system. These outlets are most commonly installed in the bathroom or vanity areas of a hotel room, where high-voltage usage (such as high wattage hairdryers) or high moisture levels can cause electrical power interruptions.

Gas leaks or smell of gas. This is a very serious situation because sparks from equipment or appliances (and even cell phones) can ignite gas. Immediate shut-off is required in a situation of known gas leakage. If appropriate, the hotel's natural gas provider should also be contacted in such emergencies.

Interior flooding. In most cases, the action required in these emergencies involves shutting off the water at the source of the leak and then making the appropriate plumbing repair. In most cases, repairs of this type must be made quickly to avoid damaging furniture, flooring materials, and other guest rooms or public areas of the hotel.

Toilet stoppage. This extremely common situation always requires prompt maintenance attention. A guest may tolerate a slow drain in a sink or tub, but a toilet stoppage emergency is quite a different matter. To avoid further problems including flooding, these emergencies must be addressed immediately.

While minor maintenance-related emergencies are not typically brought to the attention of the hotel's general manager, the chief engineer should notify the general manager or other appropriate hotel management staff when doing so is necessary to protect the well-being of guests and the reputation of the hotel.

Emergency repairs are expensive. They sometimes require the authorization of overtime for maintenance staff or outside repair personnel. In addition, needed repair parts that might normally be purchased through customary sources may need to be secured quickly (and at a premium price) from non-customary sources. While it is not possible to avoid all emergency maintenance, effective routine and PM programs reduce the number of times emergency maintenance is required and the total cost of property maintenance.

MANAGING UTILITIES

Utility management is an important part of a hotel's overall operation. Utility costs in hotels include expenses for water and sewage, gas, electricity, or other fossil fuel for heating and cooling the building, fuel for heating water, and, in some cases, the purchase of steam or chilled water. Hotels with active programs to conserve energy find that the procedures they use are not only environmentally friendly, but also save money.

Energy-related expenses that were once taken for granted by the public and most hoteliers became very important and costly during the energy crisis of the early 1970s. Since then, these costs have moderated somewhat. When the cost of utilities is relatively low, few Americans, including hoteliers, take strong measures to conserve resources and implement **energy management** programs. Alternatively, when energy costs are high, managers have a heightened sense of awareness about these costs. Every hotel manager, and every hotel staff member, should always practice energy-effective management.

LODGING LANGUAGE

Energy management: Specific engineering, maintenance, and facility-design policies and activities intended to control and reduce energy usage.

It is important to remember that, in most cases, the utilities cost for lighting, heating, and operating hotel equipment will be incurred regardless of occupancy levels. While it is true that higher hotel occupancy will result in some incremental increase in utility costs, (e.g., more rooms sold will result in increased water consumption for bathing), as much as 80 percent of total utility costs for a hotel are actually fixed. A hotel's original design and construction and the age of its buildings significantly affect its energy usage. Its usage is most affected, however, by the regular maintenance and **calibration** of the equipment consuming energy.

Managing and conserving utilities is very important because they represent one of a hotel's largest operating costs.

LODGING LANGUAGE

Calibration: The adjustment of equipment to maximize its effectiveness and operational efficiency.

Depending on the location of the hotel, energy costs can represent as much as 3–15 percent of total operating costs. In addition, energy is a valuable resource, and as responsible members of the hotel industry, all hoteliers should be committed to energy conservation. Because that is true, it is easy to see why an effective maintenance department should be very concerned with conserving energy and controlling utility costs.

Electricity

Electricity is the most common and usually the most expensive form of energy used in hotels. To be effective, the hotel's electrical source must be dependable, and it will be if the maintenance department maintains the hotel's electrical systems in a safe manner. While some hotels have a **back-up generator** for use in an emergency outage situation, most will rely on one or more local power providers to deliver electricity.

LODGING LANGUAGE

Back-up generator: Equipment used to make limited amounts of electricity on-site; utilized in times of power failure or when the hotel experiences low supply from the usual provider of electricity.

In some locations, electric bills account for more than 50 percent (and sometimes as much as 80 percent) of a hotel's total utility costs. Controlling electrical consumption can really pay off for hoteliers interested in lowering utility bills.

Electricity is used everywhere in a hotel. It powers the administrative computers, operates fire safety systems, keeps food cold in freezers and refrigerators, and provides power for security systems, to name but a few uses. When considering the total electrical consumption of hotels, however, the two most important uses of electricity, and, therefore, those the chief engineer must manage most carefully, are related to lighting and HVAC systems.

LIGHTING

The lighting in a hotel is tremendously important for curb appeal, guest comfort, worker efficiency, and property security. Lighting is sometimes referred to as illumination, and light levels are measured in **foot-candles**.

LODGING LANGUAGE

Foot-candle: A measure of illumination. One foot-candle equals one lumen per square foot.

Generally, the greater the number of foot-candles, the greater the illumination. Hotels require varying degrees of illumination in different locations, and the types of light fixtures and bulbs used play a large role in producing the most appropriate light for each hotel setting.

Artificial light is produced to supplement natural (sun) light. Natural light is cost-effective and, when used properly, can reduce utility costs by limiting the amount of artificial light that is needed. When lighting must be supplemented, the hotel can choose from two basic lighting options. The first of these is **incandescent lamps**.

LODGING LANGUAGE

Incandescent lamp: A lamp in which a filament inside the lamp's bulb is heated by electrical current to produce light.

Incandescent lamps are what most people think of when they think of the older style light bulbs used in their homes. Incandescent bulbs have relatively short life spans (2,000 hours or less) and thus must be frequently changed. They are fairly inefficient since they produce only 15–20 lumens per watt. For example, a 100-watt bulb produces 1,500–2,000 lumens. Incandescent lights are popular, however, because they are easy to install, easy to move, inexpensive to purchase, and have the characteristic of starting and restarting instantly. Incandescent lamp bulbs can be made in such a way as to concentrate light in one area (these are known as spotlights or floodlights).

In cases where a conventional incandescent light is not best suited for a specific lighting need, hotels can select an **electric discharge lamp** as a second lighting option.

LODGING LANGUAGE

Electric discharge lamp: A lamp in which light is generated by passing electrical current through a space filled with a special combination of gases. Examples include fluorescent, mercury vapor, metal halide, and sodium.

Electric discharge lamps do not operate directly from electricity. They must use a **ballast**.

LODGING LANGUAGE

Ballast: The device in an electric discharge lamp that starts, stops, and controls the electrical current to the light.

Electric discharge lamps have longer lives (5,000–25,000 hours), and higher efficiency (40–80 lumens per watt) than incandescent lamps. The most common lamp of this type is the fluorescent, and it is frequently used where high light levels and low operating costs are important. If an electric discharge lamp stops working, either the bulb or the ballast may need replacing.

Other types of electric discharge lamps include those for parking areas or security lighting. In cases such as these, sodium lamps are a good choice because they can generate 200 lumens per watt used and have extremely long lives, but the cost of purchasing and installing these lights is also greater than for fluorescent lamps.

In the late 1980s, the compact version of the fluorescent light known as the **CFL** became popular in many hotels.

LODGING LANGUAGE

CFL: Short for "Compact Fluorescent Light." An alternative light source that uses less energy and lasts longer than incandescent light.

These lights are designed to combine the energy efficiency and long life of a traditional fluorescent light with the convenience and ballast-free operation of an incandescent light. For many applications, they provide an excellent blend of operational savings and convenience.

CFLs are increasing in popularity because they are:

Changing the hotel lighting system to utilize CFL bulbs will provide savings because this type of bulb uses less energy and has a longer life than do incandescent bulbs.

Energy-efficient. CFLs use about one-fourth the energy of traditional incandescent light bulbs. For example, a 26-watt CFL produces the same amount of light as a typical 100-watt incandescent bulb.

Cost-effective. Because CFLs use about one-fourth the energy of incandescent bulbs, hotels using them save money on their electric bills. While the initial

LODGING ONLINE

The proper use of indoor and outdoor lighting in a hotel is important in many ways. To obtain a better understanding of how lighting works, visit the General Electric Company's lighting Web site. Go to:

www.gelighting.com/na/

When you arrive, select "Learn about Light," and then select "Facts About Light."

purchase price of a CFL is higher than an incandescent, the bulb lasts about 10 times longer.

Environmentally friendly. Power plants that generate electricity also produce pollution. Since CFLs use less electricity to produce the same amount of light as incandescent light bulbs, reducing the amount of electricity used also reduces the amount of pollution produced.

When selecting lighting, hotels can choose from a wide choice of lamps, bulbs, and light fixtures. The proper type, the color of the light, and the operational costs must all be taken into consideration when selecting lighting fixtures and lamps. In all cases, however, lighting maintenance, including lamp repair, bulb changing, and fixture cleaning, must be an integral part of the hotel's PM program.

HVAC

Another significant user of electrical power is the hotel's HVAC system. Heating, ventilation, and air-conditioning are considered together in the hotel's maintenance program because they all utilize the hotel's air-treatment, thermostats, **duct** and **air handler** systems.

LODGING LANGUAGE

Duct: A passageway, usually built of sheet metal, that allows fresh, cold, or warm air to be directed to various parts of a building.

Air handler: The fans and mechanical systems required to move air through ducts and to vents.

A properly operating HVAC system delivers air at a desired temperature to rooms in the hotel. The efficiency with which a hotel's HVAC system operates, and thus the comfort of the building, is affected by a variety of factors, including:

- The original temperature of the air in the room
- The temperature of the air delivered to the room
- The relative humidity of the air when delivered
- The air movement in the room
- The temperature-absorbing surfaces in the room

HVAC systems can be fairly straightforward or very complex, but all consist of components responsible for heating and cooling the hotel.

Heating Components: While it is possible for all of a hotel's heating components to be operated electrically, this is not normally the case. Heating by electricity, especially in cold climates, is generally not cost-effective. Because of this, hotels heat at least some parts of their buildings using natural gas, liquefied petroleum gas (LPG), steam, or fuel oil although electricity can be used to heat small areas.

In most hotels, the heating of hot water is second in cost only to the heating of air. A hotel requires an effective furnace (or heat pump system) for heating air, and a boiler of the right size for heating water. Regardless of the heat source, fans powered by electricity move warm air produced by the furnace to the appropriate parts of the building.

Similarly, electricity often powers pumps to move hot water produced by the hot water heater. The maintenance of these two heating components can be complex, but an effective chief engineer maintains them in a manner that is safe and cost-effective, performing calibration and maintenance tasks in accordance with manufacturer's recommendations and local building code requirements.

Cooling Components: Just as a hotel must heat air and water, in most cases it must also cool them. The major cost of operating air-cooling or air-conditioning systems is related to electricity usage. Essentially, in an air-conditioning system, electrically operated equipment extracts heat from either air or water and then utilizes the remaining cooled air or water to absorb and remove more heat from the building. The effectiveness of a cooling system is dependent on several factors, including:

- The original air temperature and humidity of the space to be cooled
- The temperature and humidity of the chilled air entering the room from the HVAC system
- The quantity of chilled air entering the room
- The operational efficiency of the air-conditioning equipment

Some cooling systems are designed to produce small quantities of very cold air that is then pumped or blown into a room to reduce its temperature, while other systems supply larger quantities of air that is not as cold but has the same room-cooling affect because the quantity of air supplied is greater.

The ability of a cooling system to deliver cold air or water of a specified temperature and in the quantity required determines the overall effectiveness of a cooling system. Very often, especially in hot humid weather, the demands placed upon a hotel's cooling system are intense. The ability of the maintenance department to maintain cooling equipment in a manner that minimizes guest discomfort (and the resulting complaints) is critical to the success of the hotel. Effective routine and PM maintenance on cooling equipment is a crucial part of the chief engineer's job in climates where air-conditioning is a frequent need.

Natural Gas

In some geographic areas where natural gas is plentiful and cost-effective, hotels use it to heat water for guest rooms and to power laundry area clothes dryers. Natural gas is also used in many hotel HVAC systems to directly or indirectly provide heat to guest rooms and public spaces.

Interestingly, the overwhelming majority of chefs and cooks prefer natural gas when cooking because of its rapid heat production and the amount of immediate temperature control it allows. Cooking with natural gas is also economical. It costs about half as much to cook with a natural gas range as with a similar electric range. Although a natural gas range may cost somewhat more than an electric model, these durable pieces of cooking equipment will pay the hotel back with energy savings and years of reliable service. Many of the new models of natural gas cooking equipment use an electronic spark ignition rather than a continuously burning **pilot light**, thereby saving as much as 30 percent on energy costs when compared to a unit using a pilot light.

LODGING LANGUAGE

Pilot light: A small permanent flame used to ignite gas at a burner.

Managed properly, natural gas is an extremely safe source of energy. If a hotel is using natural gas equipment of any type, each gas hot water heater, furnace, or other piece of equipment should have a PM program designed specifically to minimize operating costs, ensure safety, and maximize the efficiency of the unit. This is especially important because the combustible nature of natural gas requires that gas leaks be avoided at all times. In addition, the calibration of the oxygen and fuel mixture required to maximize the efficiency of the combustion process must be continually and carefully monitored.

LODGING ONLINE

Gas equipment manufacturers are understandably proud of their products. For more information on gas-operated food service equipment as well as managerial tips and restaurant operations information, go to:

www.cookingforprofit.com/

Do you prefer to cook using a gas or an electric stove? Why?

Water

Aggressively managing a hotel's water consumption is very cost-effective because it pays three ways. Conserving water:

1. Reduces the number of gallons of water purchased
2. Reduces the amount the hotel will pay in sewage (water removal) costs
3. Reduces water-heating costs because less hot water must be produced

Water costs can be dramatically reduced if the maintenance department carefully monitors water usage in all areas of the hotel. Figure 12.6 lists just a few of the activities a hotel can undertake to help reduce water-related costs. Working together, the hotel staff led by the chief engineer should implement every water-saving activity that improves the hotel's bottom line and does not negatively affect guest satisfaction.

Managing Waste

Hotels generate a tremendous amount of solid waste (trash). Sources of waste include packaging materials, such as cardboard boxes, crates, and bags used in shipping hotel

Guest Rooms

- Include inspection of all guest room faucets on the PM checklist
- Inspect toilet flush valves monthly; replace as needed
- Consider installing water-saver showerheads
- Investigate earth–friendly procedures designed to enlist the aid of guests in the water conservation process

Public Space

- Include inspection of all public restroom faucets on the PM checklist
- Install automatic flush valves in men's room urinals
- Where practical, reduce hot water temperatures in public restrooms
- Check pool and spa fill levels and water pump operation daily

Laundry

- Include, as part of the PM program, the monthly inspection of water fittings on all washers
- Pre-soak stained terry and linen rather than double washing
- Use the lowest hot water wash setting possible while still ensuring clean terry and linen

Food Service

- Serve water to diners only on request
- Operate dishwashers only as needed
- Use sprayers, not faucets, to prerinse dishes and flatware intended to be machine-washed
- Use chemical sanitizers rather than excessively hot water to sanitize pots and pans
- Use sprayers (not faucets) to rinse/wash produce prior to cooking or storage

Outdoors

- Inspect sprinkler systems for leaking and misdirected spraying daily
- Utilize the sprinkler system only when critically needed. Do not overwater
- Minimize the use of sprayed water for cleaning (driveway and parking areas, for example); sweep and spot clean these areas as needed

FIGURE 12.6 Sample Water Conservation Techniques

ALL IN A DAY'S WORK 12.2

THE SITUATION

"This doesn't make any sense," said Tamara, the hotel's controller. "Occupancy was about the same this month as it was for the same month last year. But our water bill is 40 percent higher than the same time last year!"

Terrell, the maintenance chief, looked at the bill from the hotel's local water company. "I don't know what's happening either," he said. "For the bill to go up that much, something must really be wrong!"

"I'll say it's wrong," said Jack, the general manager of the hotel. "Terrell," continued Jack, "you've got to find out what's going on here. This leak is really affecting our profits!"

A RESPONSE

Unexpected increases in utility costs are always unwelcome. In this situation, a large increase in water costs indicates either a broken water line on the property, defective equipment that has resulted in excessive water usage (e.g., malfunctioning ice machines or equipment with water-cooled motors), or a large number of small waste areas (such as multiple toilets that are leaking water into their overflow valves).

Of course, it is also possible that the meter measuring the amount of water used by the hotel is defective. In all cases, however, it is the responsibility of the maintenance chief to systematically identify and eliminate these potential sources of wasted water and their effect of "draining" the hotel's profits!

supplies, kitchen garbage, guest room trash, and even yard waste generated from the hotel's landscaping efforts. Increasingly, the hotel industry has come to realize that excessive waste and poorly conceived waste-disposal methods are detrimental to the environment and represent a poor use of natural resources. In addition, as landfills become scarce, the cost of solid waste disposal has risen. Because of this, hotels have encouraged manufacturers that ship products to them to practice **source reduction** and have aggressively implemented creative programs to reduce the generation of their own solid waste.

LODGING LANGUAGE

Source reduction: Efforts by product manufacturers to design and ship products in a way that minimizes packaging waste resulting from the product's shipment to a hotel.

Source reduction involves decreasing the amount of materials and/or energy used during the manufacture or distribution of products and packages. Since it stops waste before it starts, source reduction is the top solid waste priority of the U.S. Environmental Protection Agency.

Source reduction is not the same as recycling. Recycling is collecting already used materials and making them into another product. Recycling begins at the end of a product's life, while source reduction takes place when the product and its packaging are being designed.

One way to think about source reduction and recycling is that they are complementary activities: when combined, source reduction and recycling have a significant impact on preventing solid waste and saving resources. Source reduction conserves raw material and energy resources. Smaller packages and concentrated products, such as detergents and other cleaners, typically use fewer materials and require less energy to transport. In addition, source-reduced cleaning products take up less storage space and are easier to use. Recycling, minimizing waste generation, and wise purchasing can all help reduce waste disposal costs and should be implemented wherever possible.

In addition to improving conservation efforts and controlling costs, effective waste management means keeping inside and outside trash-removal areas clean and, to the greatest degree possible, attractive. This can be achieved by proper sanitation procedures and by enclosing the trash-removal areas with fencing or other eye-appealing materials.

Poorly maintained trash-removal areas are unsightly and can attract insects, rodents, and other scavenging animals. The chief engineer should regularly inspect these areas for PM of fencing or other surrounds and for the quality of sanitation in the trash-removal areas.

Lodging Language

Asset
Preventive Maintenance
Routine Maintenance
Emergency Maintenance
Engineering
HVAC
POM
FF&E Reserve
Restoration
Case Goods
Chief Engineer
Maintenance Chief
Outsource
Replace as Needed
Total Replacement
Work Order
PM (Preventive Maintenance) Program
PM Checklist
GFI Outlet
Energy Management
Calibration
Back-up Generator
Foot-candle
Incandescent Lamp
Electric Discharge Lamp
Ballast
CFL
Duct
Air Handler
Pilot Light
Source Reduction

For Discussion

1. Many chief engineers find that maintaining an older hotel is more challenging than maintaining a newer property. Name five areas in a hotel you think might become more difficult to manage as the hotel ages.
2. Many hotel general managers require the entire maintenance staff to go through extensive guest-service training programs. Why do you think they feel this training is important?
3. For many routine maintenance replacement items, a hotel manager has a choice between doing all of the maintenance at once (such as changing air filters in all guest rooms quarterly) and doing it as needed (such as replacing hot water heater pumps when they stop working). In other cases, such as replacing parking lot light bulbs or fan belts on motors, the manager has a choice between systematic total replacement and a "replace as needed" approach. Assume that you were required to decide on a replacement program for exterior parking lot lights in a hotel with parking for 150 cars. What factors would influence your decision?
4. In some hotels the cleaning of exterior sidewalks and parking areas is the responsibility of housekeeping. In others it is the responsibility of maintenance. Name three factors that would influence which department you would assign to this important task.
5. In most hotels, a representative from the maintenance department must be available 24/7 in case of a hotel emergency. How do you think such employees could be fairly compensated for this responsibility?
6. Lawn care is an example of a maintenance task that can be done in-house or outsourced. Assume that you operate a 135-room hotel with three acres of total lawn and landscape area. Identify three factors that might influence your decision to select an outside lawn care service for your hotel's lawn and landscape work as compared to maintaining it in-house.
7. Maintaining food service equipment often requires specialized skill and replacement parts. Name three factors that you would consider before deciding to outsource the preventive maintenance of such equipment rather than performing it in-house.
8. Water conservation is important in a hotel. List three things you could do as a hotel guest to help conserve water. How do you think hoteliers could inform guests about activities like the ones you listed?
9. Maintenance staff are often highly skilled at specific building-related trades (e.g., plumbing, electricity, carpentry, or HVAC repair). What are some steps a maintenance chief could undertake to ensure that the skills of his or her staff were kept up-to-date?
10. Many hotels have implemented aggressive recycling programs. What factors would influence your decision to begin such a program?

Team Activities

TEAM ACTIVITY 1

For major hotel repairs that cannot be done by in-house staff, some hoteliers prefer to establish a relationship with one prime contractor in each field or trade (e.g., plumbing, heating, and electrical) and then employ that contractor as needed.

Other managers prefer to solicit competitive bids for each major project and then select the best bidder. Identify three advantages and three disadvantages to each approach. Which approach would you suggest at a hotel managed by your team?

TEAM ACTIVITY 2

Maintenance staff members must often enter occupied guest rooms to address rooms-related emergency repairs. The result is often interaction with unhappy guests.

Write a script two team members can present in a role-play format. In the role-play, assume it is a hot summer day, and a maintenance staff member is explaining (correctly) to an unhappy guest that the air-conditioning unit in the room is actually working properly. However, the guest continues to complain that the room is too hot and implores the staff member to make the AC work immediately.

Chapter

13

Food and Beverage Operations

Full-Service Hotels

Chapter Outline

Chapter Overview

Full-service hotels offer food and beverage products and services to guests staying at the hotel and to others living in the community or visiting the property. People attending conventions and meetings as well as other groups desiring food and beverage service can also enjoy à la carte or banquet meals at these hotels. As a result, managers at these properties must accommodate the diverse needs of a wide range of guests when planning their food and beverage offerings.

The organization of a hotel's food and beverage department typically depends upon the volume of revenue it generates. Smaller properties may have a food and beverage manager who directs the work of the employees responsible for food production and beverage service. As the department grows in size, specialized positions (e.g., specialized chefs for the dining room, room service managers, beverage managers, and banquet managers) become necessary.

The food management process begins with menu-planning efforts that focus on what guests want to purchase and what the operation can profitably produce. After menus are planned, ingredients must be purchased, received, stored, issued, and produced. Finally, meals must actually be served to guests.

Taken from *Foundations of Lodging Management,* Second Edition, by David K. Hayes, Jack D. Ninemeier and Allisha A. Miller

Full-service hotels will typically have one or more dining areas (e.g., a casual coffee shop and a more formal dining room). In addition, other retail sales outlets such as pool snack bars, lobby kiosks offering coffee, and various beverage outlets may be operated to meet the needs of the hotel's guests. Many full-service hotels also offer room service, a distinct type of food service not generally available in limited-service hotels. Because of its complexity, a wide range of menu-planning factors, operating issues, and guest-related concerns must be addressed to effectively manage this unique food service operation.

In most communities, full-service hotels offer the widest range of banquet facilities available to guests. A full-service hotel's banquet room can range from a small space accommodating 50 people or less to large convention/conference facilities that may seat several thousand people. There is significant profit opportunity in banquet operations when hoteliers manage them effectively. As with any other type of food service operation, the first managerial consideration is menu planning driven by the identification of the guests to be served.

A successful banquet event is the result of hard work and coordination of effort. Two tools—*banquet event orders* and *banquet contracts*—help minimize misunderstandings between managers in different hotel departments and with guests. Other banquet concerns, including issues relating to the provision of alcoholic beverages during events, are also very important. These will be addressed in this chapter.

As you read this chapter, you will learn that the food and beverage operation in a full-service hotel is much more complicated than that found in a limited-service property. Food and beverage managers with specialized knowledge of the hotel business, guest relations skills, and food and beverage experience are required. The profitability of food and beverage operations in full-service hotels is a direct result of their efforts.

Chapter Objectives

1. To show the organizational structure used in smaller hotels' food and beverage operations.
2. To show the organizational structure used in larger full-service hotels' food and beverage operations.
3. To examine how hoteliers assess guest needs when planning food and beverage offerings.
4. To review important operating procedures related to purchasing, receiving, storing, issuing, and producing food and beverage products.
5. To present management concerns related to serving à la carte meals, room-service, and banquets in a hotel.

HOTEL FOOD AND BEVERAGE OFFERINGS

Full-service hotels offer à la carte and other food services for travelers who stay at the property and for others, including residents of the local community. Deciding exactly what to offer depends greatly on the hotel's location and goals. Is the hotel attempting to attract motorists on a nearby roadway traveling for pleasure or business? Is the property located in a city's business district? Does it do a large volume of convention business? Is it a resort or vacation property? In all cases, the food and beverage services offered by the hotel must be planned to meet the dining needs of those to whom the property is marketed.

Many full-service hotels also generate revenue from people living in the local community and who enjoy the same types of dining options as the hotel's guests. For example, residents of a rural community may enjoy the value-priced meals offered by a lodging property on an interstate highway exit located near the community. Residents of a large city may like to celebrate special occasions in the dining outlet of a hotel serving upscale business and pleasure travelers. It is a challenge for managers in hotel food services to identify their guests and to understand and consistently provide what they need. If they do not accomplish this, other competitive food service operations, including traditional restaurants, will provide the products and services that guests seek.

Figure 13.1 illustrates the types of food and beverage services typically offered to guests in a full-service hotel.

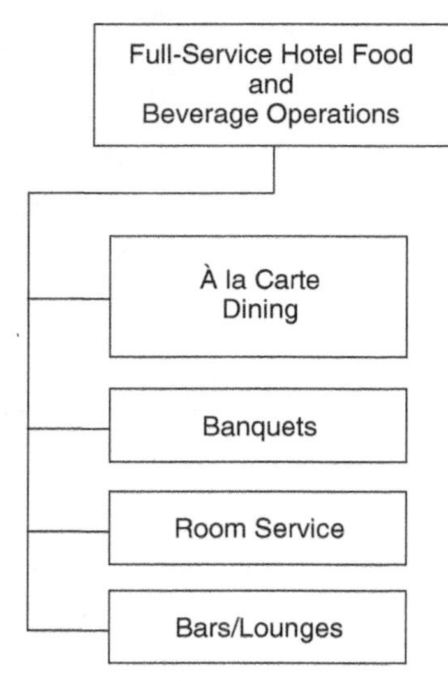

FIGURE 13.1 Food and Beverage Services Offered by Full-Service Hotels

À la Carte Dining. Depending upon its size, a full-service hotel will have one or more à la carte dining alternatives. For example, a small property might have a coffee and pastry stand or a single dining room. A very large property may have several theme restaurants and other casual dine-in options. It may also offer one or more quick-service outlets in its lobbies and/or in a swimming pool area or other locations around the property.

Banquets. Many hotels offer **banquet** functions for groups of guests meeting at the property and for others celebrating special occasions.

LODGING LANGUAGE

Banquet: A food event held in a hotel's privately reserved function room.

Room Service. Some hotels deliver food and beverage products to guest rooms. This type of food and beverage service is unique to lodging properties.

Bars and Lounges. Some hotels have a bar or lounge located near the à la carte dining room. In some cases, bar and lounge guests may also order food items in these areas. Sometimes all of the hotel's à la carte menu items can be served in the bar or lounge while in other properties a separate and more limited bar menu may be offered.

In addition to its guest-oriented food and beverage operations, some very large full-service hotels provide food services to their employees. Large hotels may employ hundreds or even thousands of staff members. Employee cafeterias are sometimes available for staff use, and a low-cost or even no-cost meal is offered.

Hoteliers must decide what type of food and beverage services to offer, such as à la carte, banquets or room service.

ORGANIZATION OF HOTEL FOOD AND BEVERAGE OPERATIONS

The organization of a food and beverage operation in a full-service hotel depends upon its size and the revenue it generates. Smaller hotels tend to generate lower revenues from food services than their higher-revenue counterparts. In the United States, the average full-service hotel can generate 25 percent or more of its total revenue from food and beverage sales. Some properties, especially those with large-volume convention/meeting/banquet business, can generate food and beverage revenues approaching 50 percent of total hotel revenues. Regardless of a hotel's size, the organizational structure of its food and beverage operation must support its revenue-generating efforts.

Smaller Hotels

Figure 13.2 shows how a food and beverage operation might be organized in a smaller hotel. The hotel's general manager supervises a food and beverage manager who, in turn, manages the work of someone responsible for food production (the head cook/chef), dining room service (the restaurant manager), and beverage production and service (the head bartender).

In a smaller full-service hotel, managerial functions are typically combined into just a few positions. For example, the food and beverage manager

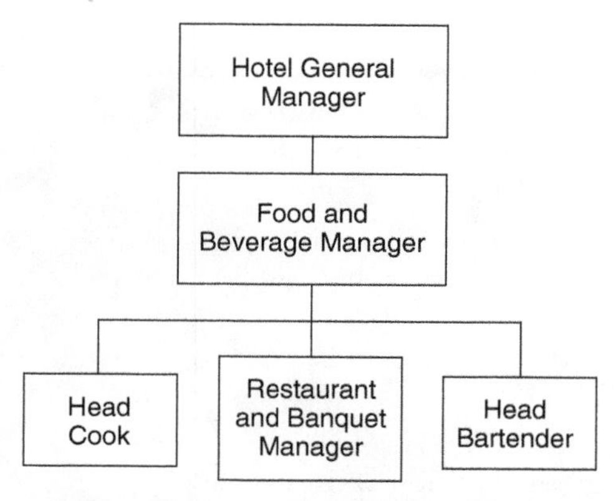

FIGURE 13.2 Organization of Food and Beverage Management Positions in Small Hotels

may be responsible for food and beverage purchasing, some accounting and control activities related to the operating of the department, and the management of banquet operations, among other duties. In hotels with larger food and beverage departments, each of these specialized tasks would be performed by a designated staff member with full-time responsibility for completing them.

Larger Hotels

As a hotel's food service operation becomes larger, additional managerial positions are needed. This is illustrated in Figure 13.3.

Note that in a large hotel, the food and beverage manager's position shown in Figure 13.2 is now titled "Director of Food and Beverage Operations." The individual filling that position supervises the work of an executive chef who, in turn, supervises a sous chef (with responsibility for food production for à la carte dining and room service) and a banquet chef (with responsibility for food produced for group functions). The director of food and beverage operations may also direct the work of a catering manager (who interacts with clients and sells group functions) and a banquet manager (who is responsible for banquet set-ups/tear-downs and service at banquets). Other **direct reports** of the director of food and beverage operations are the restaurant manager (responsible for service in the à la carte dining room[s]), the room service manager, and the beverage manager (who is responsible for the head bartenders at each beverage outlet).

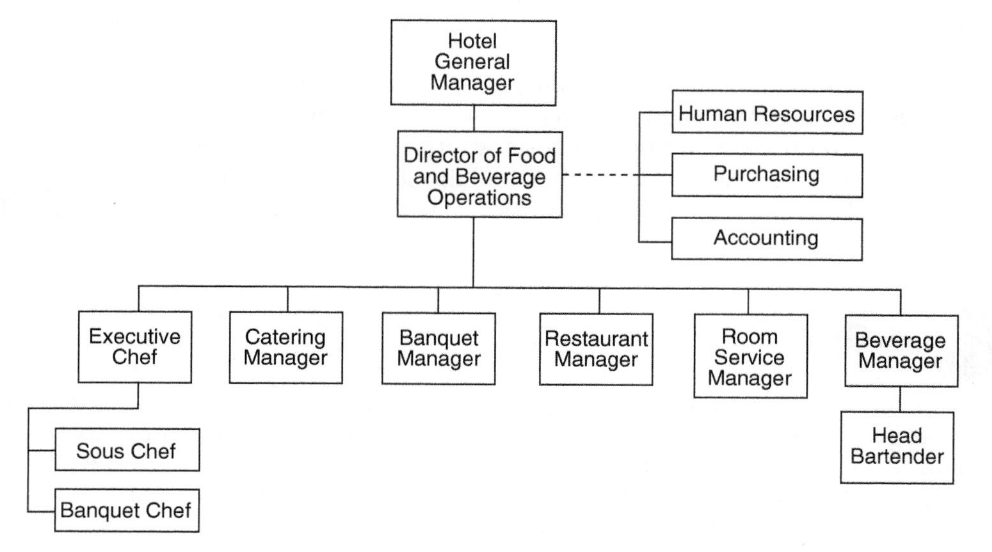

FIGURE 13.3 Organization of Food and Beverage Management Positions in Large Hotels

The size of the food and beverage operation will determine the size of staff and their specific responsibilities.

LODGING LANGUAGE

Direct report: An employee over whom a supervisor has immediate authority. For example, a sous chef is a direct report of the executive chef.

The director of food and beverage operations in a large hotel also has the benefit of technical assistance from personnel whose specialties involve human resources (including recruitment, selection, orientation, compensation/benefits administration, and interpretation/implementation of the ever-expanding body of legal issues relating to employment), centralized purchasing, and accounting/financial management.

MENU PLANNING

Food service managers in a hotel or any other type of organization must be consistently concerned about several important processes if their operations are to be successful. These processes are illustrated in Figure 13.4. They are presented here to emphasize that they are sequential, and that the first on the list, menu planning, is, according to many industry experts, the most important. In their view, "it all starts with the menu!"

Menus must offer the items guests want to buy. Managers must use marketing principles to learn what guests will buy and the prices guests will pay if they are to effectively differentiate their businesses from their competitors. In other words, an effec-

LODGING ONLINE

Hotel F&B Executive is a trade magazine addressing the managerial and operational concerns of those who manage food and beverage (F&B) departments in lodging properties. You can check out its home page at:

www.hotelfandb.com/

Do you think food service professionals working in the lodging industry must possess different skills than those working in commercial restaurants? Why or why not?

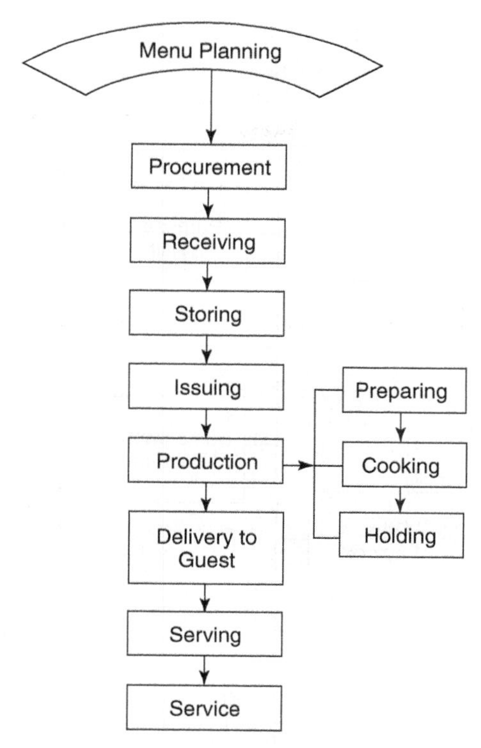

FIGURE 13.4 Overview of Food Service Processes

tive menu focuses on the guests. Entire books have been written on the topic of **menu planning.**[1]

LODGING LANGUAGE

Menu planning: The process of determining which food and beverage items will most please the guests while meeting established cost objectives.

Two of the most important menu planning considerations relate to the guests (what they want and will pay for) and to the resources available to provide menu items that consistently meet established quality standards.

Guest Concerns

The guests are the most important consideration when planning the menu, and it is critical to know what items they will order. What guest-related factors should be considered in planning a menu? Figure 13.5 helps answer this question.

PROBLEMS AND PROFITS IN HOTEL FOOD SERVICES

Food service departments in hotels have some unique challenges. One of the most important is the inability of many to be profitable. At most full-service hotels, food and beverage sales bring in fewer revenue dollars and bottom-line profits than the rental of guest rooms. As a result, financial management concerns create an umbrella under which hotel food services must constantly operate.

[1]See, for example, Jack Ninemeier and David Hayes, *Menu Planning, Design and Evaluation 2nd. Edition.* (Richmond, Calif.: McCutchan Publishing Corp., 2008).

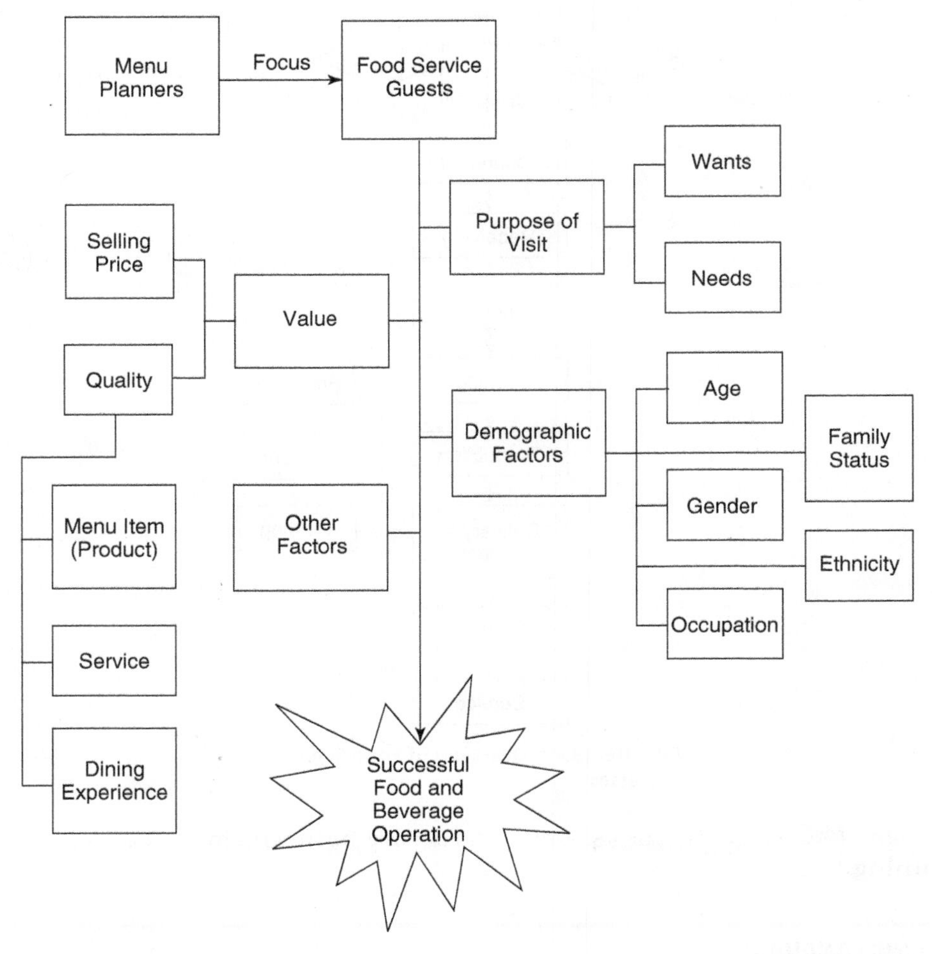

FIGURE 13.5 Menu Planning: Focus on Guests

Figure 13.5 lists many guest-related factors that must be considered when planning menus:

Purpose of Visit. Guests want an experience in line with the purpose of their visit. They may just be hungry (e.g., when travelers on an interstate highway stop at a roadside hotel), they may be discussing business, or they may be a couple or a family visiting an upscale hotel restaurant to celebrate a special occasion.

Value. The concept of **value** relates to a guest's perception of the selling price of an item relative to the quality of the menu item, service, and dining experience. Guests want to get what they pay for; they do not want to feel cheated, and, increasingly, many guests will pay more for a higher perceived quality of dining experience.

LODGING LANGUAGE

Value (foodserivce): The guest's perception of the selling price of a menu item relative to the quality of the menu item, service, and dining experience received.

Demographic Factors. Concerns such as the guests' age, marital status, gender, ethnicity, and occupation are likely to impact menu item preferences. Knowing the answer to the question "Who will be visiting our hotel's restaurant?" will help in planning the menu.

LODGING LANGUAGE

Demographic Factors: Characteristics such as age, marital status, gender, ethnicity, and occupation that help to describe or classify a person as a member of a group.

Other Factors. Social factors such as income, education, and wealth may influence what a guest desires. Other factors, including guests' lifestyles and even their personalities (e.g., the extent to which they like to try "new" foods) can be relevant to menu-planning decisions.

The goal of every menu planner is to offer items that please the guests. When guests are satisfied, they are more likely to provide repeat business. At the same time, they will tell their friends, and word-of-mouth advertising helps the food and beverage operation to remain successful.

Food and beverage operators face many guest-related concerns when planning a menu, such as who will visit their establishments and why.

Operating Concerns

Figure 13.6 highlights some of the ways that the menu, once planned, impacts the food services operation.

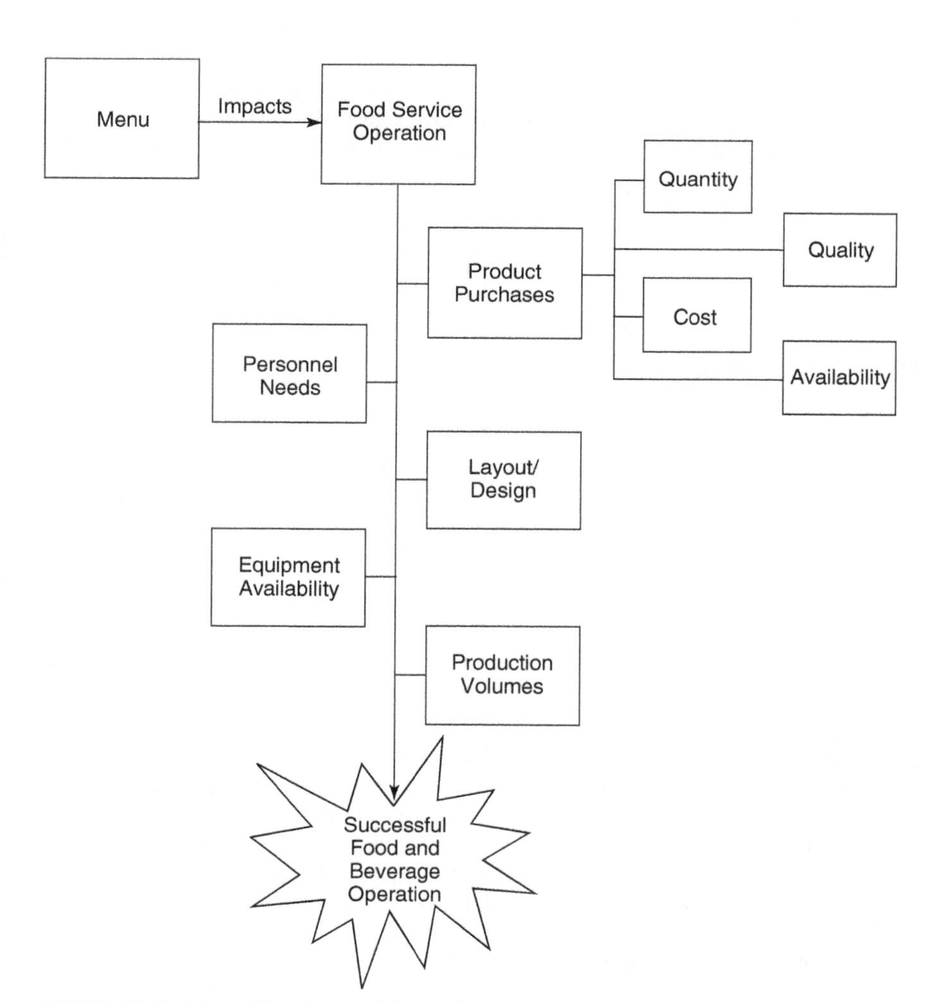

FIGURE 13.6 Menu Planning and Operations

These aspects include:

Product Purchases. All of the ingredients required to produce all the menu items offered must be consistently available in the required quantity and quality and at the right cost. Otherwise, guests may be disappointed because desired items are not available. Moreover, there will likely be significant operational disruptions when alternative menu items need to be produced.

Personnel Needs. Trained staff members must be available to produce and serve the items offered on the menu. Consider, for example, the differences in the experience and skill level necessary for an effective server in a hotel's coffee shop compared to a server preparing **flambé** dishes tableside in an upscale hotel restaurant.

LODGING LANGUAGE

Flambé: A cooking procedure in which alcohol (ethanol) is added to a hot pan to create a burst of flames.

Layout/Design Concerns. If a menu specifies a self-service salad bar, the space must be available for the serving counters and to accommodate guest movement around the salad bar area. A menu featuring fresh-baked breads requires the space necessary for an on-site bake shop or for the placement of specialized baking equipment such as proofers and ovens.

Equipment Availability. If the menu includes fried foods and grilled items, deep-fat fryers and grills will be necessary based upon anticipated business volume. The space needed for the equipment and adequate ventilation as required by fire safety codes must also be considered.

Production Volumes. The volume of menu items to be prepared must match the equipment availability to produce them. For example, if there is only one oven in the kitchen, the production of baked appetizers, entrées, desserts, and breads in any significant volume would be difficult. As a result, the menu planner in this operation must be careful not to exceed the production capacity of the available oven.

LODGING ONLINE

After the menu is planned, it must be designed. An excellent resource to help you learn more about menu design is:

www.themenumaker.com/

Do you think the average hotel food service manager should design his or her own menu or should the services of a professional menu designer be secured?

MENU DESIGN IS ALSO IMPORTANT

Most people are familiar with the type of physical menus handed to guests in a sit-down restaurant's dining room. In a hotel, the physical menu can include a place card positioned at a banquet seat or a sign identifying the item available next to each help-yourself serving dish on a buffet line.

Most hotel restaurants, whether upscale or casual, and most room service operations make a menu available to guests. Traditionally, the purpose of providing a menu was simply to inform guests about available items. Today, however, menus can be powerful in-house selling tools. They can be designed carefully to encourage guests to select items that are popular and profitable.

Menus should always be attractive, clean, and easy-to-read.

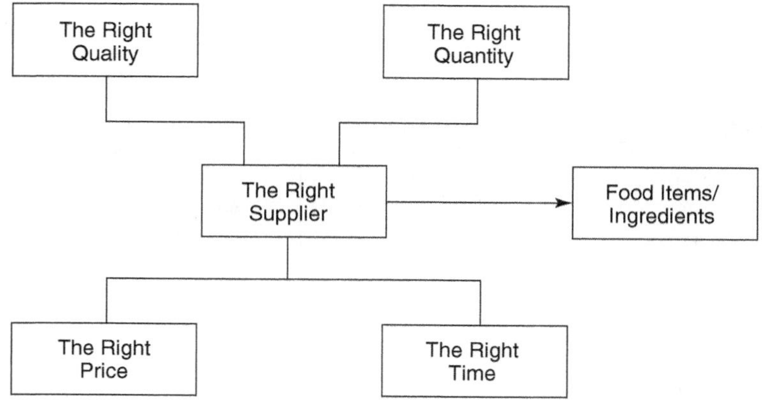

FIGURE 13.7 Five Special Purchasing Concerns

FOOD SERVICE CONTROL POINTS

After the menu is planned, other processes must be effectively managed to help the hotel's food and beverage operation be successful. Figure 13.4 indicates the processes that must occur after the menu is planned. They include:

Procurement

After the menu is planned, the **ingredients** needed to produce the items on it will be known.

LODGING LANGUAGE

Ingredients: Individual components of a food or beverage recipe. For example, flour and sugar are ingredients in pastries.

All ingredients must be procured (obtained) using effective purchasing procedures. Figure 13.7 identifies five special concerns in the food service purchasing process.

Quality is perhaps the single most important concern when purchasing food and beverage items. The purchaser must consider the intended use of the items; the closer an item is to being suitable for its intended use, the more appropriate is its quality.

For example, bright red maraschino cherries might be required at the bar for a drink garnish and in the kitchen as an ingredient in a fruit gelatin salad. A whole cherry with stem (at a relatively higher cost) may be needed at the bar because it is attractive. Cherry halves or chopped cherry pieces (at a relatively lower cost) might be best in a gelatin salad. Quality, in most cases, can best be determined only if one first knows how the product will be used.

Another purchasing factor relates to the quantity of items needed. If too much product is purchased, money that could be utilized for other purposes is tied up in inventory. As well, the quality of some products can deteriorate in storage, space must be available to house excess inventory, and when too much product is held in inventory there could be an increased chance of spoilage, **theft** and **pilferage**.

LODGING LANGUAGE

Theft: Stealing all of something at one time; for example, a thief might steal a case of liquor.

Pilferage: Stealing small quantities of something over a period of time; for example, a thief might steal one bottle from a case of beer.

By contrast, when too little product is available, **stockouts** can occur. Guests may be disappointed because a desired menu item is not available, and operating concerns can arise if substitute items must be produced.

LODGING ONLINE

Today, there are numerous ways that computerized systems can help with purchasing, receiving, storing, and issuing. To learn about some of these systems, go to:

www.calcmenu.com/

www.foodtrak.com/

www.tracrite.net/

Do you think the average food service manager working in a hotel should be specially trained in the use of food service-related software programs available today? How could they receive such training?

LODGING LANGUAGE

Stockout: The condition that arises when a food/beverage item needed for production is not available on-site.

The price is right when the cost of a food item or ingredient provides a good value. Wise purchasers realize that they are buying more than just products from a supplier. They also receive product information and service. The perceived value of these three factors (product quality, information, and service) should most influence the purchasing decision.

The right time for product delivery must also be considered. Suppliers offering a good deal on an item for tomorrow's banquet that is delivered next week are not providing value. Purchasers who frequently have problems securing the right products at the right time should look first at their operation to determine whether there is an internal problem. If not, they should select suppliers who consistently deliver required products on a timely basis.

The right supplier consistently delivers the right quality and quantities of product at the right price and at the right time. Some food services managers like to have only a few suppliers so that they can eliminate paperwork and enhance their relationship with suppliers. Other managers believe that interactions with many suppliers are beneficial to the operation. Whichever of these approaches is used, the importance of professional procurement including supplier selection and purchasing cannot be overlooked.

Receiving, Storing, and Issuing

After products are purchased, they must be received, stored, and issued to production areas. Receiving occurs when products are physically delivered to the operation. Storing is the process of holding products in a secure space with proper temperature, humidity, and product rotation until they are needed. **Issuing** involves moving products from the storage area to the place of production. Basic receiving, storing, and issuing procedures are similar for food and beverage products. These products must be protected until used so that menu items can be produced at the lowest possible cost and highest quality.

LODGING LANGUAGE

Issuing: The process of moving stored products to the place of production.

Production

Production is the process of readying products for consumption. It involves cooks working in the kitchen and bartenders working in bar areas.

LODGING LANGUAGE

Production: All of the cooking and preparation processes used to ready menu items for consumption.

Effective food or beverage production requires the use of **standardized recipes** to indicate the type and quantity of ingredients, preparation methods, and portion tools along with production instructions.

LODGING LANGUAGE

Standardized recipe: A written explanation about how a food or beverage item should be prepared. It lists the quantity of each ingredient, preparation techniques, portion size, and other information production personnel need to ensure that the item is always prepared in the same way.

Some menu items may be produced from **scratch** while others can be purchased in a **convenience food** form.

LODGING LANGUAGE

Scratch (food production): The use of basic ingredients to make items for sale. For example, a minestrone soup may be made on-site with fresh vegetables, meat, and other ingredients.

Convenience food: Food or beverage products that have some labor "built in" that otherwise would have to be added on-site. For example, a minestrone soup may be purchased pre-made in a frozen or canned form.

In many cases, a **make or buy analysis** should be performed to determine which items should be made from scratch and which should be purchased as a convenience food.

LODGING LANGUAGE

Make or Buy Analysis: The process of considering quality, costs, and other factors in scratch production and convenience food alternatives to determine which form is best for the operation.

The production of food items generally requires more elaborate and extensive preparation skills than are needed for beverages. A menu may offer a range of items requiring different levels of preparation skills. For example:

- Hamburger patties that must be grilled or that must be formed and then grilled
- Combination dishes that involve the need to clean, pre-prepare (clean, cut, and chop), and cook a variety of ingredients
- Elaborate sauces that require experience in stock reduction and preparation to prepare a sauce that in itself is an ingredient (**chained recipe**) in another menu item
- Menu items that are produced can be made individually (such as a single broiled steak) or in batches (such as a large quantity of soup).

LODGING LANGUAGE

Chained recipe: A recipe for an item such as a sauce that is itself an ingredient in another recipe (such as a tomato sauce used in a pasta dish).

Serving and Service

When a hotel has a dining room, food items prepared by cooks are transferred to employees who then serve them to guests. Bartenders preparing drinks may also produce the drinks and then transfer them to other employees who actually serve the drinks to guests. The process of moving products from production to service personnel is called

serving. Service personnel then deliver food and beverage products to guests in a process called **service**. Both serving and service procedures must be professionally planned and executed.

LODGING LANGUAGE

Serving: The process of moving prepared food or beverage items from production staff to service personnel.

Service (food and beverage): The process of transferring food and beverage products from wait staff to the guests.

Systems for food and beverage serving must be effectively designed to minimize service bottlenecks that can lower food quality (such as cold food) and lengthen guest waits (e.g., when many slow-to-prepare ice cream drinks containing alcohol hinder the production of other drinks). The speed and manner in which products are delivered to guests is very important because the perceived quality of service is just as important as product quality when guests evaluate their overall food service experiences.

À LA CARTE DINING

À la carte food services allow guests in a hotel's restaurant to order and pay for the specific menu items they desire. These meals are typically served in a designated dining area, such as a dining room, pool snack bar, or coffee shop. There are many activities included in preparing for and providing service to guests in à la carte dining operations. Some of the most important of these activities include getting ready for service and service procedures.

Getting Ready for Service

When food is prepared, it can be served in a variety of styles, including:

American (Plated) Service. In this serving style, food is pre-portioned onto serviceware (e.g., plates or bowls) in the kitchen and is then served to guests seated at tables in the dining area.

Traditional French Service. In this service style, menu items such as a classic Caesar Salad or a flaming Steak Diane are prepared and cooked at the guests' tables.

Russian (Platter) Service. In this style, food is placed on serviceware in the kitchen, brought to the guests' tables by servers, and individual portions are then placed onto the guests' plates by the servers.

English (Family) Service. In this style, food is brought to the table by the server in serving dishes that are placed on the guests' tables so that they can pass food items to one other.

Buffet (Self-Service). In this popular serving style, guests help themselves to a variety of food items that have been positioned for easy access by guests.

Counter (Bar) Service. In hotels this style of service is most common in bars and lounges. Guests place orders with service personnel behind a counter area who prepare and serve menu items to guests who may be seated at the bar.

American (plated) service is a very common à la carte servicing style. In it, guests place their individual orders, which are prepared in the kitchen and delivered to their tables.

Service styles can be combined in the same meal. For example, a Caesar Salad may be prepared tableside (French Service), and the entrée may be pre-plated in the kitchen (American Service).

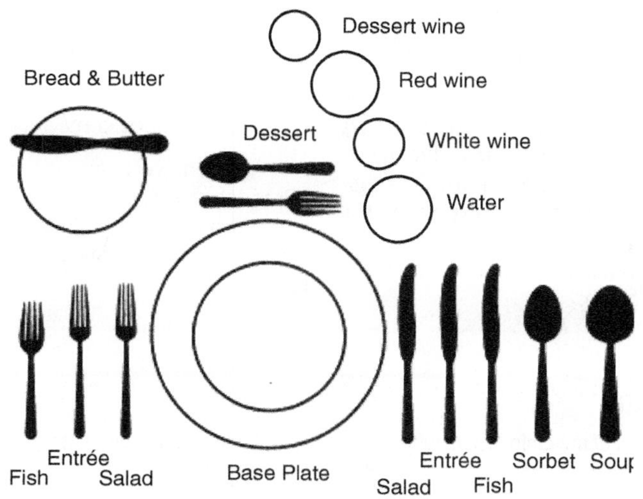

FIGURE 13.8 Example of Place Setting in an Up-Scale Dining Room

Service Procedures

Preparing to serve food properly requires staff to undertake a variety of activities including:

- Ensuring tables, chairs, and booths are clean, safe, and steady
- Checking to assure that tablecloths, if used, are correctly placed and are clean and free of burns, holes, and tears
- Ensuring **place settings** are positioned according to the hotel's standards (see an example in Figure 13.8). Note that serving pieces are typically placed such that guests use the outside items first and then move toward the center of the place setting. When reviewing Figurer 13.8, note the arrangement of the forks. Guests will first enjoy a fish course, followed by the entrée. Since a formal European meal is being served, the salad course is served after (not before) the entrée, so the salad fork is placed closest to the center of the place setting.
- Confirming that there are no water spots or fingerprints on glassware, flatware, or other serviceware.

LODGING LANGUAGE

Place setting: The arrangement of plates, glasses, knives, forks, spoons (flatware), and other service items on a dining table for one guest.

Preparing for service extends beyond checking guest dining areas. Preparing service staff is equally important. Because this is true, many food service managers implement a mandatory staff **line-up** prior to the beginning of service.

LODGING LANGUAGE

Line-up (training): A brief informational training session held before the work shift begins.

Topics discussed in the daily line-up typically include:

- Specific **server station** assignments
- Daily specials
- New menu item introductions (including opportunities to sample new items)
- Estimates of business volume during the shift based upon reservations and/or other information
- A mini-training session on a topic such as procedures to resolve service-related problems

LODGING ONLINE

Advanced technology systems can help servers place orders from the guest's table directly to the food/beverage production areas. One system uses a palm device that sends a wireless signal to the kitchen through an access antenna. To learn about this example of tableside order placement, go to:

www.rmpos.com/

When you arrive at the site, click "Products," then select "Write-On Handheld."

What are possible advantages of placing food orders for guests directly from the dining room?

LODGING LANGUAGE

Server station: An area of the dining room where all tables and booths have been assigned to a specific server.

Many steps are involved in the interaction between wait staff and guests as the dining process evolves. These steps are identified in Figure 13.9.

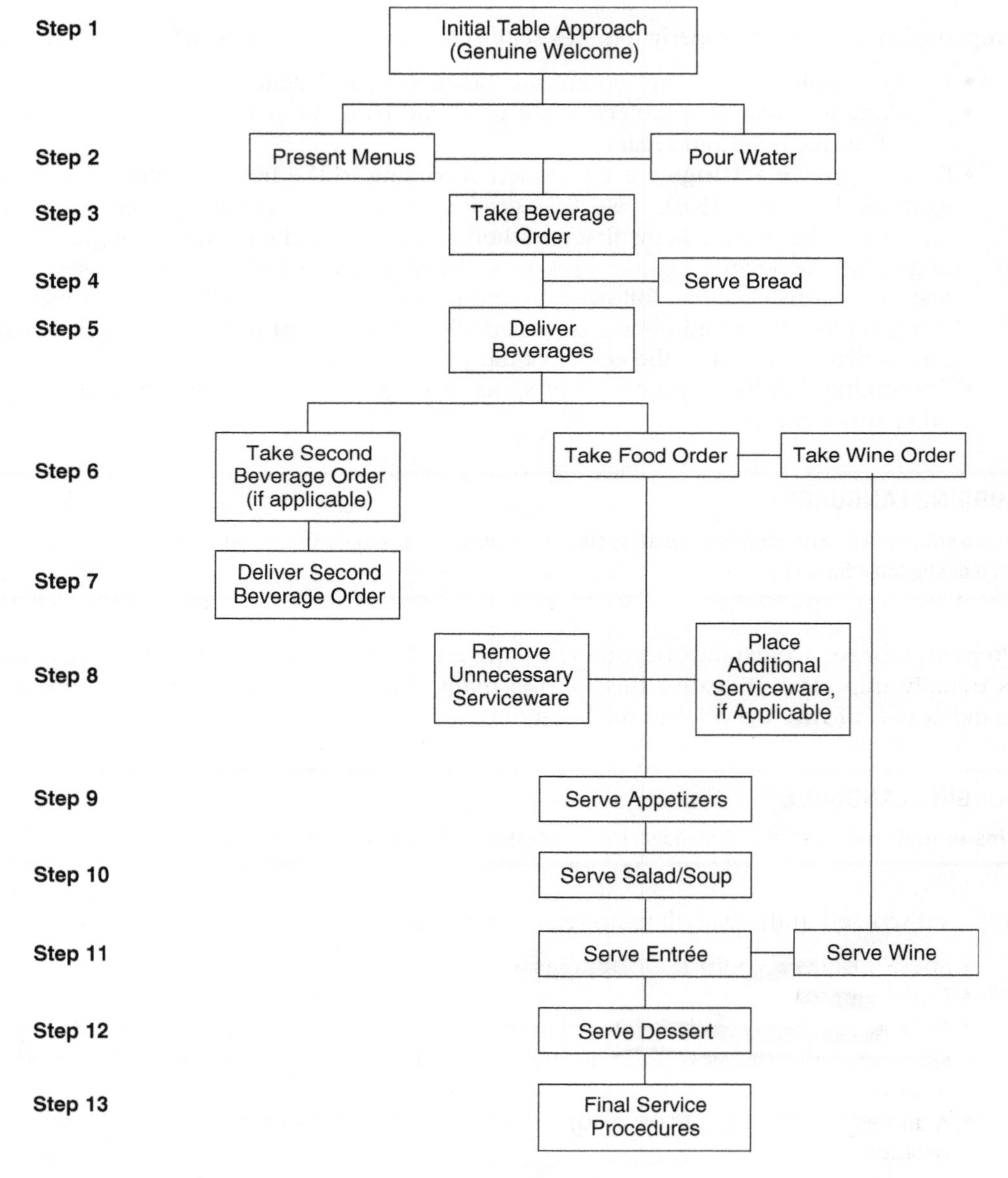

FIGURE 13.9 The Service Sequence

"WHO GETS THE SPAGHETTI?"

"Who gets the spaghetti?" or any other ordered item, is a question that will never need to be asked, and should never be asked, in a well-managed dining area. Servers should use a numbering system so that they know who gets the spaghetti. Each table in the dining room should be assigned a number (this helps with server station assignments), and each table's seats should also be numbered. When that is true, there should be no question about who gets the spaghetti because the server will have written or entered the table and seat number corresponding to the guest ordering the spaghetti on the order pad when the guest's order was placed.

The server's first step is clear; the next several steps may not be. It is important to approach the table as soon as possible after the guests are seated (Step 1).

A hospitable and genuine greeting is important. ("Hello, welcome to Vernon's Restaurant. We are pleased that you're here, and my goal is to make your visit a memorable one.") Eye contact, a feeling of self-confidence, and a genuine spirit of hospitality are helpful in this initial guest contact.

Step 2 in the service sequence will vary by property. Guests may be provided with menus by a host or hostess as they are seated, and a busperson may serve water to them before their server reaches the table. When presenting the menu, the server can mention any specials available in addition to what is listed on the menu.

A beverage order can be taken (Step 3), and bread (if offered) can be brought to the table after the beverage order is taken (Step 4). Trays should be used to carry beverage orders (and everything else!) to the table. If possible, beverages should be served from the guest's right side with the server's right hand. Service trays should not be placed on the guest's table when the server takes or delivers an order.

After beverages are delivered (Step 5), three activities become important (in Step 6) when the server next returns to the table:

- Take a second beverage order (if applicable).
- Take the food order.
- Take a wine order.

As orders are taken, servers should:

- Be thorough and ask questions. If, for example, a guest orders a steak, the server must inquire about the desired degree of doneness. If a guest orders a baked potato, they should be asked about preferred toppings.
- Repeat orders to help ensure accuracy.
- Be alert to guests' needs. For example, if they appear rushed, suggest items that can be prepared and served quickly.
- Pick up the menus after each guest has placed an order, and return them to their proper storage location.

After food/wine orders are taken, a second round of beverage orders can be delivered, if applicable. In Step 7 and Step 8, servers should remove items that will not be needed, such as pre-set wine glasses if no wine is ordered. Additional service items that will be needed after orders are known should be brought to the table. These may include special knives (if steaks are ordered) and special condiments, such as tartar sauce for seafood.

Steps 9–12 review the sequence of serving appetizers, salads/soups, entrées wine, and desserts. In these steps, attention to detail is very important. Does a guest need more water or other beverage, was an item of flatware dropped on the floor and thus needs replacement, or does someone have second thoughts about a condiment not requested earlier?

Step 13 notes the importance of final service procedures. These include:

- Presenting the check
- Assisting the guests with payment
- Ending the meal experience with a sincere "*Thank you; I enjoyed serving you; please visit us again.*"

ALL IN A DAY'S WORK 13.1

THE SITUATION

"Whose job is it, anyway?" asked Francis, a frustrated food server at the Barkley Grill in the Mountain View Hotel, to Louis, the dining room manager.

"I'm glad we're very busy tonight, and I'm working as hard as I can to provide the quality of service that our guests want," Francis continued. "When I go to one table, however, the guests already have a menu. When I go to another, they don't. The same with water. Sometimes guests have their waters before I arrive and sometimes they don't. I'm glad when they have a menu and water; it helps speed service. But, I have to waste a lot of time picking up menus and preparing water glasses to bring to the table because I never know whether guests will have them when I arrive. If they do, I look silly, and I have to return the extra glasses to the server station before I can take the order. I don't save time; I actually waste time, which could be better spent on more productive tasks."

A RESPONSE

Francis is right about the problem. The policy may be that the host or hostess staff should provide menus to the guests and that a busperson should bring water. However, if staff are not properly trained, what actually happens may not be what policy dictates. Louis can confirm the problem ("Let's talk about this at the end of the shift when we are better able to do so. In the meantime, I'll try to help out wherever I can so that you and the rest of the staff will not have to waste time.")

Francis has a legitimate complaint and did the right thing by discussing the problem with his supervisor. Louis should make it a priority to meet with dining service staff and agree upon who does what. Once this is determined, effective training programs can help to implement the agreed-upon procedures.

LODGING GOES GREEN!

What does it really mean to be a green food operation? Much of the focus on green foodservice has been placed on sustainable food options, reducing packaging wastes and emphasizing local food sourcing. Those are all important, but full-service hoteliers must also manage their food service operation in a way that is water use and energy efficient. Interestingly, the views of restaurateurs and consumers toward water have changed substantially over the past decade. In fact, water usage in food service operations serves as one good example why hoteliers must continually monitor their own and their guests' evolving views of acceptable operating practices.

For those hoteliers operating food programs in full-service hotels, the following green practices commonly utilized by restaurateurs can make a significant and positive impact on hotel profits and the environment.

1. Watch the "Bottled" Water: The decade from 2000-2010 saw an explosion in the consumption of bottled water in the United States. Increasingly, however, consumers became aware of the cost to the environment of the millions of used plastic bottles required to meet this increased demand. In hotel meeting rooms across the country, guests began to request that the hotel *not* provide bottled water. Environmentally conscious meeting planners who feel strongly on this and other green practices issues remind hoteliers of the importance of following trends in consumer perceptions of acceptable green practices.

2. Watch the "Tap" Water: Water is the single most important finite resource on earth. Foodservice operations, in general, sometimes do a poor job of water conservation. Water conservation practices along with efficient plumbing fixtures and equipment can save the hotel industry millions of dollars each year. Kitchen water fixtures, aerators, pre-rinse spray valves, urinals and toilets are all areas where tight seals and modern design can yield big savings.

3. Replace Candescent Lights with Light-Emitting Diode (LED) Lighting. The savings to hotels of replacing traditional incandescent lighting with LED or compact florescent lighting (CFL) can be significant. Not only are lighting costs reduced, but the cost of labor required to replace burned out bulbs is also reduced.

4. Check the Label: Buying appliances, electronics, and equipment that have been tested by the Environmental Protection Agency

(EPA) and that display their Energy Star label is a good way to reduce energy costs. The Energy Star label was created as a U.S. government program in 1992. Manufacturers in Canada, Japan, New Zealand, and the European Union have since adopted it. Devices carrying the Energy Star label operate using 20%-30% less energy than required by Federal standards.

5. Think Farm to Fork: Farm to Fork is a way of considering the environmental impact of transporting food from the area in which it is grown or produced to the area in which it is consumed. Minimizing the time from Farm to Fork not only reduces impact on the environment, it helps ensure ingredient quality. For many foodservice operators, a commitment to buy (whenever possible) baked goods, fresh produce, and even meats within a 150-mile radius of their operation is a way to recognize the importance of the Farm to Fork concept.

ROOM SERVICE

Many full-service hotels offer room service. Room service is the hotel term that describes the entire process of delivering menu items to guests in their rooms. Some hotels offer room service 24/7 (24 hours per day, 7 days per week). Guests of all types utilize room service, ranging from the business traveler wanting a quick breakfast, to small groups desiring a lunch during their meetings in guest room suites, to couples wanting to enjoy a romantic meal alone.

Large hotels generally employ a room service manager with total responsibility for this specialized guest offering. In such hotels, room service staff may work in a separate food preparation area designed especially for room service orders. Also, employees in these properties who deliver menu items to guest rooms may do so on a full-time basis.

In smaller hotels, the food and beverage manager will most often plan to have room service items produced by the same cook who produces the restaurant meals. In these smaller properties, room service items are typically delivered to guest rooms by a restaurant server.

Profitability

Guests noting the seemingly high prices on room service menus sometimes think that hotels make a lot of profit on room service. In fact, this is not typically the case.

If room service is not profitable for the hotel, why is it offered? There are several answers. First, it is a service to guests and some guests may select a property based on its availability. Among this type of guests are those arriving on late night airline flights and others wanting food and beverage services for small business meetings in guest rooms.

Providing quality room service requires careful planning and execution.

Secondly, the offering of room service (especially on a 24/7 basis) can add significantly to guests' perceptions of a hotel's exclusiveness and attention toward guest needs. Finally, some hotel rating services, such as the American Automobile Association (AAA), only assign their highest ratings to hotels that offer room service.

Why does room service frequently lose money? High labor costs are one reason. Much time is needed to transport food from the kitchen to guest room areas. The capital costs incurred to purchase equipment, such as delivery carts and warming devices, can be significant. If costs were allocated for elevators to transport items, for staging areas to store room service carts and to prepare them for deliveries, and for similar costs, the expenses would even be greater. Finally, items such as glasses, cups, flatware, and serviceware increase room service costs.

The need to return soiled room service items to kitchen areas often creates other problems. For example, questions of "*whose job is it to return dirty dishware items?*" to the food and beverage area can arise. Unfortunately, while those questions are being addressed, unsightly guest trays may remain in hotel hallways for longer than desirable periods of time, and some serviceware items (which can be costly to replace) may be stolen.

In some hotels, the room service department provides food and beverage service in **hospitality suites** and for other group functions in a guest room. In convention properties, vendors and exhibitors may invite customers to visit hotel rooms for **hosted events**. When these services are provided by room service staff rather than by banquet service staff, the likelihood of room service profitability increases.

LODGING LANGUAGE

Hospitality suite: A guest room rented by a supplier/vendor, usually during a convention/conference, to provide complimentary food and/or beverages to invited guests.

Hosted event: Functions that are complimentary for invited guests; costs are borne by the event's sponsor. A hosted bar may offer free beverages to wedding party guests, and a corporate sponsor may pay for a hosted reception in a hospitality suite.

Menu Planning

Special concerns are important when planning room service menus. As with any other food service alternative, quality is important. Room service menus should only offer items that can be transported relatively long distances from food preparation areas without decreases in quality. Because guests may perceive room service prices to be high, they expect food quality to be high to help justify the prices. Unfortunately, some popular items (fried eggs and french fries, for example) are not ideal room service menu items because of quality problems that can arise when they are held at serving temperatures for long periods of time during transport to guest rooms.

A food and beverage manager in a hotel can easily check food quality in the hotel's restaurant or a banquet setting by sampling various items. However, room service managers have less access to products served in room service. Efforts to solicit feedback from guests are a critical way of seeing whether quality requirements are consistently attained.

Creative hoteliers know that room service menus can be used to sell other hotel products and services. For example, a room service breakfast menu can indicate that the hotel's Sunday brunch in the dining room is very popular. An invitation on the room service breakfast menu to call about daily dinner specials in the dining room can also interest guests in thinking ahead about their evening dinner plans.

Hotels located near some airports and other tourism areas attracting international guests have another room service challenge: language barriers. A non-English-speaking guest alone in a guest room with a menu written in English will have great difficulty in ordering. Alternatives such as pictures and menu item descriptions written in the languages most used by the hotel's international guests may be solutions. If there are minimum order charges, mandatory tipping policies, or other requirements for guest room orders, these should be clearly indicated on the menu and may also be stated by the order taker.

Operating Issues

Trained room service order takers are needed regardless of whether this is full-time position or only one part of many responsibilities. Communication problems occur all too frequently in room service. If the employee fails to take a complete order, guest dissatisfaction is likely. The same types of questions that are asked in an à la carte restaurant must be asked by the room service order taker. For example:

- How would you like your steak prepared?
- Would you like sour cream with your baked potato?
- Would you like a glass of wine to complete your dinner? Tonight's special wines would go well with your entrée, and they are a great value!

It is difficult to correct errors in any food service operation. However, an inaccurate order in the dining room can sometimes be quickly corrected. For example, if catsup for french fries is omitted, it can be immediately provided. However, if catsup is omitted from the room service tray, a relatively long and time-consuming trip back to the kitchen will be necessary. Should the guest wait with cold food as a result? Alternatively, should the guest consume the meal without the desired condiments? Either way, guest dissatisfaction can result, and the negative impression may carry over to other hotel experiences. At the same time, servers who must spend additional time on this work task will be unavailable to serve other guests who, in turn, may become dissatisfied as the wait for their room service order increases. A minor problem, then, can create a ripple effect that impacts the perceptions of many guests about their entire lodging experience.

Opportunities for **suggestive selling** are plentiful in room service. The room service **guest check average** can be increased if guests are informed about items they may not have initially ordered, such as appetizers or desserts because they didn't know or think about them.

LODGING LANGUAGE

Suggestive selling: Information suggested by an order taker (in a room service operation) or by a server (in an à la carte dining operation) to encourage guests to purchase additional items or higher priced items they might otherwise not have ordered. This is commonly referred to as *up-selling*.

Guest check average: The average amount spent by a guest for a room service or dining room order. The formula for calculating Guest Check Average is:

Total Revenue ÷ Total Number of Guests Served = Guest Check Average.

Room service orders, like those in à la carte dining operations, are entered into the operation's **point-of-sale (POS) system**. Orders can then be viewed on a screen or printed on hard copy tickets to be given to the room service cook(s). A copy of the order is also given to the server when the order is transported to the guest room.

LODGING LANGUAGE

Point of Sale (POS) system: A computer system that maintains a record of guests' food and beverage purchases and payments.

In all cases, it is important for the room server to carefully note whether the items that have been plated (portioned) and placed on the room service cart for delivery are, in fact, the ones that were ordered.

POS systems with software applications designed especially for room service have greatly improved room service order taking. Modern systems typically indicate the room number and the name of the guest registered in the room from which the order is placed. Using the guest's name is an effective selling tactic, and it has become easy for the order taker to do so. When orders are placed, these systems provide information about whether

LODGING ONLINE

Significant advances have been made in the development of hotel-specific POS systems. To see one such system, designed by Microsoft, go to:

http://www.micros.com

When you arrive at the site, click on "Products," then select "Hotels and Resorts," and then select "Restaurants."

How can food and beverage managers in the hotel industry be encouraged to stay abreast of rapidly changing POS system technology?

guests are permitted to charge meals purchases to their room folios or if the meals must be paid for at the time of delivery.

In-Room Service

From the guests' perspective, room service does not end when the food and beverage order reaches the guest room. In fact, delivery of the menu items ordered by a guest is just the beginning. Room service attendants must be adequately trained in service procedures that include:

- Asking guests where the room service meal should be placed
- Explaining procedures for retrieval of room service items
- Presenting the guest check and securing signature or payment
- Opening bottles of wine
- Inquiring if the guest needs anything that has not been delivered
- Providing an attitude of genuine hospitality (rather than appearing rushed to make another room service delivery)

Managers must continually assess how room service in their hotels can be improved. Guest feedback is crucial in this effort. Sometimes, a section relating to room service is included in a general guest rating form used to evaluate the entire property. Alternatively, a specific evaluation form provided when room service is delivered can be used.

The results of guest feedback should be randomly requested from the room service manager and reviewed by the property's general manager. When results are favorable, affected personnel should be recognized and rewarded. If challenges arise, the general manager should work with those in the food and beverage department to resolve the issues. Follow-up is important so that the same problem or others related to it do not re-occur.

BANQUET OPERATIONS

The availability of a wide variety of types and sizes of banquet events sold by a hotel's **catering** sales staff is an important factor separating hotel food and beverage departments from many of their counterparts in other segments of the food service industry. The volume of banquet business helps determine whether banquet operations are the responsibility of food production and service staff or, alternatively, whether employees with specialized banquet duties are utilized.

The hotel's marketing and sales staff will normally be responsible for generating banquet business and for negotiating contracts for specific banquet events. The delivery of the promised products and services, however, falls to the food and beverage department.

LODGING LANGUAGE

Catering: The process of selling a banquet event.

Hotels with extensive convention/meeting business have special banquet needs. Large properties often have a separate convention services department whose personnel plan and coordinate all activities (including those that are food- and beverage-related) for the groups visiting the hotel. General managers of smaller hotels in which the food and

ALL IN A DAY'S WORK 13.2

THE SITUATION

Mr. Vuki, the hotel's GM, was chairing the weekly executive committee meeting. The current topic was guest data generated from a newly implemented on-screen feedback system assessing performance in guest rooms, the dining room, and at the front office. Some department heads expressed satisfaction (or at least relief!) because the guest comment scores were 90 percent "Positive," on every factor assessed. "We must be doing a good job," said the food and beverage director. "There are no consistent complaints about anything."

Mr. Vuki, however, had a different thought. "Yes, at least nine guests out of ten think we are doing an excellent job. However, we should not be satisfied until every guest says we are doing a good job. The difference between where we are now and a perfect score represents improvements we can still make."

"Let's look at room service, for example," Mr. Vuki said. "Last week we had two complaints about cold food, and one guest indicated that the order was incomplete. Also, I am carrying more room service trays back to the kitchen that I find in the hallways as I walk around on the guest room floors."

"Yes," said the executive housekeeper. "My housekeepers tell me that they are also making more frequent calls to the kitchen to pick up room service trays left from the night before as well as from breakfast."

Suddenly, the food and beverage director was on the defensive. "We are short of employees in every service position. We have just hired and are now training several waiters and waitresses who, we hope, can work both in the dining room and in room service if we need them. In the meantime, I'm going to need your help in addressing these issues."

A RESPONSE

Mr. Vuki is correct to emphasize the opportunities to improve the operation still further even in times when guest comment scores are relatively high. The executive committee meeting provides an excellent opportunity to discuss issues impacting more than one department. However, the food and beverage director should have explored service staffing issues with affected department heads as soon as he became aware of the problem. It was not necessary to wait until comments were made in the executive committee meeting.

Mr. Vuki should discuss issues of communication, teamwork, and cooperation among all department heads and their employees. He should also facilitate a discussion and agreement about what can be done to address the issues of cold food and unreturned room service trays.

beverage director administers the banquet function and their counterparts in larger properties with specialized banquet managers have something in common: they must all know and understand how banquet functions work, how they can be evaluated, and how banquets can better meet the hotel's profitability and guest-related goals.

Profitability

Banquets are generally more profitable than restaurant (dining room) operations in hotels for several reasons:

- Banquets are frequently used to celebrate special events. This provides the opportunity to sell menu items that are more expensive and, therefore, higher in **contribution margin**.
- The number of meals to be served is known in advance; in fact, there is a formal **guarantee**. Also, the event will have known starting and ending times. This makes it easier to schedule production and service labor and to reduce the "peaks and valleys" in labor requirements that often occur during, respectively, busy and slow periods in à la carte dining room operations. Finally, in a banquet, there is less likelihood of overproduction of food and subsequent waste.
- Banquet planners are frequently able to sell a **hosted bar** or a **cash bar** that enables increased sales of alcoholic beverages to guests desiring them.
- There are opportunities to rent banquet rooms in addition to selling food and beverage products.
- Servers like working banquet events because, typically, mandatory service charges increase their income.

LODGING LANGUAGE

Contribution Margin: The amount of revenue remaining from a food sale after the cost of the food used to generate the sale is paid for.

Guarantee: A contractual agreement about the number of meals to be provided at a banquet event. The event's sponsor agrees to pay for the number of guests served or the guarantee, whichever is greater.

Hosted Bar: A beverage service alternative in which the host of a function pays for beverages during all or part of the banquet event. Also known as an "open bar."

Cash Bar: A beverage service alternative where guests desiring beverages during a banquet function pay for them personally.

The banquet business is very desirable, and hotel managers should do everything possible to gain a significant market share of the community's banquet business for their hotels.

Menu Planning

Most of the factors involved in planning a menu for the hotel's restaurant(s) are important when planning banquet menus. These can include concerns about:

- guest preferences
- the ability to consistently produce items of the desired quality
- the availability of ingredients required to produce the menu items
- production/service staff with appropriate skills
- equipment, layout, or facility design issues
- nutritional issues
- sanitation
- peak volume production capabilities
- the ability to generate required profit levels at the selling prices that are charged

In addition to these concerns, there can be other planning issues related to banquet menus. The menu planner must be confident that the items to be offered can be produced in the appropriate quantity, at the appropriate level of quality, and within the required time schedule. The old saying that "the customer is always right" must be tempered when banquet menus are planned. The hotel, not the banquet buyer, will be criticized if there is a failure to deliver according to anticipated standards. For example, consider a banquet host desiring a flambéed entrée, table-side-prepared Caesar salad, and handmade pastries for hundreds of guests. These items are very labor-intensive, and a large amount of specialized service would be required to deliver the items. Personnel in the sales and marketing department of most hotels would be setting up a no-win situation if they booked this event as described. If the hotel accepts the business and does not effectively deliver the promised banquet event, the guests will be upset. If the banquet buyer could not be convinced to choose a more practical menu, his or her business may be lost. However, it is likely in the hotel's best short- and long-term interest to refuse such banquet business if it cannot be delivered according to high-quality standards.

To ensure the menu items offered to guests are ones the hotel can readily produce, many properties have pre-established banquet menus that take into account the hotel's production limitations and its profitability goals. These menus are an excellent starting point for negotiations with prospective clients. Often these menus can be used without change. In other cases, relatively minor changes, such as the substitution of a specific vegetable or dessert for the ones listed on the banquet menu can be easily made.

On other occasions, a menu designed specifically for a special event is needed. A talented banquet planner, working with the property's executive chef, can develop a menu that meets the guests' expectations and the hotel's financial requirements. By contrast, without close cooperation between the catering sales staff and the food and beverage department, conflict over what can and cannot be profitably offered to guests can easily occur.

LODGING ONLINE

Hotels often market their banquet services as critical part of their larger online presence. To see an example of one hotel's banquet menu marketing efforts, go to:

www.hiltoncs.com/

When you arrive at the site, click "Banquet Menus."

Have you ever attended a banquet event at a hotel? In your opinion, how did the product and service you received at that event compare to what you have experienced at stand-alone restaurants?

Banquet Event Orders and Contracts

Banquet planning involves paying attention to numerous details. Most hotels utilize a **banquet event order (BEO)**. A sample BEO is shown in Figure 13.10. It summarizes banquet details and helps to prevent communication problems between hotel staff and the event's sponsors.

LODGING LANGUAGE

Banquet Event Order (BEO): A form used by sales and food service personnel to detail all the requirements for a banquet event. Information provided by the client is summarized on the form, and it becomes the basis for the formal contract between the client and the hotel.

The information in the BEO describes specific details about the event to be held. In some cases, it is used to form the legal contract between a hotel and a banquet buyer. However, in other cases, a separate document may be used. In either case, it is best to have a written and signed contract that clearly identifies:

Time of Guarantee: The date when an attendance guarantee (guest count) must be received.

Cancellation policies: This should include an explanation of fees to be assessed if the banquet contract is canceled. For example, there may be a cancellation fee of 50 percent of the anticipated billing if the contract is voided 60 or more days before the event was to be held, and a 100 percent fee may apply if a cancellation occurs 60 days or less from the scheduled date of the event.

Guarantee-reduction policy: For example, if the final guarantee is less than a specified percentage of the initial guarantee, an additional per-person charge may be assessed.

Billing: Information about the amount and schedule for guest payment would be addressed in the section of the agreement.

Other Banquet Concerns

Banquet room setup, service styles, and control of beverage functions are among the other special concerns of hotel banquet managers.

BANQUET ROOM SETUP

A hotel's banquet rooms (also called **function rooms**) must be set up by the hotel's staff to reflect the type and purpose of the event to be held. For example, the room setup required for a business seminar would be very different from that of a formal wedding dinner.

Prior to arrival, service staff should pay careful attention to the details included in a group's BEO to ensure a smooth and successful event.

EVENT DATE:	BANQUET EVENT ORDER (BEO) #:
Organization:	
Billing Address:	Business Phone #:
	Business Fax #:
Contact Name:	Business E-Mail
Account Executive:	Room Rental: $
Guaranteed: ( ) persons	
BEVERAGES	ROOM SET UP
❑ Full ❑ Limited ❑ Hosted bar ❑ Non-hosted bar	❑ Classroom ❑ Theater ❑ Other: ____
❑ With bartender ( ) bars ❑ Cash bar ( ) cashiers	❑ Diagram below
❑ Premium ❑ Call ❑ House	Need:
( ) per drink ( ) bar package ( ) hours of operation	❑ Registration table / chairs: ____ ❑ Wastebasket
Time: Room:	❑ Easels ❑ Podium: ❑ standing ❑ tabletop ❑ Pads / pencils / pens / mints ❑ Water / glasses
Bar Opening/Closing Instructions: Bar to close at: ____ AM / PM Bar to reopen at: ____ AM / PM	Diagram:
Wine with Lunch / Dinner ____ with entrée, ____ servers Time: Location:	
Additional Instructions:	Linen: ❑ White ❑ Other: ____
FOOD MENU	Skirting:
____ baseplates ____ waterglasses ____ butter rosettes on lemon leaves	Napkin: ❑ White ❑ Other: ____
❑ Introduction ❑ Invocation ❑ Nothing before meal	Music:
First Course Served at: ____ AM / PM Meal Served at: ____ AM / PM	AUDIO/VISUAL
	❑ Microphone: ____ ❑ Slide Projector - package: ____ ❑ Overhead Projector - package: ____ ❑ VHS / monitor / package: ____ ❑ Mixer, ____ channel ❑ AV - cart ❑ White board / markers ❑ Screen ❑ Flipchart/pads/tape/pens ❑ LCD projector
	COAT CHECK
	❑ Hosted ❑ Cash: ____ ( ) Attendant(s) ( ) Coat Racks
BEVERAGE MENU	PARKING
	❑ Hosted ❑ Cash: $____ Fee per car: $____
	BILLING (METHOD OF PAYMENT)
	Deposit received: $____

FIGURE 13.10 Sample Banquet Event Order (BEO)

LODGING LANGUAGE

Function room: A designated hotel space that can accommodate different types of special events.

In most cases, function room setup is a very straightforward activity. The space assigned for the banquet is normally determined when the banquet event is booked and at the appropriate time the room will be set up as specified. Numerous details are typically involved in setting up a banquet room. The room's size is determined by the number of guests expected (although local fire safety codes or ordinances may also impact this decision). The type (round, square, or rectangular, for example) and size of tables; the number of seats per table; and the required space for aisles, dance floors, head tables, reception/buffet lines, or other purposes should be noted on the BEO and will affect room set up. Timing may also become critical when the same space must be used for different functions throughout the same day or when a very large evening event precedes a very large breakfast event in the same space the following day.

BANQUET SERVICE STYLES

Banquet events can involve numerous ways to serve food and beverage products to guests. Most of these serving styles (American, French, Russian, English, and Buffet) are applicable to dining room service, and several were discussed earlier in this chapter. Another style sometimes used at banquets is called Butler Service: appetizers and pre-poured champagne, for example, can be passed by service personnel circulating among guests standing at a reception. Frequently more than one service style is used during a single banquet event.

Service styles can differentiate an elegant and higher-cost banquet from its less-elegant and lower-priced counterpart. For example, a Caesar salad might be prepared tableside as a demonstration for those seated at a **head table**; then, pre-portioned servings of the Caesar salad could be served to those guests seated at all other tables. Alternatively, vegetables for a soup course could be brought to the table in individual bowls for each guest (American service); service staff could pour broth from a sterling pitcher into each guest's bowl at table side (modified Russian service). These are examples of simple ways to make a banquet appear more elegant.

LODGING LANGUAGE

Head table: Special seating at a banquet event reserved for designated guests.

CONTROL OF BEVERAGE FUNCTIONS

Many banquets include the offering of alcoholic beverages. Examples include receptions before an event, wine service during a function, and continuing service of beverages during and after the meal service has concluded. Banquets offer increased opportunities to sell **call brand** or **premium brand** beverages in addition to or in place of the property's **house brand beverages**.

LODGING LANGUAGE

Call brand beverages: High-priced and higher-quality alcoholic beverages sold by name (such as Johnnie Walker Gold Scotch) rather than by type of liquor (scotch) only.

Premium brand beverages: Highest-priced and highest-quality beverages generally available, such as Johnny Walker Black Scotch. Also referred to as "super call."

House brand beverages: Alcoholic beverages sold by type (scotch) rather than by brand that are served when a call or premium brand beverage is not requested, also called "speed-rail," "well," or "pour brand."

There are several common ways that beverages sold at banquet events can be charged for and priced. They can be sold on a per-drink basis at a cash bar where guests desiring beverages pay for them personally. Many events offer hosted (open) bars in which beverages are paid for by the host for all or part of the banquet order.

Still other events have a combination of a cash and open bar where guests are issued drink tickets for complimentary drinks and then can purchase additional beverages. Another variation occurs when drinks are complimentary for a specified time period (e.g., before dinner) and are purchased (cash bar) by guests after that time.

There are a variety of ways that beverage charges can be assessed:

Individual drink price. Cash or a ticket sold for cash is collected when each drink is sold. Alternatively, a manual or electronic tally can be made of the number of each type of drink sold, and the host is charged at an agreed-upon price-per-drink basis at the end of the event.

LABOR CHARGES

Costs for the labor required to produce and serve food is normally included in the banquet charge. Sometimes, especially when the number of guests is small and the variety of services requested is large, additional charges for the following types of labor are assessed. These can include charges for:

- bartenders and barbacks (bartender assistants)
- beverage servers
- cashiers
- security personnel
- valet (parking) staff
- coat room employees

Bottle charge. Often used with an open bar, beverages are charged on a by-bottle basis for each bottle consumed/opened. Normally, every bottle opened is charged for at a full, agreed-upon rate; guests are not allowed to take open bottles away from the hotel.

Per-person charge. This method involves charging a specific price for beverages based upon event attendance. The same number of guests used for the guarantee (discussed earlier) may become the basis for the per-person charge. A deduction from the guarantee is made for minors attending the event because they will not consume alcoholic beverages.

Hourly charge. This method involves charging the host a specific price for each hour of beverage service. To establish the hourly charge, properties must determine the number of guests to be present (the guarantee can be used with adjustment for minors) and then estimate the number of drinks to be consumed per guest for each hour of the event.

Some hotels may charge a **corkage fee** for alcoholic beverages brought into the property by guests for use during an event. Although this is often misunderstood by guests, hotels *do* incur fees when pre-purchased beverages are brought in. The beverages must be served (labor costs are involved) and the bar/dining areas must be cleaned; glasses subject to breakage are used and washed; stir sticks, cocktail napkins, appropriate garnishes, if applicable, and other supplies will also still be necessary.

LODGING LANGUAGE

Corkage fee: A charge assessed when a guest brings a bottle (e.g., of a special wine) to the hotel for consumption at a banquet function or in the hotel's dining room.

Lodging Language

Banquet
Direct Report
Menu Planning
Value (foodservice)
Demographic Factors
Flambé
Ingredients
Theft
Pilferage
Stockout
Issuing
Production
Standardized Recipe
Scratch (food production)
Convenience Food
Make or Buy Analysis
Chained Recipe
Serving
Service (food and beverage)
Place Setting
Line-up (training)
Server Station
Hospitality Suite
Hosted Event
Suggestive Selling
Guest Check Average
Point-of-Sale (POS) system
Catering
Contribution Margin
Guarantee
Hosted Bars
Cash Bars
Banquet Event Order (BEO)
Function Room
Head Table
Call Brand Beverages
Premium Brand Beverages
House Brand Beverages
Corkage Fee

For Discussion

1. Assume that you are the food and beverage manager in a hotel in New York, San Francisco, New Orleans, or Honolulu that attracts guests from all over the world. What menu-planning tactics could you use that recognize the diverse food preferences of the international markets served by your property?
2. Assume that you are interested in a career in a hotel food and beverage operations. What would be the pros and cons of starting work in a smaller full-service hotel? In a larger hotel?
3. Assume that you are a food and beverage director working with the hotel's chef to plan a new menu. You want to add a vegetarian item to the new menu. What information would the chef want from you before implementing such a change?
4. It has been said that a hotelier will pay for food items of the quality purchased even though food items of the same quality are not received. What are some procedures that you as a food service manager would use to help ensure that proper receiving procedures are in use in your hotel?
5. You have learned about several service styles in common use in hotel à la carte dining and banquet operations. How would you determine which style(s) to use for your operation?
6. There are numerous tasks that servers must perform in order to make their guests' dining experience a memorable one. What are some basics you would use as a hotel restaurant manager to train new service staff in the proper way to perform these tasks?
7. Some hotels use dining room servers and room service attendants interchangeably. What special training would a room service attendant need to become an efficient dining room server?
8. Communication problems often impact the effective planning and delivery of banquets. It is natural for marketing and sales department personnel to want to do whatever they can to fill the hotel's guest rooms and public function spaces. It is also natural for food production staff to be concerned about banquet events being sold to guests. What are some types of issues that can cause conflict between personnel in these two hotel departments?
9. The food and beverage department and its housekeeping counterpart employ the vast majority of the employees in a full-service hotel. These departments are very labor-intensive because it is not practical to use technology to replace human workers in these areas. To what extent do you think technology will replace employees in the food and beverage department in the future? Why?
10. Assume that you are an overnight guest eating a hotel's complimentary breakfast the morning of your departure. Assume also that you are a businessperson staying in a five-star hotel about to dine in the property's high-check dining room on the 60th floor of the property. What are some expectations you would have that would be the same for both dining experiences?

Team Activities

TEAM ACTIVITY 1

Today all large hotel organizations use the Internet to advertise products and services to prospective guests. Find the Web sites for several of your favorite full-service hotel organizations. To what extent do they advertise their à la carte dining opportunities? Their room service and banquet operations? Do their advertising messages give any suggestion about the importance their guests place on food and beverage alternatives when making hotel-selection decisions? While reviewing these sites, check out the "employment opportunities" or similar section, and review the types of positions for which the organizations are currently recruiting. Are there position vacancies in food and beverage operations?

TEAM ACTIVITY 2

Visit a full-service hotel in your area and request permission to borrow a menu from the à la carte dining room. Pretend that you are a consultant to the property who has been asked to make improvement suggestions. Carefully study the menu from the perspectives of both the guests and the property managers. What suggestions would you make to improve the effectiveness of the menu?

Chapter

14

Hotel Technology

Thirty years ago, it was easier for hotels to impress their guests, because the hotel room was usually more advanced than the guest's own home. The challenge today is to provide a hotel room which is more technologically sophisticated than guests' homes. And that has grown increasingly difficult in light of the Wii-, PS3-, Xbox-, Netflix-, Hulu-, iPad-, Kindle-, iPhone-, and Droid-generation of today!

State-of-the-art hotels have virtually eliminated the front desk, opting instead for handheld devices. These tablets perform all the functions of a traditional desk without the space constraints. The staff member host can check the guest into the hotel room, swipe the credit card, and even provide a keycard or RFID doorlock program while walking the guest toward the room, or enjoying a coffee in the lobby, or driving toward the property in the hotel's courtesy limo.

The hotel room greets the guest upon arrival by opening the curtains, turning on the lights, and setting the television to a welcome screen. Upon entry, the guest readily programs one-touch settings which manipulate the room to their personal preferences (see Exhibit 14-1). The guest might program a "good morning" setting, an "evening" setting, or a "bedtime" setting. The bedtime setting, for example, would close the drapes, turn-on the privacy function at both the door lock and telephone, power-off the 50+ inch high-definition television and all lighting (except the one nightlight in the bathroom which this guest prefers to remain on all night long), adjust the HVAC system, and turn-on the radio to a very low volume. Whether or not the privacy setting is in place, the guest doorbell features a housekeeping "silent doorbell" feature which allows housekeeping to scan the room with an infra-red sensor to determine whether or not it is occupied.

Newly built properties are wiring today's hotel rooms with fiber optics that carry at least one gigabit of bandwidth. This allows a fully integrated Internet Protocol property, whereby each room acts as an antenna providing wireless speed across the facility which is at least eight times faster than the best traditional hotel rooms. Enough to play games on-demand, download video, and work seamlessly online. But the property's IP network provides so much more than Wi-Fi; it also accesses better than 3,000 global television channels, thousands of world radio stations, assorted professional tools which integrate to the hotel's business center, electronic concierge assistance, and hotel and local area information. Additionally, the Internet Protocol infrastructure interfaces a number of hotel applications like VoIP telephony; point-of-sale tablets; in-house music; and locking, property management, back-of-house, energy, and fire-safety systems. In the lobby, the guest might find an electronic pad the size of a table-top surface on which to view and share weather, jogging maps, and citywide attractions. Heck, even the hotel's wall art is electronic: able to change themes, artists, and genres at a moment's notice.

TECHNOLOGY IN THE GUEST ROOM: HISTORICAL VIEW

Innkeepers have never been technology leaders. Lodging is so segmented that no one company has had the resources for research and technological innovation. The hotel industry was at the forefront of the credit-card revolution, but was unable to sustain its leadership; it lacked capital. The hotel industry was quick to adopt the computerized advantages of property management systems, but relied on outside industries to make them work; it lacked technical know-how.

Guests are pleasantly surprised to find cutting-edge technology in their hotel rooms, but they shouldn't be. Innkeepers have always marched ahead of their times. Hotels had bathtubs before the White

Taken from *Check-In Check-Out: Managing Hotel Operations*, Ninth Edition, by Gary K. Vallen and Jerome J. Vallen

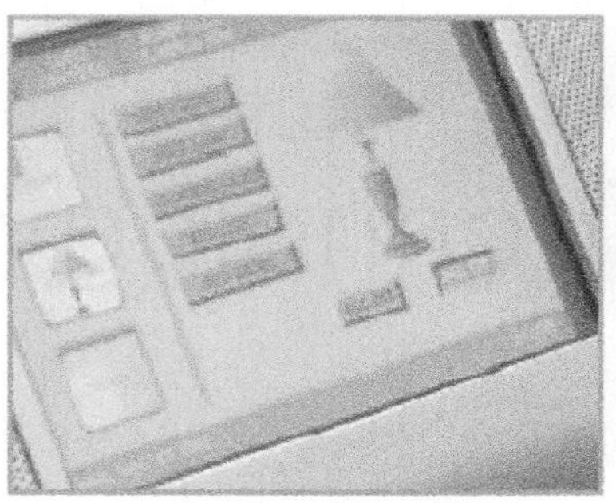

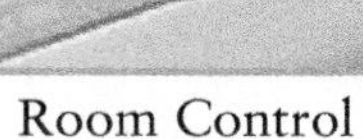

Room Control

Guest Services

Alarm Clock & Digital Radio

2-Line Speakerphone

EXHIBIT 14-1 Guest-controlled touch panels are the wave of the future. Newly built properties are hard-wiring the hotel room so that one-touch panels can control everything from the curtains to the lights; the television(s) to the locking system; the telephone to the sound system; and the coffee maker to the minibar. Imagine a guest who likes a certain "sleep" setting; he programs the touch panel accordingly (let's say one of his preferences is to dim the light above the bathroom sink) and enjoys a one-touch sleep mode each night of his visit. How much brand loyalty will there be when he visits a different property in the chain and finds that his one-touch sleep mode setting follows him property-to-property through the guest database! *Courtesy of INNCOM International Inc., Niantic, Connecticut.*

House; elevators were first tested in hotels; "tubular connectors" (mail chutes) sped letters down from the upper floors; telephones first appeared in New York City's Netherland Hotel in 1894. Hoteliers have always seized the moment, but they slipped behind over the past decade as the electronic technology revolution crossed the nation's threshold.

A Look Back

Neither the general public nor the lodging industry experienced much change in in-room technology before 1970. Small refrigerators with ice-cube makers were one early innovation. In part, this was a means of reducing labor, as the uniformed services division was responsible for delivering ice to guest rooms. Like other innovations (massage beds and television sets) either an extra charge was made for the room or a coin was needed to activate the equipment.

New telephone systems were introduced early in the decade of the 1970s (see Exhibit 14-2). Previously, hotels often had but one trunk line (outgoing connection to the telephone company's lines). Long waits for connections, especially for long-distance calls, were not unusual. Although nothing like today's cell phones, the in-room telephone soon became ubiquitous. HOBIC (Hotel Outward Bound Information Center) was a 1980 telephone innovation (see Exhibit 14-2), which enabled front desks to track calls originating in guest rooms and charge them to folios. That was sweetened in 1981 when it became legal for hotels to add service charges, especially for interstate calls. Telephone profits rose even further after AT&T's telephone monopoly was broken up in 1981. Those decades were the heyday for hotel telephone profits. Today, hotel telephone systems are a cost center, not a revenue center. And one which many experts predict will be all but gone from the hotel room landscape with a decade.

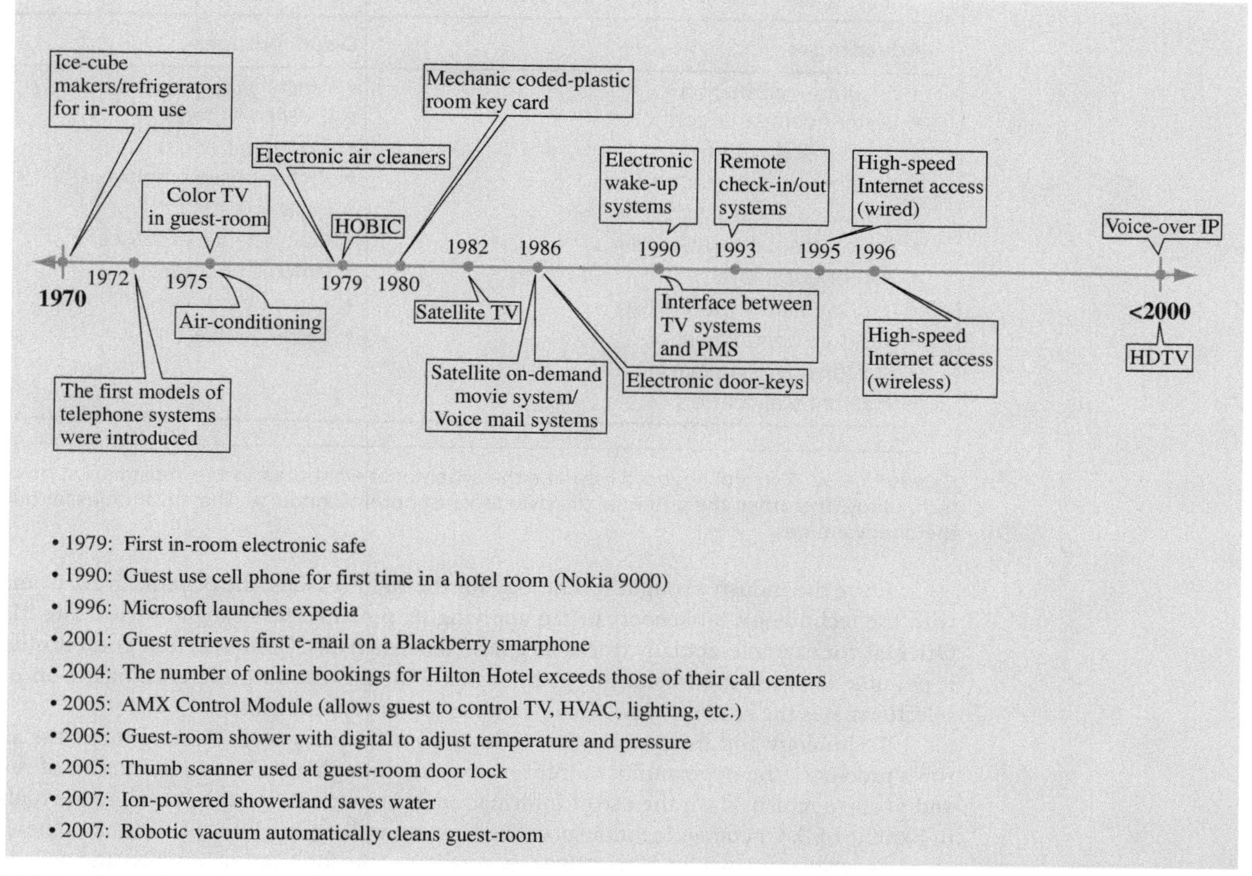

EXHIBIT 14-2 Almost four decades of technological innovations ranging from in-room refrigerators (1970) to robotic vacuums (2007). Since 2007, the rate of innovation has been too rapid to include in this small chart. This chapter describes literally dozens of enhancements which have become standard fare over the past several years.

Color television sets were well established in private homes before the industry introduced them. In 1975, hoteliers intent on differentiating their property from the competition, began installing them in special guests rooms and eventually throughout the property.

Electronic key systems came on the scene in 1986 and with them increased security and convenience. The 1990s brought new ideas. Television sets were interfaced with the hotel's PMS, enabling guests to view their folios. Guests began using the television for speedy check-out and by the mid-decade this had replaced the pencil-and-paper zip-out check-out.

The technology revolution accelerated as the new century began. High-speed Internet access (1995) was widely available. Gaining ground were Voice-over Internet Protocol (VoIP) telephone systems, high-definition TV, wireless Internet access, interactive entertainment systems, and more (see Exhibit 14-2).

Costs and Benefits

Technology is part of today's culture; so is innkeeping. Technology increases the efficiency of the staff and enhances the experience of the guest. Technology can be overdone, however, and detract from the guest experience (just try holding on through minutes of automated telephone directions before reaching, a live voice, if ever).

At first, hotels were notorious buyers of products that failed to work as promised, or worked but provided no real benefit to the operation. Most of the companies that foisted products on the industry during the 1990s are no longer in business or no longer support the product that they once sold. Only three of the original 12 technology vendors that placed advertisements in the first issue of *Hospitality Upgrade* are still in business. That is a function of the rapid rate of innovation—technology vendors matured as their products matured. Early efforts seemed to focus on buying technology just to buy technology.

The Pluses and Minuses of Hotel Technology	
Advantages	**Disadvantages**
• Accurate information	• Amenity creep
• Better operational controls	• Crashed systems
• Closer fiscal scrutiny	• Ergonomic issues
• Ease of use; minimal training	• Higher-priced employees
• Enhanced guest satisfaction	• Initial investment
• Environmental sustainability	• Maintenance expenses
• Higher guest loyalty	• Periodic upgrades
• Improved labor productivity	• Rapid obsolescence
• Reduced operating costs	• Security losses
• Speedier decision making	
• Tighter fiscal controls	

EXHIBIT 14-3 Two alphabetized lists: one the advantages attributed to the implementation of hotel technology. The other, the potential disadvantages of hotel technology. The advantages far outweigh the disadvantages.

Once the industry sought technology for the right reasons, the benefits grew. Comfortable with the technology, innkeepers began applying its potential to a range of uses. The Mandarin Oriental, for example, actually tracks its guests' favorite fruits. Computerized guest profiles make it possible to stock the welcoming fruit basket with the guest's preference based on previous selections. It is the kind of "wow" factor that makes for repeat business.

Technology and the systems that it develops offer many tools. Among them, the ability to solve problems; the opportunity to improve profits through an effective utilization of resources; and positive returns from the use of information management. These advantages are highlighted in Exhibit 14-3. Of course, technology carries costs as well, and Exhibit 14-3 itemizes these also.

Security is on that list of negatives because it is at the forefront of business and governmental concerns. This places it high on the industry's watch list. One example is wireless Internet. It is a service that hotel guests expect. But private conversations are subject to security breaches. Guest credit-card information carries a similar risk. Hotel IT managers must assess these risks and implement steps to protect the hotel. Either a wireless security protocol such as Wi-Fi protected access (WPA) must be installed, or at a minimum, guests must be asked to sign a disclaimer at registration.

Ergonomics, the study of the relation between machines and humans, is another worry linked to increased technology. For the lodging industry, it focuses primarily on the employee who may be exposed to eight hours of poorly designed office facilities, or even worse, radiation from computer monitors. Management must attend to both issues, lest the potential for expensive litigation.

Cost plays a role in technology, as it does with every management decision. The relative price of technology has been in a downward spiral for many years, but new products come into the market at high initial cost. The operation may need to invest today even though the cost will be lower in the future. Waiting may be too late. Systems must be updated and maintained if they are to contribute to the bottom line. With technology, the outlay is evident; the gains much less clear. Technology investment is similar to marketing and advertising: Will my investment pay off? It is a management conundrum.

TECHNOLOGY IN THE ROOM: THE NEW GENERATION

This review of the latest technologies in hotel guest rooms will take you across a number of interdependent categories. From locking systems to minibars, energy management to fire alarm systems, each plays an important role in guest satisfaction, attraction, safety, and/or profitability. Some systems are a necessity in the modern hotel (locking systems) others an amenity (televisions which feature 3-d and/or interactive technologies). But whether a necessity or amenity, every system necessarily goes through a cost/benefit analysis. Does it improve the hotel's bottom-line? Does it positively impact guest satisfaction? Will it enhance our competitiveness? Is it legally necessary (as with locking systems, below)?

EXHIBIT 14-4 Old-fashioned iron keys and mortise locks were used by hotels into the 1960s. They were replaced with brass keys that could be cut on property for economy and convenience. Likewise, traditional locks were eventually designed with a quick replace feature allowing the hotel's maintenance department to pull one lock out and replace it with a different lock. Locks had to be replaced each time a guest failed to return the room key. That's why key inventory control (see Exhibit 14-5) was so important to guest safety. *Courtesy of Getty Images, Inc.*

Locking Systems

Just as the in-room telephone will eventually disappear in favor of the smartphone, so too have guest-room locking systems evolved from key and mortise locks to electronic, RFID, and biometric locks. A look at these futuristic locking systems is all the more valuable when first starting with a look back through history.

TRADITIONAL MORTISE LOCKS Colonial innkeepers roomed several parties together. Indeed, strangers often slept in the same bed. Keys were not part of an early inn's inventory. Room security and personal space improved when locks and keys were introduced (see Exhibit 14-4). But maintaining key inventories became a full-time job split between engineering, which made them, and the desk, which inventoried them (see Exhibit 14-5).

Iron keys had several issues. Made of metal with hanging metal tags, they were very heavy. The weight encouraged guests to return them each time they left the building. This approach is

EXHIBIT 14-5 Compared to a manual key system, which requires tracking thousands of keys, mechanical locking systems, electronic locking systems (ELSs), and today's audible key technology are easier to manage. Mechanical locking systems (keycards with numerous small holes which match a mechanical lock code) were the first invention, following several highly publicized security lawsuits. Electronic locking systems quickly became the standard in the 1970s and 1980s, and remain the minimum standard for guest safety in today's industry.

still seen in Europe today, where smaller inns request guests to hand over their bulky room keys each time they exit the property.

Brass keys became the standard for several decades from the 1950s through 1970s. Because they were less cumbersome, brass keys disappeared at an alarming rate. Way back in 1980, when a dollar had real value, Holiday Inn reported key replacement reached $1 million annually. And since the hotel had several keys already cut and waiting in inventory for a given room, when one key was not returned by the guest, hotels were reluctant to change the door locks. Thieves knew this, and readily burglarized rooms with found keys.

The American Hotel Association, forerunner of the American Hotel & Lodging Association, convinced postal authorities to accept keys in the mail and return them to the individual hotel, which would pay postage due. That information was printed on the key tag. When such keys fell into unauthorized hands, it wasn't difficult to figure out to which hotel room the key belonged.

Something needed to be done. Plastic tags was the first modification (see Exhibit 14-5). Though there were a number of variations, plastic tags all worked around one main premise. Keys followed the lock, not the room. When a room was rekeyed, the plastic tags would be quickly changed and the previous keys, retagged, now worked the lock in the new room. This provided substantial key savings to hotels.

MECHANICAL LOCKING SYSTEMS In the early 1980s, plastic keys (not plastic tags) encoded with punched holes forever changed guest lock security (see Exhibit 14-6). Locks were now available which allowed a series of keys to be produced in an established hierarchy. The first key in the hierarchy opened the lock for as long as it was used—possibly through a succession of guests. But when that key was eventually kept by a guest and not returned to the hotel, the next key in the hierarchy would be handed out. At this time, the lock accepted the new key in the hierarchy and was designed to reject the previous key(s) in the hierarchy. In other words, the design of the lock establishes which keys will open the door (this key and anything higher in the order); previous keys are rejected by the lock.

Not only did guests like these keys because plastic was lighter and easier to carry, especially to the beach or the pool, but hotels favored them since they carried no hotel identification. They were inexpensive enough that the hotel did not worry about the costs of unreturned keys. Room numbers were still required for the convenience of the guest and because keys returned to the desk were recycled for the next occupant of that room. They were also popular with hotel lawyers because they exceeded the standard of care previously provided through the traditional brass key and mortise locks.

The best thing about the key code hierarchy is that it allows a number of parallel levels to operate in conjunction with each other. So, even as the guest continues to use the assigned

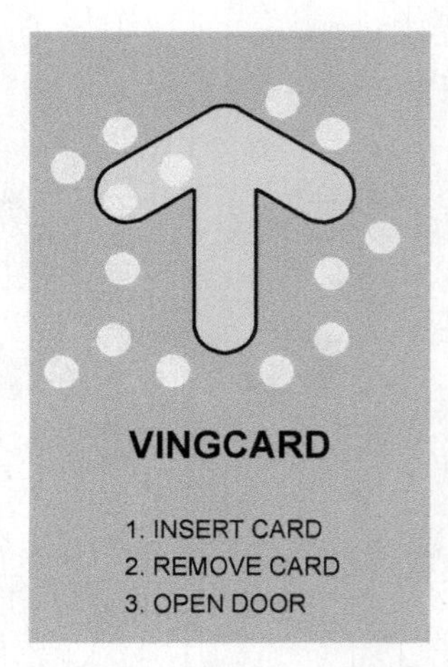

EXHIBIT 14-6 An example of the first type of keycard available to hotels. Rather than an encoded magnetic stripe (as with electronic locking systems), these mechanical locking system keycards were encoded with punched holes. In terms of hierarchical locking systems—whereby the next card used invalidates all previous cards used—these keycards represent the first generation. Even so, many of the benefits associated with today's most sophisticated electronic locking systems were still available to hotels using these keycards in the early 1980s. Many hotels still utilize these systems. *Courtesy of VingCard Elsafe, an ASSA ABLOY company, Connecticut, U.S.A., and Stockholm, Sweden.*

key during a several-day stay, housekeeping can enter the room without disrupting the guest's key code. In fact, mechanical locking systems and electronic locking systems (discussed below) carry a number of parallel level hierarchies. From the lowest level, these usually include guest hierarchy, a guest failsafe hierarchy, housekeeping, hotel security, and hotel management. Even the deadbolt will open when keys are deployed from the highest two levels—allowing access to a room where a sick or injured guest may be unable to unlock the deadbolt from within.

ELECTRONIC LOCKING SYSTEMS (ELS) The electronic lock became the third generation of locking systems. About 85% of all U.S. hotels now use one of the two versions of electronic locking systems: hard wired or microprocessor based.

Hard-Wired Systems Hard-wired electronic locking systems are ideal for properties designed from the ground-up. They provide the highest levels of security and the most flexibility for adaptation to other in-room systems being developed in this age of technology. But hard-wired systems are extremely expensive to retrofit, because virtually every door lock across the property is physically wired to a central master console at the front desk. That is why they make the most sense for new construction.

The guest-service agent programs a new key (usually a set of two keys) for each arrival and transmits that code to the room door through the hard-wired installation. By the time the guest reaches the assigned room, the key lock has the new code and accepts the guest's key. Key codes issued to previous guests are invalidated simultaneously.

Microprocessor-Based Systems Microprocessor-based systems are ideal for retrofit hotels because they function as stand-alone installations. The door lock is actually a miniature computer or "microprocessor." Microprocessor-based ELS's come in two forms: one-way or two-way communications.

One-way communication systems These utilize an ELS console which functions as an electronic key encoder. This console is not very large—about the size of a shoe box—and sits at the hotel front desk. The console encodes a sophisticated lock combination on new guest keys at the time of guest registration. Minutes later, when the key is inserted into the guest-room door-lock (see Exhibit 14-7), the one-way communication is complete; the door lock accepts the new

EXHIBIT 14-7 There are dozens of electronic locking system vendors available to the hotel industry. Here are two examples. The one on the left is Onity's brass-plated micro-processor-based ELS. The one on the right is ILCO's Solitaire 710-11. *Courtesy of Onity, A UTC Fire & Security Company, Duluth, Georgia. And courtesy of Kaba Lodging Systems, ILCO, Montreal, Canada.*

EXHIBIT 14-8 A keycard with operating instructions for the three types of locks available through this vendor. Notice the front of the key carries a DoubleTree logo. Hotel chains have experimented with all kinds of graphics; calendars, local area maps, etc. in an attempt to give the keycard a second life with the guest after check-out. It is the same logic hotels use with amenities (e.g., shampoo bottles) so guests hold on to them, re use them, and hopefully generate a bit of brand loyalty. *Courtesy of Kaba Lodging Systems, ILCO, Montreal, Canada.*

combination and automatically cancels any previous codes. This is very similar to the keycode hierarchy discussed above under mechanical locking systems.

ELS's featuring one-way communication systems offer several advantages over mechanical locking systems. Each is unique; every guest gets a new key (as many as they need). The keys are light weight; with a magnetic stripe that is generally not affected by water, sun, or sand; inexpensive (about 10 cents per key); and recyclable. Keys that are returned can be reprogrammed for another room and another guest (see Exhibit 14-8).

The door lock contains a battery-powered microprocessor (see Exhibit 14-9) and a card reader. And stored in the microprocessor is information related to previous users who accessed the room. Storing at least a few dozen of the last entries into the room, some ELS microprocessors store substantially more information than that. As guests and staff members enter the room (say the bellperson, housekeeping, or a security officer), they leave an auditable trail which can be downloaded from the lock using a special "interrogator" device available to hotel management (see Exhibit 14-10). In the case of burglarized rooms or any number of other reasons, the hotel

EXHIBIT 14-9 Electronic locking systems are either hard wired or microprocessor based. Hard-wired systems rely on electricity to operate (though they have a battery back-up for continuous operation during power outages). Microprocessor-based systems are retro-fitted and cannot use in-house electricity. They depend on a long-life battery to be a practical installation. *Courtesy of Kaba Lodging Systems, ILCO, Montreal, Canada.*

Guest Cards

Check-in:
Issue card to guest with relevant information.

Parking:
Access to parking facilities.

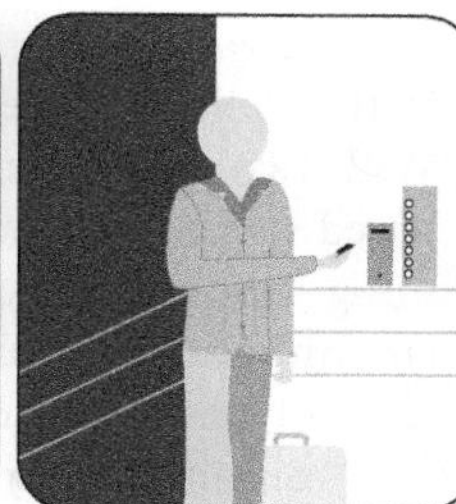

(Elevator) access:
Access to specified areas only.

Enter room:
Lock verifies that keycard has correct information (room #, unique hotel code, time frame etc.).

Payment:
Use keycard to pay for services at hotel (restaurant, souvenir shop etc.).

Other areas:
Guests have access to conference room, gym, etc., with keycard.

Lost keycard:
Hotel issues new keycard.

Enter room w/new keycard:
New keycard replaces previous guest keycard in lock.

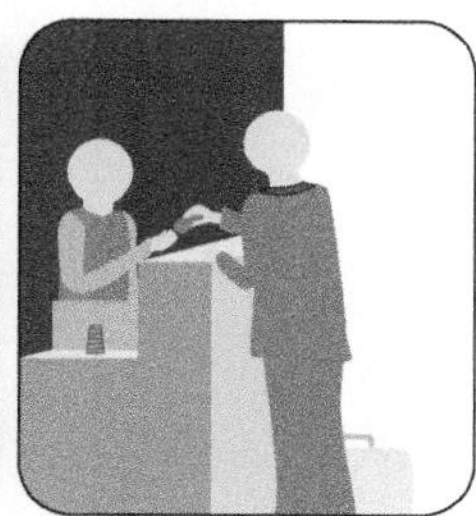

Check-out:
Hotel system reports what to bill (restaurant, etc.). Guest leaves and keycard is cancelled for access upon departure.

Staff operations

Issue keycard to employee:
Employee gets individual keycard.

Access:
Only access to specified areas.

Locklink/program lock:
Upload software and data to lock (room #, unique hotel code, set clock).

Housekeeping:
Not able to access room if privacy function is turned on by guest.

Low battery:
When low battery, employees will get 3 yellow flashes.

Lock link/read events:
Download lock events.

EXHIBIT 14-10 The advantages of two-way communication systems, whether hard wired or wireless, are highlighted here. Both guests and staff access various areas and services throughout the hotel. Security is increased, customer service enhanced, and an audit trail provided. *Courtesy of VingCard Elsafe, an ASSA ABLOY company, Connecticut, U.S.A., and Stockholm, Sweden.*

can know who entered, at what time the entry occurred, and even when the next time the door was opened from within (as when someone later exits the room).

One-way communication systems have disadvantages, as their name implies. There is no security alert if the wrong key is inserted in the lock. It also takes a trek to the desk for a new key if the party changes rooms. Their chief limitation is the "one-way" flow of information, as the following section on two-way communications explains.

Two-way communication systems Two-way communication represents the next step in the evolution of electronic locking systems. Consequently, they are more expensive to install. With two-way systems, a central database communicates to each lock through either a hard-wired system or a wireless one. A major advantage of the two-way system is two-way programming—the guest key can open various locks throughout the hotel (this is not true with one-way communication). Guest-room keys can access the parking garage, the fitness room, the pool, the elevator, and the concierge floor (see Exhibit 14-10).

Similarly, floor housekeepers who are assigned to different stations can gain access remotely to both areas of the hotel. Once a two-way system is in place, interfaces can be installed with the property management system and the point-of-sale system,

KEY CARDS Key cards are an essential element of every mechanical and electronic locking system. But even here, there are variations. Magnetic stripe cards (see Exhibit 14-6) are the most common of the four types.

Magnetic Stripe Cards These cards contain three stripes or tracks embedded into the one ABA magnetic strip. Hotels use the first track to encode the ELS. In addition to the lock access codes, key cards also carry an expiration date. Most keys automatically stop accessing the room at 2 PM on the date of departure. Cards can also be created for one-time access, as when the bellperson escorts the guest to view a room before he or she decides to stay. Magnetic stripe cards can be encoded further to facilitate charges in dining rooms, lounges, and retail outlets. Personal information such as the guest's credit-card number is not on the key cards, although rumors abound that it is.

Memory Cards As their name suggests, memory chips store data such as lock-access codes and other information. The smallest card stores about 2 kilobytes (Kbs) of data, enough to store 25 different key lock codes. Memory goes up from there: 8 Kbs can carry 125 different key lock codes; 64 Kbs as many as 1,350 key lock codes. Memory cards well serve staff members and managers who need access to multiple locks, .and hotels have locks everywhere. A memory card costs between $2 and $4 each, in contrast to 10¢ for a stripe card.

Smart Cards Smart cards, chip cards, or integrated-circuit cards are any pocket-sized card with embedded, integrated circuits. They are capable of processing information. Smart cards store more information than memory cards. Because they also process data, smart cards can serve as an electronic purse or personal identification (ID). Their cost is upward of $10 each.

RFID Cards Radio frequency ID (identification) is the fourth class of cards and the last of the group. We examine them next.

Radio Frequency Identification (RFID)

Identification using radio frequency is a recent innovation which appears perfectly suited to the hospitality industry. RFID technology stores and remotely retrieves data from devices called RFID tags or transponders. With RFID locking systems, the transponders or tags function as the room keys.

Because each transponder has a unique code, hotels have been experimenting with providing permanent tags to their frequent guests. Frequently they mail these RFID tags, but however they receive them, guests are encouraged to hold on to their RFID tag for each subsequent visit to the chain. This provides a major step in guest service, because it allows the frequent traveler direct access to the guest room while bypassing the front desk check-in process.

RFID-capable guests receive a text message upon arrival at the property. The message tells the guest which room number has been downloaded with the RFID code. The loyal customer walks right past the crowded front desk!

RFID LOCKS RFID locks are known as "contactless" locking systems, because there is no need to slide a keycard into a slot (see Exhibit 14-11). Rather, the RFID lock only needs the transponder to be in close proximity to the lock. Many front desks instruct guests to tap the tag against the lock. But a nearby wave is really all it takes. Although the tag can look like a plastic keycard, it is more fun to make it into a key fob, wristband, necklace, or any number of creative ideas.

EXHIBIT 14-11 A radio frequency identification (RFID) lock contains no keycard slot. Access is made over radio waves with the encrypted code carried on a tag or transponder. Close proximity to the lock is all it takes for the door to open. Guest satisfaction has been extremely high in those properties which have converted from an ELS to an RFID system. No more demagnetized keys requiring the guest to trek all the way back to the desk! *Courtesy of Kaba Lodging Systems, SAFLOK, Troy, Michigan.*

A careful look at Exhibit 14-11 shows why RFID locks are quickly gaining popularity. There is no keycard slot and no keyhole. That provides the guest a number of advantages:

- No need to fumble for the lock opening in a dimly lit corridor
- Ease of access for the handicapped
- Less maintenance because dirt doesn't clog the aperture
- Less sensitivity to humidity, freezing temperatures (for motel rooms with outside access), and salty sea air.
- No more complaints about keycards failing to work at the guest-room door (such an inconvenience)
- No problems with keycard codes being erased when kept in the same pocket as the guests' cell phone
- "Open Sesame," even with hands full of suitcases or packages

OTHER RFID USES The RFID transponder has a number of other uses in the hospitality industry. It can identify where a guest has been (and when) across the hotel facility. This is especially handy with conventions, seminars, and conferences. For example, imagine a guest who is attending a medical training seminar. In order to receive continuous education points, the guest needs attend at least 7 hours of the 8-hour training. RFID would provide that information, tracking each time the guest left the seminar room and again when he returned to the training session. If a hotel wanted to promote a particular restaurant or lounge, it could market directly to those RFID guests who had entered the lounge over the previous 60 days. A trade show booth might want to send promotional materials to any RFID attendee who walked past the booth and lingered longer than 15 seconds. The potential for creative ideas using RFID technology is endless!

Biometric Locking Systems

The first generation of biometric ELSs was launched by Saflok in 2004. Saflok was one of the earliest companies to work in biometrics. Arriving guests register their fingerprints or iris scans during the registration process. The front desk forwards the information to the lock. And the guest enters without delay when he or she reaches the room. Similar to all two-way communication systems, access is easily made to other locks across the property: the pool, concierge floor, and so on.

In 2006, IBM introduced a biometric locking system that scanned the user's iris. *Guestroom 2010* featured IBM's system in an exhibition sponsored by the Association of Hospitality Financial and Technology Professionals. This organization was predicting success with biometric systems in just four short years.

The science might be in place, but its guest acceptance is not. Guests do not feel comfortable giving up sensitive information such as fingerprints and iris scans. Aversion grew greater after it was learned that even CIA and FBI files have been hacked. Replacing a key card is one thing; retrieving hacked iris IDs is something else entirely. Guests also do not feel comfortable staring into an iris scanner as other guests watch them enter their room or access the pool. Even as the extreme cost of such technology decreases with time, it may prove a hard sell for guests to accept biometric devices. Still, Boston-based Nine Zero Hotel uses an iris scanner to monitor access to its Cloud Nine suite.

Smartphone Applications

In 2011, the number of smartphone users in America finally equaled the number of mobile phone users, about 140 million for each category. Another way to look at this statistic is to understand that 91% of Americans carry some form of cell phone. And half of these are smartphones. No wonder the number of smartphone apps specific to the hospitality industry have been growing so rapidly.

GUEST-ROOM LOCK APPLICATIONS Although RFID-capable locking systems have grown in popularity, it may be short-lived. Many lodging brands believe smartphones provide a better answer for tech-savvy travelers. You see, the service bottleneck for travelers—especially corporate guests—has always been the key hand-off, which is accomplished through the front-desk check-in. The RFID transponder (described above) has the potential to save the guest a major step in the check-in process by providing a key substitute through the mail, which becomes the guest's dedicated key. Yet critics suggest this only works in a perfect world. In a perfect world, the guest remembers to bring the transponder and has it readily available for access to the guest room. But those guests who leave the transponder at home, forget it in their car, or realize that it is buried in their luggage (and therefore can't place it in close proximity to the door lock)—those guests do not exist in the perfect world. The smartphone answers all of these issues. No longer does the industry need to burden its guests with additional items (keys, for example). The smartphone, which is practically attached to the ear of so many current travelers, provides access to the guest room. Once the guest downloads the free application (app) for the lodging brand, it is a simple matter to call up the confirmation for this particular reservation. With the confirmation displayed on the phone, a remote check-in completed, and a room number assigned, the guest needs to merely point the phone toward the door lock.

OTHER HOSPITALITY INDUSTRY SMARTPHONE APPLICATIONS The airline industry has developed a seamless system: make an online reservation, print your boarding pass or arrive at the airport and print it at a self-serve kiosk, walk past airport security, and then turn over your printed boarding pass as you enter the plane. Seamless, with one small hitch—why make the customer print, retain, and hand over a boarding pass? The smartphone has proven to be even more seamless, because it hosts a unique barcode which was emailed to the phone after the reservation was booked. Pass the smartphone (barcode) in front of the scanner and enter the plane, easy as pie.

Other Airline Conveniences The smartphone is as versatile as the Internet. Want to check the seat configuration on the airplane you are about to board? Use your smartphone. Want to reschedule your flight to a more convenient time? Use your smartphone. Want to receive delayed flight notices? Use your smartphone. Want access to special fares reserved *only* for smartphone users? Use your smartphone!

Hotel Check-In Some chains are already boasting that 25% of their guests check in via smartphone. A simple email from the hotel to the user's phone the morning of arrival invites the soon-to-be guest to use a remote check-in app. The benefits are substantial. As more guests choose this smartphone remote check-in option, less guests wait in line, less employees are needed at the front desk, and better are the levels of service that can be provided to both types of guests.

Upselling and Suggestive Selling Even as reduced staffing has tremendous advantages to the bottomline, there are other benefits which accrue from smartphone check-in. Upselling is one such benefit. In a traditional face-to-face check-in, upselling is only as good as the employee training and willingness to attempt an upsell. Many employees are timid in this regard and either ignore the opportunity to upsell or, when they do try an upsell, quickly cease their attempt at the guest's first—"no thanks." The smartphone app is far less shy. With a top-down approach, the smartphone offers the guest the best room category (read: most expensive), requiring the guest to actively turn down the room choice option. Then, of course, the next category is offered. And so on, until the guest eventually makes the room choice. Research demonstrates great success with upselling via smartphone apps.

Additionally, chains are loading room service menus, spa services, and dining room reservations as follow-up apps to the guest check-in. These supplemental sales have been hitting record levels in recent months. There is something almost sci-fi like in being able to order— a steak cooked to your specifications, delivered according to your travel schedule, complete with a glass of wine and salad—before you even take off for your destination city!

Tap to Pay A number of vendors (Google, Visa, MasterCard, and Citibank, to name a few) have developed "single-tap" or "wave and pay" payment solutions. More secure than credit or debit cards, the smartphone becomes the vehicle for payment at the front desk, restaurants, or any number of various outlets across the property. While it is not uncommon to hear a guest exclaim, "I left my wallet (credit card, cash, debit card) in the room," guests are never far from their smartphones. That is what makes this system so attractive—the incredible convenience of having all systems work through one device. For a quick coffee at the snack bar, a single tap or wave might be all the operation requires. When closing a guest folio for potentially thousands of dollars, a signature on the screen is still recommended.

Single-tap systems don't really require the "tap" to process a transaction. Rather, they utilize "near field communication" hardware and software. An NFC chip comes standard in most smartphones, allowing the user to simply wave the phone (no tap actually required) within a few inches of the payment terminal.

The real question will be who is in the driver's seat with regard to smartphone transactions in the coming years. Although Visa and MasterCard have been experimenting with single-tap as well as wave and pay systems, the leaders may end up being the big four smartphone providers: AT&T, T-Mobile, Verizon, and Sprint. But other experts are betting on Google, Apple, and other Internet leaders to become the primary beneficiaries of smartphone transactions through clearing houses like Google Checkout and Apple iTunes.

While some paranoia still exists with users, smartphone transactions are actually safer than carrying a wallet. NFC-eavesdropping technology does exist. Yet it is not as advanced as some people fear, where the would-be thief can simply brush against your smartphone and steal the money in your accounts. NFC eavesdropping devices need to be physically inserted between the wave and the pay. That is unlikely except with a sophisticated inside job and a relatively naïve consumer. Anyway, consumers can simply encrypt their data transmissions for added security. Or they can voluntarily require the payment terminal to ask for a password for transactions above, say $50. The last point should certainly set users at ease; when your wallet is lost or stolen there is little you can do but contact each of your credit card companies and stop their usage. But with a smartphone, you can locate the phone by GPS and/or remotely deactivate the smartphone and/or require a password to access the phone.

Mobile Apps for the Meetings Industry Conventions, conferences, trade shows, and corporate meetings have benefited substantially from smartphone apps. A recent collaboration of key executives identified at least 500 different apps specific to the meetings industry. Many are designed to provide convenience to the user by replacing the conference program (often a bulky multi-paged program that is both a hassle to carry as well as expensive to print) with a smartphone app. Now the attendee can search the day's agenda, identify last-minute room changes, confirm events for which he or she is registered, read personal bios of key speakers, and chat with other attendees. Other features include a searchable list of all conference attendees, access to the conference's social media feeds like Twitter and Facebook, scheduling assistance programs by which to plan your conference day, brief synopses of each of the day's seminars, an interactive map of the exhibit hall, and an area map of local attractions. Maybe the coolest feature for networking during a conference is an app called "Bump," whereby two new friends can exchange contact details and personal information simply by bumping their individual smartphones together!

Proximity-Based Promotion Apps Although it can be a bit unnerving the first time a smartphone user realizes how smart the phone really is, the advantages are mind-boggling. Proximity-based marketing is founded on the idea that the user—let's say John Smith, an executive in Las Vegas for two days of meetings—is interested in reading promotions specific to where he might be standing at the time. Walking through the lobby of Caesar's Palace, John's smartphone alerts him to a happy hour currently in progress at Payard's Patisserie & Bistro. How convenient, he is literally standing in front of the bistro right that moment. Later, as he walks past the Colosseum (Caesar's event center and showroom), his phone again alerts him; this time there are discounted show tickets available for this evening's show which starts in just 20 minutes. This is the concept behind proximity-based promotions.

While on the subject of casinos, there are a number of new casino gaming applications which are also proximity based. These apps allow the user to bet on sporting events, keno games, and a number of similar options provided he or she is ... you guessed it, within a certain proximity to the casino floor!

Energy Management and Climate Control Systems

After labor, energy is the industry's second largest operating expense, as it is for the nation's airline industry. According to the Environmental Protection Agency (EPA), the lodging industry spends nearly $5 billion annually on energy. And costs are rising. Energy usage in the guest room consumes 40–80% of the total utility expenditure, depending on the size, type, and class of hotel. The guest-room contribution to total energy usage is lower in those hotels which boast large public areas (spas, casinos, meeting space, etc.).

Utility usage spans a number of delivery formats, each with their own unique cost structures. Hotels use water, hot and cold, across the property in both the guest room as well as throughout the facility in such areas as laundry, kitchens, public restrooms, meeting rooms and banquets, landscaping, spa and pools, as well as décor (as in decorative fountains). Electricity, the largest single utility category for a hotel, is used in the guest room as well as all of the areas listed above. Additional sources of electricity usage would also include exterior and interior lighting; signage; all audiovisual uses across the property from the guest-room television to lobby background music; computers at the front desk, executive offices, and point-of-sale locations; fire and security systems; and the list goes on and on. Hotels are also large users of natural gas (less commonly, heating oil or steam systems) which is needed for hot water boilers; in-room and public space heating, ventilation, and air-conditioning systems; kitchen appliances; and other similar uses.

Energy costs vary by the time of day. Utility rates peak just about the time that guests leave their rooms. Signage that prompts guests to turn off the lights, television, and HVAC system when they leave the room has not been effective. Hotels began testing energy management systems (EMS) at the time of the first oil embargo in 1973. Now the industry has moved beyond the testing phase, using one of three approaches: centrally controlled systems, individually controlled systems, or network controlled systems.

Centrally controlled systems have not been well received and are, therefore, not in widespread use. Guests cannot adjust the room temperature. Control of the entire hotel rests with the engineering department. It sets a standard that old guests and young, northern guests and southern, national and international guests must all accept. They don't do so happily.

PTACS Individually controlled units are commonly referred to as PTACs, or packaged terminal air conditioners. Individually controlled systems have been in place for a long time, because they have been the guests' preference. Guests have the comfort of setting their own in-room temperatures even as hotel management anguishes over controlling utility costs.

PTACs are an especially good fit for the lower- and mid-tiered lodging segments. This is because they have a low up-front cost in terms of initial investment, they require relatively little maintenance, and what maintenance is required is comparatively simple—ideal for the skill-set

EXHIBIT 14-12 PTACs are typically installed in hotel rooms. And while the manager of the property is concerned with energy efficiency, the typical guest usually is not. Here's the drill. It's a hot summer day and when the guest arrives in the hotel room, just before he throws himself onto the bed, he cranks up the air-conditioning. Then later, when he gets hungry, he heads out to the nearest restaurant. But did he remember to turn off the PTAC before he left?

The maker of this product, Amana, claims a 35% reduction in energy usage when their DigiSmart system is used. The bulk of these savings comes through the occupancy sensor, which shuts down or sets back the PTAC unit when no one is in the room. Additional savings come from setting certain heating and cooling limits on each unit. Establishing preset limits saves both utility costs as well as extends the life of the PTAC units. One unit for one room can cost up to $800. *Courtesy of Goodman Manufacturing, Houston, Texas.*

found in many hotel engineering departments. When a unit does become inoperable, repairs are often straightforward because key parts are readily replaceable. When eventually a unit can no longer be repaired, the engineering staff merely slides out the old unit from its sheath underneath the guest-room window and replaces it with a new unit.

Newer PTAC installations have several advantages over the older units. They run quieter, control humidity better, and are more energy efficient (see Exhibit 14-12). They also allow for remote thermostatic control, a major step toward controlling energy usage in the guest room.

NETWORK-CONTROLLED ENERGY MANAGEMENT SYSTEMS Connecting an in-room thermostat to a motion detector or infra-red sensor is an important first step to developing a network-controlled energy management system. Network-controlled systems strike a balance between centrally controlled and individually controlled systems. Guests control their own comfort even as hotel management is controlling propertywide energy costs. Guests have complete control over the HVAC/PTAC system while they are in the room. The hotel controls the temperature (and lighting, television, and power outlets) when guests leave the room. They do so with in-room sensors that operate across four levels of occupancy: sold, sold and occupied, sold but unoccupied, and unsold. Ceiling sensors electronically communicate the status of the room to the EMS. Three types are commonly in use.

Keycard Control Systems As the guest enters the room, a wall-mounted unit at the entrance controls all electrical and HVAC systems. Aside from a single light shining inside the entrance to the room, nothing else operates until the guest inserts the keycard (see Exhibit 14-13).

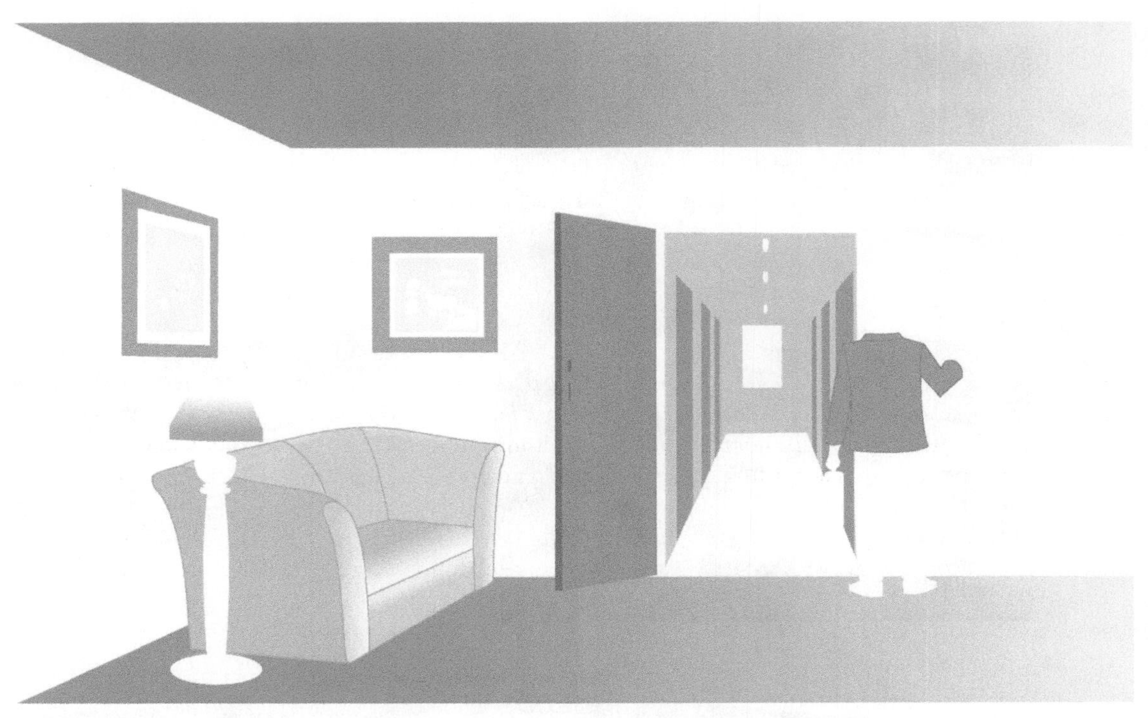

EXHIBIT 14-13 A keycard-controlled system places the responsibility for energy conservation on the guest. It is the guest who needs to insert the keycard to turn on the electrical units across the room. It is the guest who, retrieving the keycard prior to exiting the room, actively shuts down guest-room utility usage. Though there are ample problems with keycard-controlled systems, they are inexpensive to install and work better than having no energy management system at all.

Conversely, when the guest exits the room and takes the keycard, everything turns off. A one- or two-minute delay allows the guest ample time to exit. Likewise, HVAC systems do not really shut down completely. Rather, they readjust to an energy savings setting. Shutting down completely would require too much recovery time (and energy) to return the room to a comfortable temperature each time the guest returns. The system recalls the last-entered temperature and operates until that is achieved.

Keycard control systems are the simplest energy control systems. They need no in-room sensors, installation costs are minimal, and energy savings are substantial. The downside with keycard control systems, however, is lack of guest satisfaction. Everything stops operating while guests are gone. They may return to find their cell phone has not charged while they were gone, their coffee pot did not brew, or any number of other electricity-based inconveniences.

Additionally, control is the system's weakness. The wall-mounted unit takes any card with a magnetic stripe. Savvy guests get two cards at check-in or carry one from another hotel and leave the extra in the slot. Then everything runs without disruption, defeating the very purpose of the system. For environmentally sensitive guests, it works well enough.

Motion Detection Systems A motion detection system requires the installation of in-room sensors. Hallway sensors are also commonly used, because the system is often extended beyond the guest rooms. When the ceiling sensor(s) detects no motion, lights, power, and the HVAC/PTAC system are shut down. These are sensitive instruments able to detect motion from adults, children, and pets. The chief disadvantage of motion detection systems is cost. The chief advantage is that the system does not require input (e.g., a keycard) from the guest. The system is on when it detects motion; it is off when no one is in the room.

Motion detection systems are not limited to guest rooms and corridors. They work well in public space such as banquet rooms, restrooms, and even offices. Here, too, nothing is absolute. Lights and temperatures are reduced, but a minimum of both assure safety for anyone passing through.

Like any equipment, the system doesn't work unless it is properly installed. Hidden angles and nooks in the room and bath may convey a nonoccupancy mode, which might shut down the system even when guests are present. Quiet sleepers may also fail to trigger the motion detector and wake surprised because the television they left on is now off. There are anecdotal cases, probably "urban myths," of such quiet sleepers waking hot and sweaty because the entire night passed without once triggering the HVAC.

Infra-Red Heat Detection Systems Body heat detection systems are similar to motion detectors except they work from body heat generated by guests and pets rather than motion. Infra-red heat detection systems are thought to be more reliable. Although again, there are stories (myths) about guests who pull their bedcovers up so efficiently that they capture all the escaping heat. And, you guessed it, the infra-red heat detection system fails to register anyone occupying the room!

Both types of detection systems can and should be interfaced with the hotel's property management system. In this way, the EMS operates in conjunction with the PMS. The PMS provides the first important piece of information—that is, is the room occupied or not. If the room is unsold, the system will operate only at minimum levels. If the room is sold, energy utilization will be regulated according to the room's immediate status: sold and occupied or sold but unoccupied.

Housekeeping and engineering are the exception. When housekeeping enters a room, no matter what the status (sold or unsold), electrical outlets need to function, lighting needs to turn on, and HVAC systems need to power up. The television, however, will not operate when the room has been accessed by a housekeeping employee. Similarly, engineering maintenance visits, room tours by the sales department, and similar access to unsold rooms need to override the PMS's occupancy status.

"True" Detection Systems A new dual-detection energy management system was recently developed by *Smart Systems International*. Increased accuracy and reliability are achieved by combining body-heat detection and motion detection systems (see Exhibit 14-14). The result is a truer, more accurate detection system. An added feature, an adaptive learning system, controls the amount of time needed to return the temperature to the guest's set point once the room is reoccupied. Recovery time is typically set at 12 minutes when the system is installed, but hotels have the option to change the program at any time. Unlike fixed setback thermostats, drifting recovery time around outside weather conditions enhances guest comfort.

EXHIBIT 14-14 The best of both worlds, a "true" detection system regulates guest-room energy consumption by providing both types of occupancy detection; motion detection as well as body heat detection. Wireless signals are then sent to the in-room energy controller regulating and conserving usage. Dual sensory systems such as this one increase reliability and guest satisfaction, but at a higher per room installation cost than single-sensor systems. *Courtesy of Smart Systems International, Las Vegas, Nevada.*

EXHIBIT 14-15 Programmable digital thermostats designed for the lodging industry efficiently manage the guest-room temperature and operating cycles of HVAC and PTAC systems. Because these thermostats are programmable, they provide the hotel management team the ability to tailor usage to the unique operating requirements of their geographical setting.

For occupied rooms, hotel management can establish preset air-conditioning and heat levels designed to conserve utility usage while still providing a degree of guest comfort. Using the up/down buttons, the guest can fine-tune management's preset levels to match their particular comfort requirements. When the room registers unoccupied, the system defaults to a more conservative setting—a bit warmer in the summer or a bit cooler in the winter. Some hotels take an even more aggressive stance a day later; if the room remains unoccupied for the next day (and subsequent days), the system resets the temperature to levels outside of the comfort range to maximize energy savings. *Courtesy of Smart Systems International, Las Vegas, Nevada.*

Digital thermostats are integral to all types of EMSs (see Exhibit 14-15). Digital thermostats can be hard wired or wireless. They are standard equipment in many homes, so customers recognize them and easily use them to control their guest-room temperature. Because these thermostats are programmable, they provide the management team flexibility in tailoring HVAC usage to the unique operating requirements of the hotel.

For occupied rooms, managers establish preset air-conditioning and heat levels to conserve utility usage. Using the up/down buttons, the guest can fine-tune management's preset levels to match their particular comfort requirements. However, the guest's comfort range has limits—programmable digital thermostats allow management to establish parameters to prevent guests from overcooling or overheating the room.

By the way, all bets are off when the guest props open any of the doors or windows. Either through a hard-wired sensor or a remote sensor, both the front guest-room door as well as sliding glass door(s) and window(s) are linked with the HVAC system. An open door or window automatically turns off the system. No sense in heating or cooling the whole outside! (See Exhibit 14-16.)

Fire-Safety Systems

A 1946 fire in Atlanta was the nation's worst hotel conflagration until 1980, when an inferno at the MGM Grand in Las Vegas killed 85 and injured 700 persons. Unburned areas that were protected by a sprinkler system contrasted sharply with sections of the hotel which were not. Knowledge gained from the disaster spawned tighter fire regulations for hotels across the

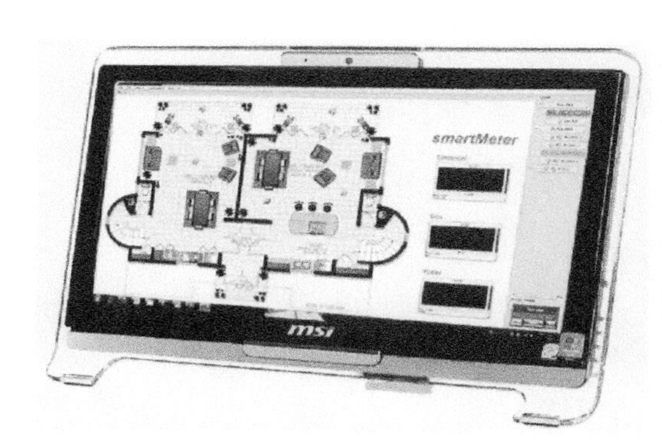

EXHIBIT 14-16 Here are some examples of products provided by one of the leading hotel energy management companies: Magnum Energy Solutions.

The motion sensor (left photo) is self-powered, using solar or ambient room light, and requires no hard-wiring. Because it requires no wiring, the hotel can place each sensor in its preferred location, providing maximum efficiency. And talk about efficiency, this product supports a "Fresnel" lens which allows the hotel to set various zones of detection. In that way, for example, traffic in the hallway or outside the guest-room windows won't accidentally trigger the parallel or perpendicular motion sensors.

The middle photo shows another wireless product for use at each window or guest-room door. These window contact sensors work in conjunction with the HVAC and/or other electrical units in the room. The sensor(s) sends a signal every 15 minutes updating the occupancy status of the room. When used on windows and sliding glass doors, the device automatically shuts down HVAC systems the moment a window or glass door is opened.

The hotel's energy management system all comes together with an energy management control module (right photo). This system allows the hotel numerous options. For example; management can visualize any single sensor anywhere on property; each sensor can be individually controlled and limits can be re programmed as warranted; timers can be set or any other event can be planned and programmed on an individual, zone, or property wide basis. The system also supports load-shedding, by reducing or shutting down in-room electrical usage during periods of peak demand and therefore peak utility costs. The control module alerts management to HVAC theft (an issue prevalent in the industry). And best of all, it is even controllable from the managers' cell phones or smartphones. *Courtesy of Magnum Energy Solutions, Hudson, Ohio.*

nation. Several technologies were developed both to help control the spread of a blaze and to communicate the double danger of smoke and fire.

The Hotel and Motel Fire Safety Act was a delayed spinoff of the Las Vegas tragedy. Federal employees on official government business must stay in fire-safe accommodations. For the purpose of the act, every guest room must have no less than an AC-powered (hard-wired) smoke alarm. Installation must be in accordance with the National Fire Protection Association (NFPA) Standard 72. Battery-powered smoke alarms do not meet that criterion. Batteries wear out and guests "borrow" them. An AC-powered alarm with a battery backup is even more desirable, but is not mandated. Under the act, buildings of four stories or more must also have fire-suppression sprinkler systems. In-room sprinkler systems represent a significant safety upgrade. The fire code in Las Vegas was changed so all hotels in that city now have in-room sprinkler systems.

Stand-alone alarms, similar to those used by homeowners, are not adequate for hotels with public space and hundreds of guest rooms. Large areas of hotel buildings are unattended for long periods. Lodging facilities need a networked fire-alarm system. An integrated fire-safety system saves lives, reduces fire damages, lowers insurance premiums, and minimizes costly litigation. Components of such a system include a centralized computer or fire-command console that uses electronic and audiocontrol devices for fire alert, response, and protection.

A good fire system connects smoke detectors (see Exhibit 14-17) to a central management system by means of a wireless network. Sensing smoke, the detector notifies the closest receiving unit, which transmits the information to the central management system. Taken up a level, the fire system is also interfaced with a paging system. Security is paged and directed to the area or

EXHIBIT 14-17 Increased safety results when smoke detectors are interfaced to a central fire-control network. The federal Hotel and Motel Fire Safety Act requires these devices to be hard wired, not merely battery operated. *Courtesy of INNCOM International Inc., Niantic, Connecticut.*

specific room to check the status. (False alarms do occur; see the case incident at the end of this chapter.) Well-managed hotels respond with trained fire teams composed of individuals from several departments. The manager on duty also responds and decides whether or not to call the public fire department.

If there is a fire, management needs to determine if the property should be evacuated. When an evacuation is necessary (always erring on the side of safety—when in doubt, evacuate), the well-trained front-desk staff initiates the property's emergency evacuation procedures. The interfaced fire-safety system automatically communicates a calm, prerecorded message to every guest-room telephone.

The message asks the guest to remain calm, but leave the room immediately (grab your room key before leaving). The first stop for the guest is the fire evacuation route posted behind the guest-room door. A quick review of this map establishes the guest's evacuation route and proximity to the nearest exit. The map and the telephone recording both remind the guest not to use elevators. The recording also instructs the guest to feel the hotel room door before opening it. A hot door should never be opened—telephone the front desk immediately, seal the bottom of the door with a wet towel, close the window(s) or leave open a crack if fresh air is needed, turn off all ventilation (HVAC and/or ceiling fans), and fill the bathtub and/or sink with water (water pressure drops when the fire department arrives; a full bathtub becomes a valuable commodity should the guest need to actually battle the fire). Even if the hotel room door is cool, the guest should get low to the floor, brace his or her shoulder against the door and open it slowly—being ready to close it quickly if there are flames on the other side. During the exit, the guest should crawl low in the smoke to the nearest exit; the freshest air is near the floor.

FIRE-SUPPRESSION SPRINKLER SYSTEMS Hotels are equipped with fire-suppression sprinkler systems across the property. There are one or more such sprinklers in every guest room (depending on square footage and room configuration). There are sprinklers in all guest hallways, lobbies, executive offices, convention space, and public spaces. In the event of a fire, sprinklers are the first line of defense, working in conjunction with fire doors, fire walls, and ventilation systems to contain the fire and minimize its impact.

There are numerous types of fire-suppression sprinkler systems, including wet pipe, dry pipe, deluge, preaction, foam, and spray. However, most hotels use either wet or dry pipe systems (the other systems are designed for special applications like factories, hazardous storage facilities, warehouses, museums, etc).

Wet Pipe Systems Wet pipe sprinklers are the most common systems installed in hotels. They are reliable, simple, and the only operating components are the automatic sprinkler heads and the alarm check valve. A continuous water supply provides water under pressure to the pipes. When an automatic sprinkler head is exposed for a sufficient time to a temperature at or above the temperature rating, the heat sensitive element (a glass bulb or fusible link) releases, allowing water to flow from that sprinkler.

Dry pipe systems are installed in hotels located in cold climates. Otherwise, in the winter, the cold external temperature could freeze the static water in a wet pipe system. There are numerous stories of this type of damage occurring. Flawed or cracked sprinkler systems have the potential to flood hotels in a matter of minutes, costing hundreds of thousands of dollars in water damage, drywall repair, and lost business. It even happens when the would-be bride—seeking something high above the floor on which to hang her wedding dress—finds the fire-suppression sprinkler head. She hangs her dress, inadvertently breaks the sprinkler head, and finds her room (not to mention her gown) soaked in minutes!

Dry Pipe Systems Dry pipe systems are used in outdoor applications (in parking garages, above the porte cochere, or underneath canopies and awnings) as well as in ceiling installations above the insulation (above the heat source). There is no water present in the "dry" piping until the fire system calls for it. The piping is filled with air, designed to hold back the pressurized water. When one or more of the automatic sprinklers is exposed, for a sufficient time, to a temperature at or above the temperature rating, it opens, allowing the air in the piping to vent from that sprinkler and the water to flow in behind it (see Exhibit 14-18).

Industry Practices in Case of Fire

Before a Fire:

Management should have all front-office employees:

- Become familiar with the hotel's fire and life safety systems.
- Know where to locate and how to use:
  - Manual pull alarms.
  - Fire extinguishers.
  - Smoke detectors.
  - Fire alarm monitoring service.
  - Exit doors & stairwells.
  - Voice alarm system and/or intercom.
  - Sprinklers.
  - Fire doors.
  - The main water shut-off valve.

At the Time of a Fire:

The front-office employee should:

- Treat every alarm as though it is a real emergency (even if the initial source is unknown).
- Call the Fire Department immediately if the alarm sounds, or a fire is suspected. Never wait to investigate the situation before notifying the Fire Department. Any delay will allow a fire to grow and further endanger the building occupants and property.
- Send two employees with walkie-talkies and flashlights to the alarm's location to investigate whether it is a real fire or not.
- Call 911 and relay information to the Fire Department, if it is determined that there is no fire, but rather a malfunction of fire safety equipment or simply a false alarm.
- Not silence the alarm until given permission to do so by Fire Department personnel or by the emergency operator.
- Not reset the alarm until the Fire Department arrives and has investigated the source of the alarm.
- Remember to provide 911 calls the following information; hotel name, problem being reported, location of the problem, hotel address, nearest cross streets.

EXHIBIT 14-18 Some good industry practices to follow before and during a fire emergency.

- **Retrieve the most up-to-date room status reports and be ready to provide such reports to the Fire Department.**
- **Contact each guest room (which may be an automatic feature of the interfaced fire-safety system) and keep track of any guest room which does not answer the telephone. Provide this list and master key(s) to the Fire Department.**

In Case of Evacuation:

The front-office employee should:

- **Be prepared to turn over operations to the hotel's fire director, an individual with sufficient knowledge of the hotel who has been preassigned and trained for this emergency.**
- **Be prepared to turn over floor responsibilities to floor wardens, preassigned employees who will locate themselves by exit doors on each floor to assist guests as they are exiting their hallways.**
- **Retrieve the most up-to-date room status reports and be ready to provide such reports to the Fire Department.**
- **Contact each guest room (which may be an automatic feature of the interfaced fire-safety system) and keep track of any guest room which does not answer the telephone. Provide this list to the Fire Department.**
- **Provide master key(s) and any assistance as requested by the Fire Department.**

EXHIBIT 14-18 Continued

Minibars

Minibars have changed over time as technology improves and the cost and degree of automation makes new investment worthwhile. Some are still not automated; others are completely automated utilizing microprocessor-based technology. In between are semiautomated models.

The convenience of minibars plays an important role in guest satisfaction, especially in full-service hotels. They must be important because guests willingly pay a handsome premium for the soft drinks, candy, beer, wine, liquor, snacks, and personal items that minibars dispense. The minibar is a good profit center for the hotel. Mindful of guest expectations, some hotels provide (without charge) an empty refrigerator that occupants stock as they prefer. Complimentary bottled water is another step toward exceeding guest expectations.

TRADITIONAL (NONAUTOMATED) MINIBARS Early versions of the minibar (see Exhibit 14-19)—and they are still popular—require a daily, manual count by a minibar employee. Minibar operations fall under the guest services department in most hotels, rarely under housekeeping. The minibar employee—armed with a master key and a rooming list—must enter every occupied room, open the refrigerator, and inventory the contents. Each room entry imposes on the guest and the guest's

EXHIBIT 14-19 Earlier versions of minibars—many are still in use—require daily, manual inventories to determine what charges need be posted to the guest's folio. Newer versions are interfaced directly to the property management system, so posting occurs automatically (see Exhibit 14-20). Even restocking is improved with automated minibars, because the minibar employee can prepare a dedicated bin for each room knowing in advance exactly which products were consumed and removed from inventory. *Courtesy of Minibar North America, Inc., Bethesda, Maryland.*

privacy. The minibar employee prepares a voucher for all the items consumed, restocks the minibar back to par, and later delivers the voucher to the front desk so charges can be made to the folio .

To minimize labor costs some hotels tried eliminating the employee, relying on a honor system instead. It was penny wise and pound foolish. Labor was still needed to restock consumed items. Honor remains part of the procedure, nevertheless. The minibar inspector works during the day. Guests return to their rooms and use the minibars at night; they check out the following morning. Guest-service agents/cashiers routinely ask departing guests whether they used any minibar items in the past 24 hours. Some pay up; some do not.

Putting a "seal" on the minibar reduces labor costs. Guests must break the seal in order to retrieve an item. The staff member need only make a quick survey from the door. If the seal is intact, the associate moves on quickly to the next room. If broken, the count and restocking proceed as usual.

SEMIAUTOMATED SYSTEMS Vendors came up with semiautomated minibars and completely automated ones in response to the several disadvantages of the initial equipment. One innovation built upon the "seal" idea used on the nonautomated equipment. Whenever the minibar door is opened, a door alert is posted to the property management system. Staff members get a report that shows which rooms have used the minibar (or, at least have opened the door to the minibar) and which rooms have not. If there is no activity, the room is skipped. This reduces both labor costs and imposition on guests.

Even this small amount of automation pays for itself quickly. This is because only one in four guests, on average, uses the in-room minibar. Knowing which rooms accessed their minibar and which did not saves dramatically on labor.

MICROPROCESSOR-BASED AUTOMATED SYSTEMS Automated minibars monitor and process sales transactions electronically. Each tray in the minibar is programmed to inventory a certain item (see Exhibit 14-20). A weight-sensitive timer or electronic eye tracks whenever a product is removed from its designated space. The timer gives the shopper some 10–60 seconds (the amount of time is programmable to the hotel's wishes) for "inspection time." If the product is returned to its place in sufficient time, the system assumes the guest was curious but ultimately not interested in the purchase. For items which are not returned, a charge is automatically posted to the guest's folio.

Posting is accomplished through an interface between the automated minibar and the property management system. The PMS sends an unlocking signal to the in-room minibar as soon as the guest checks in. Some hotels actually ask guests if they would like to utilize their minibar during their stay. Such a query, though offered in the spirit of guest service, actually reduces spur-of-the moment purchases from hunger cravings, thirst, or forgotten toiletry items, thereby doing the guest a disservice. It is best to just unlock the minibar as a standard operating procedure with every new guest.

EXHIBIT 14-20 Each item in an automated minibar sits on a pressure-sensitive tray (some systems use an electronic eye). Guests have time to examine the product and return it if unused. Once the time is exhausted, a charge for the product is automatically documented to the guest's PMS folio. A record is maintained and quickly printed out should the guest protest the charges. *Courtesy of Bartech System International, Millersville, Maryland.*

The automated minibar identifies each item removed for purchase, the time of purchase, the price of the removed item, and its tray location. A quick printout of minibar activity is possible if the guest disputes any charge at check-out. Here is usage for the guest in room 701:

Total Purchases
Minibar

Minibar Bill for Room: 701 **Time:** 12:54 **Date:** Sunday 15 April

Date	Time	Contents	Price (US $)	Tray Location
13 April	17:32:45	Imported Beer	5.50	Location 11
13 April	18:45:41	Tonic Water	2.50	Location 08
13 April	18:45:50	Beefeater Gin	6.50	Location 07
13 April	19:01:12	Mixed Nuts	7.00	Location 13
14 April	09:02:12	Spa Still Water	2.50	Location 15
14 April	09:03:01	Orange Juice	4.00	Location 17
14 April	16:32:34	Domestic Beer	4.50	Location 10
		Total Purchases	**32.50 (inc tax)**	

Guest checked in 11:25 13 April
**************THIS BILL FOR VERIFICATION PURPOSES ONLY*************

Relocking the minibar is an automatic function of the PMS's check-out procedure. Locking the minibar is performed as part of the same check-out procedure as putting the room on change. One side benefit is that housekeeping employees are no longer able to access the minibar prior to inspection and restocking by the minibar employee. This is another valuable benefit of automated minibars—no more theft loss from housekeeping employees!

Some systems even track expiration dates on products, alerting the department to items which have not sold in 30, 60, or 90 days. The interfaced microprocessor-based minibar system even helps with labor. A daily report of total minibar consumption is one of many reports generated by the PMS during the night audit. Minibar employees use the report to requisition and draw refills for the following day.

REFILL REQUIREMENTS REPORT
Automated Minibar System
Date: 15 April

Refill requirements report for the following rooms/groups/zones:
ALL

Item	Unit
Mixed Nuts	7
Spa Still Water	82
Beefeater Gin	12
Canada Dry Tonic Water	14
Orange Juice	48
Skyy Vodka	25
Coca-Cola (Can)	46
Evian Water (50ml)	76
Seven-Up (Can)	14
Domestic Beer	45
Imported Beer	23
Dorito's Cool Ranch Chips	17
Baked Lay's BBQ	11
Pretzels	3
Toothpaste	3

A refill requirements report, also produced during the previous night's audit, identifies which rooms get which inventory replacements from the total draw listed above. By way of our continuing the example, this refill requirements report shows the first few rooms from the seventh floor (including the guest from room 701, as discussed above). Note the usage of bottled water, still the most popular item sold in minibars. Bottled water sells four times more product than the next closest minibar purchase!

REFILL REQUIREMENTS REPORT
Automated Minibar System
Date: 15 April

Refill requirements report for the following rooms/groups/zones.
ALL

Seventh Floor/Room By Room

	Quantity	Item	Tray #
Room: 701	1	Mixed Nuts	13
	1	Spa Still Water	15
	1	Beefeater Gin	7
	1	Canada Dry Tonic Water	8
	1	Orange Juice	17
	1	Domestic Beer	10
Room: 702	1	Spa Still Water	15
	4	Coca-Cola (Can)	1
	1	Dorito's Cool Ranch Chips	3
Room: 703	1	Spa Still Water	15
	1	Seven-Up (Can)	2
	1	Pretzels	5
Room: 704 +++	1	Mixed Nuts	13
	1	Evian Water (50ml)	16
	1	Toothpaste	27

Minibars began life as refrigerators. Guests still like to use them as such. They are perfect for storing half a sandwich, a baby's formula, or some medicine. Sometimes space is so tight that an item must be removed to make room for the guest's personal needs. Newer models need to accommodate this secondary use because getting charged for an unused item is irritating, and trying to obtain an offsetting allowance is frustrating and time-consuming.

In-room Safes

State laws require every hotel to maintain a safe or lose the protection of the limited-liability innkeeper statutes that each state has enacted. Large steel safes and safe-deposit boxes behind the desk were the standard until small, personal, in-room safes were introduced in 1979 (see Exhibit 14-2). Modern and secure, in-room safes need to be large enough to hold the personal electronics and jewelry, including the latest 17-inch monitors, carried by today's corporate (and leisure) travelers.

Initially, most hotels charged a fee for the use of their in-room safes. Purchase contracts were often based on a revenue split between the hotel and the safe provider. Hotels kept all the income after the purchase price (plus interest) was eventually recovered. Most dropped the charge thereafter, offering the in-room safe as another amenity. It was a messy arrangement otherwise; early safes did not interface with the PMS, so there was really no way to track their use or lack of use. So an "in-room safe fee" was charged to every folio during the night audit. Guests complained loudly about the charge, as they do still about "resort fees."

Use of in-room safes reduces theft. Electronic locking systems battle external theft; in-room safes reduce internal losses. Theft by employees (internal theft) is usually an impulsive act caused by temptation. Valuables in the safe remove the temptation. They also undercut the guest's effort at defrauding the hotel. Reduced insurance premiums are another savings. The safe is very heavy, almost impossible to carry, but bolted down nevertheless.

EXHIBIT 14-21 Located in closets, built into dresser doors, designed as end-tables, or free-standing, electronic safes are an important in-room guest amenity. This closet-located safe is opened by the guest's credit card or any other magnetic stripe card, including guest-room keycard or smart card. *Courtesy of VingCard Elsafe, an ASSA ABLOY company, Connecticut, U.S.A., and Stockholm, Sweden.*

Just as guest-room locks started with mechanical keys, so did in-room safes. Not nearly as heavy as the original door keys, guests signed for and obtained keys to fit the safe lock in their particular room. Lost keys required a locksmith to open the safe and rekey the lock at the guest's expense. Today's electronic safes carry an override feature. Management can override the guest's code or credit-card code if an emergency arises (like a forgotten PIN number). It takes two inputs: an instrument that looks like a cell phone and maintains an override audit trail, and an override security code.

Electronic in-room safes progressed through several steps since their introduction.

CREDIT-CARD ACCESS Many guests like the option of swiping their credit card for access to the safe. Credit cards are more user-friendly than the personal identification number (PIN) option (discussed below) and don't require the guest to memorize a particular code. Additionally, some guests are skeptical about using a PIN number because of exaggerated traveler stories suggesting there are hidden cameras, waxed keypads, or some other way for housekeeping to spy the guests' PIN. The credit card provides the most personal access. However, it means the guest must carry the credit card when leaving the room, even when going to the pool or spa (see Exhibit 14-21).

PIN-BASED ENTRY Exhibit 14-22 illustrates the PIN-based in-room safe. Digital safes are more common than lock and key or credit-card access safes. Some feel they are the best option, because

EXHIBIT 14-22 Digital code-based safes operate on a PIN number that each guest creates. This is the most popular type of in-room electronic safe. A well-designed safe, like this one, provides an easy-to-use override feature. In an emergency, hotel staff readily overrides the guest's PIN or credit-card code with an external processor (looks like a cell phone) and override security code. An audit trail is provided for each override performed, in case the guest should complain of unauthorized access. *Courtesy of VingCard Elsafe, an ASSA ABLOY company, Connecticut, U.S.A. and Stockholm, Sweden.*

EXHIBIT 14-23 Biometric safes use the same technology as biometric door keys. Neither is yet in widespread use. The reasons are two-fold. Biometrics is an expensive technology, one in which hotels are hesitant to invest. And guests appear to be reluctant to use biometrics because they are generally uncomfortable surrendering such highly personal data. Someday, biometric safes may be the ideal product for hotel in-room security; there is no key, PIN, or magnetic stripe card to lose or forget! *Courtesy of Minibar North America, Inc., Bethesda, Maryland.*

there is no secondary element (the metal key or credit card) to be lost. Each new guest enters a PIN. Although PIN encoding is a common exercise today, one would be surprised how many times hotel management (security or bell department) is called to open an in-room safe because the guest has forgotten the PIN. Safes lock out the guest after some few attempts at entry. So, a guest who is trying to guess his wife's PIN or has simply forgotten which of a series of various PINs he might have used today can easily be locked out of subsequent attempts.

Electronic safes must be easy to use. Directions need to be clearly present on the exterior of the safe. Large keypads are a must. Additionally, the LED display should be clearly legible and designed to display the guest's PIN code for a moment prior to the safe's lock being activated. This ensures the guest can verify the code and has not inadvertently entered a wrong digit. A lack of such simple features means hotel staff will be spending more time assisting guests with entry to their safes than appropriate.

BIOMETRIC SAFES Biometric safes use the same technology as biometric locking systems. Guests register either their fingerprint or their iris scan before using the safe. Biometrics are the most convenient of the systems because there is no key to lose or PIN code to forget. However, not all models accommodate multiple users at this time, so double occupancy poses an issue. The iris or fingerprint of one guest will not trigger the mechanism that was created with the biometrics of the room's companion. Exhibit 14-23 displays a biometric safe.

COMMUNICATION SYSTEMS

The in-room guest telephone may be one of the great hotel technology failures of the past decade. The dramatic increase in use of personal cell and smartphones, coupled with the ever-decreasing in-room telephone revenues, has led to a dim future for the guest-room telephone. Unlike most technologies, where the cost of purchasing equipment decreases with time, the cost of equipping a hotel room with telephone equipment has seen virtually no decrease over the past twenty years. That is why many industry experts predict the ultimate demise of the in-room guest telephone. This devise will be replaced by in-room one-touch programmable pads as well as by the guest's own mobile phone.

A Brief History of Telephone Service

Between the early 1980s and the late 1990s, the telephone department was a big contributor to the hotel industry's bottom line. Departmental income exceeded 2.5% of total hotel revenues. Telephones were profitable because they were deregulated and automated. But hotel telephone revenues fell victim to technological innovation. Departmental profits now contribute less than 1% of total industry revenue. In many hotels, the telephone department is a cost center more than it is a revenue center. Part of the decline was no fault of the hotel industry, but caused by the introduction of the now ubiquitous cellular phone. Part of the decline was due to the hotel industry's greed—that is, due to the excessive charges hotels levied on in-room telephone use.

To encourage the growth of hotel telephones, the Federal Communications Commission (FCC)—which regulates *inter*state calls, not *intra*state calls (calls within a state)—issued a 1944 ruling. Telephone companies were directed to pay a 15% commission for all calls originating in hotels. Before the installation of direct-dial telephones, hotel operators connected guest callers to the telephone company's operators. After the call was completed, the company's operator would call the hotel operator and quote "time and charges." To those charges, the hotel added its 15% commission and posted the total to the guests' folio.

The introduction of in-room direct-dial guest telephones bypassed the telephone company's operator. Now, guest telephone charges could be routed directly through the call accounting system (CAS). The CAS tracked the calls and the charges and reported them to the front-office cashier by means of a printer located at the front desk. Initially, such charges were posted manually to the guest folios. As progress continued, the CAS was interfaced with the PMS, and telephone calls were automatically charged to guest folios.

For almost 40 years, the hotel industry had to be satisfied with this paltry 15% telephone commission structure. But in 1981, the FCC changed the rules again. This time, the simple 15% commission structure was dropped, allowing each hotel to set its own surcharge. And charge they did! Revenue zoomed. Many hotels began charging 100–500% of their cost to the guest. In other words, a call which cost the hotel, say $5, would show up on the guest's folio at a rate of $10 to $30. Guests became irate.

At first, guests began utilizing payphone booths to avoid the excess surcharges. But even here, management was ahead of its guests because hotels were now legally allowed to own the lobby payphone (and charge whatever long-distance fee they wanted to). Some chains—understanding that telephone profits were not worth risking the reputation of the brand—began offering telephone services with no additional surcharges. That proved popular with corporate travelers, albeit short-lived. The cell phone was not far behind; the first cellular telephone usage by a hotel guest was in 1990 (see Exhibit 14-2). As the 20th century ended, in-room guest telephone revenue was becoming nonexistent.

Internet Access

Initial introduction of Internet access in hotel rooms followed much the same path as telephone systems. Some hotels charged excessive rates for Internet service in the guest room, hoping to quickly recover investment and make a profit. Other hotels saw guest-room Internet access as an amenity—and like all amenities, there is a cost to the property for providing such a service—a cost which is often not recovered through specific charges, but rather through increased brand loyalty.

Internet access is clearly an important element in the guest's overall satisfaction. Recent travel statistics suggest that more than 75% of corporate travelers carry their laptop when traveling. And 62% of corporate travelers spend at least 25 minutes per day online in the hotel room. These statistics are likely to change as the 45-year-old and under crowd quickly embraces smartphone technology as their preferred source of online access while away from home.

The interesting dichotomy of recent travel is that cheaper hotels (e.g., limited service) usually provide free Internet access, while higher-end (full-service) properties are more likely to charge for such service (see Exhibit 14-24). But the trend toward free Internet is growing, and has increasingly become one of the complimentary services offered to members of hotel loyalty programs. For those hotels which still do charge for Internet access, the charges for a 24-hour daily rate range from as little as $6.99 to as much as $49.99. One explanation for the rate spread is the type of access.

DIAL-UP ACCESS The first generation of Internet access was dial-up. An in-room connection to the Internet provider was made by means of a computer modem and data port built into the telephone. Speed was poor; transmission was limited to 56 kilobits per second (Kbps). Even today, a few users, especially business travelers, prefer dial-up access because of the heightened security, and willingly trade away speed to get security.

Parent Company	Chains Where Internet Access Is Free-of-Charge	Chains Where Internet Access Is Charged a Fee
Hilton Hotels & Resorts	Hampton Hotels & Suites Hilton Garden Inn Hotels Homewood Suites by Hilton	Conrad Hotels & Resorts Hilton Hotels & Resorts Waldorf Astoria Hotels & Resorts
Hyatt Hotels & Resorts	Andaz Hotels by Hyatt Hyatt Place Hyatt Summerfield Suites	Grand Hyatt Hotels Hyatt Regency Park Hyatt Hotels
Marriott International	Courtyard by Marriott Fairfield Inn & Suites by Marriott Residence Inn by Marriott Springhill Suites by Marriott	JW Marriott Hotels & Resorts Marriott Hotels & Resorts The Ritz-Carlton Hotel Company
Starwood Hotels & Resorts	None	Aloft Element by Westin Four Points by Sheraton Le Meridien Sheraton Hotels & Resorts St. Regis Hotels & Resorts The Luxury Collection W Hotels Westin Hotels & Resorts

EXHIBIT 14-24 A frustrating dichotomy in the lodging industry; limited service chains are more likely to offer free Internet access than are full-service brands. Here is a brief sampling, in alphabetical order.

HIGH-SPEED HARD-WIRED ACCESS Depending on the type of cable and bandwidth used by the hotel, the speed of the hard-wired Internet connection can vary between 1 Mbps and 1,000 Mbps (a gig per second). The cost outlay for the hotel varies as well, but hard-wired high-speed Internet is costly. Like all hard-wired systems (locking systems, energy management, minibars, etc.) the cost is associated with wiring every room to the main server. For existing construction, wireless is almost always the right choice. For new construction, there are current and future benefits associated with hard-wiring every room.

With wired access, guest rooms are furnished with an Ethernet cable. Guests attach their laptops by means of a network interface card. To minimize the hotel's liability, guests are asked to sign a liability waiver before using the equipment. Most hotels require the waiver, whether the wired access is free or not.

HIGH-SPEED WIRELESS ACCESS Lodging managers prefer wireless access to wired access for two reasons. Guests transact much of their business in public settings, such as lobbies and meeting rooms, where wired access is difficult to install and monitor. And, as discussed above, a wireless Internet installation is much less costly than a hard-wired one. That brings the issue back to security.

Wireless means just that: The data is transmitted through the air. The information can be captured by anyone and used for his or her personal gain. The user-guest as well as the innkeeper knows that, but security fears have not deterred the very rapid growth of wireless access.

The Institute of Electrical and Electronics Engineers (IEEE) has recommended standards for wireless and wired network communications. They are known as 802.11b, 802.11g, and 802.11a. Code 802.11b was one of the first standards for transmitting data up to 11 Mbps. The other two, newer standards, transmit at higher speeds.

TIERED BANDWIDTH The lodging industry has recently begun experimenting with tiered bandwidth options for guests. Like the menu of options high-end properties offer with regard to soaps, pillows, and room categories, Internet access appears to be taking a similar path. For those guests who just want to check their emails, Internet access at lower speeds is available free of charge. But those guests who need real surfing power to stream video, play interactive games, and access rich content would be charged for their access to premium bandwidth.

In early studies, tiered bandwidth seems a most satisfying arrangement for guests. They get what they pay for, or what they choose not to pay for. By the way, it is not uncommon for one guest room to consume more bandwidth today than an entire hotel did just three years ago!

CLOUD COMPUTING Another reason one guest room today can consume more bandwidth than an entire hotel of a few years ago is devices. Yes, that's plural—"devices," because today's guests travel with far more than one single laptop. Increasingly, guests arrive with multiple devices, each with its own particular need to access the network. The old logic suggested that Wi-Fi was the best technology for using a laptop and cellular service was best for voice. Today, both technologies are coupled together and embedded in such devices as laptops, smartphones, tablet PC's, gaming devices, Netbooks, and iPads.

The answer to this multitasking is just beginning to take shape: the cloud. Cloud computing is simple enough; it means that all your data is stored in a hazy cloud which hovers above all your devices. Really, it means that large computer companies (Apple, for one) provide—for fee or free—central servers on which all your data is stored. To the user, this means no device falls behind any other device. Download a movie on your PC but watch it on your Netbook, because each accesses the cloud and remains up to date with all your other devices. This provides a huge convenience for users, a large potential revenue source for computer providers, and an increasingly expensive trend for hoteliers, who will find their bandwidth demand growing faster than ever!

Future of Hotel Telephones

As telephone revenues are falling ever lower, the search is on for new revenue sources. Guests might be enticed back to paying for hotel services through one-price, telecommunications bundling. In their personal homes, guests are already accustomed to bundled rates. Wyndham was among the first to launch the format, testing it within their frequent-guest program. Currently, all *Wyndham By Request®* members get free Internet access and free local and long-distance calls. The Westin at Chicago's O'Hare Airport charges $9.99 for 24-hour Internet access, but also offers a "Telecom Bundle." Its $16 per-day package includes high-speed Internet access, long-distance calls within the United States, local calls, and operator assistance. Other properties are joining in the bundling, because they too are taking advantage of the rapid technical advances of VOIP.

VOICE-OVER-INTERNET PROTOCOL (VOIP) This upgrade is so new that the language has not yet solidified. One hears it called *VoIP, VOIP, IP telephony, Internet telephony, Broadband telephony, Broadband Phone,* and *Voice over Broadband.* Whatever the name, it routes voice conversation over the Internet or through any other IP-based network instead of the analog (twisted-pair-cable) phone lines. Improvements in VoIP have been rapid. Sound quality, which initially was poorer than analog transmission, has quickly reached analog levels.

Hotels need a broadband, high-speed Internet connection if they want to use VoIP in conjunction with their call accounting system (CAS). Hotels within a chain are usually connected by an IP network that supports the chain's data service. Telecommunication costs are drastically reduced if the individual hotel uses that same network for guests' long-distance calls. The property most likely pays a flat, monthly fee to the ISP (Internet service provider) for unlimited use of the network. Therefore, long-distance calls originating in the guest room add virtually no cost to the hotel. In return, the hotel can offer long-distance calls as a free amenity service, or can charge a reasonable price so guests are encouraged to consider this option.

Switching from traditional telephone lines to VoIP is not complicated. The traditional, handset telephone can be reconfigured to the new technology by an analog adaptor, which converts analog signals to digital signals. The cost is minimal, about $50 per handset. This is much less costly than the $500 needed to replace handsets with VoIP digital phones. As the text mentioned earlier, technology costs continue to fall, so both figures will likely be lower in short order.

EXHIBIT 14-25 Telephone equipment that accepts VoIP (Voice-over-Internet Protocol) looks no different from the traditional instrument. Lower fixed costs to the hotel (for equipment) and virtually no variable costs for long-distance calls are driving its spreading use. And ideally, will return the hotel's telephone department to a revenue center as opposed to a cost center. *Courtesy of Cisco Systems, Inc., San Jose, California.*

VoIP telephones don't look much different than their analog cousins (see Exhibit 14-25), but they are a world apart. They are the future of hotel telephony. VoIP phones are a service and application delivery system all by themselves. The installation provides digital voice mail; alarm clocks; room service, spa, and golf interfaces; high-speed Internet access; an entry to interactive gaming; guest-room control of lighting, television, and temperature control; a digital hotel guide; and conference-call capability. A list which continues to grow as VoIP becomes more widely accepted.

Emergency 911 Calls VoIP telephone systems are found to be lacking accurate data with regard to emergency 911 calls. This is because the 911 caller-identification system was developed for traditional landline telephones. Using a computer processor–based VoIP system leaves the 911 operator without knowing from where the call was placed. In some cases, the operator may see the address of the computer (say the hotel's address) but not understand that the call is originating from a hotel and, even if that information is available, not know from which of hundreds of the hotel rooms the call is being made.

The problem is exacerbated with cellular phones and smartphones. These phones draw their transmissions from cell towers. As the cell phone moves, the tower routing the call also shifts. Additionally, during periods of busy cell phone usage, less-busy towers handle cell calls from further distances. As such, in 911 emergencies, the 911 call center receiving the call is not always the closest call center to the guest's physical location.

As technology advances, certain basic infrastructures, like the emergency 911 system, fall behind. Maybe that is another reason to keep the traditional guest-room telephone in place.

Wake-Up Systems

Most telephone installations include both voice mail and wake-up service, of which there are four types.

MANUAL WAKE-UP SYSTEMS There is an extended history of manual wake-up systems because they have been in use long before any technological advances. Guests used to call the telephone operator requesting a wake-up call. The operator then noted the room and time on a specially designed time sheet and set a special alarm clock (the brand name was Remind-O-Timer) that accommodated five-minute increments. At the appropriate time, the alarm would ring and the operator would call the room. Sometimes the call was early and sometimes it was late, depending upon the operator's call volume that morning.

SEMIAUTOMATIC SYSTEMS These systems are one step up in automation. The guest still calls the operator, who manually enters the room number and time into the system. It is the system, not the operator, that makes the wake-up call. A prerecorded message might say, "This is your wake-up call. Today's weather is a brisk 37 degrees. Enjoy your day." Other options provide the date and day of the week and a marketing message (breakfast served until 10 AM). The message is repeated every five minutes until the guest answers. After four or five tries, the system either shuts down or—the preferred approach—alerts security to physically visit the room and make certain the guest is not in distress.

FULLY AUTOMATED AND INTERACTIVE TV-BASED WAKE-UP SYSTEMS With fully automated wake-up systems, guests bypass the hotel's telephone operator and set their request by simply pushing a "wake-up" button on the guest-room telephone. A digital voice walks the user through the several simple steps. For example, for 7:00 AM, the instruction asks the guest to punch in 0700. Then it asks for a confirmation. The telephone rings at the desired time and an automated message similar to that of the semiautomated system plays its tune and/or delivers its message.

Interactive TV-based wake-up systems utilize an interface between the call accounting system and the guest-room television. Guests set the wake-up call with the TV remote. Technologically advanced or not, every hotel furnishes bedside alarm clocks. Paranoid guests, or those who have critical early-morning meetings, are known to set all three: their smartphone, the hotel's CAS wake-up system, and their bedside alarm clock!

Voice Mail

Voice mail enables a caller to leave a message for an absent guest. Historically, a telephone operator took such a message, wrote it down, and left it in the guest's mailbox (by room number) at the front desk; hence the term—*voice mailbox*. Technology has removed the operator from the message procedure, as it has with wake-up calls. By so doing, the system improved the accuracy of the message, reduced labor costs for the hotel, and made delivery more timely. A blinking light on the telephone alerts the guest to the waiting message. No longer is there any need to trek to the front desk.

The advantages of automated voice mail are numerous. Guests can leave messages as well as retrieve them. Messages can be forwarded to another room, in case one message were intended for several travelers. Messages can be personal and in the guest's native language. Access can be restricted, requiring callers to use a special PIN number that the guest has created.

Pressing the call-message button activates the system when the guest returns to the room. The guest is told there are a given number of messages, some old, some new. Messages can be saved or deleted.

The system is activated when each new guest checks in. Some systems hold messages up to 24 hours after check-out, unless the room is assigned to a new guest in the interim. In all cases, messages are deleted and a fresh, empty voice mailbox is initiated with each new check-in.

Where's My Phone?

The guest-room telephone may or may not be around in the future. On one side of the coin, experts predict the demise of the guest-room telephone because it is a costly piece of equipment which provides minimal revenue, it is readily replaced with an interactive television center and/or guest-room touch-screen tablet, and any emergency situations can be communicated through an in-room enunciator.

On the other side of the argument are experts who predict the guest-room telephone is here to stay. They argue that there are legal reasons for guest-room telephones (see 911 discussion above), they are critical in an emergency, and they remain convenient as a means of communication between guest and desk. Additionally, foreign guests are returning to the guest-room telephone for their international calls, which, when the hotel offers VoIP pricing, are cheaper than international calls on their cell phone/smartphone.

OTHER TECHNOLOGIES

In-room Entertainment Systems

Color television came to the hospitality industry in 1975 (see Exhibit 14-2). Within five years, almost every property offered it as an amenity. Today's generation of travelers expect rooms to have the same multimedia and entertainment choices that they use at home. In-room entertainment is a fast-growing revenue center. Visitors are willing to pay for movies, video-on-demand, in-room games, and high-speed Internet access. Hoteliers have shifted their offerings from conventional cable to high-tech options such as 3D televisions, high-definition, flat panel monitors, and video-on-demand equipment. Guests want to watch what they want and when they want. So when interfaced with other systems, "entertainment" systems offer:

- Personalized welcoming messages on the TV screens for new arrivals.
- Video-on-demand by means of pay-per-view (films and programs) that guests special order with options such as pause, rewind, and fast forward.
- High-speed Internet, which usually includes free news and weather.
- Wake-up calls interfaced to the television as explained previously.
- Room service with pictures of the menu items displayed on the television screen.
- Live feedback to management from surveys. Survey items that guests mark very low alert the manager on duty by means of a paging interface. Here's a unique opportunity for the hotel to "make it right".
- Different language options, especially useful as international tourism booms.
- Internet Protocol-based radio that captures broadcasts over the Internet from around the world. Thus, say, a Turkish guest can tune in Power FM, a popular radio channel from Turkey.
- Folio viewing, billing, and settling as part of the departure process. Folios can follow guests to their homes or offices by land mail or Internet.
- Parental control of programming, blocking adult material from their children's sets.
- Compatibility with a multitude of portable devices that many guests now carry.
- Other two-way communication services like book spa appointments and golf tee times.
- Flash- and Java-capable systems which can deliver a full-range of graphics, content, and services.

And this is just the start of what is still to come. Some hotels are now experimenting with in-mirror televisions. Literally, as the guest combs her hair in the mirror she can see both her own face as well as the built-in television screen. The level of opaqueness can be adjusted—from maximum television viewability to more mirror and less TV. And, of course, the in-mirror television can be turned off completely if it proves too invasive. Who knows what else is on the horizon?

PROPERTY-BY-PROPERTY CUSTOM PROGRAMMING One of the most efficient improvements found in the newest in-room entertainment systems comes in the form of labor-savings. Today's most sophisticated television systems are now controllable through one central server. A hotel which chooses to reprogram channel numbers, remove certain channels from viewership, or arrange the television so that all like-channels are grouped can do so across all televisions from one central controller. Whether the room is occupied or not; the television is on, off, or switched to standby; or the television is located in the lounge, spa, or workout center, all televisions can be centrally reprogrammed.

This degree of controllability came in handy for Marriott International recently, when they began to deliver on a controversial decision to remove the availability of adult content from their new properties. The chain also plans to phase out adult content from existing Marriott properties as it switches them from traditional video systems to video-on-demand (VOD) systems. While Marriott International's official position states the move is due to declining revenues from in-room movies, many industry insiders believe it reflects a personal commitment by leaders of the chain. Bill Marriott has shared, for many years, his disdain for pornography. Although the largest, Marriott is by no means the first—Omni Hotels decided adult content was "not the way it wanted to make money" as far back as 1999!

STREAMING ON DEMAND More and more guests are opting away from video on-demand services provided by the hotel in favor of streaming their own video. Providers like Hulu, Netflix, and YouTube allow guests to view TV programs, movies, and videos through their laptops, iPads, and smartphones. The hotel's role in the experience: to provide bandwidth and televisions compatible with everything and anything the guest is carrying!

At the Desk

Maybe technology's greatest impact has been at the desk. The property management system has quickened the speed of service, reduced labor costs, improved accuracy, and modernized the look and flow of the lobby. The PMS has been with us throughout the text, from the chapters on reservations and arrivals to those dealing with billing and auditing. Because—contradictory as it seems—the nonpersonal, self-service aspects of an electronically supported hotel strengthen the guest's perception of a caring management. Guests know that staff is available—that desk personnel will respond when needed. Knowing help can be summoned, guests appreciate the speed and anonymity of self-service. Travelers (especially business travelers) dislike waiting in line, whether they are arriving or departing. So the self-service kiosk that speeds the guest along simultaneously saves the hotel labor. One study estimated the labor savings to be between 15% and 20%! Another anomaly: Self-service kiosks may actually increase revenue. Unlike self-conscious guest-service agents, kiosks easily prompt guests to buy up to higher rate rooms. Without awkwardness, kiosks promote the ancillary services of restaurants, lounges, spas, and nightclubs. Advertising revenue from lobby concessionaires and external merchants has proven to be another unexpected plus.

As explained, self-check-in equipment accommodates arrivals with a swipe of their credit cards (see Exhibit 14-26). It accepts registrations, distributes keycards, and prints instructions for finding the room. Property management systems continue handling guests' records during their stay, tracking everything through point-of-sale(POS) terminals, telephone call-accounting systems (CASs), in-room minibars and safes, electronic locks (ELSs), and fire systems. And then the guest can return to the kiosk and its PMS interface for an electronic check-out.

Internet-based systems push the process forward. Check-ins via the hotel's website are accepted as early as seven days before arrival. Radisson Hotels led with this idea: "Express Yourself" features a three-step process. (1) Guests make reservations through any of the means, for example, telephone, Internet, agents, and so on. (2) Seven days before arrival the system sends emails inviting guests "to express" themselves by checking in. Personal preferences are accommodated: room location, no-smoking, king bed, and so on. (3) The key is waiting when the guest arrives and offers identification. And as discussed throughout the chapter, many hotels are now offering Internet-based check-in by smartphone or personal digital-assistant (PDA).

EXHIBIT 14-26 Guests dislike front-desk queues. Strategically located self-serve kiosks get the guests into their rooms (and out of their rooms) more quickly with self-check-in and self-check-out services. The exhibit shows the benefits; a guest in the foreground is handling his account while guests in the background monopolize the front-desk agent. *Courtesy of Micros Systems, Inc., Columbia, Maryland.*

Similar handheld devices are used by guest-service agents. Cross-trained staffers exit the desk. Then from the middle of the lobby, the rear of the line, by the curb, or in the parking lot or garage, guests are registered by wireless equipment that communicates with the PMS. It is service with a technological smile.

STANDARDIZATION: FROM HITIS AND BEYOND Lodging now employs many technologies, but getting to this stage has been a bumpy road. Early systems were unable to talk to one another. That incompatibility was an industrywide issue that slowed progress. Initially, the industry lacked knowledge of the subject. Eventually, a decision was made to adopt an industrywide approach. The American Hotel & Lodging Association launched an initiative called Hospitality Industry Technology Integration Standards (HITIS).

The HITIS committee created a unified programming and hardware architectural structure for the PMS and all property-related interfaces. Previously, compatibility between, say, the PMS vendor and the POS vendor (or any other combination; PMS and CAS or PMS and ELS, etc.) did not exist. HITIS created standards and hoteliers were urged to specify them as part of their requests for proposal (RFPs) as early equipment was upgraded. And they did with good success.

OTA, Open Travel Alliance, the next generation of cooperative effort, expanded the horizon from "hospitality" to "travel." Its goal states: "...our primary focus is the creation of electronic message structures to facilitate communication between the disparate systems in the global travel industry." The organization's website goes on to identify membership, including "travel suppliers, defined as any company with primary control of inventory, including air carriers, car rental companies, hotel companies, railways, cruise lines, insurance companies, golf course owners, motorcycle, water or bicycle tour companies, etc."

Clearly, OTA's interest doesn't focus on lodging exclusively, but rather as one of its cross-industry sectors. Within the definition of a travel supplier, the hotel industry isn't as large as hoteliers imagine. As industry-buyers learned with HITIS, it takes cooperation among the immediate user-buyers to force uniformity from the manufacturer-sellers. A new association, Hotel Technology Next Generation (HTNG), returned the momentum to the lodging industry.

HTNG, a nonprofit organization, is more like HITIS than is OTA. All three organizations bring manufacturers, suppliers, consultants, and end-users together. HTNG's narrower universe concentrates on lodging, whereas lodging is but one segment within OTA. Within itself, lodging's focus is all inclusive, embracing the full scope of lodging technology: operations, telecommunications, in-room entertainment, customer information systems, and electronic installations.

Employing the initiatives of both of its predecessor organizations as well as its own, HTNG has begun certifying products, identifying them with an HTNG label and special logo. In so doing, it rejuvenates the work of HITIS. By using standardized interfaces rather than reinventing, as was done in the early effort, vendors save time and money. Knowing that larger companies will interface with them, smaller vendors are encouraged to participate. This broadens the scope of progress.

Whatever the organization one subscribes to, it works only when hoteliers buy from vendors that comply with universal standards. They have; so progress continues unabated.

Summary

No longer is hotel technology viewed as necessary cost. Today, it is a strategy which finds itself at the core of the entire operation. Technology impacts guests from the moment of reservation, through their arrival and departure, and into their next stay. It tracks, implements, and facilitates so many parts of the guest's stay and the hotel's operation that no summary list is practical.

For an industry as old as innkeeping, technology is the new kid. Still, it has shaken traditions and reformulated the delivery of "guest service." Few would say that service has diminished with the use of PMSs, or in-room technologies, or improved fire and security systems. Technology is a great differentiator, separating the "Mine Host" profile from the modern hotel executive. We find it in more than a dozen applications in the guest room alone. Just as the single bed with a connecting bath has been replaced with supreme bedding and multiple shower heads, so has the operator-assisted telephone and the open window been replaced by VoIP phones and sophisticated PTAC systems.

Resources and Challenges

Web Assignment

Visit http://www.hitec.org and report on either the next or the previous HITEC meeting. Explain what HITEC means, where the meeting was held (or will be held), the number of vendors, and two interesting aspects of the meeting's content.

Interesting Tidbits

- In 2011, Starbucks became the first major retailer to allow single-tap smartphone payment applications across all 6,800 of its stores.
- In a step toward regulating energy conservation, the U.S. government will no longer allow the manufacture of incandescent, halogen, and linear fluorescent bulbs. Beginning in 2012, the U.S. legislation begins phasing out certain bulbs—starting with the incandescent 100-watt bulb—the most common bedside light bulb in the lodging industry.
- The Lock Museum of Orange Country is located in Garden Grove, California. Among the exhibits are classic prison hardware such as leg irons and handcuffs, including those of the famous escape artist Houdini. Closer to the hotel industry are old keys and locks, including the lock from Elvis Presley's dressing room at the MGM Grand in Las Vegas.
- Robotics were not discussed in this chapter, but Hotelier Grace Leo-Andrieu, whose hotel company is based in Paris, and is a consultant for *Travel + LeisureMagazine,* foresees their use as part of an in-room vacuuming and disinfecting system, as a back-and-foot massage amenity, or even as a food and beverage delivery system!
- Marriott has launched an employee recruiting tool—a game found on Facebook called "My Marriott Hotel."

Challenges

True/False

Questions that are partially false should be marked false.

_____ **1.** By changing the name of their "Telephone Departments" to "The Department of Communications (DOC)," hotels have been able to stop the decrease in revenue that began about 1990, caused partly by hotels overcharging for in-room calls.

_____ **2.** Biometrics, the price of which has dropped substantially with time, has been widely adopted by the lodging industry, and is the best means yet of increasing security of both guests' assets and persons.

_____ **3.** "True" detection systems are energy detection systems that sense both body heat and body motion, and therefore achieve a truer reading of room occupancy than utilizing just one or the other alone.

_____ **4.** Four nonprofit organizations (in alphabetic order: HITIS, HTNG, OTA, PIN) have been launched during the past several years to establish standards for the manufacture and sale of hotel technology.

_____ **5.** The hotel PMS has been interfaced with the POS, the CAS, the ELS, and the HVAC to provide better service to guests and improved costs for the business.

Problems

1. The relationship of the telephone and hotel industries has changed significantly since the 1960s. List three major pieces of legislation, court rulings, findings by the FCC, or decisions by members of either industry that caused or contributed to the changes. How did each alter the way in which the hotel's telephone department operates?
2. Undoubtedly, some PMS vendors will comply with HITIS standards and others will not. What are the benefits to a hotel manager who purchases software from a vendor in compliance? Are there any disadvantages to using a vendor in compliance with HITIS standards?
3. Most hotel operations charge a premium for the convenience of placing long-distance phone calls directly from the room. The text discussed international guests who prefer to use the guest-room telephone rather than their own cell phone because international calls are so expensive by cell phone. If such calls are placed through the hotel's VoIP, what is the cost per call to the hotel? If you were running the chain, would you charge a fee for in-room long-distance calls or give the calls away as just another amenity? Explain your logic.
4. Using professional terminology correctly is important to understanding and being understood. Identify the following acronyms or abbreviations and briefly discuss what they represent:

   a. HOBIC **b.** WATS
   c. PMS **d.** FCC
   e. ELS **f.** OCC
   g. AT&T **h.** PBX
   i. RFID **j.** POS
   k. CAS **l.** AH&LA
   m. PPC **n.** VoIP
   o. HVAC **p.** PTAC
   q. Tap to Pay **r.** Bandwidth
   s. Smart cards
5. Be creative and imagine the hotel room of the future. Describe several guest-operated interfaces or devices that might be available in your fictitious hotel room of tomorrow.

AN INCIDENT IN HOTEL MANAGEMENT

The Bare Facts

Stay Today, a small West-coast limited-service chain, decided to market themselves toward the Asian traveler. It used a well-respected Asian marketing firm to create the "buzz." Among the hype: a fully electronic hotel. The effort had already showed positive results when a Japanese couple arrived one afternoon. Luckily—because they spoke no English—all their reservation papers were in order, including a four-day deposit. After much nodding and smiling, they were provided a keycard to room 1714, a nonsmoking room as prescribed by the reservation.

As they let themselves into the room, they realized there were no lights operating, except one single light above the front door. They walked back downstairs and were escorted to the room by an employee who showed them that inserting the keycard would turn on all in-room systems. They thanked the employee.

After a while, they sensed the room was growing very warm. Yet they could not determine how to adjust the temperature. Again, they walked downstairs and were escorted to the room by a different employee. This time they were shown how to access the temperature control setting on the one-touch guest-controlled tablet. They thanked the employee.

Late that evening, as they prepared for bed, they realized there were no light switches anywhere on the walls. The husband removed the keycard from the control slot, the lights turned off (except the annoying single bulb above the front door), and they went to sleep. An hour later, they were awake because the room was growing too warm. The husband reinserted the keycard, but then all the lights came back on. They decided to sleep with all the lights on. The next morning they tried to make themselves understood at the front desk.

Questions

1. Was there a management failure here; if so, what?
2. What should be the hotel's immediate response to this morning's complaint?
3. What further, long-run action should management consider?

Answers to True/False Quiz

1. False. Changing the name is meaningless. Hotels need to change the structure in order to woo guests back, if that is even possible. Two strategies are being tested: (1) Bundle all telecommunications together to increase sales; and (2) Use ISPs (Internet service providers) to carry VoIP calls at a lower cost.
2. False. Guests are reluctant to surrender very personal attributes such as fingerprints and eye scans, and until that changes, biometric security systems will not gain position in hotels. Additionally, biometrics still remain relatively expensive even as other forms of technology decrease in price.
3. True. However, the more accurate sensing comes at a higher initial cost, because the hotel is supporting two systems (infra-red and motion detectors) rather than just one.
4. False. This is a "catch question." HITIS, HTNG, and OTA are organizations working to standardize equipment interfaces. PIN is a well-known abbreviation for one's personal identification number. So it doesn't belong in the grouping.
5. True. And these four interfaces are just the start of a long list of current and potential systems (minibars and fire-safety, for example) and many more to come.

INDEX

Q

R